Introduction to Int͘ ͗l Property Law

Introduction to Intellectual Property Law

Fourth edition

Jeremy Phillips BA (Cantab), PhD (Kent)

Intellectual Property Consultant, Slaughter and May;
Professor, Magister Lventinvs, University of Alicante;
Visiting Professor at the Faculty of Laws, University College London;
Visiting Professor, School of Finance and Law, Bournemouth
University.

Alison Firth MA (Oxon), MSc

Barrister;
Senior Lecturer, Intellectual Property Law Unit,
Queen Mary & Westfield College, University of London.

Butterworths
LexisNexis™

Members of the LexisNexis Group worldwide

United Kingdom	Butterworths Tolley, a Division of Reed Elsevier (UK) Ltd, Halsbury House, 35 Chancery Lane, LONDON, WC2A 1EL, and 4 Hill Street, EDINBURGH EH2 3JZ
Argentina	Abeledo Perrot, Jurisprudencia Argentina and Depalma, BUENOS AIRES
Australia	Butterworths, a Division of Reed International Books Australia Pty Ltd, CHATSWOOD, New South Wales
Austria	ARD Betriebsdienst and Verlag Orac, VIENNA
Canada	Butterworths Canada Ltd, MARKHAM, Ontario
Chile	Publitecsa and Conosur Ltda, SANTIAGO DE CHILE
Czech Republic	Orac sro, PRAGUE
France	Editions du Juris-Classeur SA, PARIS
Hong Kong	Butterworths Asia (Hong Kong), HONG KONG
Hungary	Hvg Orac, BUDAPEST
India	Butterworths India, NEW DELHI
Ireland	Butterworths (Ireland) Ltd, DUBLIN
Italy	Giuffré, MILAN
Malaysia	Malayan Law Journal Sdn Bhd, KUALA LUMPUR
New Zealand	Butterworths of New Zealand, WELLINGTON
Poland	Wydawnictwa Prawnicze PWN, WARSAW
Singapore	Butterworths Asia, SINGAPORE
South Africa	Butterworths Publishers (Pty) Ltd, DURBAN
Switzerland	Stämpfli Verlag AG, BERNE
USA	LexisNexis, DAYTON, Ohio

© Reed Elsevier (UK) Ltd 2001

A CIP Catalogue record for this book is available from the British Library.

ISBN 0 406 99757 8

Printed in Great Britain by Cromwell Press, Trowbridge, Wiltshire

Visit Butterworths LexisNexis *direct* at www.butterworths.com

Preface to fourth edition

The first edition of this book was hand-written in black ball-point pen. The second edition was largely typed; the third edition was word-processed. This fourth edition, a product of modern times, is the result of a thousand emails, attached documents, phone messages and not a little telepathy between two authors who have seen each other just once during its period of gestation. The next edition, if there should be one, will no doubt be founded on a veritable coral reef of text messages.

That we were able to combine to write this book is even more surprising when one considers how different are our personalities and approaches to the law. The first author employs metaphor and simile as his preferred pedagogic techniques and belongs to the school of thought that is happy to accept that the impression that users receive of the law is itself part of the law. The second author demands a sharp and critical focus on the law as the starting point for legal study and believes that personal enthusiasms should be the servant, not the master, of legal analysis. The second author charitably accepts that it is upon the authors alone that rests the full responsibility for mistakes and omissions in the following text, while the first author is content to let the blame lie where it properly belongs: with publishers, printers, proof-readers, inappropriate use of the spell-check and inexplicable deviations in the normally predictable law of nature. And so on.

We are however united in our hope that, by reading this *Introduction*, readers will succeed in being introduced to intellectual property. This book is not a substitute for any of the comprehensive IP textbooks or practitioners' manuals, those potent proofs that paper-based titles can be joyously lucrative even in the electronic age. Read it, enjoy it and move on to the next thing in your life.

Now for the 'honours' section:

Jeremy's credits: my gratitude to (i) the many generations of students whose questions and comments have served to enrich my understanding and enjoyment of IP law, providing the initial motivation for writing this book and (ii) my friends and colleagues at Slaughter and May, especially Nigel Swycher and his partners Susie Middlemiss and Cathy Connolly, for demonstrating how many extraordinary things you can do with IP, once you understand the law.

Alison's credits: special thanks are due to my son Will Thompson, for his patience and IT expertise and to the UK Patent Office for help with facts and figures. Colleagues and students have provided insights and encouragement. I am also grateful to the team at Butterworths for their efficiency and good humour.

Joint credit: a big thank you to Julia Locklan, who has worked so hard on the proofs – and in such a very short time frame too.

Jeremy Phillips	Alison Firth
Temple Fortune	Dulwich
November 2001	*November 2001*

Preface to first edition

There is something a little paradoxical about the subject of intellectual property. This is because, while there is scarcely any human behaviour which its laws do not touch, intellectual property is inherently intangible. It is an invisible estate which may be created or inherited, an invisible estate which some may enjoy and from which others will be eternally barred.

If I may be permitted a further metaphor, it has long been my view that intellectual property is the Carmen of commercial law; it is a subject with charm, personality and a force of character, attributes which are more tellingly depicted by the impressionistic strokes of the artist's brush than by anatomical dissection. This metaphor has dominated my approach to the writing of this book, for it will soon be apparent to the reader that the subjective, frequently impressionistic view of the field of study has been chosen in preference to the precise enunciation of legal rules. *Introduction to Intellectual Property Law* is designed to whet the appetite, and not to sate it.

In writing this book I owe an immense and incalculable debt to the late Harry Bloom. An enthusiastic, impatient man, Harry refused to distinguish the lawyer from the prophet, the prescription from the prediction or the message from its medium. As a teacher he was by turns inspirational and infuriating, and usually controversial. He maintained that intellectual property law could not be properly understood without recourse to economics, politics, cybernetics, psychology, sociology, industrial relations or the natural sciences: the study of the sum and total of human knowledge and experience. This book does not pretend to encompass the full range of disciplines which Harry Bloom would have required but it does, however, seek to achieve one of Harry's less lofty aims, that of making the subject sufficiently interesting for others to wish to get involved in it too. If I have achieved this aim I shall be well satisfied.

A number of my learned and respected colleagues, students and former students have read parts of the text and have offered criticism and

Preface to first edition

encouragement in equal parts; they are of course no more responsible for my thoughts than for my debts. They include Allison Coleman, Nigel Swycher, Sam Ricketson, Rob Merkin and Richard Pratt. Particular gratitude is due to Shelley Lane, with whom I have shared my intellectual property LLB teaching over the past two years, and from whom I have gained so many new and unorthodox perspectives, and to Suzanne Emmery, who has toiled long and hard over my manuscript. I should also mention Hugh Brett and the many other 'IP' aficionados who have given encouragement and support to much of my work on intellectual property.

Jeremy Phillips
Finchley
April 1986

Contents

Contents

Contents

Contents

Table of statutes

References in this Table to *Statutes* are to Halsbury's Statutes of England (Fourth Edition) showing the volume and page at which the annotated text of the Act may be found.

References in the right-hand column are to paragraph numbers.

Paragraph numbers in **bold** indicate where the material is reproduced in the text.

Table of statutory instruments

References in the right-hand column are to paragraph numbers.

Paragraph numbers in **bold** indicate where the material is reproduced in the text.

Table of treaties

References in the right-hand column are to paragraph numbers.

Paragraph numbers in **bold** indicate where the material is reproduced in the text.

List of cases

List of cases

List of cases

xli

Part I

Introduction

Chapter 1

What is intellectual property?

Is it 'intellectual'? Is it 'property'?

1.1 To this question there are two answers, one is based on an ordinary colloquial understanding of the literal meanings of the words 'intellectual' and 'property'; the other is legal. The ordinary common-sense description of intellectual property is that it simply comprises all those things that are 'intellectual' because they emanate from the use of the human brain, for example Lara Croft, websites, mobile phones, lists of names and addresses, the way to make genuine Coca-Cola or a suitably seductive name for a new brand of perfume.

1.2 Some may take pedantic exception to the stipulation that it is specifically from the human brain that intellectual property must be taken to originate; what, for example, of the computer which exercises its own 'intellect' in printing out the results of its own calculations, or of the hypothetical monkey shackled eternally to a presumably indestructible PC, hammering the keyboard at random until it writes the next Harry Potter book? Are these also intellectual property? If the answer to this question is answered in the affirmative, it is not because of any inherent vice in the definition offered above, but rather because of a subtle appreciation that there is a low level of human intellectual activity which we are inclined to regard as enjoying the status of 'property'. After all, not only activities of monkeys or computers but also the programming of the intelligent computer, the cunning juxtaposition of monkey and typewriter can be regarded as part of the process of intellectual endeavour. But there is a level below which intellectual activity is not capable of being treated as 'property'. Thus the decision to play Dwight Yorke up front alongside Andy Cole in the Manchester United football team may be the result of an intellectual process but most people would not consider the result of that process as being 'property'.

1.3   The legal description of intellectual property differs from the colloquial in that it focuses upon the rights which are enjoyed in the produce of the mind, rather than upon that produce itself. In legal terms we call a piece of land, a painting or a motor car 'property' not because it is a solid, physical thing in itself but because individuals or legal entities such as companies can assert a right in it against some or all other persons. The word 'property' itself comes from the Latin word *proprius*, which means 'one's own'. If we bear this in mind, we can take the expression 'intellectual property' to mean the legal rights which may be asserted in respect of the product of the human intellect, for example Chanel's right to stop people filling bottles with home-made concoctions and selling them on the street corner as CHANEL No 5. It is also convenient to treat as intellectual property the rights and powers which one may enjoy over another's work, such as the manufacturer's right to be allowed to use someone else's invention where a patent for that invention has been granted to that other person but has not been industrially exploited.

1.4   The intelligent observer of human behaviour will have spotted that the fruits of exercise of human intellect would exist even if they enjoyed no legal protection – in the same way as a plot of land or a bar of chocolate would exist even if no one could claim the legal right to own or possess it; but it is the existence of such a right to do so which entitles us to refer to such physical things as 'property'. The ordinary words which form the component parts of our day-to-day conversation are not generally regarded as intellectual property, even if a great deal of thought went into their being coined: words such as 'chair', 'banana' and 'Tarzan' do not exist in nature – they have all been created by the use of the human intellect – but we do not regard them as 'property' because the law does not provide a right to prevent their expropriation. The opposite is true of words such as 'Pepsi', 'champagne' or 'Darth Vader', all of which are carefully guarded items of property notwithstanding the frequency with which they find their way out of people's mouths. Confusingly, some words are sometimes property and sometimes not, for example 'aspirin', 'marigold' and 'Pocahontas'.

What is intellectual property law?

1.5   The intelligent and logical reader may regard this question as superfluous once the phrase 'intellectual property' has been defined in legal terms. Can he not safely conclude that intellectual property law is the aggregate of rights and duties which pertain to the control of intellectual property? This assumption would be incorrect, because the demands of practical reality have supplanted the strict rules of logic. On reading this book, our logical reader will find reference to rules and remedies that appear to have no relevance whatsoever to ownership or control of the product of the human intellect. For example, intellectual property law as widely understood by its devotees includes such topics as whether the London and Provincial Law Assurance Society could stop the London and Provincial Joint Stock Life Assurance Company from trading under that name,[1] whether a manufacturer of wine in the Champagne region of France could stop a British manufacturer of a non-vinous substance from advertising it as 'Babycham, the genuine Champagne Perry'[2] or whether a milk roundsman employed by a dairy could be prevented from soliciting his employer's customers prior to his leaving the dairy's employment.[3]

1. *London and Provincial Law Assurance Society v London and Provincial Joint Stock Life Assurance Co* (1847) 17 LJ Ch 37.
2. *H P Bulmer Ltd and Showerings Ltd v J Bollinger SA* [1978] RPC 79.
3. *Wessex Dairies Ltd v Smith* [1935] 2 KB 80.

1.6 There are two explanations as to why such apparently irrelevant or extraneous legal material is traditionally included within the corpus of intellectual property law. The first is that the traditional manner of protecting the owner of intellectual property against encroachment by others is the grant by the state of an exclusionary, and in some cases exclusive, right to the exploitation, for a limited duration, of the creative output of the intellect. The owner of such rights naturally seeks to derive the greatest benefit from them. One effective means of doing this is by finding other legal means of extending the limited duration of his rights. Thus an inventor normally has a maximum legal monopoly of just twenty years of the right to stop others making a product protected as a patented invention; but if he can find an attractive name for that product people may continue to buy it from him, even though others can compete with him in the manufacture and sale of it after his patent has expired.[1] Accordingly the law of marks and names as applied to goods and services and to the companies that market them is of great importance to the person who wishes to exploit his intellectual produce; the overall legal control of monopolies (whether generated by statute or not) will be important when it is considered whether the intellectual owner can sustain his market dominance even once his patent or copyright has expired.

1. Eg the LIBRIUM and VALIUM trade marks, which protect their proprietor's market dominance in the manufacture of sedative drugs for which the patents have expired; cf *Linoleum Manufacturing Co v Nairn* (1878) 7 Ch D 834.

1.7   Second, whether a person enjoys a monopoly over his intellectual property or not, he knows that his exploitation of it will be free from the terrors of unwanted competition if he can persuade his likeliest competitors not to compete against him, or if he can persuade his employees, most intimately acquainted with his trade secrets and practices, not to leave him and work instead for a competitor. Both of these aims are capable of being achieved by means of the law of contract. Thus the making of contracts, with regard to the result of intellectual endeavour, and the validity of those contracts once made, inevitably become subjects of interest to the intellectual property lawyer.

Is intellectual property law an important subject?

1.8   Devotees of intellectual property law can take comfort in the fact that their subject is no longer perceived as a niche, an arcane professional craft of no genuine significance. While the topic was scarcely known as late as the beginning of the 1980s, it has finally assumed its position as the jewel in the crown of legal practice. Universities and colleges vie with each other for the privilege of offering the most attractive IP programmes, which exist in ample supply for both graduates and undergraduates. Advertisements in lawyers' magazines and on the Internet proclaim the many rewards bestowed on even relatively junior specialists in the art. No fewer than three professions – lawyer, patent agent and trade mark attorney – exist to serve the burgeoning and lucrative demands of clients. Intellectual property is a benign parent; it feeds the hungry, occupies the idle and neglects the needs of none of its children.

1.9   The reason for this is not hard to find. Intellectual property is the currency of our time. The production of commodities was replaced by the supply of services as the dynamo that propels the engine of the economy; now the supply of services has itself been superseded by the provision of information. This is the age of satellite and cable transmission, of broadcast, of interactive media, of computers and the internet, of data creation and transfer, of entertainment and education, fact and fancy: all of this is intellectual property. While a minority of the UK's population consists of home-owners, virtually everyone owns some intellectual property. Traders pick their way warily through the myriad trade mark monopolies that govern the import and sale of goods and the supply of services in this land. Literally hundreds of millions of copyright works are created daily; many are infringed. Our feet may be planted on the ground but our heads are in cyberspace.

1.10 Even if one chooses to dismiss as insignificant a claim for greater teaching of intellectual property law which is based on practical professional expediency, one should not treat so lightly the claim that intellectual property law plays a vital part in the physical well-being of the individual and in the commercial vitality of the economy. For it is an important function of intellectual property law that it encourages (if such is possible) the creation of ideas and inventions, their disclosure for the benefit of all, not to mention their commercial exploitation so as to facilitate the greatest potential exploitation of their practical or concrete embodiments. The positive, as well as potential negative, effects of intellectual property on global well-being appear to be recognised in Art 16.5 of the Convention on Biological Diversity,[1] which states:

> 'the Contracting Parties, recognizing that patents and other intellectual property rights may have an influence on the implementation of this Convention, shall cooperate in this regard subject to national legislation and international law in order to ensure that such rights are supportive of and do not run counter to its objectives'.

1.   Of 5 June 1992, signed in Rio de Janeiro by more than 150 states at the United Nations conference on the environment and development. See M Chandler *The Biodiversity Convention: Selected Issues of Interest to the International Lawyer* (1993) 4 Colo J Int Env L and P, 141 at 161.

1.11 Where land is purchased, the purchaser can often derive immense financial advantage without actually doing anything to, with or under the land he buys. In contrast, a person who acquires an intellectual property right can derive no financial benefit from it except by using it commercially. If he secures, for example, a patent for a new product, he will gain advantage only by making that product and selling it, or by charging others who wish to exploit his patent. This use is capable of benefiting more than merely the patent's owner. For example, a patent's user may derive profit through his use of it, the consumer will benefit through the ability to acquire a product manufactured under it, members of the country's available workforce will gain employment, the government will take its taxes and all will (in theory) be happy. If a person who creates intellectual property subsequently derives some benefit from its use, he will (in theory) be encouraged to endeavour to repeat the process by which the pleasure of that benefit was previously obtained. An economy which is incapable of creating its own intellectual property must import it. It is thus imperative for the economic well-being of any country that it guard against a massive outflow of funds[1] by providing a commercial environment in which the creation of intellectual property is rewarded; and it is this which has been perhaps the most important function of intellectual property law.

1. For an interesting insight into this danger see D Morgan 'Cable, Computers and Canadian Culture' (1985) 6 Journal of Media Law and Practice 138.

Intellectual property and moral rights

1.12 Aside from its practical and economic aspects, intellectual property law fulfils functions which have a purely moral content: for it is ideally capable of providing (i) that no one other than the inventor, author or other intellectual creator is falsely described as being such; (ii) that the creator of a work may make legal objection to the distortion of his work by others, and (iii) that the author who has changed his mind about the validity of his intellectual product can retract it prior to the embarrassment he incurs by reason of its publication by any other person. The rights described above are sometimes referred to as moral rights, since they protect the creator's moral rather than his pecuniary interest in his work.[1] In those countries which share with the UK a common law heritage these rights are often vestigial or non-existent, but the intellectual property laws of many other countries (notably those influenced by civil law principles) accord them a good deal of jurisprudential content. In principle, moral rights are the author's non-transferable 'birthright' and cannot be sold. This non-transferability is wise if one considers that their function is to protect the creator's integrity as a human being, which is not an appropriate subject of sale. It is only necessary to reflect upon the plot of *The Phantom of the Opera*[2] to appreciate the benefits which can accrue from such rights, and the distress resulting from their absence.

1. On moral rights see Ch 18 below. Those accorded to authors by the Copyright, Designs and Patents Act 1988 can be waived but not actually transferred.
2. Briefly, the 'phantom' is a brilliant but impecunious composer whose work is published in the name of his rich and much-despised patron; because he has no *droit moral*, the 'phantom' turns to evil deeds in order to satisfy his feelings of injustice.

Intellectual property means and ends

1.13 The Universal Declaration of Human Rights would appear to depend upon intellectual property law for the realisation of at least some of its objects. For example, no one is to be subject to arbitrary interference with his or her privacy,[1] and everyone has a right to own property[2] and to make a living.[3] Professor C G Weeramantry, however, in *The Slumbering Sentinels*,[4] lists 'intellectual property in scientific knowledge' as a source of possible denigration of the right to share in scientific advancement and its benefit.[5] Whether one takes this assertion seriously or not (and intellectual property rights are characteristically circumscribed by rules relating to the protection of the public interest), it does indicate that intellectual property rights – in common with all other legal rights – are capable of abuse or, more accurately, of use in a manner which may be regarded as prejudicial either to competing private interests or to the public interest. This is no mere hypothetical matter. In *Service Corpn International plc v Channel Four Television Corpn*[6] Lightman J based a decision not to grant an injunction to suppress an alleged infringement of copyright on a direct application of the European Convention on Human Rights' commitment to freedom of speech.

1. Universal Declaration of Human Rights, art 12.
2. Ibid art 17.
3. Ibid art 23.
4. *The Slumbering Sentinels* (1983).
5. Ibid p 17, table 2.1.
6. [1999] EMLR 83: see Jeremy Phillips, 'Forebodings and a Funeral' [1998] Ent LR 211-215.

1.14   It is proper to emphasise the importance of intellectual property law as an academic discipline and as a driving force in the economic life of the new millennium. However, it must be recognised that, despite its importance, intellectual property law is not a sacred cow; it is merely a body of laws which is intended to act as a means of achieving a particular set of ends. Where such laws do not achieve their stipulated ends, or the price which is paid for their doing so exceeds the value of achieving those ends, then intellectual property law is as much an object of scrutiny, criticism, amendment or repeal as is any other set of normative or distributive rules. In the UK at any rate, each brand of intellectual property law evolved as a result of essentially practical considerations; those same considerations could lead to its death. In many foreign jurisdictions, in contrast, intellectual property rights are not dependent upon considerations of practical utility but are superior (and possibly anterior) to them. At the time of writing, the shifting sands of necessity and the adoption of policies of international harmony have brought British intellectual property laws close to those of other countries; whether this state of affairs is purely temporary, or not, is a matter for speculation beyond the covers of this book, which has been written with the British reader particularly in mind. Where subsequent chapters review and examine the law, they will therefore give more scope to the investigation of their relation to the ends achieved than to the irresoluble question of their metaphysical link between man, his creations and his relations with others.

Chapter 2

Protectability of intellectual property

How, in practical terms, can intellectual property be protected?

2.1 The easiest way to protect intellectual property is to keep it in one's head. If a person possesses in his head a good idea, he runs no risk that anyone else will see or find it, and thereby appropriate it. Such intellectual property may be preserved thus until its owner chooses to divulge it; if the idea consists of a process of doing something, it even remains securely in the possession of its owner if he performs that process when no one is looking. And, like the old countess in *The Queen of Spades*,[1] the possessor of such property can take it to the grave with him, safe in the knowledge that no one will inherit it. A similar means of protecting intellectual property is that of locking it away in a safe. Unfortunately there is relatively little potential for the commercial exploitation of intellectual property while it remains thus protected. This is because the keeping of an idea to oneself and the commercial utilisation of that idea are inherently contradictory notions. Moreover, the possessor of an idea will find that there is nothing he can do if any other person independently happens upon the same idea and decides to make it public. Independent discovery of ideas is an unsurprisingly frequent occurrence, since people working at the 'rock face' of any theoretical or applied science tend to direct their attention at the same problem.[2]

1. In Tchaikovsky's opera (1890), based on a story by Pushkin, the old countess dies rather than reveal her secret, but then posthumously appears to the young gambler in a dream.
2. On the phenomenon of independent discovery see R Epstein 'Industrial Invention: Heroic or Systematic?' (1926) 40 Quarterly Journal of Economics 232. See also Mustill LJ's account of the race to synthesize t-PA in *Genentech Inc's* Patent [1989] RPC 147.

2.2 Apart from the expedient of a refusal to divulge it, intellectual property is not practically protectable by any other physical means. This is not to say that human ingenuity has not been concentrated upon the practical means of its protection. Advanced research has been conducted into purely physical means of guarding against such unauthorised uses of intellectual property as the illicit copying of pre-recorded CDs, the duplication of computer software, the unlicensed reception of broadcasts and cable diffusion and hacking into valuable and confidential databases. In all these instances the purely physical expedient has been turned to only when the law has been regarded as incapable of providing sufficient protection by means of the rights it accords to intellectual property holders.[1] The physical restraint upon unauthorised dissemination is, however, subject to one important weakness: it would currently seem that there is no electronic device or process so sophisticated that it cannot be neutralised, eroded or reversed by the exercise of sophistication equal to that of its original conception.[2] Then the technological measure itself requires the protection of law.[3] A further drawback to some forms of technological protection is that they block access to the material.[4] This is as unattractive to the rock band seeking maximum publicity as it is to the researcher trying to collate medical studies on Alzheimer's disease. For these reasons the legal protection of intellectual property is regarded as being more valuable than the physical embodiment of it.

1. A Thomas 'Online Music Piracy, Anonymity and Copyright Protection' [2001] Ent LR 1. On the adequacy of copyright see J Phillips 'The Risk that Rewards: Copyright Infringement Today' [2001] Ent LR 103.
2. This logical assumption, accepted long ago by G Davies 'Private Copying of Sound and Audio Visual Recordings' ESC 1984, pp 147-148, does not seem to have inhibited ever more complex technical solutions: see P Akester, 'Survey of Technological Measures for the Protection of Copyright' [2001] Ent LR 36.
3. See World Intellectual Property Organisation 1996 Copyright Treaty, Art 11.
4. T Vinje 'A Brave New World of Technological Proptection Systems: Will There Still be Room for Copyright? [1996] EIPR 431.

Legal protection of intellectual property

2.3   If it is preferable to enjoy an enforceable legal right to one's property rather than to put a fence of barbed wire around it, we must examine the means by which the law can benefit the holder of intellectual property. There are five essentially different means by which it may do so: they are, in descending order of legal cogency, an absolute monopoly of the market, a qualified monopoly, a monopoly of the use of one's creation within the market, a compulsory licence and a body of disparate principles linked together by the concept of unfair competition. Let us look, in outline, at each.

(i) The absolute monopoly of the market

2.4   This is the right of the intellectual property owner to prevent all other persons from using that property within the market place governed by the law which protects it. An example of the absolute monopoly can be found in the rights enjoyed by the holder of a patent for an invention. Not only can he stop anyone copying the novel product or process covered by his patent, but he can also prevent him from utilising the practical embodiment of his idea as described in the patent specification even if that person has independently invented it himself during the currency of the first inventor's patent.[1] As may be imagined, the holder of an absolute monopoly wields considerable commercial power in any market when others actually want to buy or use his invention. For this reason it has been found necessary to mitigate the effects of the right-holder's potential ability to abuse his absolute power. Thus the patentee who stops others using his patent but refuses to use it himself may find his economic kingdom placed in the benign stewardship of the Comptroller of Patents,[2] who will oversee the terms of its use by others.[3]

1. On the scope of the patent monopoly see Chs 7 and 8 below.
2. The full title of the Comptroller (pronounced 'Controller') is 'Comptroller-General of Patents, Designs and Trade Marks'. For administrative purposes, she also enjoys the more prosaic title of 'Chief Executive'.
3. Patents Act 1977, ss 48-59.

2.5   Since the holder of an absolute monopoly right can prevent subsequent independent conceivers of the same invention from using it, the effect of such protection of the first inventor is not merely to accord to him a property right. For example, once an idea is embodied in the form of a patent, it cannot be the subject matter of intellectual property – at least for the purposes of patent law – of any later act of invention. The subsequent inventor of the same invention is thus not only deprived of the right to patent his invention; he is unable, for the duration of the patent, to derive any recognised legal benefit at all from its exploitation, and has no claim to be known as its inventor.[1] However, a person who privately and independently conceives and uses an invention *before* the date from which the patent was granted can continue doing so, on the basis that what he has once done lawfully should not be allowed to become unlawful.[2] This same principle is applied in trade mark law. Once a trade mark registration is granted it confers an exclusive right upon its owner,[3] but this too is subject to the ability of prior users to continue their use.[4] Honest concurrent users may be able to obtain concurrent registration to protect theirs.[5]

2.5 *Protectability of intellectual property*

1. Cf Patents Act 1977, s 13.
2. Patents Act 1977, s 64.
3. Trade Marks Act 1994, s 9(1).
4. Ibid, s 11(3), which contemplates use in a particular locality.
5. Ibid, ss 7, 11(1).

(ii) The qualified monopoly

2.6 This is the right which a creator of intellectual property enjoys in respect of works which command an absolute market monopoly subject to one major qualification: he cannot stop another party 'stripping down' his creation and thus effectively using it as the basis for his own creation. This species of monopoly protects the topographies of semiconductor chips,[1] as well as new plant and seed varieties.[2] The justification for this sort of protection is that it prevents the out-and-out 'free rider' from making gratuitous use of the creator's efforts, while enabling the serious, painstaking competitor to build upon the creator's efforts in the knowledge that his scientific advances too can be utilised in turn by the creator. It is significant that both in the field of semiconductor topography protection and in that of plant varieties, this qualification upon the absolute monopoly – usually referred to as 'reverse engineering' – was introduced upon the insistence of intellectual property creators themselves. Why was this so? It was because they feared that the impact of a single dominant monopoly at the inception of a new shift in industrial development could snuff out competition with subsequent damage being inflicted upon scientific research and, ultimately, consumer choice.

1. Copyright, Designs and Patents Act 1988, s 226(1A)(b), as provided for in the Design Right (Semiconductor Topographies) Regulations 1989 (SI 1989/1100) reg 8.
2. Section 8 of the Plant Varieties Act 1997 permits the reproduction of protected plant varieties for the purpose of breeding further varieties.

(iii) The monopoly of use of one's personal creation

2.7 This is the right of the creator of intellectual property to prevent others from copying or otherwise exploiting the work actually produced by him, but without the right to prevent the exploitation of an identical or similar work produced through the independent intellectual endeavour of another. Such a 'relative monopoly' is exemplified by the protection most frequently given by copyright law. In theory this protection appears far less adequate a form of protection than that given by the absolute monopoly, since there exists the possibility that two or more persons may independently conceive identical or highly similar songs, paintings or dramatic sketches. In

14

practice, however, the lesser degree of protection is only infrequently a cause of serious discontent on the part of the first creator of the intellectual property. This is because, when two people write, for example, an identical passage of prose, our own subjective reaction to the statistical probability of such coincidence is to infer that the later of the two writers copied the work of the earlier unless he can show fairly clearly that he did not. Additionally, one effect of the technical sophistication of the Western world (currently the main constituent of the 'global village'[1]) is that the mass performance and reproduction of works renders the statistical possibility of true coincidence even less likely. If a song tops the charts in the UK, its subsequent saturation of the live and media audiences for popular music is so great that the British traveller abroad does not feel surprised to hear it frequently in Stockholm, Madrid, Rome or Vienna. He would, however, feel surprised to hear that a composer of popular songs had, quite independently of the first writer and without copying, conceived the identical or similar song in any of those cities after the date in which that song had achieved commercial success – unless the similarities between the two were basically just commonplace expressions.[2]

1. This term, much in vogue in the late 1960s and early 1970s, was coined by Marshall MacLuhan in his book *The Media is the Message* (1967).
2. See Isobel Brown, 'Sounds Familiar? The "Chariots of Fire" Case' [1987] EIPR 244.

2.8 Where there is a high likelihood that identical or similar works have indeed been independently produced, without any trespass upon the original creator's intellectual endeavour, it is probable that, in the vast majority of cases, the original creator's financial or moral position will not be seriously threatened by the competition of others for the provision of similar or identical works. For example, the Eiffel Tower, Big Ben, the Statue of Liberty and Mr and Mrs David Beckham are all such popular targets for photographers that it is quite likely that many different photographers have succeeded in taking virtually identical photographs of those subjects. The first photographer to record his particular perspective upon the subject, or to publish it, cannot claim to be able to prevent others from taking, and indeed exploiting, their own photographs, even if it was his idea to take such a picture. The idea of taking the photograph is free to all: it lies in the 'public domain' of human intellectual activity. One could indeed say that the idea of taking a photograph of any specific subject was itself inherent in the concept of the use of a camera for taking photographs. What is protectable here is the exercise of the individual's skill and aesthetic appreciation in the taking of a particular

15

photograph. Where a multitude of photographers all independently produce profoundly similar end-products, this mass similarity is evidence that the degree of skill and aesthetic appreciation which has gone into the making of the photograph is relatively small, so that the value of each photographer's intellectual result is also small. The position which photographs of the Eiffel Tower or Big Ben occupy within the spectrum of works entitled to copyright protection is thus a relatively humble one. Another example of a relative monopoly is the database right.[1] Here the justification for protection – substantial investment[2] – is a purely economic one. The right permits its owner to control the extraction and re-utilisation of data contained in a structured database.

1. Copyright in Databases Regulations 1997, SI 1997/3032, regs 12-25, implementing Directive 96/9/EC of 11 March 1996 on the legal protection of databases, [1996] OJ L77/20.
2. Ibid, reg 13.

(iv) The compulsory licence

2.9 This is a form of benefit to the intellectual property owner which can scarcely be called protection, for it relinquishes his control over his intellectual product, yet it has much to commend it when viewed from an economic rather than a moral standpoint. The compulsory licence is a right to use the intellectual property which is enjoyed by all who wish to use it. This licensed trespass is, however, not gratuitous. For just as the creator of the intellectual property is compelled to allow all to use his creation, so equally are all who avail themselves of this facility compelled to pay to him in return a sum which, ideally, bears some relationship to the extent or value of that use. Design and patent law are both familiar with forms of this device. For example, anyone who wishes to make use of an unregistered design during the final five years of the duration of design right may do so of right, so long as he pays the right's proprietor a sum agreed between the two or fixed by the Comptroller.[1] Likewise, a manufacturer who wishes to use a patent which has lain dormant in the hands of its holder may apply to the Comptroller for a compulsory licence to do so[2] – though such an application may be resisted by the holder of the patent. Some rights simply do not confer exclusive powers on their owners; the phrase 'equitable remuneration' is often associated with these.[3]

1. Copyright, Designs and Patents Act 1988, s 237.
2. Patents Act 1977, s 48.
3. Such as musical performers' rights to share in the proceeds of playing and broadcasting their recorded performances to the public: Copyright, Designs and Patents Act 1988, s 182D.

2.10 The compulsory licence has its critics who argue that, if intellectual property is to be treated as property at all so as to accord to its creator the rights and responsibilities appropriate to the fact that he has created what did not exist before, it must possess the legal characteristics of property. These characteristics include the right to exclude others from the use or possession of it. After all, one may not enjoy a right to use without permission another's car, nor may one help oneself to a right of way over a neighbour's garden. On the other hand, it is argued that the recognition by law of intellectual property rights is made by relation to their subservience to the requirements of commercial efficacy and economic principle, one of which is that the grant of such rights must favour the most widespread manufacture and availability of products among the consuming public which collectively suffers the correlative detriment of not being the intellectual property right holder. If there is no benefit to the consumer through the exploitation of intellectual property, there is no justification for its collective detriment. These arguments are not *ad idem*, for that of the property owner is moral, while that of the supporter of compulsory licences is economic. The one can therefore never formally rebut the other.

(v) Unfair competition

2.11 The protection of the creator of intellectual property by means of unfair competition laws is rather less precise (but not necessarily less adequate) than the grant of, say, an absolute or qualified monopoly. The idea behind the grant of an absolute or qualified monopoly in the exploitation of intellectual property is that the right to the sole exploitation of that property is the reward for creating or divulging it. The owner of the monopoly so granted can exploit it himself, or sell or license its exploitation by another, or he may do nothing with it at all. The vast majority of works susceptible to copyright protection, and a regrettably large proportion of those covered by patent protection, are never in fact exploited by means of commercial manufacture and sale. Now, rather than encourage the establishment of monopolies which will never be commercially utilised, the argument runs, why not dispense with the grant of a monopoly and simply render unlawful those activities by others which unfairly prejudice the ability of the intellectual property creator (or his successor in title) to get a fair profit from such intellectual property as he wishes to exploit? The acceptance of this argument entails the implementation of 'unfair competition' rules, which do not exclude others entirely from the use of any identifiable intellectual property, but which do ensure that their use of that property should be fair.[1]

1. J Lahore, 'Unfair Copying: Old Concepts, New Ideas' [1992] EIPR 428.

2.12   UK law does not have a recognised doctrine of unfair competition, and attempts to establish it formally within the common law have always failed.[1] This is not to say that the rules of UK law do not operate as a de facto set of unfair competition rules. The law of passing off, for example, can be used in order to protect from simulation by one trader the appearance, name, style and trading or advertising techniques of another;[2] and the 'springboard' doctrine in breach of confidence law, which prevents a recipient of a trade secret from exploiting it prematurely even once that secret becomes common knowledge and ceases to be intellectual property,[3] are all examples of the operation of principles of unfair competition While 'unfair competition' can, therefore, play a role similar to that of the traditional intellectual property monopolies, it may be criticised on the ground that it is more vulnerable to the vicissitudes of subjective evaluation than is the arbitrary statutory monopoly. It is relatively easy to decide whether a patent or copyright monopoly exists, and the ascertainment of infringement is effected by reference to primarily factual criteria; but whether acts complained of constitute 'unfair' competition depends on one's individual notion of what constitutes 'unfair', and that – however carefully the law seeks to prescribe its parameters – is always likely to be the subject of uncertainty. Where 'unfair competition' may seem the most attractive means of protecting intellectual property rights is where it is contemplated as a replacement for less certain means of legal protection such as passing off. In other countries it is also used to prevent repeated insubstantial takings of protected subject-matter; something which will not usually amount to infringement of the intellectual property rights concerned,[4] but which nonetheless may undermine the right owner's position in the marketplace.[5]

1. See eg the comments of the Privy Council in *Cadbury-Schweppes Ltd v Pub Squash Co Pty Ltd* [1981] RPC 429. Renewed calls for specific laws against unfair competition were made during the passage through Parliament of the Trade Marks Act 1994. An amendment to prohibit 'lookalikes' – imitations of product get-up – was not adopted: Hansard, 16 May 1994, col 301. See, further Ch 19 below.
2. See Ch 20 below.
3. See eg *Saltman Engineering Co Ltd v Campbell Engineering Co Ltd* (1948) 65 RPC 203; *Yates Circuit Foil Co v Electrofoils Ltd* [1976] FSR 345; *Speed Seal v Paddington* [1986] 1 All ER 91.
4. See *Electronic Techniques (Anglia) Ltd v Critchley Components Ltd* [1997] FSR 401.
5. This is recognised in the context of databases: Copyright and Rights in Databases Regulations 1997, SI 1997/3032, reg 16(2).

The significance of contract law

2.13 As already mentioned, the creator of intellectual property may either wish to exploit it himself or he may by contract allow someone else to exploit it instead of (or as well as) himself. In such cases he can protect his own commercial interests by inserting such terms into the contractual licence as he can persuade his licensee to accept. The role played by contract law in the protection of intellectual property rights is not, however, uniform. Where the intellectual property consists of confidential information such as a trade secret, the contract under which it is disclosed to a licensee will give its owner some protection against acts which, under the terms of the contract, the licensee promises not to do (such as disclosing the secret without permission), but it offers little scope for protection against the use of the contents of his secret by a person with whom he has made no contract. The role played by contract in licensing the use of a trade marked, patented, or copyright work is quite different; there the licensor already has full protection against the copying of his work by others, and it is because he already has such protection that he can (in theory) command the sort of licence fee he desires. The purpose then of granting a contractual licence may not be to gain protection but to gain money. It may thus be seen that, while the transmission of intellectual property rights by contract may have the function of protecting such rights, it may not be accurate to regard contract law as being a principal device for the protection of intellectual property. Furthermore, the extent to which contract law may be used is limited by anti-trust or competition laws, in particular Art 81 of the EEC Treaty[1] and the Competition Act 1998.[2]

1. See para **27.5** below.
2. For an early and unsuccessful attempt to undermine a contractual licence between an intellectual property owner and its subsidiary as being anticompetitive and an abuse of a dominant position see *Claritas (UK) Ltd v Post Office and Postal Preference Service Ltd* [2001] ETMR 679.

Restitution, economic torts and intellectual property

2.14 Allied both to the contractual approach and that of unfair competition is the law of restitution.[1] This area of the law deals with concepts such as unjust enrichment, which share some characteristics with the subject matter of this book. A number of commentators have noted parallels.[2] It should also be borne in mind that passing off and infringements of intellectual property may be regarded as economic torts, to be seen in the context of such torts in general.[3]

2.14   *Protectability of intellectual property*

1. For a refreshingly helpful appreciation of this body of law see G Virgo *Principles of the Law of Restitution* (1999), P Jaffey *The Nature and Scope of Restitution* (2000).
2. Eg A Kamperman Sanders *Unfair Competition Law* (1977); W Gordon 'On Owning Information – Intellectual Property and the Restitutionary Impulse' (1992) 78 VLR 149.
3. For which, see H Carty *An Analysis of the Economic Torts* (2001).

Part II

Inventions

Chapter 3

Protecting inventions

Inventions in nature

3.1 Leaving aside for a moment the activities of *homo sapiens*, the act of invention – whether as a result of an intellectual process or as an apparently random consequence of evolution – would seem to be a well-recognised phenomenon. Thus the weaver bird, endowed with apparently scant intellectual apparatus and without the benefit of a prehensile thumb, conceived and taught itself how to weave a nest of great intricacy, while the bee constructs the honeycomb, the spider its web and the termite its labyrinthine towers. Moving from products to processes we note the ability of primates to utilise sticks and other raw materials as tools, and the constructional skills demonstrated by the beaver in constructing its lodge. In none of these cases is there any natural tendency towards the appropriation of property, in the sense of the assumption of any individual rights in the invention so devised. Indeed, the well-being of the species is in some cases enhanced by, and in others entirely dependent upon, the free copying or adaption of such products or techniques. Natural inventions, it may be noted, are not necessarily antecedent to the development of animal self-expression, but would appear to be established prior to the adoption of perceptible norms of intra-species communication which, in the model of *homo sapiens*, are protectable by the laws of copyright. Thus we hold invention in nature to be antecedent to the acquisition of literary or verbal skills.

3.2 An interesting perspective has been offered by Michael Pendleton,[1] who has pointed out that, at least as far as human beings are concerned, all inventions can be regarded as being comprised of units of information. Under this view, that which appears to our eyes to be an 'invention', a creation of something new, is no more than a synthesis of known units of information, not really an invention at all. Correlative to this view is the assumption that, if each unit of information is a community resource, part of the common heritage of mankind, no edifice constructed from such communal blocks should be able to constitute a privately-owned invention. The modern intellectual property lawyer finds it difficult to accept this, unless he can persuade himself that there is no difference between a palace and the pile of bricks from which it is built.

1.   Michael Pendleton, 'Intellectual Property, Information-Based Society and a New International Economic Order – the Policy Options?' [1985] EIPR 31.

Why protect?

3.3   Since it is man, and man alone, who has required that his inventions be protected from unauthorised emulation by others, it is worth pausing to enquire as to why this is so. The lawyer who has been educated within the great human rights traditions of the civil law of continental Europe would hold an invention to be an appropriate subject of property by virtue of the fact that it has been created by the skill and labour of an individual. Such a right might be accorded him along with his other natural rights such as freedom of association, liberty or equality, by virtue of his essential humanity. The common lawyer of the Anglo-American tradition would probably disagree, and say that property in an invention was not a natural right to which all are inherently entitled so much as a right which exists only to the extent that a deliberate legal act has made it so, and which should only exist to the extent that it confers a practical advantage or use on one party which outweighs the detriment of it to others.[1] Which of these positions is correct is a matter of personal taste and of jurisprudential speculation;[2] the former is little more than an unverifiable assertion, while the latter pursues an understanding of law by abandoning the pursuit of any higher morality. Perhaps there is justification for adopting a position which seeks to recognise the essential attractive force of each, by maintaining that the continental approach emphasises the importance of man's aspirations to justice under the law, while the common law approach focuses firmly upon the concept of *lex lata* as the final arbiter of man's claims to justice. The rotation of the earth around its axis does not, however, depend upon the resolution of this issue.[3]

1.   Note eg 'functional' approaches recorded in the title of the 1709 Copyright Act ('An Act for the encouragement of Learning by vesting the Copies of Printed Books in the Authors or Purchasers of such Copies during the Times herein mentioned') and the United States Constitution, art 1, para 8 ('The Congress shall have Power . . . to Promote the Progress of Science and Useful Arts, by securing to Authors and Inventors the exclusive Right to their Respective Writings and Discoveries').

2. For a sustained analysis, see P Drahos *A Philosophy of Intellectual Property* (1996).
3. See also, D Vaver 'Some Agnostic Thoughts on Intellectual Property' (1991) 6 IPJ 125.

How to protect?

3.4 Consideration of the previous chapter[1] reveals that there are five potential means of turning an invention into legal property. One could grant an absolute right to the inventor to use it, and to prevent others from doing so; one could qualify this right by allowing senior competitors to strip an invention down to its basic components and then re-engineer it into their own products, while ordinary copying remains forbidden; one could grant a right to prevent the copying of the invention, while leaving it free to another inventor to make the same invention independently; one could simply allow the inventor the privilege of raising a levy on use of his invention, without his having any right to prevent its use; or one could give him no right save that of objecting to any unauthorised use which interfered with his legitimate expectation of being able to derive a reasonable benefit from the invention. Curiously enough one finds in current British patent literature little discussion either of whether inventions should be treated as property at all,[2] or of which of the five legal approaches mentioned above best fits the needs of inventors and potential users of the invention. So far as international patent protection is concerned, however, there is a wealth of literature on the subject, largely devoted to the heated issue of whether a patent owner's right to prevent others working an invention in another country, in which he (the patent owner) chooses not to manufacture the invention himself, is a natural property right or an abuse of his monopoly.

1. See paras **2.3-2.12** above.
2. Cf the rich nineteenth-century literature on the subject, such as R Macfie, *Copyright and Patents for Inventions: Pleas and Plans for Cheaper Books and Greater Industrial Freedom* (1883); N N *On Intellectual Property* (1876). A bibliography of the writings of McFie and his contemporaries may be found in M Coulter *Property in Ideas* (1990).

3.5 The basic argument in favour of protecting inventions through the grant of absolute monopoly runs as follows: (i) it costs money to make and test an invention;[1] (ii) the money thus laid out ought to be recouped by the inventor when he exploits his invention; (iii) if others could emulate that invention without having encountered the same primary cost, they could exploit the invention by copying it more cheaply, thus obtaining a profit for themselves while depriving the inventor of the opportunity of recouping his outlay.[2] To counter the argument that it is unfair to deprive all but the inventor of the opportunity of making or using the subject of the invention, it is stipulated under the law of the UK and in most patents systems that:

(i) an invention which is the subject of a monopoly should be novel and not therefore previously known or available to the monopolist's competitors. Those competitors would not therefore be prevented from doing anything which they were previously doing;[3] and

(ii) the monopoly should in any event be limited in time, and not perpetual.[4] This limitation is unparalleled in other forms of property law, where plots of land, buildings, jewellery and kitchen utensils do not simply cease to be property after the passage of a number of years, and it indicates the economic basis for treating inventions as property: once a set number of years has elapsed, the monopoly owner is deemed to have had sufficient opportunity to exploit his commercial advantage and recoup his expenses. His competitors are therefore enabled to utilise his invention too, and it becomes part of the 'public domain'.[5] Note that if the true basis for treating inventions as property is moral, rather than practical and economic, it becomes difficult to justify the temporary duration of its proprietary nature.

1. Eg *The Innovations Report: a Buyer's Guide*, Autumn/Winter 1990, p 26, where the Space Pen, developed at a cost of $1m, was advertised at just £14.95.
2. For a good account of protection philosophy see J Aubrey 'A Justification of the Patent System' in J Phillips (ed), *Patents in Perspective* (1985).
3. Patents Act 1977, s 1(1); see also *The Clothworkers of Ipswich* (1614) Godb 252, where Coke CJ said '... for when the trade is become common ... there is no reason that such should be forbidden to use it'.
4. Patents Act 1977, s 25(1).
5. 'Public domain' is regarded for patent purposes as a domain to which the public has free, unlimited access. The same is true for copyright, except that in some countries the public domain may be regarded as being a property which is held in trust for the benefit of authors and others, and may not be used without payment: see eg Italy's Law No 633 of 22 April 1941 on the protection of copyright and other rights, arts 175ff. For the purposes of unregistered design rights, the public domain consists of designs which are commonplace – a peculiarly subjective criterion by which works may move from the public domain to private ownership, or vice versa, in response to whims of fashion. See, generally, J Phillips 'The Diminishing Domain', [1996] EIPR 429.

3.6 The economic argument in favour of the absolute monopoly apparently acts against the adoption of any qualified or limited monopoly principle; for if any of the first inventor's competitors is free to utilise the same invention by virtue of his having independently conceived of it himself, or through a legitimate form of 'reverse engineering', then the first inventor will once again be deprived of the benefit of the monopoly as a means of recouping his research and development (R & D) expenditure. On the other hand, it can be seen that any limited monopoly principle works to the benefit of the second inventor who, in the case of the absolute monopoly principle, has also incurred R & D expenditure but has, once the first inventor's monopoly is established, no expectation of being able to recoup his R & D costs at all. What would happen if both the first and second inventor were each to enjoy a qualified monopoly in their invention, each being able to use, sell or license to others? In theory each could exploit the invention and exclude others from doing so, which would give each a chance to recoup his R & D costs and gain a reasonable expectation of profit. Each would still, of course, be in competition with the other, which would mean that a prospective licensee could 'shop around' between them until he obtained a licence on terms most favourable to himself. In reality, though, the operation of two separate monopolies in respect of the identical invention would produce grave problems with regard to enforcement, proof and damages, and could so devalue the monopoly as to render investment in its exploitation an even more risky and uncertain business than it is at present.

3.7 How does the 'compulsory licence' proprietary interest compare with that of the monopoly? It is clear that the inventor who has no exclusive right of control over his invention cannot exclude rivals from manufacturing or using it; but he could expect an income commensurate with the extent of the use of his invention by others. Where revenue derived from this use very substantially exceeds his R & D costs, it may provide him with a substantial benefit; but it may well be that product competition will deprive him of the incentive to secure the sort of profit, in a market controlled by him, which could have tempted him (or his shareholders) to put up the capital for R & D activity of uncertain outcome. It has been asserted that only with the establishment of a firm legal monopoly will any capitalist – whether the inventor or not – feel confident about bringing a new product into a market which has not yet been proved to exist for it. This assertion may certainly be true in individual cases, but it is difficult to derive from it a principle that innovation will be stifled without monopoly protection. If one looks, for example, at the expansion of the biotechnology industry, one sees the result of huge R & D expense being incurred in a market where the extent of the availability of legal protection by patent monopoly was unclear and where the effectiveness of protection by patent law had not yet been satisfactorily established.

3.8 The 'compulsory licence' solution has two further points to commend it. First it renders largely unnecessary the sort of destructive litigation which has for so long characterised the patent system, where one party sues the other for patent infringement and the other counterclaims that the patent is invalid.[1] If the patent-monopolist wins, he drives the infringer from the market; if he loses, then his property in his invention is destroyed. The high stakes of this 'winner-take-all' litigation may not be seen to favour an out-of-court settlement, especially since the monopolist's failure to act in defence of his property in his invention may be an encouragement to others to infringe it, and may even be viewed as tacit admission that his monopoly would not stand up to the severe judicial scrutiny of the court. 'Compulsory licence' litigation would be much less vicious since it would not be determinative of the sole right to operate within a market; instead, it would be for the patentee to show that the invention in issue has been used by another party, and then to sue for the payment of a reasonable licence royalty. Invalidity proceedings would still be available, but the defendant's right to use the invention would no longer depend upon their outcome. Moreover, to the extent that the availability of a compulsory licence encourages the manufacture and use of inventions among competing firms, it would appear to benefit the consuming public through the provision of greater customer choice and through price competition.[2]

1. For a further mention of these tactics see para **8.1**.
2. This point was effectively argued with regard to industrially exploited copyright in the Monopolies and Mergers Commission's Report, *Ford Motor Company Ltd*, Cmnd 9437 1985, especially at para 6.70. It is, however, not accepted by owners of pharmaceutical patents, who successfully lobbied for the life of their patents in Europe to be extended by the use of supplementary protection certificates under Council Regulation (EEC) 1768/92 of 18 June 1992, OJ L182/1 of 2 July 1992: see para **27.7**.

3.9 Against the compulsory licence has, however, been raised the objection that there is no simple and arbitrary manner by which the amount of the royalty can be calculated.[1] Should it take into account the expense of initial R & D or the commercial value of its exploitation, or both? Should it have regard to the circumstance that the manufacturing capacity of the licensor is greater than that of the licensee, or vice versa? Should it take into account the length of the unexpired term of the property right, at the end of which the invention may be used without cost by the public, or should it not? And should it take account of the social value of the invention? If a means of fixing a level of royalty payments acceptable to licensor and licensee cannot be easily found, then the expense of referral of the matter to an arbitral body, and the resulting uncertainty, may detract from the advantages of the 'compulsory licence' system.

1. Analysis of cases suggests that the Patent Office tends to look for a 'going rate' in the industry concerned. See, eg, A Firth 'Licences of Right: "New Existing Patents" under the Patents Act 1977' [1986] EIPR 168.

3.10   A further means of protecting the interest of the owner of the invention, that of allowing its use by others to the extent that such use does not conflict with his reasonable commercial expectation, would seem to offer or facilitate an insufficiently precise or reliable degree of recompense to merit serious consideration. This is not to say that it is entirely without relevance to the question of the extent of the monopolist's protection, because criteria which may be described as corresponding to the principles of unfair competition have been pressed into service as a means of limiting the extent of the inventor's absolute monopoly.[1]

1. Patents Act 1977, ss 60(5)(a)-(c), 64(1). Note that Art 82 of the EC Treaty may also limit rights where they are exercised to prevent the development of new markets: see, further, para **27.5** below.

3.11   Which of these competing varieties of patent protection is the right one? To this question there is no easy answer. This is because what suits one economic system is not necessarily apt for another. The competition-oriented economies of Western Europe, the United States and Japan, for instance, have hitherto favoured the absolute monopoly as a means of encouraging free enterprise and technological growth. The successful inventor is rewarded with his monopoly. With it he may do nothing, or he may exploit it. If he exploits it, his competitors are forced to challenge the validity of his patent, or to compete by making their own inventions from which the original inventor is excluded, or to seek a fresh market entirely (or they may go to the wall).

3.12   In the formerly socialist eastern European economies, where the resources allocated for commercial and industrial enterprise were for the most part controlled by the state, private monopolies were viewed with ideological suspicion and the inevitable waste through duplicated research, market saturation and so on was regarded as an unjustifiable extravagance. They therefore tended to favour the 'compulsory licence' approach in the form of 'inventors' certificates'. This form of invention recognition no longer enjoys support and has been largely superseded by the traditional monopoly.[1] In the less industrialised regions of the world there is a preference for a monopoly-based system of invention protection but, in truth, in many such countries, where resources and capital are unfortunately scarce and the market is small, simply to be the first supplier on the market is often to establish one's own de facto monopoly, for the market may not be large enough to give the second competitor even a viable toehold.[2] This fact has not, however, prevented countries from adopting patent systems as a means of complying with the 'TRIPs' agreement, on Trade-Related aspects of Intellectual Property Rights, in order to join the World Trade Organization.[3]

1. See Dr A von Füner, 'Perestroika and Patents' (1990) 23 Patent World 30.
2. For an account of the non-impact of intellectual property rights upon a developing country, see *Transfer and Development of Technology in Rwanda*, UNCTAD Report No UNCTAD/TT/511982; P Drahos cites a number of studies in 'Intellectual Property and Human Rights' [1999] IPQ at n 53.
3. See para **28.2** below.

Innovation warrants

3.13   The protection of inventions not yet intellectually conceived, and existing only as a desirable end, may seem fanciful; yet there is some similarity between such protection and the age-old custom of granting mineral rights over land. The holder of such a privilege is given the right to search a particular area and, if he finds anything, to keep and exploit his find. Just as only one enterprise at a time can physically dig down under the earth in any given location in search of gold or whatever, so (the analogy goes) only one party should be permitted to work in a particular intellectual property field. Thus one would imagine the world divided up not physically but commercially, into markets, and the right to protection within a particular market not yet in existence could be sold off to an appropriate prospector. An example could go as follows: electric-cum-petrol powered cars are, as all agree, a good idea, but the expense of R & D, coupled with the knowledge that even a successful end-product would not necessarily be patentable,[1] would act as a disincentive to innovate. An exclusive right to 'prospect' the area would preserve the worth of one's R & D risks and make one less vulnerable to competition from the second-on-the-market producer who gets a 'free ride' on the pioneering innovator's hard-earned experience. The holder of a 'prospecting licence' would also be able to co-ordinate R & D of others, leading to the development of new products with one manufacturing standard instead of many (as in the case of microcomputers, video cassette recorders and cellular telephone systems). This approach to the protection of innovation, through granting a monopoly in a market and not in a product or process, is however open to objections. Protection of the market itself would inhibit competition and the benefits which competition brings; there is also the question of how one should evaluate a potential monopolist's competence to hold such a right; should the grantee be the first person to identify an unexploited market, or the first person to prove himself capable of performing the R & D necessary to bring the market's demands to fruition?

1. Patents Act 1977, s 1(1), discussed in Ch 5 below.

3.14 In contrast to the existing patent system's criteria of protection, and with the proposal outlined in the previous paragraph, there lies the possibility of granting protection only to such inventions as are actually marketed. Since no patent confers a genuine benefit upon mankind in the absence of commercial or industrial exploitation, and since mankind charitably grants far more patents than are actually exploited, there is a case for saying that the benefit conferred upon society by the product innovator should be a condition precedent of his deriving protection in return for it. The 'innovation warrant', hypothesised and forcibly argued by William Kingston,[1] derives some sustenance from this notion. This warrant would be accorded to the first to market a product (not a process); it would grant monopoly rights which, in terms of their duration and extent, would be carefully tailored to the industrial and commercial milieu of the product in question. Kingston's proposals have enjoyed some support amongst the business and economic communities, but have not been popular amongst lawyers and administrators. This is because legal protection would be a function of what is presumed to be justice in the individual case, and it is difficult to build up legal rules, or to advise clients, on the basis of principles which do not enjoy general application or the support of a doctrine of precedent. It is also difficult to see precisely how 'innovation warrant' protection would respond to the particular challenge of, say, the pharmaceutical industry, when currently patent protection is most important for a very long period of time, when a product is in a 'limbo' state between having been invented and having satisfied the health administration as to its safety and therefore its marketability.

1. See W Kingston 'Innovation Patents and Warrants' in J Phillips (ed) *Patents in Perspective* (1985); 'Recognizing the Difference' *The Times*, 22 August 1983. On the relationship between innovation and invention and other proposals, see further W Kingston 'The Patent System – Unexploited Potential' in CIPA Centenary Lectures (1992), Queen Mary & Westfield College.

Petty patents or utility models

3.15 Many countries have a 'petty patent' or 'utility model' system,[1] to reward and protect small inventions – for example, functional improvements in hand tools or other useful articles. Under many laws, utility models do not protect processes or subject matter such as chemical formulae. Local novelty is usually required, but often no degree of inventive step. The UK does not at present have a system of utility model protection. The fact that it, along with Luxembourg and Sweden, does not do so is regarded as distorting the single European market, which is why there now exists a draft harmonisation directive,[2] the effect of which would be to compel the UK to adopt a utility model system. Although there is considerable scepticism in the UK as to the value of such an instrument,[3] other countries appear to have benefited enormously from it. Since in almost every country that offers utility model protection the preponderant majority of rights are held by local businesses against foreign competitors, it is paradoxical that the implementation of national utility model systems throughout the EU may make it more difficult, not less, for manufactured products to move freely within the single European market.[4]

1. U Suthersanen 'A Brief Tour of Utility Model Law' [1998] EIPR 44.
2. Proposal for Directive approximating the legal arrangements for the Protection of Inventions by Utility Model [1998] OJ C36/13; amended proposal COM (99) 309, adopted by the Commission on 30 June 1999.
3. See the arguments set forth in M Llewelyn 'The Model Myth' Patent World, February 1996, p 32; R Jacob 'Industrial Property: Industry's Enemy' [1997] IPQ 3; C Lees 'Utility Models: a Question of Balance' Patent World, May 1999, p 20.
4. For example, WIPO's filing figures for 1999 show that in Spain 3,094 utility models were filed by domestic applicants, but just 170 by foreigners; in Italy the figures are 2,804 and 158 respectively.

3.16 Only harmonisation of national laws is proposed, not a Europe-wide system of protection. National offices would examine applications as to form, but not carry out any substantive examination of the merits of the application – whether it met the requirements of novelty, and low inventive step, viz 'presenting an advantage and not very obvious'.[1] The advantage presented could be practical and technical or educational or of value in entertainment. The latter would seem to stray towards the realm of copyright. A search of 'prior art' would be optional during application, but compulsory in the event of legal proceedings for enforcement. Maximum duration would be ten years.[2] Involuntary licensing would follow the practice for patents in the state concerned.[3] These features were presented as advantageous to small and medium-sized enterprises. However, large businesses would be as likely as small to apply for protection.

1. Art 6.1; see para **3.15**, n 2.
2. Art 19.
3. Art 20.6; see Beier 'Exclusive Rights, Statutory Licences and Compulsory Licences in Patent and Utility Model Law' (1999) IIC 251.

Chapter 4

Inventions and the patent system

Introduction to the patent system

Where did the patent system come from?

4.1 The practice of granting monopolies by letters patent has a long history which it is not necessary to record here.[1] Suffice to say that the patent system as we know it today was not conceived until 1852.[2] Prior to that there is a period of over 500 years in which patent monopolies were granted, quite often to inventors but not necessarily because they were inventors.

1. See eg N Davenport *The United Kingdom Patent System* (1979); J Phillips *Charles Dickens and the 'Poor Man's Tale of a Patent'* (1984); H Fox *Monopolies and Patents: a Study of the History and Future of the Patent Monopoly* (1974).
2. The Patent Law Amendment Act 1852, which established a Patent Office, reduced and rationalised application fees, required the printing and serial numbering of patent specifications and introduced the concept of the 'provisional' application.

What is a patent?

4.2 Nowadays the word is synonymous with a monopoly right in an invention, but its use results from a colloquial abbreviation. When the Crown granted any right to an individual, it could do so by writing out a document to which the king's or queen's seal was appended. If anyone challenged that individual's right to do what was within the terms of his royal privilege, the holder of the document could show it to the objector by way of proof of his entitlement to do it. Such a grant was therefore evidenced by 'letters patent', ie a document which was not sealed up, but which was rolled up, with the seal being appended at the bottom. It was thus open (or 'patent' from the Latin). While 'letters patent' were granted for a number of other purposes, for example, the appointment of High Court judges or the grant of mining rights, they were most frequently granted to inventors, so the word 'patent' was eventually used to describe the inventor's monopoly.

4.3 *Inventions and the patent system*

How is 'patent' pronounced?

4.3 The word 'patent' may be pronounced with either a long or short 'a' without causing undue offence. It appears to this author that, as a rough generalisation, the short 'a' is more frequently employed to refer to the inventor's monopoly (ie a patent; the patent system), while the long 'a' is reserved for other adjectival uses (eg 'patent leather', 'patent stupidity'). Another commentator has referred to a hybrid pronunciation which is presumably prevalent in some areas of East London,[1] but the Latin etymology of the word would favour a short 'a' throughout.

1. P Meinhardt *Inventions, Patents and Trade Marks* (1971) at p 20.

When did patents start?

4.4 The first English patents were granted from 1331 to foreigners who wished to practise their crafts in England. There was no conception of their having to invent anything: they needed merely to come and work, and the patent would act as a sort of 'safe-conduct pass' if they were threatened by local rivals or guildsmen. Eventually in 1559 the talented Jacobo Aconcio, an elderly Italian emigré who fortified Berwick against the Scots and attempted the drainage of Plumstead Marshes, asked for a patent not because he was a foreigner who wanted protection but because, he pleaded, it was unfair that anyone who wished could copy his invention to his detriment.[1] From this date onwards the Crown would seem to have granted patents of two distinct kinds: monopolies in inventions, which were favourably viewed by Parliament and the public, and monopolies over things which were already invented, including a number of consumer staple products, which were viewed with great resentment by frustrated traders and distressed citizens.

1. On the activities of Aconcio see J Phillips 'The English Patent as a Reward for Invention' [1983] EIPR 41.

4.5 After the *Case of Monopolies* in 1602[1] (which struck down a royal monopoly on the manufacture of playing cards) and the Statute of Monopolies 1623,[2] the Crown's prerogative to grant patent monopolies was restricted to the extent that, while monopolies for new and useful inventions could be granted, unproductive monopolies for the benefit of court favourites could not.

1. *Darcy v Allen* (1602) 11 Co Rep 84b, noted by D Seabourne Davies 'Further Light on the Case of Monopolies' (1932) 48 LQR 396.
2. 21 Jac 1 c 3.

34

The disclosure of inventions

4.6　During the sixteenth and seventeenth centuries the would-be monopolist had to plead with the king or queen for the right to acquire protection for his invention, often offering the Crown some sort of financial inducement in return. During this period there was no general principle that the patent applicant had to tell anyone else the details of his invention. But by the early eighteenth century, when the monarch spoke little English and many of his functions were dealt with by officers of the state, a change took place. A monopoly in any invention would be granted automatically to any applicant who claimed to be the true and first inventor and who deposited with the Crown's officers a description of his invention. This description, later known as the 'specification', became the *raison d'être* of subsequent patent philosophy: the patent monopoly ceased to be an exercise of the royal whim and became instead an effective 'contract' between the Crown and the inventor. Under the terms of this contract the inventor had to disclose to the Crown (and therefore to the public, on whose behalf the Crown rules) the details of his invention, in return for which the Crown granted absolute protection against the unauthorised copying of that invention for a stated term of years.[1]

1.　The 'contract' theory is reflected in a number of old patent decisions, eg *R v Wheeler* (1819) 2 B & Ald 345; *Harmer v Plane* (1807) 14 Ves 130; *Patterson v Gas Light and Coke Co* (1875) 2 Ch D 812.

Rationalising the patent system

4.7　Once the granting of patents was dependent not upon royal patronage but upon the making of an application in appropriate form to the Solicitor General or Attorney General,[1] the patent system remained, until the time of the Great Exhibition in 1851, more a means of collecting a multiplicity of fees from inventors than the procedure for the systematic examination of applications and storage of information contained in specifications which is familiar to modern inventors. The inadequacies and expense of the patent granting process were pilloried by Charles Dickens in his short story, *A Poor Man's Tale of a Patent*.[2] Dickens' pungent exposé, together with the unanswerable case for the efficient storage, cataloguing and publication of patent specifications,[3] led to swift legislative reform in 1852 when the responsibility for the patent system was taken away from the Law Officers of the Crown and vested in independent Commissioners for Patents.[4] In 1855 the Patent Office Library[5] was opened and, for the first time, it became possible for inventors and other users to get some idea of the scientific developments which had taken place in their own fields of interest. Though the patent system has changed radically since the 1850s in terms of its details of operation and function (as will be explained below), many of its currently recognisable aims and objects stem from that period.

1. On which see Vindicator 'On the Fees and Charges upon Patents for Inventions', (1829) 2 London Journal of Arts and Sciences 311.
2. First published in *Household Words* 19 October 1850; reprinted in J Phillips *Charles Dickens and the 'Poor Man's Tale of a Patent'* (1984).
3. On the first publication of specifications see J Hewish *The Indefatigable Mr Woodcraft* (1982) pp 22-29.
4. See para **4.1**, n 2 above.
5. The Patent Office Library is now part of the British Library.

The modern patent system

4.8　A series of statutory reforms, culminating in the Patents Act 1949, gave the United Kingdom a relatively streamlined and sophisticated patent system, but it was superseded in 1977 by new legislation which was only partially concerned with the state of domestic patent law. The principal effect of the Patents Act 1977[1] has been to draw UK patent law closer to that of its major European trading partners, in accordance with the provisions of the European Patent Convention.[2] The implementation of this Convention by its Member States (Austria, Belgium, Cyprus, Denmark, the Republic of Ireland, Finland, France, Germany, Greece, Italy, Liechtenstein, Luxembourg, Monaco, the Netherlands, Portugal, Spain, Sweden, Switzerland, Turkey and the United Kingdom as of August 2001[3]) has resulted in the establishment of more or less common criteria of patentability and in the operation of a European Patent Office (EPO) in Munich. If an applicant wishes to take out patents in three or more of these countries, he can do so more cheaply and efficiently by making a single application through the EPO than by making separate applications to the countries concerned. As can be imagined, this facility has substantially reduced the attractiveness of the purely national patent application,[4] but it is safer for the cautious applicant to seek national patent protection on a state-by-state basis if the patentability of his invention is in doubt; once the EPO rejects an application, it automatically fails in all its Member States unless any individual Member State provides by its domestic law that it should not do so,[5] but state-by-state applications may leave him with at least some patents at the end of the day. A Diplomatic Conference in November 2000 agreed revisions to the European Patent Convention, in particular relating to the assessment of novelty and infringement.

1. For a critique of the operation of the 1977 Act, see R Jacob (now Jacob J) 'The Success of the 1977 Act' [1993] EIPR 312.
2. Convention on the Grant of European Patents, Munich, 5 October 1973 (Cmnd 5656).
3. A number of European countries from the former Eastern bloc have been invited to join the Convention on 1 July 2002: Bulgaria, Czech Republic, Estonia, Hungary, Poland, Romania, Slovakia, Slovenia: EPO Press Release 1/99.
4. The Comptroller's Annual Reports indicate that the volume of UK patent applications diminished from 54,423 in 1977 to only 27,178 in 1992. Recently, there have been modest increases, to 30,467 in 1999, probably assisted by the Patent Office's decision to reduce fees: see para **6.14** below. Other patent offices were harder hit. For example, the Netherlands received 3,226 patent applications in 1977 but only some 595 direct in 1991.
5. European Patent Convention, art 135(1)(b).

The European Community and the world

4.9 There is not yet a single patent for the whole territory of the EC, but the Patents Act 1977 was 'geared up' for the future coming into force of the Community Patent Convention[1] (CPC). This instrument has been amended,[2] but to date has not been implemented[3] and is now likely to be superseded by a Community Patent Regulation by analogy with the successful model of the Community Trade Mark Regulation.[4] The Community Patent will be achieved by providing that the EC is a single designated state for the purpose of granting European patents, and that a patent granted under the EPC route in respect of any EC country will take effect throughout the EC.[5] The Community patent is designed to complement the existing national patents.[6] The Patents Act 1977 also provides for the operation of the facility of the Patent Co-operation Treaty (PCT), which simplifies and cheapens the whole business of obtaining a multiplicity of patents across the globe.[7] Currently the PCT facilitates the making of applications in over 100 countries.[8] Under the terms of the PCT it is possible to file for international patent protection, designating as many PCT member states as the applicant seeks protection in. The EPC countries can be designated together through a PCT application; indeed this happens in about 95% of applications.

1. See Patents Act 1977, ss 86-88.
2. Community Patent Agreement 1993.
3. A major obstacle has been the issue of languages: whether the system should use English only, the three official languages of the EPO (English, French, German) all the official languages of EC Member States (which would involve much expensive translation work) or some other combination.
4. Council Regulation No 40/94.
5. Unless the applicant requests otherwise.

6. For a proposal to combine the EPC and CPC see van Benthem 'The European Patent System and European Internality' (1993) 24 IIC 435.
7. See Patents Act 1977, s 89.
8. An up-to-date list of countries which belong to the PCT (administered by the World Intellectual Property Organization) is printed in each month's issue of WIPO's PCT Newsletter or may be found on the WIPO website at www.wipo.int.

What is an invention?

4.10   Curiously enough, the Patents Act 1977 does not define the word 'invention' in an intelligible manner at all; it assumes that everyone knows what an invention is, and then qualifies this assumption by declaring that, for its purposes, some things are not inventions. Some may feel that this is a bit like defining an elephant as anything which is generally accepted to be an elephant but excluding cows, dogs and hens; however, the failure to define 'invention' is, probably, not merely excusable but even justifiable. First it should be noted that from the Statute of Monopolies in 1623 to the Patents Act 1949, 'invention' was defined as 'any manner of new manufacture', a vague definition which may be regarded as providing a necessary condition without which something is not an invention, but which does little to help one to identify one of any given set of facts. Second, it is hard to conceive of a precise definition of a word such as 'invention' which is capable of denoting, in colloquial terms, both the act of inventing and the result of that act, and which can extend to physically tangible things, to processes or methods as applied to them, and to processes by which they are applied to other things (eg to a new insecticide, or to a new and more effective means of applying insecticides to insects). Third, one rarely needs to know whether something is an invention or not, for legal purposes, unless it is to ascertain whether it is patentable.[1] The criteria of patentability are stringent and often difficult to fulfil but they at least are concisely defined. In purely practical terms no good purpose can be served by refusing to grant a patent to something which fulfils the criteria of patentability but which is not, on the basis of any legal definition, capable of being regarded as an invention, unless that refusal is justified by the fact that the would-be invention is already susceptible to legal protection outside the Patents Act. Lastly, it might be illogical to suppose that something previously unknown could be defined in advance.

1. An important exception is the Patents Act 1977, s 39, which determines the ownership of inventions, not merely of patents: considered in *Re Viziball Ltd's Application* [1988] RPC 213. The term 'invention' was considered in *Biogen v Medeva* [1997] RPC 1 at 31.

What is not an invention?

4.11   According to the Patents Act 1977, section 1(2), the following are not inventions:

(i)   A discovery – therefore merely to find a hitherto unknown substance which exists in nature is not to make an invention; nor is it an invention to discover a physical property of such a substance (eg that it is magnetic, water-soluble or has good heat conduction properties).[1] However, a discovery may lead to a product or process which is patentable. It has been argued that discoveries themselves should be included in the category of patentable inventions, since discovery is itself a meritorious and often arduous endeavour and since the discoverer may need the stimulus of a monopoly as an incentive to disclose his find,[2] but the patentability of discoveries would result in man's expropriation of nature itself, and it is difficult to justify the expropriation by one of what is already the natural legacy of all.[3]

(ii)   A scientific theory – this means that Einstein's theory of relativity and the various accounts of 'black holes' in space cannot be inventions. This exclusion is entirely sensible since, being no more than hypotheses or explanations as to how physical events occur, theories cannot as such be realistically exploited industrially. On the other hand, a device which operates through the practical application of a scientific theory will be regarded as an invention.

(iii)   A mathematical method – thus a means of calculating square roots, or of resolving equations, would not be considered an invention. At best it is no more than a useful idea, which cannot of itself be monopolised. Once again, though, a device for the performance of such methods will be an invention.[4]

(iv)   A literary, dramatic, musical or artistic work – since these are all covered by Part I of the Copyright, Designs and Patents Act 1988, there seems no need to provide a dual system of legal protection, especially when the copyright protection is of substantially greater duration than that of the Patents Act.[5] Sometimes a product which is undeniably an invention (eg a cigarette lighter or a safety belt harness clasp) will have a certain aesthetic appeal or arresting visual quality. The mere fact that it does so will not disentitle it to any protection offered under the Patents Act, but to the extent that it has any visual appeal it is protectable only by copyright or industrial design law.[6]

(v)   Any aesthetic creation not included under (iv) above – in other words, films, sound recordings and such like. This is not to say that a new type of CD is not capable of being an invention, for it will be if it is a new product. It is merely to establish that a known type of CD cannot be regarded as an invention if the only thing which distinguishes it from previously existing CDs is the item recorded on it (sound recordings are, however, protected by copyright under the Copyright, Designs and Patents Act 1988).[7]

(vi) A scheme, rule or method for performing a mental act – it would be unrealistic to expect any law to be able to stop a person from thinking or performing, for example, mental arithmetic, in a particular manner. In *Fujitsu's Application*,[8] a means of analysing and visualising the structure of crystals was computer-aided, but still unpatentable as a mental act. On the other hand, the cynic might argue, there is no reason to exclude them from being inventions for, even though any resulting patent would be useless to its holder, it would provide revenue for the Patent Office which issues it.

(vii) A scheme, rule or method of playing a game or doing business – thus a formula for success in 'Monopoly', a new chess opening or a new cost-effective scheme for the re-stocking of merchandise are not inventions, although the form of their presentation may be protected by copyright and they may in any event be protected by the laws relating to trade (and other) secrets.[9]

(viii) A program[10] for a computer – this exclusion is based upon the analogy between the computer and the human brain. Just as matter processed or a thought-process utilised by the latter cannot be regarded as invention, so the computer's 'mental' instructions are likewise treated as being methods for performing a mental act. This analogy is not a compelling one,[11] but there is sound legal policy to support it: the conception of a computer program is a matter of the application of programming techniques (which are frequently within the common professional expertise of the programming industry) to a particular problem. It has been thought unfair to treat as an invention (and therefore as something capable of being 'property') anything which depends for its unique nature upon the scope of the problem which the programmer sets out to solve, rather than upon any inventive thought-process of the programmer. The protection of computer programs has most commonly been regarded, both in the UK and elsewhere, as a matter for copyright law.[12] However, a computer which has been programmed in a particular manner may be regarded as an invention, provided that it produces a concrete, technical result.[13] Conversely, if the computer as programmed merely performs an excluded task, such as the performance of a mental act[14] or a method of presenting information or doing business,[15] it is not patentable. The distinction between a standard computer, programmed to produce a technical effect and thus patentable, and the program itself or on a carrier, became difficult to sustain. In the light of EPO practice and UK case law, the UK Patent Office has announced[16] that it will grant patents for computer programs having a suitable technical effect. In the US[17] a more sympathetic attitude has been taken towards the patentability of computer programs per se.

(ix) The presentation of information – a new scheme for presenting what is already known is not treated as an invention although a device which embodies that scheme may be. Once again, it is the law of copyright which is thus open to protect the particular form taken by such a presentation.

1. See eg Lindley LJ in *Lane Fox v Kensington and Knightsbridge Electric Lighting Co* (1892) 9 RPC 413 at 426 ('When Volta discovered the effect of electric current from a battery on a frog's leg he made a great discovery, but no patentable invention').

2. Plant breeders' rights, however, are available to the discoverer of a new plant variety, even if he had no hand at all in that variety's development. On those rights see Ch 25.

3. This argument is also used against the patenting of life forms – see paras **5.29** and **5.31** below.

4. *Re Gale* [1991] RPC 305.

5. On the duration of copyright see Ch 14.

6. On the protection of industrially applicable designs see Ch 24.

7. Discussed in Ch 12.

8. [1997] RPC 608.

9. See Chs 19 and 20. Contrast the position in the US, where business methods are considered patentable: J Thomas 'An epistemiology of appropriation: patentable subject-matter after State Street Bank' [2000] IPQ 1.

10. Parliament has adopted the American spelling 'program' for computers, while preserving the traditional English 'programme' for cable and broadcast emanations; the *Shorter Oxford English Dictionary* however shows that 'program' is the original English spelling, 'programme' being a more recent French import.

11. The word 'computer' is itself a metaphor. Thus the third edition of the *Shorter Oxford English Dictionary* (revised to 1968) gives as the only meaning of 'computer': 'one who computes', and 'one employed to make calculations in an observatory'.

12. See eg *VICOM/Computer-related Invention* [1987] 2 EPOR 74, subsequently followed in a number of UK and European Patent Office cases, most influentially in EPO cases T0935/97 [1999] EPOR 301 and T1173/97 [2000] EPOR 219 (both applications by *International Business Machines Corpn (IBM)*. See Laakonen & Whaite 'The EPO Simplifies Software Patenting' [1999] IPQ 487; K Beresford 'The Patenting of Software in Europe and the UK' Patent World, April 1997, p 14.

13. *Raytheon Co's Application* [1993] RPC 427; *Fujitsu's Application* [1997] RPC 608.

14. *Merrill Lynch's Application* [1989] RPC 561.

15. See Ch 23 below; G Lea 'Software Protection Trends in the 1990s' [1995] Ent LR 276.

16. See Practice Note [1999] RPC 563; R Davis 'Patentability of Computer Software' [2000] NLJ 65.
17. M J Lennon 'US Software Patents', Managing Intellectual Property, June 1994, p 31.

4.12 The exclusions from the definition of an invention may be categorised into two main groups: those things which are actually or inherently protectable by copyright law, and those things which are no more than disembodied ideas, schemes or formulae and which have no practical, physical dimension in which they can be commercially exploited. So far as the first category is concerned, protection of literary and aesthetic works by copyright is the sign of a relatively highly developed body of legal theory. In more primitive legal systems, such as those of Venice[1] or England[2] in the early days of printing, the grant of a patent monopoly was happily regarded as a suitable means of protecting rights in books. So far as the second category is concerned, the regarding of disembodied ideas as not being inventions reflects a greater legal concern with functional considerations, and with the practical and economic implications of the patent system, than with the acknowledgement of the merits of the mental processes by which 'concrete' inventions arise.

1. See H Brown *The Venetian Printing Press* (1891).
2. See eg the Queen's Printer's patent to print the Authorized Version of the Bible and the 1662 Book of Common Prayer, noted in *Copyright and Designs Law* Cmnd 673 1977, para 650. Such patents are still in force.

4.13 The list of 'non-inventions' under the Patents Act 1977 is not closed. The Secretary of State for Trade and Industry may lay an order before both Houses of Parliament, by which he may make additions to or deletions from that list for the purpose of maintaining it 'in conformity with developments in science and technology'.[1] Under previous legislation it was not possible to patent, for example, a perpetual motion machine, since such a concept is in defiance of well-accepted laws of science.[2] Nowadays an inventor who, by virtue of his invention, is able to prove that a well-accepted law of science is wrong will not be barred from seeking a patent for it; but the Secretary of State's power may be used so as to redefine 'invention' by excluding it.

1. Patents Act 1977, s 1(5). No orders have yet been made under this provision.
2. On the fallacy of *perpetuum mobile* see Giancarlo Notaro, 'The Eternal Illusion', (1989) 13 Patent World, pp 41-43. In *Newman/Perpetual Motion* [1988] EPOR 301 the European Patent Office refused such an application on the ground of insufficiency – the specification would not enable readers to overcome the law of conservation of energy. See, also, *Webb's Application* IPD 11078.

Chapter 5

The patentability of an invention

What is a patentable invention?

5.1   Once something has satisfied the criteria of invention, it must then be shown to be patentable before it is capable of attracting an exclusive monopoly in its exploitation. The UK's criteria for patentability are those which it has adopted from the European Patent Convention;[1] given the normative influence of the EPC, it is not surprising that British criteria for patentability are shared by many other countries both in the developed economies and elsewhere.[2] For an invention to be patentable:

(i)   it must be new,
(ii)   it must involve an 'inventive step',
(iii)   it must be industrially applicable, and
(iv)   it must not be excluded from patentability by reference to the Patents Act 1977, section 1(3), discussed below.[3]

Let us examine in turn each of the criteria for patentability, bearing in mind that they are cumulative; each must be satisfied before a patent can be granted.[4]

1.   The Convention on the Grant of European Patents, Munich, 1973, art 52(1) closely corresponds to the Patents Act 1977, s 1(1).
2.   See eg *WIPO Model Law for Developing Countries on Inventions* (1979), vol 1 (Patents) Ch 2, s 113; and see Agreement on Trade-Related Aspects of Intellectual Property Rights ('TRIPs'), arts 27-34.
3.   See paras **5.29-5.31**.
4.   Patents Act 1977, s 18(2).

(1) The invention must be new

5.2   Taking the invention's 'priority date', which is usually the date on which an application is first made for a patent for it,[1] one looks back at 'the state of the art',[2] that is to say, the sum and total of human knowledge which has at any time been made available to the public, anywhere in the world and in any way. If the invention does not appear to be already part of the state of the art, or if it is not possible to infer that it was implicitly part of the state of the art,[3] the invention is new. This is so even if the invention has been secretly known and used by someone else for hundreds of years,[4] because 'new' means, in this context, 'new to the public'. We accept that the grant of the patent monopoly is therefore the price which the public pays for the disclosure to it of what was not previously known to it. Where more than one person arrives at an invention, the first to initiate disclosure by filing a patent application is entitled to the reward, in the UK and most other countries.[5] The public, for these purposes, means not just the public at large but the aggregate of all individuals (and presumably corporations) which comprise it. If one highly specialised scientist publishes an article fully and accurately describing his invention in a journal, it still forms part of the state of the art because it has been made available to the public, even though the man on the Clapham omnibus would have no idea that it had been made available to him.

1. Patents Act 1977, s 5.
2. Ibid, s 2(2).
3. See *Molins v Industrial Machinery Co Ltd* (1938) 55 RPC 31, cf *Re Mobil Oil/ Friction reducing additive* [1990] OJ EPO 93; [1990] EPOR 73; explained in *Bristol-Myers Squibb v Baker Norton Pharmaceuticals Inc* [2001] RPC 1.
4. Prior secretly-used inventions do not undermine novelty but cannot themselves be suppressed by a subsequent patent grant to another: see Patents Act 1977, s 64(1).
5. The United States has fought a valiant rearguard battle to defend the notion of awarding a patent to the first to invent, but the principle of making the grant to the first to file has now been conceded.

When is an invention 'made available to the public'?

5.3 Availability may be achieved by publication in written or oral form, or it may be made by public use. Not every public use of an invention is, however, capable of making its inventive content available to the public. It is plain that anyone who sails down the river Thames on a new-style 'windsurfer' will be disclosing its shape, format and inventive design features to all who watch it.[1] Equally clearly, the circuitry of a computer – being concealed from the public's gaze – cannot be said to be 'made available' merely by virtue of the computer's use in public.[2] Between these two extremes are many factual situations which may give rise to a public suspicion that something has been invented, a suspicion which cannot be clarified in the absence of a further supply of information. In such cases it will be unclear whether public use has made the invention available, each case being decided on its own facts.[3] If the public has in fact freely enjoyed all the benefits of an invention, knowing that it works but not necessarily exactly how, a patent will not be granted to foreclose access to those benefits.[4] In relation to documentary disclosures, the House of Lords has sensibly held[5] that, if an invention is to be taken as being 'available to the public', the public must be able to avail itself of the invention. In other words the disclosure must be 'enabling', a criterion which is applied in the European Patent Office[6] and in the UK.[7]

1. See *Windsurfing International Inc v Tabur Marine (Great Britain) Ltd* [1985] RPC 59.
2. *Quantel Ltd v Spaceward* [1990] RPC 83. Both types of use were present in *Lux Traffic Controls v Pike Signal* [1993] RPC 107.
3. On the criteria which are likely to influence a finding that an invention has been made available to the public, see *Guidelines for Examination in the European Patent Office*, Part D, Chapter V.
4. Thus in *Merrell Dow Pharmaceuticals Inc v Norton* [1996] RPC 76, the patent for a metabolite of terfenadine, a successful anti-histamine, was held invalid. Terfenadine, disclosed in an earlier, expired, patent, was shown to have worked because it was converted into the metabolite by the patient's liver. Following the teaching of the earlier patent would have made patients well by reason of the metabolite, even though its chemical identity was unknown at the time. A German Court reached a similar result by holding the metabolite patent valid but not infringed – see V, C & T Vossius 'Prior Written Disclosure and Public Prior Use under German Law and the EPC' [1994] 3 EIPR 130; and see Taucher 'Reflections on the German Terfenadine case', Patent World, April 1999, p 19.
5. In *Asahi* [1991] RPC 485.
6. Eg *Re ICI/Pyridine Herbicides* [1986] EPOR 232, 'Availability to the public' [1993] OJ EPO 277.
7. *PLG Research Ltd v Ardon International Ltd* [1993] FSR 197 at 225. For an example of a disclosure which was not enabling, see *Genentech Inc's (Human Growth Hormone) Patent* [1989] RPC 613. See also A Perkins and A Stebbing, 'Artful Determination: State of the Art and *PCME v Goyen*' [1999] EIPR 377.

5.4 Historically, the reason for according patentable status solely to new inventions was simple: if there were no criterion of novelty, then one man could obtain a monopoly for that which another man was already publicly using, and that would be unfair in two respects. First he would be getting a monopoly but would not have given the public anything which, broadly speaking, it did not already have, and second, he would be able to stop the other man doing that which, before the patent grant, was perfectly permissible.[1]

1. See *Clothworkers of Ipswich* (1614) Godb 252; the same philosophy can be detected in the 'right to work' novelty test of Sachs LJ in *General Tire and Rubber Co v Firestone Tyre and Rubber Co Ltd* [1972] RPC 457 at 485-486.

5.5 In practice our perspective upon the requirement of novelty is not as simple as the previous paragraphs indicate. Since the 'public domain', the sum total of man's past and present knowledge, keeps growing, it becomes more and more difficult to devise something which is entirely novel[1] and, as technology advances, it becomes more costly to investigate and exploit those areas in which invention is made. While it may or may not be true to state that all the 'easy' inventions have been made, it is true to state that inventions of the simple 'gadget' type form only an insignificant part of the innovation industry,[2] and that the vast majority of patent applications are far too complex to be understood by most laymen. The determination by the inventor's professional advisers and by the Patent Office as to what constitutes a 'new' invention is thus an expensive, intellectually sophisticated and time-consuming operation, which more closely resembles the Glass Bead Game[3] than the establishment of an economic monopoly and which leads to no certain result; for even the most exhaustive search of the state of the art can fail to locate published materials which 'anticipate' the applicant's invention. Since a patent once granted can be invalidated if any subsequent investigation of the prior art reveals that the invention is not, after all, novel, it is often worth a trade rival's effort to hunt for anticipatory skeletons in the invention's conceptual cupboard.[4] Indeed, it has frequently been asserted that the majority of patents granted are either invalid for want of novelty, or could be described as such if enough money were spent on the search for their antecedents.[5]

1. Between 750,000 and 1 million new patent documents were published annually. According to C Oppenheim 'Information Aspects of Patents' in J Phillips (ed) *Patents in Perspective* (1985) at p 55.
2. For a recent example, see *Haberman v Jackel* [1999] FSR 683.
3. H Hesse *The Glass Bead Game* (Penguin edn 1972); the game's flavour can be sampled in 'A General Introduction to its History for the Layman'.
4. For a good example of an exercise in undermining a patent see *Windsurfing International Inc v Tabur Marine (Great Britain) Ltd* [1985] RPC 59.
5. See T Blanco White *Patents for Inventions* (3rd edn 1982), p 98; the BountyQuest.com web site encourages people to come forward with 'prior art' to invalidate US patents.

5.6 Accordingly the suggestion has from time to time been made that the requirement of novelty be abandoned, or at any rate relaxed, as a strict condition of patentability. The Patent Office would be spared the task of examining each application's novelty, and no harm is done in granting a patent for an invention which is not novel, so long as no one other than the patent applicant is actually using (or contemplating using) it at the time the application is made. This proposal also has the merit that it takes into account the fallibility of human memory; for technology can be lost or forgotten quite easily. Why, the argument concludes, should a patent for a device invented in 1985 be rendered invalid because an archaeologist in 1986 finds records of a similar device during an archaeological excavation of an Inca settlement in the jungles of Peru? Is its commercial or social value any the less, and is its value to the public as a publication of a piece of intellectual property diminished? The patentee's award would be received, in such a case, not for giving the public something new, but for finding something which it had lost.[1]

1. Information which enters the public domain but is later 'forgotten' can in principle be protected by the laws of breach of confidence: see Ch 20.

5.7 Allied to the question of novelty per se is that of novelty and the 'technology gap'. If an invention is sufficiently novel in its conception, the patent which protects it may be impotent as a means of rendering effective reward to its holder. First, the state of technology may not be sufficiently developed to enable the invention to be manufactured to an acceptable standard, or to enable an invention to be usefully exploited (as was the case with the sapphire stylus with a ground point, which preceded by some years the development of 'microgroove' long-playing records).[1] Second, the invention may be so novel that it may not be possible to persuade those whose accomplishments lie within a particular field of expertise that the invention has any service value or advantage to it: this was one of the problems faced by Frank Whittle when he invented the jet engine.[2] In each case the patent is likely to expire without being used and therefore without either the public or the private right-holder deriving much, if any, benefit from it. In such cases, especially where R & D costs are high and the market is small, even once technology and industrial receptivity have developed to the stage of being able to deal with the invention, the risk of developing it may appear unacceptable if there is no 'posthumous' monopoly in respect of the expired patent.[3] In such cases, should novelty be waived so that a second monopoly be granted? In purely commercial terms the answer should be 'yes', but in moral terms it may not be so easy, since to grant a monopoly on an expired patent is to deprive the public of its right to the free exploitation of that which, by way of the initial patent grant, it has already paid for. However, the effective life of pharmaceutical and agrochemical patents in the European Union may be extended for up to five years, where exploitation has been delayed by the need to obtain regulatory approval, under a system of supplementary protection certificates.[4]

1. See *Killick v Pye Ltd* [1958] RPC 23.
2. See eg A Feldman and P Ford *'Scientists and Inventors'* (1979) pp 300-301.
3. In the UK it is no longer possible to obtain an extension of a patent grant: cf Patents Act 1949, ss 23 and 24.
4. Regulations 1768/92 and 1610/96, implemented in the UK by SI 1992/ 3091 and SI 1996/1320. See R Whaite and N Jones 'Pharmaceutical Patent Term

Restoration: the European Commission's Regulation' [1992] EIPR 324. See, also, J Adams 'Supplementary Protection Certificates: the "Salt" Problem' [1995] EIPR 277.

5.8 Can this particular dilemma be resolved by allowing a second patent grant? To argue that, once a patent expires, the invention is in the public domain and should therefore belong to the public, is to place greater value upon the property itself than upon the reasons for according rights in it. If the net result of acknowledging the claim of the public domain is to keep the invention suspended in a sort of unexploitable limbo, it should be necessary to iterate the consequential benefits which would accrue to that same public from its exploitation, even by a monopoly holder. The new, enhanced or cheaper product which results from its exploitation becomes available to the public at large, employment is created, profit is (possibly) enjoyed and taxes are gathered. The European Patent Office practice[1] of granting patents for inventive new uses of known compounds might be regarded as a step in this direction. However, the UK Court of Appeal has pointed out[2] that use for the previously known purpose should not be prevented by such a patent.

1. Eg *Re Mobil/Friction reducing additive* [1990] EPOR 73.
2. *Bristol-Myers Squibb Co v Baker Norton Pharmaceuticals Inc* [2001] RPC 1, CA.

5.9 An alternative solution which has been proposed is to change the conditions of patentability so that the patent monopoly be awarded to the first person to market its subject matter, not the first person to disclose it.[1] This proposal would radically restructure the patent system; the race to the Patent Office engendered by the need to prove novelty would be replaced by the race to the market place. This proposal is not, however, free of criticism. For example, without the confident expectation of being the winner in the race to the market place, the industrialist may not wish to expend R & D funding and effort in the first place; and those who conceive of marginal improvements in the patented product will be unable to protect their ideas by patent law if they could not market the product without being considered infringers of the original patent.

1. See H Kronz 'Patent Protection for Innovations: a Model' [1983] EIPR 178 and 206.

5.10 Perhaps an ideal compromise solution would be the retention of the novelty-oriented patent system as we know it, but to accord a separate and distinct monopoly also to products marketed for the first time, whether they have been the subject of previous patent applications or not. This solution would encourage the disclosure and exploitation of improvements and modifications of existing products, which may themselves be so close to the prior art as to be incapable of patent protection (sometimes referred to as 'incremental innovation').[1] This proposal would also benefit the large number of developing countries whose indigenous manufacturers can rarely if ever satisfy the criterion of absolute novelty which the WIPO Model Law for Developing Countries requires for even its least industrially mature adherents.

1. See W Kingston 'Innovation Patents and Warrants' in J Phillips (ed) *Patents in Perspective* (1985) and para **3.14** above.

(2) The invention must involve an 'inventive step'

5.11   The invention must not simply be something which has not previously existed, but it must also owe its existence to the exercise by the human intellect of a creative thought-process.[1] To use the parlance of the Patents Act 1977 an invention shall be taken to involve an inventive step if 'it is not obvious to a person skilled in the art ...'.[2] This indicates, sensibly, that the yardstick by which 'inventive step' is measured is not that of what appears obvious to the man in the street since, measured by that low standard, it is difficult to imagine many modern patent applications which would ever appear obvious to him.[3] Instead, one consults the hypothetical 'person skilled in the art'. He is, of course, reasonable, but that is not the attribute with which we are principally concerned. He is British, is taken to possess a familiarity with the state of the art which may be 'active' or 'passive' (ie he will know the details of latest developments within his speciality, or will know where to look for them), but he lacks any ability to make inventions.[4] His German counterpart, however, has only reasonable knowledge of the prior art, but is taken to be capable of original thought.[5] The harmonisation of national patent laws within the scope of operation of the European Patent Convention has had the effect of drawing all Member States, and the European Patent Office itself, closer together: the EPO 'person skilled in the art' is cautious, risk-averse, though prepared to do minor modifications.[6]

1. The human element of inventiveness may be quite minimal: see eg Charles Goodyear's invention of the vulcanisation of rubber, in A Feldman and P Ford *Scientists and Inventors* (1979).
2. Patents Act 1977, s 3.
3 Although simplicity and inventive step are not mutually exclusive: *Haberman v Jackal* [1999] FSR 683.
4. See eg *Beecham Group Ltd's (Amoxycillin) Application* [1980] RPC 261.

5. See E Pakuscher 'Examination for non-obviousness – a Response' (1981) 12 IIC 816. Note that in Germany, and now in numerous other countries, lesser inventions may be protected by registration as utility models.
6. *Genentech/Expression in Yeast* [1996] EPOR 85.

5.12 Once we have identified our person skilled in the art,[1] we then give him the problem which the inventor has claimed to solve by means of his patent, and ask him to apply, uninventively, the state of the art to it. If he comes up with the same answer as that contained in the patent specification, then it is 'obvious' and does not therefore merit monopoly protection. In other words, we pose a subjectively loaded question ('Is the solution obvious?'), and pretend to answer it objectively ('Yes, if the hypothetical person skilled in the art could have conceived it without inventive thought'); but all we have done is to add further subjective variables: the state of mind and the thought-processes of an idealised and non-existent person.

1. For judicial scepticism as to this character's usefulness, see *Société Technique de Pulverisation Step v Emson Europe* [1993] RPC 513 at 519 per Hoffmann LJ. However, since the 'person skilled in the art' is mentioned in the Act and Convention, he or she is hard to ignore.

5.13 The requirements of novelty and inventive step reflect different objectives which the patent system claims to seek. Rewarding the disclosure to the public of that which was not previously known is a policy which justifies the requirement of novelty, in that what is not new to the public cannot be said to be disclosed to it. On the other hand, the rewarding and encouragement of the meritorious art of inventing is promoted by insisting upon the requirement of inventive step, since what has not been obtained by intellectual creativity is not regarded as an appropriate subject for reward. The inventive step requirement also provides, in theory, valuable protection for the competitors of the patent applicant; for if, it is argued, something is obvious, it is already part of man's common stock of intellectual resources, and should remain open for all to use. The grant of a monopoly in a product or process which is new but obvious is tantamount to the undesirable prohibition, or at any rate to the inhibition, of competition in any field of industrial activity in which a new product or process is utilised.

5.14 It should not be thought that the case for a requirement of inventive step is unanswerable. Whether a product is new or not can be ascertained by a process which is, at base, objective: the comparison of the new with the old. If the two are essentially the same, or if the old clearly anticipates the new, the result will not be patentable. In contrast, whether an invention is obvious or not is, in principle, subjective, and any pretence at making the test of obviousness objective is abandoned by the concession that it is impossible for any rational and intelligent human being to 'unknow' what he already knows. Since that which has already been disclosed so frequently seems obvious once it is explained[1] (as many an enthusiast who has ever spent quarter-of-an-hour contemplating a crossword puzzle clue will agree, once the solution is manifested to him), it is clear that the assessment of inventive step is a procedure which potentially threatens the achievement of justice in the granting of patents. This is because, by the time the sufficiency of an inventive step is discussed in legal proceedings, the alleged invention may have become not merely commonplace but obsolete during the period of time which has elapsed since its initial conception, and it is so difficult to view it in the context of a prior art which has long since been superseded.

1.   For the problem of hindsight in this enquiry, see *Beloit Technologies Inc v Valmet Paper Machinery Inc* [1997] RPC 489.

5.15   Both British and European law have done their best to define tests and guidelines as to what is, or is not, obvious,[1] and they have striven valiantly to apply their tests accurately and consistently where they can, but the definition and identification of inventive step would seem to be a task beyond the wit of man. It is submitted that the means of identifying inventive step, described below, should be consigned to oblivion by the bold process of abolishing the inventive step requirement. Any application for a patent for an invention which can satisfy a stringent criterion of novelty should be sufficiently meritorious of legal protection. Indeed, the very act of creating and identifying that which is new – whether or not it is sufficiently 'inventive' to satisfy current 'obviousness' requirements – would seem to be an intellectual task of sufficient inherent merit to deserve protection on its own account.

1.   The most influential analysis of this topic, *Windsurfing*, para **5.5**, n 3, was actually decided under the Patents Act 1949 but its methodology has been used in a number of cases under the 1977 Act: eg *Boehringer Mannheim v Genzyme* [1993] FSR 716; *Mölnlycke AB v Procter & Gamble Ltd (No 5)* [1994] RPC 49, CA; *Union Carbide v BP* [1999] RPC 409; *Re Palmaz's European Patent (UK)* [2000] RPC 631. The European Patent Office has published a set of detailed but non-binding guidelines which indicate how EPO examiners will be likely to respond to any question of inventive step. The EPO's approach is said to be more demanding than that which has prevailed in the UK Patent Office: B Reid *A Practical Guide to Patent Law* (3rd edn 1999) pp 186-189.

5.16   How is inventive step discerned? In *Windsurfing*,[1] the Court of Appeal dealt with the inquiry in a number of stages, which can be paraphrased as follows:

(a)   identify the inventive concept of the patent;
(b)   identify the person skilled in the art and clothe him with the general knowledge common at the relevant date;[2]
(c)   ascertain the differences – the 'step' - between the alleged invention and the 'prior art' – matter cited as available to the public by disclosure or use;
(d)   decide whether taking the step represented by those differences would have been obvious to the skilled person, without knowledge of the invention.

The inventive concept may be very specific – the solution to a known specific problem – or very general – identifying a fresh goal which opens up a new field of technology. Or it could be somewhere in between the two – finding a new route to achieve a known goal.[3] In the first and third cases, the patent is likely to be framed in the 'problem/solution' manner[4] beloved of the European Patent Office and the first stage of the *Windsurfing* inquiry is relatively easy. Where the patent identifies a fresh goal, or formulates a previously unrecognised problem, identifying the inventive concept may be a less mechanical exercise for the court, although these types of patent usually involve a greater degree of invention.

Common sense and case law suggest a variety of approaches for detecting inventive step, and they have met with varying degrees of support.[5] Let us examine some of them:

(i) *Would a person versed in the art assess the likelihood of success of the as yet unmade invention as sufficient to warrant its actual trial?*[6] This test, which may be regarded as 'appropriate' only where the hypothetical man skilled in the art had a particular problem in mind, raises its own problem. If the answer is 'no', one may infer that the invention was not obvious, but there is nothing from which an inference of obviousness may be drawn from the answer 'yes'.[7] This is particularly the case in respect of 'selection patents'[8] discussed below.[9]

(ii) *If the invention involves a substantial advance in the state of the art, why was it not done before?*[10] The nature of this test is to raise a presumption of inventiveness where a substantial development of the art takes place, rebuttable by a reasonable explanation[11] which accounts for the 'gap' in more practical or prosaic terms than that of non-obviousness. Unlike the previous test it is equally applicable whether or not the skilled man has a particular problem or goal in mind but it only applies where a substantial advance in the state of the art is achieved.

(iii) *Does the invention satisfy a long-felt want?*[12] If so, it may be assumed that the invention is not obvious, otherwise it would have been utilised sooner in response to the compelling pressure of demand. This test, which is easier to apply than its predecessors, does not depend so strongly upon the substitution of uncertain values (a long-felt want is easier to identify than a likelihood of success or a substantial advance in the state of the art) but is incomplete in the same way as the first test; the answer 'yes' encourages the inference that the invention is not obvious, but the answer 'no' does not discourage it. This is particularly important if one considers that the reason why an invention does not satisfy a long-felt want may be that the invention is not made in order to 'satisfy' demand but in order to 'create' it.

(iv) *Is the invention merely the application of a well-known product (or process) for a well-known purpose?*[13] If so, then the end result is the product of base analogy, rather than of inventive step. Thus the use on the front wheels of a horse-drawn carriage of a variety of suspension which was already used on the rear wheels did not result in that carriage, despite its novelty, being a patentable invention.[14] Conversely, it may be inventive to solve a problem in one field of technology by importing a solution from another, unrelated, field.[15]

(v) *Is the invention commercially successful?* The implication of this consideration is that the commercial success of an invention is an indication that a hitherto unexploited market has been stimulated and satisfied; and one should be entitled to assume that anyone, in this era of vigorous competition in capitalist economies, who satisfies such a market with a new product has done something which was not obvious, at least to his competitors.[16] Unfortunately, the same implication of inventive step can be derived from the failure of a product or process to achieve any commercial success, where, for example, a product is so advanced that manufacturers or the general public cannot be persuaded that it is of any benefit to them.[17] There is also something of a logical difficulty in trying to infer the non-obviousness of the product of intellectual thought from the (non-)obviousness of its market. Furthermore, commercial success may be due to factors other than invention.[18]

(vi) *Is the invention merely a collocation of features which already exist in the prior art?*[19] Such novel devices as a digital clock-cum-pencil-sharpener, an electric toothbrush with a detachable head which could function as an egg-whip, or a combination of hair-restorer and laxative, would not attract patent protection on the basis that the addition of one well-known thing to another does not constitute an advance in the prior art. The lack of patent protection for such products has been the subject of critical comment[20] and has certainly disappointed a number of amateur inventors, but conventional wisdom dictates that the patent system would be debased by the patentability of such objects, for whom a more appropriate form of protection may in any event be sought under design law.[21]

1. *Windsurfing International Inc v Tabur Marine (Great Britain)* [1985] RPC 59; see para **5.15**, n 1 above; Griffiths '*Windsurfing* and the Inventive Step' [1999] IPQ 160. In *David J Instance Ltd v Denny Bros Printing Ltd* (2001) Times, 22 June, the Court of Appeal said that the *Windsurfer* approach, though useful, were not mandatory and that a trial judge could therefore go straight to the heart of the issue without going through the motions of applying it.
2. See paras **5.11** and **5.12**, above. The court usually has a real person, in the shape of an expert witness, as a model for the 'person skilled in the art'.
3. See *Biogen v Medeva* [1997] RPC 1 at 34 per Lord Hoffman.
4. The World Intellectual Property Organisation has defined 'invention' as the 'an idea which permits the practical solution of a specific problem in a field of technology' *Introduction to Intellectual Property: Theory and Practice (1997)*; however, the European Patent Office does not always adhere to a problem/ solution approach: *ALCAN/Aluminium Alloys* [1995] EPOR 501.
5. Whether or not a particular approach was obvious to try would depend upon the tenor of the prior art: *Johns-Manville Corpn's Patent* [1967] RPC 479.
6. The courts sometimes criticise these approaches as straying from the main enquiry set out in the Patents Act 1977 and the European Patent Convention: eg *PLG Research Ltd v Ardon International Ltd* [1995] RPC 287. However, asking such questions can provide useful pointers.
7. Thus in *Boehringer Mannheim GmbH v Genzyme* [1993] FSR 716 a formula had been disclosed, but not how to make the product. The latter might have been obvious to try, but the Court held that the patent would lack inventive step only if it was obvious *how* to obtain the product. (It was.)
8. See eg *Du Pont de Nemours & Co's (Witsiepe's) Application* [1982] FSR 303.
9. Para **5.20**.
10. *Technograph Printed Circuits Ltd v Mills and Rockley (Electronics) Ltd* [1969] RPC 395 at 405 (per Harman LJ). See also *Re Shoketsu Kinzoko Kogyo KK's Patent* [1992] FSR 184.
11. See, eg *Optical Coating Laboratory Inc v Pilkington* [1995] RPC 145 at 166.
12. *Parks-Cramer Co v G W Thornton & Sons Ltd* [1966] RPC 407 at 418.
13. *Longbottom v Shaw* (1891) 8 RPC 333.
14. *Morgan & Co Ltd v Windover & Co Ltd* (1890) 7 RPC 131.
15. *IBM/ Enclosure for Data-Processing Apparatus* (T09/82) [1997] EPOR 303.
16. See *Parks-Cramer* above.
17. *Technograph*, n 10, at p 416 (per Widgery LJ).
18. Eg *Hallen v Brabantia* [1991] RPC 195.
19. *Williams v Nye* (1890) 7 RPC 62.
20. See P G Cole 'Obvious and Lacking in Inventive Step' [1982] EIPR 102 and 142.
21. See Ch 24.

5.17 The elimination of collocations from the patent application procedure is achieved by a process of casting around the prior art and identifying each element of the would-be patentable invention as being already contained within the public domain.[1] In the case of the digital clock which doubles as a pencil-sharpener, that is a simple task, because there is nothing inherently original in the collocation; the clock is always a clock, the pencil-sharpener a pencil-sharpener, and the collocation of them both has no function not already inherent in their well-known separate functions. But what of the collocation which consists of a number of well-known items, some of which are now used in a new manner, or which is used to solve a problem which had not previously been apparent? This was the issue at stake in the patentability of the well-known Black & Decker 'Workmate', a portable work-bench consisting of a number of component parts, all of which were known to the prior art and which were used in well-known ways, but which were combined to form a new object which achieved a result far greater than that which was apparent to anyone objectively surveying its many parts. The 'Workmate' patent was regarded as valid,[2] since the inventive step came in the conception of the new product and in the fact that it could be achieved by the cunning juxtaposition of features which already belonged to the prior art.

1. For the dangers of the one-at-a-time approach, see *Re Shoketsu Kinzoko Kogyo KK's Patent* [1992] FSR 184.
2. *Hickman v Andrews* [1983] RPC 147.

Proof of lack of 'inventive step'

5.18 As a matter of pure common sense, the degree of ease with which the case against inventive step is made will have a substantial impact upon its success. If one can show that an invention is merely an analogous use of something already used, one's point is easy to grasp, and thence to accept (or reject). If, on the other hand, it is necessary to resort to the practice of 'mosaicing',[1] one inevitably runs into difficulty. Regarding the prior art as a vast quantity of tesserae, one is entitled to piece the tesserae together in order to form a mosaic, by way of replication of the alleged invention and to claim, therefore, that since there was nothing in that invention which did not also appear in the mosaic, it was firmly based upon the prior art and was therefore obvious. This approach is not, however, warmly welcomed by litigants or the judiciary, since it is a time-consuming and expensive exercise, and since the more effort goes into the making of the mosaic, the less obvious the disputed invention appears.[2]

1. *Allmänna Svenska Electriska A/B v Burntisland* (1952) 69 RPC 63.
2. For good examples of a contrived attempt to mosaic an invention see *Hickman v Andrews* [1983] RPC 147; and *Pfizer Ltd's Patent* [2001] FSR 201.

5.19   A useful checklist of factors relevant to the question of inventive step was provided by Laddie J in *Haberman v Jackel*:[1]

(a)   What was the problem which the patented development addressed?

(b)   How long had that problem existed?

(c)   How significant was the problem seen to be?

(d)   How widely known was the problem and how many were likely to have been seeking a solution?

(e)   What prior art would have been likely to be known to those expected to have been involved in finding a solution?

(f)   What other publications were put forward in the period leading up to the publication of the patentee's development?

(g)   To what extent were there factors which would have held back the exploitation of the solution even if it were technically obvious?

(h)   How well had the patentee's development been received?

(i)   To what extent could it be shown that the commercial success was due to the technical merits of the development?

1.   [1999] FSR 683.

Selection patents

5.20   An interesting problem which spans both novelty and inventive step is that of the 'selection patent'.[1] The term 'selection patent' will not be found in the Patents Act 1977, but is a convenient term of reference for the following phenomenon. Let us say that a particular substance can be synthesised by means of the application to a certain metal of any acid in certain conditions, and that this is well known and is part of the prior art. An inventor then discovers that the selection, from the entire range of acids, of one or more specified acids will confer a particular advantage in that process, either by synthesising the end product more quickly, or in safer conditions. Is his invention patentable?

1.   For an account of the development of this concept, see J Jeffs 'Selection Patents' [1988] EIPR 291; for an example, see *RHONE POULENC/Ester Production* [1999] EPOR 443. R Spangenberg 'The Novelty of Selection Inventions' (1997) 28 IIC 808 describes the approach of the European Patent Office.

5.21   So far as novelty is concerned, one may feel that the inventor has thrown the prior art into a clearer perspective without actually extending it; he has, by analogy, not so much created a new intellectual tool as sharpened an old one. With regard to inventive step, once it is known that any acid will produce the end result, it is trite science to say that inevitably some acids will do the job more efficiently than others; why then allow that the performance of an obvious process, that of testing plausible alternatives to see which works best, should result in a patentable invention? On the other hand, the person who goes to the time and trouble of sifting through alternative substances, forms or other variables in order to establish which is the best, or who genuinely seeks the possibly unforeseen benefits which he discovers, should not go unrewarded for his efforts. The balance of this argument between competing claims to justice is confused, in most cases, by the fact that the prior art is itself the subject of a valid patent, and that opposition to the selection patent's claim to patentability may come from an earlier patentee who is anxious to bring the later invention within the scope of his earlier discovery in order to stop it.

5.22 So far as the law is concerned, the selection patent is legitimate, so long as the following conditions are satisfied:

(i) the invention must relate to a substantial advantage which is derived from the selection of the chemicals, polymers, or whatever, which form the class selected;
(ii) all the members of the class selected must be able to convey that advantage;
(iii) none of the unselected variables should be able to confer the same advantage.[1]

1. *IG Farbenindustrie AG's Patents* (1930) 47 RPC 289 at p 322; see also *Hallen v Brabantia* [1991] RPC 195 at 217.

(3) The invention must be capable of industrial application[1]

5.23 This requirement emphasises the importance of practical application to the patent system. However good an idea is, or however elegant its explication, it cannot be patented unless it is a thing which can be made (ie a product) or a means of making a thing, or of achieving a concrete end result (ie a process). This same requirement is already implicit in the exclusion of discoveries, mental processes, ways of presenting information and suchlike from the status of 'inventions' under the Patents Act 1977.[2] One wonders whether the general requirement of industrial applicability is in fact superfluous to the Act, given that it is difficult to think of any examples of intellectual endeavour which would not be excluded by section 1(2) and which would only be deprived of patentability by section 4(1). Section 1(2) is in fact wider than section 4(1) in its scope; it excludes, for example, computer programs *per se* from patentability, notwithstanding the strong claim they make for having industrial applicability.

1. Patents Act 1977, ss 1(4), 4.
2. Ibid, s 1(2).

5.24 'Industrial applicability' was phraseology new to the Patents Act 1977, but its germ may be found in the traditional requirement that a patentable invention be a 'new manner of manufacture'.[1] From an examination of what failed to satisfy the criteria of 'manner of manufacture' under the old law, we may get an idea of that which is incapable of industrial applicability under the current law. Examples include a scheme for the laying of public utility pipes and cables so as to minimise the disruption caused by the digging up of roads,[2] new systems of indexing[3] and of musical notation,[4] and a method of marking buoys as an aid to navigation.[5] The criterion of industrial applicability could perhaps be used to refuse a patent for something which cannot possibly work, such as a perpetual motion machine,[6] but should not be equated with a requirement of utility.[7] Rather, the patent should disclose a use in technology, including agriculture.[8] Consequently, a broad patent claiming a large class of biological entities of unknown and varied operation cannot be sustained,[9] nor a patent claiming a gene sequence of undisclosed function.[10]

1. 'New manner of manufacture' formed part of the definition of 'invention' under the Patents Act 1949, s 101(1).
2. *Hiller's Application* [1969] RPC 267.
3. *Ward's Application* (1911) 29 RPC 79.
4. *M's Application* (1924) 41 RPC 159. Cf *Pitman's Application* [1969] RPC 646.
5. *W's Application* (1914) 31 RPC 141.
6. The headnote to *NEWMAN/Perpetual Motion Machine* (T05/86) [1988] EPOR 301 suggests this, although the decision appears to have been based on lack of sufficient disclosure: art 83 EPC.
7. The former requirement of utility was not carried over to the 1977 Act; see also Franzosi 'Patent Inventions:Technical and Social Phases: Industrial Character and Utility' [1997] EIPR 251.
8. Patents Act 1977, s 4(2).
9. A problem discussed in *Chiron Corp v Murex Diagnostics Ltd* [1996] RPC 535.
10. Directive EC 98/71 on the Legal Protection of Biotechnological Inventions [1998] OJ L213/13, art 5(3), implemented in the UK by the Patents Regulations 2000 (SI 2000/2037); see AIPPI 'Report Q150 – Patentability Requirements and the Scope of Protection of ESTs, SNPs and Entire Genomes' [2000] EIPR 39.

5.25   A further provision (section 4(2)) excludes from 'industrial applicability' any 'method of treatment of the human or animal body, by surgery or therapy'[1] and any 'method of diagnosis practised on the human or animal body'. The apparent reason for this is founded in a concession that the protection of life and health are universally recognised objectives which transcend the sordid realm of proprietary rights. Every individual has a right to expect that his physician or surgeon will be able to ply his craft so as to serve the paramount aims of restoring health and decreasing pain, and it would be preposterous for a third party to hold it within his power, by virtue of a patent grant, to prevent the man of medicine from performing his vital skills to the best of his knowledge and ability. Since man is but one humble species of animal, it is only logical to extend to the whole the protection claimed in justice by but one naked and unrepresentative part; therefore no patent may be granted for the treatment or diagnosis of man or beast.

1. For a discussion from a European perspective, see R Moufang 'Methods of Medical Treatment under Patent Law' (1993) 24 IIC 18; *Visx v Nidex Ltd (No 4)* [1999] FSR 405.

5.26 However, the conclusion against patentability is dubious,[1] for the reasoning by which such inventions are denied industrial applicability could justify the retention of their patentability, subject to the trifling proviso that their use, other than by the patentee, cannot be stopped; the use would then instead be subject to a compulsory licence, and the surgeon or other supplier of the treatment would pay a small royalty to the patentee. This would at least encourage anyone of a moderately philanthropic cast of mind to disclose his invention; the current effect of section 4(2) indicates that the person who invents such forms of treatment or diagnosis may be best served by keeping it to himself and securing a de facto monopoly in his skills which will benefit no one else's patients but his own.

1. For the position elsewhere, see Cuthbert 'Patent Law Reform in New Zealand: Should Methods of Medical Treatment be Patentable?' Patent World, May 1997, p 32; Kell 'Expanding the Frontier of Patentability: Methods of Medical Treatment of the Human Body [1995] EIPR 202 (Aus).

5.27 The same subsection raises a number of interesting legal problems on account of the imprecision of its drafting:

(i) Does 'treatment' or 'diagnosis' imply the existence of an actual disease or illness to be diagnosed? If they do, then contraceptive devices and pregnancy tests would be patentable; since neither conception nor pregnancy are illnesses, their inhibition or diagnosis would not be exempted from patentability under section 4(2). This is indeed the case,[1] and this conclusion is not inconsistent with the exclusion from patentability of methods of immunisation or vaccination.[2] The latter, while applied to a body which enjoys good health, are intended to prevent future disease, and the law makes no distinction between treatments which are precedent or antecedent to the disease they are intended to combat.

(ii) Does section 4(2) prevent the patentability of methods of treatment or diagnosis which are industrial or commercial, rather than medical, in their nature? In other words, the treatment of an animal with hormones so as to fatten it up for profitable slaughter, or the means of diagnosing whether an oyster contains a pearl, are not intended to confer any benefit upon the objects of their application; they are intended to lead to the swifter despatch of those objects. Should they thus be patentable? In general, the answer would appear to be that they may be[3] but this answer is given with some hesitation since the distinction between these inventions and those described in the previous paragraph is not indicated by the text of the section.

(iii) Does 'treatment' or 'diagnosis' imply the existence of a live object? To give examples, would a process of embalming a dead body, or a means of diagnosing the cause of a corpse's demise, be excluded from patentability? The public policy argument in favour of the patient's interests, which provides the *raison d'être* of the exclusion, does not apply here; a different public policy argument may be raised against patentability, in that the refusal to allow the use of a post-mortem diagnostic technique could result in the spread of a virulent disease – but it is difficult to imagine that a court would ever exercise its equitable jurisdiction so as to restrain the autopsy process, or grant anything other than nominal or trivial damages for such an infringement.

(iv) Does 'treatment' or 'diagnosis' imply the existence of an organic body? It may be speculated as to whether a new method of replacing the worn parts of prosthetic limbs, or a new system for the diagnosis of structural weaknesses in artificial joints, would be excluded from patentability. What little case law there is suggests exclusion,[4] but it is difficult to point to any coherent principle which would lead to the resolution of this issue.

(v) Does the treatment of ectoparasites, for example headlice, fall within the scope of section 4(2)? If one is treating the human by ridding him of an unhealthy infestation, then section 4(2) will remove the method of treatment from patentability. However the courts have been prepared to accept that there is at least an arguable case for saying that, if it is the ectoparasite which is being 'treated' by extermination, there is no human or animal treatment, and, accordingly, such treatment may be patentable.[5]

1. See eg *Schering's Application* [1971] RPC 337.
2. *Unilever's (Davis's) Application* [1983] RPC 219; In *SALMINEN/Pigs III* [1989] EPOR 125 at 128 the EPO defined 'therapy' as 'any non-surgical treatment which is designed to cure, alleviate, or lessen symptom or prevent or reduce the possibility of malfunction of the animal body'.

3. *R v Patents Appeal Tribunal, ex p Swift & Co* [1962] RPC 37. The EPO has distinguished between beauty therapy and 'treatment by therapy': *Du Pont/ Appetite Suppressant* [1987] EPOR 6; *Roussel-Uclaf* [1986] OJEPO 295.
4. *Tectronics/Pacemaker* [1996] OJ EPO 274.
5. *Stafford-Miller's Application* [1984] FSR 258.

5.28   It must be observed that, however one interprets section 4(2), it clearly applies only to methods and processes. If a product is made which can be used for the purposes of treatment and diagnosis, its patentability as a product is in no way impaired.[1] This means that the pharmaceutical company which develops a new[2] drug for the cure of an illness can patent both the drug itself and the method of manufacturing it; only the methods of administering it (eg intravenously at three-day intervals, or five times a day before meals) cannot be patented. The manufacturer is thus safe from competition in the disclosure, maintenance and marketing of his product, and there is little obvious justification for extending legal protection beyond this point. Likewise the manufacturer of surgical apparatus can enjoy similar privileges, but his patent will not be construed as extended to methods of use.[3]

1. Eg *Siemens/Flow Measuring Apparatus* [1989] OJEPO 171; *Bristol-Myers Squibb Co v Baker Norton Pharmaceuticals Inc* [2001] RPC 1.
2. The first medical indication of a known substance is rendered patentable by s 2(6) of the Patents Act 1977, which eases the requirement of novelty in this situation. In *EISAI/Second Medical Indication* [1979-85] EPOR B 241, somewhat reluctantly followed in *John Wyeth & Brother Ltd's Application*; *Schering's Application* [1985] RPC 545, it was held that use of the so-called 'Swiss Claim' enabled a patent to be obtained for a second medical indication. A revision to art 54 of the European Patent Convention will ease the way to patenting second and subsequent medical indications of known compounds: Diplomatic Conference, November 2000.
3. *Visx Inc v Nidex Co Ltd (No 4)* [1999] FSR 405.

(4) Inventions excluded from patentability

5.29   Even once the patent applicant has climbed the small mountain of proof that what he has conceived is an invention, and has then scaled the rather higher mountain of showing that his invention is patentable, he must still negotiate two final trip-wires, as it were: his invention must not be found to be:

(i)   one the commercial exploitation of which would be contrary to public policy or morality; or
(ii) any variety of animal or plant, or any essentially biological process for the production of animals or plants, not being a microbiological process or the product of such a process.[1]

1. Patents Act 1977, s 1(3), as amended by Patents Regulations 2000 (SI 2000/ 2037) reg 3, reflecting art 53(a) and (b) of the European Patent Convention.

5.30   So far as inventions which are contrary to public policy or morality are concerned, it is likely that any invention which causes substantial annoyance, inconvenience or danger to the physical or moral welfare of the public will be included. Examples which spring to mind are patent applications for implements for use in the process of torture, electronic machinery for causing electricity meters to under-record a user's electricity consumption and for chemicals which may have an aphrodisiac or other behavioural impact upon the person into whose drink they are surreptitiously imparted. Contraceptive devices are no longer considered to encourage immoral behaviour;[1] although they may lessen the risks of immoral behaviour, they are presumably not regarded as increasing the pleasure which may be derived from it. Two further points to note with regard to such inventions: (i) the mere fact that a particular form of behaviour is illegal in the UK or in any part of it does not necessarily mean that an invention which facilitates it will necessarily be unpatentable,[2] which means that a new skateboard is not barred from patentability merely because its use is banned in all parks under the supervision of the Nowhereshire County Council, and (ii) the words 'contrary to public policy or morality' are a paraphrase of the concept of acts contrary to *ordre public*, the untranslatable French term left in the English version of the European Patent Convention.[3] This received considerable attention in the course of Harvard University's application to patent the 'Onco-mouse' – a creature[4] genetically engineered to be particularly susceptible to cancer. Such a mouse is of great commercial and scientific interest to those who test potential carcinogens. The EPO's Board of Appeal[5] directed the Examining Division to weigh up the issues of morality; it did so and granted the patent.[6] However, a large number of parties filed oppositions on moral and other grounds.[7] It has been argued that the patent system is neither apt nor adequate to deal with moral and environmental issues and should not be required to do so.[8] Certainly, refusal of a patent does not prevent use of the invention for which it is sought; grant of a patent provides a control mechanism only to the patentee. However, moral consideration is built into the system by Art 53(a)[9] and section 1(4).[10] It appears that the EPO is setting a high threshold, that of abhorrence, for exclusion from patentability on moral grounds.[11] The EC Directive on Biotechnological Inventions[12] provides a list of inventions considered unpatentable. These include the cloning of human beings, the use of human embryos for industrial or commercial purposes and processes for modifying the genetic identity of animals, which are likely to cause them suffering without any substantial benefit to man or animal.

1. Cf *Riddlesbarger's Application* (1935) 53 RPC 57, where the royal prerogative was exercised so as to refuse the grant of a patent for a contraceptive.
2. Patents Act 1977, s 1(4).
3. Art 53(a).
4. Harvard's claims were actually to modified non-human mammals and rodents rather than to mice specifically.
5. *Harvard/Onco-mouse* [1990] 12 OJ EPO 476; [1990] EPOR 501.
6. [1992] 10 OJ EPO 590.
7. For a summary see H-R Jaenichen and A Schrell 'The "Harvard Onco-mouse" in the Opposition Proceedings before the European Patent Office' [1993] EIPR 345.
8. See, for example, R Nott 'The Proposed EC Directive on Biotechnological Inventions' [1994] 5 EIPR 191.
9. Para **5.29**, n 1 above. For analysis of the legal and moral issues, see D Beyleveld and R Brownsword, *Mice, Morality and Patents* (1993); B Sherman and L Bently 'The Question of Patenting Life' in L Bently and S Maniatis (eds) *Intellectual Property and Ethics* (1998) Vol 4, Perspectives on Intellectual Property; P Drahos 'Biotechnology, Patents, Markets and Morality' [1999] EIPR 441. See also *NOVARTIS/Transgenic Plant* [2000] EPOR 305.
10. For a survey of cases where the patent system has been used as a 'social filter' see A Wells 'Patenting New Life Forms: an Ecological Perspective' [1994] 3 EIPR 111.
11. Eg *Lubrizol Genetics*, cited in H-R Jaenichen and A Schrell 'The European Patent Office's Recent Decisions on Patenting Plants' [1993] EIPR 466.
12. Directive EC 98/71 on the Legal Protection of Biotechnological Inventions [1998] OJ L213/13, art 6(2). These principles were adopted into the Implementing Regulations to the EPC, as Rule 23d. The Patents Regulations 2000 (SI 2000/2037) imported them into the Patents Act 1977 as s 76A and Sch A2.

5.31   So far as plant and animal inventions are concerned, plant varieties are excluded because the plant variety legislation,[1] designed specifically to protect them, was intended to be mutually exclusive of the patent system. In March 1991, however, the UPOV Convention on plant variety rights was amended to remove this mutual exclusion. Animal varieties, which are excluded for no good economic or moral reason, are not excluded from patentability in a number of other common law jurisdictions.[2] In the *Onco-mouse* case,[3] the European Patent Office interpreted the exclusion narrowly and proceeded to grant a patent for genetically modified mammals. The situation was complicated by the fact that 'animal variety' has no precise scientific or legal meaning and by the fact that the German text of the European Patent Convention appears to exclude 'species' rather than 'varieties'.[4] Greater certainty has been achieved through the intervention of the EC. First of all, Regulation (EC) No 2100/94 on Community Plant Variety Rights introduced a definition of 'plant variety'.[5] The European

Community Directive on Biotechnological Inventions[6] then adopted this definition and provided for the patentability of both plant[7] and animal[8] inventions, provided the technical feasibility of the invention is not confined to a particular plant or animal variety. The European Patent Office then incorporated these changes into its Regulations.[9] Micro-biological products are patentable,[10] even though they bear the characteristics of animal or plant-hood when viewed under a microscope, they look like a test-tube full of chemicals to the human eye and are often created under what, to the ignorant lawyer, appears to be the same sort of laboratory conditions.

1. The Plant Varieties Act 1997, discussed in Ch 25.
2. See discussion at para **25.3** below.
3. Para **5.30**, nn 5 and 6 above.
4. For an explanation of these problems of interpretation, see Beyleveld and Brownsword, para **5.30**, n 9 above. For countries within the EC, guidance is now given by art 2.3 of the Biotechnology Directive, n 5 below, which in turn refers to art 5 of Regulation 2100/94 on Community plant variety rights [1994] OJ L 227/1.
5. Art 5.
6. Directive EC 98/71 on the Legal Protection of Biotechnological Inventions [1998] OJ L213/13, given effect in the UK by the Patents Regulations 2000 (SI 2000/2037).
7. Art 4(2). See Funder 'Rethinking Patents for Plant Innovation' [1999] EIPR 551.
8. Art 4(2). See, also, M Llewelyn 'The Patenting of Biological Material [2000] EIPR 191.
9. Implementing Regulations, rules 23b and c.
10. Patents Act 1977, s 1(3)(b).

Chapter 6

Obtaining a patent

Introduction

6.1   The rules which govern the procedure leading to the grant of a patent are not normally the subject of close academic scrutiny or comment. Some have generated comment, but most are written off as arbitrary and tedious detail, of interest only to the pedant or the bureaucrat. The dismissal of this body of rules is, perhaps, unfair, if one considers that any brand of political, social or economic policy is, at the last resort, only as good as the rules which establish it. Patents as a reward for making or disclosing inventions are an attractive notion, but it is the substance of the mind-befuddling minutiae which in the end enables the intentions of Parliament to succeed or fail. This chapter will not give a full and detailed account of the regulation of patent application and grant.[1] It will, however, paint with a broad brush a general picture of the whole process, commenting where appropriate upon the impact of this body of rules upon the world around it.

1.   At the time of writing, the Patent Rules 1995 (SI 1995/2093) had been amended by a number of subsequent statutory instruments (SIs 1999/1092, 1999/1899, 1999/3197 and SI 2001/1412). The best place to consult the amended Rules is probably to use the 'unofficial' consolidated version, which is available on the Patent Office website at www.patent.gov.uk. For a full account of the regulation of patent application and grant, the reader is referred to the *CIPA Guide to the Patents Act 1977* (5th edn 2001) pp 128-311.

Who can apply for a patent?

6.2   Any natural or legal person may apply for a patent, whether he is the inventor or not, and whether or not he has any right to the invention.[1] This does not mean that any resulting patent will belong to the applicant. In the first place the applicant has to state the identity of the inventor.[2] If the applicant is someone other than the inventor, he must give an explanation as to how he came to be the applicant;[3] if he cannot do so, the application will be unlikely to proceed unless the person entitled to the invention takes it over.[4] If it transpires that a patent has been granted to someone who is not entitled to it, the person who is entitled to it can have the patent revoked,[5] or he can have it transferred to him.[6]

1. Patents Act 1977, s 7(1).
2. Patents Form 1/77, in the Patents Rules 1995, Sch 1.
3. See Patents Form 7/77.
4. Patents Act 1977, s 8 provides for the determination of disputes as to who should be entitled to be the applicant.
5. Patents Act 1977, s 72(1)(b).
6. Ibid, s 37.

To whom is the patent granted?

6.3 The grantee[1] of a patent is the inventor,[2] unless someone else (his employer, in about nine out of every ten cases[3]) has a better claim to it, or unless either the inventor or his employer has transferred the invention to anyone else.[4] It is assumed that the person who takes the trouble to apply for a patent and who claims to be entitled to do so is the person who is actually entitled to it, unless the contrary is apparent.[5]

1. Patents Act 1977, s 72(2). Neither of the words 'grantee' or 'patentee' are used in the 1977 Act, which employs the term 'proprietor' to cover any person entitled to a patent or an application for a patent.
2. 'Inventor' is explained in para **6.4.**
3. This is an estimated figure which has been widely accepted by commentators: see eg M Ruete, 'The German Employee Invention Law: an Outline', in J Phillips *Employees' Inventions: a Comparative Study* (1981) at p 180.
4. See Patents Act 1977, s 7(2)(c); for a case of dispute, see *Buchanan v Alba Diagnostics* [2000] RPC 367.
5. A challenge under the Patents Act 1977, s 8 may, however, be made on Patents Form 2/77.

Inventors and joint inventors

6.4 The Patents Act, which does not define 'invention', does define 'inventor'. By section 7(3) the inventor 'in relation to an invention means the actual deviser of the invention'. In the context of a Patents Act one wonders in respect of what, other than an invention, an inventor can be an inventor of. It is also open to speculation as to whether there is a subtle but significant difference between a deviser and an actual deviser. Since the Patents Act indicates that 'an invention ... shall, unless the context otherwise requires, be taken to be that specified in a claim of the specification ... as interpreted by the description and any drawing claimed in that specification'[1] one could argue a trifle facetiously that the actual deviser of such an invention is the patent agent who drafts the claim and describes the invention in terms of its patentable features

– but this is certainly not what the Act intended. Rather, the first step is to use the information in the patent to identify the inventive concept.[2] The inventor is the person who devises or contributes this. Depending on the relative importance of the concept and its execution, the inventor may be the 'ideas' person, the person who overcomes problems in reducing the ideas into practice, or a combination of the two.[3]

1. Patents Act 1977, s 125(1).
2. *Henry Bros (Magherafelt) Ltd v Ministry of Defence* [1999] RPC 442; in that case 'key joint' means for joining sections of prefabricated, blast-proof, buildings.
3. See, variously *Hickton's Patent Syndicate v Patents and Machine* (1909) 26 RPC 339; *Norris's Patent* [1988] RPC 159; *Goddin and Rennies' Patent* [1996] RPC 141; *Staeng Ltd's Patent* [1996] RPC 183.

6.5   The Act allows for the mental act of one brain to be credited to more than one body: references to 'inventor' include 'joint inventor'.[1] Organisations in which original research is performed by teams of scientists and technicians strongly favour the concept of 'joint invention'. Taking a lengthy temporal perspective of the period between the commencement of a project and the maturation of a recognisable invention, they claim that all those who participated positively in the maturation process are to be regarded as 'joint inventors'. This approach has much to commend it in terms of good industrial relations, for it rewards team effort with a team accolade, encouraging *esprit de corps* and reducing the tensions of jealousy and the prospect of selfish non-disclosure by one or more individuals within the team. It also renders unnecessary the difficult procedure of deciding which of, say, ten researchers was the actual deviser. On the other hand, logic does not support the concept. Invention is a mental process, and minds do not behave as bodies. Two men can jointly carry a trunk, sing a song, or rent a plot of land, but they cannot jointly think a thought, dream a dream, or feel a pain. Where two or more people work together and an invention occurs, there are in logic two possible results; one is that one is the inventor and the other is not; the other is that, the same thoughts and perceptions having occurred individually to each, they are each separate individual inventors with nothing except a common aim or common research environment to experience jointly. Fortunately the law has waxed its ears against the Siren-song of logic to pursue instead the practical demands of human fallibility.[2] Joint invention may lead to joint ownership of patent rights – a legally tricky situation which, the Court of Appeal has said, 'calls for clarification'.[3]

1. Patents Act 1977, s 7(3).
2. Thus the law regards effectively as joint inventors two men, neither of whom is able to satisfy the court that he is entitled, to the exclusion of the other, to be regarded as the sole inventor: see *Re Russell's Patent* (1857) 2 De G & J 130.

3. *Henry Bros (Magherafelt) Ltd v Ministry of Defence* [1999] RPC 442 at 451. See D Marchese 'Joint Ownership of Intellectual Property' [1999] EIPR 364.

What is a patent application?

6.6 Since the Patent Office is, inevitably, a bureaucracy, the maintenance of efficient order dictates a proliferation of rules which determine the nature of a valid patent application. Gone are the days when a would-be patentee could put quill to parchment and beseech the monarch to exercise in his favour the royal prerogative of granting a patent.[1] This is because the sheer volume of patent applications, and the complexity of inventions, require that the Patent Office be able with ease to process, store, retrieve and comprehend each application with a minimum of delay. Every aspect of the patent application is thus closely prescribed by law, right down to size of paper and the width of margins which surround the text.[2] Much of today's application procedure is conducted upon standard forms which may be obtained from the Patent Office, patent agents and from some patent depository libraries which stock them.

1. The royal prerogative, preserved by the Patents Act 1949, s 102(1), has been suspended or abrogated by the Patents Act 1977, s 18(4), which lays down that the power to grant a patent lies with the Comptroller alone.
2. See eg Patents Rules 1995, rr 18-20.

6.7 The Patents Act itself prescribes that every application contains (i) a request for a patent grant, (ii) a description of the invention (its 'specification'), (iii) a claim[1] which establishes what the invention actually does, and (iv) a potted description of it (the 'abstract'), which enables the Patent Office to decide (without needing to read it in full) who should ultimately examine it.[2] Of these requirements only the first can confidently be fulfilled by every applicant. The others are more difficult. Fortunately, the quality of the abstract has no bearing upon the success or failure of the application (the Comptroller can rewrite it), but the specification and claim must be got exactly right if the applicant is not to fail miserably. If the specification is faulty, then the invention and its description will be different; the resulting patent may be invalidated,[3] or may validly protect a different invention from that which the patentee thought he had protected. If the claim is faulty, the patent may be invalid because the inventor claims the invention can do something which it can't,[4] or (almost worse) the patent may be valid but useless, because the claim fails to state that the invention *can* do something; if what is done by an alleged infringer does not fall within the claims of a valid patent, it may not be regarded as an infringing act, which means of course that the patentee will be powerless to stop it. The drafting of claims and specifications is a tricky business for those who do not regularly practise it. If you do not believe that this is so, get a piece of paper and try describing any simple object (eg a ball-point pen, an egg-timer or a watch-strap) in such a way that any person skilled in the art could rely upon your description of it in making an end-product which conforms to the object you started off with. Then get two objects with similar functions, and try identifying precisely what the advantage of the one over the other actually is.

1. A White 'Function and Structure of Patent Claims' [1993] EIPR 243.
2. Patents Act 1977, s 14(2).
3. Ibid, s 72(1)(c) and (d).
4. Ibid, s 72(1)(a), with reference to s 4(1).

6.8   The timing of an application is a matter of great concern to the inventor or his successor in title. This is because a premature application may result in the disclosure of an idea which has been only imperfectly and incompletely realised, the specification describing only a primitive form, the potential uses of which may not be appreciated when the claims are drafted. On the other hand, any delay in filing an application may result in a competitor getting in first with his own application for an identical or similar invention. For this reason the application need not be filed all at once. The applicant can secure a 'filing date' (the date from which his patent will run, and after which no one else's disclosures will be considered as part of the prior art by which to test his novelty[1]) by sending the Patent Office (i) identification of the applicant, (ii) an indication that he will be seeking a patent, (iii) a description of the invention, and (iv) a filing fee.[2] From the filing date the applicant then has twelve months in which to formalise his application by submitting the specification, claims and abstract.[3] This period may be used profitably in working out the full ramifications of the invention. If, by the end of it, no formalisation has taken place, the application is treated as having been withdrawn.[4]

1. Patents Act 1977, s 5(1).
2. Ibid, s 15(1); the prescribed fee is now £0, see para **6.14**.
3. Patents Rules 1995, r 25(1).
4. Patents Act 1977, s 15(5).

6.9   The application, when made, is in effect a secret shared by the applicant and the Patent Office. If the applicant has second thoughts about proceeding with his application, he is entitled to withdraw it and keep his invention as a piece of confidential information.[1] Even though he has shown his invention to a public body, he is not considered to have made his invention available to the public, which means that if A applies for a patent and then withdraws his application, B can later secure a patent for the identical invention; it does not matter that B is not the invention's first inventor (or his successor in title). If an application is not withdrawn, it will eventually be published by the Patent Office.[2] Once it is published, it will be known to potential licensees, infringers and trade rivals. It becomes a matter of public knowledge.

1. Patents Act 1977, s 14(9) permits the withdrawal of an application at any time prior to grant. If the withdrawal takes place before publication of the application under s 16(1), the invention remains secret.
2. Patent Rules 1995, r 25 prescribes that publication will take place 18 months after the filing date, or from the so-called 'priority date' if earlier: see para **5.2**.

What happens to the patent application?

6.10 Until the coming into force of the Patents Act 1977, a patent application would be published for all to inspect; if no objector raised his voice, and if the applicant's invention had not already been patented within the previous fifty years, the application would then proceed more or less automatically to grant.[1] There was thus little in the way of 'quality control', except so far as opposition proceedings could eliminate invalid applications. This was favoured by those who felt that the patent grant procedure should be as simple as possible in order to expedite the protection and development of publicly disclosed inventions, but it was opposed by those who disliked the 'weak' nature of the patents then granted; since applications were not scrutinised by experts in order to ascertain their patentability, many patents were granted for old or obvious inventions simply because it was not worth anyone's while to object at the time that the application was still in the pipeline. Such patents were 'weak' in that, once they became of any commercial significance, their validity could be easily impugned by a competitor or prospective licensee who did not favour the terms under which he was offered a licence. 'Weak' patents had one further objection: they did not impress financiers from whom R & D investment funding was solicited. Moreover, whether resulting patents were 'weak' or 'strong', the opposition procedure was disliked by all save those whose livelihood benefited from it. Opposing an application could delay grant by many years, and could involve expensive litigation on more or less the same legal grounds upon which the validity of the patent, once granted, could be challenged.[2]

1. On the old procedure for obtaining a patent see *The British Patent System* (Cmnd 4407) 1970, paras 28-33 and Figure 1.

2. See Patents Act 1949, s 14 (opposition) and s 32 (revocation). Oppositions may be lodged in the European Patent Office, as in *Onco-mouse* and the other cases discussed under paras. **5.29-5.30** above.

6.11 The Patents Act 1977 abolished opposition proceedings, but seeks to safeguard the interests of the applicant, his competitors and the public at large[1] by subjecting all applications to a rigorous examination as to their validity. Modern information technology has provided the skilled examiner with the assurance that the prior art is often no more than a button-press away, which facilitates the examination of the novelty of an application. The examination of inventive step is, however, more in the nature of a subjective assessment; one may wonder whether there is any practical benefit to be derived from such an exercise.[2]

1. Who may lodge their observations on patentability under s 21 of the Patents Act 1977.
2. See discussion at para **5.14** above.

6.12 What form does the search and examination procedure take? First there is a preliminary examination and search,[1] where the examiner makes sure that the numerous formalities of application have been complied with; he does not actually analyse the issues of novelty and inventive step, but instead identifies the documentary sources to which he thinks reference will later be made when a full examination takes place.[2] The logic of this is that the applicant can himself have a look at these documents and decide whether there is sufficient likelihood of success to warrant his perseverance with his application. If a preliminary examination shows that his invention has been anticipated, he can cut his losses and retreat discreetly to the drawing-board. The same documents may reveal that, while his invention probably is patentable, the market for similar products or processes is so well served that his novel product could not be sold successfully under normal commercial conditions; in this case too, he will be well advised to direct his energies elsewhere.

1. Patents Act 1977, s 17(1).
2. Ibid, s 17(4).

6.13 Once the preliminary search and examination has indicated that it is worth the applicant's while to proceed with his application, he must request a substantive examination[1] of his invention's novelty and inventive step. This is in fact an interactive process, the examiner indicating his objections and the applicant suggesting amendments which will prove acceptable to him. If this second stage of examination is successfully negotiated, the application will proceed automatically to the grant of patent.[2] For a straightforward patent application, the procedure may be accelerated by filing a request for examination at the same time as asking for the search and preliminary examination. The applicant also asks for publication and early grant. Not surprisingly, this is called 'combined search and examination'.

1. Patents Act 1977, s 18(1).
2. Ibid, s 18(4).

How much does it cost to get a patent?

6.14 It costs nothing to keep an invention secret, but patent costs can be a severe burden to the successful applicant, not least because he usually has to pay them all before his invention – which itself may have been expensive to test and develop – earns him a single penny. In the first place he must pay official fees. As a rough generalisation the Patent Office will talk to an applicant, give him information and allow him to file a patent application without cost, but it will not perform any further act for him unless it receives the due fee. An idea of some of the Patent Office's fees may be gleaned from the following table:[1]

	£
Filing of the initial application	0
Preliminary examination and search	130
Substantive examination	70
Amendment of application	40
Alterations of name and address	0
Correction of an error or mistake	40

Renewal fees vary from £50 (to 5th year) to £400 (20th year).

1. Patents (Fees) Rules 1998 (SI 1998/1778).

6.15 Apart from Patent Office fees, the applicant may incur patent agents' fees. The drafting of patent applications and the giving of incidental legal, technical, scientific and commercial advice will vary according to the client's demands and the complexity of the invention, but recent estimates indicate that the applicant will pay more for his patent agent's services than for his package holiday, his television set or his house purchase fees.[1] It should not be forgotten that these fees will be incurred irrespective of the invention's success or failure. Many commentators have argued that the cost of applying for a patent should be made less burdensome,[2] at any rate for the private inventor and the small business. Successive governments have claimed to be sympathetic to this call, and have pledged to do all they can to alleviate the hardship of the small-time patent applicant, short of actually helping him.

1. For a fairly simple invention, which can be described in a few pages, the Chartered Institute of Patent Agents estimates £750 + VAT for filing the initial application, £1,200 + VAT for preparing and filing the full specification and claims, with additional fees for dealing with the examiner's report and objections (figures cited on the Chartered Institute's website at www.cipa.org.uk, 2001). The Chartered Institute offers patent clinics, usually by appointment, where members of the public can seek preliminary advice. Again, details can be found on the web site.

2. See eg A Buckley 'A Creative Alternative to the Private Inventor's Patent' in J Phillips (ed) *Patents in Perspective* (1985).

Chapter 7

The consequences of obtaining a patent

A monopoly is secured

7.1 The successful patentee acquires a right to exclude others from using or exploiting his invention for a period of not more than, and usually very much less than, twenty years from the priority date of his patent application.[1] The duration of the patent grant is initially four years from the priority date[2] and the patentee has the option of renewing his monopoly, annually, upon the payment of progressively steeper renewal fees.[3] If he fails to renew his patent and does not take advantage of the 'kiss of life' provisions whereby a lapsed patent may be resuscitated on the payment of the appropriate guilt-offering,[4] then the invention formerly protected by it falls irrevocably into the public domain.

1. Patents Act 1977, ss 25, 28 and 29.
2. Ibid, s 25(3); Patents Rules 1995, r 39(1).
3. The current fee scale is imposed by the Patents (Fees) Rules 1998 (SI 1998/1778).
4. Patents Act 1977, s 28.

7.2 Some curiosities regarding the patent term may be noted. In the first place, while the monopoly term extends from the filing date of the application, infringers of the patent cannot be sued until the application has first been granted in fact,[1] and has then been taken to be granted in law, once notice of its grant has been published in the *Patents and Designs Journal*.[2] Thus a patent grant, like the Queen, enjoys two birthdays. Second, since the actual grant may well not occur until more than four years from the priority date, the ingenuity of the country's legal draftsmen has been employed in the creation of special rules facilitating the renewal of patents which have not yet been granted.[3] Third, there is no general[4] means of prolonging beyond 20 years the duration of the term prescribed by the Patents Act 1977. Under the Patents Act 1949, the proprietor of a patent could apply for the extension of his sixteen-year term by up to ten years if, despite its merits, it had yielded him an insufficiently rewarding return or if its exploitation had been inhibited on account of a war.[5] This provision, which was not in fact greatly used,[6] was less praised for its flexibility than criticised for causing industrial uncertainty.[7] In fact the European Patent Convention, which calls for a standard twenty-year term,[8] does not prevent the UK from extending patents, so long as it does not discriminate between its own patents and those granted by the European Patent Office;[9] but this would appear to assume the possibility of extending all patent terms by state decree, rather than the provision of a scheme for the consideration of the claims of individual patentees.[10]

1. Patents Act 1977, s 25(1).
2. This journal is published by statutory authority: Patents Act 1977, s 123(6); Patents Rules 1995, r 115 as amended by Patents (Amendment) Rules 1999 (SI 1999/1092), r 16.
3. Patents Rules 1995, r 39(1), proviso.
4. See para **7.3** below for the special regime of supplementary protection certificates applicable to pharmaceutical patents.
5. Patents Act 1949, ss 23 and 24.
6. Between 1959 and 1968 only 48 applications were made for patent extensions, of which 23 were granted: *Patents, Designs, and Trade Marks* the 86th Report of the Comptroller of Patents (1968).
7. *The British Patent System* Cmnd 4407, 1970, paras 347-348.
8. European Patent Convention, art 63(1); the TRIPs agreement specifies a minimum term of 20 years: art 33.
9. European Patent Convention, art 63(2).
10. The text of art 63(2) would seem to refer to blanket extensions of all patents in the case of war or 'similar emergency conditions'.

7.3 Within the pharmaceutical industry, where stringent requirements with regard to the trial of drugs must be fulfilled before marketing can take place, the patent may have only a few years to run before the patented product is actually available to the public. This led pharmaceutical manufacturers to argue forcefully in favour of an extendible term – or of an automatically longer term – for pharmaceutical patents. While this plea was received favourably in the United States,[1] it was not initially viewed sympathetically in most other jurisdictions. In particular it has been felt by many that the protection accorded by the patent is truly enjoyed from the date of publication of grant, from which the patent's proprietor – even though he cannot sell the patented product himself – can prevent others from taking advantage of it. More to the point, from a commercial point of view, is the fact that the strength of the goodwill in any trade mark under which the product is marketed will ensure that the patent proprietor's dominant market position will persist after other manufacturers have been able to bring on to the market their 'generic' products (ie products with the same properties and active ingredients as the patent proprietor's but without the same trade mark). As a concession to pharmaceutical patent owners, however, Regulation 1768/ 92/EEC created a system of supplementary protection certificates for medicinal products.[2] This entitles the owners of pharmaceutical patents to an extended regime of effective protection where regulatory delays of more than five years have been experienced. The maximum available extension is five years.[3] The scheme was subsequently extended to patents for agro-chemicals, which also have to await marketing authorisation.[4]

1.   Generic Animal Drug Patent Term Extension Act 1988.
2.   Given effect within the administration of UK patents by the Patents (Supplementary Protection Certificate for Medicinal Products) Regulations 1992 (SI 1992/3091) and Patents (Supplementary Protection Certificates) Rules 1997 (SI 1997/64. There must be a valid authorisation to market the product in the state concerned *Yamanouchi Pharmaceuticals Co Ltd v Comptroller-General* [1997] RPC 844, ECJ.
3.   See R Whaite and N Jones 'Pharmaceutical Patent Term Restoration: the European Community's Regulation' [1992] EIPR 324.
4.   EC Regulation 1610/96 concerning the creation of a supplementary protection certificate for plant protection products; Patents (Supplementary Protection Certificates for Plant Protection Products) Regulations 1996 (SI 1996/ 1320); *BASF AG's SPC Application* [2000] RPC 1.

Is the twenty year patent term too long?

7.4   Table A shows the rate at which UK patents are renewed; from it we can infer that a preponderant majority lapse prior to the expiry of their full term. The data as to the extent of non-renewal is open to a number of plausible explanations. For example:

(i)   The number of patents renewed declines as a consequence of the gradual obsolescence of technology; only in areas of relative technological stagnation will an invention still be in commercial demand two decades after the initial application is made.

(ii)   The number of patents renewed into their final year comes close to representing the true total of profitably exploited patents. The attrition rate between the fifth and subsequent years is merely an index of the rate at which unsuccessful patentees lose hope of attracting licensees or venture capital.

(iii)   Even with increasingly stringent examination of novelty and inventive step, far too many non-meritorious intellectual conceptions are accorded patentable status. Non-renewals reflect a gradual awareness that the patent would be invalid if challenged.

(iv)   The prime functions of the patent system for industry are to publicise inventions so as to attract trade interest and to give the patent applicant a measure of security in negotiating the realisation of such interest. Both these functions are generally effectively fulfilled well before the expiration of even the initial four-year period. Thereafter, renewal only becomes necessary where the circumstances of the invention's exploitation particularly demand it.

(v)   The renewal of patents is inhibited by the increasing expense of renewal fees (a complaint often heard among independent inventors). Without wishing to be unduly sceptical, one may wish to consider whether the expense of £400 – the maximum renewal fee – would ever realistically deter a trader from purchasing an absolute monopoly to sell or make a commodity in the UK, a market of nearly sixty million souls[1] with a gross domestic product of some £935billion.[2] The cost of such a monopoly is actually less than that of purchasing a packet of twenty cigarettes a day.

None of these explanations is self-evidently true, and each may be apt in respect of particular patentees, industries or periods of technological development. It must be recognised, however, that it is extremely difficult to perform from the data above any reasoning which can convincingly argue the case for either extending or decreasing the maximum term of grant.

1.   Office for National Statistics, 2000.
2.   HM Treasury figure for 2000.

7.5   If non-renewal is viewed in terms of time, it can be seen that the rate of the non-renewal of granted patents is slowing down. Once again a number of explanations are possible. For example:

(i)   There has been a gradual improvement in the quality of granted patents, as applicants have given their own patent applications a greater degree of critical scrutiny in the light of the increasing need to control their expenditure during an economic recession.

(ii)   Professional standards have risen among patent agents, who are thus better able to detect weaknesses in applications and advise their clients accordingly.

(iii)   Increased reliance on more efficient techniques of on-line patent search has resulted in fewer patents being sought for inventions which have been anticipated by the prior art.

(iv)   Increased reliance has been placed upon the protection of inventions in certain fields, for example household gadgets, electronic circuits and functional manufactured goods by means of unregistered design right[1] or registration of shapes as trade

7.5 *The consequences of obtaining a patent*

Table A: Patent renewals

Patents renewed into

Year	5th	8th	11th	14th	16th	17th	18th	19th	20th
1988	22,675	23,048	15,473	8,818	7,477	5,991	5,032	3,879	3,181
1989	20,427	24,226	15,048	9,320	7,072	6,248	5,040	4,164	3,070
1990	20,637	25,561	16,796	10,110	7,011	6,073	5,564	4,354	3,395
1991	18,227	25,572	17,179	10,762	7,539	5,794	5,342	4,702	3,332
1992	18,205	25,829	17,555	10,416	7,431	6,199	4,868	4,223	3,633
1993	17,281	24,898	17,117	10,450	7,469	5,973	4,940	3,668	3.086
1994	19,628	25,081	17,720	10,825	7,218	6,174	4,830	3,885	2,731
1995	20,180	25,572	18,552	11,216	7,761	6,185	5,217	3,949	3,093
1996	21,151	29,496	18,623	11,615	8,375	6,752	5,309	4,363	3,196
1997	20,933	32,258	19,478	12,476	8,523	7,280	5,812	4,384	3,504
1998	20,040	30,054	21,102	12,831	8,718	7,138	6,036	4,554	3,325
1999	20,333	31,573	23,551	13,617	9,864	7,999	6,390	5,243	3,777

Figures taken from Patent Office Annual Reports

marks.[2] Any patents granted for such inventions or devices would naturally be allowed to lapse once the product concerned was rendered technologically obsolete or became unfashionable to domestic consumers so removing these from the pool of patented products would leave inventions with a longer commercial life.

(v)   The figures indicate a reversal of the long-accepted notion that the rate of growth of scientific knowledge, or of its industrial application, is exponential.[3] Such a reversal can be explained, at any rate in the UK, as a natural consequence of the shrinkage of industrial research operations, the diminution of educational standards or opportunities, the concentration of skilled endeavour upon the service industries to the detriment of the innovation sector, and so on.

(vi) The overall number of surviving patents remains roughly constant but the annual crop of grants from which they are derived grows smaller as it becomes increasingly difficult to make new inventions. According to another opinion, modern inventions have a far briefer life-cycle than their predecessors. If this view were correct we should expect to see a far more rapid rate of non-renewal, which would be against the present trend. Nonetheless, it is hoped that the assessment of full and correct implications of patent statistics, may result from effective scrutiny by economists,[4] and not be left to the mere unskilled lawyer.

1.   See para **24.10**, below.
2.   See para **21.11**, below.
3.   In the long term, since 1900, the rise in patenting has been exponential: see L Rymer 'The Future of Industrial Property' (1998) 9 AIPJ 113 diagram at 116.
4.   See eg C Taylor and Z Silberston *The Economic Impact of the Patent System* (1973); J Schmookler *Invention and Economic Growth* (1966); C Freedman *The Economics of Industrial Innovations* (2nd edn 1982); A Silberston *The Economic Importance of Patents* (1987); O Granstrand *The Economics and Management of Patents* (1999); P Drahos, ed *Intellectual Property* (1999). U Roy, R D Tuch, J E Clark in 'Global Assessment of Patents, Research and Development, Invention and Economic Output' (1997) 79 JPTOS 110 and 157 chart the correlation between patenting and a number of other economic indicators.

A property is born

7.6   A patent is a piece of personal property.[1] It therefore partakes of many of the characteristics of any other type of property you care to consider. It can be sold, leased, mortgaged, given away or willed. Unlike most other types of property, however, the potential date of its death is fixed at the date of its conception, which means that it is difficult to find a customer for a patent which is nearing its expiry date.

1.   Patents Act 1977, s 30(1).

7.7   The consequences of obtaining a patent

7.7   There are a number of rules which attend the disposal or passage of patent rights, and they are a good deal more technical than their description in this book may suggest. In brief, any assignment or mortgage of a patent is, quite simply, void if it is not in writing and signed both by the patentee and by the person who acquires the patent from him.[1] This is a sensible arrangement which makes it easier for a lawyer to advise as to who is actually entitled to the patent.

1.   Patents Act 1977, s 30(6). *Baxter International v Nederland Produktie Laboratorium voor Boledtransfusieapparatur* [1998] RPC 250.

7.8   If you want to know who holds the rights in a particular patent, you must consult the Patent Office register.[1] This register contains the details of every patent (and application) operative within the jurisdiction, and also of any official act which has a bearing upon it, such as a 'licence of right' endorsement, the grant of a compulsory licence or a determination that it be revoked.[2] In addition, a person who acquires someone else's patent, or secures a licence to use someone else's patent, must take the trouble to have the entry in the register concerning that patent amended by the recording of his acquired interest.[3] If he fails to do this, the consequences for him may be particularly serious; for example, a court of law will not be inclined to believe that he owns a patent if someone else's name is listed as proprietor by the register,[4] and he may find that he cannot mulct an infringer of damages in respect of infringements carried out more than six months prior to the registration of his interest.[5]

1.   Patents Act 1977, s 32(1).
2.   Ibid, s 32(2), and the rules made under it.
3.   Ibid, s 33(1).
4.   Ibid, s 32(9)-(11).
5.   Ibid, s 68.

7.9   If a patentee doesn't want his patent, can't sell it or give it away, and can't even wait for it to expire, he can actually surrender it to the Comptroller.[1] If he does so, the patent ceases to have any effect from the date the Comptroller accepts the surrender. This provision is little used,[2] which is not surprising since the patentee has little or nothing to gain from surrendering a patent which will automatically lapse if it is not renewed. Unlike other sorts of unwanted property, the patent takes up little shelf-room and needs no dusting; its surrender may enable its holder to avoid undesirable litigation,[3] but so may the simple procedure of letting the patent lapse. Incidentally, the surrender of a patent is one of the Patent Office's free services to its customers.[4]

1.   Patents Act 1977, s 29.

2. The Comptroller's Annual Report for 1999-2000, for example, indicated that in 1999 there were nine applications for surrender and that one was allowed.
3. For example, a petition for revocation, which publicises the patent's defects to the possible detriment of equivalent patents in other countries; see *SmithKline Beecham v Connaught* [1999] FSR 284; D Sternfeld 'Open Justice: A Court of Appeal Decision' [2000] EIPR 95.
4. There is no cost involved in surrendering a patent by means of form 2/77.

The use of the patent may be offered to other traders

7.10   When a patent is applied for, its grant is secured on the basis of a 'contract' theory:[1] the inventor or his successor discloses to the Patent Office an invention which it was within his power to keep secret and the Patent Office gives him a monopoly in return if the invention is new (there being no risk that existing users would be inconvenienced) and non-obvious (otherwise the benefit obtained by the inventor would greatly exceed that obtained by the public). Once the patent is granted, however, the public demands a further benefit: that the patent be exploited so that the country's industrial economy be enriched by the use or manufacture of the subject of the invention.

1.   See para **4.6**, above.

7.11   When a patentee effectively exploits his invention, he can with a good conscience prevent others from seeking to exploit it also. On the other hand, there seems something of the 'dog in manger'[1] about the patentee who owns property which he neither uses himself nor is prepared to let others enjoy. In considering how to resolve the issue, the law distinguishes between two types of patentee – he who cannot, and he who will not, exploit the patent himself.

1.   V S Vernon-Jones, *Aesop's Fables* (1912, reprinted 1974), p 60.

7.12   The patentee who cannot exploit the patent himself may be unable to do so for any number of reasons: lack of industrial manufacturing capacity, absence of marketing skills, shortage of R & D funding, and so on. In such circumstances the patentee will derive no benefit from his patent unless he can rectify his own shortcomings or find someone else to use his patent instead of him in return for a suitable monetary payment. The second of these alternatives is usually the far more attractive as a business proposition since it involves less risk and a near-certainty of deriving some profit or of recouping some loss, from the patenting process; the law attempts to facilitate it by means of the 'licence of right'.

7.13   *The consequences of obtaining a patent*

What does the law provide?

7.13   The law provides simply that, at any time after the patent grant, the patent's proprietor can ask the Comptroller to make an entry in the patent register that a licence in his patent be made available as of right to anyone who wishes to exploit it himself.[1] When this is done, the Comptroller will check the register and in particular satisfy herself that licensing is possible because no one is already registered as an exclusive licensee.[2] This check having been made the register will be amended so as to make the patent subject to a 'licence of right'. From the patent proprietor's point of view the 'licence of right' endorsement is attractive for two reasons: the renewal fees of a patent so endorsed are halved,[3] and the advertisement of the 'licence of right' in the *Journal* provides publicity which may catch the eye of a potential licensee. These inducements are not, in practical terms, of very great value. Reduced fees are only a worthwhile saving if the proprietor is very poor, or if the invention is so advanced that it is contained in a number of patents all of which are endorsed 'licence of right' simultaneously. Moreover, the advertisement of all endorsed patents in the *Journal* is a far less scientific and far more chancy way of finding a licensee than would be the employment, for a small fee, of any of the commercial innovation and development services or databases compiled and operated by invention brokers, or any of the 'technology transfer' bulletins.[4]

1.   Patents Act 1977, s 46(1).
2.   Ibid, s 46(2).
3.   Ibid, s 46(3)(d).
4.   Eg World Business Publications' *Technology Transfer International.*

What is the position of the licensee who wishes to exploit a licence of right?

7.14   Ideally the licensee and the patent owner will settle by negotiation such terms as are mutually agreeable[1] (the most important being the amount the licensee is to pay), the resulting licence being indistinguishable from one which is granted under a regular patent. If this does not occur, then the licensee is still entitled to use the patent under terms imposed upon both parties by the Comptroller.[2] A licensee under a patent which is subsequently metamorphosed into a 'licence of right' patent can exchange his freely negotiated licence for a licence of right on terms imposed by the Comptroller,[3] and this is likely to occur when licences of right are granted on terms more favourable than those enjoyed by an original non-exclusive licensee. Termination of licences of right is possible if circumstances change.[4] Note that 'new existing patents' in the pipeline at commencement of the Patents Act 1977 were given an extra four years' life, subject to licence of right provisions.[5]

1. Patents Act 1977, s 46(3)(a).
2. Ibid. For the bases on which the Comptroller will settle royalties and other terms, see *Smith Kline & French Laboratories Ltd's (Cimetidine) Patents* [1990] RPC 203; *Cabot Safety Corpn's Patent* [1992] RPC 39.
3. Patents Act 1977, s 46(3)(b).
4. *Smith Kline & French Laboratories Ltd v Harris Pharmaceuticals Ltd* [1992] FSR 110. Two licences of right were cancelled in 1995, 25 in 1998 and 7 in 2000.
5. Patents Act 1977, Sch 4, para 1. See, further, para **7.3**.

7.15   The number of patents endorsed 'licence of right' is not great. Table B gives an idea as to their relative frequency. The patentee who has problems attracting licensees will have to face the choice of either cutting his costs and letting his patent lapse or seeking a 'licence of right' endorsement. A comparison of Tables A and B indicates that, right or wrong, they overwhelmingly opt for the former.

Table B: Licences of right

Year	No. of applications for licence of right status	No. allowed
1992	561	557
1993	553	545
1994	549	536
1995	1,755	1,732
1996	387	379
1997	1,332	1,305
1998	2,511	2,455
1999	1,011	884

The use of the patent may be seized by other traders

7.16   Every schoolboy knows the tale about the light-bulb manufacturer who, on hearing of a means of making a perpetually illuminable light-bulb, purchases the patent and suppresses it, thus forcing the public to purchase, to the manufacturer's great benefit, the traditional, frequently-replaced variety. Indeed, the same tale is told, *mutatis mutandis*, of multiple-strike matches and indestructible hosiery. These tales are a collective defamation of the patent system which, displaying great prudence in its judgment, has so ordered its priorities as to provide machinery which has the potential to prevent the occurrence of such abuses of the monopoly grant.

7.17   The means so employed by the patent system is that of the compulsory licence.[1] Once there has elapsed a period of three years from the date of the patent grant, anyone who wants to use someone else's patent may apply to the Comptroller for the patent to be forcibly endorsed 'licence of right', or for a compulsory licence to work or make the invention in question.[2] Broadly speaking the Comptroller may not break the patentee's statutory monopoly unless the applicant for a licence can show that the invention is being unused or under-used in relation to demand or that failure to grant a licence voluntarily and on reasonable terms has hamstrung the exploitation or development of other British industries. The grounds on which a compulsory licence may be sought depend upon the status of the patentee. If the patent owner is a 'WTO Proprietor',[3] section 48A applies. Under this section the applicant must show that it has attempted over a reasonable period to obtain a licence. Where the applicant needs a licence to work his own patent, the Comptroller must be satisfied that he is prepared to grant a cross-licence on reasonable terms. Compulsory licences are non-exclusive and there are limits on their assignment; they are predominantly for supply to the UK market and must provide adequate remuneration to the patentee.[4] Additional grounds for grant of a compulsory licence apply when the patentee is not a 'WTO Proprietor'.[5]

1.   On the compulsory licence, see paras **3.6-3.9** above.
2.   Patents Act 1977, s 48; new ss 48, 48A and 48B were inserted into the Patents Act 1977 by the Patents and Trade Marks (World Trade Organisation) Regulations 1999 (SI 1999/1899) with effect from 29 July 1999.
3.   Ie he, she or it has a connection with a member country of the World Trade Organisation by nationality, domicile, or real and effective industrial or commercial establishment: s 48(5). This includes all the countries of the European Union, indeed, most countries of the world apart. By putting the UK and other EC countries on an equal footing, it appears to satisfy the principles of equal treatment and free movement of goods under the EC Treaty. See, further, paras **27.1** and **27.5** below. Cf *EC Commission v United Kingdom and Italy* [1993] RPC 283, [1993] FSR 1; *Gebhardt's Patent* [1992] RPC 1.
4.   Patents Act 1977, s 48A(6).
5.   Ibid, s 48B.

7.18   Until 1984 the Patent Office kept no separate statistics on the frequency of compulsory licence applications, presumably because they were so rarely made. In 1990 only four such applications were filed;

in 1991-1994 and 1998-99, not a single one. Of three applications in 1995, four in 1996 and one in 1997, none were allowed. As might be expected the explanation of such scant use depends upon one's viewpoint; a variety of plausible reasons exist, each of which may be valid up to a point:

(i) The three-year wait before a compulsory licence may be sought – established in order to give the patentee a reasonable time in which to exploit his patent himself – is too long. Three years from grant means five or more years from the original priority date, by which time many initially attractive and marketable inventions have become technologically obsolete, ecologically undesirable or commercially non-viable.

(ii) The examination of these figures in isolation creates a misleadingly pathological impression of commercial practice. The reality is that the threat of a compulsory licence encourages patentees to work their inventions or to license them on the most favourable terms they can secure by negotiation, the potential licensee's negotiating hand being strengthened by the availability of a compulsory licence. The statistics therefore only record the failures, not the successes, of the compulsory licence provision.[1]

(iii) The criteria for establishing that a compulsory licence should be granted are not so much legal as economic or commercial, which means that the patentee who is reluctant to succumb to a compulsory licence application has ample opportunity for indulging in tactics of delay and obfuscation. This being the case, a prospective licensee will not invoke the compulsory licence procedure unless he has a long purse and infinite patience.[2]

1. The Green Paper *Intellectual Property Rights and Innovation* Cmnd 9117, 1983, doubted this explanation at para 5.13.
2. And even then he may well fail, eg *Monsanto's CCP Patent* [1990] FSR 93.

The Crown can make use of the monopoly it grants

7.19 Ever since the Venetian Senate passed the first coherent patent litigation in 1474,[1] it has been considered prudent policy on the part of governments to ensure that they are not unduly fettered by the exercise of monopolies which they themselves have granted. This fairly simple principle has been preserved in the Patents Act 1977, where it occupies eight and a half sides of detailed, complex prose.[2]

1. See J Phillips 'Origin of the Patent System' (1980) The Inventor no 4, p 8, and 'The English Patent as a Reward for Invention' (1982) 3 Journal of Legal History 71.
2. Patents Act 1977, ss 55-59.

7.20   Painting again with a broad brush, we may distinguish two essentially different situations in which the Crown may wish to act unhindered by private patent rights. The first is where the good order and smooth running of the nation's affairs requires that products be made (such as medicines or armaments), or processes employed (such as water purification or energy production), which if it were to fall within the province of any individual to deny, or to concede only in return for a promise of a king's ransom it may well be reckoned unfair that a person who is given by the state, as a reward for disclosing his invention, a market monopoly, should then be able to secure a second reward against his original benefactor. On the other hand, if the patent grant is perceived as a reward for the disclosure of a meritorious invention, the sale or use of the subject of the patent may be seen as a wholly distinct benefit for which the Crown should be expected to pay the full market price; and, since the market for many products or processes may consist largely or entirely of agencies of, or funded by, the Crown, it can be asserted that the protection of the Crown's interest against the realities of the market effectively neuters the patent grant.

7.21   The second situation in which the government may (indeed, will) transgress the invisible fence which maps out the province of the patent grant is where there exists a state of emergency. In such a situation the contemplation of market factors and the niceties of intellectual property etiquette are swept aside. When London Bridge is falling down, the capital is engulfed in flames or triffids beset the beleaguered nation, even patent lawyers will generally agree – without prejudice to their clients' interests – that it is wise to act first, pay later.

7.22   The provisions of the Patents Act which deal with Crown use do not distinguish these two categories of use overmuch, for the same principles apply to each. They are that:

(i)   an act will be regarded as Crown use if it is performed 'for the services of the Crown';[1]

(ii)   use may be made of the invention both by the government and by anyone authorised in writing by the government;[2]

(iii)   the patentee will be entitled to compensation in respect of such use.[3] Courts have concluded that the amount of compensation is such sum as would have been paid by a willing licensee to a willing licensor;[4]

(iv)   the amount of compensation will take into account both the patentee's loss of commercial advantage *qua* patentee and the additional detriment inflicted upon him *qua* manufacturer[5] and loss of supply contracts;[6]

(v) a legitimate exclusive licensee can also receive compensation for his loss of market expectation.[7]

1. Patents Act 1977, s 55(1). Eg the construction of a blast-resistant prefabricated building for use as a police station in Northern Ireland: *Henry Bros (Magherafelt) Ltd v Ministry of Defence and Northern Ireland Office* [1999] RPC 442, CA.
2. Patents Act 1977, s 55(1). Note that retrospective authorisation by the Crown may 'purge' infringement: *Dory v Sheffield Health Authority* [1991] FSR 221.
3. Patents Act 1977, s 55(4), (5).
4. See *Patchett's Patent* [1967] RPC 237 (under the Patents Act 1949, ss 46-48).
5. *Re Generics (UK) Ltd's Application* [1986] 2 FTLR 100.
6. Patents Act 1977, s 57A.
7. Ibid.

7.23 It is interesting to consider what constitutes 'the services of the Crown'. The statutory definition is not exhaustive but merely inclusive, with specific mention of the supply of anything for foreign defence purposes, the production or supply of specified drugs or medicines, and for the atomic energy industry.[1] The reference to drugs and medicines is particularly controversial; for it allows the government-run National Health Service (the largest single purchaser of medical goods in the world) not only to manufacture for itself a medicine patented by another, but also to invite non-licensees of the patent to submit tenders for the supply of such medicine and then to sanction what would otherwise be an infringing manufacture and supply.[2] Pharmaceutical manufacturers regard such a facility as a gross and unjustifiable interference with the exercise of their monopoly, citing the recouping of massive research, testing and plant installation costs as the reason why they should be allowed to sell drugs and medicines at very much more than what a Department of Health accountant might regard as an acceptable profit per manufactured unit.[3] Governments, on the other hand, are responsible not merely for the health of their citizens but also for the wise administration of the money provided by, or seized from, the public which they serve. The public's view of its own best interest is confused to the point of incoherence: no one enjoys paying taxes or contributing to pharmaceutical companies' massive profits, while good health and the enjoyment of corporate dividends are regarded as inalienable human rights. Until the two economic and moral perspectives of this debate are capable of decisive synthesis, the present law seems as good an arbitrary and unacceptable compromise as any other.

1. Patents Act 1977, s 56(2).
2. Cf *Pfizer Corpn v Ministry of Health* [1965] AC 512. This possibility led the court to reject a defendant's arguments against grant of an injunction in *Biogen v Medeva* [1993] RPC 475.
3. For a trenchant account of the virtues of the unfettered pharmaceutical patent

7.23 *The consequences of obtaining a patent*

see E Jucket *Patents – Why?* (2nd edn 1988).

7.24 When there is a period of emergency,[1] the same provisions apply but the scope of 'services of the Crown' is greatly enhanced. The Act specifies[2] that inventions may be used:

(a) for the efficient prosecution of any war in which Her Majesty's Government may be engaged;

(b) for the maintenance of supplies and services essential to the life and well-being of the community;

(c) for the promotion of the productivity of industry, commerce or agriculture, and for redressing the balance of trade;

(d) for generally ensuring that the whole resources of the community are employed in the manner best calculated to serve the community's interests; and

(e) for the relief of suffering and the provision of essential supplies anywhere in the world which is in grave distress as the result of war.

1. Patents Act 1977, s 59.
2. Ibid, s 59(1).

7.25 How often does the Crown seek to rely upon its right to take a licence in a grantee's patent? The Patent Office keeps no statistics on this topic but it seems that the right is but rarely exercised, even in times of war. This is presumably because, in the first place, so many major patents of use to the government – especially in the defence industries – already belong to it, and secondly, because only a relatively small proportion of patents outside the defence and pharmaceutical sectors are likely to be of direct relevance to most of the activities in which a government would be likely to indulge during a state of emergency.

Chapter 8

Infringement and revocation

A question of context

8.1   Before examining the substantive issues of infringement and revocation, it is worth asking why revocation should be dealt with in the context of infringement rather than as an adjunct of patentability: after all, if a patent grant is to be revoked, its lack of patentability is the surest and most obvious ground upon which it may be attacked, and there is a certain symmetry inherent in the juxtaposition of the criteria for creating and then destroying a legal monopoly. Against this it may be stated that lack of patentability is in fact only one of five grounds upon which a patent may be impugned.[1] It is also a fact of life that revocation is generally raised, not in the abstract by some kind and disinterested soul who wishes to rid the economy of an undeserved monopoly, but by an infringing defendant against whom the full legal force of the patent has been unleashed and whose only realistic means of escaping liability is by killing the claimant's monopoly before it kills him.

1. Patents Act 1977, s 72(1).

The notion of infringement

8.2   The lawyer will note that the concept of patent infringement owes much to an imperfect analogy with that of trespass to land. The patent is a sort of property, the specification being the site-plan which delimits the property-owner's borders; anyone doing any act which falls within the scope of the patentee's legitimate claims is a trespasser, who must be driven off. But while the Englishman's home is his castle, his patent is virtually sovereign domain, as will be seen later.

8.3   What acts constitute infringement? Under the law prior to the Patents Act 1977, it was an infringement to 'make, use, exercise or vend' a patented product, or a product made by means of a patented process, without the authorisation of the right holder.[1] 'Make', 'use' and 'vend' gave the lawyer relatively little trouble, although the word 'exercise' seems, in retrospect, to have been more appropriately applicable to what a proprietor does with his dog than with his patent. This old notion of infringement was, despite its simplicity, the subject of criticism in that it was too narrow, and did not protect the patentee against activities which, it was argued,[2] were both morally culpable and commercially detrimental to his position as a legally protected monopolist. When the Patents Act 1977 employed a wider definition of infringement, the old-style infringing acts were often referred to as 'primary infringements', the new infringing acts being 'secondary infringements'. This terminology is not employed by the statute itself.

1. Form of Patent Grant (Patents Rules 1958-61 Sch 4, Form A), made under the Patents Act 1949, s 21(3).
2. *The British Patent System* Cmnd 4407, 1970, paras 269-273.

Infringement under the Patents Act 1977

8.4   The following acts are regarded as infringements of a patentee's monopoly right if they are performed without his actual or implicit authorisation:[1]

(i)   making, disposing of, offering to dispose of, importing, using or keeping (whether for disposal or otherwise) a patented product;

(ii)   doing any of the same acts in relation to a product derived directly from a patented process;

(iii)   using or offering for use in the UK a patented process in the knowledge that its use by an unauthorised person or anyone to whom it is offered would be an infringement. Note that, for this purpose, actual knowledge need not be proven; it is sufficient that it would have been obvious to the 'reasonable person in the circumstances' that the use would have been an infringing one. The characteristics of this particular 'reasonable person' have not yet been established by case law and are not apparent from the Act itself. One wonders what level of knowledge of patent law, commercial practice and of the state of the art itself will be imputed to him;

(iv)   supplying or offering to supply any unlicensed person with 'any of the means, relating to an essential element of the invention, for putting the invention into effect', in the knowledge that those means are suitable for putting the invention into effect.[2]

1. Patents Act 1977, s 60(1), (2).
2. P Mes 'Indirect Patent Infringement' (1999) 30 IIC 531 discusses German cases on this form of infringement.

8.5 Of these four groups of infringing acts, the first probably comprises the most common and the least problematic kinds of infringement; difficulties mainly arise as to whether what the defendant is doing actually falls within the scope of the patentee's monopoly.[1] If the 'repair' of a patented product is so extensive as to amount to making it afresh, that activity will infringe.[2] 'Disposing' is a comprehensive term, which presumably includes destruction. It has been held that an advertisement constitutes an 'offer to dispose of', notwithstanding the distinction in English law between offers and invitations to treat.[3] Whether 'keeping' infringes seems to depend upon whether the defendant has an interest in the nature of the product: a mere warehouseman may not infringe, but an import-export company will.[4] Doing any of these acts in relation to a product derived directly from a patented process infringes even if the process is operated outside the UK. However, the requirement of 'directly' is strictly applied.[5] The last group has attracted attention since it is a 'secondary' or 'indirect' infringement, an act previously permitted under patent law.[6] The intention of Parliament was that, following the recommendation of the Banks Committee,[7] a person who sells a patented product in 'kit' form will be liable for patent infringement even though he has not made the product itself and even though he may have advised a real or potential purchaser that the assembly of the invention's parts should not be done except under licence from the patent holder. This section has still not yet been subjected to full judicial scrutiny,[8] but it is imagined that it will prove to be fraught with difficulties in its application. In the first place, does the word 'means' indicate only the physical ingredients which, assembled together, embody the patented product, or does it also embrace the process of know-how required before the invention is put into effect? In similar vein, does 'secondary infringement' apply to all types of patented invention, whether product or process, or is only the former assumed to be protected? A more difficult question relates to the interpretation of the word 'essential'; does it mean 'essential' in the sense of 'essential for the putting into effect of the invention', or 'essential in order for the invention to have acquired the status of a patentable invention'? The Act does, however, resolve one question, when it specifies[9] that to (offer to) supply a staple commercial product – presumably coal, water, oil, electricity and the like – will not be actionable as a patent infringement, even if the supplier knew it was to be used for infringing purposes, unless the (offer to) supply is made for the purpose of inducing the person supplied to perform a 'primary infringement'.

1. See paras **8.9-8.15**, below.
2. *United Wire Screen Ltd v Screen Repair Services (Scotland) Ltd* [2001] FSR 365, HL.
3. *Gerber Garment Technology Inc v Lectra Systems Ltd* [1995] RPC 383 at 411-412.

4. Contrast *Smith Kline & French Laboratories v Harbottle (RD) Mercantile Ltd* [1979] FSR 555, [1980] RPC 363 with *Smith Kline & French Laboratories v DDSA* [1978] FSR 109.
5. *Pioneer Electronics Capital Inc v Warner Music* [1995] RPC 487; affd [1997] RPC 757; H Hurdle 'What is the Direct Product of a Patented Process?' [1997] EIPR 322. For biotechnology processes, Directive 98/44 on the Legal Protection of Biotechnological Inventions [1998] OJ L213/13, art 8(2) further protects further generations of product.
6. But now rendered infringing by Patents Act 1977, s 60(2).
7. *The British Patent System* Cmnd 4407, 1970.
8. In *Helitune Ltd v Stewart Hughes Ltd* [1991] FSR 171, the offer to supply the means relating to an essential element of the invention was admitted; the only disputed issue was that of knowledge. In *Merrell Dow Pharmaceuticals Inc v Norton* [1994] RPC 1, contributory infringement was alleged but the case was concluded on a preliminary finding of invalidity, which ultimately went to the House of Lords (see [1996] RPC 76, para **8.5**, above). Suppliers to rubber planters were held by the Malaysian court to have infringed in *Rhône Poulenc v Dikloride Herbicides* [1988] FSR 282.
9. Patents Act 1977, s 60(3).

Defences

8.6 The alleged infringer enjoys a wide range of defences to a patent infringement action, so much so that the patentee who wishes to enforce his monopoly may feel that the odds are stacked heavily against him. From the patentee's point of view the defendant's armoury of potential defences is particularly daunting when it is remembered that the patentee may already have bled his finances white in the research, development, patenting, market testing, staff training, tooling and manufacturing processes in order to sell his product or use his process, under the leaky umbrella of the Patents Act's protection. Human nature being what it is, one fully understands why the serious industrial innovator should be so much attracted towards the operation of cartels, the establishment of restrictive trade practices or the security-blanket of the merger; for each (in the absence of legal intervention by competition or by the state)[1] offers benefits far too infrequently derived from the exercise of the patent right.

1. For a full account of legal constraints upon unfettered anticompetitive activities see Whish, *Competition Law* (4th edn 2001).

8.7 On the other hand the law is concerned with principles of justice that lie uneasily around the perimeter of commercial practice. One such principle is that like cases have to be treated in like fashion. It is on this principle that the same law must govern the commercially successful giant who, with his perhaps spurious patent, stalks his industrially insignificant prey with intent to drive him from the market place and, on the other hand, the fair-minded small patentee, whose undoubtedly deserved monopoly is trampled underfoot by a multinational rogue competitor. Distributive justice assumes that those two cases are identical, because in each the subject of a patentee's grant is encroached upon by another. It is not acceptable to distinguish the two on the ground that the first case is 'villain patentee versus hero infringer' while the second is 'hero patentee versus villain infringer'. This is because, while 'patentee' and 'infringer' are objectively verifiable states of being, 'hero' and 'villain' are subjective evaluation, and each man is a hero in his own eyes. The law does possess procedures for discriminating between 'hero' and 'villain' in commercial practices, but the Patents Act is not one of them.

8.8   What, then, are the defences to patent infringement? Broadly they are as follows:

(i)   the act complained of is not an infringing act (discussed at paragraph **8.9** below);

(ii)   the infringement has been performed privately and for purposes which are not commercial,[1] such as taking apart and reassembling a patented device to show a student how it works;

(iii)   the act is done for experimental purposes relating to the subject matter of the invention,[2] such as performing a patented process in a laboratory to see if it really works, or if it can be done better. Sometimes, however, an 'experiment' is not carried out to uncover new knowledge but to demonstrate something to somebody. If the demonstration is for the purposes of legal proceedings it falls within the defence.[3] Commercial demonstrations to impress regulatory authorities or potential customers do not;[4]

(iv)   the act complained of is simply the extemporaneous making up in a pharmacy of a medicine described in a doctor's or dentist's prescription.[5] Note that, in such a case, the defence extends only to the preparation or use of the medicine, so would not protect the doctor who writes out the prescription; but the Patents Act does not define 'infringement' in such a way as to make the author of the prescription liable. This is because in contrast to copyright[6] it contains no provision that authorisation of an infringement by another is itself an infringement;

(v)   the infringement is committed in relation to a foreign-registered ship, hovercraft or aircraft[7] which temporarily or accidentally enters United Kingdom territorial waters or air-space;[8]

(vi)   the defendant used to do such acts before the priority date of the claimant's patent;[9] after all, while the patent is a reward for the disclosure of information, a party which already possessed and used such information as a trade secret has gained nothing from the patent applicant's disclosure and should not be expected to forfeit the right to do what was already his practice;

(vii) the claimant had already expressly or implicitly licensed the defendant to perform the act complained of. The most important instances of this defence occur when the claimant sells patented goods to the defendant. The court will generally be willing to imply a licence under which the defendant can carry out acts which would otherwise constitute infringements of patent. Formerly this extended to carrying out repairs, but the House of Lords has held that these cannot be so extensive as to amount to remaking the product, the act for for which a licence would be required;[10]

(viii) the claimant's entitlement to stop the defendant performing otherwise infringing acts would be a 'derogation of grant' in respect of the supply of patented products to third parties. This defence has been applied in copyright infringement proceedings.[11] Although there seems no good reason in principle why it should not equally apply to patent law, the Privy Council has held it to be of limited application;[12]

(ix) the claimant's rights have been 'exhausted'. Exhaustion is a continental notion which has proved decisive in the limitation of the extent to which all intellectual property rights, particularly trade marks, can be exercised in European Community law.[13] The idea is simple. A is a patentee of a product; he sells a quantity of such products to wholesaler B, who in turn sells them to retailer C. If there were no principle of exhaustion, A would be able to stop B selling to C, or C selling his product to the general public, since he could point to the fact that his patent grant gives him the exclusive right to sell his patented product. Common law purists would argue that no doctrine of exhaustion is needed; A's sale to B contains an implicit licence that B can resell,[14] and A and C have entered into an implied contract under which A licenses C to sell the goods in consideration of C's act of purchasing the goods from B, which benefits A since B would not have purchased from A if he had no expectation of selling the goods later. This is a little clumsy. It is much easier to say, as does the Draft Community Patent Regulation,[15] that all the patentee's rights in each individual item made in accordance with his patent remain enforceable until the first authorised putting of each good on to the market. Once the patentee has notionally dealt with each unit of production in such a manner, his right is 'exhausted' in respect of it and he has no further interest in the fate of that product, unless there are legitimate grounds on which to oppose the further commercialisation of the product;

(x) the claimant has engaged in anti-competitive activity,[16] such as abuse of a dominant position contrary to Art 82 of the EC Treaty.[17]

(xi) the claimant is not the person entitled to sue; for example he may be only a non-exclusive licensee, or he may not have been the proprietor of the patent at the time the patent was infringed;

(xii) the patent is not valid; this is discussed below, at paragraph **8.18**;

(xiii) more than six years elapsed between the infringement of the patent and its grant, in which case the English period of limitations expires.[18] This piece of tragi-comedy was not removed by Parliament in 1988 when a large-scale overhaul of intellectual property law was effected. However, it is unlikely to recur since the maximum period between publication of a patent application and grant of the patent in the UK is now 36 months. Post-grant oppositions in the European Patent Office may drag on for long periods, but the patentee is entitled to sue for infringement while the opposition is pending, although the court may reluctantly grant a stay of proceedings pending the outcome of opposition.

(xiv) the patent relates to a plant or animal and the defendant is a farmer saving seed or breeding from his own animals, where he has previously obtained his stock from the patentee or a licensed source.[19]

1. Patents Act 1977, s 60(5)(a). Note the conjunctive 'and'.
2. Patents Act 1977, s 60(5)(b).
3. *Smith Kline & French Laboratories Ltd v Evans Medical* [1989] FSR 513. Experiments done for a mixed purpose would not be spared from infringement by s 60(5)(a).
4. *Monsanto Co v Stauffer Chemical Co* [1985] RPC 515; *Auchincloss v Agricultural & Veterinary Supplies* [1999] RPC 397. See Van de Merwe 'Experimental Use and Submission of Data for Regulatory Approval' (2000) IIC 380. In Germany, the experimental use defence has been interpreted more generously.
5. Patents Act 1977, s 60(5)(c).
6. Copyright, Design and Patents Act 1988, s 16(2). However, it is an open question whether a physician is a joint tortfeasor; cf *CBS Songs Ltd v Amstrad* [1988] AC 1013.
7. The vehicle in question must belong to, or be registered in, a country which is a party to the Paris Convention on Industrial Property 1883.
8. Patents Act 1977, s 60(5)(d)-(f).
9. Patents Act 1977, s 64(1). See *Lubrizol Corpn v Esso Petroleum Co Ltd (No 5)* [1998] RPC 727, CA; I Davies and S Cohen 'Section 64 of the UK Patents Act 1977: Right to Continue Use Begun before Priority Date' [1994] EIPR 239.
10. *United Wire Ltd v Screen Repair Services (Scotland) Ltd* [2001] FSR 365.
11. *British Leyland Motor Corp Ltd v Armstrong* [1986] RPC 279.
12. *Canon Kabushiki Kaisha v Green Cartridge Co (Hong Kong)* [1997] AC 728, [1997] FSR 817.

13. See eg *Revlon Inc v Cripps and Lee Ltd* [1980] FSR 85; *Sterling Drug Inc v CH Beck Ltd* [1973] RPC 915; N Gross 'Trade Mark Exhaustion' [2001] EIPR 224.
14. See *Betts v Willmott* (1871) 6 Ch App 239; *SA des Manufactures de Glaces v Tilghman's Patent Sand Blast Co* (1883) 25 Ch D 1.
15. Proposal for a Council Regulation on the Community Patent COM (2000) 412 final, art 10.
16. Contrary to Chapter II of the Competition Act 1998; see para **8.6**, n 1 above.
17. Allegations of this sort were rejected in *Philips Electronics v Ingham* [1999] FSR 112; see M Cunningham 'How Far Can a Patent Holder Go? [1999] EIPR 469 For art 82, see para **27.5**.
18. *Sevcon Ltd v Lucas CAV Ltd* [1986] 2 All ER 104.
19. Patents Act 1977 s 60(5)(g) and (h), inserted by Patent Regulations 2000 (SI 2000/2037).

Has the defendant trespassed?

8.9   The claimant's patent has been analogised to his real estate; the patent specification marks out the claimant's territory, and infringement takes place whenever it is established that the defendant has encroached upon it. Unfortunately, the reality is not as simple as the analogy suggests, not least because it is first necessary to interpret the specification before one can decide whether infringement takes place, and the specification is drafted with the primary object of securing the patent examiner's approval, as well as being a means of fending off subsequent infringements. Because the specification is addressed to the examiner rather than to the would-be competitor, its emphasis is upon distinguishing the inventor's conception as clearly as possible from the prior art, which might otherwise be said to anticipate the application or render it obvious. If the same invention's specification were addressed primarily to the potential infringer, one feels that it would be drafted so as to draw the innovations within it as close as possible to the prior art, to make it more difficult for its addressee to evade infringement by establishing that what he has done, while closely related to the contents of the specification, lies between the prior art and the subject of the patent in question.[1]

1.   A line of argument sometimes described as the 'squeeze' or '*Gillette*' defence, after *Gillette Safety Razor Co v Anglo-American Trading Co* (1913) 30 RPC 465 at 480.

8.10   When considering the meaning and extent of a patent specification, it is impossible to ignore the fact that the courts have struggled for centuries with the same issue – construction – in a very similar context: that of the interpretation of statutes. The court is charged with giving effect to the intention of Parliament, and can do so in one of three ways:

(i) by giving each word its literal meaning;[1]
(ii) by giving each word its literal meaning but presuming that, since Parliament does not intend to reach a result which is absurd, a more reasonable construction should be adopted if possible;[2] or
(iii) by examining Parliament's aims and objects, and reading the statute in the light of them.[3]

Faced with these three choices the reader may intuitively opt for one or other which pleases him, or which he regards as the most likely to do justice. The courts themselves have found over the years that each of the three canons of construction is invaluable within a legal context which requires it. Broadly (and thus unreliably) speaking, the first approach is favoured when the words of the statute are unambiguous; the second when they may be construed in one of two or more ways; the third when the whole context of their applicability or extent is unclear.

1. Eg *Salomon v A Salomon Co Ltd* [1897] AC 22 at 38.
2. See *Heydon's Case* (1584) 3 Co Rep 7a at 7b.
3. Eg *Re Lockwood, Atherton v Brooke* [1958] Ch 231.

8.11 Judges in patent cases[1] have used three analogous canons of construction: patent specifications may be construed literally;[2] they may be subjected to the 'pith and marrow' procedure of focusing upon the elements of the specification which are most essential;[3] or a 'purposive' construction may examine the function which integers described in a specification are to fulfil, rather than solely the words which convey those functions.[4] The literal interpretation owed its existence to the principle that the patent applicant has the opportunity to draft the extent of a monopoly which will enjoy the force of law for a term of years. Since he has the benefit of being able to prescribe, as widely as he wishes, the limits of his terrain, he also has to endure the burden of the *contra proferentum* rule: any words he uses will be construed as narrowly as their meaning allows, since it is presumed that a person has not claimed for himself that which he has left for the benefit of others. This approach to the interpretation of specifications, which owes more to the influence of literature[5] than the requirements of justice, is no longer insisted upon. If there *is* literal infringement, the patentee's case will be easy to prove. If not, the court will proceed to a broader canon of construction.

1. In *Daily v Etablissements Fernand Berchet* [1993] RPC 357, [1992] FSR 533, Balcombe LJ opined that the construction of patent specifications merely involved the usual canons of construction applied by the courts to any written document.
2. For a view of literal interpretation see *Rodi and Weinenberger AG v Henry Showell Ltd* [1969] RPC 367 at 380 (per Lord Upjohn), citing *Van der Lely NV v Bamfords Ltd* [1963] RPC 61.

3. *Clark v Adie* (1877) 2 App Cas 315 at 320.
4. See A Walton 'Purposive Construction' [1984] EIPR 93.
5. On the literal interpretation see eg W Shakespeare *The Merchant of Venice* Act IV, scene I, especially lines 306-313, 325-333.

8.12 The 'pith and marrow' principle, on the other hand, was of great importance. It dictated that, where an invention as described in the specification consists of a number of separate integers, an industrial rival may be considered to have infringed his monopoly even if only, say, seven out of ten of those integers are copied, so long as the elements common to each are those which are regarded as the 'pith and marrow', the real substance, of the patented invention. None of the elements of the 'pith and marrow' need be novel if taken by itself, but the combination of those vital elements must be that which effectively distances the patentee's invention from the prior art. If it is those elements which have been taken, the other elements will be treated as if they were inessential components of the invention's patentability, however essential they may be in the functional role played by them in the concrete realisation of the invention itself. Another way of describing the non-'pith and marrow' elements is that they may be no more than physical or mechanical equivalents of other elements which could perform the same function, though perhaps in a manner which was not exactly the same.[1] The pith and marrow technique of construction has been superseded by purposive construction, the mode held[2] to correspond most nearly to the Protocol on construction of Art 69 of the European Patent Convention, which exhorts courts to adopt constructions which balance the requirements of fair reward to the inventor and certainty for third parties.[3] It has been suggested that the concept of 'equivalents' may be given a new lease of life by a second Article added to the Protocol in November 2000.[4] This states that 'for the purpose of determining the extent of protection conferred by a European patent, due account shall be taken of any element which is equivalent to an element specified in the claims'. Unfortunately, while we are mandated to take due account of equivalents, the Article does not say *how* we are to take due account of them. This will doubtless be a rich source of litigation at home and abroad, once the changes to the Protocol have been ratified.

1. On the 'Doctrine of mechanical equivalents' see *Marconi and Marconi's Wireless Telegraph Ltd v British Radio-Telegraph and Telephone Co* (1911) 28 RPC 181 at 217.
2. Eg *Kastner v Rizla Ltd* [1995] RPC 585.
3. A uniform interpretation of Art 69 is important since infringement of patents granted by the European Patent Office is at present a matter for national courts. See D Stauder 'History of Art 69(1) EPC' (1992) 23 IIC 311.
4. See R Nack and B Phélip 'Diplomatic Conference for the Revision of the European Patent Convention' (2001) 32 IIC 200.

8.13 'Purposive' construction is the favoured approach to the interpretation of a specification, and is best illustrated by the notable House of Lords decision in the *Catnic* case.[1] The patentees' invention was a load-bearing lintel (figure 1); the patent specification indicated that the principal support be supplied by a metal face which was vertical to the base.

The defendants' lintel (figure 2) was similar, except that the support was not quite vertical. The reason why the claimants' support was specified as 'vertical' was that a vertical support has greater load-bearing propensities than any other, as anyone who has squashed flat a slightly crooked drawing pin will know. The defendants' support would therefore bear less weight; but, because that support was not far from the perpendicular, the difference between the load-bearing capabilities of each was almost insignificant.

Fig 1 The plaintiff's lintel   Fig 2 The defendant's lintel

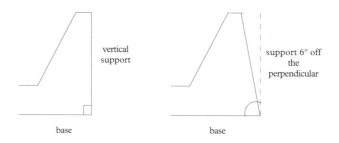

1. *Catnic Components Ltd v Hill and Smith Ltd* [1982] RPC 183. This case related to a patent granted under the Patents Act 1949. The same approach was applied in relation to a patent granted under the Patents Act 1977 by Hoffman J in *Improver Corpn v Remington Consumer Products Ltd* [1990] FSR 181 to navigate between what has been described as 'Scylla, the rock of literal construction; and Charybdis, the whirlpool of guided freedom as required by the Protocol' *Hoescht Celanese Corpn v BP Chemicals Ltd* [1999] FSR 319 at 324, per Aldous LJ .

8.14 The defendants maintained that they had not infringed the claimants' patent. In the first place, they argued, there was no literal infringement, since they had not exactly reproduced the features of the claimants' product. Second, they submitted, there was no 'pith and marrow' infringement; the perpendicularity of the patented lintel's support was essential to its function and ultimate character, and no lintel which lacked this essential characteristic could be said to be an infringement. Against this the claimants argued that 'vertical' was not to be understood in a literal manner, since the vicissitudes of manufacture in the non-precision engineering sector would rarely result in the product's being possessed of an exact perpendicularity even if such were sought; they also suggested that there had been a 'pith and marrow' infringement in that the essential element of the support was that it be a support, not that it be entirely upright.

8.15   In the event, the House of Lords held the patent to have been infringed.[1] The decisive feature of the supporting strut was that it fulfilled the purpose of supporting a load. In this context the word 'vertical' meant 'vertical or sufficiently close to vertical to be able to perform the same functions as it would have done if it were vertical'.[2] Their Lordships did not consider that there was anything novel in their decision, or that there was more than one legal means by which an allegedly infringing article could be measured against an existing patent specification;[3] but in adopting what Lord Diplock described as a 'purposive' approach, they opted for what had been called the 'signpost' interpretation of patent specifications in preference to the 'fencepost' approach. Put another way, the patent specification does not mark out the perimeter of the patentee's claims, but merely points the reader in the direction in which he may not travel without a licence. It may be observed that the scope of patents and the available defences to infringement will have profound economic effects.[4]

1. *Catnic Components Ltd v Hill and Smith Ltd* [1982] RPC 183.
2. Ibid at p 244.
3. Ibid at p 242.
4. Merges and Nelson 'On the Complex Economics of Patent Scope' (1990) 90 Columbia L Rev 839; P Cole 'Pioneering Pays – or Does it?'[2000] EIPR 534; B Domeij 'Patent Claim Scope: Initial and Follow-on Pharmaceutical Inventions' [2001] EIPR 326.

Revocation

8.16   On the principle that the best form of defence is attack, the manufacturer or importer who faces infringement proceedings will often be advised to bring into dispute the validity of the patent. This advice is frequently sound for the following reasons:

(i)   it will lengthen the proceedings and make them more expensive, thus inconveniencing the patentee who, even if successful, will not recover from the defendant the full extent of his costs;[1]

(ii)   it may, by increasing the delay and expense suffered by the patentee, facilitate an out-of-court settlement on terms favourable to the defendant;

(iii) it may inhibit any further action on the part of the patentee whose patent looks quite valid on the surface, where the patentee is himself aware of its potential vulnerability[2] and suspects that the defendant may genuinely have spotted it too;

(iv) it may encourage other potential infringers to enter the market, or at any rate to threaten to do so,[3] thus providing the patentee with a further incentive to secure a discreet out-of-court settlement.

1. The successful litigant can expect to recoup 60%-65% of his infringement action costs: see *CIPA Guide to the Patents Act 1977* (2nd edn, 1984), pp 305-306. (Recent editions of the *Guide* omit such estimates.)
2. This may be particularly so where the grant of a patent owes less to the inventiveness of the inventor than to that of his patent agent.
3. On which see *Conder International Ltd v Hibbing Ltd* [1984] FSR 312 at p 315.

8.17 None of this is apparent from a perusal of the Patents Act itself, which is concerned with the identification of grounds upon which a patentee is morally disentitled to wield his monopoly and with the legal mechanism for effecting the consequent legal disentitlement. It should not, however, be thought that the patentee's hands are tied entirely behind his back where, in seeking to defend his rights, he finds them challenged. This is because the Patents Act 1977 has substantially tilted in his favour the balance of tactical considerations which pertained under the Act of 1949. The improvements are two:

(i) It is no longer possible for the validity of a patent to be challenged at the application stage, through opposition proceedings.[1] This significantly reduced the degree of expense, inconvenience and delay inflicted upon the patentee;

(ii) The fact that patents are now examined for inventive step as well as novelty should mean that the resulting patent has a 'strong' presumption of validity.

1. Although it is possible for third parties to file observations on patentability during processing of the application: Patents Act 1977, s 21; European Patent Convention, art 115. In the European Patent Office it is also possible to file opposition for nine months after grant of a European Patent. Art 99 EPC.

The grounds of revocation

8.18 On what grounds may a patent be revoked? The Patents Act 1977, section 72 provides that a patent may be revoked *only* on any of the following grounds:

(i) *The invention is not a patentable invention.*[1] In other words, the invention is not novel, lacks inventive step or industrial application, or falls within the categories of intellectual creations which are statute-barred from being 'inventions', or which may not be patented'. Judging by the evidence of the law reports, lack of novelty or inventive step are the most common grounds upon which revocation is sought, both because they are the grounds which genuinely most often give rise to objection to a patent, and because of their tactical nuisance-value in resisting infringement proceedings.

(ii) *The patent was not granted to the right person(s).*[2] Curiously enough, the frequency of disputes as to the grantee's entitlement would seem to have diminished over the last century or so, although the proportion of patents granted to a person other than the inventor has persistently risen. Perhaps this is a tribute to the efficiency of lawyers, whose duty it is to ensure that the assignee of an invention (or its initial owner, if he is the inventor's employer)[3] does not face any objection to the patent application raised by the original inventor. The frequency of revocation proceedings on this ground has been further reduced by the imposition of further conditions, (a) that only a person entitled to the patent can bring proceedings under it and in the course of an action must establish that he is entitled to be granted that patent, and (b) that such a complaint may not be made if the action was commenced more than two years from the date of grant, unless it can be proved that the grantee knows that he was not entitled to be granted the patent.

(iii) *The specification does not disclose the invention clearly and completely enough for it to be performed by a person skilled in the art.*[4] Since the quid pro quo for the grant of a patent monopoly is the disclosure of the totality of the invention, it would not be right for a person to enjoy a monopoly for a term of years if he did not disclose enough of his invention to enable any of his trade rivals to put it into effect once the term of years had expired. This is not to say that the patent applicant has to spill all the beans; for the obligation is only one of disclosing enough information to provide a basic blue-print for making or operating his invention,[5] and he need not disclose (as was the case under the Patents Act 1949) the best way of putting the invention into effect. Critics of the patent system have pointed out that the most valuable part of the patentee's intellectual property is not the invention itself but the 'know-how' behind its successful production;[6] thus a patent may disclose a new means of synthesising a chemical, but the really important information – how to do it cheaply, efficiently and on a large scale – is concealed and can thus be separately licensed by the patentee for a high price. This argument, others claim, misses the point. The 'know-how' is only of primary importance once the substance of the invention itself is known; and, however valuable 'know-how' may be, it is the novelty and non-obviousness which provide the *sine qua non* for the realisation of any new product or process. The debate continues. Note that a former argument against validity, that the claims were not fairly based on the information disclosed in the specification, is not available under the 1977 Act.[7]

(iv) *The specification disclosed matter which extends beyond that disclosed in the patent application.* This and the following point are included only for the sake of completeness. They are technically complex and fall outside the scope of this book.

(v) *The protection conferred by the patent has been extended by an amendment to it which should not have been allowed.*

1. Patents Act 1977, s 72(1)(a).
2. Ibid, s 72(1)(b), amended by s 295 and Sch 5, para 18 of the Copyright, Designs and Patents Act 1988; applied in *Henry Bros (Magharafelt) v Ministry of Defence* [1999] RPC 442 .
3. Patents Act 1977, s 39.
4. Ibid, s 72(1)(c); in *Biogen v Medeva* [1997] RPC 1 the 'litmus test' was whether the claims covered other ways of working the invention which owed nothing to the teaching or principles disclosed in the patent specification.
5. The addressee of the patent can be expected to engage in routine trials to make the invention work and to correct obvious errors: *Mentor Corpn v Hollister Inc* [1993] RPC 7.
6. See eg Lord Nathan 'Invention and Protection – the New Dimension' (1979) 19 *The Inventor* no 4, p 7.
7. *Genentech Inc's Patent* [1989] RPC 147. This argument may however be used to support an application to amend: *Schering Biotech Corpn's Patent* [1993] RPC 249.

The mechanics of revocation

8.19   The revocation of a patent may be sought by anyone, subject to the restriction to would-be grantees of the right to seek revocation on the ground that the patent was granted to the wrong person.[1] Under the Patents Act 1949 revocation proceedings could only be instituted by a party who could establish sufficient *locus standi* through being materially affected by the patent grant, such as a rival manufacturer.[2] That view was, it is submitted, unreasonably restrictive, since every member of the public is affected by the impact of every monopoly, to the extent that it determines the availability of goods and services and the price which he must pay for them. On the other hand, it is unusual for a party to instigate revocation proceedings if he has no vested interest in their outcome so it is not likely that the wider availability of such proceedings makes a great difference in practice.

1. Patents Act 1977, s 72(2).
2. Patents Act 1949, s 32(1).

8.20   The applicant to revoke a patent has a choice of forum; he may apply to the Comptroller or to the court.[1] The Comptroller in fact possesses wider powers than the court in at least one respect: he can act *suo motu* in order to revoke a patent – even if no one has asked him to do so – if it lacks novelty through its anticipation by an earlier patent application which was not published until after the date of that patent's application.[2] It is appropriate that the Comptroller, whose functions are both administrative and judicial, should be able to combine these functions in order to effect a revocation on administrative grounds; he may not, however, do so without giving the proprietor of the patent an opportunity to amend his specification so as to exclude anything which formed part of the state of the art by virtue of the earlier patent application.[3]

1.   The High Court or the Patents County Court.
2.   Patents Act 1977, s 73(1).
3.   Ibid.

How frequently is revocation sought?

8.21   The table below indicates that revocation is relatively infrequently the subject of formal proceedings, but this takes no account of the tactical value of the threat of such proceedings as a means of compromising an infringement action or of obtaining a favourable licence. The substantive majority of patents revoked in recent years have been revoked under the Comptroller's powers[1] to revoke a UK patent when both European and UK patents have been granted for the same invention. This power was enhanced in 1988, when the patent proprietor was given the opportunity to elect to have either the UK patent or the European patent revoked.

Year	Application to revoke	Patents revoked
1992	84	52
1993	99	93
1994	94	77
1995	107	84
1996	119	96
1997	111	92
1998	118	97
1999	98	81

Source: Patent Office annual reports and accounts.

1.   Patents Act 1977, s 73(2): 78 out of 98 applications in 1999.

Other defensive tactics

8.22 Mention may be made of two other procedures which are available to protect the public against unwarranted claims of patent infringement. First, it is possible to apply to the court or to the Patent Office for a declaration that specific activities do not infringe the patent.[1] This has the advantage that a prospective defendant may seize the initiative in prospective litigation. Where unjustified threats are made to sue for infringement (otherwise than by using a process, manufacturing or importing) an aggrieved person may bring proceedings to restrain the threats and also obtain damages and a declaration that the threats are unjustifiable.[2] Since patent litigation is notoriously expensive, the mere whiff of proceedings may deter dealing with someone against whom allegations are made. It is the policy of the Act to encourage patentees to stem infringements at source, rather than to harry those down the chain of commerce who may have little interest in challenging claims.[3]

1. Patents Act 1977, s 71. See, eg *Rohm & Haas Co v Collag Ltd* [2001] FSR 426.
2. Patents Act 1977, s 70. See, eg *Siegfried Demel v C&H Jefferson* [1999] FSR 204
3. See Lim HG 'The Threats Section of the UK Trade Marks Act 1994' [1995] EIPR 138 for a discussion of this mischief.

Chapter 9

The patent and legal policy

The lawyer's role

9.1   Now that the five preceding chapters have given a brief idea
of the nature of patent law, it is worth looking at the patent system
from a different standpoint. The law, as many lawyers view it, is
little more than a series of rules which must be taken into account
when advising clients on the extent of their rights, duties and
liberties; but the law, as enacted by Parliament, is an organism of
the greatest complexity. The desirability of monopolies, and the
degree of control which may be exercised over them, is a subject
which falls within the specialist knowledge of the economist; the
likely effect of market incentives and stimuli is properly the subject
of the industrial psychologist; the ideological acceptability of rules
which promote private privilege falls to be gauged by the political
scientist; the likely shop-floor consequences are noted by the
industrial sociologist; the value of the patent grant is weighed by
the investment consultant, and so on. By the time a measure such
as a Patents Act has obtained the Queen's signature, it is likely
that every one of these disciplines will have registered its opinion
as to the appropriateness (or otherwise) of the measure, and the
end product will represent a compromise between their frequently
conflicting demands.[1] It is the lawyer who is the author of this
compromise. He is, at the last resort, little other than a hired hand,
and it is only through the exercise of his unique skills that
economic, social and industrial policy, not to mention morality,
are metamorphosed into law. The Patents Act's aims are not, then,
primarily legal, which means that it is by reference to non-legal
criteria that the Act's success (or failure) stands to be judged.

1.   Some measure of the breadth of conflicting interests may be gathered from
     the Banks Report, *The British Patent System* Cmnd 4407, 1970, Appendix A,
     which lists four pages' worth of parties sufficiently interested in the shape of
     patent reform that they submitted written or oral evidence.

The patent as an incentive to invent

9.2 One of the best-known justifications of the patent system is that it encourages invention by providing an incentive for people to invent. Sadly, it is submitted, there is not one shred of evidence that any patent system has provided an incentive which leads an otherwise uninventive person to perform acts of invention.[1] It is an inescapable fact of the human condition that not every person possesses the necessary mental ability to originate a scientific solution to a problem by intellectual creation, or by reordering existing knowledge in a new and hitherto unappreciated manner. There is no doubt that one can make a person want to invent, even if he has no inventive capacity at all, but by doing so one merely stimulates a yearning for a desired end, without reference to the means by which it may be achieved.

1. On the psychological impact of the patent system see J Phillips 'Patents and Incentives to Invent' (1984) Endeavour (ns) 90; J Phillips (ed) *Employees' Inventions: a Comparative Study* (1981), Ch 1.

9.3 Even where a person is fortunate enough to be endowed with the faculty of invention, the existence of a patent system does not in general seem to be a crucial factor in enhancing his determination to invent. In an estimated 90% of granted patents the inventor is employed to make the invention and the resulting patent will belong to his employer. To say that, in such cases, the potential availability of a patent actually stimulates invention is a bit like saying that you can spur on a donkey by offering a carrot to his rider.

9.4 Where the inventor has both the faculty of invention and the desire to become incredibly rich, one suspects that the lure of a patent will provide a measure of encouragement. But here even the hardened cynic may find it difficult to escape confusion with the reasonable man when he points out that the road to hell is paved with good intentions. The cost of obtaining a patent is high; patent agents, the Patent Office, industrial and commercial advisers and makers of prototypes will all want to be paid whether the invention is successful or not; even if the invention is successful, the patentee will usually have to pay his patenting and related costs before he sees so much as a penny in return for his effort; and, at the end of the day, most patents are not profitably exploitable and would not be worth holding even if they were given away.[1]

1. Few books on innovation management and marketing treat patents seriously. See eg A Berridge *Product Innovation and Development* (1977), which devotes only 70 words to the patent system within the context of overseas sales strategy,

and P Drucker's *Innovation and Entrepreneurship* (1985), the index of which lists references to (inter alia) Bagehot, Cicero, da Vinci, Goethe, Saint-Simon and Women, but not to patents. Tidd, Bessant and Pavitt *Managing Innovation* (1997) do refer to patents, but use them as as indicators of innovative activity. There are honourable exceptions, eg P H Sullivan et al *Profiting from Intellectual Capital* (1998); J Pierce and I Purvis *Working with Technology* (2001).

9.5   When people do invent, there is some evidence that they do so because they are trying to solve a problem.[1] In the case of employee inventors the problem (like any resulting patent) usually belongs to the employer,[2] while the independent inventor is trying to solve a problem of his own. Viewed in psychological terms the inventor is not so much motivated by the patent system to make an invention as stimulated by a particular problem to find a way round it. To put it another way, when a rat is in a maze, he is trying to solve the problem of how to get out and find his dinner, rather than to fulfil his desire to solve maze-based problems. If any conclusion may be drawn from the foregoing, it is that the encouragement of invention is more likely to be achieved by educating people in the prior art and by stimulating them with unsolved problems, than by holding out the prospect of a right to pay for the privilege of stopping someone else from developing or marketing your invention, which is what a patent grant is.

1.   See S MacDonald 'Australia – the Patent System and the Inventor' [1983] EIPR 154.
2.   On employees' inventions generally see J Phillips and M Hoolahan *Employees' Inventions in the United Kingdom* (1982); W Cornish 'Rights in Employees' Inventions – the UK Position' (1990) 21 IIC 298; P Chandler 'Employees'Inventions: Inventorship and Ownership' [1997] EIPR 262.

9.6   Before leaving this topic, it is worth casting further shadow upon the thick black pall of ignorance by wondering why it is that the law, which regards invention as a laudable and desirable activity, should be so greatly at odds with the public image of the inventor. The popular conception of the inventor is that of an eccentric buffoon, devoid of practical common sense, financial awareness and finer human feeling; he is derided by cartoonists, shunned by 'sane' industrialists, peed on by doggies in the street, and avoided by respectable bank managers. It is notable that the insurance clerk who pens detective stories does not scruple to call himself a writer; the schoolboy who takes his sketch-pad to the Lake District for a half-term hike is pleased to be described as an artist; the mother-of-three at her weekly evening class will vaunt her status of sculptor and the parlours of a hundred thousand dwellings from Dundee to Dorset resound to the quill-scratching of smugly self-proclaimed poets – but how few admit without apology to being inventors! In British eyes, to be an inventor is to bear a greater stigma than even the teacher or the engineer. No incentive to invent, it is submitted, is as sorely lacking as is the tolerance or respect of the wider public, and a society which denigrates its inventors' failures while begrudging them the fruits of their success will be the poorer for it.

The patent as an incentive to disclose

9.7 Even if the advocate of the patent system were to concede to his opponents the case against the justification of the patent system as an incentive, he might still defend that system more convincingly in terms of its incentive effect upon those who, having already made inventions, wonder what they are going to do with them. The 'contract' theory of patents, it will be recalled,[1] portrays the grant of a patent as a reward or, in contractual terms, 'consideration'[2] for the disclosure to the public of the new invention. This theory is illustrated in figure 3.

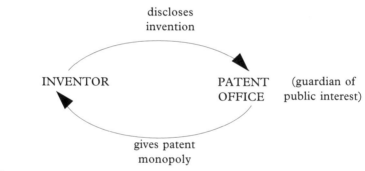

fig. 3

In the vast majority of cases this model is inappropriate because, as has been indicated above, the employer should be interposed in the manner suggested by figure 4.

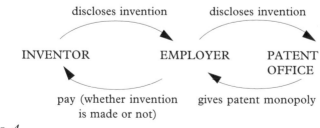

fig. 4

It does not require a profound analysis of figure 4 to recognise that, while the reward of a patent monopoly may provide an excellent incentive to the employer to disclose the invention in return for it, the patent does not impinge upon the inventor at all. As a hired hand, as it were, he will almost certainly enjoy his wages and experience the same vicissitudes of employment whether he invents or not, and whether – if he invents – he discloses his invention to his employer. The 'employees' inventions' code of the Patents Act 1977, sections 39-43, recognises that the patent system *per se* has little incentive impact upon the inventor; it therefore seeks to provide further incentives. Let us briefly examine it.

1. See para **4.6** above.
2. On the concept of 'consideration' see G Treitel *The Law of Contract* (10th edn 1999) Ch 3.

The 'employees' inventions' code – an outline

9.8 The Government in 1977 accepted a number of principles, which were incorporated into the Patents Act[1] even though they might be more appropriately viewed as part of the Employment Protection legislation. The principles are as follows:

(i) an employee inventor whose employer successfully exploits his invention should share some of the fruits of that success;

(ii) the right to claim such a share should not depend upon the mere chance of whether the invention belonged originally to the inventor or to his employer;

(iii) the size of the employee inventor's reward should be calculable by reference to the relative worth of his and his employer's efforts and expectations;

(iv) the employer should not be allowed to deprive the inventor, by means of a term to that effect in the contract of employment, of his entitlement to any legal rights which would otherwise be his;[2]

(v) the employer should not be able to claim that an employee's invention belongs to him unless he pays the inventor to do the sort of work from which that invention is expected to result, or unless the inventor enjoys such an exalted and trusted position that it simply would not be fair to allow him to exploit his invention to the exclusion of his employer.

None of these principles was novel, since they had been implemented into Swedish[3] and West German[4] law many years previously. What was novel was the implicit recognition by the UK legislation of the fact that inventors needed some greater form of encouragement to invent or to disclose an invention than the law previously offered.

1. Patents Act 1977, ss 39-43.
2. The common law was already tending in this direction: see *Electrolux Ltd v Hudson* [1977] FSR 312, discussed by J Phillips in 'Ownership of Employees' Inventions in Ireland' (1976) 11 *Irish Jurist* (ns) 331.
3. Act of 18 June 1949 regarding the Right to Inventions of Employees (Swedish Code of Statutes no 1949: 345), discussed by F Raussing 'The Swedish Law of Employees' Inventions' in J Phillips (ed) *Employees' Inventions: A Comparative Study* (1981).
4. See M Ruete 'The German Employee-Invention Law: an Outline' in J Phillips, op cit, n 3.

9.9   These principles, broadly drawn and easily comprehensible in their generality, became complex and difficult to apply by the time they had been rendered into statutory form. They also lost much of their potential force as stimuli. For example, the inventor whose invention initially belonged to his employer could only sustain a claim for compensation if he could show that the employer received, or was expected to receive, from the exploitation of the patent (not the invention) an 'outstanding benefit'.[1] Further, whoever owns the invention, it seems that the amount received by the inventor will depend upon such peculiarly non-commercial criteria as the difficulty with which the invention was made[2] as well as the degree of help and assistance received by the inventor in its subsequent development.[3]

1. Patents Act 1977, s 40(1). The almost impossible burden of establishing 'outstanding benefit' is shown by three cases in which employees' claims were unsuccessful: *GEC Avionics Ltd's Patent* [1992] RPC 107; *British Steel plc's Patent* [1992] RPC 117 and *Memco-Med Ltd's Patent* [1992] RPC 403.
2. Patents Act 1977, s 41(4)(b).
3. Ibid, s 41(4)(c) and (d).

9.10   Sadly, there is little evidence that this statutory award scheme has had any incentive impact in the UK. The figures for published successful award claims by employee inventors based upon the 1977 code are as follows:[1]

Awards made when first owner of the invention is

	(i) the employee	*(ii) the employer*	*Claims lodged with the Comptroller*
1982	0	0	0
1986	0	0	5
1990	0	0	2
1994	0	0	1
1998	0	0	0

Curiously enough, there is little to suggest that even those countries where employees' inventions award schemes operate successfully have a higher degree of inventive activity than those which do not. Table C, which lists United Kingdom applications originating from a number of industrial countries, illustrates the rate at which patent applications are forthcoming.

Apart from Japan, where the active encouragement of invention is enthusiastically pursued,[2] and the United States,[3] where employee inventors only get what they can bargain for (ie little or nothing),[4] the pattern suggests that those countries which do not operate award schemes actually encourage more inventive activity than those which do.

1. UK Figures are taken from the Comptroller's Annual Reports.
2. On the Japanese position see T Doi 'Employees' Inventions: the Law and Practice in Japan' in J Phillips *Employees' Inventions: a Comparative Study* (1981).
3. United States' practice was criticised by N Orkin 'The Legal Rights of the Employed Inventor in the United States' in J Phillips op cit; it was defended by F Harter 'Statutorily Decreed Awards for Employed Inventors: Will they Spur Advancement of the Useful Arts? (1971/2) 42 IDEA 575.
4. This meets with the approval of some employee inventors who believe that the contract of employment offers the best chance for the employee to negotiate his market worth: see J Rabinow 'The Employee Inventor – an Inventor's View' (1965) 47 JPOS 469.

9.11   If the employee's best chance of reward for invention lies in being paid to invent by his employer, patent law can assist this process by ensuring that the employer is not otherwise entitled to employees' patents. That is the tenor of section 39(1) and (2). Subsection (2) ensures that inventions belong to the employee, unless the conditions of subsection (1) obtain. Subsection (1) describes two classes of situation where and invention made by an employee in the course of his duties belongs to the employer. In the first,[1] invention falls within the employee's normal duties, or those specifically assigned to him, *and* the circumstances are such that invention might reasonably be expected. This is illustrated by the decision in *Greater Glasgow Health Board's Application.*[2] An opthalmic registrar employed by the Board to treat patients was held, as against his employer, to be entitled to an optical spacing device which he had invented for use with an opthalmoscope. Although he was invited to avail himself of research facilities in his Department, he had little time to do this in view of his heavy clinical load. The second situation is that of a very senior employee. Section 39(1)(b) states that an invention made by this class of employee, who has 'a special obligation to further the interests of

Table C: Proportion (%) of foreign-originating UK applications

Country	1978	1980	1982	1984	1988	1990	1992	1994	1996	1998	Are employee invention rewards schemes provided by law or encouraged by the State?
Japan	11.8	19.4	20.6	22.5	23.5	24.1	20.8	19.4	17.2	15.2	Yes
Taiwan	0.2	0.5	0.8	1.1	2.4	3.3	4.3	3.1	3.3	4.2	No
Canada	1.7	1.5	1.5	1.9	4.0	4.4	5.7	5.6	4.9	4.6	No
Hong Kong	0.4	0.6	0.8	0.8	2.1	1.9	2.0	1.6	1.5	1.0	No
Italy	3.2	4.2	3.7	3.8	3.2	3.1	2.8	2.1	1.8	1.2	No
Australia	1.2	1.0	1.1	1.5	1.4	1.4	1.4	1.5	1.3	1.2	No
Norway	0.4	0.2	0.4	0.4	0.8	0.9	0.9	1.0	1.1	1.6	Yes
Spain	0.5	0.5	0.5	0.7	0.8	0.9	1.2	1.0	0.8	0.5	No
S Africa	0.4	0.5	0.5	0.6	0.7	1.0	1.0	0.5	0.5	0.5	No
N Zealand	0.3	0.3	0.3	0.4	0.4	0.3	0.2	0.3	0.3	0.4	No
USSR	1.1	0.7	0.8	0.7	1.0	1.0	0.04	0.04	0.07	0.02	Yes
Switzerland	5.2	5.0	4.1	4.8	5.0	4.4	5.1	4.2	4.0	3.9	No
Austria	0.7	0.7	0.4	0.7	0.4	0.5	0.5	0.4	0.5	0.2	Yes
Denmark	1.2	0.7	0.8	0.8	0.8	0.6	0.5	0	0.6	0.8	Yes
Sweden	2.8	2.6	1.8	1.8	0.8	0.9	1.0	1.6	1.3	2.1	Yes
France	7.4	5.0	3.5	3.5	3.3	3.2	3.1	3.2	2.5	2.4	Yes
Germany	19.7	16.4	13.8	13.8	12.6	11.7	11.8	12.7	10.1	10.2	Yes
USA	33.1	30.7	29.7	29.8	25.0	23.4	23.0	27.5	29.0	29.4	No

the employer's undertaking' at the relevant time, shall belong to the employer. The inventor in *Staeng Ltd's Patents*[3] was a 'Product Development Manager' who solved a problem posed by a customer.[4] He was responsible directly to his company's managing director and had considerable power. The Patent Office held that his share of the invention belonged to his employer by virtue of section 39(1)(b).[5]

1. Patents Act s 39(1)(a).
2. [1996] RPC 207.
3. [1996] RPC 183.
4. The manager and the customer's employee were held to be joint inventors.
5. The Hearing Officer also held that the employer was entitled to the patent by virtue of s 39(1)(a). For criticism of this finding, and that of joint inventorship, see A Chandler 'Employees' Inventions: Inventorship and Ownership' [1997] EIPR 262.

The patent as an incentive to investment

9.12 One further incentive feature of the patent system should not be overlooked: its arguable function as a stimulus to investment in the development of a new product or process. After all, if the person who offers the necessary finance for the development and commercial promotion of a product knows that it is protected by a patent, it would seem reasonable for him to place great store upon the fact that no other trade rival can market that same product without running the risk of patent infringement proceedings.

9.13 In reality the grant of a patent is not the commercial attraction which it might seem to be, for at least the following reasons:

(i)   the grant of a patent is no guarantee of its continued validity, since lack of novelty or inventive step may give rise to the revocation of the patent at any time;

(ii) even the cast iron validity of a patent would provide no guarantee of its commercial viability. In many cases the patent covers an invention for which there is no ready market, or for which the market is already satisfied by an inferior product which could not be displaced on account of the great expense of developing the new product;

(iii) the mere fact that a patent has been applied for and its specification published will alert market rivals and may thus rob the patentee of the valuable assets of surprise and being first on the market;

(iv) the risk of the patented invention being superseded by the subsequent art cannot be ignored;

(v)   failure to exploit a patent swiftly and successfully may lead to compulsory licence proceedings being instituted and to the critical division of a potentially monopolistic market.

9.14   Taking the foregoing points into account, it is not surprising that the majority of financiers who offer risk or venture capital are reluctant to back a project unless it involves little real element of risk,[1] and that pension fund managers contrive instead to purchase paintings by the old masters, high-grade office premises and 'blue-chip' company shares. To be fair, the government has recognised that the private investment sector is reluctant to throw its hard-earned cash after speculative hunches, which is why generous tax benefits were introduced for those who run such risks.[2] The British Technology Group[3] (now privatised) was charged with financing the most promising invention developments put before it; but since until recently it was a public body risking public money on projects which, historically, had originated largely from the public sector anyway, it was difficult to conclude that its activities were either determined or encouraged by any incentives provided by the patent system. It is worth noting, *en passant*, that the British Technology Group's average royalty income, derived from each of the patented inventions held by it, is only in the region of £4,000.[4] If successfully exploited and carefully pruned[5] patent portfolios bring in revenue of this average relative paucity, it is not difficult to understand why so few inventors grow rich on the fruits of their patents.

1.   The finance house may try to protect its investment by taking security over patents and other intellectual property: D Townend 'Intellectual Property as Security Interest' [1997] IPQ 168; Besant and Punt 'The Use of Intellectual Property as Security for Debt Finance' [1997] IPQ 279; J Phillips 'The Use of Intellectual Property as Security for Debt Finance – a Time to Advance' [1997] EIPR 276; Guthrie and Orr 'Fixed Security Rights over Intellectual Property in Scotland' [1996] EIPR 597. However, this security will be illusory if the patents, etc, are worthless.

2.   The Business Start-up and Business Expansion Schemes, introduced by the Finance Act 1983, enabled individuals to obtain substantial tax relief when investing in new or small, expanding businesses.

3.   BTG was formed through the coming together of two earlier public bodies, the National Research Development Corporation and the National Enterprise Board.

4.   In its accounts to 31 March 1998, BTG reported revenues of £19.82 million. It currently hold about 5,000 patents, in 300 groups, or 'technologies'. These are licensed under some 350 licence agreements. (Information obtained from the BTG web site at www.btgplc.com).

5.   BTG state on their web site 'We bring a ruthless focus to our existing portfolio, maintaining the diversification and balance, terminating failed or unproductive technologies while continuing to attract high quality, innovative and leading edge inventions that will have a lasting impact in the areas of life sciences and physical sciences'.

9.15   *The patent and legal policy*

Reforms and proposals

The United Kingdom

9.15   The Government's Green Paper of 1983, *Intellectual Property Rights and Innovation*,[1] took a critical look at the innovation industry. The innovation industry, however, took an even more critical and substantially better-informed look at the Green Paper,[2] with the result that most of the mooted reforms (listed in **9.16**) stood little or no chance of being introduced and were substituted by the more realistic reform proposals of the 1986 White Paper[3] (listed in **9.17**). The reforms introduced in the Copyright, Designs and Patents Act 1988, listed in **9.18**, bore no similarity to the earlier list.

1.   Cmnd 9117.
2.   See eg A Staines 'Some Thoughts on the 1983 Green Paper' in J Phillips (ed) *Patents in Perspective* (1985); K Hodkinson and B Quest 'Further Reform of the Patent Laws? The Case Against Petty Patents' [1985] EIPR 108.
3.   *Intellectual Property and Innovation*, Cmnd 9712.

9.16   The principal proposals for reform of the substantive patent law, propounded by the Green Paper, were as follows:

(i)   the introduction of an ex parte right of re-examination of a patent[1] at any time after its grant, so that the validity of a patent could be tested in full in a hearing before the Comptroller without the need to embark upon revocation proceedings or to trespass upon the subject-matter of the challenged patent so as to invite infringement proceedings. Despite its efficacy in the United States, ex parte re-examination was reckoned to be unworkable in the United Kingdom and was therefore abandoned.

(ii)   the establishment of a low-cost 'petty patent' system for the registration of inventions.[2] Unlike the fully-fledged patent, the registered invention would not be subjected to the lengthy and expensive search and examination procedures; it would, however, confer a monopoly upon its owner for a limited period of five years, and would form the basis for an infringement action similar to that already operating for patents, so long as its validity (in terms of novelty and inventive step) is confirmed by the Comptroller before infringement action is commenced. This proposal would provide low cost protection for the small inventor who could not otherwise afford a patent, but it was not warmly welcomed by its intended beneficiaries. This is because most small-scale innovators do not have the industrial capacity to develop their inventions themselves and must therefore seek the co-operation of a manufacturing licensee; the latter would be acutely aware that the subject matter of the licence would fall within the public domain within five years, and that its novelty and inventive step were untested. This would make the investment of risk capital an even less attractive proposition than it is at present. Many other European Community Member States have petty patents or 'utility models',[3] however, and the Commission has proposed a harmonising directive, which would compel the UK to introduce such a system.[4]

(iii) Employee inventors were to be given the right to take title to an invention which belongs to an employer who fails to exploit it.[5] The employer faced with the threat of 'use it or lose it' will in probability opt for the latter course if he is already established in his market, which means that the employee inventor will have to make a difficult choice between establishing his own enterprise and casting his lot with his employer. The likelihood of the inventor making a success of his employer's unexploited invention is so slender that the 'use it or lose it' principle could be justified on moral, but not economic, grounds.[6]

(iv) The compulsory licence provisions of the Patents Act[7] were to be made more effective by requiring the transfer, to the would-be licensee, of any unpatented and unpatentable 'know-how', which would facilitate the exploitation of the invention, at any rate where there is a clear abuse of monopoly.[8] This proposal, which would be impossible to implement, gained no support.

1. Cmnd 9117, para 5.10 and Annex C.
2. Ibid, para 4.3 and Annex B. This proposal remained in abeyance until 1993, when the Government embarked on a consultation exercise.
3. U Suthersanen 'A Brief Tour of "Utility Model" Law' [1998] EIPR 44.
4. Proposal [1998] OJ C36/13; amended proposal COM (99) 309 adopted by the Commission on 30 June 1999.
5. Ibid, para 5.31.
6. An employee's alleged freedom to take an 'unwanted' invention with him to a new employer was rejected in *Triplex Safety Glass v Scorah* [1938] Ch 211, (1938) 55 RPC 21, a breach of confidence case.
7. See para **7.16** above.
8. Green Paper, Ch 5, paras 5.11-5.22.

9.17 The 1986 White Paper proposed as follows:[1]

(i) The 'hiving-off' of the Patent Office which, it was believed, would operate more efficiently outside the civil service under the control of a Board appointed by the Secretary of State for Trade and Industry.[2] This proposal was dropped when it became apparent that the Patent Office would be unlikely to run on a financially viable basis outside the civil service. The question of privatising some or all of the Patent Office's function resurfaced in 1993 but as yet the Office and its functions remain in the public sector.[3]

(ii) The giving of far greater publicity to the importance of intellectual property.[4] This has been done most effectively by the Patent Office, with the result that far more people in the United Kingdom now know about the patent system, even if they don't understand very much about its substance and modus operandi.

(iii) The commencement of invalidity proceedings before the Comptroller in the case of infringement, revocation, threats and certain other proceedings,[5] and the giving of wider powers to the Comptroller to grant relief.[6] The reasoning behind this proposal was that it would reduce the expense and increase the speed of contested proceedings. In the face of heavy criticism from specialist practitioners, the proposal was withdrawn.

(iv) The critical examination of the virtual monopoly enjoyed by patent agents[7] in the prosecution of patent applications. This was done by the Office of Fair Trading[8] with the result that now any person can practise the patent agent's profession for gain[9] – but restrictions still exist with regard to how an unqualified patent agent may describe himself[10] and communications between the unqualified patent agent and his client are not the subject of any privilege against disclosure.[11] At the time of writing, the OFT was again subjecting the legal professions to scrutiny.

1. *Intellectual Property and Innovation*, Cmnd 9712.
2. Ibid, para 1.6.
3. For a criticism see C Morcom 'Privatisation and the Patent Office' [1994] 4 EIPR 143. The Patent Office now has 'Agency' Status within the Department of Trade & Industry, see Annual Reports, passim.
4. Ibid, para 1.12. The Patent Office's web site at www.patent.gov.uk and the intellectual property 'portal' provide effective information and links.
5. Ibid, para 4.7.
6. Ibid, para 4.9.
7. Ibid, para 4.36.
8. 'Review of Restrictions on the Patent Agents' Profession', 25 September 1986, see K Weatherald 'The OFT and DTI versus the British Patent Profession', Patent World, July 1987, p 50.
9. Copyright, Designs and Patents Act 1988, s 274(1).
10. Ibid, ss 276 to 279.
11. Ibid, s 280.

9.18 The Copyright, Designs and Patents Act 1988 introduced, inter alia, the following amendments:

(i) The Lord Chancellor was given power to designate any county court as a patents county court and to confer upon it the jurisdiction to determine such matters pertinent or ancillary to patents as he might specify.[1] This move, designed to offer a less expensive mode of litigation and to reduce the pressure of patent litigation in the High Court, has been implemented.[2]

(ii) Procedures for filing applications for UK patents from abroad via the Patent Co-operation Treaty were clarified.[3]

(iii) It became easier to obtain the restoration of a lapsed patent.[4]

1. Section 287.
2. See A Poore 'The Patents County Court', Managing Intellectual Property, March 1994, p 45; P Ford 'The Patents County Court, London – Four Years' Experience' (1996) 27 IIC 235.
3. Sch 5, paras 24-25.
4. Sch 5, para 6.

European patents and litigation

9.19 As well as enjoying a choice of courts in which to litigate infringement of a UK patent,[1] a patentee with a number of equivalent patents in Europe and elsewhere might have to choose where, under which patent and legal system, to sue an infringer. Factors influencing this choice of forum would include (i) likelihood of success, including availability of defences, (ii) speed of resolution of the dispute,[2] (iii) availability of remedies, both interim and final,[3] (iv) whether the defendant could challenge the validity of the patent in the infringement proceedings, (v) appeal procedures, (vi) the cost of the proceedings. By suing successfully in one jurisdiction, the patentee would hope to encourage that infringer and also third parties to refrain from working the invention in all jurisdictions where it was patented. However, if litigation in several states proves necessary, it is possible that the different courts will reach different decisions,[4] even with patents granted by the European Patent Office and therefore containing identical claims. Indeed, not only do the bundle of national patents which the European Patent Office grants to a successful applicant fall to be interpreted by national courts, but they may diverge in scope if they are amended in the member states concerned. These facts may be regarded as a weakness of the present system.

1. In England and Wales, the Patent Court (within the Chancery Division of the High Court) or the Patents County Court (see para **9.18** above). In Scotland, infringement proceedings are brought before the Court of Session, in Northern Ireland, the High Court: see Patents Act 1977, s 130(1).
2. A jurisdiction may be chosen for the slowness of its proceedings, for tactical reasons, as with the 'Italian Torpedo'. This is a tactic whereby a potential defendant sues in Italy for a declaration of non-infringement in order to found jurisdiction there and 'sink' actions elsewhere. The Italian courts are 'not particularly quick', so litigation is postponed almost indefinitely: M Franzosi 'Worldwide Patent Litigation and the Italian Torpedo' [1997] EIPR 382.

3. For some time the District Court of The Hague, Netherlands, was rather popular with claimants because of its willingness to grant extra-territorial orders in 'Kort Geding' – short proceedings. See PA Haas 'Extra-territoriality in Patent Infringement Issues' [2001] IPQ 187; M Rijsdijk 'Patent Cases: 1994 to the Present' [2000] EIPR 120.
4. See, eg C Gielen 'Dutch Court Disagrees with English Court in Rapamycin Case' [2000] EIPR N-127. In fact the English Court of Appeal subsequently allowed an appeal from the High Court's Rapamycin decision: *American Home Products Corpn v Novartis Pharmaceuticals UK Ltd* [2001] RPC 159. Gielen's note remains of interest in highlighting the differences between English, Dutch and German proceedings.

9.20 Within Europe, spice is added to the forum-shoppers' menu by the Brussels and Lugano Conventions[1] on civil jurisdiction and enforcement of judgments. These provide that a defendant may be sued for a tort (a) in the state of his domicile[2] or (b) in the state where the harmful event occurred.[3] Under Art 2, the court can reach a decision and award relief on a Europe-wide basis; under Art 5(3) only in relation to the state concerned. However, in the case of a registered right, Art 16(4) stipulates that validity may only be put in issue in the state where the right is registered. Thus, for example, the English Court could not rule on the validity of a European Patent (Germany). Since the issues of infringement and validity are inextricably linked in litigation under the Patents Act 1977, our Courts are reluctant to exercise their jurisdiction under Art 2 in patent cases.[4] Not all countries' courts have the same qualms, however. Indeed, in Germany the courts are accustomed to separate consideration of infringement (heard at first instance by the *Land* courts) and validity (a Federal matter). Application of the jurisdiction Conventions becomes even more complex when multiple defendants and causes of action are concerned, and in relation to interim orders, or 'provisional measures'. Such matters are beyond the scope of this book.[5] Suffice it to say that international patent litigation is far from straightforward or uniform in its outcomes.

1. The Brussels Convention governs jurisdiction as between members of the European Community; the equivalent Lugano Convention as between members of the European Free Trade Association. These are given effect in the UK by the Civil Jurisdiction and Judgments Act 1982. See LJ Cohen 'Intellectual Property and the Brussels Convention: An English Perspective' [1997] EIPR 379. As of 1 March 2002, the Brussels Convention will be replaced by a Council Regulation to largely similar effect: (EC) No 44/2001, of 22 December 2002, on jurisdiction and the recognition and enforcement of judgments in civil and commercial matters. Happily the main article numbers are retained, but art 16(4) will become art 22(4).
2. Art 2 in both Conventions.
3. Art 5(3) in both Conventions.
4. In *Fort Dodge Animal Health Products v Akzo Nobel* [1998] FSR 222, the Court of Appeal held that a claim for infringement as well as a counterclaim for

revocation were 'principally concerned' with validity. This meant that they were matters for the courts in the state of registration of patent; Art 19 of the Brussels Convention therefore required the English court to decline jurisdiction.

5. See, further, eg C Wadlow *Enforcement of Intellectual Property in European and International Law* (1998).

9.21 A number of proposals have been made for reform to ease the difficulties described above:

(i) a procedure for centralised amendment of patents granted by the European Patent Office. Since patents can only be amended to reduce their scope, this has been described as a 'central limitation procedure'.[1] New Arts 105a-105c to the European Patent Convention were agreed at a Diplomatic Conference in November 2000. When these are ratified by EPC Member States, the proprietor will be able to apply at any time to the EPO to limit or revoke all patents resulting from a single grant;

(ii) improved convergence in the decision-making of the national courts, by making systematic arrangements for national patent judges to sit on an Enlarged Board of Appeal at the European Patent Office;[2]

(iii) the establishment of a European Patent Court, combining the legal and technical expertise of national patent judges and members of the EPO Boards of Appeal, to hear questions of interpretation by referral;[3]

(iv) creation of a unitary Community Patent;[4] this would apply only in the countries of the EU, so does not obviate the need for co-operation amongst the wider community of EPC members. Furthermore, if questions of infringement and validity were left to national patent courts of first instance, the problems of unpredictable interpretation and forum-shopping would remain;[5]

(v) the establishment of a Community Patent Court;[6]

(vi) the establishment of a European Patent Court to hear disputes relating to European Patents at first instance and on appeal. This would be by way of a Protocol under the European Patent Convention;[7]

(vii) replacement of the EPC with a Community Patent system, administered by the EPO. Association agreements would enable non-EU countries to participate. National patents would be abolished but infringement and validity would be heard together by national courts. Care would be taken to ensure that national judicial systems had patent expertise at the appeals level if not at first instance. This could be achieved in part by drafting judges on to the EPO Boards of Appeal, as in (ii).[8]

Readers will note that the proposals overlap. More than one European Patent Court would increase, rather than decrease, the complexity of litigation in this field.[9] Furthermore, in view of the actual or alleged lack of experienced patent judges in a number of Member States, it is difficult to see how one, let alone two, such courts could be manned.[10]

1. See R Nack and B Phélip 'Diplomatic Conference for the Revision of the European Patent Convention' (2001) 32 IIC 200.
2. R Jacob 'The Enlarged Board of Appeal of the EPO: A Proposal' [1997] EIPR 224. This would have the added advantage of increasing the independence of the Enlarged Board of appeal from the EPO examination structure.
3. J Brinkhof 'The Desirability, Necessity and Feasibility of Co-operation between Courts in the Field of European Patent Law' [1997] EIPR 226.
4. The current Proposal for a Council Regulation on the Community Patent was published by the EC Commission on 1 August 2000 as COM (2000) 412 final.
5. See P Leith 'Revision of the EPC, the Community Patent Regulation and "European Technical Judges"' [2001] EIPR 250. Leith proposes a decentralised system whereby members of the EPO Boards of Appeal would participate in the decisions of the national courts, thus reversing the flows proposed by Jacob and Brinkhof, nn 2 and 3 above; COM (2000) 412 final at para 2.4.5.1.
6. The proposed Community Patent Regulation, above, n 4, envisages a Community Intellectual Property Court to hear cases on patent infringement and invalidity proceedings, at first instance and on appeal.
7. See Structure Paper of the Working Party on Litigation reproduced by A Addor and S Luginbuehl 'The First Steps towards and Optional Protocol under the European Patent Convention on the Settlement of Litigation concerning European Patents [2000] EIPR S-1.
8. J Willens 'The EPC:The Emperor's Phantom Clothes? A Blueprint instead of a Green Paper' [1998] IPQI.
9. For a comparison, see P Cole 'Centralised Litigation for European Patents: New Proposals for Inclusion in the EPC Revision Package' [2001] EIPR 219.
10. J Pagenberg 'The First Instance European Patent Court – a Tribunal without Judges and Attorneys?' (2000) IIC 481.

European patents – other reforms

9.22   The Diplomatic Conference for the Revision of the European Patent Convention agreed a number of other items.[1] These included:

(i)   empowering the EPO Administrative Council to amend the Convention in response to international treaties and EC law (Art 35)

(ii)   retention of the exclusion in Art 52(2)(c) for computer programs 'as such';[2]

(iii) moving the exclusion of methods of medical treatment from Art 52 (industrial application) to Art 53 (public policy exceptions) and confirming that first and second medical uses of known compounds can be claimed (new Art 54(4) and (5));[3]

(iv)   mention of 'equivalents' in the Protocol to Art 69;[4]

(v)   introducing a procedure for judicial review of Board of Appeal decisions within the EPO where a fundamental procedural defect or criminal act has vitiated a decision;[5]

(vi) paving the way for filing in any language, with postponement of the need to translate into one of the official languages of the EPO.

1.   See para **9.21**, n 1 above.
2.   See para **4.11**, above.
3.   See above, paras **5.25-5.28**.
4.   See above, para **8.12**.
5.   Art 112a. For the dearth of review procedures, see *Lenzing AG's European Patents (UK)* [1997] RPC 245.

9.23   However, the cost of translations under the European Patent Convention remains high. Applications may presently be made in one of the three official languages: English, French and German,[1] or one of the 'allowable languages'[2] – official languages of contracting states – provided the application is translated into an Office language within three months. Claims are translated into the other two official languages of the EPO for publication at grant.[3] Many contracting states have opted to require further translation into their national languages.[4] The total cost of these translations was estimated in 1992 as £7,500 for 12 languages.[5] More recently the typical cost of translation into eight languages has been put at 12,600 euros (somewhat less than £9,000), a significant proportion of the total lifetime cost of a patent (estimated at 49,900 euros).[6] Despite a report that there was little interest in reducing translation costs,[7] they are seen as marring the competitiveness of Europe's industry.[8] The proposed Community Patent would not require translation into national languages in order for the patent to take effect unless translation were required for the purposes of litigation.[9]

1.   EPC, art 14(1).
2.   EPC, art 14(2); if translation is not filed, the application is deemed to have been withdrawn.
3.   EPC, art 14(7).
4.   Failure to do so being fatal to the patent rights; *BASF* Case C-44/98, ECJ.
5.   J Neukom 'What Price the Community Patent' [1992] EIPR 111.
6.   S Stokes 'Commission Proposes the Creation of a Community Patent' [2000] EIPR N-155; COM (2000) 412 final. For translations into 11 EU official languages, the cost goes up to 17,000 euros, about £12,000.
7.   P Leith *Harmonisation of Intellectual Property in Europe: A Case Study of Patent Procedure* (1998) Vol 3 Perspectives on Intellectual Property, ed A Chandler, p 137, citing an EPO survey of 1994.
8.   See n 7, above.
9.   M Franzosi 'Save Your Translation expenses: follow the Clear Teaching of the Unclear) Art 69 EPC' [1998] EIPR 36 argues that claims only need be translated.

Part III

Copyright

Chapter 10

The concept of copyright

A brief historical introduction

10.1 Instances of legal intervention in order to punish one person for copying the literary or aesthetic output of another were known even before the concept of copyright took shape; indeed, there is a fair amount of literature on the subject.[1] There was no systematic legal protection against acts of copying, however, until three features, one technological and two cultural,[2] became coincident. The first of these features was the development of means of large-scale production of works, in particular the printing press. Once the potential for the profitable exploitation of printed works was finally recognised, the right to extract profits from printing was worth fighting over; and once it was worth fighting over, the need arose for the legal resolution of such disputes. In this context it is no accident that the demand for the exclusive right to make copies of a work was made not by authors, but by printers and publishers.[3] The second necessary feature of a copyright-conscious environment was the emergence of a sufficiently large literate audience for it to be worth anyone's while to print works in quantity. The third feature was the change which took place with regard to man's attitude towards copying; for many generations the imitation of a classical style or form of expression had been regarded as the ultimate degree in the attainment of aesthetic excellence but, once the expression of original thought supplanted the faithful adherence to accepted cultural norms, the act of imitation became less and less acceptable, and could not expect the law's encouragement or acquiescence.[4] Once these three features combined, they provided a necessary condition for the development of copyright, even if they could not actually have been said to have caused its emergence.[5]

1. See eg M-C Dock 'The Origin and Development of the Literary Property Concept' (1975) *Revue Internationale du Droit d'Auteur* 126; J Phillips 'St Columba as Copyright Infringer' [1985] EIPR 350. See also the historians of copyright cited in K Bowrey 'Who's Writing Copyright's History?' [1996] EIPR 322.
2. See, also, D Burkitt 'Copyrighting Culture: The History and Cultural Specificity of the Western Model of Copyright' [2001] IPQ 146.

3.   See eg A Birrell *Seven Lectures on Copyright* (1898) pp 78-93; J Feather 'Authors, Publishers and Politicians: the History of Copyright and the Book Trade' [1988] 12 EIPR 377.
4.   For a general explanation of this proposition see B Kaplan *An Unhurried View of Copyright* (1967).
5.   For the effect of political climate, see L Gimeno 'Politics, Patents and Copright in 20th Century Spain' in A Firth (ed) *Prehistory and Development of Intellectual Property Systems* (1997), Vol 1, Perspectives in Intellectual Property, p 159.

10.2   In the United Kingdom copyright, when it did emerge, was – as its name suggests – the right to make a copy of a work and, by implication, to stop others doing so. From the manner of the growth of copyright it is easy to see how the English lawyer maintained a remarkably consistent view of copyright as a right to stop the making of copies, despite the extension of that right from 1709, when all it covered was books and sheet music,[1] to the first great consolidation of copyright in 1911,[2] by which time the law could be seen to protect such diverse objects as photographs, sculptures, gramophone records and telegram codes. The word 'copyright' is not an accurate translation of the equivalent term used in countries of the civil law tradition. To render into English the notion of *droit d'auteur* (France), *Urheberrecht* (Germany), *derecho de autor* (Spain) or *diritto d'autore* (Italy) one must employ the phrase 'author's right'.[3] This distinction reflects not so much a matter of terminological chance[4] as a profound chasm between common law and civil law approaches to copyright. Common law protects a work because it can be copied with undesirable results, while civil law protects an author because he has a moral entitlement to control and exploit the product of his intellectual labour.[5] Despite this apparent divergence, Ginsburg[6] has shown that copyright and author's right had similar beginnings. Of the two terminologies, that of the common law seems nowadays to be the less appropriate. This is because acts such as the unauthorised performance of a song, broadcast of a poem or cable transmission of a play are all infringements of copyright, although they have nothing to do with the making of copies at all. Furthermore, since 1842 at least, the author has been a main point of reference for copyright law.[7]

1.   Copyright Act 1709, s 1; *Bach v Longman* (1777) 2 Cowp 623.
2.   Copyright Act 1911 (1 & 2 Geo 5, c 46).
3.   Y Gendreau 'The Copyright Civilisation in Canada' [2000] IPQ 84, gives a view from as country which enbraces the common law and civil law.
4.   On terminology, see J A L Sterling, 'Challenges in the Context of Copyright and Digital Technology' (2000) IIC 508.
5.   On the effectiveness of authors' rights see C Le Stanc 'The Practical Scope of the Intellectual Rights of the Author in French Law' [1988] 3 EIPR 88.
6.   J Ginsburg 'A Tale of Two Copyrights: Literary Property in Revolutionary France and America' (1990) 64 Tulane Law Review 991. Drahos notes that in pre-revolutionary France, during the 1750s, 40% of those in the Bastille were

there because of offences relating to the book trade: 'Intellectual Property and Human Rights' [1999] IPQ 319. As for his title, Drahos remarks that the historical connections [between intellectual property and human rights] were thin at best.

7. C Seville 'Talfourd and his Contemporaries: the Making of the Copyright Act 1842' in A Firth (ed) 'The Prehistory and Development of Intellectual Property Systems' (1997) Vol 1 Perspectives on Intellectual Property, at p 47.

Copyright as a temporary property right

10.3 Over the years a great debate has been conducted, largely over the unconcerned heads of copyright owners, as to whether copyright is 'property' or not. This issue is quite sterile so far as English law is concerned, since the nature and extent of copyright is defined almost exclusively by the express provisions of the statute law which governs it; the only issues which involve consideration of copyright's status as property are peripheral ones such as whether it is possible to commit a criminal theft of a copyright, whether copyright belongs to a partnership when works are created in the course of the partners' business, or whether the testamentary disposition of one's 'property' to a favourite nephew includes the disposition of one's copyright as well as one's golf clubs and fishing rods.

10.4 The Copyright Act 1956 was conclusive that copyright is property.[1] The Copyright, Designs and Patents Act 1988 describes copyright as 'a property right'.[2] Most property is categorised by English law as being either 'real property' (or 'realty') or 'personal property' ('personalty'), the subtle distinction being that real property is the property in land, while personal property is the property in one's moveable possessions ('chattels'), or in 'choses in action' such as debts owed to one.[3] Although copyright most resembles 'personal property' under the statute and is said to be transmissible as personal or movable property,[4] it is really *sui generis* since its assignment and inheritance, in fact, follow rules specially laid down for it, and not just the normal laws of personal property. The most important of these rules is that the transfer of a copyright is only legally recognised if the transaction is recorded in writing and signed by the seller;[5] this rule does not apply to the sale of other personal property such as a toothbrush or a packet of cigarettes. Furthermore, ways of exploiting copyright are far more interesting and varied than methods of exacting payment of a debt.

1. Copyright Act 1956, s 36(1).
2. Copyright, Designs and Patents Act 1988, s 1(1).
3. On whether copyrights and other intellectual property may be regarded as 'choses in action', see J Fitzgerald and A Firth, 'Equitable Assignments in Relation to Intellectual Property' [1999] IPQ 228 at 231-232.

4. Copyright, Designs and Patents Act 1988, s 90(1).
5. Ibid, s 90(3).

10.5 Nonetheless, the debate as to whether copyright is 'property' rumbles on, largely because there exists a sizeable body of otherwise intelligent persons who argue from the mistaken premise that something cannot truly be 'property' unless it is solid and has the attributes of a physical presence. Real and personal property, they assert, are property because they exist in fact; copyright has no existence except in law, and is therefore an abstraction which, whatever its utility, is simply not property. This position reflects a misunderstanding of the use to which lawyers put the word 'property'. The word is derived from the Latin word *proprius*, meaning 'one's own'; something is therefore property if someone is entitled to enforce rights in it. To talk of concepts such as 'ownerless property' (an inappropriate translation, it is submitted, of *res nullius*) is to apply to the notion of 'property' in its legal sense a meaning which is more appropriate to the natural sciences, where one talks of a substance having one or more 'properties', of which its physical dimension is but one. However, recourse to the physical rather than the metaphysical is a well-known practice of common lawyers, and its results should not be entirely criticised. One consequence of the ambiguity inherent in the word 'property' is that it is not an act of theft to steal another's copyright, even though (i) it is an appropriation of another's property and (ii) the word 'property' is defined under the Theft Act 1968, section 4(1), as including 'intangible property'. One might have thought that copyright was 'intangible property' but for the recognition by the courts that the phrase is applicable only to intangible but physically existing property such as gas, vapour or air.[1]

1. *Oxford v Moss* [1979] Crim LR 119; *R v Absolon* (1983) Times, 14 September. See also K Gray 'Property in Thin Air' (1991) 52 CLJ 252.

10.6 Once it is conceded that copyright is property, although it may be of no more substance than the hole in the Polo mint, it is apparent that it suffers from a degree of transience. A plot of land usually stays 'property' forever, and a tea cup remains an ownable commodity to eternity; a pet budgerigar is a chattel even after its death and, when a set of wooden cricket stumps is incinerated, the resultant ashes are regarded as being not merely transmissible but indeed as a desirable property.[1] The same cannot be said of copyright, which expires and dies at the stroke of midnight, leaving not so much as a corpse behind it.[2] If copyright is property, it has been argued, then why should it be artificially and arbitrarily limited in time? This is an argument which is easier to reject than to disprove, and it rests upon the unspoken major premise that all types of property should be treated in the same manner by virtue of their status as property. In fact, the reason why real and traditional personal property are property for an unlimited duration is that, since their ability to be possessed by one person to the exclusion of others is coterminous with their physical existence, the law must provide rules which determine the entitlement to their possession for the duration of their existence. No such demand is made of copyright, which has no existence outside the four walls of the Copyright, Designs and Patents Act. To put it another way, ownership of copyright is only a legal right to exercise a legal right, and has no existence except as a legal right.

1. The Ashes, the symbolic remains of English cricket, have been the subject of fierce competition between the English and Australian cricket teams for more than a century.
2. On the duration of copyright see Ch 14.

Copyright and unfair competition

10.7 The United Kingdom's common law has never been able to develop an actionable wrong of 'unfair competition', although it has from time to time been invited to do so. It is quite possible that one of the reasons for this lies in the fact that the concept of copyright was already established[1] before competition law had developed beyond the stage of rejecting the capricious royal grant of harmful monopolies,[2] and before unfair competition law had progressed beyond the simple prohibition of a trader's marking his own goods with another's identifying mark.[3] Early copyright litigation reveals that, in the minds of the judiciary in the eighteenth century, the concept of copyright was not so much related to the promotion of the good of the author as derived from the fundamental notion that no one person should be able to compete unfairly against another by appropriating the fruits of his intellectual labour.[4]

1. On the early history of copyright see eg A Birrell *Copyright in Books* (1899), Ch 2 ('The Origin of Copyright').
2. *Darcy v Allen* (1602) 11 Co Rep 84b.
3. *The Clothier of Gloucester's case,* cited in *Southern v How* (1618) Poph 143.
4. See eg *Millar v Taylor* (1768) 4 Burr 2303 at pp 2334 to 2335.

10.8 The inhibition of an unfair competition law by the early emergence of a dynamic statute-based copyright concept had a number of interesting consequences. The first was that, as each new form of abuse of another's intellectual endeavour became apparent, the common law could not safely be invoked so as to right even a manifest moral wrong, which in turn meant that each such abuse required a remedy in the form of a petition to Parliament for the creation of additional statutory copyright laws.[1] The second was that the categories of work protected under British copyright law were widely construed, to the extent that a drawing of an industrially exploitable motor exhaust pipe,[2] or a sketch of working parts of a vacuum cleaner,[3] could fall within the provisions of the copyright law which protected 'artistic works'; in most other countries such artefacts would not be protected by an 'author's right', and would instead fall to be protected by 'slavish copying' rules,[4] or by utility model registration.[5,6] Similarly, literary copyright in compilations was used to protect lists and databases.[7] This area has now been harmonised by the EC Directive on the legal protection of databases.[8] Copyright protects the architecture of a database, and a *sui generis* right prohibits the unfair extraction or re-utilisation of items of information contained in the database. Third, the lack of a body of unfair competition law deprived would-be plaintiffs of a useful ground outside copyright law upon which there could be founded a claim that their legitimate commercial expectations were being interfered with by competition from exploitation of non-infringing copies of their works (for example, the losses caused to authors through library loans,[9] or the damage to pre-recorded video cassette sales through the availability for hire, at an attractive rate, of lawfully recorded tapes[10]) or by repeated takings of insubstantial and therefore non-infringing amounts.[11] Fourth, the assessment of damages for copyright infringement was traditionally calculated by reference to the loss or harm inflicted upon the owner of an intellectual property right as such, rather than as the competitor in a trading market.[12] Finally, the paucity of case law authorities with regard to the unfair utilisation by one man of another's image, reputation or appearance has made it unlikely that a tort of wrongful appropriation of another's personality will ever emerge through the courts.[13] It is not surprising that calls are periodically made[14] for the UK to introduce a tort of unfair competition. The interface between copyright and competition law – that area of the law which seeks to promote a competitive market by prohibiting restrictive practices and abuses of dominance – will be discussed later at paragraphs **14.22-14.25**.

1. For an account of pre-1911 statute law at its most complex see T Scrutton *The Law of Copyright* (4th edn 1903).
2. *British Leyland Motor Corpn Ltd v Armstrong Patents Ltd* [1986] AC 577.
3. *Hoover plc v George Hulme (Stockport) Ltd* [1982] FSR 565.
4. See eg the Austrian Supreme Court decision of 17 April 1984, 4 Ob 331/83, noted at [1984] EIPR D-207; for unfair competition in other European countries, see: Schricker 'Twenty Five Years of Protection against Unfair Competition' (1995) 26 IIC 166; Clauss 'The French Law of Disloyal Competition' [1995] EIPR 550; Henning Bodewig 'International Protection against Unfair Competition (1999) 30 IIC 166.

5. Eg West German Utility Model Act of 2 January 1968, as amended to 13 June 1980. See also C Rohnke 'Protection of External Product Features in West Germany' [1990] 2 EIPR 41.
6. For a comparative survey of utility model regimes U Suthersanen 'A Brief Tour of "Utility Model" Law' [1998] EIPR 44.
7. Eg the list of lawyers names and addresses in *Waterlow Directories Ltd v Reed Information Services Ltd* [1992] FSR 409.
8. Directive 96/6; [1996] OJ L77/20, implemented in the UK by the Copyright and Rights in Databases Regulations 1997 (SI 1997/3032).
9. Now compensated by the Public Lending Right Scheme, discussed in Ch 15.
10. On which see the Governmental Green Paper *The Recording and Rental of Audio and Video Copyright Material: A Consultative Document* Cmnd 9445, 1985. A rental right was introduced into copyright law in 1988 and rental and lending rights are now harmonised within the EC: see para **13.21**.
11. *Electronic Techniques (Anglia) Ltd v Critchley Components Ltd* [1997] FSR 401.
12. On copyright damages see para **14.11**.
13. See eg *McCulloch v May* (1948) 65 RPC 58; *Sim v Heinz* [1959] RPC 75; *Lyngstad v Anabas Products Ltd* [1977] FSR 62; *Tolley v Fry* [1931] AC 333. The plaintiff's success in *Kaye v Robertson* [1991] FSR 62 was based on malicious falsehood. The advance of digital technology has made the misuse of personal images particularly troublesome – see K Schilling '"Wapping Woman in Court Porn Shock!" or Computerised Rape: Is it Actionable in Libel?' [1994] 3 Ent LR 98; P Jones 'Manipulating the Law against Misleading Imagery: Photomontage and Appropriation of Well-known Personality' [1998] EIPR 28.
14. For citations of calls from academics and practitioners, and discussion of possible pitfalls in introducing a civil law wrong into a common law system, see J Adams 'Unfair competition: Why a Need is Unmet' [1992] 8 EIPR 259; Robertson and Horton, 'Does the UK or the EC Need an Unfair Competition Law?' [1995] EIPR 568. See, also, A Kamperman Sanders 'Unfair Competition Law – Some Economic Considerations' in J A L Sterling (ed) *Intellectual Property and Market Freedom* (1997) Vol 2, Perspectives on Intellectual Property, p 131. C Gielen, 'WIPO and Unfair Competition' [1997] EIPR 78 summarises WIPO's proposal. This does not deal in detail, however, with the kinds of unfair competition outlined above.

The copyright monopoly

10.9 It should be remembered that the copyright monopoly is only a limited, qualified sort of monopoly[1] and that, while the holder of the copyright is entitled to stop anyone else copying or otherwise unlawfully exploiting the work he enjoys rights in, it offers him no vestige of protection against the person who designs or writes his own independent work without recourse to the act of copying. It is also worth considering that the economic impact of any individual copyright will be, at least in theory, markedly different from the economic impact of a patent monopoly. The patentee's market control is often well-nigh absolute when he holds a patent for a product, since no one else can make or exploit that product at all; where a patent covers a process, the patentee's market power is only absolute where the market is for the process itself (eg if he is the only person who can offer a particular dry-cleaning technique), and is often weak when the patent covers a process of manufacture for a product which is already available through other processes.

1. See para **2.6**. Sir Hugh Laddie took a different view in 'Copyright: Over-strength, Over-regulated, Over-rated' [1996] EIPR 253.

10.10 In copyright, the qualified monopoly is usually fairly weak in economic terms. The author of a detective story may enjoy the sole right to authorise its publication and sale for seventy years following his death, but he is unlikely to be the sole purveyor of detective stories.[1] Likewise, the manufacturer of a new pop record will find that his monopoly offers him no protection in a market in which over 100 different and competing products are launched each week.[2] Because of this relative weakness in the copyright monopoly, it is not surprising that the Copyright Act 1956 had few provisions[3] to compare with the compulsory licence, Crown licence and abuse of monopoly provisions of the Patents Act 1977. However, criticism of failure by industrial copyright owners to license spare parts[4] led to a change in Parliament's attitude and the 1988 Act contains a number of provisions[5] to limit unfettered exploitation of copyright works.

1. See A McGee and G Scanlan 'Genre as an Intellectual Property Right' [1999] IPQ 471.
2. See G Davies *Piracy of Phonograms* (1981), Table 12 at p 144.
3. See eg Copyright Act 1956, ss 8 and 23-30.
4. See the Monopolies and Mergers Commission's Report, *Ford Motor Co's Replacement Parts Policy* Cmnd 9437, 1985 reported at [1986] ECC 106 and summarised at [1986] FSR 147.
5. See, eg Copyright, Designs and Patents Act 1988, ss 66, 121, 126, 137, 140-141, 144.

10.11 Attempts have been made to evaluate and quantify the effects of the copyright monopoly, but their influence on its development has been slight, despite lip-service to economics and competitiveness in reforms from the Whitford Report of 1977[1] through to the programme of copyright harmonisation measures introduced by the European Community.[2] Sir Albert Plant's study,[3] cited even today by economists, is more than sixty years old and relates to an industry in which television was unknown and new technologies scarcely imaginable. Stephen Breyer's controversial questioning of the traditional assumptions underlying the copyright monopoly[4] was the work of a critical and incisive lawyer, not an economist. Further glimmers of light have been provided by authors such as Phillips,[5] Gordon,[6] Power[7] and MacQueen.[8] Van den Bergh,[9] considers the 'economic optimal size' of copyright in order to achieve a desirable balance of incentives for the production of information and for its dissemination. Interestingly, he concludes that vague norms applied by judges may do a better job than detailed statutory rules. Sadly, the days of vague norms are numbered in the European digital market. This is because the European Community has given a detailed prescription for exceptions and limitations to copyright.[10] The Competition Commission, formerly the Monopolies and Mergers Commission, makes economic analyses of particular market sectors when reporting on alleged anti-competitive behaviour,[11] as does the European Commission,[12] but what is needed is an economic overview of the effects of copyright in general.[13] Unfortunately, the march of technology tends to ensure that market characteristics change almost as quickly as they can be measured, so the insight provided by empirical studies tends to be retrospective.

1. Copyright and Designs Law (Cmnd 6731, 1977).
2. Foreshadowed in the 1988 Green Paper *Copyright and the Challenge of Technology* COM (88) 172 final, and *Follow-up* COM (90) 584 final. See also J Rodriguez Pardo 'Highlights of the Origins of the European Union Law on Copyright' [2001] EIPR 238, stressing earlier and cultural background.
3. A Plant 'The Economic Aspects of Copyright in Books' (1934) *Economica (n.s.)* 167.
4. S Breyer 'The Uneasy Case for Copyright' (1970) 84 *Harv LR* 281.
5. Jennifer Phillips *The Economic Importance of Copyright* (1985), revisited in 1994 by T Price.
6. W Gordon 'Fair Use as Market Failure: a Structural and Economic Analysis of the Betamax Case and its Predecessors' (1983) 30 Journal of the Copyright Society of the US, 253.
7. T Power 'Digitisation of Serials and Publications: The Seminal Objective of Copyright' [1997] EIPR 444.
8. H MacQueen (ed) *Special Issue: Innovation, Incentive and Reward: Intellectual Property Law and Policy,* (1997) 5 David Hume Papers on Public Policy
9. R van den Burgh 'The Role and Social Justification of Copyright: a "Law and Economics" Approach' [1998] IPQ 17.
10. Directive 2001/29/EC on Copyright and Related Rights in the Information Society, 22 June 2001, OJ L167/10; implementation date, 22 December 2002.
11. *Ford Motor Co Ltd* Cmnd 9437, 1985.
12. Eg *Eurofix-Bauco v Hilti* [1988] FSR 473.
13. But see H Cohen Jehoram 'Critical Reflections on the Economic Importance of Copyright' (1989) 20 IIC 485.

10.12 An extensive survey of the literature on the economics of copyright has been carried out by Watt,[1] who goes on to develop models for the economic analysis of copyright and copyright transactions such as licensing. He makes mention of a number of factors often left out by economists, such as recycling and second-hand sales. Watt reaches a number of interesting, if not always surprising, conclusions. These include the following:

135

(i) unlicensed copying is not always adverse to society and can even be beneficial (in limited doses) to the producer of 'legitimate' product;

(ii) to protect its position, that producer may use strategies other than enforcement of copyright, including apt pricing of originals, delivering intellectual property on a good which is complementary to a product which cannot easily be copied,[2] or delivering copyright product in some way that makes copying more expensive;[3]

(iii) optimal modes of royalty payment are likely to include a significant 'up-front' payment;

(iv) the socially optimal degree of regulation by copyright law is less than the maximum possible. He acknowledges that it is difficult in real life, with so many variables, to determine the appropriate level;

(v) regarding collecting societies, social welfare is not likely to be enhanced by competition between rival societies. It is better to have one society with close regulation;

(vi) patent economics may be different, since product patents tend to protect capital goods.

1. R Watt *Copyright and Economic Theory*, 2000.
2. So-called 'bundling'.
3. Such as technological protection. Watt suggests that this is economically inefficient: it tends to raise the price of 'originals' and to lead to a 'technology race' with the copyist. Another option is to issue frequent updates.

Copyright as moral property

10.13 Neither real nor personal property depends for their continued existence upon any criteria of inherent or functional morality, nor is there any reason why they should. A plot of land cannot be inherently immoral and, even if morally outrageous acts take place upon it, it remains property, while a transparent négligée is governed by the same rules of transmissibility and devolution on the death of its owner as any other chattel, without regard to the fact that it may have been used for the most brazen acts of prostitution. Copyright, being *sui generis*, does not follow this rule because, as a matter of law, it does not operate to protect any work which is of an obscene or immoral nature.[1] The justification for this rule, which lies outside the Copyright Act itself, is that the courts should not lend their hand to the enforcement of any right in any work the substance of which is immoral, for to do so is to legitimise that immorality.[2] The practical consequence of such a rule, of course, is that the dissemination of immoral works is incapable of being restricted unless those works are so immoral as to fall within the narrow scope of 'obscene publications' under the criminal law.[3]

1. For a discussion of this topic see J Phillips, 'Copyright in Obscene Publications: some British and American Problems' (1978) 6 AALR 138.
2. See *Stockdale v Onwhyn* (1826) 5 B & C 173.
3. Obscene Publications Act 1959, s 1, discussed in G Robertson and A Nicol *Media Law* (1985) pp 69-75.

10.14   At one time this principle, which originally impeded the enforcement of copyright in defamatory,[1] blasphemous[2] and seditious[3] works, as well as the merely immoral, was applied to the extent of rendering unenforceable the copyright in Elinor Glyn's novel *Three Weeks*,[4] which (per Younger J) portrayed in an attractive light the institution of adultery. Glyn succeeded in shocking the Great War generation by peering through, but not actually lifting, the veil of physical intimacy behind which her characters exercised their corrosive influence upon the nation's readership. Measured by such exacting standards it is difficult to imagine that the works of John Fowles, Lawrence Durrell or Gunther Grass would be sure of legal protection. Fortunately for those authors, public standards of morality have eased. It is now many years since a work was last deprived of copyright protection on the grounds of immorality and in at least one case when such an intervention might have been expected, the moral standing of the work was alluded to in deprecatory terms neither by the court nor by the defence.[5] In the *Spycatcher* case,[6] the House of Lords was divided as to whether Peter Wright, the author of the book, was owner of unenforceable copyright or was not the owner of copyright at all. The 'moral rights' of authors, which refer not to the moral standard of their works but to mechanisms for sustaining the authors' reputation and honour, are discussed in Ch 18.

1. *Walcot v Walker* (1802) 7 Ves 1.
2. *Burnett v Chetwood* (1720) 2 Mer 441n.
3. *Hime v Dale* (1803) 2 Camp 27 n.
4. *Glyn v Weston Feature Film* [1916] 1 Ch 261, reviewed in J Phillips 'Elinor Glyn and the "Three Weeks" Litigation' [1982] EIPR 336.
5. *Ekland v Scripglow Ltd* [1982] FSR 431 ('Electric Blue' cinematograph film).
6. *A-G v Observer Ltd* [1990] 1 AC 109.

Chapter 11

Authors' works

The concept of the original work of authorship

11.1   The Copyright, Designs and Patents Act 1988 gives protection to a wide variety of works, which are listed in section 1(1). This approach, that of listing the types of work which may attract copyright, might be labelled the 'pigeon-hole' approach. In its favour, it has certainty and clarity, but it does have disadvantages.[1] First, a creative expression which does not fit into any of the 'pigeon-holes' will be denied copyright protection.[2] Conversely, a creation may fall into more than one category, in which case the Court has to decide whether to give it the protection afforded to both,[3] or one only.[4] This makes a difference because the modes of infringement differ from work to work. Third, new categories have had to be devised from time to time to cater for new forms of expression. Finally, since many works are digitally recorded, reproduced or used, the distinctions between the categories are becoming obsolete.[5]

1.   A Christie 'A Proposal for Simplifying United Kingdom Copyright Law' [2001] EIPR 26 cites structural complexity and other difficulties; see also S Ricketson 'Simplifying Copyright Law: Proposals from Down Under' [1999] EIPR 537.
2.   The probably artistic and certainly original positioning of a Rolls Royce in a swimming pool in *Creation Records v News Group* [1997] EMLR 444 is a case in point.
3.   As in *Norowzian v Arks Ltd (No 2)* [2000] FSR 363 – 'jump edited' sequence of images protected as both a film and as a dramatic work.
4.   *Electronic Techniques (Anglia) Ltd v Critchley Components Ltd* [1997] FSR 401.
5.   S Perlmutter 'Convergence and the Future of Copyright' [2001] EIPR 111 discusses this in the context of technological and structural changes in the copyright industries.

11.2   Returning to the 'pigeon-holes' of the 1988 Act, the first grouping – original literary, dramatic, musical and artistic works – lists the classic types of authors' works for which copyright protection has been available for a century or more. Such works provide the raw material which is refined and exploited commercially by the various media, publishing and information-distributing industries. This category of work includes the written word, the composer's sheet music, the playwright's sketches and dialogues and the artist's drawings. Such works were accorded special status under the 1988 Act's predecessor. Being treated in the first part of the Copyright Act 1956, they used to be described by commentators as 'Part I works'. Since they share the requirement that they be 'original' they are sometimes called 'original works'. The original work of authorship may be distinguished from the second species of work, the tangible or intangible vehicle for the dissemination of informational subject matter. This second species includes the compact disc upon which a song is recorded, the film of a successful play, the televised broadcast of an aircraft hijacking and the published edition of a set of poems. These tangible or intangible vehicles were described as 'Part II works' from their place in the Copyright Act 1956 and are sometimes referred to as 'derivative' works, because their value is not in their form or substance so much as in the information which can be derived from them. They may also include or be based upon a pre-existing literary, dramatic or other work. Thus a film may be based on a screen-play, a sound recording may include the words and music of a song and when a television broadcast is made, literary and dramatic works, films and sound recordings can be transmitted.

11.3 Sometimes the term 'neighbouring rights' is used to describe the protection of the second species of work. This use is made by analogy with a distinction recognised in many civil law jurisdictions, and in the Berne Convention of 1886,[1] between rights in works of authorship and rights in works which could not be described as directly emanating from the exercise of a creative human intellect but which bordered upon works of authorship. Strictly speaking, to include films within the term 'neighbouring rights' is inaccurate, because those continental systems which employ that term regard cinematograph films[2] as original works of authorship in their own right. (Since 1908, films have enjoyed the status of works under the Berne Convention.) To avoid confusion and anomaly, the adoption of a terminology to iron out these differences has been suggested.[3]

1. On the history, evolution and current condition of the Berne Convention see S Ricketson *The Berne Copyright Convention* (1986).
2. See A Dietz *Copyright Law in the European Community* (1978), pp 50-62. There is curious divergence in the way that different countries define films for the purpose of copyright: A Firth 'Film, Ciné and Audio-visual Works: Questions of definition' in Barendt and Firth (eds) *The Yearbook of Copyright and Media Law* Vol V (2000) p 221.

3. J A L Sterling, 'Harmonisation of Usage of the Terms "Copyright", "Author's Right" and "Neighbouring Rights" '[1989] 1 EIPR 14.

11.4   Copyrights in the different species of work are cumulative; that is, inclusion in a later work does not affect the existence of copyright in an earlier work. The record company making a sound recording, the producer of a film, or the corporation transmitting a broadcast will (usually) have obtained permission from the owner of copyright in any work recorded, filmed or broadcast. But a consequence of the concurrent nature of copyright in included and derivative works is that a person who copies her favourite operatic recording on to tape may find that she is infringing, at the press of a button, copyright in the opera's libretto and musical score, as well as copyright in the sound recording.

11.5   Authors' works and derivative works, copyright and neighbouring rights, are given equal status under the 1988 Act.[1] However the four types of authors' work have the same requirement of originality and are discussed in the rest of this chapter. The other types of work have less stringent and more specific criteria of originality, and are discussed in the next chapter.

1.   Copyright, Designs and Patents Act 1988, ss 1, 2 and 16.

What is an original work?

11.6   Copyright protects any literary, dramatic, musical and artistic phenomenon if it can be regarded as an 'original work'.[1] Anything which is 'original' but not a 'work', or vice versa, will fail to measure up to the criteria for protection. 'Author' is defined[2] as the person who creates a work, but neither 'original' nor 'work' are defined, so it is to case law that we must turn for elucidation.

1.   Copyright, Designs and Patents Act 1988, ss 1(3) and (5).
2.   Ibid, s 9(1). Authorship is discussed below in para **11.12ff**.

What is a 'work'?

11.7   The prerequisite of a 'work' is that it be the product of human endeavour, be that endeavour ever so slight, and not simply something which occurs in nature. A sculpture would thus be a 'work', but not a sandstone monolith so eroded by the elements as to take on apparently human features. A cloud pattern is not a work but a photograph of the cloud pattern would be a work, as would weather predictions generated by computer from the photograph. The human element of a work may take one or more of a number of forms: it may be found in the skill, judgement and effort involved in the act of creation,[1] in the time required for its production,[2] in the length of the resulting product,[3] in the cost required for its construction,[4] or even in the construction of a computer program which selects, apparently at random, the features of its printout.[5]

1. *University of London Press v University Tutorial Press* [1916] 2 Ch 601 at 608-9.
2. Ibid at 609.
3. *Sinanide v La Maison Kosmeo* (1928) 44 TLR 574 at 575.
4. *Macmillan & Co Ltd v Cooper* (1923) 93 LJPC 113 at 117; investment is the criterion for subsistence of database right, see para **11.17**.
5. *Express Newspapers plc v Liverpool Daily Post and Echo plc* [1985] FSR 306, noted in (1985) JBL 491.

11.8 To the objective bystander it may seem that, in non-technical language, work can be directed into one of three channels. It can be regarded as an intellectual input from which the end product results (eg as mental thought which shapes the conception of a painting), as a physical act combined with intellectual input and which directly shapes its final form (eg as the manual guidance of the paint-brush across the artist's canvas) or as a purely physical act devoid of intellectual input (eg as in the operation of an X-ray machine). Since copyright is a right which protects a creator's intellectual product, and which is part of a body of law known as 'intellectual property', it should be plainly obvious that the law treats 'work' in the first, as well as the second, of its meanings, but not the third. In fact, nothing is further from the truth. You can have enough lofty ideas to fill a think-tank and yet find that you have not produced an original 'work' until you have given those ideas an appropriate form. Literary works[1] may be written, spoken or sung to a tune, but copyright cannot subsist until the literary work is recorded, in writing or otherwise.[2] A dramatic work may be of dance or mime, but must be recorded for copyright to subsist. So there must be a physical expression to constitute a 'work', and fixation in some reproducible form before that work can be copyright. Often physical expression and fixation will be simultaneous, as where a novel is written longhand or created and stored in a word processor. In other cases there may be a time lag. For example, a composer may work out a new piece of music on the piano; the work has been created in perceptible form and may have been heard by a number of people but needs to be recorded on to tape or in musical notation before it can attract copyright. Artistic works cannot exist except in some visually perceptible form, and so have caused few problems apart from three-dimensional holograms projected into space, which were not contemplated by the legislature in 1956. The 1988 Act defines 'photograph' in very broad terms[3] so as to ensure that holograms are included. Holograms which cause a moving image to be seen are however protected as 'films' under section 5(l).

1. Copyright, Designs and Patents Act 1988, s 3(1).
2. Ibid, s 3(2). For the wide definition of 'writing', see s 178. See, further. D J Brennan and A F Christie 'Spoken Words and Copyright Subsistence in Anglo-American Law' [2000] IPQ, 309.
3. See Copyright, Designs and Patents Act 1988, s 4(2).

What is 'original'?

11.9   A literary, dramatic, musical or artistic work is only protectable by copyright if it is 'original'. This requirement is, fortunately for the author, much easier to satisfy than the apparently synonymous requirement of novelty in patent law. It is clear that novelty has no place in copyright law; if this were not so, then an enormous quantity of copyright-protected work would be thrown into the public domain. Originality in the copyright sense simply means that there is a direct causative link between the author's mental conception and the work which emanates from his hand.[1] Thus, where twenty artists all make a sketch of the Changing of the Guard, what gives them each an entitlement to copyright, even if their works are identical, is the fact that each has executed his work by reference to his own judgement and not by copying another; and the completion of the first artist's sketch does not form part of a 'prior art' against which the nineteen subsequent sketches are measured and found wanting through anticipation. A laboriously traced drawing by which no visually significant new matter is introduced will not, however, qualify as 'original'.[2] Many works exist in various draft forms before they are completed. The existence of drafts does not rob the final product of originality,[3] even though the drafts of partially completed works may enjoy copyright by virtue of their authors' skill, labour and judgement.[4]

1. *University of London Press Ltd v University Tutorial Press Ltd* [1916] 2 Ch 601 at 608.
2. *Interlego AG v Tyco Industries Inc* [1989] AC 217.
3. *LA Gear Inc v Hi-Tec Sports plc* [1992] FSR 121.
4. *Art Direction v USP Needham* [1977] 2 NZLR 12; *Ray v Classic FM* [1998] FSR 622.

11.10   How far the notion of originality extends is open to doubt. In *Walter v Lane*[1] it was accepted by the House of Lords that a newspaper reporter's record of a speech by the Earl of Roseberry could be an original literary work by that reporter, although the authority of this decision is reduced by the fact that it involved the application of a very much older copyright law, which contained no explicit requirement that a work be original. In enacting the Copyright, Designs and Patents Act 1988, Parliament seems to have taken the view that *Walter v Lane* is still good law;[2] its effect is preserved in sub-section 3(3). A shadow of doubt was cast over the rationale of this case in *Roberton v Lewis*,[3] where the claimant could not satisfy the court that his arrangement of a long-established folk-tune was an original work rather than a work which was 'copied' from the public domain.[4] In *Antiquesportfolio.com plc v Rodney Fitch & Co Ltd*[5] it was held that a photograph of an antique piece of furniture was original and hence protected by copyright. It is perhaps not surprising that photography, a genre which almost inevitably records pre-existing images, provides a test-bed for notions of originality.[6] Of one thing we can be sure – a work which actually incorporates large tracts of another's work – even without a vestige of consent – can still be regarded as original to its author.[7] The consequence of this is that if a skilful author goes through a John Fowles novel, rewrites passages of prose and dialogue which he considers aesthetically ill-conceived, and then publishes his work as an improved edition, he will undoubtedly be successfully sued for copyright infringement by John Fowles; and if that august writer were so impressed by the rewriting that he wished to publish the revised version as having been written by himself, he could not do so without infringing copyright in a book, the vast bulk of which was, in truth, 'original' to him since it had been written by himself.[8]

1. [1900] AC 539.
2. Reporter's copyright was present in *Express Newspapers v News (UK)* [1991]FSR 36.
3. [1976] RPC 169.
4. In *Christoffer v Poseidon Film Distribution Ltd* [2000] ECDR 487, it was argued unsuccessfully that the claimant's reworking of a Greek myth was not original. For the difficulties raised by copyright protection of a decipherment of Dead Sea Scrolls, see M D Birnhack 'The Dead Sea Scrolls Case: Who is an Author?' [2001] EIPR 128.
5. [2001] FSR 345.
6. For discussions of originality and authorship in relation to photographs, see R Deazley 'Photographing Paintings in the Public Domain: A Response to Garnett' [2001] EIPR 179, K Garnett 'Copyright in Photographs' [2000] EIPR 229; K Garnett and A Abbott, 'Who is the "Author" of a Photograph?' [1998] EIPR 204; K Lupton 'Photographs and the Concept of Originality in Copyright Law' [1988] 9 EIPR 257; Byrne 'Photography and the Law of Copyright' (1989) 20 IIC 37. Art 6 of Council Directive 93/98/EEC (29 October 1993, OJ L290/9) harmonised the requirement of originality for copyright protection of photographs at 'the author's own intellectual creation' and prohibited the imposition by EU Member States of other, higher, criteria for eligibility. Member States, may however, protect photographs which fall short of this standard.

7. *Warwick Film Productions Ltd v Eisinger* [1969] 1 Ch 508.
8. See *Redwood Music Ltd v Chappell & Co Ltd* [1982] RPC 109.

11.11   In relation to computer programs,[1] UK law has applied the same standard of originality as to any author's work. This approach was not taken, however, in many other jurisdictions where programs were protected by copyright.[2] The originality requirement for computer software is now ostensibly[3] harmonised across the European Union by directive 91/250/EEC on the legal protection of computer programs.[4] Art 1(3) of the Directive states that originality is required in the sense of 'the author's own intellectual creation'. In implementing the directive, the view was taken that the UK standard already complied with this criterion. However, in implementing the more recent Database directive, the UK legislature has adopted the EC wording.[5] For further discussion of copyright in computer software see para **23.5**.

1. Literary works by virtue of the Copyright, Designs and Patents Act 1988, s 3(1)(b). For the concept of 'Copyleft', an alternative to copyright proposed in the context of computer software, see P Lambert 'Copyright, Copyleft and Software IPRs: is Contract Still King?' [2001] EIPR 165.
2. See, for example, Dreier 'Copyright Protection for Computer Programs in Foreign Countries' (1989) 20 IIC 803 at 809-815.
3. Debate continued as to the level at which originality has been set: Fuerkoda 'Dutch Implementation of the EEC Directive on Computer Programs' [1992] 8 EIPR 289.
4. 14 May 1991, OJ 1991 L122/42.
5. Copyright, Designs and Patents Act 1988, s 3A(2), inserted by the Copyright and Rights in Databases Regulations 1997 (SI 1997/3032).

Who is the author of a work?

11.12   'Author' is defined as the person who creates a work. It is generally agreed that the creator is the person who actually writes or draws the original work, but this principle is subject to important – if infrequently litigated – exceptions. In the first place it is tempered by the notion of the amanuensis; that is, the person who writes or draws, not on his own initiative but as if his hand belonged to another. This notion antecedes copyright, for it is generally well known that Bede was too ill to write his famous vernacular translation of St John's Gospel and dictated it instead to a faithful copyist.[1] The businessman who dictates letters to a shorthand typist so that they may be typed up is to be regarded as the author, even though the typist's skill at shorthand caused the letters to take the physical form necessary for copyright to subsist. It is unlikely that the shorthand typist's skill and labours cause any further copyright to come into being by faithfully transcribing the spoken word. The shorthand typist, for the purposes of copyright (but not defamation[2]), is regarded therefore as being no more than a mindless pair of hands. Similarly with artistic works, a person who cannot draw or make designs may find that he is credited with authorship of the work if he has so motivated another as to have deprived the latter of any substantial artistic judgement in that execution of the work.[3] In the case of photographs too, the selection and arrangement of subject-matter may contribute considerably to the creative effort even where the person who performs that selection and arrangement is not the actual photographer.[4]

1. See the account of Bede's life which prefaces his *Historia Ecclesiastica* (1896).
2. On the status of secretarial functionaries see *Riddick v Thames Board Mills Ltd* [1977] QB 881.
3. See *Kenrick & Co v Lawrence & Co* (1890) 25 QBD 99; *Stannard v Harrison* (1871) 19 WR 811.
4. See para **11.10**, n 6, above.

11.13 A copyright work may be created by a computer in circumstances where it is neither realistic nor feasible to identify one or more specific individuals as the author in the sense of that word described in the previous paragraph. This reality is recognised by the law, which describes them as 'computer-generated' works.[1] In such a case the 'author' is regarded as the person who undertakes the arrangements necessary for creation of the work.[2] It is not wholly certain who this person will be,[3] but it is clear that a human being who controls the generation of a work may be regarded as its author.[4] Since a computer can be regarded either as the progenitor of a work or as a mere tool in the hands of a real human author, a distinction has been drawn between 'computer-generated' and 'computer-aided' works.

1. Copyright, Designs and Patents Act 1988, s 178.
2. Ibid, s 9(3).
3. It appears most likely to be the person who makes the economic arrangements: *A&M Records v Video Collection* [1995] EMLR 25.
4. *Express Newspapers plc v Liverpool Daily Post and Echo plc* [1985] FSR 306.

11.14 Other miscellaneous points to note on the subject of authorship are as follows:

(a) A 'ghosted' work, one which purports to have been written by a celebrity but which has actually been penned by a biographer or reporter on the basis of knowledge gleaned from interviews, is authored by the 'ghost' writer, not the celebrity.[1]
(b) The fact that the text or form of a work has been allegedly dictated by the spirit of a dead person will not affect its authorship;[2] thus the piano pieces penned by Rosemary Brown at the behest of

Beethoven, Schubert and others were her own works of authorship
for copyright purposes.

(c)   Two or more persons can jointly be regarded as authors of the
same work, so long as their separate intellectual efforts cannot
be distinguished.[3]

(d)   The 'person' who creates a work is frequently a human individual.
In the case of computer-generated works, sound recordings, films,
broadcasts and cable transmission, that person may also be a
company. An amusing scenario, in which it was argued that a
corporation could be the author of a literary work, was penned
by A P Herbert in one of his *Misleading Cases*.[4]

(e)   In theory, the Copyright Act mainly protects works first published
in the UK or created by an author who was a 'qualified person' (ie
British or Irish) at the time the work was created or at other specified
times.[5] The works of authors of most other countries are, however,
protected as well. This is because the UK grants reciprocal protection
to the authors of those countries which share its membership of the
Berne Copyright Union,[6] or the Universal Copyright Convention,[7]
and which therefore protect the works of British authors in return.

(f)   A work which is created by an animal – for example, the literary
product of monkeys chained to typewriters, or the pictures painted
by ducks walking across a canvas[8] – cannot, it is submitted, be
regarded as a work of copyright unless there is a specifically human
contribution to the execution of the work.

1.   *Donoghue v Allied Newspapers Ltd* [1938] Ch 106; cf *Chaplin v Leslie Frewin
(Publishers) Ltd* [1966] Ch 71; *Heptulla v Orient Longman Ltd* [1989] FSR
598.
2.   *Cummins Ltd v Bond* [1927] 1 Ch 167.
3.   Copyright, Designs and Patents Act 1988, s 10(1). See also s 10(2) on
broadcasts.
4.   *Mackintosh v Haddock: Uncommon Law* (1969) p 326.
5.   Copyright, Designs and Patents Act 1988, s 1(3) and 154.
6.   Ibid, s 159.
7.   Ibid.
8.   The Daily Telegraph, 1 October 1983, relates the saga of a painting purchased
by Mrs Gladhill from an artist, Brian Burgess. The painting had in fact been
executed by a stray duck belonging to one Ernest Cleverley. The matter was
reported to the Merseyside Trading Standards Office, which considered that
Mrs Gladhill was not entitled to the return of her purchase price since there
was no warranty that the picture had been painted by Burgess.

Literary works

11.15   The first type of work protected by the law of copyright was
the literary work, since the Statute of Anne in 1709 was passed in
response to a demand from printers that their profitable book

monopolies be preserved. In the eighteenth century it was not thought necessary to seek to define the scope of what the law protected, since books were so much at the heart of the copyright-based industries, but by the latter part of the twentieth century it has become apparent, first, that books represent only one of many elements in British intellectual property transactions, and second that works of a very diverse nature are now treated to the protection enjoyed by the 'literary work'. It takes only a brief survey of recent reported copyright infringement actions involving literary works to see how few of them deal with the making of copies of books.

11.16 Having defined a literary work as one which is written, spoken or sung,[1] the Copyright, Designs and Patents Act goes on to say that this accordingly includes 'a table or compilation'.[2] This formula, which has been held to include such prosaic items as lists of pronounceable five letter words[3] (but not individual five letter words[4]), logarithmic tables,[5] football pools coupons[6] and television programmes,[7] makes it crystal clear that when Parliament chose the word 'literary', it was not searching for a laudatory epithet as in the phrase 'literary masterpiece'. The following textual works give examples of which oeuvres enjoy the status of literary works: examination questions,[8] instructions for the use of herbicide,[9] lists of names of horses[10] and letters to newspapers.[11] To this list is added computer programs[12] which were generally accorded copyright protection as literary works even before explicit statutory provision was made.[13]

1. Copyright, Designs and Patents Act 1988, s 3(1).
2. Ibid, s 3(1)(a). This has afforded protection to databases in the UK, as in *Waterlow Directories Ltd v Reed* [1992] FSR 409.
3. *D P Anderson & Co Ltd v Lieber Code Co* [1917] 2 KB 469; *Ager v Peninsula and Oriental Steam Navigation Co* (1884) 26 Ch D 637.
4. *Exxon Corpn v Exxon Insurance Consultants International Ltd* [1982] Ch 119.
5. *Baily v Taylor* (1829) 1 Russ & M 73.
6. *Ladbroke v William Hill* [1964] 1 WLR 273.
7. *Independent Television Publications Ltd v Time Out Ltd* [1984] FSR 64.
8. *University of London Press v University Tutorial Press* [1916] 2 Ch 601.
9. *Elanco Products Ltd v Mandops (Agrochemical Specialists) Ltd* [1979] FSR 46.
10. *Weatherby & Sons v International Horse Agency and Exchange Ltd* [1910] 2 Ch 297.
11. *Springfield v Thame* (1903) 89 LT 242.
12. And preparatory design material for computer programs: Copyright, Designs and Patents Act 1988, s 3(1)(b) and (c) (as amended by the Copyright (Computer Programs) Regulations 1992: SI 1992/3233). On computer programs generally see para **23.5**.
13. Eg *Sega Enterprises Ltd v Richards (No 2)* [1983] FSR 73, which predated the Copyright (Computer Software) Amendment Act 1985. Some doubt appears to have been entertained by the Court of Appeal in *Milltronics Ltd v Hycontrol Ltd* [1990] FSR 273.

11.17 A close relative of the table or compilation is the database.[1] This is 'a collection of independent works, data or other materials which (a) are arranged in a systematic or methodical way, and (b) are individually accessible by electronic or other means'. Many tables and compilations will fall within this definition. Some, however, will fail to meet the criterion of 'independent' or possibly that of 'systematic or methodical' and will continue to be governed by the old law. If the selection and arrangement of the data elements in a database, as defined, shows originality in the sense of an author's own intellectual creation, it attracts copyright. Regardless of this, if substantial investment is made in the creation or revision of the database, its contents will be protected against unauthorised extraction or re-utilisation of data.[2]

1. Copyright, Designs and Patents Act, s 3A, see para **23.20**.
2. Copyright and Rights in Databases Regulations 1997 (SI 1997/3032), reg 16.

11.18 How short may a literary work be and yet retain the protection of law? In one old case[1] the slogan 'a social necessity not a luxury' was regarded as not being a literary work, but the reason why it was not is regrettably unclear. The court undoubtedly regarded the phrase as having an insufficiently substantial identity to constitute a literary work, which is why it was mis-described as lacking 'originality'. If it had rhyme and metre (eg 'A Mars a day helps you work, rest and play'), it might well have been considered to be a literary work, by analogy with Ogden Nash's well-known poem:

'Candy is dandy
But liquor is quicker'[2]

and the even briefer poem on microbes,

'Adam
Had'em'.[3]

So far, no English court has yet accepted that copyright might subsist in a single word. In *Exxon Corpn v Exxon Insurance Consultants International Ltd*[4] the argument that 'Exxon' might be protected by copyright was rejected on two grounds. The first was that nothing could be a literary work unless it conveyed information, provided instruction or gave pleasure; 'Exxon' failed to satisfy any of these criteria and could not therefore be a literary work.[5] The second was that 'Exxon' was a name and, since other statutory means exist for the protection of names, the Copyright Act 1956 could not (as a matter of probability rather than as a matter of law) be taken to have been intended to provide protection for 'denominative' works.[6] These two grounds are contradictory; anything which is a name is, almost by definition, information, as anyone who has ever tried to locate a novel from a public library without recourse to the author's identity will readily concede. But if the first argument is wrong, so is the second, since no principle of depriving 'denominative' works of their copyright status operates in respect of symbols which are allowed the protection of artistic copyright even though they are registered as trade marks.[7] The only conclusion to be drawn from this is that it is easier to recognise intuitively a literary (or non-literary) work than it is to define one.

1. *Sinanide v La Maison Kosmeo* (1928) 44 TLR 574. Two factual sentences were held not to constitute a work in *Noah v Shuba* [1991] FSR 14, unlike the paragraph to which they were wrongly appended.
2. Ogden Nash *On Ice-Breaking* (1931).
3. Anonymous *Oxford Dictionary of Quotations* (2nd edn).
4. [1982] Ch 119.
5. Ibid at 143 (per Stephenson LJ).
6. Ibid at pp 130 to 131 (Graham J), cf pp 143-144.
7. See eg *Sobrefina SA's Application* [1974] RPC 672, in which a registered design was not regarded as being barred from trade mark protection.

Dramatic works

11.19 The Copyright, Designs and Patents Act 1988 does not indicate what constitutes a dramatic work beyond laying down that such work includes works of dance and mime.[1] A theatrical play, which is obviously a dramatic work in the colloquial sense of the word, contains a great deal of literary matter. Literary work is defined, however, so as to exclude dramatic (or musical) works.[2] A play's dialogue does not, therefore, enjoy protection as a dramatic work, as opposed to a literary work.

1. S 3(1).
2. Ibid.

11.20 Sequences of manoeuvres performed by aerobatic pilots are often devised on the ground with the aid of a specific notation, the Aresti notation. It is interesting to speculate whether these should be regarded as dramatic works. Other types of activity of which records are made, and which may be copied by reference to those records, are gymnastic, ice-skating and synchronised swimming routines. While the governing bodies of these sports (or quasi-sports) insist that these routines have nothing to do with copyright, a plain reading of the Copyright, Designs and Patents Act 1988 would suggest that they are clearly dramatic works.[1] Arnold[2] questions whether a less pre-meditated sporting event such as a football match might be regarded as a dramatic work. Although he considers this unlikely, he argues that an edited film of a match could attract copyright as a dramatic work, applying *Norowzian v Arks Ltd.*[3]

1. See Vicki Pasek 'Performers' Rights in Sport: Where does Copyright Stand?' (1990) 8 Copyright World 13.
2. R Arnold 'Copyright in Sporting Events and Broadcasts or Films of Sporting Events after *Norowzian*' in E Barendt and A Firth (eds) *Yearbook of Copyright and Media Law 2001.*
3. [2000] FSR 363.

11.21 An early application of the principle that a dramatic work is not protectable unless it is recorded in appropriate form can be seen in *Tate v Fullbrook.*[1] The claimant in that case wrote a dramatic sketch in which the dialogue of the actors was clearly recorded but the stage directions were not. In the sketch as performed, a knock-kneed street urchin was required to place a firecracker beneath the foot of another actor; this 'gag', but not the dialogue, was reproduced in the defendant's sketch. The court held that the performance of this dramatic incident could not constitute any infringement of copyright since there was no written record of it which could have been read and repeated by others. Now, recording of dramatic incident in any form – for example a video recording – will suffice to bring a 'gag' or stage routine within the ambit of copyright protection.[2] This will also be the case if the character of the drama is achieved by editing of the recording.[3]

1. [1908] 1 KB 821.
2. S 3(2); cf *Green v Broadcasting Corpn of New Zealand* [1989] RPC 700, where a television show format was held not to be protected by copyright. The claimant's arguments in Green appear to have concentrated on the format as a literary work. See S Lane and R Bridge 'The Protection of Formats under English Law' [1990] Ent LR 96 and 131.
3. *Norowzian v Arks Ltd (No 2)* [2000] FSR 363. This finding, that the content of a film is protected also as a dramatic work, has had a mixed reception. T Rivers 'Norowzian Revisited' [2000] EIPR 389 points out that the decision gives no guidance as to which of many possible characters involved in the making of a film, should be regarded as author of the dramatic work. In *Norowzian* itself the claimant was the only person involved. Cf M James 'Some Joy at Last for Cinematographers' [2000] EIPR 131.

Musical works

11.22 The Copyright, Designs and Patents Act offers no indication at all as to what constitutes a 'musical work', wisely leaving to the good sense of the would-be claimant the decision as to whether his work is musical or not. The *Concise Oxford Dictionary*, much favoured by the British judiciary, asserts that music is the 'art of combining sounds with a view to beauty of form and expression of emotion; sounds so produced; pleasant sound…',[1] but the Controller of BBC Radio Three and the organisers of the Sir Henry Wood Promenade Concerts would find such a definition intolerably narrow. For some, at any rate, music is a branch of physics or a form of psycho-therapy rather than an aesthetic art form. Little can usefully be added to the speculations of musicologists,[2] but it may be profitable to note that no claim by a claimant that his work is musical has ever been rejected by a British court,[3] although not every claimant is accorded the status of author.[4]

1. The multi-volumed full *Oxford English Dictionary* conveys further the information that 'music' is a form of noctuid moth, while 'musical' is a term for a horse which suffers from defective respiration.
2. Note that neither the twenty-volumed *New Grove Dictionary of Music and Musicians*, (ed) S Sadie (1980), nor E Blom's Everyman's *Dictionary of Music* (1946), include an entry under 'music'; cf *Encyclopaedia Britannica* 15th edn, vol 12, pp 662-667, which provides an intellectually complex account of some of the more important definitions. For an example of the evidence of musicologists, see *Williamson Music v Pearson Partnership* [1987] FSR 97.
3. For further citations as to the nature of musical works, see A Firth 'Authorship, Ownership and Infringement in Music Copyright' [1992] Ent LR 211.
4. Eg *Hadley v Kemp* [1999] EMLR 589; R Arnold 'Are Performers Authors?' [1999] EIPR 464.

11.23 The following further points may also be noted:

(i) There is no formal *de minimis* principle which operates in the field of musical works. While it is improbable that a single note, however carefully selected, arranged and orchestrated by its author, will ever be considered a musical work, there is some small evidence that a distinctive motif consisting of only four chords will be so regarded.[1]

(ii) The question whether a musical motif or sound logo, by possessing the attributes of an audio-identificatory device, is 'denominative' and therefore potentially excluded from copyright protection by analogy with arguments raised in the *Exxon* case,[2] has yet to be judicially considered. Distinctive sound motifs are registrable as trade marks[3] in the United Kingdom.

(iii) Any form of recording, whether on tape or in musical notation, will suffice to fix a musical work for copyright purposes.[4]

(iv) A song consists of two separate works: the tune is a musical work while the lyrics are a literary work.[5] However, certain statutory defences to an infringement action treat the words of a song like the accompanying music, rather than as literary works in general.[6]

1. *Lawton v Dundas* (1985) Times, 13 June noted in (1985) 13 Commercial Law Bulletin, para 16.
2. *Exxon Corpn v Exxon Insurance Consultants International Ltd* [1982] Ch 119. See para **11.18**.
3. Trade Marks Act 1994, s 1 requires that a registrable mark be distinctive and capable of graphical representation.
4. Copyright, Designs and Patents Act 1988, s 3(2).
5. On the independence of word and music see *Rubens v Pathé Frères Pathephone Ltd* (1912) 29 TLR 174. The status of lyrics as separate literary works is confirmed by s 3(1) of the Copyright, Designs and Patents Act 1988.
6. Copyright, Designs and Patents Act 1988, s 31(3).

Artistic works

11.24 The Copyright, Designs and Patents Act 1988, section 4(1), divides 'artistic works'[1] into three entirely self-contained categories which are best taken in turn. The categories are: (i) graphic works, photographs, sculptures and collages; (ii) works of architecture (buildings and models for buildings), and (iii) works of artistic craftsmanship.

1. See, generally, S Stokes 'Categorising Art in Copyright Law' [2001] Ent LR 179.

Graphic works, photographs, sculptures and collages

11.25 These works are protected by copyright whether or not they possess any artistic quality,[1] which indicates that, in this context if no other, the word 'artistic' is not a laudatory epithet but instead imports a reference to the creative input of the author or artist. 'Graphic work' is defined as including (a) any painting, drawing, diagram, map, chart or plan, and (b) any engraving, etching, lithograph, woodcut or similar work.[2] Since graphic works can carry a substantial volume of literary data in the form of place-names on maps or textual explanations of diagrams, charts and plans, it is clear that the same works can be both 'literary' and 'artistic'.[3] The concurrence of literary and artistic work is fraught with potential legal difficulties because both the modes of infringement and the statutory defences to infringement are different. The practical consequences of this are considered below.[4] 'Photograph' is defined[5] very generally as a recording of light or other radiation on any medium whereby an image is, or from which an image may be, produced. Thus X-rays and holograms fall within the definition. 'Photograph' does not include a part of a film but a still or single frame is regarded as part of a film: see para **12.8** below. 'Sculpture' expressly includes any cast or model created for the purpose of making the end product.[6]

1. Copyright, Designs and Patents Act 1988, s 4(1)(a).
2. Ibid, s 4(2).
3. Affirmed in *Macmillan Publishers Ltd v Thomas Reed* [1993] FSR 455; see also *Anacon v Environmental Research* [1994] FSR 359.
4. Paras **13.16-13.18**.
5. Copyright, Designs and Patents Act 1988, s 4(2).
6. Ibid, but not if the end product is other than a sculpture: *J &S Davies Holdings Ltd v Wright Health Group Ltd* [1988] RPC 403.

11.26 Is there a *de minimis* principle with regard to drawings, paintings and the like? Works by artists such as Mondrian and Picasso have been generally hailed as works of genius despite the fact that they may seem, to the objective observer, to be comprised of no more than a small number of straight and curved lines respectively.[1] The decision in *Kenrick & Co v Lawrence & Co*[2] came close to laying down a *de minimis* principle when Wills J declined to recognise copyright in a simple drawing of a hand holding a pencil over a ballot sheet, but that case was decided in relation to an earlier piece of legislation known as the Fine Arts Copyright Act 1862, which – as its title suggests – was intended to protect works of a more refined and (in its laudatory sense) artistic nature than the 1988 Act with its commitment to protect drawings irrespective of their artistic quality. Wills J also rejected the claimant's claim on the grounds that any copyright in a simple or commonplace work could be infringed only by an 'exact literal reproduction'. To this extent, *Kenrick v Lawrence* still represents the law. In *British Northrop v Texteam*,[3] copyright protection was recognised for drawings of simple engineering components. In *Solar Thomson v Barton*[4] it was conceded that copyright existed in simple design drawings for a pulley wheel. Such cases, however, were complicated by the fact that the drawings almost invariably carried quite a lot of information in literary form – dimensions, tolerances and so forth. While such literary matter would not suffice to 'beef up' the drawings' claim to artistic copyright,[5] it could be relevant to whether copyists come sufficiently close to infringe.[6] In the last three cases mentioned, artistic copyright in production drawings was being used to achieve a monopoly for the design of functional articles shown in the drawings. This development in copyright law was criticised in *British Leyland Motor Corpn Ltd v Armstrong Patents*[7] and has been reformed by the Copyright, Designs and Patents Act 1988.[8]

1. See eg P Picasso *Head*, 1928 (New York); P Mondrian *Composition with red, black, blue yellow and grey*, 1920 (Amsterdam, Municipal Museum).
2. (1890) 25 QBD 99.
3. [1974] RPC 57.
4. [1977] RPC 537.
5. In *Entec v Abacus* [1992] FSR 332, the drawings in question were said to be an aid to the understanding of dimensions.

6. *Interlego AG v Tyco Industries Inc* [1989] AC 217. In *Anacon v Environmental Research* [1994] FSR 659, Jacob J held that literary copyright in a 'net list' of components for an electronic circuit diagram was infringed by the defendant's list.
7. [1986] FSR 221.
8. See paras **14.21** and **24.3**, below.

Buildings and models for buildings[1]

11.27   While the 'irrespective of artistic quality' tag is not explicitly extended to cover buildings and models for them, it must be assumed that those words be read in. Most buildings are protected by copyright because they are three dimensional reproductions of two dimensional architects' plans which are of course protected as drawings; and if the plans enjoy copyright irrespective of their artistic quality, it follows that even the much-despised public sector tower blocks of the 1960s are secure from the unlikely threat of an infringement. It is difficult to imagine that Parliament intended to set a higher aesthetic standard for the vesting of copyright in buildings not erected from architects' plans than for the protection of buildings which were so constructed. Although Parliament has responded to the *British Leyland* decision by subverting[2] the mechanism whereby copyright in drawings for *articles* was used to protect the shape of the articles, a building is unlikely to fall within the meaning of 'article'. One further point is that the phrase which follows buildings is 'models for buildings', not 'models of buildings'. It is clear from this phrase that Parliament intended to bring within the ambit of copyright such three dimensional models as were referable to buildings not yet made, rather than to miniature copies of buildings already in existence. 'Building' is further defined in section 4(2) as including any fixed structure, and part of a building or fixed structure. Thus bridges, piers, oil rigs and (*per* Alison Firth, Jeremy Phillips *dubitante*) probably landscaped gardens, but not ships or floating pontoons, are works of architecture. Just how small a 'part' can be, while still qualifying as a work of architecture, is debatable. For example, a built-in bedroom wardrobe or a modern 'designer' kitchen with fitted units could be described as 'part of a fixed structure'– but it is unlikely that Parliament was intending to protect them as artistic works. In *Mark Wilkinson Furniture Ltd v Woodcraft Designs (Radcliffe) Ltd* the claimants relied successfully upon design right in fitted units.[3]

1. Copyright, Designs and Patents Act 1988, s 4(1)(b).
2. Ibid, s 51.
3. [1998] FSR 63; for design right, see Ch 24.

Works of artistic craftsmanship

11.28   This category of work[1] has been a great disappointment to its authors and copyright owners. Typical works of artistic craftsmanship might include Fabergé eggs, the fancy icing on a cake, the lace-work on a wedding dress, a Chippendale chair and the handtooled patterned leather binding of a precious book. Items excluded from this category are factory mock-ups of industrially manufactured furniture,[2] weatherproof rain capes for babies and peasant-inspired garments for grown-ups,[3] sets of coloured plastic rods for educational use[4] and almost certainly all mass-produced items, especially if they are made of plastic or nylon and can be purchased without financial embarrassment by anyone who earns less than a judge.

1. Copyright, Designs and Patents Act 1988, s 4(1)(c). For a comparative survey of this type of work in its economic context, see M Rushton 'An Economic Approach to Copyright in Works of Artistic Craftsmanship' [2001] IPQ 255.
2. *Hensher v Restawile Upholstery* [1976] AC 64.
3. *Merlet v Mothercare plc* [1984] FSR 358; *Guild v Eskander Ltd* [2001] FSR 645.
4. *Cuisenaire v Reed* [1963] VR 719.

11.29   How does one define a 'work of artistic craftsmanship'? The Copyright, Designs and Patents Act 1988 gives no direct clue as to the meaning of the phrase but hints at its intention where, in protecting such works, the words 'irrespective of artistic quality', which apply to paintings, sculptures and drawings, are omitted. By the canon of statutory interpretation known to Latin speakers as *inclusio unius, exclusio alterius*,[1] it may reasonably be inferred that nothing could be a work of artistic craftsmanship unless it satisfied some unspoken criterion of artistic quality; and this is indeed the conclusion which the great majority of judges have, rightly or wrongly, accepted.

1. For a discussion of this interpretational device see *Maxwell on Statutory Interpretation* (12th edn 1969), p 193.

11.30   The problems of defining a work of artistic craftsmanship by reference to an unstated element of artistic quality are nowhere better illustrated than in *Hensher v Restawile*,[1] a case which spawned a plethora of conflicting approaches even where it was widely felt that the subject at the heart of the litigation – a model of a particularly vulgar suite of furniture – was not, and could never be, a work of artistic craftsmanship. The views of the judiciary on this topic are as follows:

(i)   Graham J, at first instance,[2] felt that it was not possible for him to devise a definition of 'artistic', nor was it appropriate to do so where Parliament had left the matter undefined. To him, that which made any work 'artistic' was the presence of those elements in it which distinguished it from other works. The furniture before him was nothing if not distinctive, and therefore 'artistic'. To say that it was a work of craftsmanship was, however, more difficult, since the claimant's prototype was really just roughly cobbled together out of odd materials lying around in the workshop.

(ii) Russell LJ, who delivered the judgment of the Court of Appeal,[3] was struck by the fact that the finished product, once derived from the prototype, was bought for its functionality, not for the inherent aesthetic attraction or value of its appearance. In order for a work to be of artistic craftsmanship, he suggested, it should be purchased for its aesthetic and not its functional qualities. In other words, one can gauge whether a work is of artistic craftsmanship by examination, not of the work itself but of the motives of its purchasers.

(iii) Lord Reid, the first of five judges to speak in the House of Lords, took the view that one can ascertain whether a work is of artistic craftsmanship by conducting, in effect, an opinion poll. If most people regard an item as a work of artistic craftsmanship, then the law should treat it as such.[4] This approach is logically preferable to that of Russell LJ, since it takes into account the impressions not only of those who purchased the product (who may be a small minority whose purchase results from a shared delusion that the work is aesthetically attractive), but of the great and wise majority who fail to make such purchase. Unfortunately this approach begs the question, if one asks any number of people whether a work is of artistic craftsmanship, one does not know whether their 'yes' or 'no' responses are a consequence of the application of the same standard. The only way one can avoid this is by first instructing the common herd as to what, in law, such a work is, and it seems a little circular to say to a person 'A work of artistic craftsmanship is a work which most people would consider to be a work of artistic craftsmanship. Do you consider that this work before you would be so considered?'

(iv) Lord Morris rejected the populist extreme proposed by Lord Reid. Since most men in the street are unable to distinguish their Ars from their El Greco, it would be more sensible, he suggested, to take a consensus only of those who are expert in the area of works of artistic craftsmen.[5] The objection to this suggestion is that, if Lord Reid's test begged the question, Lord Morris's proposal double-begs it. Until one knows what a work of artistic craftsmanship is, one cannot say who is, or is not, an expert in such works.

(v) Lord Dilhorne's approach was not so much to cut the Gordian knot as to bypass Gordium completely: any given object either is, or is not, a work of artistic craftsmanship, and the way one finds out which is the case is not through seeking the philosopher's stone of a workable definition. If one consults one's intuition, one simply knows that something is or is not artistic, and that is an end to the matter.[6] The suite of furniture in the instant case was not a work of artistic craftsmanship because his Lordship knew it wasn't. In fact there is much to commend Lord Dilhorne's approach, if viewed from the point of view of the American Realist school of jurisprudence.[7] Since judges, either with a full or an impaired consciousness, have an observed tendency to decide cases in accordance with their own personal opinions and preferences[8] (the word 'prejudices' is not used because it gives offence), it is honest for them to say that they are finding for one party against another because it satisfies their desire to do what seems fair on the facts. The conventional requirement that a judge gives legal reasons for his intuitively fact-based decisions is not only dishonest, it may be said, but unnecessarily complicates the law. At the last resort, though, Lord Dilhorne's approach causes an undesirable degree of uncertainty to a claimant who cannot discover whether his work is of artistic craftsmanship without taking an alleged infringer to the highest court in the land.

(vi) Lord Simon of Glaisdale, observing acutely the verbal formula employed by the Copyright Act, pointed out that 'work of artistic craftsmanship' is, literally, a work the craftsmanship of which is artistic;[9] he chided those whose interpretations, in his view, relied upon the formula 'artistic work of craftsmanship'. In this case the furniture, being no more than a cobbled-together industrial prototype, could in no sense be said to be a work made by a process of artistic craftsmanship, and did not therefore enjoy copyright protection. This view has been criticised[10] on the semantic ground that the words 'of craftsmanship' are most intelligently construed as an adjectival phrase by means of which the clumsy and non-current word 'craftsmanship-like' is avoided. A work of artistic craftsmanship is thus an artistic craftsmanship-like work. If this objection is correct, it is not then necessary to establish how 'craftsmanship' may be identified as being 'artistic'. This approach is also to be preferred because it can cope with the situation where the artistry and craftsmanship are provided by different authors collaborating jointly to produce the work.[11]

(vii) Lord Kilbrandon, finding no help from the approaches of his brethren, struck out upon a novel path along which, as a criminal

157

lawyer, he was peculiarly equipped to venture. Just as one determines the guilt of a criminal by looking at his state of mind ('Did the accused intend to inflict grievous bodily harm on the deceased?'), so one determines the status of a work of artistic craftsmanship by examining the state of the craftsman's mind ('Did the craftsman intend to commit an artistic work?'). If the craftsman did so intend, the work is one of artistic craftsmanship;[12] here there was no evidence of such intent and, even if the old presumption were current that a man intends the natural and probable consequences of his actions, the suite in issue was not the natural and probable consequence of a craftsman's intending to make an artistic work.

1. *Hensher v Restawile Upholstery* [1976] AC 64.
2. [1973] 1 WLR 144.
3. [1976] AC 64.
4. Ibid at 78.
5. Ibid, at 82. However, the decision of experts to include garments in a fashion exhibition at the Victoria and Albert Museum did not persuade the court that the garments in *Guild v Eskander Ltd* [2001]FSR 645 were works of artistic craftsmanship.
6. Ibid, at 85-86.
7. On American Realism see Lord Lloyd and M Freeman *Lloyd's Introduction to Jurisprudence* (5th edn, 1985) pp 679-803.
8. On the vulnerability of US Supreme Court judges to their cultural milieu see eg G Schubert *The Political Role of the Courts: Judicial Policy-Making* (1965), pp 113-125.
9. [1976] AC 64 at 90.
10. J Phillips ' "Artistic" Copyright' (1975) 38 MLR 86.
11. A possibility contemplated in *Vermaat and Powell v Boncrest Ltd* [2001] FSR 43; in that case there was insufficient contact between a designer in England and craftswomen in India for such a finding.
12. [1976] AC 64 at 97.

11.31 This approach, which has been applied subsequently in *Merlet v Mothercare plc*,[1] suffers from four drawbacks. The first is that the craftsman may have intended to make a work of artistic craftsmanship but the end product falls short of his lofty aspirations. In such a case, Lord Kilbrandon felt, the fact that the craftsman's co-workers would not have thought that the author was producing a work of artistic craftsmanship would remove the work from copyright protection despite the author's intention.[2] This qualification does meet the objection, but one is left with the feeling that it is rather artificial and that it lies far from the words of the Act itself. The second objection is that no other author's work depends for its status upon the intention of its author.[3] The third objection is that it may be difficult or impossible to establish or assess the craftsman's intention if, for example, an infringement action is brought by an assignee in respect of a work the author of which has died, emigrated, or cannot be traced. The fourth objection is that the other Lords of Appeal in Ordinary gave it little support. Even Lord Reid, who kindly describes the artist's intention as 'important', goes on to say that it is neither a sufficient nor a necessary criterion of the work's status.[4]

1. *Merlet v Mothercare plc* [1984] FSR 358.
2. [1976] AC 64 at 98.
3. Y Gendreau, 'Intention and Copyright Law' in Pollau-Dullian, ed, *The Internet and Author's Rights* (1999) Vol 5 Perspectives on Intellectual Property, p 3, gives a lucid account of the role of intention in other aspects of copyright.
4. Ibid, at 78.

Chapter 12

Derivative works

Introduction

12.1   Copyright in the works described in the last chapter protects the author or creator of a work against plagiarism of his intellectual product. However, copyright in the other types of work generally protects the investment of the entrepreneur who encapsulates an author's work in a form in which it can be commercially exploited or otherwise disseminated to its consuming public. This is not to say that a derivative work is devoid of the sort of actual or potential intellectual merit which is regarded by many as the justification of copyright protection; after all, the technical skills and aesthetic appreciation required by the sound recording engineer, when turning a simple song into a chart-busting disco dance, is nowadays almost invariably greater than the skill and effort involved in composing or performing that song in the first place. It is important to understand, however, that copyright in a derivative work does not exist as a response to a demand that a meritorious form of expression be protected; it exists instead as a response to a demand that the entrepreneur's investment be protected.

12.2   It is for this reason that, for these works, the definitions of authorship appear somewhat artificial. The initial owner of copyright in a sound recording, film, cable programme, broadcast or typographical arrangement of a work is its 'author' but, as is shortly to be discussed below,[1] conceptual resemblance between these 'authors' and creators of classic works is discernible only by means of a concerted effort at self-deception. Ownership of broadcasts or cable programmes has nothing to do with authorship or creativity at all, while copyright in published editions of works vests in an 'author' who is defined as the 'publisher'. It is not therefore surprising that, while the British talk of 'copyright' in derivative works, lawyers whose education lies within the civil law traditions of continental Europe find it difficult to refer to the protection of those works (with the exception of films) as forming part of the 'author's right'.

1.   See para **12.25**.

12.3 The first British copyright legislation to confer an explicit copyright upon sound recordings was the Copyright Act 1911.[1] Prior to the passage of that Act, the status of sound recordings was unclear; they were not regarded as musical (or any other) works,[2] and it was not accepted that the making of a sound recording would constitute an infringement of copyright in a musical work if it were done without the authorisation of the owner of copyright in the work recorded.[3]

1. Copyright Act 1911, s 19(1).
2. Minutes of Evidence taken before the Law of Copyright Committee, Cd 5051, 1910. The matter was not, it seems, determined by case law.
3. *Boosey v Whight* [1900] 1 Ch 122; *Monckton v Gramophone Co* (1912) 106 LT 84.

Sound recordings

12.4 As the modern reader will appreciate, there are many different means by which a sound may be recorded. Until the late 1980s, the most commercially significant recording technique employed the cassette tape; by 1988 an estimated 85% of British homes possessed at least one cassette player/recorder,[1] and nearly £400 million was spent on prerecorded tapes in that year.[2] By 1989, sales of longplaying CDs had already overtaken those of vinyl LPs[3] and in 1994 CDs first outsold cassettes on a global basis.[4] By 1998, CD players were found in 87% of British households.[5] At the time of writing, the CD was still the most popular medium for sound recordings in the UK[6] and worldwide.[7]

1. British Phonographic Industry Ltd's (BPI's) Annual Report, p 56 (British Market Research Bureau Statistics).
2. BPI estimate; ibid, at p 42.
3. M Hung and E Garcia Morencos *World Record Sales 1969-1990*, IFPI.
4. IFPI *The Recording Industry in Numbers 99*, p 4.
5. Ibid, pp 62-63.
6. Ibid.
7. IFPI *The Recording Industry in Numbers 99*, p 4 reports CDs as representing 66% of all albums, although the CD was in its early stages of penetration in many countries, especially in the less developed Asian and Eastern European countries.

12.5 The first sound recording which most people own is likely to be a musical toy, often operated by a clockwork or other wind-up mechanism, by which the same tune may be unceasingly repeated to the child's delight and to the annoyance of all proximate adults. Empirical research reveals that the dissection of such toys may well expose a sound recording in the form of a disc or cylinder which contains rubber, metal or plastic nodules which 'programme' the operation of percussive or other sound-producing media. In the toys of previous generations, the same sound-producing media were often programmed by mechanically legible perforated rolls of paper. The most modern toys are now programmed by tiny 'music chips', which enable birthday cards to perform the tune of 'Happy Birthday to You' when opened. With regard to all such devices, the faithful rendition of a set of sounds by means of fairly robust apparatus is generally paramount while for the sound-recording media referred to in the previous paragraph, the quality of the sound reproduction is a matter of the greatest importance. This distinction is of significance when considering the industrial and commercial applications of copyright, but it has no current bearing upon the applicability of the criteria of copyright protection.

Definition of 'sound recording'

12.6   Since it is clear that there are many different types of sound which can be the subject of a recording, and many different ways in which each sound can be recorded, the Copyright, Designs and Patents Act 1988 provides a broad definition of 'sound recording' from which no sound which may be the subject of a worthwhile commercially marketable venture has been arbitrarily excluded. In section 5A(1), therefore, the statutory draftsman has defined 'sound recording' as:

'. . . (a) a recording of sounds, from which the sounds may be reproduced, or

(b) a recording of the whole or any part of a literary, dramatic or musical work, from which sounds reproducing the work or part may be produced . . .'

This makes clear that the content of a sound recording may, but need not, be a work or part of a work. The definition then goes on:

'... regardless of the medium on which the recording is made or the method by which sounds are reproduced or produced...'

Use of the words 'reproduced or produced' provides strong evidence that Parliament intended piano rolls and mechanical musical toys to fall within the definition, as was the case under the 1956 Act.[1] Against that, however, is the use of 'recording' in (a) and (b), which suggests that 'sound recording' must be derived from actual sounds, rather than from mere electronic impulses or sound ratios computed by mathematical calculations. It is likely that section 5A of the 1988 Act will be construed to change the law as little as possible,[2] especially as section 172(2) says 'A provision which corresponds to a provision of the previous law shall not be construed as departing from the previous law merely because of a change of expression'.

1. S 12(1).
2. Ss 5A and 5B were introduced in place of s 5 by the Duration of Copyright and Rights in Performances Regulations 1995 (SI 1995/3297). This did not change the basic definition of 'sound recording' but ensured that sound tracks accompanying films could be treated as part of the film, to comply with Directive 93/98/EEC harmonising the term of protection of copyright and certain related rights. Under s 5, the sound track was treated separately. S 5B(5) makes clear, however, that the sound track may still be protected as a sound recording.

12.7   So far as 'sound' is concerned, we assume that what we can hear is a sound; but what about that which we cannot hear? For example, would a tape recording of dog-instructions in the form of high-pitched whistles, inaudible to the human ear however great their amplification, be protectable? In view of the breadth of the definition set out in para **12.6**, you are invited to consider whether a parrot trained to recite the poems of Milton, or a schoolchild chanting his multiplication tables, could be regarded as a 'record'. What would be the 'medium' required by section 5A(1)?

Films

12.8   The Copyright Act 1956, section 13, provided the first means of protection for the film *per se* under British law. Prior to it, each of the film's component parts was separately protected: each frame of the film was protected as a photograph, the script was a literary work, the soundtrack a sound recording, and so on. This compartmentalised form of protection could be defended in strict logic, since the finished product which is viewed on the cinema or television screen is a vehicle which contains numerous distinct species of intellectual and industrial product, but compartmentalised protection was not ideally suited to the commercial environment in which licences are granted, rights assigned and permissions sought. It is not, therefore, surprising that the replacement of the previous multitude of rights by a single right vesting in the film's maker met no serious opposition. However, two European Directives[1] have stipulated that the principal director of a cinematographic or audiovisual work shall be considered as author or at least one of the authors.[2] It was argued[3] that films should also enjoy protection as dramatic works under the Copyright, Designs and Patents Act 1988. This has been held to be the case in *Norowzian v Arks Ltd (No 2)*.[4] It is not clear from that decision who should be regarded as the author of the dramatic work in the general case.[5] Kamina suggests[6] that the director, perhaps the script or scenario writers and other contributors should be considered as joint authors of the drama. If these persons are employees of the film producer, the latter will be entitled automatically to the dramatic copyright.[7] If they are freelance, however, the producer would need to take assignment of the dramatic rights to concentrate the rights in single ownership.

1. Council Directive 92/100/EEC on rental right and lending rights and on certain rights relating to copyright in the field of intellectual property, art 2.2 (implementation date 1 July 1994); Council Directive 93/98/EEC harmonising the term of protection of copyright and certain related rights (implementation date 1 July 1995). The Copyright, Designs and Patents Act 1988, s 9(2)(ab), inserted by the Copyright and Related Rights Regulations 1996 (SI 1996/2967), changes the authorship rules for films made from 1 July 1994 onwards.
2. See, further, G Dworkin 'Authorship of Films' [1993] EIPR 157.
3. P Kamina 'Authorship of Films and Implementation of the Term Directive: a Tale of Two Copyrights' [1994] EIPR 319.
4. [2000] FSR 363, CA. See para **11.20**.
5. A criticism levied by T Rivers in 'Norowzian Revisited' [2000] EIPR 389.
6. See above, n 3.
7. Copyright, Designs and Patents Act 1988, s 11(2).

12.9 Section 5B(1) of the Copyright, Designs and Patents Act 1988 defines 'film' as meaning (not 'including'):

'... a recording on any medium from which a moving image may by any means be produced...'

Thus the definition covers not only the home video, the pre-recorded television documentary and the classic celluloid 'film', but also the technology of a bygone era. Many museums display models consisting of a large, rotating cylindrical drum around the external circumference of which are affixed a sequence of still illustrations of the different phases of a particular action – for example, the galloping of a horse.[1] When the drum is rotated at speed, and the sequence of images is viewed from one vantage point, the rapid passage of the stationary images creates the illusion of motion.

1. For a discussion of early cinematography see *Encyclopedia Britannica* (11th edn 1910-1911), vol 6, pp 374-375 or Ceram, *Archaeology of the Cinema*, (1965, Thames and Hudson).

Broadcasts

12.10 Copyright subsists in certain television and sound broadcasts under the terms of the Copyright, Designs and Patents Act 1988, section

6. Prior to 1 July 1957 no broadcast enjoyed copyright protection. The subject matter of the broadcast is irrelevant to the issue of its protectability under copyright law; thus the subject matter may be a poetry recitation, a sound recording of bird calls from the Orkneys, a derivative work which incorporates authors' works (eg a film embodying a written script and accompanying songs), or not a work at all (eg live camera coverage of a volcanic eruption).

Definition of 'broadcast'

12.11 In section 6 of the Copyright, Designs and Patents Act 1988 appears a pragmatic and comprehensive definition. First of all, broadcasting involves a transmission by 'wireless telegraphy', a phrase which means the sending of unchannelled electromagnetic energy, 'over paths not provided by a material substance constructed or arranged for that purpose'.[1] Thus transmissions by wire or optical fibre are excluded.[2] Next, a transmission which passes the first test may be characterised as a broadcast either if it is capable of being lawfully received by the public (an objective test) or if it is transmitted for presentation to members of the public (a subjective test which depends on the intention of the person making the transmission).[3] In other words, a typical BBC World Service news bulletin is 'broadcast', as is a sinking ship's 'May-day' signal, while a set of instructions issued to an aircraft's pilot by an air traffic controller is not.

1. Copyright, Designs and Patents Act 1988, s 178.
2. Such transmissions may attract cable programme copyright – see para **12.18** below.
3. 'Broadcast' is in fact a metaphor borrowed from agriculture; in its original context it referred to the sowing of seed, not to the seed as sowed.

Encrypted transmission

12.12 A problem arises with transmissions which are sent out in encoded or 'encrypted' form, so that only people with appropriate decoders may make sense of them. Some encrypted transmissions, such as pay television, are directed at members of the public – provided they pay for the privilege of using the decoder. Others are encrypted precisely to prevent members of the public from gaining access to the information transmitted. Subsection 6(2) attempts to deal with the varying aims of encryption by stating:

'An encrypted transmission shall be regarded as capable of being lawfully received by members of the public only if decoding equipment has been made available to members of the public by or with the authority of the person making the transmission or the person providing the contents of the transmission.'[1]

Thus an encrypted pay television transmission can be said to be 'broadcast' while a telephone call sent from a car over a radio network is not.

1.   This is consistent with art 1.2(c) of Council Directive 93/83/EEC on cable and satellite: OJ 1993 L248/15.

What is transmitted?

12.13   The definition in section 6(1) refers to transmission of 'visual images, sounds or other information'. This includes not only ordinary television and video broadcasts, but also teletext services. It is not clear whether the words 'or other information' protect anything not already covered by the words 'visual images' or 'sounds' at least as far as today's technology goes. It would, however, seem that 'other information' would include transmitted data pertinent to the receiving equipment's ability to synchronise sounds and visual images, but which is not itself capable of being seen or heard.

Where does transmission take place?

12.14   Since the 1988 Act protects broadcasts within the territories to which the Act applies or extends, it is important to establish which broadcasts are covered by that Act's protection. For example, we would expect the Act to govern a broadcast made in Birmingham and received in Bristol, but not one which was made in Bali and received in Brunei. The general principle which governs jurisdiction is that broadcasts are protected by the law of the country in which they are made, even if – as in the case of BBC World Service programmes – they are intended primarily for an audience of foreign news-addicts, as well as British insomniacs. Where a broadcast is made via a satellite, the situation becomes more complex; for example, if a broadcast is beamed up from Brighton to a geostationary satellite over Bordeaux, from which it is then beamed down to Bilbao, has the broadcast been made in England, where the 'uplink' signal leaves the earth, or in France? Now that the UK has implemented Council Directive 93/83/EEC,[1] section 6(4) ensures that the broadcast is deemed to be made in the State where, under the control and responsibility of the person making the broadcast,[2] the signals are introduced into an 'uninterrupted chain of communication' to the public. In the case of a satellite broadcast, this is the chain which leads up to the satellite and back to earth. If, according to that definition, a satellite broadcast occurs outside the EEA, in a state providing inadequate protection, the next two contenders are the Member State where the 'uplink' station is located or (failing that) the state where the broadcasting organisation has its principal establishment in the EEA.

1. Of 27 September 1993, OJ 1993 L248/15; implemented by The Copyright and Related Rights Regulations 1996 (SI 1996/2967).
2. The person making the transmission, if he has any responsibility for the content and the person providing the programmes who makes arrangements for transmission; see paras **12.28-12.29**.

The definitions and infringement

12.15 The definitions of 'broadcast' and 'cable programme' are not just important for establishing whether copyright subsists or not. Broadcasting and inclusion in a cable programme service are listed in section 16 of the 1988 Act as ways in which copyright in other works may be infringed. Thus the issue of infringement will depend on whether the activity concerned falls within the relevant definitions; the same definitions applying to infringement as to subsistence.

Cable programmes

12.16 When Parliament was considering its new copyright law back in 1956, the possibilities of the so-called 'new technology' had not been appreciated. Computers did exist,[1] but their impact upon copyright had not been recognised at all; indeed, the only facet of computing which was firmly grasped by laymen at that time was its potential as a scapegoat for human failure. Cable transmission of programmes for reception in the home was also then extant, but it was seen primarily, if not solely, as a means of enhancing the distribution of programmes already broadcast. Some 10% of potential television viewers in the UK live in locations which are physically inappropriate for the reception of wireless broadcasts, perhaps because a mountain or high building comes between the transmitters and their domestic reception apparatus, or because they live in an enclosed valley; cable transmission was seen as a convenient way of 'piping' broadcast programmes into the home from receiving apparatus situated in a more auspicious location. Cable TV was only recognised in the UK as having a valuable independent function to play in the dissemination of once the number of operators in the United States showed how they could create viewer choice through the multiplication of channels, thereby stimulating competition between programme providers, while making attractive profits into the bargain. Cable is now regarded as an economically desirable means of disseminating information in places where populations are concentrated, satellite television having to a great extent solved the problem of transmission to large areas of sparse population or to countries such as Indonesia where no other means of transmission is feasible.

1. The early history of computers is chronicled in S Hollingdale and G Toothill *Electronic Computers* (1965), Chs 1-3.

12.17 The Cable and Broadcasting Act 1984, section 22, first created copyright in cable programmes (except 'repeats'). The protection of cable programmes under copyright law is a long way removed from the original function of copyright as a means of protecting the author of a literary work against the unauthorised copying and publication of the intellectual property which was created by his labour. Many of those who speak of 'author's rights' and 'neighbouring rights' abhor the 'dilution' of the concept of copyright which results from regarding ephemera such as cable programmes and broadcasts as 'works' protectable by copyright. On the other hand, it is clear that all species of right protected under the Copyright Act share in common a golden principle: they are all derived from the notion that it is unfair for one person to take unfair commercial advantage of the resources of another, whether those resources be expended in a physical, intellectual, temporal or financial sense. This notion may be found explicitly in copyright's oldest 'leading case', *Millar v Taylor*,[1] where Willes J said:

'It is certainly not agreeable to natural justice, that a stranger should reap the beneficial produce of another man's work',

and it enjoys no less support today, when the concept of 'unfair competition' is strongly invoked wherever true intellectual property rights appear ineffectual.

1. (1769) 4 Burr 2303 at 2334 to 2335.

Cable programmes under the 1988 Act

12.18 Cable transmission involves the sending of signals along designated material paths. This is spelt out[1] by specifying the use of a telecommunications system[2] and excluding wireless telegraphy, which in turn excludes[3] transmission over paths constructed or arranged for the purpose. The use of a double negative is not very elegant, but it does ensure that the definitions of 'broadcast' and 'cable programme' are complementary. Whether a cable transmission constitutes a cable programme or not depends upon whether it is included in a cable programme service.[4] Apart from the means of transmission, such a service is defined[5] in the following way: the service must involve the sending of visual images, sounds or other information for reception either at two or more places (simultaneously or not)[6] or for presentation to members of the public.[7] The definition thus has an objective limb (the requirement that there be two or more recipients) and a subjective limb (one must consider the purpose of the transmission). If either of these criteria are satisfied, one then goes on to consider whether the service is taken out of the category 'cable programme service' by the exceptions in subsection 7(2). These are designed to insure that private or in-house or truly interactive transmissions are not caught by the definition. Thus telephone communications between only two individuals, conference calls and the operational services of cable companies do not constitute cable programme services. An individual buying goods by 'teleshopping' would receive catalogue pages as a cable service, despite the fact that he was choosing which pages to view. The transmission of his or her subsequent order and its acceptance would not, however, be part of a cable programme service.

1. Copyright, Designs and Patents Act 1988, s 7(1).
2. Defined in s 178 of the 1988 Act as a system for conveying visual images, sounds or other information by electronic means.
3. Copyright, Designs and Patents Act 1988, s 178.
4. Ibid, s 7(1).
5. Ibid, s 7(1).
6. Ibid, s 7(1)(a).
7. Ibid, s 7(1)(b).

Cable programme services and the Internet

12.19 An earlier edition of this book suggested that providers of database services might be able to rely upon cable programme copyright to protect their creations against misuse. Database operators now have their own regime of copyright and *sui generis* protection.[1] However, in *Shetland Times v Wills*,[2] the operators of a newspaper web site sought to rely upon the definition of 'cable programme service' to protect their news pages from 'deep linking' by a competitor. The defendant's news site had hypertext links that enabled users to go straight to the relevant page of the Shetland Times site, bypassing the claimants' home page and thus avoiding advertising. The Scots Court of Session, without deciding the point, was prepared to assume that it was arguable that the defendant was including the claimant's copyright material in a cable programme service, contrary to section 20 of the Copyright, Design and Patents Act 1988 and, on that assumption, granted the Scots equivalent of an interim injunction. This case was settled shortly before the appeal was due to be heard, so the point was never formally considered. In contrast with the *Shetland Times* case, the argument that the establishment of a hypertext link constituted the inclusion of material in a cable programme transmission was not considered sufficiently meritorious to be raised before the court in the subsequent Dutch *kranten.com* case.[3]

1. See para **12.19A.**
2. [1997] FSR 604.
3. *Algemeen Dagblad BV v Eureka Internetdienst*, 22 August 2000 (to be reported in the ECDR, 2002).

Database right

12.20 This *sui generis* right is closely related to the entrepreneurial copyrights; it is triggered by a 'substantial' investment in obtaining, verifying or presenting the contents of a database.[1] 'Database' itself is defined for copyright purposes; where the selection or arrangement of data items is original, the architecture of the database attracts copyright.[2] 'Database right', however, protects those contents against unauthorised use in ways unfair to the owner of the right.[3]

1. Copyright and Rights in Databases Regulations 1997 (SI 1997/3032), reg 13.
2. Copyright, Designs and Patents Act 1988, s 3A.
3. Copyright and Rights in Databases Regulations 1997 (SI 1997/3032), reg 16. See, further, para **23.20-23.23.**

Published editions of works

12.21 Just as a cassette or film may enjoy copyright protection even though it may be no more than, or not even, a vehicle for the dissemination of a work, such as a trumpet sonata or a film script, so too a book can find itself protected from unauthorised copying even when the works it contains are separately protected, or not protected at all, from copying. This result follows from the Copyright, Designs and Patents Act 1988, section 1(1)(c), which accords copyright protection to the typographical arrangement of published editions. 'Published edition' is defined in section 8 as meaning a published edition of the whole or any part of one or more literary, dramatic or musical works. In *Newspaper Licensing Agency v Marks & Spencer plc*[1] the claimants complained of duplication by the defendants of clippings of single newspaper articles. In order to decide whether the defendants were taking a substantial part of the claimant's copyright creation, it was necessary to decide whether 'edition' referred to each individual article, the newspaper as a whole, or something in between, such as a page. The House of Lords held that 'edition' referred to the whole newspaper and that the defendants had not infringed. In other words, sections 1 and 8 create a copyright in the manner in which the letters and other typographical elements which make up a literary or other non-artistic work are designed to appear upon the printed page.[2]

1. [2001] 3 WLR 290, HL.
2. The issues in the case and the decisions below are analysed by T Baloch 'Typography in Law: From Mechanics to Aesthetics' [2001] Ent LR 78.

12.22 It is usually assumed that the function of this copyright is twofold: to prevent a person making use of another's labour-intensive effort in page-setting through the use of photographic or reprographic techniques and to prevent another's adoption of the same lettering typeface in setting up his own print run. In fact, there is nothing in the definitions to indicate that it is the *appearance* of the page, rather than its typographical *arrangement*, which is protected. The significance of this distinction lies in the fact that matters such as the arrangement of lines of text so as to produce felicitous word-breaks at the end of lines, well-spaced words, a justified right-hand margin and an absence of 'rivers' (vertically connected runs of interverbal spaces) are more pertinent to the typographical arrangement of the work than is the choice of one typeface in preference to another. If this view is correct, it is an infringement of copyright under this section to make an edition, in Roman type, of a work published in Gothic type, if the same spacing and typeface organisation has been adopted.

12.23 Note that there is no protection for the typographical arrangement of unpublished works, whether or not they are intended for subsequent publication. This is strange, since the damage which may be caused in each case is broadly the same, and the man whose edition has not yet been published stands to suffer greater loss. Like the whereabouts of the crew of the *Marie Celeste* and the explanation of the popularity of Pokémon, the reason for distinguishing between published and unpublished works in this way is one of the great unsolved mysteries of our time.

Publication right

12.24 This entrepreneurial right protects investment by the first person who brings to the public[1] a previously unpublished authorial work or film whose copyright has expired.[2] It is a mandatory element of the European Community's 'Term Directive'.[3] Since UK copyright in most unpublished works does not expire until the end of 2039,[4] its effects have not greatly been felt to date. Nonetheless copyright in certain unpublished artistic works, such as photographs, has already expired in the UK and elsewhere. Publication right would presumably be available for these. If a 'lost work' of a very early author, such as a Canterbury Tale of Geoffrey Chaucer, were discovered and published, would it be eligible for publication right? Since the tale was never in copyright under statute, could publication be treated as 'after expiry of copyright', as stipulated in Art 4? Any such argument would have to be based on common law copyright in unpublished works, an uncertain concept which was definitively abolished by the Copyright Act 1911.[5]

1. For these purposes, publication not only means issuing copies to the public or making available by an electronic retrieval system, but also rental or lending of copies, public exhibition or performance, broadcasting or cable-casting: Copyright and Related Rights Regulations 1996 (SI 1996/2967), reg 16 (2).
2. H Laddie, P Prescott and M Vitoria, A Speck and L Lane *The Modern Law of Copyright and Designs* (3rd edn 2000) rather dub these 'derelict works': Ch 16. Those authors question a number of aspects of publication right, including the validity of the Community legislation on which it is based (n 3, below).
3. Council Directive 93/98/EEC of 29 October 1993 harmonising the term of protection of copyright and certain related rights, [1993] OJ L290/9, implemented as to publication right in the UK by The Copyright and Related Rights Regulations 1996 (SI 1996/2967), regs 16 and 17. For implementation elsewhere, see G Lea, 'The Term Directive and its Implementation' in E Barendt and A Firth (eds) *Yearbook of Copyright and Media Law 1999,* p 177.
4. Copyright, Designs and Patents Act, 1988, s 170 and Sch 1, para 12.
5. S 31.

Originality and derivative works

12.25 To attract copyright, literary, dramatic, musical and artistic works must be 'original'[1] in the sense of originating from their authors, who have expended independent skill and labour, and not just copied.[2] Derivative works, too, need a kind of originality, which is spelt out for each type of work. Thus no copyright subsists in a sound recording or film which is a copy (infringing or not) taken from a previous sound recording or film.[3] Nor does copyright subsist in a broadcast insofar as it infringes copyright in another broadcast or cable programme.[4] Cable programmes do not enjoy copyright if they involve reception and immediate re-transmission of a broadcast, or insofar as they infringe copyright in other cable programmes or broadcasts.[5] The result of these latter provisions is that repeat broadcasts and cable programmes now enjoy their own copyright. The duration of that copyright, however, expires at the same time as copyright in the original broadcast or cable programme.[6] Copyright subsists in typographical arrangements of published editions only insofar as they do not repeat the typographical arrangement of previous editions.[7]

1. Copyright, Designs and Patents Act 1988, s 1(1).
2. See para **11.9** above.
3. Copyright, Designs and Patents Act 1988, s 5(2).
4. Ibid, s 6(6).
5. Ibid, s 7(6).
6. Ibid, s 14(2).
7. Ibid, s 8(2).

Creatorship and ownership

12.26   So far as literary, dramatic, musical and artistic works are concerned, the treatment of creatorship and ownership follows a close pattern: the author of such a work is the person who first renders it into an appropriate tangible form, and copyright vests in the author unless some other party has a better claim to it, such as, for example, an employer who had paid the author specifically to make it.[1] While derivative works do not follow this pattern, some of the underlying principles are broadly the same.

1. Copyright, Designs and Patents Act 1988, s 11(2).

Sound recordings and films

12.27   Copyright in sound recordings and films vests in their 'author'.[1] This may sound much like the 'author' of a literary, dramatic or musical work, but this is not so, since the word 'author' is given specific definitions by section 9(2) of the Copyright, Designs and Patents Act 1988.[2] Subsection 9(2)(aa) states that the author of a sound recording is its producer, whilst subsection 9(2)(ab) confers the status of author of a film jointly upon the producer and director. Turning to section 178, we find that 'producer' means 'the person by whom the arrangements necessary for the making of the recording or film are undertaken'. The maker of a film was previously defined in similar terms for copyright purposes.[3] 'Arrangements' could refer to economic arrangements,[4] physical arrangements, or both.[5] Although film producer and director are both declared authors by section 9(2)(ab), it is not clear that this applies to the dramatic copyright in a film.[6] Only the director enjoys moral rights.[7]

12.27 *Derivative works*

1. Copyright, Designs and Patents Act 1988, s 9(1).
2. Amended in relation to films and sound recordings by the Copyright and Related Rights Regulations 1996 (SI 1996/2967), reg 18(1).
3. Copyright Act 1956, s 13(10).
4. *A&M Records Ltd v Collection International Ltd Century* [1995] EMLR 25 (sound recording); *Century Communications Ltd v Mayfair Entertainment Ltd* [1993] EMLR 335 (film, Hong Kong).
5. *Beggars Banquet Records Ltd v Carlton Television Ltd* [1993] EMLR 349 (film).
6. See para **11.20-11.21**.
7. Ch 18.

Ownership of copyright in broadcasts

12.28   Under the 1956 Act,[1] only transmissions made by the British Broadcasting Corporation (BBC) and the Independent Broadcasting Authority (IBA) attracted copyright. Now the transmissions of 'pirate' stations (as well as those of the many legitimate stations permitted to broadcast) will apparently be protected by copyright. It may be, however, that an old principle – no enforcement of copyright in an iniquitous work[2] – would apply to hamper 'pirate' broadcasters in the unlikely event that they brought proceedings for infringement of copyright.

1. Copyright Act 1956, s 14(1).
2. *Glyn v Weston Feature Film Co* [1916] 1 Ch 261. Recently referred to in *A-G v Observer* [1990] AC 109, sub nom *A-G v Guardian Newspapers Ltd (No 2)* [1988] 3 All ER 545.

12.29   Ownership of copyright in broadcasts is conferred[1] upon the person providing the programme and upon a person transmitting who has responsibility to any extent for content. Thus broadcasting copyright will frequently vest in joint owners. This addressed a complaint by independent television companies[2] that they, and not the transmitting authority (who might have a lesser interest in enforcement), should own broadcasting copyright.

1. Copyright, Designs and Patents Act 1988, ss 6(3) and 9(2)(b).
2. See *Copyright and Designs Law* Cmnd 6732, 1977, paras 585-586.

12.30   The owner of 'typeface' copyright is not the person who makes the typographical arrangement of the work but the person who publishes it.[1] It is clear from this that the interest protected is not the typesetter's labour but the publisher's investment.

1. Copyright, Designs and Patents Act 1988, s 9(2)(d).

Chapter 13

Infringement

The concept of infringement in copyright law

13.1   Unlike patent infringement, which depends upon the patent applicant sketching out by means of claims a 'territory' for himself upon which others may not trespass, copyright infringement knows no concept of the claim. Each work, upon and by virtue of its creation, determines the extent of the monopoly which its copyright owner will enjoy, subject to the principle of the 'restricted act': so far as each type of copyright work is concerned, the Copyright, Designs and Patents Act 1988 specifies those acts ('restricted acts') which a person other than the copyright owner cannot perform without making himself liable to copyright infringement proceedings.[1] It is *not* an infringement to create an identical or similar work independently. In the 1988 Act, an attempt has been made to put the infringement of copyright in the different types of work on a uniform footing. The 1956 Act spelt out the restricted acts work by work, which led to difficulty. However, there still remain differences in the modes of infringement of the various types of work as, indeed, is necessary to do justice. This chapter will highlight some of the major issues arising from the following species of infringement:

(i)   making a copy
(ii)   issuing copies to the public[2]
(iii) performing
(iv)   broadcasting
(v)   transmitting by cable
(vi)   adapting
(vii) but not authorising any of (i) to (vi) above (which is discussed in Ch 26).

1.   S 28.
2.   This includes even the temporary issue of copies by way of rental (cf lending, which is discussed in Ch 15).

13.2   It is an infringement to copy a work without licence from the copyright owner.[1] Copying is an act restricted by copyright in every

175

description of work,[2] as is suggested by the very name 'copyright'. The 'copy' must be derived from the protected work, but the process of copying can be direct or indirect, complete or partial.[3] Not everything which derives from a copyright work is necessarily a copy; however, section 17 describes various specific forms of copying:

(i)   reproducing a literary, dramatic, musical or artistic work in any material form;[4] including

(ii) making a three-dimensional copy of a two-dimensional artistic work, and vice versa;[5]

(iii) photographing an image contained in a film, broadcast or cable programme (copying for these works is defined inclusively);[6]

(iv) making a 'facsimile copy' of the typographical arrangement of a published edition;[7]

(v)   making a transient copy of any type of work.[8]

1.   Copyright, Designs and Patents Act 1988, s 16(2). See paras **13.9, 13.13**.
2.   Ibid, s 17(1).
3.   Ibid, s 16(3)(a).
4.   Ibid, s 17(2).
5.   Ibid, s 17(3).
6.   Ibid, s 17(4).
7.   Ibid, s 17(5).
8.   Ibid, s 17(6).

13.3   The widest of these categories is 'reproducing ... in any material form'[1] a literary, dramatic, musical or artistic work, since the concept of 'reproduction' for this purpose is far wider than that accorded to it by normal dictionary or colloquial usage. It is easy to think of the splendid Constable painting, *The Haywain*, hanging in the dentist's waiting room as a reproduction of the identical picture hanging in London's National Gallery; it is less easy to label a picture postcard of the Venus de Milo as a 'reproduction' of the statue, although copying includes the rendering into two-dimensional form of a three-dimensional object. Even more difficult is the conception that a videotape of a mime artiste's routine is a 'reproduction' of a piece of paper upon which that artiste's dramatic instructions are printed.

1.   Copyright, Designs and Patents Act 1988, s 17(2).

13.4   'Reproducing in any material form' includes 'storing the work in any medium by electronic means'.[1] Thus storage on the hard disc of a computer, or by means of a computer on to a separate floppy disc or CD can infringe. The 1988 Act may be said to prevent 'digital' as well as 'analog' copying.[2] Since that the definition of reproduction includes even transient copying,[3] it is especially difficult to predict how far copyright protection extends. *Laddie et al*[4] observe it may be scientifically correct (if absurd) to say that a person reading a newspaper over someone else's shoulder stores an unlicensed reproduction in his or her brain by electronic means, and so infringes copyright. It would be even more bizarre if the copyright-infringing reader had a poor memory, so that the reproduction was not even stored to be recounted later to colleagues at work. *Laddie et al* suggest that the puzzle may be solved by purposive interpretation. 'Copy' and 'store' suggest that a reproduction is being saved for future use, while 'any medium by electronic means' is clearly aimed at computer memory, including temporary 'RAM'. Questions such as these taxed the collective mind of the Diplomatic Conference which concluded the World Intellectual Property Organisation Copyright Treaty in 1996; unable to agree on treaty language to cope with electronic copying, they resorted to a mere statement that the right to restrict copying applies in the digital environment.[5] Ultimately it must be a matter for judicial common sense. Note that the exhibition of original works or of legitimate copies is not an act restricted by copyright. This suggests that the right to control digital reproduction should not be construed in such as way as to enable the copyright owner to control the display of works on a computer monitor. [6]

1. Copyright, Designs and Patents Act 1988, s 17(2).
2. For the difficulties inherent in controlling digital copying, see H Rosenblatt 'The Impact of New Technology on Composer and Music Publishers: Policing the Superhighways' [1994] Ent LR 89.
3. Copyright, Designs and Patents Act 1988, s 17(6).
4. *The Modern Law of Copyright* (3rd edn 2000) paras 14.10-14.11.
5. J Reinbothe, M Martin-Prat and S von Lewinski 'The new WIPO Treaties: A First Resumé' [1997] EIPR 171 at 172; T Vinje 'The New WIPO Copyright Treaty: A Happy Result in Geneva' [1997] EIPR 230.
6. Cf *Bookmakers' Afternoon Greyhound Services v Wilf Gilbert (Staffordshire) Ltd* [1994] FSR 723.

13.5   Under the Copyright Act 1956, infringement of copyright in sound recordings and cinematograph films was only achieved if either was copied in like form.[1] Thus it was not an infringement of copyright in a sound recording, or a cinematograph film, to make a literary or musical work. Sound recordings are not mentioned at all in section 17 of the 1988 Act and the copying of films is defined only as including photographic images. The question therefore arises as to whether the definition of copying has been extended for sound recordings and films. The answer is 'no'.[2] The 1988 Act was designed 'to restate large parts of existing law unchanged but in a much plainer and more easily understood form'. Furthermore, copying by change of medium is spelt out for artistic works. By inference, other changes of medium would not involve copying. In practice this rarely leads to problems. Any works embodied in a sound recording or film will enjoy their own copyright; so that if a new ballet is first recorded on film, the choreographer will enjoy dramatic copyright. It is the choreographer who should be in a position to prevent others from performing or recording the dance. The film-maker deserves protection against those who would exploit the film as such. However, in *Norowzian v Arks,* the dramatic effect was achieved by editing the film sequence after shooting. An independently made film which imitated the content could not infringe copyright in the film as such, but it might infringe copyright in the film as a dramatic work.[3]

1. Ss 12(5) and 13(5).
2. *Norowzian v Arks* [1998] FSR 394.
3. *Norowzian v Arks (No 2)* [2000] FSR 363, CA.

13.6 Broadcasts and cable programmes have no tangible and corporeal form at all: they are no more than airwaves or electronic impulses travelling along pieces of wire. The making of a film or sound recording from them is an infringement of copyright even if, for example, in the case of a live broadcast or cable programme, the recording of the programme by a domestic viewer is the first making of a permanent copy of that programme. Owners of domestic recording equipment are, however, relieved to learn that the making of a hard copy of a broadcast or cable programme is only an infringement of copyright if it is done other than privately for the purpose of time-shifting.[1]

1. Copyright, Designs and Patents Act 1988, s 70.

13.7 Published editions of works are only infringed by the making of 'facsimile copies', which includes reductions or enlargements.[1] This species of infringement through copy-making is noteworthy in that there is no stipulation of material form: it is not known whether this omission holds any legal significance. In any event, transient or incidental copying may infringe.[2]

1. Copyright, Designs and Patents Act 1988, s 178.
2. Ibid, s 17(6).

Reproduction: a matter of form or content?

13.8 A person who makes an identical version of another's work has clearly reproduced it. This is the sort of reproduction which most commercial piracy and counterfeiting employs, since the printer's customer expects to enjoy all the aesthetic and functional benefits which accrue from the original product. The fact that the defendant's product is identical to the claimant's is greatly appreciated by the latter in copyright infringement proceedings; this is because, although the claimant may well not be able to prove that an actual copying took place, he can show the court that his work and the defendant's are identical and leave it to an embarrassed defendant to explain how his work and the claimant's turned out to be the same.[1] If the claimant's work was made and published prior to the defendant's, and is not of a commonplace nature, infringement is a natural inference even if copying cannot be proved. The same is true where copying is partial; complete identity between the taking and the relevant part of the original will provide a strong inference of copying. In order to establish infringement it will only be necessary to establish that the part taken is a substantial part of the original,[2] in quality as well as quantity.[3]

1. See *Corelli v Gray* (1913) 29 TLR 570.
2. Copyright, Designs and Patents Act 1988, s 16(3)(a). See para **13.30**, below.
3. Thus in *Warwick Film Productions Ltd v Eisinger* [1969] 1 Ch 508, the material taken was not original to the author of the work in issue and therefore not a substantial part of that work.

13.9 An inexact reproduction[1] of another's work may or may not be a copyright infringement: it is all a matter of degree.[2] If one takes the opening lines of the well-known music-hall song,

'Show me the way to go home.
I'm tired and I want to go to bed.
I had a little drink about an hour ago,
And it's gone right to my head',[3]

their meaning is the same as the sesquipedalian circumlocution

'Indicate the way to my abode.
I'm fatigued and I wish to return.
I imbibed a small refreshment sixty minutes ago
And it's percolated to my cranium'

even though different words are used. One might consider therefore that the latter was an infringement of the former, in that it had reproduced the *content* of the first even though it had not reproduced the *form*. This reasoning by analogy is attractive and commercially essential, but it cannot be extended indefinitely. After all, the words

'How do I get home?
I'm tired and drunk'

179

also reproduce the content of the message without reproducing the original form, but any copyright lawyer who was not also tired and drunk would advise his clients that no infringement has taken place.

1. Sometimes referred to as 'altered copying' to distinguish it from 'partial copying', as in *Designers Guild Ltd v Russell Williams (Textiles) Ltd* [2001] FSR 113, HL.
2. See further para **13.30**.
3. I King and H Swaine 'Show Me the Way to Go Home' (1925).

13.10 The question of the content/form dichotomy, as the above problem is often described,[1] is still the subject of much debate. This is because there are situations in which it may not be possible to copy the content without also copying the form. One such situation can arise when a set of television programme schedules is published in a magazine such as *The Radio Times*. The magazine's content, information as to which programme follows which, is free for all to use, but it is unlikely that anyone who wishes to make use of that information by publishing it in his own newspaper can do so without being regarded as having infringed copyright in the *form* in which the information was published.[2] An extreme example of a similar effect may be seen in *Elanco v Mandops*[3] (an interlocutory proceeding upon which no great reliance should be placed): manufacturers of a patented herbicide did a good deal of experimentation with their product so that they could advise its users as to how much herbicide to apply, and in what manner. When the patent expired a rival manufacturer sought to sell the same herbicide and to provide the same factual information as to its use, though in different words. Obviously influenced by the fact that the defendant was enjoying without payment the benefits of the claimant's research, the Court of Appeal found the use of that factual data to be an infringement of copyright in the form in which it was expressed. The result would, however, have been different if the defendant, having read the claimant's herbicide instructions, conducted its own researches and independently collated identical data; this being so, one wonders whether what masquerades as a noble protection of the claimant's research endeavours is really just a waste of time, effort and money for a would-be commercial rival.

1. Also known as the 'idea/expression dichotomy'.
2. *Independent Television Publications Ltd v Time Out Ltd* [1984] FSR 64. There is now an obligation to supply programme listings to independent publishers for a reasonable fee: Broadcasting Act 1990, s 176 and Sch 17. The Copyright Tribunal has jurisdiction over terms, exercised in *News Group Newspapers Ltd v Independent Television Publications Ltd* [1993] RPC 173.
3. *Elanco Products Ltd v Mandops (Agrochemical Specialists) Ltd* [1979] FSR 46.

13.11 One final note on form and content. A parody is a work which consciously mimics and 'sends up' the form of another work, while its content may be entirely different. Should the fact that the original work and its parody are aimed at different audiences and fulfil different aesthetic functions excuse the parody from being stigmatised as a copyright infringement? At one time it was thought[1] that no infringement was committed if the amount of effort and skill which the parodist expended upon his work was so great that the parody could be regarded as an original work in its own right. This view, which was only *obiter*, was founded upon the misapprehension[2] that a work was either an original work or an infringing one. Since a work can be both original *and* infringing,[3] it is not surprising that, in *Schweppes Ltd v Wellingtons Ltd*,[4] Falconer J held that parody could not of itself affect the question of infringement: either a substantial part of a work was copied or it was not (the substantiality of an infringement is discussed below at para **13.30**). In rejecting a defence of parody in *Williamson Music v Pearson Partnership*,[5] the court took account of the commercial nature of the parody. This pragmatic approach may be contrasted with the position in the United States, where constitutionally based arguments have given the defence of parody a strong position in copyright and other intellectual property litigation.[6] Is the UK approach consistent with Article 10.1 of the European Convention on Human Rights? That principle of freedom of expression entered the UK statute book by way of the Human Rights Act 1998, section 1(1). At the time of writing there were no decisions on copyright in parodies under the Human Rights Act, but in *Ashdown v Telegraph Group Ltd*,[7] the Court of Appeal considered the relationship between Art 10 and the defences[8] available under the Copyright, Designs and Patents Act 1988. The 1988 Act, containing as it does a balance between the rights of copyright owners and those of users,[9] was held to provide the kind of balance between freedom of expression and responsibility envisaged by the Convention for a democratic society. Although there might be rare occasions where the public interest demanded the reproduction of a work,[10] these occasions are unlikely to involve parody.

1. *Joy Music Ltd v Sunday Pictorial Newspapers (1920) Ltd* [1960] 2 QB 60.
2. A misapprehension which still crops up from time to time. See, for example, *Ashmore v Douglas-Home* [1987] FSR 553.
3. See *Warwick Film Productions Ltd v Eisinger* [1969] 1 Ch 508.
4. [1984] FSR 210.
5. [1987] FSR 97.
6. See, for example, R Bernstein 'US Supreme Court Rules on Parody and Fair Use' [1994] Ent LR 95; A Langvardt 'Protected Marks and Protected Speech: Establishing the First Amendment Boundaries in Trademark Parody cases' (1992) 82 TMR 671; E Gredley and S Maniatis 'Parody: A Fatal Attraction?' [1997] EIPR 339 and 412.

7. [2001] EMLR 1003, upholding [2001] EMLR 20.
8. See paras **14.16-14.21**; non-commercial or journalistic parody could constitute fair dealing for the purpose of criticism or review.
9. For examples, see G Johnston 'Copyright and Freedom of the Media: A Modest Proposal' [1996] EIPR 6.
10. *Ashdown v Telegraph Group Ltd*, n 7.

Indirect infringements and 'reverse engineering'

13.12   When one makes a three-dimensional product for commercial use, that product is usually constructed at the end of a chain of closely linked intellectual property developments. For example, if one makes a new type of folding tubular-steel-framed garden chair, it is normal to start out with drawings and sketches which indicate the approximate appearance and proportions of the chair. From those sketches one may make an exploded diagram which indicates how each of the chair's parts relates to the other. Next one may construct a wooden 'mock-up' or model which gives some idea of the appearance and shape of the end product. Moulds or casts will then be prepared, and the separate manufactured components will be assembled into a chair which, in probability, will not in itself be a copyright-protected work. However, a copy of the chair will be an indirect, three-dimensional copy of the sketches and diagrams.

13.13   It is considered desirable, by those who wish to make a copy of another's product, that they should be able to 're-design' or 're-originate' that product. The process by which this re-design is effected is known by the polite and dignified term 'reverse engineering'.[1] In three fascinating cases in recent years the courts held, on the facts, that particular varieties of 'reverse engineering' have constituted copyright infringement through reproduction of the work which it was sought to emulate. While two of the three leave one with the feeling that justice has been done, all three leave one with the distinct impression that the Copyright Act 1956 was forcibly applied to situations which Parliament did not consider when the Act was passed, and that the judges have practised a technique which, politely, we may describe as 'reverse legislation'. Parliament has now struck back by removing the reverse engineering of industrial design from the scope of copyright infringement.[2] The legislature has, however, adopted certain general principles which emerged from the cases.

1.   A term first used in British litigation as recently as *Weir Pumps v CML Pumps* [1984] FSR 33.
2.   Copyright, Designs and Patents Act 1988, s 51. See below at para **14.19**(ix).

13.14   In *House of Spring Gardens v Point Blank*[1] the Irish High Court and Supreme Court had to consider a remarkable attempt to circumvent the concept of reproduction by breaking the chain of causation which normally links an infringing product to its legitimate antecedent. The facts, greatly simplified, were as follows: A made, from copyright drawings, a bullet-proof vest which B wished to copy. B made a careful study of the features of A's vest and passed them on to a barrister, C. C instructed a fashion designer, D, to design a vest which would possess all the features and attributes required by B. D set about this task and came up with a design for a vest which was substantially the same as A's. Could D be said to have copied A's pattern when he had not seen it and when he had exercised his own skill and judgement in fulfilling his client's order?

1.   *House of Spring Gardens Ltd v Point Blank Ltd* [1985] FSR 327, affirming the full legal analysis at first instance, reported at [1983] FSR 213.

13.15   The judges were all agreed that D's design was an infringing copy of A's, because the degree of detail specified by B to C, and thence to D, was such that D's skill and judgement were only exercised in following his instructions; no skill or effort was expended in the act of independent creation, and D was therefore no more than a machine or amanuensis by means of which B's description of A's design could be converted into a reasonable facsimile of it. One cannot quarrel with this result, but it is tempting to speculate as to what might have happened if, say, B had specified twelve out of twenty salient features of A's design and D, who could have exercised his professional judgement so as to create a variety of different designs in accordance with B's specifications, happened to produce an end result which (to B's delight) resembled A's. In any event, Parliament has approved the decision's logic; section 16(3) of the Copyright, Designs and Patents Act 1988 stipulates that it is immaterial (to the issue of indirect infringement) whether any intervening acts themselves infringe. If a trader emulated another's product selection (not infringement of copyright) it is quite likely that the emulators' catalogue would infringe literary copyright in the first trader's catalogue.[1]

1.   Cf *Purefoy Engineering Co Ltd v Sykes Boxall & Co Ltd* (1955) 72 RPC 89.

13.16   In *British Leyland Motor Corpn Ltd v Armstrong*[1] the British courts were faced with a more difficult problem of causation. BL designed an exhaust pipe; the 'design' consisted of a number of drawings of the pipe, which were accompanied by a list of co-ordinate measurements of its various features. Anyone who sought to make a three-dimensional version of any of the illustrations would have found them useless; the co-ordinates, on the other hand, gave the exact scale and dimensions of the exhaust pipe. The defendants manufactured an exhaust pipe which was nearly identical to BL's product, having compiled for their own use, from one of BL's exhaust pipes, a set of co-ordinates of their own (thus 're-originating' BL's literary work). This was an intentional act of copying, but it was not clear whether it was a copyright infringement. This is because, although it is an infringement of an artistic work to make a three-dimensional version of it, it is not an infringement of a literary work to do the same, and it was the literary more than the artistic features of BL's design which had been the subject of the reverse engineering process.

1.   *British Leyland Motor Corpn Ltd v Armstrong Patents Co Ltd* [1986] RPC 279.

13.17   All of the courts, from Whitford J to the House of Lords, agreed that there had been a copyright infringement, and all found it difficult to give a convincing account as to why this should be so. Literary works and artistic works are governed by separate sets of laws with regard to infringement and there is no means by which it can be concluded that, where the same subject matter is both an artistic and a literary work, the separate laws applicable to each suddenly become applicable to the other.

13.18   In *Interlego v Tyco Industries*[1] the Privy Council went some way towards clarifying the dilemma. The literary content of engineering drawings may be taken into account when deciding whether infringing use has been made of a *substantial*[2] part of a copyright *artistic* work. But the presence of literary matter such as dimensions and tolerance does not of itself confer copyright on an unoriginal artistic work. There is no infringement by three-dimensional use of literary information. This squares with the decision in *Brigid Foley v Elliott*[3] where a knitted garment was held to be an execution of a literary work (the knitting pattern) but not a *reproduction*.

1.   [1989] AC 217.
2.   See para **13.30**, below.
3.   [1982] RPC 433.

13.19   The final 'reverse engineering' case under consideration is that of *Plix Products Ltd v Winstone*,[1] a decision of the New Zealand High Court. The claimants manufactured green plastic kiwifruit trays, known as 'plixes', which were so successful as a means of grading and accommodating kiwifruit that the Kiwifruit Marketing Authority made it a requirement that persons packing kiwifruit for export had to use trays of an identical dimension, capacity and weight to the claimants' product. The defendants, who wished to manufacture kiwifruit trays for the export market, obtained from the Kiwifruit Marketing Authority the specifications which had to be met and instructed a consultant to design a tray which complied with them. The resulting tray was held to constitute an infringement of the claimants' artistic copyright in (inter alia) their drawings, models and moulds. The judge regarded the events which led to the defendants' reproduction of the claimants' product as being indicative of a single and unbroken chain of causation, although the Kiwifruit Marketing Authority played a peculiar role of intermediary when it 'translated' the claimants' artistic work into a literary work from which the defendants' artistic work could be constructed. A non-lawyer, looking at this decision, would probably conclude that the defendants were rather hard done by since it was all the fault of the Kiwifruit Marketing Authority. This view is in fact supported by the law, which provides that it is an infringement of copyright for a person to 'authorise' the doing of a restricted act by another if he does not have the authority to do so. This is discussed below in Ch 26.

1.   [1986] FSR 63.

Issuing copies to the public

13.20   Under previous legislation the publication of literary, dramatic, musical or artistic works was restricted by copyright.[1] 'Publication' meant the issue of copies to the public for the first time in the United Kingdom.[2] Once a work had been published, the copyright owner had no control over the circulation of legitimate copies of the work. Section 18(2) of the Copyright, Designs and Patents Act 1988 gives the copyright owner the right to put each and every copy of a work into circulation for the first time. Once a copy has been issued to the public within the European Economic Area,[3] the copyright owner can no longer use the issuing right to control the importation or circulation of those copies within the UK. If the copies are infringing, however, their import or circulation may involve 'secondary infringement' of copyright.[4] Section 18 deals with the launching of products onto the market on a permanent basis. Temporary issue is restricted by rental right and lending right – see para **13.21** and Ch 15 below. The 'issuing right'[5] or distribution right[6] provides an important exception to the principle that the owner of a chattel may dispose of it as he or she pleases. The issuing right applies to every description of copyright work. If the BBC broadcasts a television drama, such as 'Eastenders', many millions of viewers may see and possibly tape the programme. But the owners of copyright in the broadcast and the included dramatic work will still have the right to control the release of commercial videotapes of the programme. Section 18(2)(b) is surprising since it purports to give the owner of UK copyright and issuing right outside the EEA. Some have thought that this provision is firmly contradicted by s 16(1), which states that copyright restricts acts in the United Kingdom and must therefore be the result of a rare error by the Parliamentary draftsman.[7] A more charitable, though less probable, conclusion is that s 16(1) does not rule out the possibility of a copyright owner having the exclusive right to control restricted acts outside the UK but is merely declaratory of the fact that the copyright owner does have that right within the UK.

1. Copyright Act 1956, ss 2(5), (6), 3(5), (6).
2. Ibid, s 48(1) and *Infabrics Ltd v Jaytex Ltd* [1982] AC 1.
3. Copyright, Designs and Patents Act 1988, s 18(2)(a). This is consistent with the principle of free movement of goods: see ch 27. S 18(2) as originally enacted seemed to embrace a principle of 'international exhaustion'. Once a copy had been issued to the public anywhere in the world, its further issue to the UK public could not be prevented.
4. Copyright, Designs and Patents Act 1988, ss 22 and 23; see para 26.9, below.
5. Sterling [1989] 8 EIPR 295 proposes the term 'issuing right'.
6. As it is described in art 9 of Council Directive 92/100/EEC (the rental right directive) which obliges member states to confer such rights upon performers, phonogram and film producers and broadcasting organisations.
7. Section 18 has been amended twice since 1988, by the Copyright (Computer Programs) Regulations 1992 (SI 1992/3233) and the Copyright and Related Rights Regulations 1996 (SI 1996/2967). See, further, Laddie et al *The Modern Law of Copyright* (3rd edn 2000), ch 15.

Rental

13.21   In the case of sound recordings, films and computer programs, the issuing right was initially extended[1] to enable the copyright owner to control the rental[2] of copies commercially or for reward. Although commercial rental of vinyl records was practised to a certain extent,[3] its economic impact was limited by the rapid deterioration of the discs. With the development of compact discs, however, came the possibility of almost limitless copying from a single disc. By 1988 it was estimated that compact discs were available for rental from more than a thousand outlets in the UK.[4] A blank tape levy to provide recompense for copyright owners whose works are copied was mooted and was adopted in some jurisdictions.[5] However, Parliament rejected the tape levy in favour of a rental right, a mechanism also found at the time in other countries.[6] Subsequently, the UK implemented Council Directive 92/100/EEC,[7] providing more comprehensive rental and lending rights in respect of author's works, performances, phonograms and films (but not buildings or works of applied art). 'Rental' means making the original[8] or a copy available to the public on terms that it will or may be returned, for direct or indirect economic or commercial advantage.[9] 'Economic or commercial advantage' would appear to be a polite way of saying 'profit'.[10] Neither 'rental' nor 'lending' includes lending for such activities as performing or exhibiting in public, broadcasting or making a work available for on-the-spot reference.[11] These purposes are either non-infringing, in which case it is legitimate for the work to be hired out or lent, or infringing in their own right, in which case the lender may or may not be liable for authorising the infringement.[12]

1. Copyright, Designs and Patents Act 1988, s 18(2), as originally enacted.
2. At the time, 'rental' was defined in s 178.
3. See, for example, *CBS Inc v Ames* [1982] Ch 91, where the hirer was held not to authorise infringement.
4. Davies [1988] EIPR 127.
5. For example, Australia: Copyright Amendment Act 1989, Part Vc.
6. For example, Denmark: see *Warner Bros Inc v Christiansen*: 158/86 [1988] ECR 2605.
7. Of 19 November 1992 on rental right and lending right and on certain rights related to copyright in the field of intellectual property OJ 1992 L346/61. This Directive, known to wholefood enthusiasts as the 'lental' directive, was implemented by the Copyright and Related Rights Regulations 1996 (SI 1996/ 2967).
8. Copyright, Designs and Patents Act 1988, s 18A(6); for the meaning of 'copies', see s 17 and paras **13.2-13.7**.
9. Copyright, Designs and Patents Act 1988, s 18A(2).
10. Ibid, s 18A(5).
11. Ibid, s 18A(3).
12. See ch 26.

Performing

13.22   It is an infringement of copyright in a literary, dramatic or musical work to perform it in public without the copyright owner's permission.[1] 'Performance' is defined as including:

'(a) delivery, in the case of lectures, addresses, speeches and sermons, and
(b) in general any mode of visual or acoustic presentation including presentation by means of a sound recording, film, broadcast or cable programme ...'[2]

In other words, if I stand on top of a hill with a flag in each hand, and signal in semaphore one of Philip Larkin's poems, I would seem to be performing it.

13.22 *Infringement*

1. Copyright, Designs and Patents Act 1988, s 19(1).
2. Ibid, s 19(2).

13.23 An interesting question which arises from this inclusive definition is whether 'performance' presupposes the existence, or the attention, of an audience, or whether 'presentation' in a public place is sufficient. In deciding questions of infringement by performance under earlier legislation, the courts have regarded the character of the audience as a criterion more important than the size of the audience or the place of performance. In *Duck v Bates*,[1] a free performance at Guy's Hospital for the entertainment of nurses and others connected with the hospital was held not to infringe dramatic copyright. There was not present 'a sufficient part of the public who would go to a licensed performance'. The hospital show was quasi-domestic in character. In *Jennings v Stephens*[2] 'a performance before Women's Institute members in a Northamptonshire village' was held to be 'in public'. The audience could fairly be considered as part of the copyright owners' public. This approach was approved in *Turner Electrical Instruments Ltd v Performing Right Society Ltd*[3] (where the 'public' were workers in a factory). In *Performing Right Society v Harlequin*[4] the playing of a record over loudspeakers in a shop was held to be in public; the music was audible from the street. In *Performing Right Society v Glasgow Rangers Football Club*[5] the playing of music before a football crowd was held to be a performance in public, even though the crowd had gathered to watch a match and not listen to the performance. It seems therefore that *an* appropriate audience is required, but not necessarily their attention. This conclusion is supported by considering the meaning of 'presentation'; if 'presentation' suggests the gerund as an 'act of presenting', then an audience to whom the presentation is made would seem to be implicit. If, on the other hand, 'presentation' really means 'means by which a presentation may be affected', then the performance would seem to be an infringing act whether it is for the benefit of an audience to whom it is presented or not. The first of the two interpretations is, it is submitted, the correct one; since 'delivery' and 'mode of presentation' fulfil similar roles within the definition and since 'delivery' requires a recipient, it should be accepted that a presentation requires an audience. As a postscript to this discussion it should be stated that it is often unwise to examine literally the words of the Parliamentary draftsman and to conclude that Parliament actually intended what it said: for if 'performance' truly included 'any mode of visual... presentation', a man could 'perform' a work by writing it down on a piece of paper. In the 'Music on Hold' case,[6] the Australian courts have considered whether music played to unwitting telephone callers awaiting attention was being transmitted by cable or broadcast to the public by the telecommunications operator, Telstra. In deciding both these questions against Telstra, the courts took the view that 'music on hold' involved dissemination to the public, even though this occurred during large numbers of essentially private calls. The fact that the callers really wanted to speak to someone rather than listen to the music did not prevent their being part of the copyright owners' public.[7]

1. (1884) 13 QBD 843.
2. [1936] Ch 469.
3. [1943] Ch 167. The Performing Right Society (PRS) is established for the collective administration of performing rights in copyright works.
4. [1979] FSR 233.
5. [1975] RPC 626.
6. *Telstra Corpn Ltd v Australian Performing Rights Association Ltd* (1997) 146 ALR 649, Fed Ct.
7. See K Weatherall 'An End to Private Communications in Copyright? The Expansion of Rights to Communicate Works to the Public' [1999] EIPR 342, 398 especially at 401.

13.24 It is not infringement of an artistic work to perform it. This means that one is entitled to dress up (or down) actors and position them on a stage, before an audience, so that they present the collective appearance of the 'Déjeuner sur l'Herbe' or the like.[1] Curiously, if such a 'tableau vivant' constitutes a 'variety act',[2] it may be wrong to film it without the performers' consent.

1. Cf *Hanfstaengl v Empire Palace* [1894] 2 Ch 1.
2. Within the meaning of s 180(2)(d) of the Copyright, Designs and Patents Act 1988. See ch 17 below.

13.25 Where the work is a sound recording, film, broadcast or cable programme, the equivalent activity restricted by copyright is its playing or showing in public.[1] In all cases it is the organiser of the public performance, playing or showing who is liable; section 19(4) exempts performers and those who operate a sound or projection system from liability, for example the disc jockey who is engaged to play recordings of popular music at the behest of the proprietor of premises in which a public performance takes place.

1. Copyright, Designs and Patents Act 1988, s 19(3).

Broadcasting and cabling

13.26 With the exception of published editions of works, every work in which copyright vests is protected against its unauthorised inclusion in a television broadcast or cable programme; any work which has a sound is also protected against unauthorised inclusion in a sound broadcast.[1] It is not, however, an infringement of copyright in a broadcast,[2] or in work contained in it, to include that broadcast in a cable programme which immediately follows the broadcast and which is transmitted for reception in an area in which that broadcast is intended to be received.[3] This may seem like common sense since all that the person who re-transmits broadcasts does is to improve the accessibility of what is already available to all to receive, but copyright owners have deep-rooted objections, both in principle and in international law, to the notion that a cable programme provider can derive pecuniary benefit from a use of copyright-protected material for which he has not paid. This debate may be sterile since, in financial terms, it is unlikely that the copyright owner would receive a greater total revenue if he were allowed to extract royalties for the authorisation of immediate re-transmissions of broadcast works. This is because the total number of intended receivers is the same, whatever the mode of transmission and reception; a recognition of the value of the cable programme's audience would therefore be likely to be equated with a corresponding diminution in the size, and therefore value, of the receiving audience of the broadcast. If, however, the broadcast itself infringes copyright in a work the fact of retransmission by cable may be taken into account in assessing damages.[4] If the retransmission extends beyond the area for which the broadcast is licensed, the copyright owner may claim a royalty, to be settled by the Copyright Tribunal if it cannot be agreed.[5] These arrangements reflect Council Directive 93/83/EEC,[6] which provides for the collective administration of cable retransmission rights.[7]

1. Copyright, Designs and Patents Act 1988, s 20.
2. Ibid, s 73(2); ss 73 and 73A were inserted by the Broadcasting Act 1996, Sch 9, para 1.
3. Ibid, s 73(3).
4. Ibid, s 73(3) proviso.
5. Ibid, ss 74(4) and 73A.
6. Of 27 September 1993 on the coordination of certain rules concerning copyright applicable to satellite broadcasting and cable retransmission.
7. Arts 8-12.

Making an adaptation

13.27 So far as literary, dramatic and musical works[1] (but no others) are concerned, it is an infringement of copyright to make an unauthorised 'adaptation' of it. The word 'adaptation' should not be allowed its colloquial meaning, since it is the subject of a detailed and inclusive definition.[2] It is (i) a translation of the work, (ii) the dramatisation of a non-dramatic work, (iii) the non-dramatisation of a dramatic work, (iv) the rendering of a work into strip-cartoon form, or (v) the arrangement or transcription of a musical work. 'Adaptation' in relation to a computer program or database means an arrangement or altered version or translation of it.[3] The conversion of a computer program from one language to another – whether that language is intelligible to, and discernible by, machine or man – is a 'translation' of the program for the purposes of infringement.[4]

1. Copyright, Designs and Patents Act 1988, s 21(1).
2. Ibid, s 21(3).
3. Computer program: Copyright, Designs and Patents Act 1988, s 21(3)(ab), inserted by the Copyright (Computer Programs) Regulations 1992 (SI 1992/3233); database: Copyright, Designs and Patents Act 1988, s 21(3)(ac), inserted by the Copyright and Rights in Databases Regulations 1997 (SI 1997/3032).
4. Copyright, Designs and Patents Act 1988, s 21(4).

13.28   Three points should be noted with regard to adaptation. First, it is impossible that anything which is an adaptation of a work is not also a substantial reproduction of it; to that extent, the 'adaptation' provisions of the Copyright Act may be viewed as a rather sophisticated form of inclusive definition of reproduction.[1] Second, when one is considering the case of a work other than a computer program, it is necessary to distinguish translation from transliteration: the copying out of a short story in Pitman's short-hand or Gothic script would thus be a reproduction but not an adaptation, as would be the presentation of a popular tune in terms of doh-re-mi rather than traditional notation. Third, the copying, performance and so on of an adaptation infringes copyright in the original work. This is so even where the adaptation has not previously been recorded.[2] Thus a performer who publicly translates the novel *Bonfire of the Vanities* into French outside the London Stock Exchange would infringe copyright in the novel, even though the performance is of an adaptation which has not been recorded.

1. Although insofar as it enables the copyright owner to control treatment of the work, it can be seen as an economic cousin of the moral right of integrity: see para **18.12** below.
2. Copyright, Designs and Patents Act 1988, s 21(2).

Must infringement be intentional?

13.29   While the Copyright, Designs and Patents Act sometimes takes a lenient attitude towards the liability of accidental and non-intentional infringers,[1] an infringing act is no less an infringement, so long as a causal connection exists between the original work and the infringing work, whether the defendant has deliberately set out to pirate the claimant's work or has subconsciously imbibed and then reproduced it.[2] Any other conclusion would make it even more difficult for the copyright owner to protect his invisible estate than it is at present. In principle, since intention to infringe need not be proved, what the claimant must do is to show enough similarity between his work and the alleged infringing work to raise a prima facie case of infringement. Once he has done so, it is for the defendant to explain his work away. This he may do by persuading the court that both works copied a common source, or that the two works were independently composed without reference to each other; or that the claimant in fact copied his work. If the defendant cannot do this, he will be presumed to have infringed the claimant's copyright.[3] To guard against disputes of this nature, many authors try to lay up a store of evidence; poor designers may post copies of drawings in registered packets, which remain sealed. Wealthier creators may post copies to their solicitors, who can record and store upon arrival.

1. See eg the requirement of knowledge for 'secondary' infringement and criminal offences – ss 22-26 and 107 – and the 'innocence' defence to a claim to damages – s 97(1). On the role of intention in copyright more generally, see Y Gendreau, 'Intention and Copyright Law' in Pollaud-Dullian, ed, *The Internet and Author's Rights* (1999) Vol 5 Perspectives on Intellectual Property, p 3.
2. *Francis, Day and Hunter Ltd v Bron* [1963] Ch 587.
3. *Corelli v Gray* (1913) 29 TLR 570.

Complete and partial infringements

13.30 The law of trespass to property is clear in its assertion that you need only put one unlicensed foot on your neighbour's property in order to be considered a trespasser upon it; it would be absurd to regard a person as a trespasser only if he had tramped all over it. Similarly, in copyright, it is not necessary for a person to copy, perform, broadcast or do any other restricted act to the whole of a protected work before he is considered to have infringed it: he need only trespass upon a 'substantial part' of it.[1] It goes almost without saying that a term such as 'substantial part' is difficult to define in theory or identify in practice. Perhaps the following rules of thumb will assist: (i) a large proportion of a work will almost certainly be regarded as a 'substantial part' of it[2] (for example the first 300 pages of a 600 page telephone directory); (ii) a small proportion of a work will be a 'substantial part' if it possesses any commercial value;[3] (iii) even a tiny proportion of a work may well be a 'substantial part' if it possesses key features by which the whole is identified or recognised[4] (for example the first four notes of Beethoven's Fifth Symphony, or the words 'Twas Brillig, and the Slithy Toves/Did Gyre and Gimble in the Wabes' from Lewis Carroll's story *Through the Looking-Glass*). It must, however, be stressed that the question whether a part of a work is a 'substantial part' is inherently subjective, and does not therefore lend itself to consistent resolution. An example of this can be seen in the reversals in *Designers Guild Ltd v Russell Williams (Textiles) Ltd (No 2)*[5] as between High Court, Court of Appeal and House of Lords. The House of Lords stressed the importance of separating out the questions of proof of copying (evidenced by similarities between claimant's and defendant's works) and of substantiality (comparing what has been taken with the totality of the claimant's work).

1. Copyright, Designs and Patents Act 1988, s 16(3)(a).
2. For an actual instance of the application of principles of proportionality see *Sillitoe v McGraw-Hill* [1983] FSR 545.
3. Thus 'what is worth copying is prima facie worth protecting', per Peterson J in *University of London Press v University Tutorial Press* [1916] 2 Ch 601 at 610. In *Express Newspapers plc v Liverpool Daily Post and Echo plc* [1985] FSR 306 Whitford J found that one seven-hundredth of a literary work was a 'substantial part' of it.
4. See eg *Spelling Goldberg Productions Inc v BPC Publishing Ltd* [1981] RPC 283.
5. [1998] FSR 803, HCt; revsd [2000] FSR 121, CA; revsd [2001] FSR 113, HL.

Chapter 14

Subsistence, protection and erosion of copyright

The copyright term – a summary

Duration: literary, dramatic, musical and artistic works

14.1   The life of a work or other subject matter protected by
copyright will frequently be nasty and brutish, but rarely short.
Formerly, literary, dramatic, musical works and engravings which
were unpublished on their author's death could enjoy copyright
protection in perpetuity but fell into the public domain at the end of
fifty years from the end of the year in which they were first
posthumously published, publicly performed, sold in the form of
records, broadcast or included in a cable programme.[1] The author
and his assignee were unlikely to derive much commercial benefit
from this potentially perpetual protection; perpetual copyright has
now been abolished by the Copyright, Designs and Patents Act 1988.[2]
For those works which remained unpublished on the commencement
of the 1988 Act, copyright will expire at midnight on 31 December
2039.[3] If the work is published for the first time after expiry of
copyright, Council Directive 93/98/EEC[4] confers upon the lawful
publisher rights 'equivalent to the economic rights of the author'
for a further period of 25 years.

1.   Copyright Act 1956, ss 2(3), 3(4)(a). J Griffiths 'Copyright in English
     Literature: Denying the Public Domain' [2000] EIPR 150.
2.   Copyright, Designs and Patents Act 1988, s 12(2).
3.   Ibid, Sch 1, para 12(4). For extension of the term of copyright generally, see
     para **14.2**.
4.   Of 29 October 1993 harmonising the term of protection of copyright and
     related rights OJ 1993 L290/9. See para **27.8**.

14.2   The UK copyright term for literary, dramatic, musical and
artistic works is now the same whether they are made available to
the public in the author's lifetime or not. The 1988 Act provided
that such works would fall into the public domain at the end of the
fiftieth year from the end of the calendar year of the author's death.[1]

Even this period may be regarded as over-generous, given that so small a proportion of protected works have any commercial value or cultural utility even fifteen or twenty years after their creation.[2] However, in order to harmonise copyright terms across the European single market, and noting that authors' heirs live longer these days, Council Directive 93/98/EEC[3] has increased the term to 70 years from the author's death. This affected any work still in copyright anywhere in the European Union on the implementation date, 1 July 1995. This extension of term applies to works of EEA origin or authorship. For other works the Directive and Regulations introduced what is known as 'comparison of term' – a work will be entitled to the full UK term of 70 years from the author's death only if it is protected for at least as long in its country of origin.[4] If that country protects for a lesser term, the lesser term will apply in the UK.[5] There are special provisions for anonymous or pseudonymous works.[6] The extension of term meant that copyright in some existing works was extended or even revived. This caused a degree of consternation among users.[7] The 1995 Regulations make provision for ownership and exercise of extended and revived copyright.[8] In particular, notice may be given to the owner of revived copyright as to a proposed use. If notice is given, the use is treated as licensed. The Copyright Tribunal may be asked to set a reasonable royalty if that cannot be agreed.

1. Copyright, Designs and Patents Act 1988, s 12(1). Where there are joint authors, the last to die sets the copyright term: s 12(4).
2. Cf the relatively small proportion of registered designs (c 15%) and patents (c 8.5%) renewed into their final periods. For an interesting discussion of the copyright term see K Puri [1990] 1 EIPR 12. Note the special term of Crown copyright – the lesser of 50 years from publication or 125 years from creation; likewise special terms of copyright apply to Parliamentary copyright, that in Acts and Measures and the copyright of international organisations: Copyright, Designs and Patents Act 1988 ss 163-168.
3. See para **14.1** at n 4; implemented by the Duration of Copyright and Rights in Performances Regulations 1995 (SI 1995/3297). J Adams and M Edenborough 'The Duration of Copyright in the United Kingdom after the 1995 Regulations' [1996] EIPR 590 give a helpful table at pp 595-596. See also A Robinson 'The Life and Terms of UK Copyright in Original Works' [1997] Ent LR 60.
4. Defined in Copyright, Designs and Patents Act 1988, s 15A.
5. Copyright, Designs and Patents Act 1988, s 12(6). This does not shorten existing copyrights, however.
6. Copyright, Designs and Patents Act 1988, s 12(3)-(5).
7. Eg P Parrinder 'The Dead Hand of European Copyright' [1993] EIPR 391.
8. Duration of Copyright and Rights in Performances Regulations 1995 (SI 1995/3297), regs 17-26. B Lindner 'Revival of Rights and Protection of Acquired Rights' [2000] EIPR 133.

Duration: other works

14.3   Other works are protected for the following durations (in years to end-year):

Type of medium	Unpublished	Published/disseminated
Sound recordings	50 years from making	50 years from release[1]
Cinematograph films	70 years from the last to die of: principal director, author of screen-play, author of dialogue, composer of specially created music used in the film[2]	
Broadcasts ⎫ Cable programmes ⎬ Repeat broadcasts & cable programmes	Not applicable	⎧ 50 years ⎨ 50 years[3] 50 years from original broadcast/inclusion[4]
Published editions		25 years[5]

1. Copyright, Designs and Patents Act 1988, s 13A. 'Release' means that the work is published, broadcast, cabled, or played in public: s 13A(3). Again, 'comparison of term' applies, subject to the UK's international obligations: s 13A(4) and (5).
2. Copyright, Designs and Patents Act 1988, s 13B, again, subject to 'comparison of term' and special provisions for anonymous films.
3. Copyright, Designs and Patents Act 1988, s 14(1)-(4), including 'comparison of term'.
4. Copyright, Designs and Patents Act 1988, s 14(5)-(6). It is not clear whether an encrypted broadcast can be given a new lease of life by being broadcast in unencrypted form or whether the latter is just a 'repeat'.
5. Copyright, Designs and Patents Act 1988, s 15.

14.4   It has been argued by some[1] that the value of copyright-protected works is such that they should not cease, on the expiry of the copyright term, to possess a fiscal dimension. If they fall into the public domain, should they not be held in trust, as it were, for the benefit of the public? On this basis it would still be necessary for users to pay for the exploitation of works which fall into the public domain, but the revenue so derived would be channelled into the public purse for the purpose of encouraging young authors with prizes, keeping old authors from starvation, financing the publication of commercially unattractive works, and so on. A number of countries have adopted laws on a 'paying public domain'[2] (usually known as the *domaine publique payant*). While on the subject, the reader may wish to consider two points of no legal consequence at all, being matters which instead reflect upon the human psyche. The first is that *domaine publique payant* is one of a number of instances of the English giving French names to rights which do not exist, or are persistently ignored, under English law.[3] The second is that to talk of works 'falling' into the public domain[4] is to employ vocabulary which suggests that, somehow, private ownership of monopoly rights is a more elevated value than that of the public's free access to educational and informational sources. If we were to talk instead of works 'ascending' into the public domain, we might provoke more thought about it, even if we cannot raise the general level of the great debate between owners and consumers of copyright works.

1. On the *domaine publique payant* see eg D Lipszyc 'Intellectual Works in the Public Domain' [1983] EIPR 100; cf A Barr-Smith 'Domaine Publique Payant' (1983) 1 International Media Law 38.
2. See D Lipszyc, n 1 above, at p 101; A Dietz, 'Term of Protection in Copyright Law and Paying Public Domain: A New German Initiative' [2000] EIPR 506.
3. Eg *droit de repentir, droit de suite*: see para **18.2**.
4. On the public domain as an endangered resource, see J Phillips, 'The Diminishing Domain' [1996] EIPR 429.

Sudden death of copyright

14.5   In theory, copyright protection may disappear at a stroke if a work is adjudged to be obscene, at any rate if a two-hundred year accretion of authorities is not to be entirely disregarded.[1] The high water-mark of this doctrine was reached in 1916 in *Glyn v Weston Feature Films*,[2] where Elinor Glyn's novel, *Three Weeks*, was adjudged to be deprived of copyright protection on the ground that it condoned and encouraged adultery and was apt to lead chaste young maidens astray. Times, however, change. When *Three Weeks* was televised in 1977[3] the British viewing public watched it without a single recorded adverse reaction, which no doubt indicates that, over the intervening 62 years, the typical viewer would have found adultery a preferable activity to moral censure. The principle that an iniquitous work may not enjoy copyright (or at least that copyright will not be enforced) was recently referred to in litigation concerning *Spycatcher*,[4] a book written by a former member of MI6, the British Secret Service.

1. For a detailed legal analysis see J Phillips 'Copyright in Obscene Works: some British and American Problems' (1978) 6 Anglo-Am LR 138.
2. [1916] 1 Ch 261; see also para **10.12**.
3. *Three Weeks* was televised on 9 March 1977 as part of Thames Television's Romance series.
4. *A-G v Observer Ltd* [1990] 1 AC 109.

14.6   The Copyright, Designs and Patents Act 1988 at sections 11 and 91, like its predecessors, is silent as to the impact of obscenity upon the vesting of property, which leaves one open to conclude that, in juridical terms, copyright does vest in obscene works but the courts will not permit their procedures and remedies to be used for the purpose of enforcing proprietary rights in that which is immoral.[1] This seems to be the preferable view of the authorities, including *Spycatcher.* The House of Lords' opinions in *Spycatcher* were delivered while the 1988 Act was completing its journey through Parliament; it received the Royal Assent on 15 November 1988. Section 171(3) states 'Nothing in this Part[2] affects any rule of law preventing or restricting the enforcement of copyright, on grounds of public interest or otherwise'. If this view is correct, one senses the employment of double standards by the judiciary. The court which is prepared to reject a copyright claim made with respect to a book condoning adultery is the same court which grants a proprietary interest in a domestic home to a partner in such a relationship;[3] and it seems difficult to maintain with conviction that literature which described various sexual activities should be deprived of its copyright status as property while physical aids to sexual gratification should be items of personal property just as if they were book-cases or desk-lamps.[4] In all events, it may well be that the judges of today are less eager to protect public morality than they were in Edwardian times. While Younger J did not wait to be asked but acted *suo motu* in decopyrighting *Three Weeks*, Peter Gibson J in *Ekland v Scripglow*[5] made no effort to raise the status of the subject matter before him and certainly the law report leaves the reader in no doubt that the film, 'Electric Blue', was something other than a documentary account of a lively address given at the Conservative Party Conference. In *Stephens v Avery*,[6] a case involving disclosure of personal secrets, the Vice-Chancellor said:

> 'If it is right that there is now no generally accepted code of sexual morality applying to this case, it would be quite wrong in my judgment for any judge to apply his own personal moral views, however strongly held, in deciding the legal rights of the parties. The court's function is to apply the law, not personal prejudice. Only in a case where there is still a generally accepted moral code can the court refuse to enforce rights in such a way as to offend that generally accepted code.'

1.   See *Stockdale v Onwhyn* (1826) 5 B & C 173. The same may apply to libellous and seditious works: see *Walcot v Walker* (1802) 7 Ves 1; *Hime v Dale* (1803) 2 Camp 27n.
2.   The part dealing with copyright.
3.   Eg *Backhouse v Backhouse* [1978] 1 WLR 243.

4. *Conegate Ltd v Customs and Excise Comrs:* 121/85 [1987] QB 254.
5. [1982] FSR 431.
6. [1988] 2 All ER 477 at 480-481.

Remedies for infringement

14.7 The length of a copyright term is only a matter of concern to the proprietor of the copyright if the copyright is capable of conferring some description of benefit upon him. What benefit, then, can copyright confer upon the proprietor with regard to the activities of an actual or potential infringer? In brief, the proprietor – and the holder of an exclusive licence to exploit a work in a particular manner[1] – can stop an actual infringement being repeated, prevent a potential infringement from occurring, secure damages to compensate him for the commercial and other damage inflicted upon him, get an 'account of profits' and claim the possession of certain infringing copies and devices used for making them; he can also seek a declaration that an infringement has occurred. All of those remedies are available under civil law. Additionally, the copyright owner may call in the police and have the infringer prosecuted;[2] once criminal process has commenced, the court may order[3] that infringing copies be delivered up to the copyright owner or some other person (usually a solicitor). Alternatively, in sentencing a person convicted of infringing copyright, the court may make an order for compensation.[4] If all else fails, the copyright owner can grab infringing goods which are exposed for sale and walk off with them, although this remedy is strictly limited in its scope.[5] This chapter will discuss some aspects of these remedies.

1. Copyright, Designs and Patents Act 1988, s 101.
2. Copyright, Designs and Patents Act 1988, s 107. Ss 296 and 297A discourage the fraudulent receipt of transmissions and the supply of unauthorised decoders by making these activities criminal offences. S 297A was revised in accordance with Directive 98/84/EC on the legal provision of services based on, or consisting of, conditional access, [1998] OJ L320/54.
3. Copyright, Designs and Patents Act 1988, s 108.
4. Powers of Criminal Courts Act 1973, s 35. The court may also award costs against the person convicted.
5. Copyright, Designs and Patents Act 1988, s 100.

14.8 Most of these remedies are available in civil proceedings, which have been subject in England and Wales to the so-called 'Woolf' reforms (named after their judicial progenitor, Lord Woolf). New Civil Procedure Rules are designed to achieve the 'overriding objective' of dealing with cases justly, that is to say, fairly, in a manner proportionate to the case but as expeditiously and cheaply as possible.[1] Litigation is to be regarded as a last resort. To this end, 'pre-action protocols' are being devised. Consultation on draft protocols for intellectual property[2] was starting as this edition went to press. The Woolf reforms also introduced allegedly 'public-friendly' changes in terminology, such as calling 'plaintiffs' , 'claimants' and so forth.[3] In this chapter we attempt to use terminology current in England and Wales; Scotland has rather different procedural terminology.

1. J Lambert, 'IP Litigation after Woolf' [1999] EIPR 427.
2. Currently available for inspection on www.richardsbutler.com.
3. This change, supposedly introduced for the benefit of the public, has baffled most laymen who, reared on a diet of American TV court dramas, wonder what the problem was with 'plaintiff'.

Some international aspects of copyright litigation

14.9 In civil cases (but not criminal) it may be possible to sue for copyright infringements committed in other European countries. This is not because the 1988 Act extends overseas, nor because there is such a thing as 'European copyright'. It is because the Brussels and Lugano Conventions on Civil Jurisdiction and Judgments[1] give jurisdiction over defendants domiciled in this country, in respect of activities elsewhere in Europe.[2] In *Pearce v Ove Arup Partnership Ltd*[3] the claimant was allowed to pursue his case in England in respect of alleged infringements of architectural copyright by construction of a building in the Netherlands. Consideration is being given in several forums to an international convention governing jurisdiction in intellectual property cases.[4] In disputes with an international dimension, arbitration may be an attractive alternative to litigation: the World Intellectual Property Organization offers an arbitration service.[5] In the case of 'hosting' of copyright material by Internet service providers, the European Commission is funding a pilot 'notice and take-down' procedure[6] whereby rights owners can submit requests to a neutral body, Rightswatch.[7] If that body considers a request well-founded, it will ask the ISP which is holding the material on-line to take it down.

1. Discussed in relation to patents in para **9.20**. For all Member States except for Denmark, the Brussels Convention will be replaced by Council Regulation (EC) No 44/2001 which enters into force on 1 March 2002, OJ [2000] L12/1 of 16 January 2001. See para **14.17**
2. E Jooris 'Infringement of Foreign Copyright and the Jurisdiction of English Courts' [1996] EIPR 127. Other bases for jurisdiction include interim measures and proceedings against multiple parties. The Civil Jurisdiction and Judgments Act 1992 implements these and also governs jurisdiction as between the various parts of the United Kingdom.
3. [1999] FSR 525, CA.
4. For jurisdictional problems, see, eg PE Geller 'International Intellectual Property, Conflicts of Laws and Internet Remedies' [2000] EIPR 121. For

the question as to which law should be applied, especially to Internet uses, see S Plenter 'Choice of Law Rules for Copyright Infingements in the Global Information Infrastructure: a Never-ending Story? [2001] EIPR 313.
5. P Nutzi 'Intellectual Property Arbitration' [1997] EIPR 192.
6. In anticipation of implementation of Directive of 22 June 2001 on Copyright and related rights in the information society. Initially the project will cover music rights only.
7. Info@rightswatch.com offers further information by e-mail.

The injunction or restraining order

14.10 An injunction is a court order, directed at a named person or group of persons, which demands that a particular course of action be undone (if completed), be stopped (if incomplete), or that it should not be started. The phrase 'restraining order' describes the last two kinds of order, which are far more common than mandatory injunctions. Copyright injunctions obey much the same rules as injunctions granted under all other areas of law, and are not discussed in detail here.[1] In procedural terms it is worth noting that the 'interim' or 'interlocutory' injunction, which prohibits a particular use of copyright material on a temporary basis until such time as a full trial may be heard, is that which is most frequently the subject of litigation. Since a person who is stopped from using someone else's copyright work for maybe two or three years, pending the full trial, will usually lose interest in that work and find something else to perform or copy, the trial of the interlocutory motion is sometimes treated by the parties (and by the court) as if it were the trial of the full action. Other interim orders include the 'freezing' order, to retain assets within the jurisdiction and keep them available to satisfy an order for damages, and the 'search and seize' order, designed to preserve vulnerable evidence. Occasionally, the copyright owner may need the help of the court in identifying an infringer. In *Coca Cola Co v British Telecommunications plc*,[2] the claimant had evidence that the infringer was using a particular mobile telephone number, but did not know whose number it was. The court ordered BT to disclose the identity of the subscriber. The award of an injunction, whether interim or final (permanent) is discretionary. The court may decline to make the order where damages are an adequate remedy for the claimant. This has long been recognised for interim injunctions. Recently, however, the courts have refused final injunctions on the grounds that equitable damages in lieu would be appropriate.[3]

1. For a good account of copyright remedies, see H Laddie, P Prescott, M Vitoria, A Speck and L Lane *The Modern Law of Copyright and Designs* (3rd edn, 2000), ch 39.

2. [1999] FSR 518.
3. Eg *Ludlow Music v Williams* [2001] FSR 271; G Harbottle 'Permanent Injunctions in Copyright Cases' [2001] EIPR 154; J Phillips 'The Risk that Rewards: Copyright Infringement Today' [2001] Ent LR 103.

Damages

14.11   A person who is held liable for copyright infringement can expect to face the consequences by being made to pay a sum of money in reparation for the harm which he has inflicted upon the economic interests of the copyright holder. Like any other damages for civil wrong, copyright infringement damages are calculated by reference to the amount of money which, so far as money can, puts the victim in the position he would have been in, had the copyright not been infringed.[1] Where the copyright owner has lost sales and therefore profits to the infringer, the infringer must make good those losses.[2] Where little or trivial damage has been inflicted, the award of damages is said to be 'nominal' which, many people forget, means 'damages in name only'. In copyright circles an award of £100 has been said to have been 'nominal',[3] although a sum of such magnitude could, at the time of writing, have purchased 250 chocolate bars from a standard automatic vending machine or enough postage stamps to finance the second class delivery of 500 Christmas cards. Where the infringed copyright has been licensed to other users, the quantum of damages will usually be calculated by reference to what would have been a reasonable licence fee.[4]

1. *Fenning Film Service Ltd v Wolverhampton, Walsall and District Cinemas Ltd* [1914] 3 KB 1171 at 1174.
2. G Moss and D Rogers 'Damages for Loss of Profits in Intellectual Property Litigation' [1997] EIPR 425, commenting on *Gerber Garment Technology Systems Inc v Lectra Systems* [1997] RPC 443, CA (a patent case).
3. *Infabrics Ltd v Jaytex Ltd* [1985] FSR 75, noted in (1985) JBL 244.
4. *Performing Right Society Ltd v Bradford Corpn* (1921) Macg Cop Cas (1917-23) 309.

14.12   Sometimes the amount of commercial damage caused by a copyright infringement may be small compared with the damage caused to the copyright owner's feelings. This may happen, for example, in the case of a person who, without authorisation, publicly reads out extracts of a particularly subversive essay penned by a respectable pillar of society during the days of his rebellious studenthood. The Copyright, Designs and Patents Act 1988, section 97(2), provides that the claimant can recover damages in excess of normal compensatory damages if the court can be satisfied that justice requires it,

'... having regard ... to ... (a) the flagrancy of the infringement, and (b) any benefit accruing to the defendant by reason of the infringement...'

These extra damages are often now known as 'additional' damages.[1] Such damages were awarded to the owner of copyright in design drawings for a racing car in *Nichols Advanced Vehicle Systems Inc v Rees*[2] and for infringement of architectural copyright in *Cala Homes (South) Ltd v Alfred McAlpine Homes East Ltd (No 2)*.[3] A former precondition for additional damages, that effective relief was otherwise unavailable,[4] was omitted from section 97(2). 'Additional' has been interpreted as meaning in addition to normal damages,[5] so that an award under section 97(2) cannot be combined with an account of profits.[6]

1. C Michalos 'Copyright and Punishment: the Nature of Additional Damages' [2000] EIPR 470.
2. [1979] RPC 127.
3. [1996] FSR 36.
4. Copyright Act 1956, s 17(3).
5. *Cala Homes*, n 3.
6. *Redrow Homes v Betts Bros* [1998] RPC 793; K Campbell 'Additional Damages for Breach of Copyright: The Approaches of Scotland and England Compared' [1997] EIPR 522.

Account of profits

14.13   Where an infringement has caused the claimant little loss but has greatly benefited the defendant, an award of compensatory damages would be small. This would make it worthwhile for a defendant to adopt a deliberate commercial policy of infringement, setting aside as a business expense the proportion of his profit which must be devoted to the payment of damages. In order to remove the attractiveness of this option, the law offers the injured claimant the chance of claiming as his own the profits made by the defendant: this is known as an 'account of profits'.[1] In *Potton v Yorkclose*,[2] the court noted that an account was given to prevent the unjust enrichment of the defendant, insofar as attributable to infringement. A typical scenario for an 'account of profits' would be that of the claimant who manufactures, at full industrial capacity, 10,000 garden gnomes to a sculpture in which he owns copyright, and sells them in a market which demands the supply of 50,000 such gnomes in a year. The infringing defendant has made a huge profit on the sale of 40,000 illicit gnomes, but he has not caused the claimant any real loss since the claimant could not have sold any more gnomes if he tried. It is true that the claimant has lost the potential licence revenue on 40,000 gnomes, but this loss may be small in relation to the profitability of gnomes. The pricing of an infringing gnome at £10 might be as follows:

Manufacturer's profit	£3
Distribution cost	£1
Advertising cost	£1
Manufacturing cost	£3
Raw materials cost	£2

If the reasonable royalty attributable as a rate for calculating damages is even as high as 10% of the retail price, the copyright owner would enjoy £1 on the sale of each gnome as against the £2 worth of transactional profit retained by the infringer. In such a case, the claimant would far rather seek an account of the defendant's profits than sue for damages.[3]

1. On the relation of account of profits to damages see *Caxton Publishing Co Ltd v Sutherland Publishing Co Ltd* [1939] AC 178.
2. [1990] FSR 11.
3. For the functions and measure of the account of profits and its problematic elements, see L Bently 'Accounting for Profits Gained by Infringement of Copyright: When does it End?' [1991] EIPR 5.

14.14   An account of profits is often extremely difficult and expensive to prepare, given that it is hard even in factually simple cases to establish what proportion of the defendant's profit is derived from the copyright infringement in contrast with profits which he would have made anyway.[1] This difficulty has major tactical consequences: a claimant who is prepared to subject the defendant to the expense and inconvenience of an account may be better able to settle his action out of court, on favourable terms, than the claimant who only seeks an award of damages. To keep his options open, the claimant will normally seek an account of profits and an inquiry as to damages as alternatives. He will then have to make an election if successful at trial. At that stage he may ask for information on which to base his choice.[2]

1. See *My Kinda Town Ltd v Soll* [1982] FSR 147 and *Colbeam Palmer v Stock Affiliates* [1972] RPC 303.
2. *Island Records Ltd v Tring International plc* [1995] 3 All ER 444, [1995] FSR 560, [1996] 1 WLR 1256.

Delivery up

14.15   As part of its Equitable jurisdiction, the court may order delivery up of infringing material, either as an interim measure (the claimant's solicitor will normally give an undertaking to keep the material safe pending trial) or at final judgment (in which case delivery up for destruction may be made). This spares a defendant the temptation to use or dispose of the material, in breach of injunction, and keeps the material off the market, thereby preventing prejudice to the claimant's economic position. There is now also a discretionary, statutory, remedy of delivery up, provided by section 99 of the 1988 Act, and a right of seizure of infringing goods from persons who have no fixed place of business.[1]

1. Copyright, Designs and Patents Act 1988, s 100 and see *EMI Records Ltd v Kudhail* [1985] FSR 36; D Barron 'Roving *Anton Piller* Orders' [1996] EIPR 183.

Defences

14.16 Just as copyright in respect of each work or subject matter is a bundle of 'restricted acts', each of which has its own characteristics and foibles, so too is the law of defences to infringement a bundle of sticks of unequal length with which to beat the lawful proprietor. The defences are provided by specifying a number of 'permitted acts' – acts which are permitted notwithstanding the presence of copyright. They may be seen as serving one or more of four laudable objectives, each of which is discussed below: public administration, the advancement of education, the protection of the public's right to be informed and the fixing of limits beyond which it is unreasonable to assert a proprietary right in one's own or another's work.[1] Viewed less charitably, the same defences may be described as achieving the following results: impoverishing authors, frustrating copyright owners, appeasing parasites and enriching lawyers.

1. F W Grosheide 'Copyright from a User's Perspective: Access Rights for Users' [2001] EIPR 321 argues that the traditional balance between copyright owners and users may have to give way to something different and more suited to our digital age.

Exceptions and limitations under the 'Copyright' and 'e-commerce' Directives

14.17 The paragraphs which follow outline the 'permitted acts' in force at the time of writing. However, by the end of 2002, the UK must implement EC Directive 2001/29 on copyright and related rights in the information society.[1] Art 5 of the Directive comprises a closed, but non-mandatory, list of exceptions and limitations to copyright. The directive as a whole and Art 5 in particular have attracted criticism,[2]

205

not least because Art 5 will not significantly advance the cause of harmonisation.[3] In formulating exceptions to copyright, the EC and its Member States are bound by international treaties – the Berne Convention and the WTO agreement.[4] Exceptions and limitations must conform to the so-called 'three-step test' of the Berne Convention: the exception (i) must apply only to certain special cases, (ii) must not conflict with the normal exploitation of the work nor (iii) unreasonably prejudice the legitimate interests of the author. [5] In addition to the Copyright Directive, the UK must implement Directive 2000/31 on legal aspects of electronic commerce[6] by 17 January 2002. Arts 12-14 of the 'e-commerce' directive exempt Internet service providers from liability for certain acts of transmission and temporary reproduction of copyright material.[7]

1. Of 22 June 2001, [2001] OJ L167/10; M Doherty and I Griffiths 'Harmonising European Copyright Law for the Digital Age' [2000] EIPR 17.
2. Eg T Vinje 'Should We Be Digging Copyright's Grave?' [2000] EIPR 551; B Hugenholtz 'Why the Copyright Directive is Unimportant and Possibly Invalid' [2000] EIPR 499; T Hackett 'European Directive Compromise' (2001) 103(4) Library Association Record 191.
3. It will, however, enable EU Member States to accede to the WIPO Copyright Treaty of 1996; see ch 28.
4. See ch 28. S Ricketson, 'The Boundaries of Copyright: Its Proper Limitations and Exceptions: International Conventions and Treaties' [1999] Idea 56.
5. T Heide 'The Berne Three-step Test and the Proposed Copyright Directive' [1999] EIPR 105.
6. [2000] OJ L178/1.
7. For an analysis of the ways in which Internet service providers hold and transmit works, see B Hugenholtz 'Caching and Copyright: The Right of Temporary Copying' [2000] EIPR 482.

Public administration

14.18 Six sections appear under this heading in the Copyright, Designs and Patents Act 1988; at least three of them might also be justified as serving one of the other objectives.

(i) It is a defence to an action for infringement of copyright in any work to show that the allegedly infringing act was done for the purposes of Parliamentary or judicial proceedings or for the purposes of a report on those proceedings.[1] An equivalent defence applies to Royal Commissions and statutory enquiries.[2] However, for the purposes of reporting, it is not permitted to make free with another published report;[3] that is consistent with the *Walter v Lane* principle discussed in para **11.10** above.

(ii) Factual material open to public inspection or on an official register may be copied and used for certain purposes.[4]

(iii) Where unpublished literary, dramatic, musical or artistic works are communicated to the Crown with their copyright owners' permission, the Crown may copy and publish the material in connection with the purposes for which it was communicated.[5]
(iv) Acts specifically authorised by statute may be performed without infringement unless otherwise provided in the statute concerned.[6]

The thrust of all these exceptions is that private copyright material may be used for public purposes. The Copyright Designs and Patents Act is rather less forthcoming as to whether copyright material which has been generated by or on behalf of *public* bodies may be used for other public, or private, purposes.[7] This is more the province of the Freedom of Information Act 2000.[8]

1. Copyright, Designs and Patents Act 1988, s 45; *A v B* [2001] EMLR 1007 (copying of two pages of a personal diary for use in judicial proceedings for divorce).
2. Copyright, Designs and Patents Act 1988, s 46.
3. Ibid, s 46(2).
4. Ibid, ss 47 and 49.
5. Ibid, s 48.
6. Ibid, s 50.
7. J Griffiths 'Copyright Law and Censorship – the Impact of the Human Rights Act 1998' in E Barendt and A Firth (eds) *Yearbook of Copyright and Media Law 1999*, p 3.
8. 2000 c 36.

The advancement of education

14.19 A number of defences relate directly or indirectly to this end. Each is described briefly below.

(i) A 'fair dealing' with a literary, dramatic, musical or artistic work for the purposes of research or private study is allowed.[1] Likewise fair dealing with the typographical arrangement of a published edition for these purposes does not infringe.[2] No legal definition or authoritative explanation of 'fair dealing' for this purpose yet exists; since 'fair' is a word which the legislature selected with great care when it sought a formula which could establish a general principle without seeking to legislate for every conceivable situation in which a restricted act would be tolerated by the law, it may be best left undefined. However, in 1965 the Publishers' Association and the Society of Authors published guidelines as to the level of copying which they would not consider unfair.[3] The advent of cheap reprography resulted in the withdrawal, in 1985, of these guidelines and to the establishment of blanket licensing by the Copyright Licensing Agency Ltd.[4]

The Guidelines were subsequently reissued[5] in collaboration with the Writers' Guild. Photocopying by a reader for her/his own use will be regarded as fair if it comprises copying up to a maximum of a complete chapter in a book, or a maximum otherwise of 5% of a literary work or a short story or poem of up to ten pages. Some points to note: (a) there may be circumstances in which it is 'fair dealing' to make a copy of a larger proportion of a work, if it is for the purpose of research and private study; (b) it is generally agreed that a person who makes more than one copy of the same work cannot rely on the defence unless, which is unlikely, he needs more than one copy for the stated purpose; (c) no corresponding provision permits 'fair dealing' with other works, although it has been suggested that, even apart from the statute, a 'fair dealing' defence may still exist at common law;[6] (d) conduct which seriously undermines the proper exploitation of a copyright work is unlikely to be fair.[7]

(ii) The inclusion of a short passage from a published literary or dramatic work in a collection intended for use in schools (and other educational establishments specified by the Secretary of State[8]) is allowed if the collection consists mainly of non-copyright work and a number of other statutory conditions are satisfied. The most important of these conditions is that the excerpted work should not have been intended for use in educational establishments.

(iii) Educational establishments may make reprographic copies of up to 1% per calendar quarter of any published literary, dramatic or musical works without infringing copyright in the works or the typographical arrangements. If licences are known to be available, this provision ceases to apply.[9]

(iv) A library may make or supply a copy of an article published in a periodical for the benefit of a person who requires it for the purposes of research and private study, so long as various other statutory and regulatory conditions are fulfilled.[10] A similar provision permits the copying, or the supply of a copy, of a reasonable proportion of any other published literary, dramatic or musical work.[11] There are restrictions on librarians making multiple copies.[12] Librarians may supply copies to other libraries[13] and make copies to preserve or replace rare items which are damaged or lost.[14]

(v) A person who reproduces an unpublished work for the purposes of research or private study does not infringe the copyright in it, where the author has been dead for more than fifty years and more than one hundred years has elapsed since it was made, so long as the work in question lives in a museum, library or other publicly-accessible depository.[15] Archive works created on or after 1 August 1989 may be copied in more restricted circumstances.[16]

(vi) The fact that a work has been reproduced (a) in the course of instruction (or preparation for instruction) by instructor or student but not by means of a 'reprographic process', (b) in an examination question or (c) in an examination answer does not of itself result in a copyright infringement.[17] In other words, when a teacher gets a class of thirty children to copy out a poem as an exercise in italic handwriting, no infringement of copyright takes place; nor is it an infringement of copyright in a textbook for the diligent schoolchild to commit passages from it to his memory and repeat them in his examination answers. Instruction in the making of films or soundtracks is also protected by a similar provision permitting the use of films, sound recordings, broadcasts and cable programmes.[18]

(vii) The performance, in a classroom setting, of a literary, dramatic, or musical work, and the employment of a sound recording, cinematograph film, television broadcast or cable programme, are not to be regarded as 'public performance' or 'playing or showing in public' for the purpose of infringement.[19] Persons directly connected with the establishment's activities may be present, and an outsider may perform for the purposes of instruction.

(viii) Broadcasts and cable programmes may be recorded for educational use where licensing schemes are not available.[20]

1. Copyright, Designs and Patents Act 1988, s 29(1). Conversion of a computer program from a low-level into a high-level language ('decompilation') is excluded from fair dealing by s 29(4), but is permitted if necessary to create independent but interoperable programs: s 50B; s 50A permits the making of backup copies and other activities where necessary for the lawful use or correction of a program. These subsections were inserted by the Copyright (Computer Programs) Regulations 1992 (SI 199/3233). S 29(5) stipulates that anything done in relation to a database for commercial research purposes is not considered fair, whereas s 29(1A) confirms that fair dealing with a database for the purposes of other research or private study is permitted provided the source is indicated. These provisions were inserted by the Copyright and Rights in Databases Regulations 1997 (SI 1997/3032), reg 8.

2. Copyright, Designs and Patents Act 1988, s 29(2); *Newspaper Licensing Agency v Marks & Spencer plc* [2001] 3 WLR 290.

3. *Photocopying and the Law*, which was not in fact published until 1970.

4. For multiple copying, the Copyright Licensing Agency grants (i) 'blanket' licences, with sampling schemes to assist in distribution of revenues, (ii) transactional licences, whereby permission is granted and a fee paid for specific copyright (permission being sought via the CLA Rapid Clearance Scheme, CLARCS) and (iii) a digitisation scheme, under which material is scanned and made available on the intranets of universities and other users. The scope of reprography licensing by the CLA extends to almost all educational institutions and many governmental, professional and commercial bodies, including solicitors and fast copy outlets. The CLA now administers reprographic licences for artistic works in the catalogue of the Design and Artists Copyright Society Ltd. The

Summer 2000 issue of newsletter CLArion reported distribution of £14.9 million by the CLA in the past year from reprography licensing revenues. For further details, see H Laddie et al *The Modern Law of Copyright and Designs* (3rd edn, 2000) at 25.18-25.23 or the CLA web site at www.cla.co.uk. Other licensing schemes are available for newspapers, liturgical materials, and so forth.
5. See C Clark *Photocopying from Books and Journals* (1990), British Copyright Council, p 9; Fair Dealing and Library Privilege (pamphlet) Copyright Licensing Agency.
6. See W Cornish, *Intellectual Property* (4th edn, 1999) para 11–39.
7. Eg *Sillitoe v McGraw-Hill* [1983] FSR 545. To interpret 'fair dealing' otherwise would contravene the 'Berne three-step test' see para **14.17** above.
8. Copyright, Designs and Patents Act 1988, ss 33 and 174.
9. Ibid, s 36(3). Although the scope of licences available from the Copyright Licensing Agency and other organisations is now very wide, see n 4, this provision remains useful for publications not included in the schemes.
10. Copyright, Designs and Patents Act 1988, s 38. For brief details, see C Clark n 5 above.
11. Copyright, Designs and Patents Act 1988, s 39.
12. Ibid, s 40.
13. Ibid, s 41.
14. Ibid, s 42.
15. Ibid, Sch 1, para 16; Copyright Act 1956, s 7(6). This, being a transitional provision of the 1988 Act, was not amended when the term of authorial copyrights was extended to 70 years by the Duration of Copyright and Rights in Performances Regulations 1995 (SI 1995/3297).
16. Copyright, Designs and Patents Act 1988, s 43.
17. Ibid, s 32(1) and (3).
18. Ibid, s 32(2).
19. Ibid, s 34.
20. Ibid, s 35. Several licensing schemes have now been certified: SIs 1990/879, 1993/193 and 1993/2755.

Protection of the public's right to be informed

14.20 This notion is specifically protected by the following provisions:

(i) No fair dealing with a work (other than a photograph) for the purpose of reporting current events is an infringement.[1] Photographs are excepted to preserve the transient economic value of 'news shots'. Where the work is copied in a newspaper or periodical, there must be a 'sufficient acknowledgement' of that work, but no acknowledgement is required where the medium of reportage is that of broadcasting, cable, sound recording or film. This is presumably because the legislation assumed that the imposition of 'sufficient acknowledgement' obligations upon the visually transient media could not be fulfilled in any way which would be of any benefit to the copyright owner.[2] It would not, in any event, be possible to provide simultaneous 'sufficient acknowledgement' where live broadcasts take place. For example, the broadcasters' microphones at the FA Cup Final might catch the incidental strains of a popular song which the supporters of one or other team have adopted as a means of encouraging their heroes. Not every newsworthy event will be considered 'current'. The death of the Duchess of Windsor did not make her early life 'current', although it stimulated media interest.[3] On the other hand, it was at least arguable that the uncertain events surrounding the death of Diana, Princess of Wales, could be regarded as 'current' several years after her death.[4] It is also important to be clear what is the purpose of the use: in *Pro Sieben AG v Carlton UK Television Ltd*[5] it was investigating the practice of 'chequebook journalism' rather than covering the subject matter of that form of journalism. Since reporting of current events involves communication to the public, the fairness of use for this purpose will depend upon whether the work in question has been published or not.[6] Where the work is a database, the possibility of infringing database right, as well as copyright, must be borne in mind.[7]

(ii) It is permissible to include a work in an artistic work, sound recording, cable programme broadcast or film if its inclusion is 'incidental'.[8] However, music or songs which are intentionally included as 'incidental' are not permitted by this section. Thus the march 'Colonel Bogey' captured on news film in *Hawkes & Son (London) Ltd v Paramount*[9] could be included today without infringement, as could the capturing by sports broadcasters of snatches of a recording of Prokofiev's *Dances of the Knights* played when teams emerge to play football at Sunderland's 'Stadium of Light'. However, a piece of music chosen as 'incidental' to a discotheque scene in a film could not be used without the appropriate consent. Comparative advertising showing the front cover of the claimant's magazine could not be said to include it 'incidentally': 'incidental' should be understood in the sense of 'casual, inessential, subordinate or merely background'.[10]

(iii) Notes or recordings legitimately made for the purpose of broadcasting, cable or of reporting current events may be used in certain circumstances without infringing copyright in any literary work recorded.[11]

(iv) Publication and reproduction of any work or subject matter may be permissible on the ground of 'public interest'. There is no statutory provision to this effect, but case law has given encouragement to those who maintain its validity. For example, the Court of Appeal in *Hubbard v Vosper*[12] refused to grant an injunction to restrain the reproduction in the defendant's book of literary works, in which the claimant had copyright, which described and illustrated activities of the Church of Scientology

211

– which the defendant claimed to be detrimental to the wellbeing of members of the public. Similarly, in *Kennard v Lewis*,[13] no injunction was granted to restrain the defendant from publishing the claimant's statements relating to the policy of the Campaign for Nuclear Disarmament, at a time when the public debate as to the relative virtues of multilateral and unilateral disarmament, as against the maintenance and increase of nuclear weapons, was in full swing. In neither case did the court state that the defendant's acts were non-infringing *per se*, but it certainly seems that certain overtly infringing acts will not attract an injunctive remedy and are, therefore, only vulnerable to actions for damages, an account of profits or a declaration. The policy behind 'public interest' defences is questionable: should the fact that there is a public interest in the dissemination of the *content* of a work justify the reproduction of the *form* in which that content is expressed? The answer, it seems, is in the affirmative.[14] Section 171(3) of the Copyright, Designs and Patents Act 1988 preserves public interest as a defence to infringement. Although its scope seemed to be curtailed by the decision of the Court of Appeal in *Hyde Park Residence Ltd v Yelland*,[15] the public interest defence in copyright may be made out where it is important for the public to see for themselves the work in question, rather than be informed as to its content.[16] Once the information has been published, it seems that the defence is no longer available.[17]

(v)   The recent 'information explosion' has included a vast expansion of scientific and technical literature. To enable researchers and others to keep up-to-date without having to scan every periodical and publication in their field, a number of learned societies and commercial organisations have developed abstracting and alerting services. These rely heavily on the abstracts by which most scientific and technical periodicals require authors to indicate the contents of articles. Copying these abstracts to the public is expressly permitted by section 60 of the Copyright, Designs and Patents Act 1988, unless licences are available under a certified scheme.

1. Copyright, Designs and Patents Act 1988, s 30(2).
2. Although acknowledgment may be relevant to a finding of fairness: *BBC v British Satellite Broadcasting Ltd* [1992] Ch 141, [1991] 3 All ER 833.
3. *Associated Newspapers Group plc v News Group Newspapers Ltd* [1986] RPC 515.
4. *Hyde Park Residence Ltd v Yelland* [2000] RPC 604; J Phillips 'When is a Fact?' [2000] Ent LR 116.
5. [1999] 1 WLR 605, [1999] FSR 610, CA, see also *Hyde Park*, n 4.
6. *Beloff v Pressdram Ltd* [1973] 1 All ER 241, [1973] RPC 765.
7. J N Adams 'The Reporting Exception: Does it Still Exist? [1999] EIPR 383; J Adams 'Small Earthquake in Venezuela: The Database Regulations 1997' [1998] EIPR 129; para **23.20**.

8. Copyright, Designs and Patents Act 1988, s 31, which also covers works-within-works: s 31(2).
9. [1934] Ch 593.
10. *IPC Magazines v MGN Ltd* [1998] FSR 431.
11. Copyright, Designs and Patents Act 1988, s 58.
12. [1972] 2 QB 84.
13. [1983] FSR 346; cf *Distillers Ltd v Times Newspapers Ltd* [1975] QB 613, where the public interest in disclosure was outweighed by a public interest in preserving the confidence of documents delivered up for the purpose of litigation.
14. See *Lion Laboratories Ltd v Evans* [1985] QB 526 and Phillips [1987] 4 EIPR 108; *Ashdown v Telegraph Group Ltd* [2001] EMLR 1003.
15. [2000] RPC 604. R Burrell 'Defending the Public Interest' [2000] EIPR 394.
16. *Ashdown v Telegraph Group Ltd* [2001] EMLR 1003, doubting *Hyde Park Residence Ltd v Yelland*.
17. *Express Newspapers plc v News (UK) Ltd* [1991] FSR 36.

The fixing of reasonable limits to the copyright monopoly

14.21 A number of defences fall within this category and have no greater unifying factor than their appeal to the reasonable man. They make for efficacy in public, commercial and private life.

(i) Fair dealing with works for the purposes of criticism or review,[1] so long as sufficient acknowledgement is given of the work used.[2] The criticism or review may be of the work in question (including ideas or events described in,[3] exemplified by,[4] or concerning the use of[5]) the work), of another work or of a performance of a work. The rationale of this defence is that the quotation of a work in a critique of it does not of itself satisfy customer demand for that work;[6] it is, ideally, of a *de minimis* nature in comparison with other trespasses upon copyright property.

(ii) The public reading or recitation of a published literary or dramatic work is not an infringement of copyright if only a reasonable extract of the work is employed and sufficient acknowledgement of the source is given.[7] Such recitation may in fact enhance sales of the recited work, and is unlikely to reduce them. This defence also applies if the recitation is broadcast or included in a cable programme service.[8]

(iii) An 'ephemeral' recording of a literary, dramatic, musical or artistic work, or of a sound recording or film, is permitted if it is made by a party which is entitled to broadcast it, so that the broadcast can take place at the broadcaster's convenience. Thus if the BBC has a licence to broadcast a live concert which starts at 7.30 pm, but the transmission of the previous programme overruns its allotted time by half an hour, the BBC can record the concert and put it out at 8 pm.[9] The copy made for this purpose must be 'ephemeral' in that it must be destroyed within 28 days, and it must not have been used for any unauthorised purpose prior to its destruction.[10] Otherwise, it is treated as infringing.[11] A related activity is that of recording by broadcasting organisations for the purposes of supervision and control.[12]

(iv) The showing of a broadcast or cable programme to a public audience who have not paid for admission to the venue in question infringes copyright neither in the broadcast nor the cable programme, nor in any included film or sound recording.[13] Hotels, social clubs and the like also enjoy the benefit of this exception. In a similar vein, sound recordings may be played at meetings of not-for-profit organisations whose main objects are charitable.[14]

(v) Home taping of broadcasts and cable programmes is permitted for the purpose of 'time-shifting' – listening to or viewing the programme at a more convenient time.[15]

(vi) Once a sculpture, model for a building or work of artistic craftsmanship is permanently situated in a public place or in premises open to the public, one can draw, paint, photograph, film or broadcast it without fear of an infringement action.[16] Works of architecture may be treated in similar manner[17] even if they are not in a public place. These provisions doubtless exempt twentieth-century tourists from the dreadful prospect of having their holiday snaps delivered up for destruction. The holiday snaps or films may even be exploited by the sale of postcards, or videos, by broadcasting or cabling, without infringing copyright in the work of art concerned.[18]

(vii) An artist does not infringe copyright in his own earlier works, even if he reproduces parts of them by using moulds, plans, sketches and so on, so long as he does not repeat or imitate the main design of his earlier works.[19] This enables the artist to develop his style and rework his themes without falling foul of what, in patent law, would be termed 'prior art'.

(viii) Copyright in a building, or plans for a building, is not infringed by reconstructing that building.[20] However, extending an existing building in a way which reproduces a substantial part of the building or plans is likely to infringe if done without the architect's permission.[21] Common law extensions of this defence were thought to allow the purchaser of a piece of machinery to make replacement parts (with which to replace broken components) and to have replacement parts made by others,[22] at least where replacement was normally required during the machine's useful life. However, the Privy Council's decision in *Canon Kabushiki Kaisha v Green Cartridge Co (Hong Kong) Ltd*[23] suggests that this line of argument has limited application, especially where the manufacturer's pricing policy allows a purchaser to choose between high initial outlay and lower running costs or *vice versa*.

(ix) Section 17(3) of the Copyright, Designs and Patents Act 1988 states that 'in relation to an artistic work copying includes the making of a copy in three dimensions of a two dimensional work' and vice versa. Thus if a drawing shows the construction of a pump, copyright in the drawing may on this basis be used to prevent duplication of the pump. This principle has far-reaching consequences, and was used extensively to protect industrial design prior to the Copyright, Designs and Patents Act 1988.[24] Now, however, where a drawing or other work embodies the design for an article, sections 51 and 52 may limit the effect of copyright. Protection may be reduced or eliminated depending on the nature of the article, the nature of the design and the number of articles which are made to the design. Where the article is an artistic work, or the design is of surface decoration, full copyright protection is available until the design is 'exploited industrially' by the making of 50 or more articles or piece goods and the marketing of such items.[25] Twenty-five years after industrial exploitation, articles may be made freely to the design.[26] Where the article is not an artistic work,[27] and the design is of shape or configuration, section 51 permits anyone to make an article to the design or to copy articles made to the design. The relationship between copyright and designs is considered in detail in Chapter 24.

(x) Things done by or with the permission of the proprietor of a registered design do not infringe copyright in an artistic work.[28]

(xi) The export of works of cultural or historical importance may be restricted. Where a condition of export involves the deposit of a copy in an appropriate library or archive, that copy may be made without infringing copyright.[29]

(xii) Typefaces may be used in the ordinary course of printing.[30] Where graphic materials have been sold to enable purchasers to use a typeface, copyright protection against the production and sale of such materials lasts only 25 years.[31] This latter provision is analogous to section 52.[32]

(xiii) Where backup copies may be made of computer software and other works in electronic form, upon permitted transfer of the main copy the recipient is entitled to make or use the backup copies and the transferor's right ceases.[33]

(xiv) The person entitled to use a database may do anything necessary to access the database and use its contents without infringing any copyright which attaches to the database's structure.[34]

(xv) Literary, dramatic, musical and artistic works of unknown authorship pose a problem: nobody knows when the copyright period expires. Consequently when the author may be presumed dead for 70 years or more, the acts restricted by copyright may be carried out without infringing.[35] This of course does not apply to Crown copyright, which has its own special duration.[36]

(xvi) There is a section euphemistically headed 'recordings of folksongs'.[37] This is designed to enable archives to be created of latter-day popular culture and especially rugby and football songs. These songs typically involve the setting of new words to popular music. The words tend to be of unknown authorship and the musical copyright owner is likely to be highly conscious of the value of his asset.

(xvii) Where an artistic work is to be sold, copies may be made to advertise the sale.[38] This provision does not, however, permit art catalogues subsequently to be sold to the public without permission from copyright owners.

1. Copyright, Designs and Patents Act 1988, s 30(1).
2. On the legal interpretation of 'sufficient acknowledgement' see *Sillitoe v McGraw-Hill* [1983] FSR 545, criticised by J Phillips 'Sufficient Acknowledgement of Literary Works' (1984) 100 LQR 179.
3. *Hubbard v Vosper* [1972] 2 QB 84.
4. *Pro Sieben Media AG v Carlton UK Television Ltd* [1999] 1 WLR 605, [1999] FSR 610.
5. *Time Warner Co v Channel Four Television plc* [1994] EMLR 1: the suppression of the film *Clockwork Orange* in the UK by Stanley Kubrick, its director.
6. Cf *Sillitoe v McGraw-Hill* [1983] FSR 545.
7. Copyright, Designs and Patents Act 1988, s 59(1). See for example, *Hubbard v Vosper* [1972] 2 QB 84.
8. Copyright, Designs and Patents Act 1988, s 59(2), reversing s 6(5) of the Copyright Act 1956.
9. Ibid, s 68(1).
10. Ibid, s 68(3).
11. Ibid, s 68(4).
12. Ibid, s 69, as amended by the Broadcasting Acts 1990 and 1996.
13. Copyright, Designs and Patents Act 1988, s 72.
14. Ibid, s 67. In *Phonographic Performance Ltd v South Tyneside Metropolitan Borough Council* [2001] RPC 594, [2000] EMLR 446, this exception was held not to apply to activities organised by the Council, whose main objects were not found to be charitable or quasi-charitable. Nor was the Council an organisation similar to the 'club or society' envisaged by s 67.
15. Copyright, Designs and Patents Act 1988, s 70.
16. Ibid, s 62(1) and (2).
17. Ibid.
18. Ibid, s 62(3).
19. Ibid, s 64.
20. Ibid, s 65.
21. *Meikle v Maufe* [1941] 3 All ER 144 – the Heal's building in London's Tottenham Court Road.
22. *Solar Thomson Engineering Co Ltd v Barton* [1977] RPC 537; *Weir Pumps Ltd v CML Pumps Ltd* [1984] FSR 33; *British Leyland Motor Corpn Ltd v Armstrong Patents Co Ltd* [1986] AC 577.
23. [1997] AC 728, [1997] FSR 817. See also para **8.8**.

24. See, further, para **24.2**, below.
25. Copyright, Designs and Patents Act 1988, s 52(1), SI 1989/1070.
26. Ibid, s 52(2).
27. Or typeface.
28. Copyright, Designs and Patents Act 1988, s 53.
29. Ibid, s 44.
30. Ibid, s 54.
31. Ibid, s 55.
32. Note 25 above and see para **24.5**, below.
33. Copyright, Designs and Patents Act 1988, s 56. For the circumstances in which backup copies can be made, see para **14.19** at n 1. The acts permitted under the Copyright (Computer Programs) Regulations 1992 (SI 1992/3233) cannot be subject to contrary agreement made after 1 January 1993: s 296A.
34. Copyright, Designs and Patents Act 1988, s 50D.
35. Ibid, s 57, as amended consequent upon Council Directive 93/98/EEC by the Duration of Copyright and Rights in Performances Regulations 1995 (SI 1995/3297): see paras **14.1** to **14.3**, above.
36. See para **14.2**, n 2, above.
37. Copyright, Designs and Patents Act 1988, s 61.
38. Ibid, s 63.

Copyright and domestic competition law

14.22 We have already seen in Chapter 7 how the unfettered exploitation of a patent is inhibited by statutory provisions which enable a frustrated competitor (or would-be competitor) to secure a compulsory licence and thus mitigate the worst effects of an abuse of monopoly.

The Copyright, Designs and Patents Act 1988 provides various sanctions to possible abuses of monopoly. There is an elaborate framework[1] within which collective organisations may administer licences subject to the jurisdiction of a Copyright Tribunal.[2] The Secretary of State may order compulsory lending licences, where no licensing scheme exists.[3] The exercise of copyright may also be subject to the competition rules of the EEC Treaty.[4] The Competition Act 1998 has reformed UK competition law to make it resemble that of the EC.[5] Regulation of restrictive practices is contained in Chapter I. Section 2, which reflects Art 81 of the EC Treaty and prohibits agreements, decisions by associations or concerted practices which (a) may affect trade within the UK and (b) have as their object or effect the prevention, restriction or distortion of competition within the UK. Some agreements, including mergers (which are regulated by other provisions), planning obligations, professional rules and other designated types of agreement, are excluded from the operation of Chapter I.[6] As with Art 81 EC, restrictive agreements with beneficial effects for industry or the economy may be exempted,[7] individually or *en bloc*. Exemptions under Art 81 act as so-called 'parallel exemptions',[8] to shield the agreement from the prohibitions of Chapter I. While EC 'block exemptions' are available for many intellectual property transactions,[9] none is apt where the primary purpose of the agreement is to license or transfer copyright.[10] There are *de minimis* indications under the 1998 Act. First, 'small agreements' within the meaning of section 39 do not attract liability for fines.[11] Second, the Office of Fair Trading has indicated that its Director does not propose to apply the Chapter I prohibition to agreements where the parties' combined market share does not exceed 25%.[12] The Competition Act 1998 prohibits abuse of dominant position[13] by Chapter II, in a manner redolent of Art 82 of the EC Treaty. Conduct of 'minor significance', ie by an undertaking with a turnover of less than £50 million in the previous year,[14] is immune from penalties, although not the other effects of the Act.

Guidelines on the application of the Competition Act 1998 to intellectual property had long been promised but, at the time of writing of this edition, consultations on draft guidelines had not yet opened. In the meantime, some insight into the attitude to copyright of the UK competition regulators may be gleaned from reports of the Monopolies and Mergers Commission[15] in proceedings under earlier UK competition laws. These will continue to be of relevance for some time under the transitional provisions of the Competition Act 1998.

1. Chapters VII and VIII of the 1988 Act – ss 116-152.
2. In a report entitled *Collective Licensing* Cm 530, 1988, the Monopolies and Mergers Commission made recommendations as to how the Copyright Tribunal might carry out its statutory functions. Procedure is now governed by the Copyright Tribunal Rules 1989 (SI 1989/1129), amended by SI 1991/201 and SI 1992/467. From time to time Practice Directions and Notices are issued. See H Laddie, P Prescott, M Vitoria, A Speck and L Lane *The Modern Law of Copyright and Designs* (3rd edn, 2000) Ch 26.
3. See Copyright, Designs and Patents Act 1988, s 66(1) and (2).
4. See para **27.2**.
5. D Livingston *The Competition Act 1998: a Practical Guide* (2001).
6. Competition Act 1998, s 3.
7. Ibid, ss 3-9.
8. Ibid, s 10.
9. For example the Technology Transfer Block Exemption, reg 240/96 for patents and know-how.
10. Neither the EC block exemption for vertical agreements, Regulation 2790/1999, nor the UK exclusion order for land and vertical agreements (SI 2000/310), applies in this case.
11. These are agreements which are not price fixing agreements between parties whose combined, worldwide, turnover, does not exceed £20 million: The Competition Act 1998 (Small Agreements and Conduct of Minor Significance) Order 2000 (SI 2000/262). A transaction between an individual author and a large concern, say a publisher or broadcaster whose turnover exceeds £20 million pa, will not benefit from this.
12. Guideline OFT 401 *The Chapter I Prohibition*.
13. Competition Act 1998, s 18. Guideline OFT 415 *Assessment of Market Power* explains how the market position of an undertaking will be gauged.

14. The Competition Act 1998 (Small Agreements and Conduct of Minor Significance) Order 2000 (SI 2000/262). A group of companies will fall to be considered a single undertaking, with the result that agreements between them do not fall foul of Chapter I, but their turnover will be aggregated for the purposes of the Chapter II prohibition.
15. Now replaced by the Competition Commission: Competition Act 1998, s 45.

14.23 One such law was the Competition Act 1980. Under this Act the Director General of Fair Trading was empowered to investigate the substance of any alleged anti-competitive practice,[1] a term which was defined so broadly that it could in theory cover almost every legitimate and illegitimate business practice discussed in this book. If the Director General was of the opinion that such a practice existed, he might then refer to the Monopolies and Mergers Commission the question whether that practice operated to the detriment of the public interest.[2] For this purpose 'public interest' seemed to comprehend both the private interests of commercial rivals[3] and the interests of the public at large.[4] The Monopolies and Mergers Commission, it should be noted, was in theory better able to review the acceptability of a monopoly's enforcement than the Comptroller of Patents, since it comprised up to 32 experts drawn from the various worlds of legal practice, commerce and business economics.[5] It also heard monopoly references under the Fair Trading Act 1973, whereby the Director-General asked the Commission to determine whether a monopoly situation existed and, if so, whether the monopoly operated against the public interest.

1. Competition Act 1980, ss 2, 3.
2. Ibid, s 5.
3. Monopolies and Mergers Commission Report *Ford Motor Company Ltd* Cmnd 9437, 1985, paras 6.27-6.50.
4. Monopolies and Mergers Commission Report *The British Broadcasting Corporation and Independent Television Publications Ltd* Cmnd 9614, 1985, paras 6.12-6.25.
5. On the composition of the Commission see R Merkin and K Williams *Competition Law* (1984), pp 21-22. Details of its successor, the Competition Commission, are available at www.competition-commission.org.uk.

14.24 On four occasions when the Monopolies and Mergers Commission reported upon the enforcement of copyright, it started from the unquestionable premise that the maintenance by the copyright owner of market exclusivity was an appropriate subject for its consideration. In the first case, *Ford Motor Company Ltd*,[1] the Commission found that Ford's use of 'spare part' artistic copyright, so as to prevent rival manufacturers from selling identical parts more cheaply, was an abuse of monopoly which was contrary to the public interest. In *Independent Television Publications Ltd and British*

Broadcasting Corporation[2] it concluded that the exercise of literary copyright so as to prevent (i) the publication by any rival to the *TV Times* or *Radio Times* of a full week's advance viewing schedules and (ii) the publication by any single periodical of both BBC and IBA weekly advance programme information was an abuse of monopoly which was *not* contrary to the public interest. In *Collective Licensing*[3] it reviewed the operation of an organisation to which performing rights are assigned[4] and concluded that collective licensing bodies were the best available mechanism for licensing sound recordings provided that they could be restrained from using that monopoly unfairly.[5] A number of recommendations to achieve the latter were incorporated in the collective licensing provisions of the Copyright, Designs and Patents Act 1988.[6] In *The Supply of Recorded Music*,[7] a reference prompted by complaints about the price of CDs in the UK, the Commission considered the relationship between artists and the record industry. They concluded that there was no case for change in contractual or copyright framework governing these relationships. Furthermore, they rejected the suggestion that record companies' ability to use copyright to control parallel imports should be removed. In each of the Commission's reports there is far more discussion of market considerations than of purely legal issues; since market considerations are unique to each case, the precedential value of the Commission's view of the legal issues in any individual case is not therefore great.

1. Monopolies and Mergers Commission Report *Ford Motor Company Ltd* Cmnd 9437, 1985.
2. Monopolies and Mergers Commission Report *The British Broadcasting Corporation and Independent Television Publications Ltd* Cmnd 9614, 1985.
3. Monopolies and Mergers Commission Report *Collective Licensing* Cmnd 530, 1988.
4. Phonographic Performance Limited. Other licensing organisations were considered to be outside the Commission's terms of reference since they took licences rather than assignments from the copyright owners. See H Rosenblatt 'Copryight Assignments: Rights and Wrongs – The Collecting Societies' Perspective' [2000] IPQ 187.
5. In *Performing Rights 1996* Cm 3147 the Commission considered the operation of another collecting society, the Performing Right Society. Holding that certain of its mechanisms, policies and practices operated against the public interest, the Commission recommended changes to the management of the Society and to its relationships with its members.
6. See para **14.22**, above.
7. 1994 Cm 2599.

14.25 In *Ford*,[1] the Monopolies and Mergers Commission bemoaned the fact that its powers did not go beyond those of making recommendations; no executive or judicial action could implement its recommendations in the absence of some explicit remedy or statutory provision to that effect. The Secretary of State for Trade and Industry enjoyed some limited powers under the Competition Act,[2] but these did not extend to (i) the curtailing of an excessive duration for copyright protection (as the Commission desired in the *Ford* case, where it was felt that five years was time enough to exploit a monopoly in car spares, whatever the term of artistic copyright in other works), or to (ii) the granting of one or more compulsory licences to exploit another's copyright (which the Commission would have been perfectly content with in the Ford investigation[3]). This factor of impotence was even more pronounced in the ITP and BBC report, where the Commission was unanimous in asserting that, even if it had held the exercise of copyright to be against the public interest, it could not have agreed on any course of action which would have led to its cure.[4] In consequence came section 144 of the Copyright, Designs and Patents Act 1988, which provides for compulsory licensing where the copyright owner has refused to license on reasonable terms, or has granted licences on unduly restrictive terms and where the Monopolies and Mergers Commission has reported on that conduct as operating against the public interest. Section 144 is couched in terms very similar to those of section 51 of the Patents Act 1977.[5] In *Classified Directory Advertising Services*,[6] the Commission contrasted the position under patents and copyright, where it might be desirable to order licensing to enable techniques and know-how to pass from single use to multiple use, with that of trade marks. Since trade marks had a different kind of function – to indicate origin to consumers – a similar remedy would be inappropriate.

1. Monopolies and Mergers Commission Report *Ford Motor Company Ltd* Cmnd 9437, 1985, para 6.60.
2. Competition Act 1980, s 10.
3. See *Ford*, n 1 above at para 6.65.
4. Monopolies and Mergers Commission Report *The British Broadcasting Corporation and Independent Television Publications Ltd* Cmnd 9614, 1985, para 642.
5. See *CIPA Guide to the Patents Act 1977* (5th edn 2001) p 502.
6. 1996 Cm 3171 paras 2.109-2.110.

Part IV

Pseudo-copyrights

Chapter 15

Public lending right

Introduction

15.1 When a person writes a literary work, he finds that copyright adheres to his words as the pen leaves them, for copyright is quick to attach itself to the tangible and legible results of a person's writing. This copyright sticks fast, and remains with the author as he revises his work, takes it to a publisher, receives and corrects his proofs. Once publication has taken place, the author then discovers that, while copyright remains faithfully attached to the work he originally penned, it does not become likewise attached to that work's lawfully manufactured copies. More accurately, once he has sold a book of his work to a member of the public, he can still stop the making of further, unlawful copies, but it is more difficult to stop his purchaser doing anything else with it. While still retaining copyright, he has lost control of the published chattel. So, for example, he cannot stop the book's new owner from selling it to a second-hand book dealer, or from lending it to a friend, even though these activities will probably reduce demand for new books. The same applies to any other copyright work. This means that, if Jeff Koon were to fashion one of his characteristic sculptures, he could use his copyright to stop a purchaser from making copies of it but not to stop him taking a sledge-hammer and smashing it to pieces.[1] Furthermore, many consumers of art and literature do not have the space, money or inclination to admire their very own books lined up on a study shelf, or have their very own sculpture permanently positioned in the garden. They would prefer to borrow books from the public library and return them once read, to hire films from their local video shop and return them once watched, to hire paintings for meeting rooms at their places of work and return them once others have been suitably impressed. In these cases the users may pay fines to the library, hire fees to the video shop or subscriptions to the owner of the paintings for hire, but are unlikely to form a queue to reward the authors.

1. For limitations on an author's 'moral right' to object to derogatory treatment see para **18.13**.

225

15.2 United Kingdom and European legislation have gone some way to improving the author's lot in this regard. The rights of a copyright owner now include a 'rental right' which in theory permits him to share in the proceeds of commercial hire of any variety of work or of copies of the work.[1] There is also a lending right, imposed by Directive 92/100/EEC.[2] However, that directive permits considerable derogation in relation to lending right.[3] 'Lending' is defined in Art 1.3 as:

> 'making available for use, for a limited period of time and not for direct or indirect economic or commercial advantage, when it is made through establishments which are accessible to the public'.

Thus lending right does not cover every not-for-profit loan, but only those made through public libraries or other public institutions. The way in which the UK has implemented this aspect of the 1992 Directive[4] was coloured by the pre-existing Public Lending Right Scheme, to which we shall turn next.

1. Rental right was first conferred on sound recordings, films or computer programs and subsequently extended to all works: see ss 16(1)(ab), 18A and 93A of the Copyright, Designs and Patents Act 1988 (as amended by the Copyright (Computer Programs) Regulations 1992: SI 1992/3233) and the Copyright and Related Rights Regulations 1996 (SI 1996/2967), para **13.21** above.
2. Of 19 November 1992 , on rental right and lending right and on certain rights related to copyright in the field of intellectual property [1992] OJ L346/61.
3. Art 5. See J Griffiths 'Copyright and Public Lending in the United Kingdom' [1997] EIPR 499.
4. By the Copyright and Related Rights Regulations 1996 (SI 1996/2967).

15.3 The fact that the sale of a literary work, or a lawfully made copy of it, effectively 'exhausts'[1] the copyright proprietor's interest in its physical essence was of no concern to earlier British copyright law. Until 1979 this was a source of great complaint among authors whose books were purchased by public lending libraries. Each book purchased by a library, they argued, was liable to be borrowed on numerous occasions by library users, and each act of borrowing was an actual or probable lost sale.[2] The authors' cries of distress were both echoed and amplified by their publishers, whose detriment through lost sales was greater than authors' to the proportion that they enjoyed the benefit of sales: the less generous the publisher's royalty to the author, the more each lost sale cost him.

1. For a brief note on 'exhaustion' of rights see ch 27.
2. For an account of the statistical aspects of the loan/sale relationship see B Brophy *A Guide to Public Lending Right* (1983), pp 51-57. Authors Bridget Brophy,

Maureen Duffy and Michael Holroyd, together with MP Michael Foot and others, were particularly instrumental in the creation of Public Lending Right. See *Whose Loan is it Anyway?* (1999) published by the Registrar of Public Lending Right.

15.4 What was then to be done about this state of affairs? Libraries were adamant that the cost of paying compensation to much-borrowed authors should not fall on them, since this was in their eyes an abuse of library resources which would result in less money being spent upon new purchases, with a consequent reduction in readers' choice and the compulsory rendering ignorant of the great British public. Borrowers, too, insisted that they should not have to pay this tax upon learning, since (i) as contributors to the coffers of the local government authority which administered their library services, they had already funded the purchase of each borrowed book by the library, and had therefore, through the public library, bought the book themselves, and since (ii) less affluent borrowers would be penalised for the very act of self-betterment which libraries were intended to facilitate *gratis*.

15.5 Even if the principle of compensating authors (and/or publishers) for lost sales caused by library loans were conceded, two further bridges remained to be crossed. The first was that of deciding who should be paid what: should the most popular, and therefore probably the richest, authors get the most, on the basis that they had lost the most profit (or had provided the greatest pleasure), or should the least popular be paid disproportionately more on the basis they would probably, through a likely lack of sales, be the neediest? The second problem was that of counting, assessing or guessing the number of loans in the absence of any cheap and convenient means of doing so. This problem was resolved by the development and application of computers and it is difficult, looking back on the lending right debate through 1990s spectacles, to imagine that it could ever have been such a major stumbling-block to the development of a formal public lending right.

The public lending right

15.6 Some countries, of which the most notable is Germany, have long had a doctrine of the author's right which is so developed as to possess a 'distribution right'[1] which is infringed by the putting of a book into a library – whether public or private – without any resulting acceptance of an obligation to compensate the author for real or hypothetical borrowings. In Germany there is no practical likelihood of thousands of authors running up and down the nation's libraries, demanding with menaces the withdrawal of their works until a tidy sum is paid. This is because the 'distribution right', though a private right enjoyed by every author, is only capable of being exercised collectively by a society or other body which represents authors in general.[2] In the UK, however, the extension of copyright so as to embrace a public lending right was not viewed with favour, not so much because copyright was considered inherently unsuitable as because so many authors had already assigned their copyright to their publishers, and it was hoped that authors rather than publishers would be the prime beneficiaries of a library lending right.[3] A free-standing public lending right was devised, funded from central government. The Netherlands also developed a specific public lending right system;[4] Denmark has had a scheme since 1946 and Denmark and various other Nordic countries have 'cultural' systems to encourage authors to write in their national languages. Council Directive 92/100/EEC[5] permits the adoption or continuation of these schemes.[6]

1. Copyright Act of 9 September 1965, as amended, paras 15, 17, 27.
2. Ibid, para 27(4).
3. On author/publisher relations prior to the passage of PLR, and on authors' aspirations, see R Findlater (ed) *Public Lending Right – a Matter of Justice* (1970).
4. See *PLR Report 1999-2000*, pp 26-28. In 1995 the UK Public Lending Right Office convened an international conference at which the International PLR Network was established. The network now has a web site, www.plrinternational.com, which gives details of current activities
5. Para **15.4**, above.
6. Art 5.

15.7 Accordingly, in 1979 the UK Parliament passed the Public Lending Right Act. The Act turned out to be little more than a skeleton for public lending right (PLR), establishing the Office of Registrar of Public Lending Right[1] and providing that an author could claim PLR in his publications. PLR, like all good property rights, was to be transmissible, and would expire (like copyright) at the stroke of midnight on the last day of the fifty-first December following the author's death.[2] Subsequent rules were to determine which authors and which books were eligible for the benefits of PLR, how the quantum of PLR was to be assessed and how it was to be distributed. The significance of passing a skeleton Act and fleshing it out with subsequent rules did not lie in the principle that Acts of Parliament must be obeyed but rules are made to be broken; it was a recognition of the empirical nature of PLR. Since no one knew how (or whether) the hitherto untried scheme of PLR would work, it was easier to encapsulate the details in rules which could conveniently be amended by laying an amending order before both Houses of Parliament[3] than to set in motion the cumbersome and time-consuming procedure of statutory amendment. The wisdom of this policy has been proved by subsequent events[4] – many adjustments have been made to the Scheme.

1. A corporation sole.
2. Public Lending Right Act 1979, s 1(6). The term was increased by 20 years, to life + 70, to reflect change in the duration of copyright, see para **14.1** et seq. The PLR Advisory Committee, in reviewing the scheme, considered whether it would be possible to reduce the period for payments until 20 years after the author's death thereby making a greater proportion of the fund available to living authors. This was felt not to be feasible: *PLR Report 1999-2000*, pp 24-25.
3. Public Lending Right Scheme 1982 (Commencement) Order 1982.
4. The Scheme with amendments consolidated to 1990 formed Appendix 2 to the Public Lending Right Scheme 1982 (Commencement of Variations) Order 1990, SI 1990/2360. For subsequent changes, see the various Public Lending Right Scheme 1982 (Commencement of Variations) Orders: SI 1991/2618, SI 1992/3049, SI 1993/2049, SI 1996/338, SI 1997/1576, SI 2000/933 and SI 2000/3319 and the Public Lending Right (Increase of Limit) Order 1993 (SI 1993/799).

The PLR scheme

15.8   The Public Lending Right Scheme 1982, as amended,[1] confers PLR upon eligible authors in respect of eligible books, so long as the eligibility of each is recorded upon the Registrar's computer at Stockton-on-Tees. Eligible authors, broadly speaking, must be individuals and resident within the EEA.[2] They must be alive at the date when application for registration is sought, or have died no more than ten years previously.[3] Eligible books are those which are printed and bound,[4] are published with an ISBN,[5] are not subject to Crown copyright[6] and are written by at least one natural person.[7] Special rules govern the eligibility of editors (including compilers, abridgers and revisers), illustrators (including photographers) and translators.[8]

1. See amending orders referred to in para **15.7**, n 4.
2. 1982 Scheme, art 5 (as amended by SI 2000/933).
3. 1982 Scheme, as amended, arts 5A and 6A.
4. Paperbacks count as 'bound': art 6(2).
5. International Standard Book Number, for applications to register submitted after 30 June 1991.
6. 1982 Scheme, art 6(2)(c). 'Non-official' publications of Her Majesty's Stationery Office are published under authors' copyright rather than Crown Copyright, so that the normal PLR mechanisms may apply: PLR Review 1992-93, p 7.
7. 1982 Scheme, as amended, art 6(2)(a).
8. 1982 scheme, as amended, art 4(1).

15.9   The distribution of PLR entitlements to authors is a complicated and fascinating affair, for a variety of reasons. In the first place one is invited to contrast the precision with which distributive justice is sought by means of mathematical formulae relating to the assessment of loans and distribution of income with the apparently arbitrary manner in which the amount of money to be distributed is actually decided. Secondly, one is tempted to speculate upon the efficacy of PLR as a life-raft for financially embarrassed authors given that, the more authors who attain PLR eligibility, the less each can expect to derive from it. Thirdly, one cannot but admire the measure of altruism which is built into the system and cannot be evaded: the most frequently borrowed authors find that, however great is their moral entitlement to PLR, an arbitrary ceiling of £6,000 (raised in 1989 from £5,000) is imposed upon their legal entitlement. This £6,000, if the experience of the first ten years is anything to go by, is by way of recompense for over 300,000 loans per annum.[1] If PLR is in any way a notional consolation for lost sales one wonders whether, perhaps, the £6,000 cut-off point is not a little ungenerous. Fourthly, the use of books in public reference collections was felt to be too difficult to compensate under the scheme.[2]

1. Annual loans have reduced over the last 10 years from about 650 million to 450 million: Dr J Parker, speaking to members of the British Literary and Artistic Copyright Association, 6 September 2001.
2. From time to time studies and enquiries are made to evaluate this possibility, eg *PLR Review* 1992-93, p 8; *PLR Report 1999-2000*, p 19.

Calculation of payments

15.10   The size of the original annual PLR budget, provided out of Treasury funds, was originally fixed at £2 million.[1] Of this, approximately £400,000 was consumed by administrative expenses, leaving £1,600,000 for the authors themselves. Almost £500,000 of that sum was expected to be clawed back by the Commissioners of Inland Revenue, which meant that in cash terms the real benefit to authors was not great: before deduction of tax the average payment made under the scheme was £216 in 1985. By the year 1999-2000, the government grant had risen to over £5 million. After subtracting operating costs, the amount distributed to authors was £4.2 million. For that year operating costs represented 17%, including sums for moving office and replacing the PLR computer.[2] Despite the rate per loan in1999-2000, 2.18p, being the highest in the seventeen years of the scheme's operation,[3] the average payment per registered author was £137, as opposed to £184 in 1992-93. Authors have gained from the improved efficiency of the system but the largesse of the Department of Culture, Media and Sport is spread more thinly. In the first year of operation, only 7,562 authors registered PLR claims to 63,202 titles; a year later, in February 1985, these figures had risen to 9,395 and 77,521 respectively. By February 2000 the figures stood at 30,674 and 304,769.[4] Further gentle increases may be expected until the number of books of eligible and registered authors which appear on library shelves each year no longer exceeds the number of books by ineligible authors which disappear from them. Authors will be glad to learn that the grant is set to increase from £5 million to £7 million as from April 2002.[5] At the time of writing the minimum payment to authors was £5; this lower threshold is designed to save the administrative costs of making large numbers of very small payments, and is being kept under review.[6]

1. Public Lending Right Act 1979, s 2 (2).
2. *PLR Report 1999-2000*, p 8.
3. *PLR Report 1999-2000*, p 5 and subsequently raised to 2.49p: SI 2000/3319.
4. *PLR Report 1999-2000*, p 8.
5. *PLR Report 1999-2000*, pp 1 and 22-23.
6. *PLR Report 1999-2000*, pp 9-10.

15.11 In the UK each year there are hundreds of millions of borrowings from public libraries. Although it is now technically feasible to record the particulars of every loan, and to distribute the PLR fund on a per-loan basis between all eligible authors, it would not be cost-effective to do so. At the sacrifice of some precision in determining the PLR quantum of each eligible author and work, distributions are calculated statistically on the basis of data supplied by sample libraries from specific geographical areas.[1] Any given sampling point is used for a maximum of four consecutive years. Improvements to the PLR computing and data collection arrangements appear to have resulted in an increasing sampling rate. In 1999-2000, distribution was based upon 10.8% of UK library loans,[2] better than the long-term target of 10%.[3] In 1999-2000, the upper limit of £6,000 resulted in a redistribution of nearly 10% of the funds available; 73% of the fund was paid out in sums of £500 or more, compared with 20% in payments over £100.[4] However, by far the largest number of payments, 12,248, were made to authors receiving between £5 and £99.99.[5]

1. Public Lending Right Act 1979, Sch 2.
2. *PLR Report 1999-2000*, p 8
3. See *PLR Review* 1992-93, pp 5 and 13.
4. *PLR Report 1999-2000*, p 9.
5. *PLR Report 1999-2000*, p 8.

15.12 Note that PLR only applies in respect of loans of books from public libraries. Loans made by private libraries and university libraries,[1] and loans of other works such as audio books, CDs and video cassettes, remain entirely unaffected. Loans by public libraries of works other than books that are eligible for the Public Lending Right Scheme are not permitted by virtue of section 40A(1), but to date the copyright owners have not taken advantage of this opportunity to charge a royalty. The PLR Report of 1999-2000 reports initiatives by the Authors' Licensing and Collecting Society in connection with the licensing of audio books.[2]

1. Council Directive 92/100/EEC permits the perpetuation of this state of affairs by allowing Member States to exempt categories of establishment: art 5.3; Parliament has taken advantage of the opportunity by enacting s 40A(2) of the Copyright, Designs and Patents Act 1988, as inserted by the the Copyright and Related Rights Regulations 1996 (SI 1996/2967).
2. At p 17.

The future of public lending right

15.13 It is uncertain at the time of writing whether public lending right will be extended beyond books in printed form[1] or whether it will co-exist with other forms of collection of lending right. The PLR Registry has accumulated a considerable body of expertise in administering lending right. This is being put to use in its international PLR initiatives, and the information on UK library borrowing is available for research.[2] The future of PLR in its present form will depend upon the borrowing patterns from public libraries. Increasingly, the public is turning to new media for information and entertainment. The UK PLR Registry has already begun to consider the challenge of e-books, whereby works can be downloaded onto portable media.[3] It is hoped that its know-how will be retained and applied more widely as new forms of reward become necessary to deal with technological and political advances.

1. See para **15.12** at n 2.
2. *PLR Report 1999-2000*, pp 26-28 and 19.
3. *PLR Report 1999-2000.* These new forms of dissemination will be influenced by Directive 2001/29 on copyright and related rights in the information society. See G Cornish, 'Libraries and the Harmonisation of Copyright' [1998] EIPR 241 for view from the British Library on a draft of that directive.

Chapter 16

Resale royalty rights

The problem defined

16.1 The legal protection accorded to the British artist or sculptor in his intellectual creations has sometimes been criticised for its inadequacy.[1] The law of copyright, originally conceived as a protection against unlawful publication and reproduction of books, was extended so as to prevent infringement of publication and reproduction rights in both two- and three-dimensional art works,[2] and currently the artist or sculptor receives substantially the same degree of legal protection as does the author of an original literary work.[3] Equality of protection is not, however, a guarantee of equality of commercial opportunity and success. This is because the means by which an author exploits his written works are substantially different in practice from those utilised by artists or sculptors. The principal method by which a literary author derives financial benefit from his copyright is by making or licensing others to make copies of his works, which are then sold to the public. While there may be some intrinsic historical or substantial value in the author's original manuscript,[4] it is not from the disposal of the manuscript but from the sale of copies that the author derives income. If the work is one of literary merit or historical interest, the author may gain further from the exploitation of his copyright by making, or licensing others to make, films, cartoon strips, board games or the like from it. On the other hand, the value of copyright to the artist or sculptor is inherently limited in so far as it may be regarded as a means of generating income. In most instances he will derive his income principally from the sale of the chattel he has created, and not from the reproduction of his work. The value placed upon the artist's or sculptor's original work is usually substantially higher than that placed upon even identical reproductions of his work, both by actual or would-be purchasers[5] and by the viewing public.[6] This is not invariably the case. Much art is commissioned expressly for the purpose of reproduction (for example greetings card pictures, souvenirs of royal or papal occasions, calendar designs, illustrations and photographs for books), and for such purposes copyright law is well

233

suited to prevent, discourage or penalise illicit reproductions. The creators of popular images may be able to generate considerable income from the sale of prints of their work.[7]

1. See eg G McFarlane 'The Case for the Droit de Suite' (1981) New Law Journal 146; J Alexander Sinclair, 'Resale Royalty Rights – a Reply', [1980] EIPR 201; *Copyright and Designs Law* Cmnd 6732, 1977, paras 798-800.
2. Sculptures were first protected by the Sculpture Copyright Act 1814; paintings, drawings and photographs by the Fine Arts Copyright Act 1862. All are now covered by the Copyright, Designs and Patents Act 1988, s 4.
3. On the extent of protection of copyright works see Chs 13 and 14.
4. In July 1980 a manuscript of Tennyson's poem 'In Memoriam' fetched £100,000 at Sotheby's (The Times, 23 July 1980); in 1981 one could purchase a copy of that poet's complete works for only £7.50.
5. The reactions of the art trade to the attribution of authenticity of paintings are well revealed in T Keating, F Norman and G Norman, *The Fake's Progress* (1977) and in C Wright *The Art of the Forger* (1984). A complete exhibition has been staged at the British Museum on Fakes, Fraud & Forgery.
6. On the relative aesthetic merits of original paintings and identical reproductions see J Berger *Ways of Seeing* (1972), Ch 1.
7. J H Merryman 'The Proposed Generalisation of the *Droit de Suite* in the European Communities' [1997] IPQ 16 at p 25 claims that artists like Jasper Johns, David Hockney and others 'often have annual incomes of well into six figures from prints alone' Merryman also refers, at n 25, to the seedier end of the 'fine print' trade.

16.2 From a legal point of view there is no distinction between the producers of intellectual property in literary, artistic, dramatic and musical works: each is termed 'author' by the Copyright, Designs and Patents Act 1988,[1] there being no separate category of 'artist' or 'sculptor'.[2] In contrast with this, there is a popular and widespread apprehension of a distinction between 'author' on the one hand and 'artist' or 'sculptor' on the other. There is also a discernible appreciation in popular parlance of a distinction between an 'artist' (a laudatory term applied to one who creates a work of art) and a 'designer', 'illustrator' or 'draftsman' (terms indicating the creator of something which is either wholly or partly functional, or which is designed to be exploited through reproduction rather than through sale of a valued chattel[3]).

1. S 9(1).
2. The words 'artist' and 'sculptor' are not defined for any legal purposes in any UK statute.
3. Thus the *Collins English Dictionary* gives as one of the meanings of 'artist' a person who is 'skilled in some task or occupation'; another is one 'who displays in his work' (whether artistic or not) 'qualities required in art, such as sensibility and imagination'. The definitions of 'designer', 'draftsman' and 'illustrator' focus upon the ends achieved, rather than upon the means of achieving such ends or the skill required so as to exercise such means. M Franzosi 'The Legal Protection of Industrial Design: Unfair Competition as a Basis for Protection' [1990] EIPR 154 discusses the admirable combination of qualities in a designer – creative imagination plus logic.

16.3 In view of their different and distinctive modes of utilising copyright, and in view of their relatively low standard of remuneration, artists and sculptors have been identified as a special category of copyright producers whose interests are insufficiently protected by the law as it stands.[1] A particular element of iniquity in the remuneration of this category would appear to be that, if a work is sold which possesses especial artistic merit, the subsequent sale of it by the original purchaser of that work from its creator will attract a very much greater price than that which the original purchaser paid to its creator. The creator is not entitled to any share in an inflated price paid by a subsequent purchaser. In many cases the price paid to the original purchaser would appear to be enhanced by the fact that the creator of the work is no longer alive; in such cases the creator's dependants likewise enjoy no right to a share in the subsequent sale price. Only where the terms of the initial contract of sale include an obligation to share the proceeds of a subsequent sale will the creator or his estate be entitled to benefit from the increased value of the work. The imposition of such a term in an art sale contract is not apparently in the nature of a prevalent custom; its use, if indeed it is employed, must be quite unusual. In any event, the contract will avail the author only as against the first purchaser with whom the contract is made.

1. See, eg, the works cited in n 1, para **16.1**; L de Pierredon-Fawcett *The Droit de Suite in Literary and Artistic Property* (1991).

Proposed solutions

16.4 Could a way be found of enabling the artist or sculptor to benefit further from the exercise of his skills than he does at present? Possible reforms include (i) the extension of the duration of copyright protection, (ii) the provision of tax benefits[1] and (iii) the introduction of a resale royalty right, or *droit de suite,* such as is already in operation in some countries.[2]

1. The UK does to some extent mitigate the rigours of creation by allowing 'tax-spreading'. For a general account of the tax position see Shipwright and Price *UK Taxation and Intellectual Property* (2nd edn, 1996) esp pp 115-118; J Hickey, 'Taxation of Technology and Intellectual Property: Policy and the Law' [1997] IPQ 319; R Gallafent, N Eastaway and V Dauppe *Intellectual Property Law and Taxation* (5th edn, 1998) esp pp 198-200.
2. By 1 January 1986, 26 Berne Convention countries and two others (Ecuador and Peru) had adopted *droit de suite*: S Ricketson *The Berne Convention for the Protection of Literary and Artistic Works*: 1886-1986, para 8.50. Ten years later, the EC Commission's *Proposal for a European Parliament and Council Directive on the Resale Right for the benefit of the Author of an Original Work of Art*, COM (96) 97 final, identified 39 countries as having enacted such a right. However, many of these may not have a fully operational right.

16.5 Extension of the duration of copyright protection, beyond the period of the author's life plus 70 years laid down in Council Directive 1993/98/EEC,[1] would not seem particularly appropriate for the purpose of improving the creative artist's opportunity of enhancing his earnings, given the relatively scant relevance of traditional copyright law to the patterns of exploitation of inherently valuable chattels. The provision of significant tax benefits, such as the exemption from income tax of all money received by artists and sculptors in respect of their commissions, has already been implemented in the Republic of Ireland[2] (where authors and composers also benefit), and is attractive in its simplicity of operation; on the other hand, it confers no benefit upon the creator's estate, and is a charge upon the public purse rather than upon the seller of the valuable work, the current beneficiary of a 'windfall' profit on the sale. At the time of writing, the UK Inland Revenue was consulting on reforms to the taxation of intellectual property[3] but the proposals fell short of significant 'tax breaks' for authors and artists. Should, then, a *droit de suite* be introduced?

1. Of 29 October 1993 harmonising the term of copyright: OJ 1993 L290/9; see paras **14.1-14.2**.
2. On the Irish law see p Ussher 'Favoured Tax Treatment for Authors in the Republic of Ireland' [1979] EIPR 106.
3. Technical Notes of March 1999, March 2000, June 2000 and November 2000 were posted on the Revenue web site: www.inlandrevenue.gov.uk. In the March 2000 budget, stamp duty was abolished for intellectual property transactions.

The resale royalty right

16.6 In its simple form, the resale royalty right consists of no more than an enforceable legal claim, on the part of the creator of an aesthetic chattel, to an entitlement to a proportion of the proceeds of subsequent sales of the work. This right originated in France in 1920;[1] it is described in the Brussels text of the Berne Convention for the Protection of Literary and Artistic Works[2] in 1948, repeated in the Paris text of 1971.[3] Art 14 *ter* states:

'(1) The author or after his death the persons or institutions authorised by national legislation, shall, with respect to original works of art and original manuscripts of writers and composers, enjoy the inalienable right to an interest in any sale of the work subsequent to the first transfer by the author of the work.

(2) The protection provided by the preceding paragraph may be claimed in a country of the Union only if legislation in the country to which the author belongs so permits, and to the extent permitted by the country where this protection is claimed.[4]

(3) The procedure for collection and the amounts shall be matters for determination by national legislation.'

As may be seen, the failure to provide for resale royalty rights is not incompatible with ratification of the Paris text. Such rights are found in Belgium, Germany, France, Italy, Luxembourg and numerous countries less important from the point of view of art sales, but these countries are currently only a small minority of the Berne Union member states.

1. On the French law see R Plaisant, 'The "Droit de Suite"' (1969) 5 Copyright 157; for a brief history see S Ricketson *The Berne Convention for the Protection of Literary and Artistic Works*: 1886-1986 (1987) para 8.50. See also L de Pierredon-Fawcett *The Droit de Suite in Literary and Artistic Property: a Comparative Law Study* (1991).
2. Art 14 *bis*.
3. Cmnd 5002, 1972.
4. Ie the right may be afforded (or denied) to foreign artists on the basis of reciprocity of protection. However, this principle may not be used within the EC to discriminate on the ground of nationality: *Collins v Imtrat*: C-92/92 [1993] 3 CMLR 773, [1994] FSR 166, a case involving performers' rights. See para **27.1**.

16.7 Concerning the nature of the resale royalty right, it should be noted that it is not a part of 'copyright' law in the sense in which 'copyright' is understood in the common law jurisdictions.[1] It does not restrict the ability of any person other than the creator to make copies of, or to do anything with, the intellectual property in question. Nor is it a *droit moral*, a right the function of which is to protect the creator's reputation or integrity.[2] In short it is, to the Englishman, more in the way of an adjunct to the ordinary laws of personal property, rendering the seller of a chattel a trustee for the benefit of its creator. On the other hand, the resale royalty right is well understood in Continental jurisprudence to comprise a part of the 'author's right'.

1. On the common law notion of copyright see eg J Phillips, R Durie and I Karet *Whale on Copyright* (5th edn 1997), Ch 2.
2. On *droit moral* see Ch 18.

Is the resale royalty right practicable?

16.8 There would appear to be principally three ways in which a *droit de suite* could operate. One is a private right privately enforced by the sculptor or artist, or by his estate, against either the seller or the buyer of any work subject to the resale royalty right. The second is a private right collectively enforced through the assignment of that right to an appropriate agency which would enforce it and would channel the proceeds back to the beneficiary. The third is a state-administered system by which the proceeds of sale could be monitored and redirected as appropriate. The cost of administering resale royalties through a collecting body has been reckoned to represent about 15% of the revenue collected.[1] It is likely that developments in computing would enable marginal improvements to be made upon that figure.[2]

1. *Copyright and Designs Law* Cmnd 6732, 1977, para 797.
2. See, for example, the progressive reduction pro rata in operating costs achieved by the Public Lending Right Registry: para **15.10**.

16.9   From a practical point of view, each of these possible schemes suffers from the difficulty of tracing sales other than those conducted in public, such as auctions, or those reported in conveniently accessible media such as newspapers or art magazines. Such sources could however be more efficiently searched by a collecting agency than by individual beneficiaries of the right. It would be wrong in principle to exclude private sales from the resale royalty right, if such right be desirable; but apart from the difficulty of tracing such sales, a suitable limitation period for actions to recover the resale royalty would have to be determined.

16.10   In enacting the Copyright, Designs and Patents Act 1988, which was drafted with ratification of the Paris text of the Berne Convention in mind, the UK Parliament did not introduce *droit de suite*. Reasons for this, set out in the Government's White Paper of 1986,[1] included the difficulty of operating *droit de suite* over private sales, a recognition that justice might require the artist to share in losses as well as profits and the cost and complexity of administration. These last difficulties were expressed by a number of organisations consulted by the Australian Copyright Council in a survey[2] on *droit de suite*.

1. *Intellectual Property & Innovation*, Cmnd 9712 of 1986, paras 19.13-19.16.
2. Australian Copyright Council *Droit de Suite: the Art Resale Royalty and its Implications for Australia*, 1989; S Ricketson, 'Moral rights and the *Droit de Suite*: International Conditions and Australian Obligations' [1990] Ent LR 78.

Can the creator improve his position even without a statutory resale royalty right?

16.11   Even without a resale royalty right, the artist or sculptor can take some steps to protect his financial interest in his work. He can no longer seek membership of the Visual Artists Rights Society (VARS), which, during its brief existence, was prepared to assume the responsibility of administering his resale royalty rights overseas, in jurisdictions which provided for collective rather than purely individual administration of such rights.[1] On the other hand, he could turn his attention to the terms of the contract under which he parts with his work of art. He could require, as a term of sale, that the purchaser (i) pay to him or to his estate or assigns an agreed proportion of a subsequent purchase price, (ii) notify him of any subsequent sale and (iii) require any subsequent purchaser to accept a similar clause in his contract. Perhaps his lawyer could advise him to go even further and to insert a *Romalpa* clause into the contract,[2] to the effect that no title in the painting or sculpture would vest in the purchaser until *either* (in the event of a subsequent transfer) the payment by the purchaser of a proportion of the price he receives for it, *or* the elapsing of 70 years after the end of the year in which the work's creator died.

1. VARS was set up in the early 1980s but soon closed.
2. The *Romalpa* or 'reservation of title' clause is named after the case of *Aluminium Industrie Vaassen BV v Romalpa Aluminium Ltd* [1976] 1 WLR 676 in which that clause was drawn to lawyers' attention.

Droit de suite and the EC

16.12 It was suggested that, in so far as some EC art markets are subject to the operation of the *droit de suite* and others are not, there is a distortion in competition between these markets which is contrary to the provisions of the EC Treaty.[1] Given the relatively small amounts of money which were collected in resale royalty rights in those countries which operate it (for example SPADEM, in its time by far the most successful and prestigious resale royalty collection agency, received only two million francs on French sales in 1980,[2] and in 1972 the total sum collected worldwide was little over £100,000),[3] the operation of a *droit de suite* would appear to distort competition between art markets to no greater extent than does the disparity between the prices of restaurants and hotels at which art purchasers stay during auctions. This view was echoed by the Australian Copyright Council in recommending the introduction of *droit de suite* in Australia: the royalty should be 'absorbable along with other costs of sale (eg commission fees, etc)'.[4]

1. See, generally, Ch 27. For a criticism of this view, see D Booton 'A Critical Analysis of the European Commission's Proposal for a Directive Harmonising *Droit de Suite*' [1998] IPQ 165, at pp 176-179.
2. G McFarlane, n 1, para 16.1, at pp 146-147. SPADEM has since become insolvent and has ceased to operate: J H Merryman 'The Proposed Generalisation of the *Droit de Suite* in the European Communities' [1997] IPQ 16 at n 40. The Australian Copyright Council estimated in 1989 that a 5% resale royalty would generate $Aus 570,000: para **16.10**, n 2, above.

3. *Copyright and Designs Law* n 1, para 16.1, at para 797. A study by the US Copyright Office examined the right, which had been introduced in California by State legislation, concluded against its introduction at Federal level: *Droit de Suite: The Artist's Resale Royalty:* A Report of the Register of Copyrights of the Library of Congress (1993), cited by Merryman, n 2 above.
4. Para **16.13**, n 2, below.

16.13 The European Commission had recommended to the Council of Ministers that a *droit de suite* be generally enforced throughout its Member States.[1] But in 1981 the Commission's investigation into the harmonisation of *droit de suite* was abandoned, it being concluded that harmonisation within the EC would not prevent opportunities arising from its evasion by sales taking place outside the EC.[2] The possible effect of *droit de suite* in driving art sales outside the EC was mentioned in the 1986 White Paper 'Intellectual Property and Innovation'.[3] Nonetheless, the Commission renewed its interest in *droit de suite* and artists in the UK and elsewhere campaigned for its introduction.[4] In 1996 the European Commission made a further proposal for harmonisation,[5] which matured after much debate[6] into an EC Directive of the European Parliament and of the Council on the Resale Right for the Benefit of the Author of an Original Work of Art.[7] The title makes it clear that the proposed introduction of the right for manuscripts was not sustained.[8]

1. See *Reform of the Law relating to Copyright, Designs and Performers' Protection: a Consultative Document* Cmnd 8302, although the 'Dietz Report' (A Dietz *Copyright Law in the European Community* (1978)), commissioned by the Commission of the European Communities to examine, inter alia, the feasibility of establishing model harmonisation solutions, had explicitly excluded consideration of the *droit de suite* (see p viii).
2. [1981] EIPR D-162.
3. Cmnd 9712, para 19.15.
4. T Shapiro '*Droit de Suite*: an Author's Right in the Copyright Law of the European Community' [1992] Ent LR 118 argues in favour.
5. *Proposal for a European Parliament and Council Directive on the Resale Right for the benefit of the Author of an Original Work of Art*, COM (96) 97 final.
6. On the opposition of the UK art market and Government, see D Booton 'A Critical Analysis of the European Commission's Proposal for a Directive Harmonising *Droit de Suite*' [1998] IPQ 165.
7. Likely to be approved by the end of 2001. This chapter is based on the final draft available at the time of going to press.
8. Manuscripts not being included in the pre-existing French and German laws: S Hughes 'Droit de Suite: A Critical Analysis of the Proposed Directive' [1997] EIPR 694; and see Recital 19.

16.14 So far as the operation of the right in the UK is concerned, it is important to consider whether transfers other than the sale of an art work for money should constitute a sale for the purposes of a resale royalty claim. The equivalence of money and money's worth is recognised in the Copyright Designs and Patents Act 1988.[1] If, for example, a painting is not sold to a purchaser at an auction, but is exchanged for another painting or for services rendered, or if a painting is given to the Inland Revenue in satisfaction of an obligation to pay tax,[2] would the painter be entitled to benefit? The transferor of the painting in such instances has not actually received any money, but he has received the benefit of the appreciated value of the work. Recital 18 of the Directive[3] states that the right shall apply to 'all acts of resale', but that recital seems to be directed to the type of sale – public sales and those through a dealer attract the royalty[4] but wholly private sales do not – rather than the nature of consideration. Arts 3 and 4 refer to 'sale price' rather than 'proceeds of sale' or other more general term. The price is to be calculated net of tax[5] but presumably this refers to sales tax or value added tax[6] rather than any other fiscal obligation of the seller. A related problem is that of the applicability of *droit de suite* where the artist's work has become permanently fixed to the purchaser's building, or land, which is then sold *en bloc*: should the artist derive a share in what is essentially a sale of land?

1. Eg s 263(1) defines a commission as being for money or money's worth, in relation to ownership of unregistered design right.
2. The Inland Revenue will only accept works of pre-eminent national, historic or artistic interest.
3. Directive 2001/84 on the Resale Right for the Benefit of the Author of an Original Work of Art; [2001] OJ L272/32.
4. Ibid, art 1(2). Member States may provide that where a gallery buys a work from an artist for EUR 10,000 or less and resells it within three years, no royalty is payable: ibid, art 1(3).
5. Ibid, art 5.
6. Ibid, Recital 12 refers to harmonisation of 'turnover' or 'value added' taxes in the Community, which apply to the art market.

16.15 It is also important to consider the extent of the artist's or sculptor's share in the subsequent proceeds of sale of a work. Since the purchase of a work of art is commonly accepted to be an investment of one's money in an appreciating commodity, it should be accepted that some measure of legitimate profit can be accorded to the subsequent seller of the work in which his money is invested. To put it another way, a buyer of a £5,000 painting, selling it ten years later for £10,000, will frequently have done better to put his money into a building society or bank deposit account. Should he still have to cede a proportion of his relatively unsuccessful investment income to the artist? An affirmative answer seems harsh, and might have the unfortunate effect of depressing the price at which the creator of a work will be able to part with his creation; however, a negative answer leads us to problems of calculation of the *quantum* not only of the artist's entitlement, but also of the purchaser's. The taxation of capital appreciation in the UK already grapples with these problems;[1] only the net gain on disposal of an asset is subject to tax, after adjustments to reflect acquisition cost and the effects of inflation. Similar mechanisms have not, however, been adopted for resale royalties.[2]

1. See para **16.4**, n 1.
2. Directive 2001/84, Recital 20.

16.16 Once the question of the seller's obligation[1] is dealt with, the question of the creator's entitlement remains. It is difficult to see how any fixed proportion of the appreciated value of a work of art can be designated as appropriate for doing justice to its recipients. In one case it may be that an artist has enhanced the value of his own early work, by attracting greater recognition of his subsequent output. In another case the enhanced value of the work might itself be a consequence of the fact that a particularly distinguished art collector has purchased it, or that it has been exhibited at a prestigious exhibition. While it is not possible to deny that the great majority of creators of such intellectual property are unable to make a satisfactory living from their endeavours, it is not easy to see how the allocation of any particular proportion of the proceeds of a subsequent sale will remedy this, especially since subsequent sales may or may not occur. In this context, the provision of tax advantages for artists and sculptors in respect of the work's initial sale revenue may seem more apt for the purpose: after all, the subsequent sale may or may not take place, but the initial sale is inevitable in these instances.

1. Directive 2001/84 on the Resale Right for the Benefit of the Author of an Original Work of Art; [2001] OJ L272/32, art 1(4) provides that the seller, rather than the subsequent purchaser, shall be liable for the royalty. However there is an option for Member States to impose the liability on the 'art market professional' involved in the sale, ie the saleroom, gallery or dealer: ibid, art 1(2) and (4). See, also, Recital 25.

How will the resale royalty be calculated?

16.17 The Directive sets a sliding scale of resale royalty. Significant features are the minimum threshold, the rate bands and the maximum royalty. The minimum threshold is designed to exclude sales at the low end of the price range, where the costs of collecting and administering the royalty would be disproportionate to the benefit to the artist.[1] Member States are obliged to provide for resale royalties on sale prices in excess of EUR 3,000,[2] currently a little less than £2,000. However, a Member State may set the threshold lower than this.[3] Once the sale price exceeds the minimum threshold, the initial royalty rate is 4% on the portion of the sale price up to EUR 50,000.[4] It is not entirely clear from Art 4 that the 4% royalty applies to the whole sale price rather than to the excess over EUR 3,000. Assuming that this is the case, a seller will achieve a lower price net of royalty for sales between EUR 3,000 and 3,125 than for a sale at EUR 2,999.[5] The rates and bands are shown in Table 1.

Table 1 (all prices in EUR)

Sale Price	Royalty rate
Up to 50,000	4%
50,001-200,000	3%
200,001-350,000	1%
350,001-500,000	0.5%
500,001 upwards	0.25%

The maximum resale royalty is 12,500.[6]

1. Directive 2001/84 on the Resale Right for the Benefit of the Author of an Original Work of Art; [2001] OJ L272/32, Recital 22.
2. Ibid, art 3(2).
3. Ibid, art 3(1); Member States also have freedom to set the royalty rate in this band, provided that it is no lower than 4%: art 4(3).
4. Ibid, art 4(1)(a). However, Member States may set an alternative rate of 5% in this band: art 4(2).
5. Earlier drafts produced anomalous calculations in the bottom band: S Hughes 'Droit de Suite: A Critical Analysis of the Proposed Directive' [1997] EIPR 694 at pp 696-697. Hughes questions the wisdom of a variable rate, noting that France scrapped variable rates in favour of a fixed rate in 1957.
6. Proviso to art 4(1). Hughes, n 5 above, recommended a maximum threshold, which would produce the same effect.

To which works does the resale royalty obligation attach?

16.18 The 'original works of art' to which the resale right applies are defined in Art 2(1) as:

> 'works of graphic or plastic art such as pictures, collages, paintings, drawings, engravings, prints, lithographs, sculptures, tapestries, ceramics, glassware and photographs, provided they are made by the artist himself or are copies considered to be original works of art.'

16.18   *Resale royalty rights*

This definition elaborates in two ways upon that in Art 14*ter* of the Berne Convention.[1] First, it provides a non-exhaustive list of works which may be considered as 'art'. Secondly, it sets a rather odd standard of originality. Other copyright directives, such as the Database Directive,[2] refer to the author's 'own intellectual creation'. Resale royalty was intended to attach to limited edition prints and the like as well as to one-off works.[3] It is surprising, however, that there need be no work which meets usual the copyright standard.[4] Nor is there any guidance as to how many copies may be 'considered original works of art'. Art 2(2) merely states that copies 'made in limited numbers by the artist himself or under his authority shall be considered to be original works of art' for the purposes of the directive. Earlier drafts referred to 'professional usage' or to a maximum of 12 copies.[5] The US Copyright Office recommended in 1992 that any Federal *droit de suite* apply only to limited editions of 10 or less.[6] The EC directive appears to leave *droit de suite* open to the kind of abuse cited by Merryman, where an artist signs blank pieces of paper on which prints can be made.[7]

1. See para **16.6**.
2. Directive 96/9, [1996] OJ L77/20.
3. Directive 2001/84 on the Resale Right for the Benefit of the Author of an Original Work of Art; [2001] OJ L272/32, art 2(2).
4. See S Hughes 'Droit de Suite: A Critical Analysis of the Proposed Directive' [1997] EIPR 694.
5. Ibid.
6. US Copyright Office Report *Droit de Suite: The Artist's Resale Royalty* (1992) p 151, cited in Hughes, n 5 above.
7. J H Merryman 'The Proposed Generalisation of the *Droit de Suite* in the European Communities' [1997] IPQ 16 at n 26.

Will droit de suite really be administered, and how?

16.19   The Directive tacitly acknowledges that in many Member States, even those with legislation providing for resale royalty, the right is not effective. Recital 28 makes clear that Member States are responsible for regulating the exercise of the right, possibly by means a collecting society.[1] It goes on to insist that the Members States must ensure that amounts intended for authors who are nationals of other member states are in fact collected and distributed. The rights endure for the copyright term of author's life plus 70 years.[2] The author is entitled to receive the royalties during his lifetime, thereafter those entitled under national laws of succession.[3] Although Member States are required to implement the directive by 1 January 2006,[4] Member States which do not already have the right may postpone commencement of the right to posthumous royalties until 1 January

2010[5] or for a further two years if notice is given to the Commission.[6] To assist in collecting the royalty, the person entitled may require information from art market professionals up to three years from the relevant resale.[7] This falls short of the notification requirement recommended by Hughes.[8]

1. Directive 2001/84 on the Resale Right for the Benefit of the Author of an Original Work of Art; [2001] OJ L272/32, art 6 allows for compulsory or optional collective management.
2. Ibid, art 8.1.
3. Ibid, art 6, recital 27.
4. Ibid, art 12(1).
5. Ibid, art 8(2).
6. Ibid, art 8(3).
7. Ibid, art 9.
8. See S Hughes 'Droit de Suite: A Critical Analysis of the Proposed Directive' [1997] EIPR 694.

Conclusion

16.20 There would seem to be a substantial moral basis for seeking to improve the financial position of the creative artist and his heirs. The implementation of a *droit de suite* is one of a number of ways of achieving this end, but it is not clear whether it is, in theory or in practice, the most appropriate means of doing so.[1] In the meantime, it would be a valuable exercise if artists were to adopt the contractual expedients mentioned above.

1. See, also, details of the US Copyright Office Hearings on the *droit de suite*, published at (1992) 16 Col-VLA J of Law and the Arts 185.

Chapter 17

Performers' protection

The traditional view examined

17.1 The copyright law of the United Kingdom concerns itself with the protection not of ideas but of objects or distributional media in which those ideas are embodied or by which they are communicated. The performance of a work by an actor or musician is, in the theory, neither an idea in itself nor a medium for its embodiment or transmission; it is merely an ephemeral and insubstantial execution of the idea of another, and thus does not merit copyright protection.[1] This view is of course open to criticism.[2] Even if performers are not also authors of their material,[3] it may take the intellectual and inspirational work of a talented pianist to give shape and form to an otherwise unappreciated sonata. Likewise, a run-of-the-mill play or film script can be brought to life for its audience by the intelligent rendition of a principal part by a well-trained actor. If a performance is itself the product of intellectual effort, and each different performance of a work can be separately identified, recorded and commercially exploited, it would seem at least as deserving of protection as the motley array of bus tickets, advertising jingles, X-ray plates and jam jar labels which currently enjoy the law's patronage.

1. Cf *Copyright and Designs Law* Cmnd 6732, 1977, at para 409: the Whitford Committee felt that it was on practical, not moral, grounds that a copyright should not be granted.
2. R Arnold 'Are Performers Authors?' [1999] EIPR 464, commenting on the decision in *Hadley v Kemp* [1999] EMLR 589.
3. As was the case in *Stuart v Barrett* [1994] EMLR 448.

The Performers' Protection Acts

17.2 The vulnerability of performers was recognised at a comparatively early stage in the United Kingdom: in 1925 Parliament enacted the Dramatic and Musical Performers' Protection Act. The protection granted was that of the criminal rather than the civil law. This meant that someone whose performance of a dramatic or musical

246

work was recorded without permission could, having made a complaint, leave it to the state to bring the wrongdoer to justice. This means of protection had its drawbacks: the statute provided no compensation for aggrieved performers; the penalties faced by illicit recorders ('bootleggers') were light; to secure a conviction involved proof of the crime beyond reasonable doubt. In 1958, the 1925 Act was replaced by a broadly similar statute. Under the Dramatic and Musical Performers' Protection Act 1958 a performance still had to be of a *work* to qualify for protection and criminal penalties were again the sanction for unauthorised recording.

The Rome Convention

17.3 In 1961, representatives of 44 countries, including the United Kingdom, gathered in Rome to agree a convention for 'the protection of performers, producers of phonograms and broadcasting organisations'. Art 7(1) recited that the protection provided for performers should include the *possibility of preventing* broadcasting and fixation of performances without consent. In 1963 the United Kingdom ratified the Rome Convention[1] and enacted the Performers' Protection Act 1963. This statute supplemented the 1958 Act and contained[2] a rather nice description of performers:

> '. . . any actors, singers, musicians, dancers or other persons who act, sing, deliver, declaim, play in or otherwise perform literary, dramatic, musical or artistic works.'

Subsequently, penalties for offences were greatly increased by the Performers' Protection Act 1972. However, the countries of the world were slow to ratify the Rome Convention. Even by 15 July 2001, only 68 countries were listed on the WIPO website[3] as being parties to Rome.

1. Cmnd 2425 (1964).
2. In s 1(1).
3. www.wipo.org. As opposed to the 148 signatories of the Berne Convention and 162 of the Paris Convention. For these treaties, see ch 28.

Civil rights of action

17.4 During the 1960s and early 1970s, the UK pop record industry had burgeoned. The rewards of illicit commercial recording tempted many to run the risk of fines or imprisonment. In a number of cases, prior to 1986, attempts were made to bring civil proceedings against bootleggers for breach of statutory duty. These cases were largely unsuccessful, although in *Ex p Island Records*[1] the Court of Appeal took the view that, while the Performers' Protection Acts did not confer civil rights of action on performers or their record companies, equity might intervene to prevent the commission of crimes. The latter part of this decision was disapproved by the House of Lords in *Lonrho Ltd v Shell (No 2)*.[2] This conclusion was strengthened by the decision in *RCA Corpn v Pollard*,[3] where the performer in question (Elvis Presley) had died and was not a party to the action. The Court of Appeal confirmed in that case that recording companies could not obtain redress against bootleggers.

1. [1978] Ch 122.
2. [1982] AC 173.
3. [1983] FSR 9.

'Pink Panther' litigation: Rickless v United Artists

17.5 In 1986 the tide turned decisively in favour of performers. The personal representatives of the late Peter Sellers had brought a civil action[1] to restrain the use of clips and out-takes[2] from 'Pink Panther' films, in which Sellers had starred as the muddlesome Inspector Clouseau, to make a posthumous film. Sellers had not consented to such use of the material; indeed it was contrary to express terms in Sellers' contracts. The Court of Appeal held[3] that performers enjoyed civil rights of action under the Acts which had been passed for their protection. Furthermore, personal representatives were entitled to sue on those rights for some unspecified period after a performer's death. The injunction and substantial damages awarded by the trial judge were upheld. This result was no doubt satisfactory to the shades of Peter Sellers and to his heirs but it left the law in an unsatisfactory state. In the first edition of this book, Jeremy Phillips wrote:

> '...the term implicit in the Acts is that of the life of the performer, it being for the performer to give written permission for authorised copies and recordings to be made. The performer cannot give written consent once he has died and, since he is the "victim" of the crime whom the Acts seek to protect,[4] he is in no need of protection once he has passed away.'

That sensible view was overtaken by *Rickless*, which made it difficult for Parliament to grant lifetime-only rights of action to performers – if rights were to terminate upon death, accrued rights and expectations might have to be extinguished.[5] Other potential problems arose. The only acts spared from infringement by the Performers' Protection Acts were those carried out for private and domestic purposes; a public act of reporting or research might be permitted under copyright law but still fall foul of performers' rights.

1. *Rickless v United Artists Corpn* [1988] QB 40.
2. Unused sections of film.
3. [1988] QB 40.
4. See eg *RCA Corpn v Pollard* [1983] FSR 9 at 18-19 (per Oliver LJ).
5. Furthermore, the Rome Convention in art 14 specifies a minimum period of 20 years' protection, calculated from the end of the year in which the performance takes place.

The 1988 reforms

17.6 The Copyright, Designs and Patents Act 1988 retained criminal sanctions[1] against illicit recording and exploitation of such recordings and introduced express rights of action for performers and for those enjoying exclusive rights to record the performances. These rights enabled their owners to prevent unauthorised recording and live broadcasts and to restrain commercial use of illicit recordings.[2] Protection was extended to variety artists and the definition of 'performance' was released in most cases from the stricture that a work be performed.[3] The rights subsisted if the performer, performance or record company had an appropriate link[4] with the United Kingdom, the European Community or a Rome Convention country.[5] The performers' rights introduced by the 1998 Act were personal and inalienable during the performer's life.[6] After death they were to be administered by the person directed in the performer's will, or by personal representatives if no testamentary direction is given.[7] Thus representatives might be involved in litigation and distribution many years after a performer's death. The rights of persons enjoying exclusive recording contracts appear to be transmissible only together with the benefit of those contracts.[8] These rights remain but have been partially supplanted by so-called 'performers' property rights'.[9]

1. Copyright, Designs and Patents Act 1988, ss 180(1) and 198.
2. Ibid, s 180(1).
3. Ibid, s 180(2).
4. Copyright, Designs and Patents Act 1988, ss 181, 206.
5. As at July 1999 the Performances (Reciprocal Protection)(Convention Countries) Order 1999, Sch, Part 1, lists 47 such states (other than EC Member States). See para **17.3**, n 3.
6. Ibid, s 192, now repealed by the Copyright and Related Rights Regulations 1996 (SI 1996/2967) and replaced by s 192A, which makes equivalent provision for 'performers' non-property rights'.
7. Ibid, s 192 A(2).
8. Ibid, s 192B.
9. Ibid, s 191A-M.

17.7   *Performers' protection*

The TRIPs agreement

17.7   The Agreement on Trade-Related Aspects of Intellectual Property Rights (TRIPs)[1] requires minimum standards of protection for performers.[2] Art 14(1) provides that performers must be able to prevent the unauthorised 'fixation' (recording) of their performances and the reproduction of such bootleg recordings. They must also be able to control the broadcasting and communication to the public of their live performances. For countries outside the EC which are parties to TRIPs but not to the Rome Convention, performers' rights in the UK are limited to those required by TRIPs.[3]

1. Complementary to the World Trade Organization Agreement; see para **28.2**.
2. Art 14 also sets a minimum standard of protection for producers of phonograms and for broadcasting organisations.
3. Performances (Reciprocal Protection)(Convention Countries) Order 1999 (SI 1999/1752), reg 3. The countries concerned are listed in Part 2 of the Schedule to the order. They include the United States of America.

European Community developments

17.8   Performers were protected to differing extents in the various Member States of the EU. In the early 1990s, there were discussions at Community level about the accession of Member States to the Rome Convention.[1] Subsequently, three harmonising directives in the area of copyright and related rights were influential in extending the scope of protection available for performers within the EU. First, Directive 92/100/EEC conferred rights on performers to authorise or prohibit the rental or lending of recordings of their performances.[2] These rights were to be transferable, but the performers would retain an unwaivable right to equitable remuneration for rental.[3] The same directive further required Member States to give performers rights over the broadcasting, communication to the public or recording of their live performances and the reproduction or distribution of recordings of performances.[4] The reproduction and distribution rights, unlike their UK counterparts, were to be transferable inter vivos.[5] Second, the 'Cable and Satellite' Directive 93/83/EEC ensured that performers' broadcasting rights included satellite broadcasts[6] and allowed cable retransmission rights to be exercised only by way of collective administration.[7] Last, the 'term Directive' 93/98/EEC harmonised the duration of performers' rights.[8] Unfortunately, the term directive introduced the compulsory 'comparison of term',[9] so that where the UK protects the performances of artistes from outside the EC,[10] it must do so only for as long as performers protection lasts in the country of origin. These Directives have been implemented by the Copyright

250

and Related Rights Regulations 1996.[11] As a result, UK law on performers' protection has become highly complex.[12] What follows necessarily gives only a taste of some of the principles.

1. See, for example, Council Resolution of 14 May 1992; [1992] OJ C138/1.
2. [1992] OJ L346/61, art 2(1).For rental right, see para **13.21**. For lending right, see para **15.2**.
3. Ibid, art 4.
4. Ibid, arts 6-9.
5. Arts 7(2) and 9(4).
6. [1993] OJ L248/15, art 4
7. Ibid, arts 8 and 9.
8. [1993] OJ L290/9, art 3(1).
9. Ibid, art 7(2).
10. For the position of third countries generally, see K H Pilny and B R Eagle 'The Significance of Intellectual Property at the Community Level vis-á-vis Non-EU Trading Nations' [1998] EIPR 4.
11. SI 1996/2967.
12. For a thorough treatment, readers may consult R Arnold Performers' Rights (2nd edn, 1997); H Laddie et al *The Modern Law of Copyright* (3rd edn, 2000), ch 12.

The WIPO Treaty and proposal

17.9 The situation will become even more elaborate when the UK ratifies the WIPO Performances and Phonograms Treaty of 1996,[1] which relates to sound performances and recordings only. The main change to UK law will be the introduction of moral rights for performers.[2] However, the rules on qualification for protection will be complicated further, to the extent to which the Treaty is ratified by countries outside the EC. On the horizon is a WIPO initiative on audiovisual performances.[3]

1. Of 20 December 1996. See J Reinbothe and S von Lewinski 'The New WIPO Treaties: A First Resumé' [1997] EIPR 171.
2. See para **18.16**; for a comparative view, see A Bertrand 'Moral Rights in Performances' [1994] Ent LR 114.
3. S von Lewinski 'The WIPO Diplomatic Conference on Audiovisual Performers: A First Resumé' [2001] EIPR 333; see para **18.16**.

Consent

17.10 In contrast with the requirement in earlier Acts that valid consent be given in writing by or on behalf of the performer, consent under the 1988 Act need take no particular form.[1] It may be specific or general, retrospective or prospective. It is presumably open to a performer to give qualified or conditional consent – that a recording of the performance be used for some purposes but not others. Although this is not spelt out in the 1988 Act, any other conclusion would be inconsistent with the provisions of the Rome Convention[2] and with *Rickless*.[3] A performer's consent is effective against a record company to whom (s)he has granted exclusive rights, even though in those circumstances it will constitute a breach of the recording contract to permit a third party to record. It is a crime for someone to represent falsely that he is authorised to give consent[4] but false representation of authority is not a form of civil infringement of rights in performances.[5] The problems of obtaining consents to reproduce a previous recording where a large number of people were involved in the performance may be alleviated by applying to the copyright tribunal to give consent on behalf of performers who cannot be traced.[6]

1. Copyright, Designs and Patents Act 1988, s 193.
2. Cmnd 2425, 1964, art 7(1)(c)(ii).
3. [1988] QB 40, see also para **17.5**.
4. Copyright, Designs and Patents Act 1988, s 201.
5. Cf copyright infringement by authorisation: see ch 26 below.
6. Copyright, Designs and Patents Act 1988, s 190 as amended by the Copyright and Related Rights Regulations 1996, reg 23 (SI 1996/2967).

The meaning of 'performance'

17.11   'Performance' is defined[1] as meaning a live performance by one or more individuals which is a dramatic performance (including dance or mime), a musical performance, a reading or recitation of a literary work, or the performance of a variety act (or any similar presentation). The last category[2] was introduced for the first time by the 1988 Act. Judi Dench acting a Shakespearean role or reading a sonnet, Michael Flatley executing a lively dance sequence or Marcel Marceau silently carrying out a masterpiece of mime would all be giving 'performances'. So would Winton Marsalis improvising on the trumpet, Barbara Fusar Poli and Maurizio Margaglio doing a breathtaking ice routine and motley jugglers and street artistes at the Avignon festival. Tim Henman playing tennis at Wimbledon or Tiger Woods on the golf course at St Andrews might give fine sporting performances but they would probably not enjoy protection under the 1988 Act.[3] Somewhere between these two groups are those highly-paid Premier League footballers who perform skilled impersonations of a player being scythed down in the penalty area by a member of the opposing team. Other types of activity are difficult to categorise; for example, are the aerobatic routines of the Red Arrows flying team 'performances'? And what about a firework display arranged to accompany Handel's firework music? The Performers' Protection Acts also protected the performance of an artistic work, possibly referring to the long-gone custom of presenting 'tableaux vivants' where actors posed so as to reproduce well-known works of art.[4] If a tableau vivant were staged today it would presumably be protected as being akin to a variety act.

1. Copyright, Designs and Patents Act 1988, s 180(2).
2. The WIPO Performances and Phonograms Treaty of 1996 has 'expressions of folklore' rather than 'variety acts'.
3. See V Pasek 'Performers' Rights in Sport' Copyright World, Issue Eight, January/February 1990, p 13; but see R Arnold, 'Copyright in Sporting Events' in E Barendt and A Firth (eds) *Yearbook of Copyright and Media Law 2001*.
4. See *Hanfstaengl v Empire Palace* [1894] 2 Ch 1.

The rights conferred

17.12   A performer's rights in a qualifying performance are infringed by live broadcast or cable transmission of the whole or a substantial part of the performance without the performer's consent.[1] Other forms of infringement under section 182 are: recording directly from a live performance and recording directly from a live broadcast or cablecast.[2] Where a performance is played in public, broadcast or cablecast from a commercially published sound recording, the performer is entitled to equitable remuneration.[3] The notion of substantiality derives from copyright law,[4] where the quality of what is used is as important as the quantity. It is also an infringement without consent to make an unauthorised copy of a recorded performance.[5] So if, with sales in mind, I videotape a television broadcast of Marilyn Manson performing on tour, and make copies of the recording to sell in a street market, all the video recordings will be illicit[6] unless I obtain appropriate consent. My sales on Oxford Street will constitute infringement of another right, that of issuing copies to the public.[7] The rental and lending of the original recording of the performance, or of copies of it, also require consent: section 182C. The rights of reproduction, distribution and rental/lending are designated 'performers' property rights'. As well as being assignable,[8] they attract all the usual remedies for infringement of property rights.[9] Additional damages are also available.[10] Infringement of the other rights is actionable as a breach of statutory duty, as are the rights enjoyed by those having exclusive recording contracts with performers.[11] Apart from remedies provided by the general law, delivery up and peripatetic seizure are specifically provided for under the Act.[12]

1. Copyright Designs and Patents Act, s 182(1)(b).
2. Ibid, s 182(1)(a) and (c).
3. Ibid, s 182D, implementing art 8.1 of Directive 92/100 of 19 November 1992 on rental right and lending right and on certain rights relating to copyright in the field of intellectual property OJ 1992 L346/61. The right may not be assigned,

except to a collecting society. For criticism of the right, see A Robinson 'UK Copyright and the Communication of Sound Recordings to the Public' [1995] Ent LR 312.
4. Copyright, Designs and Patents Act 1988, s 16(3)(a); S Bate and L Abramson 'To Sample or Not to Sample' [1997] Ent LR 193.
5. Copyright Designs and Patents Act 1988 s 182B. *Bassey v Icon Entertainment plc* [1995] EMLR 596 confirmed that this was the case under previous law.
6. 'Illicit recording' is fully defined in s 197.
7. Copyright, Designs and Patents Act 1988, s 182B.
8. Where rental right is assigned, the performer retains a right to equitable remuneration for rental of sound recordings or films embodying his qualifying performance. This operates rather like the right to equitable remuneration outlined at n 3 above, except that it may be discharged by a single payment at the time of transfer of the rental right: Copyright, Design and Patents Act 1988, s 191H(4).
9. Ibid, s 191I ff.
10. Ibid, s 191J. See para **17.14**.
11. Copyright, Designs and Patents Act 1988, s 194.
12. Ss 195 and 196.

Infringing use of 'bootleg' recordings

17.13   Once a recording has been made without the performer's consent, the performer's rights may further be infringed by playing the recording in public, broadcasting it or including it in a cable programme service[1] when the infringer knows or has reason to believe that the recording was made without consent. This mode of infringement may be difficult to invoke since it requires the absence of consent twice – once at the making of the recording and once at its presentation to the public – as well as actual or constructive knowledge on the part of the infringer. It was not infringement under the 1988 Act, as originally drafted, to broadcast a legitimate recording[2] or to broadcast an illicit recording if permission to broadcast is obtained. However, the EC rental right directive[3] required Member States to confer exclusive rights upon performers to control the distribution, rental and lending of fixations of their performances, be they illicit or licit.[4] The wider rights, now contained in sections 182A-D of the Copyright, Designs and Patents Act are outlined above.[5] There are further varieties of infringement[6] – importing (not for private and domestic purposes), commercially possessing or dealing with illicit recordings.[7] Again, lack of consent must be proved on two occasions – on the making of the recording (which must or ought to be known to the infringer) and at the time of the import (or other unauthorised act). Once the illicit recording has passed through the hands of an innocent acquirer – someone who did not know and had no reason to believe that the recording was made without consent – reasonable royalty damages are the only remedy for these latter infringements.[8]

1. Copyright, Designs and Patents Act 1988, s 183 (performers) and s 187 (those having exclusive recording rights).
2. This act may however infringe copyright in the recording and in any included works.
3. Note 2, para **17.8**, implemented by the Copyright and Related Rights Regulations 1996 (SI 1996/2967).
4. Arts 8.1, 9.1 and 2.1.
5. Para **17.12**.
6. Ibid, s 184.
7. For 'recording' and 'illicit' see para **17.12**, nn 2 and 3 above.
8. Ibid, s 184(2) and (3).

Civil remedies for non-performers

17.14   Where a commercially valuable and highly sought-after performer contracts to make records exclusively for one manufacturer, that manufacturer has a particular interest in suing bootleggers. This is because any person who records and makes illicit copies of a live or recorded performance of a pop-star is likely to make sales of those copies at the expense of the record manufacturer. In business terms the legitimate manufacturer bears the cost of the artist's recording fees and royalties, the studio recording expenses, so-called value-added tax, promotion and publicity, while the illicit exploiter (a 'bootlegger') pays no royalties or taxes and conveniently rides upon the crest of the legitimate manufacturer's publicity campaign. If the investment of time, effort and money in the making of new records and the promotion of new performers is considered to be a good thing, that investment should be protected in law. The 1988 Act introduced protection for those who enjoy an exclusive recording contract in respect of the performance in question. 'Persons having recording rights'[1] are granted rights similar to those originally granted by the 1988 Act to performers.[2] However, Parliament has not seen fit to grant separate rights in performances to those who enjoy exclusive *broadcasting* rights.

1. Copyright, Designs and Patents Act 1988, s 185.
2. Ibid, ss 186-188.

Limits upon rights in performances

17.15   Just as the Copyright, Designs and Patents Act 1988 curtails the copyright monopoly by expressly permitting certain activities which might otherwise infringe,[1] section 189 and Schedule 2 provide a battery of exceptions to the statutory rights in performances. Many of the acts permitted by copyright law are reproduced in these provisions. Others such as the private study or time-shifting exception[2] are unnecessary, since private and domestic activities do not in any event infringe rights in performances. A notable exception is fair dealing for non-private research, which is spared from copyright infringement by section 29. Scientific research is a worthy activity mentioned in the Rome Convention;[3] research is not, however, referred to anywhere in Schedule 2. Thus the onus is presumably upon a researcher who wishes to reproduce substantial parts of a performance to obtain consents from all performers or to apply for substituted consent from the Copyright Tribunal[4] – an onerous task. This is despite the fact that Art 10 of the EC rental right directive[5] permits the same exceptions for performers' rights as the member state provides for copyright and makes further explicit mention of private and educational uses. Performers' property rights can be licensed, and licensing schemes can be challenged before the Copyright Tribunal,[6] as can certain matters relating to the rights to equitable remuneration.

1. See paras **14.17** and **14.19** above.
2. See s 70.
3. Art 15(1)(c).
4. See para **17.5** above.
5. Note 2, para **17.12**.
6. Copyright, Designs and Patents Act, s 205B. E Bragiel 'Is the Copyright Tribunal Showing Irrational Tendencies? [2001] EIPR 371.

Criminal provisions

17.16 In the absence of sufficient consent,[1] the commercial making, possession of or dealing with an illicit recording,[2] if the person concerned knows or has reason to believe that the recording was made without permission, may result in a substantial fine or imprisonment[3] as well as delivery up of the illicit recordings.[4] From a date yet to be appointed, section 198A imposes upon local Weights and Measures Authorities[5] the duty of enforcing these criminal provisions.

1. For a definition see Copyright, Designs and Patents Act 1988, s 198(3).
2. Ibid, s 197.
3. Ibid, s 198(5).
4. Ibid, s 199.
5. Ie Trading Standards officers.

Chapter 18

Moral rights

The concept of the moral right

18.1 The concession by Parliament that authors could enjoy the copyright in their works was founded upon a recognition that authors were engaged in the creation of culturally beneficial works[1] which would be copied without compensation if no right to control copies were established. For this reason copyright has usually been viewed in the UK as an essentially economic tool by means of which the author can carve his living. The civil law jurisdiction of continental Europe[2] did not, however, start from the same premise. Instead, the author was viewed as being entitled, by virtue of the fact that he had created a work, to control all facets of that work; and since his creation, as a form of self-expression, reflected upon his personal reputation and integrity, not merely the right of commercial exploitation of his work, but the right to sustain the integrity of his relationship with the world by means of his work was acknowledged as an appropriate subject of legal protection. The rights of commercial exploitation were often described as 'patrimonial rights'; they could be licensed, assigned, abandoned or treated in the same way as any other commercial commodity. The rights which protected the integrity of the author's reputation were called 'moral rights'; they could not be sold or eroded by the claims of commercial efficacy, and might even be regarded as vesting in perpetuity.[3] While these rights are a component of author's right and hence closely allied to copyright, they may also be seen as a means of protecting information and reputation. For other rights achieving these ends, see the following chapters of this book.[4]

1. And publishers were engaged in disseminating them. Cf P Prescott 'The Origins of Copyright: a Debunking View' [1989] 12 EIPR 453.
2. At least since the French revolution. See, eg, A Dietz 'The Moral Rights of the Author: Moral Rights and the Civil Law Countries' (1995) 19 Col-VLA J of Law and the Arts 199.
3. For good accounts of the *droit moral* as viewed by the common lawyer see S Ricketson *The Law of Intellectual Property* (2nd edn, 1999), ch 10.

4.   See, also, *Clark v Associated Newspapers* [1998] RPC 261, where the claimant succeeded in passing off and for false attribution of authorship under the Copyright, Designs and Patents Act 1988, s 84(1).

Types of moral right

18.2   A number of moral rights exist in civil law jurisdictions in one form or another. They include:

(i)   The right to be acknowledged as the author of a work (droit à la paternité): this is perhaps the most fundamental moral right, since it is the right to the acknowledgement by the world that a particular state of affairs exists. Since for most authors the financial rewards of creation are few, irregular and begrudgingly bestowed long in arrears, the spontaneous plaudits of recognition and appreciation by one's audience will warm the heart even if they do not fill the stomach. An author who has no right to insist upon the world knowing that he is indeed the author thus risks the loss of his greatest satisfaction.

(ii)   Corollary to an author's right to be identified with a work is the principle that the work should not be attributed to the wrong person as author; in these circumstances the alleged author, as well as the true author, might have cause for complaint.

(iii)   The right to determine when a work is complete, and to refuse to complete it if he is not satisfied with it: this right is of particular value to artists who may judge themselves by standards more exacting than those who have commissioned their services.

(iv)   Once a work is complete, the right to decide whether, when and how the work should be made available to the public. This may be achieved by exercising copyright appropriately, but may be bolstered by the moral right to repent of one's work and to have it withdrawn before it is published: thus the author of even a completed work may be able to claim that, since he has changed his mind about what he is saying, a work which no longer reflects his true ideas would cast a slur upon his integrity.[1] In some jurisdictions the right of repentance (*droit de repentir*) may be exercised even after publication.

(v)   Once complete, a work has its own integrity; tampering with it might reflect back unfavourably upon the author. Thus there is recognised the right to object to mutilations of one's work: since the completed work is the ultimate form of the author's expression, to tamper with it whether by adding to or subtracting from it is to cause the author's audience to draw a distorted conclusion as to the author's work. The exercise of this 'right of integrity' is the subject of great anxiety to editors and parodists, amongst others.[2]

(vi) The right to object to undesirable modes of display or exploitation: perhaps a sub-head of the previous right, this covers such acts as the broadcasting of a film with so many breaks for commercial advertising that, although the film itself is not altered in any way, the impact upon the audience is lessened.[3] Other acts under this head would be the display of a sculpture, which was designed for a particular location, in another location[4] or the adoption by a right-wing political party of an anthem composed by a left-wing composer (or vice versa).

(vii) The right to prevent the physical destruction of one's work: this right indicates the existence of a major area of conflict between the author or artist and the purchaser of his works. The purchaser expects to be able to treat a purchased artwork as his own, and thus to be able to use or abuse it in such way as he feels appropriate. He cannot do so if the artist's right to insist upon the survival of his work takes precedence over his proprietary rights.[5] Conflict is likely in cases such as that of the artist whose major *oeuvre* is a mural which has been lovingly and painstakingly applied to the wall of a building when the owner intends to demolish it in order to make way for another building.

(viii) The right to the loyalty of one's publisher: thus it is inconsistent with the *droit moral* for the publisher of an author's work to publish a work by another author which is critical or derogatory of the first author.[6]

(ix) The right to respond to criticism, especially if it is excessive.

1. Ricketson, n 3 to para **18.1** above, at para 10.5, n 7, cites the case of the artist Whistler who, being dissatisfied with a portrait, refused to hand it over to the sitter's husband; he was obliged to pay damages to the claimant, but not to deliver up the painting.
2. And film distributors: see *Argos Films SA v Ivens* [1992] FSR 547 where the moral right was used to prevent the distributor inserting an explanation.
3. This was restrained in the US as copyright infringement on the basis that the cutting and insertion involved went beyond the terms of the original licence of 'Monty Python' programmes: *Gilliam v American Broadcasting Companies Inc* 538 F 2d 14 (1976). Cf *Preminger v Columbia Picture Corpn* 149 US 872 (1966). See E Donovan, S Donovan and C Berman 'Mural Art and the Artist's Rights' (1989) Copyright World, Issue 4, p 11.
4. However in *Re Lenin's Monument* [1992] FSR 265 the right of the owner wishing to remove the monument from its place of display and preserve it by burying prevailed as against the sculptor.
5. See eg the dispute between the Bernard Buffet and the owner of a refrigerator upon which paintings had been made, as to whether the refrigerator might be sold off piecemeal: *Cour de Cassation* judgment of 6 July 1965. Ricketson, n 3 to para **18.1** above, at para 10.5, n 13.
6. A case in point is *Editions Gallimard v Hamish Hamilton Ltd* [1986] FSR 42 (estate of Camus brought successful action against publisher of subsequent critique).

18.3 *Moral rights*

The Berne Convention and United Kingdom law

18.3 Art 6*bis* of the Berne Convention for the Protection of Literary and Artistic Works[1] states:

'(1) Independently of the author's economic rights, and even after the transfer of the said rights, the author shall have the right to claim authorship of the work and to object to any distortion, mutilation or other modification of, or other derogatory action in relation to, the said work, which would be prejudicial to his honour or reputation.

(2) The rights granted to the author in accordance with the preceding paragraph shall, after his death, be maintained, at least until the expiry of the economic rights, and shall be exercisable by the persons or institutions authorised by the legislation of the country where protection is claimed...

(3) The means of redress for safeguarding the rights granted by this Article shall be governed by the legislation of the country where protection is claimed.'

The United Kingdom has been a party to the Berne Convention since 1887 but has not shown generosity to authors in the grant of moral rights.[2] It was received wisdom for many years that the protection of copyright combined with that of the general law (in particular the laws of contract, defamation and passing off[3]) plus a sprinkling of express statutory provisions[4] made sufficient provision for moral rights. The general attitude of British lawyers was typified by Danckwerts LJ in *Chaplin v Leslie Frewin Ltd*,[5] a case in which a minor wished to withdraw from publication a book which, he claimed, was defamatory, scandalous and would cause his own reputation to suffer. His Lordship felt that, since the assignment of copyright was solely a commercial matter, the transfer of property for gain, even such matters as the author's moral welfare were irrelevant. As he put it, 'The mud may cling, but the profit will be secured'.[6]

1. Cmnd 5002, 1972.
2. G Dworkin 'The Moral Right and English Copyright Law' (1981) 12 IIC 476.
3. See paras **19.6** and **20.7** ff.
4. The rights to object to publication, etc, of altered artistic works and to object to false attribution of authorship: Copyright Act 1956, s 43.
5. [1966] Ch 71.
6. Ibid at 95.

18.4 It was characteristic of the British perversity of logic that the non-author, who could hardly be expected to benefit as a class from the Copyright Act 1956, enjoyed greater protection of his integrity than did the author. If Smith wrote a novel which was published under the name of Jones, both might be offended. The French and German protect the interest of Smith, who has done the work without receiving the credit; the British, however, gave Smith no comfort but rushed to protect Jones, who had been falsely stigmatised as an author and could secure damages for this blot upon his escutcheon.[1] In one notable case[2] a singer who was seeking publicity for the promotion of her professional career was awarded small but nonetheless substantial damages when a newspaper carried an embarrassing article about her and printed it under her name. In another,[3] the action for false attribution of authorship was used to deal with misleading additions to the claimant's work. The right against false attribution has been extended.[4]

1. Copyright Act 1956, s 43.
2. *Moore v News of the World Ltd* [1972] 1 QB 441.
3. *Noah v Shuba* [1991] FSR 14 (decided under the Copyright Act 1956).
4. See para **18.14** below.

18.5   Attempts to establish the existence under British law of the sort of relief which only moral rights could provide succeeded or failed on the interpretation of contractual terms rather than upon any recognition of the moral right.[1] Thus a well-known conservative public figure was unable to prevent the publication of a radical poem written in the days of his youth,[2] and a composer of songs could not, on achieving fame, suppress the publication of second-rate works assigned to his publisher in the days of his obscurity;[3] on the other hand a playwright was able to seek compensation where the BBC had, in editing his play, removed two lines of dialogue which he claimed to be crucial to the play's dénouement.[4]

It was significant that the court regarded the contract between Frisby and the BBC as conferring a copyright licence rather than transferring copyright. Assignees of copyright were regarded as enjoying extensive editing rights whereas a licensee who strayed beyond the limited bounds of a copyright licence would be liable for infringement of copyright as well as breach of contract. Thus in *Gilliam v American Broadcasting Companies Inc*,[5] the Monty Python team successfully sued American sub-licensees ABC for copyright infringement when ABC drastically pruned a programme to make room for a large volume of advertising. The head licence, to the BBC, had permitted only minor alterations to the script.

1. G Dworkin 'Moral Rights in English Law: The Shape of Things to Come' [1986] EIPR 329.
2. *Southey v Sherwood* (1817) 2 Mer 435.

18.5 *Moral rights*

3. *Harris v Warren and Phillips* [1918] WN 173.
4. *Frisby v BBC* [1967] Ch 932.
5. 538 F 2d 14 (1976).

Remedies for moral injury under the general law

18.6

(i) *The law of contract*: in theory where an author sells a work to another, or is commissioned to execute a work for him, he can seek the inclusion in his contract of a term to the effect that each such moral right as he requires be recognised by the other party. This is, however, an opportunity of which the author can rarely avail himself. In terms of balance of bargaining power, the creator of a work is usually in a far weaker position than his publisher or commissioner,[1] and is scarcely in a position to dictate the inclusion of terms which may work to the stronger party's financial detriment. In any event, contractual protection only operates *inter partes*; any invasion of a moral right by a third party will not be repulsed by brandishing a document which evidences a contract to which he is not party and under which he does not claim.

(ii) *Defamation*: if a false attribution of authorship or the mutilation of a work has the result that the author is regarded with hatred, ridicule or contempt by ordinary right-minded folk, an action for defamation will lie. In *Moore v News of the World Ltd*[2] a false attribution of authorship was defamatory. In *Moseley v Stanley Paul & Co*[3] the publication of a serious work under an unsuitable cover was held capable of cheapening the author's reputation. Since defamation damages are usually awarded on a generous scale the appeal of a libel suit should be high. In reality, however, defamation provides no adequate defence of the author's moral right. Most transgressions of the moral right do not defame the author in the public's eyes even if they cause the author to feel that his reputation as a creator has been tarnished, and those acts which do constitute defamation are brought to count only at a very great cost to the claimant. Finally no damages will be recoverable for a *bona fide* defamation where the defendant is able to concede liability and publish an apology under the terms of the Defamation Act 1996.[4]

(iii) *Passing off*: where A passes the goods, services or works of B off as those of A, an action for passing off will lie if B can show that he owned the 'goodwill' in his reputation and that his 'goodwill' was damaged by A's acts;[5] this remedy has obvious applications where, through a false attribution, one man's work is made to appear to be another's. Passing off is, of course, scarcely coterminous with the totality of moral rights and is not a substitute for it.

1. See comments of the House of Lords in *Schroeder Music Publishing Co Ltd v Macaulay* [1974] 3 All ER 616.
2. [1972] 1 QB 441.
3. Macg Cop Cas (1917-23) 341.
4. The Defamation Act 1996, ss 2-4.
5. See para **19.**7, n 2 below.

Reform of United Kingdom law

18.7   The Whitford Committee[1] proposed in 1977 that the Copyright Act should be amended so as to provide explicit protection for the right to claim authorship of one's work and the right to object to unreasonable modifications to it, in order to bring the UK at least nominally within the terms of the Berne Convention.[2] It was recommended that these moral rights, if not actually assignable like Esau's birthright, should be capable of being deemed waived in appropriate circumstances, such as where a 'ghost writer' is hired to write the memoirs of a person whose fame exceeds his literary talents, or where a person is prepared to bear the detriment of mutilation as being a small price to pay for the glory of having his work televised. These examples indicate that, so far as any conflict of commercial and moral rights is concerned, money talks louder than morals.

1. Copyright and Design Law Cmnd 6732, paras 51-57.
2. Curiously, the United States of America acceded to Berne without feeling the need to introduce moral rights into its copyright legislation: R Oman 'Letter from the United States of America' (1991) 27 Copyright 117. In 1988 the Australian Copyright Law Review Committee deemed it unnecessary to introduce specific moral rights legislation to comply with Berne. S Ricketson 'Moral Rights and the Droit de Suite: International Conditions and Australian Obligations' [1990] Ent LR 78, argued that Australia was in breach of its obligations. In 2000, Australia introduced moral rights legislation: K Gettens, 'Australia Now Has Moral Rights: The Copyright Amendment (Moral Rights) Act 2000' [2001] Ent LR 129.

18.8   The Copyright, Designs and Patents Act 1988 introduced express moral rights, namely paternity[1] and integrity,[2] for certain works which enjoy UK copyright, extended the right to object to false attribution of authorship[3] and introduced a very limited right of privacy in films and photographs commissioned for private and domestic purposes.[4] It has been argued that the UK still does not comply with its obligations under Art *6bis* of the Berne Convention.[5] The new rights have been described as 'timid things, venturing little further than their common law forbears'.[6] They are easily lost by waiver. Although section 87(2) states that any of the moral rights conferred may be waived by instrument in writing signed by the person giving up the right, section 87(4) makes sure that the general law of contract or estoppel in relation to an informal waiver is not excluded.[7] The rights of paternity, integrity and privacy expire along with copyright in the works in question[8] while the right against attribution expires 20 years after the death of the alleged author.[9] The rights are not assignable,[10] but may be transmitted after death by express testamentary disposition, implicitly with copyright or in default to personal representatives.[11] Because copyright is a bundle of rights, such as the book publication rights, dramatisation rights, translation rights and so forth in the case of a literary work, moral rights relating to these separate activities may be transmitted separately:[12] there are provisions for moral rights to follow a testamentary split of copyright.[13]

1. Ss 77-79.
2. Ibid, ss 80-83.
3. Ibid, s 84.
4. Ibid, s 85.
5. I Stamatoudi 'Moral Rights of Authors in England: The Missing Emphasis on the Role of Creators' [1997] IPQ 478.
6. W R Cornish 'Moral Rights under the 1988 Act' [1989] 12 EIPR 449.
7. For the general law see, eg, G Treitel *The Law of Contract* (10th edn, 1999).
8. Copyright, Designs and Patents Act 1988, s 86(1).
9. Ibid, s 86(2).
10. Ibid, s 94.
11. Ibid, s 97.
12. Ibid, s 90(2).
13. Ibid, s 95(2) and (3).

The right to be identified as author or director

18.9 The first of the new rights, that of paternity, is available to authors of literary, dramatic, musical and artistic works and to the directors of films. Provided the work qualifies for copyright protection and none of the many exceptions specified in section 79 apply, the moral right to be identified as author or director vests automatically in these people. However, before it can be exercised, it must be asserted.[1] On an assignment of copyright (which must be in writing and signed to take effect[2]) a statement that the right is asserted will be effective not only against the assignee but also against anyone subsequently claiming title through the assignee.[3] Otherwise, an assertion is made by instrument in writing signed by the author or director, which takes effect against anyone who has notice.[4] Thus it is a good idea to ensure that notice of the assertion is printed on every copy of a work in circulation. There are special provisions[5] for artists, who often part with the only copy of a work without assigning copyright.

1. Copyright, Designs and Patents Act 1988, ss 77(1), 78. *Christoffer v Poseidon* [2000] ECDR 487.
2. Copyright, Designs and Patents Act 1988, s 90(3).
3. Ibid, s 78(2)(a) and (3)(a).
4. Ibid, s 78(2)(b) and (4)(b).
5. Ibid, s 78(3) and (4)(c) and (d).

18.10 The author or director may then take action, for breach of statutory duty,[1] against infringers who fail to identify the former by appropriate means[2] when putting the work before the public – by such activities as commercial publication,[3] public performance, broadcasting or including in a cable programme service.[4] There is one occasion where the right to be identified applies even though the copyright owner has no control over the event – the public exhibition of an artistic work. Conversely, not all acts restricted by copyright attract the right to be identified. The author of a musical work, or the words of a song, has no right to be identified when her work is performed in public, broadcast or transmitted in a cable programme. An architect has the right to be identified on a building but only on the first to be built to his design. Non-commercial publication does not require identification at all.

1. Copyright, Designs and Patents Act 1988, s 103(1).
2. For details see ibid, s 77(7).
3. Defined ibid, s 175(2).
4. S 77(2)-(6).

18.11 Section 79 spells out many exceptions to the right to be identified. Where copyright first vests in the author's employer, nothing done with the authority of the employer or subsequent owner of copyright infringes paternity right. Some of the acts permitted under copyright, including fair dealing for the purpose of reporting of current events, do not infringe the right[1] while it simply does not apply to computer programs, typeface design, computer-generated works, or any work made for the purpose of reporting current events. Unattributed publication in newspapers and periodicals or collective reference books does not infringe where the work was made or made available for such a purpose with the author's consent. The reader will have realised by now that the interests of many economic forces have taken precedence over the interests of authors.

1. Copyright, Designs and Patents Act 1988, s 79(4).

The right of integrity

18.12 Section 80 of the 1988 Act confers a right of integrity upon authors of copyright literary, dramatic, musical and artistic works and upon the directors of copyright films. These persons, in the words of subsection (1), have 'the right in the circumstances mentioned in this section not to have [their] work subjected to derogatory treatment'. However, it transpires that the right is infringed not by the treatment itself, but by putting a work so treated before the public[1] or possessing or dealing commercially with a work known to be mutilated.[2] 'Treatment' means any addition to, deletion from[3] or alteration to[4] or adaptation of the work other than translation or musical transcription by change of key or register. It is unlikely that placing an entire work in an inappropriate context constitutes 'treatment'. So to display an artistic work in a down-market shop window, or to set obscene words to the tune of a well-known song might affect the reputation of the artist or composer but would not infringe the right granted by the 1988 Act. Whether binding a serious work of scholarship in a luridly unsuitable paperback cover constitutes 'treatment' is also doubtful. It is irrelevant whether total destruction constitutes 'treatment'; since there is nothing left to expose to the public there can be no infringement.[5] Treatment is derogatory if it 'amounts to distortion or mutilation of the work or is otherwise prejudicial to the honour or reputation of the author or director'.[6] Thus derogatory treatment probably falls short of defamation, but not very far short. Ricketson observes in the context of the Berne Convention that '"Honour" and "reputation" are more objective concepts, being analogous to the kind of personal interests which are protected by actions for defamation'.[7] The test does appears to be an objective one; the views of the author or director would be strong evidence but by no means conclusive. In *Pasterfield v Denham*,[8] the fact that the author felt aggrieved was held insufficient to establish derogatory treatment.

1. Copyright, Designs and Patents Act 1988, s 80(3)-(6).
2. Ibid, s 83. It is also infringement to distribute non-commercially but so as to prejudice the author or director's honour or reputation.
3. In *Morrison Leahy Music Ltd v Lightbond* [1993] EMLR 144 the court considered it arguable that deletion of almost all of the claimant's works was 'treatment'; the excerpts were removed from their supporting context and placed in a 'Megamix' recording in a possibly derogatory manner. See S Bate and L Abramson 'To Sample or not to Sample?' [1997] ENT LR 193.
4. In *Tidy v Trustees of the Natural History Museum* (1997) 39 IPR 501, it was not in dispute that reduction, from A3 to postage stamp size, might amount to 'treatment'. Summary judgment was refused, however, it not being clear beyond possibility of defence that the treatment was derogatory.
5. Televising the process of destruction could well infringe, however.
6. Copyright, Designs and Patents Act 1988, s 80(2)(b).

7. *The Berne Convention for the Protection of Literary and Artistic Works: 1886-1986* (1987) p 471. See also A Dietz 'The Artist's Right of Integrity under Copyright Law: A Comparative Approach' (1994) 25 IIC 177.
8. [1999] FSR 168, citing the Canadian case of *Snow v Eaton Centre* (1982) 70 CPR (2d) 105, where the author's view was given great weight.

18.13   The right of integrity is also subject to a catalogue of exceptions.[1] It does not apply to computer programs, to computer-generated works,[2] or to works made for the purpose of reporting current events. Nor can the right be infringed by publication in a periodical or reference book if the work was made for such a publication or made available with the consent of the author. It is not infringed by anything done to avoid committing a crime or to comply with a statutory duty.[3] Anything done by the BBC to avoid offending against good taste or decency, to avoid encouraging crime or disorder or to avoid offence to public feeling is spared from infringement. If copyright in a work or film initially vests in the author's or director's employer, in the Crown, Parliament or an international organisation, the right of integrity does not apply unless the author has been identified; even then a proper disclaimer will suffice to avoid infringement.

1. Copyright, Designs and Patents Act 1988, s 81; the range of 'permitted acts' is considerably narrower than for the right of attribution. In the context of the right of integrity, it will be interesting to see whether the UK implements optional art 5(3)(k) of Directive 2001/29/EC, which provides that use of works for the purpose of caricature, parody or pastiche do not infringe the rights of reproduction and communication to the public, provided that they do not comflict with a normal exploitation of the work nor unreasonably prejudice the legitimate interests of the rightholder: art 5(5). See [2001] OJ L167/10 at 17 and para **18.16**, n 5.
2. For which there is no human author to be prejudiced by derogatory treatment: see s 178.
3. Including duties of independent broadcasters.

False attribution and privacy

18.14   The 1988 Act[1] extended the right to object to false attribution to film directors. It also removed a previous requirement that a false attribution be physically 'affixed' to a work (except where that was impracticable because the work was being performed, broadcast or cablecast). Now the actionably false attribution, express or implied, may be contained in other material issued or displayed to the public. In *Clark v Associated Newspapers*, spoof diaries by an identified author were entitled 'Alan Clark's Secret Political Diaries'. The defendants were held liable both in passing off and for false attribution of authorship. For the finding of false attribution, the court considered what would be the single meaning of the title to a notional reasonable reader. Having decided that the reader would take the diaries as having been written by the late Alan Clark, an MP with an elaborate political and private life, the court went on to decide that this was not cured by the various counter-messages printed alongside the 'diaries'. The right of privacy introduced by the 1988 Act[3] was designed to compensate for changes in provisions relating to first ownership of copyright. Under the Copyright Act 1956, copyright vested in the commissioners of certain artistic works including photographs. When these provisions were repealed, it was thought that commissioners of wedding photographs, and the like, needed alternative protection against unauthorised publication.[4] So, subject to a very few exceptions, where a person commissions a photograph or film for private and domestic purposes and a copyright work results, the commissioner is given the right not to have the work published, publicly exhibited or shown, broadcast or included in a cable programme service.

1. Copyright, Designs and Patents Act 1988, s 84. Note that the 'rental right' directive 92/100/EEC, by art 2.2, and the 'term' directive 93/98/EEC, by art 2.1, required that the principal director of a film be regarded as one of its authors. The texts of the above directives may be found at OJ 1992 L346/61 and OJ 1993 L290/9. The Copyright, Designs and Patents Act s 10 has been amended to implement these, by SI 1996/2967.
2. [1998] RPC 261.
3. Copyright, Designs and Patents Act 1988, s 85.
4. See, eg, *Mail Newspapers plc v Express Newspapers plc* [1987] FSR 90.

Weak rights, strong remedies and hard copies

18.15 Critics of the new moral rights are no doubt correct in maintaining that they are shy creatures which fall rather short of what is required by the Berne Convention. But authors and directors whose rights have been infringed do stand a chance of speedy redress. Courts in the United Kingdom are accustomed to granting immediate relief in cases of intellectual property infringement. It is unlikely that judges will be deterred from doing the same in the case of infringement of moral rights just because infringement constitutes a breach of statutory duty rather than unlawful invasion of an intangible property right. It may be suggested that a system of weak rights and strong remedies will leave authors in a position very similar to those whose jurisdiction provides strong rights but weak remedies. Strong remedies have no effect, however, where no right exists at all; the British moral armoury lacks many of the rights available in other jurisdictions. Moral rights and remedies for their breach become especially pertinent in relation to electronic uses of copyright works. Author identification may be relied upon by users as an indication of quality control, so there is a public interest in supporting the right of paternity. The ease with which works can be digitally manipulated suggests that allegations of derogatory treatment may become more widespread. But, at the same time, questions of jurisdiction and applicable law make enforcement more complex. It has been questioned whether moral rights can survive the shift from hard copy to electronic form.[1] It may be, however, that moral rights are more adaptable than economic rights. Because they are not primarily economic rights, they are more likely to remain constant while digitisation transforms the economics of copyright.

1. Y Gendreau, 'Digital Technology and Copyright: Can Moral Rights Survive the Disappearance of the Hard Copy?' [1995] Ent LR 214.

Moral rights and performers

18.16 In 1996 a Performers and Phonograms Treaty was concluded under the auspices of the World Intellectual Property Organisation. The Treaty[1] requires signatories to confer economic rights on performers in relation to exploitation of their performances in sound media. To a large extent, these are present already in UK law,[2] although amendment of the relevant provisions will be required to conform with EC law. However, the Treaty also obliges states to protect the moral rights of sound performers.[3] At the time of writing, the UK Government was engaged in consultation[4] with a view to implementing the moral rights provisions of the Performers and Phonograms Treaty at the same time as the EC Directive 2001/29 on copyright and related rights in the information society.[5] A Diplomatic Conference in December 2000 failed to conclude a Treaty for the protection of audio-visual performances, although some progress was made with drafting.[6]

1. Commentators often abbreviate 'WIPO Performers and Phonograms Treaty of 1996' to 'WPPT'.
2. See ch 17.
3. WPPT, art 5.
4. Information is available on-line at www.patent.gov.uk/copy/notices/moralperform.htm.
5. [2001] OJ L167/10.
6. S von Lewinski 'The WIPO Diplomatic Conference on Audio-visual Performers: A First Resumé' [2001] EIPR 333.

Part V

Rights in information and reputation

Chapter 19

Fair and unfair competition

Introduction

19.1 Where an intellectual creation takes on the form of one of the statutory classes of works discussed elsewhere in this book, its protection is relatively clearly determinable. Thus a painting or a song will enjoy copyright[1] and a design may be registered under the Registered Designs Act[2] while a novel and inventive product or process will enjoy patent protection.[3] Where an intellectual creation falls outside these categories, it may be protected in one of three ways: (i) it may be the subject of an express or implied contract which governs its use by one or both of the parties; (ii) if it has not yet been made available to the public it may be kept secret and thus enjoy the equitable protection of breach of confidence law; (iii) once it has been made public, it may only be protected by the laws of passing off and by other laws which protect reputations.[4] Examples of these three modes of protection are as follows:

(i)   A, who has developed a new but non-patentable technique for the rust-proofing of gardening implements, contracts to let B use that process on condition that B does not exceed an annual production quota, that he keeps the process secret and that he pays a per-unit royalty on treated items (such a contract is often referred to as a 'pure know-how licence');

(ii) A, who is writing an exposé of the scandalous administration of British universities, shows the manuscript confidentially to the Vice-Chancellor of one of the universities in order to seek his opinion as to whether it is factually correct; the unauthorised leaking by the Vice-Chancellor of the work's factual content would not infringe copyright or be in breach of contract, but it would be a breach of confidence;

(iii) A, the proprietor of the Betta-Burger fast food restaurant, can stop B from setting up across the road an identically named restaurant which imitates the 'house style' or 'get-up' of A's establishment.

19.1 *Fair and unfair competition*

From this it can be seen that contract, breach of confidence and passing off are valuable adjuncts to the statutory monopolies as means of protecting intellectual creations. These three areas of law are not, however, purpose-built areas of intellectual property, and thus have limitations which render them rather unreliable as means of intellectual property protection. This chapter will give a brief account of the role of each; breach of confidence and passing off will be treated in their own right in Chapter 20 below.

1. Copyright, Designs and Patents Act 1988, ss 1, 3, 4, discussed in Ch 11.
2. Discussed in Ch 24.
3. On criteria of patentability see Ch 5.
4. Eg injurious falsehood (*Ratcliffe v Evans* [1892] 2 QB 524), G Crown 'Malicious Falsehood into the 21st Century' [1997] Ent LR 6; defamation (on which see Bovril's successful settlement of an action in respect of a false allegation that its products contained excess sugar, The Times, 18 December 1985).

Contract

19.2   The aim of the law of contract is to give legal effect to voluntary private agreements between parties. Contract law is such a large subject that it is not possible to give even a general overview of it in a book of this length.[1] This paragraph will simply highlight a few salient points of contract law which are pertinent to intellectual property.

(i)   Contracts cannot prevent competition. If the effect of a contract is to prevent one party from trading in competition with another, that contract will be unenforceable to the extent that it does so; this is known as the doctrine of 'restraint of trade'.[2] Since the whole point of statutory intellectual property law is to protect its creator's (or his assignee's) investment of time and money in the development of new works by excluding others from trading in competition with them, it can be recognised that the objects of contract law and intellectual property monopolies are, at least *prima facie*, in conflict.[3] Actually both bodies of law shrink from absolutism: intellectual property law allows justifiable encroachments in the monopolies it grants,[4] while contract law permits a clause which reasonably prohibits competition as a necessary by-product of protecting a person's legitimate interests in his trade secrets and industrial know-how.[5]

(ii)   The unequal bargaining positions of the parties to the contract may lead to situations where the contract (or some of its terms) will be held void.[6] This is likely to occur where one party is financially powerful and can dictate unfair terms to another party who must take them or leave them, or where a vulnerable party does not obtain independent legal advice before entering into an agreement the purpose of which is to better the other party to his own detriment. Relief from contracts made whilst unduly influenced by the powerful party has proved important in the entertainment world, where impecunious composers who have signed away the exclusive rights in their music to a music publisher for a derisory sum, and without any guarantee that the work will be published and promoted, have been able to recover their copyright.[7] The exploitation of young and impressionable pop stars by their more business-minded managers has also led to the setting aside of mutually agreed contractual rights.[8]

(iii) A contract may be 'frustrated' and therefore unenforceable once its subject matter perishes or suffers a major change of status.[9] Thus a contract in which A licenses B to exploit a valuable body of secret know-how will lose its subject matter if C publishes the know-how in a trade journal; likewise if A licenses B to sell its new recipe frankfurters and those frankfurters are then banned for reasons of health and hygiene on account of their ingredients, there is no way that the contract can be enforced; it is 'frustrated'.

(iv) Remedies for breach of contract include damages[10] (but not punitive damages[11]), injunction (restraining order),[12] specific performance[13] (an order that the party in breach does what he says he should) but not an account of profits[14] or the delivery-up of unlawfully made articles.

1. For a good account of contract law see G Treitel *The Law of Contract* (10th edn, 1999). Note that Scots law differs from the contract law of England and Wales and that of Northern Ireland in a number of respects. A brief account of the differences, including the relationship with restitution, may be found in H MacQueen 'Unjust Enrichment and Contractual Liability – a Scots Perspective' in Rose, ed, *Failure of Contract* (1997).
2. On restraint of trade see G Treitel op cit pp 415-427: see also J Phillips 'The Construction of Contracts in Restraint of Trade' (1978) 13 Irish Jurist (ns) 254; M Stanton 'Absorption or Sterilisation: Restraint of Trade in the Music Industry' [1995] Ent LR 123.
3. This is particularly important in the field of trade secrets, discussed in Ch 20.
4. See eg the acts permitted by ss 28-76 of the Copyright, Designs and Patents Act 1988.
5. On the potential scope of express and implied restraints upon the use and disclosure of confidential information see *Faccenda Chicken Ltd v Fowler* [1986] FSR 291; *Poeton v Horton* [2001] FSR 169.
6. For a discussion on whether the inequality of bargaining power may of itself be regarded as a ground of invalidity see Treitel op cit pp 384-385. Note Sch 1, para 1(c) of the Unfair Contract Terms Act 1977 disapplies ss 2-4 'so far as it relates to the creation or transfer of a right or interest ...in copyright... or other intellectual property'.
7. *O'Sullivan v Management Agency & Music Ltd* [1985] QB 428, noted in J Tatt 'The O'Sullivan Case: Remedying Undue Influence in Music Contracts' [1985] EIPR 301; Treitel op cit deals with duress (common law) and undue influence (Equity) at pp 375-389.

8. See *Page One Records Ltd v Britton* [1968] 1 WLR 157. However, setting aside might not be the appropriate remedy where a claimant had acquiesced and received substantial benefits from the defendant's performance of the contract: *Elton John v Richard James* [1991] FSR 397.
9. On frustration of contract see Treitel op cit at pp 805-863.
10. On contract damages see Treitel op cit at pp 864-943 informed by Treitel's earlier *Remedies for breach of contract: a comparative analysis* 1988.
11. Cf 'additional' damages under Copyright, Designs and Patents Act 1988, s 97 (2).
12. *Warner Bros Pictures Inc v Nelson* [1937] 1 KB 209 now referred to as a 'restraining order'.
13. On specific performance see Treitel at pp 949-968.
14. Save in exceptional circumstances: *A-G v Blake* [2000] EMLR 949; cf *Nottingham University v Fishel* [2001] RPC 367.

Breach of confidence

19.3   The law of breach of confidence extends to cover any obligation not to divulge information which is not generally available to the public. Some of this information may be genuinely intellectual property, such as an invention which an inventor describes to his patent agent in order to find out whether it is worth patenting, while some of it is no more than concealed fact, such as the attributes of a set of etchings[1] or lists of a trader's customers.[2]

1. *Prince Albert v Strange* (1849) 2 De G & Sm 652, explained in J Phillips 'Prince Albert and the Etchings' [1984] EIPR 324.
2. Eg *Roger Bullivant Ltd v Ellis* [1987] FSR 172.

19.4   The legal nature of breach of confidence is unclear.[1] Suffice it to say that an obligation to keep a confidence may be imposed by the terms of a contract (in which case contract law will apply), by reference to the 'property right' of the 'owner' of the secret which is invaded by others,[2] or by the law of equity which can be involved in order to stop the doing of a generally wrongful act even if it is neither a breach of contract nor an invasion of property.[3] The Law Commission proposed a new statutory tort of breach of confidence,[4] with clearly identifiable rules and remedies, but the Commission's examination of this area led to such a degree of organisation and clarification of the existing cases and principles that the previous pressure for its general reform would seem to have abated.

1. On the legal nature of breach of confidence see F Gurry *Breach of Confidence* (1984); A Coleman *The Legal Protection of Trade Secrets* (1992) pp 37-49; J Hull *Commercial Secrecy: law and practice* (1998) Ch 2.
2. Especially in some Commonwealth jurisdictions; see eg S Ricketson 'Confidential Information – a New Proprietary Interest?' (1977) 11 Melb ULR 223 and 289; J Hull 'Property Rights in Questionnaires: an Academic Question

in the Hong Kong Court of Appeal' [1994] EIPR 404. More recently the English Law Commission proposed, in *Legislating the Criminal Code: Misuse of Trade Secrets*, 1997, Consultation Paper 150, that a proprietary basis be adopted for the purposes of criminal law.

3. See eg G Jones 'Restitution of Benefits Obtained in Breach of Another's Confidence' (1970) 86 LQR 463; In *Coco v Clark* [1969] RPC 41, the action for breach of confidence was characterised by Megarry, VC, as a 'cousin of trust', a 'pure equitable doctrine'.

4. See *Breach of Confidence* (Law Com No 110) Cmnd 8388, para 6.5.

19.5   The remedies for breach of confidence (which is discussed in greater detail in the next chapter) are quite extensive. It is now clear that compensatory damages[1] will be recoverable where an unauthorised use or divulgation of secret information has taken place.[2] In *Lac Minerals*,[3] the Supreme Court of Canada decided that the defendants held profits on constructive trust for the claimants. An injunction or restraining order will prevent not only the use or publication of secrets[4] but, in an appropriate case, the exploitation of information which, on account of the defendant's acts, has ceased to be confidential.[5] Allied to this is the 'spring-board' doctrine[6] – that no person should, by virtue of his own breach of obligation in respect of secret information, get an unfair commercial advantage when that information becomes generally available; not, at least, until he could reasonably have acquired or assembled the information for himself.[7] Like other areas of intellectual property, but unlike contract, breach of confidence is also remediable by means of an order of delivery-up of unlawful documents or materials.[8]

1. Damages in lieu of an equitable remedy have been available since Lord Cairns' Act of 1858. Lord Goff, in *A-G v Guardian Newspapers Ltd (No 2)* [1990] 1 AC 109 described damages for breach of confidence as arising from a 'beneficent interpretation' of Lord Cairns' Act. See also McDermott *Equitable Damages* 1994.

2. See eg *Seager v Copydex Ltd* [1967] RPC 349; *Fraser v Thames Television Ltd* [1984] QB 44.

3. *LAC Minerals Ltd v International Corona Resources Ltd* [1990] FSR 441; for further consideration of obligations of confidence and remedies in Canada, see the Supreme Court's decision in *Cadbury Schweppes Inc v FBI Foods Ltd* [2000] FSR 491. Lord Millett has stated, in 'Restitution and Constructive Trusts' (1998) 114 LQR 399, that the 'remedial constructive trust' does not exist in English law; rather the phrase is a misnomer for an equitable duty to account.

4. Eg *Argyll v Argyll* [1967] Ch 302.

5. See *Speed Seal Products Ltd v Paddington* [1986] 1 All ER 91.

6. Or 'head start' doctrine: Hull *Commercial Secrecy: law and practice* (1998) para 3.37 et seq.

7. See eg *Terrapin Ltd v Builders' Supply Co (Hayes) Ltd* [1967] RPC 375 at 392; *Ackroyds (London) Ltd v Islington Plastics Ltd* [1962] RPC 97; *Roger Bullivant Ltd v Ellis* [1987] FSR 172. See para **20.4** below.

8. *Industrial Furnaces Ltd v Reaves* [1970] RPC 605.

19.6   *Fair and unfair competition*

Passing off

19.6   Like breach of confidence, passing off is a legal remedy of dubious pedigree,[1] stemming from an equitable action to restrain the use of a name in circumstances in which the owner of that name might be exposed to legal actions if the use of his name was unchecked,[2] and from a mutant form of the common law tort of deceit.[3] Before the late nineteenth century there was little awareness of the availability of passing off,[4] which indeed had to wait until 1979 for a formal legal definition.[5]

1.   For a fuller account, see C Wadlow *The Law of Passing Off* (2nd edn 1995) Ch 1.
2.   *Routh v Webster* (1847) 10 Beav 561.
3.   On the relationship of passing off to deceit see J Phillips and A Coleman, 'Passing Off and the Common Field of Activity' (1985) 101 LQR 242 at 243-244.
4.   For some comments on the relative frequency of reported trade mark and passing off cases see J Phillips 'Sir Arthur Kekewich: A Study in Intellectual Property Litigation 1886-1907' [1983] EIPR 335.
5.   See *Erven Warnink B V v Townend & Sons (Hull) Ltd* [1979] AC 731, [1980]RPC 31; Carty 'The Development of Passing Off in the Twentieth Century', Ch 3 in Dawson and Firth (eds) *Trade Marks Retrospective* 2000, Vol 7 Perspectives in Intellectual Property.

19.7   In principle passing off takes place wherever one person so emulates the appearance, name, get-up or other identificatory features of another's business or trade products as to confuse the public and to lead the public to believe that his goods or business are those of the other person.[1] This cause of action may well overlap with other areas of intellectual property, for example, where one manufacturer of confectionery employs a wrapping in which, as an artistic work, a rival manufacture owns the copyright, or where a product to which a registered design is applied is exactly imitated by another, so long as the similarity causes confusion as to the product's origins at the point of sale. The value of passing off is not merely that it is an ancillary remedy to that of infringement of a statutory monopoly; it is that, since passing off protects *not* the right to make a product but the right to enjoy undisturbed the goodwill[2] in one's business reputation, one can claim passing off protection even when one's statutory monopoly has expired, so long as one still enjoys goodwill as a trader.

1.   Or vice versa – see *Matthew Gloag & Son Ltd v Welsh Distillers Ltd* [1998] ETMR 504, in which it was held that traders in 'Scotch Whisky' could arguably sue another for selling Scotch whisky as 'Welsh Whisky'.
2.   On 'goodwill' see Ch 20. For a detailed analysis see J Drysdale and M Silverleaf *Passing Off Law and Practice* (1986), paras 2.27-2.31. See also C Wadlow *The Law of Passing Off* (2nd edn 1995) Ch 2. In the absence of goodwill, no passing off action will lie, even if the defendant misleads the public: *British Broadcasting Corpn v Talksport Ltd* [2001] FSR 53.

19.8   Passing off actually enjoys its own statutory dimension in the form of the registered trade mark.[1] In many reported cases it can be seen that an action for passing off and a trade mark infringement action run parallel in the same proceedings, since the statutory registration of a mark, name or other identificatory badge does not preclude its proprietor from suing in passing off as well as, or instead of, instituting trade mark proceedings.[2] Broadly speaking, the choice between relying on passing off and trade mark infringement proceedings is analogous to the choice between pushing one's bicycle and riding it: the latter makes for a smoother, swifter journey, but there are some destinations which cannot be reached without dismounting.

1.   In passing off, business goodwill is the *intellectual* property whereas registration rights more closely resemble a proprietary interest in the mark itself: see *Reckitt & Coleman Products v Borden Inc* [1990] 1 All ER 873 at 890.
2.   Trade Marks Act 1994, s 2(2); *Jay v Ladler* (1888) 40 Ch D 649.

Economic considerations

19.9   Where a statutory monopoly is established, careful consideration is given to its economic impact. A statutory monopoly which lasts for too great a duration, which cannot be avoided by alternative products and technologies, which is unexploited or which results in an undesirable concentration of market power will therefore be subject to regulatory measures which guard against its abuse or undesirable side effects. Similar considerations are programmed into the law of contract,[1] but do not exist in breach of confidence[2] or passing off law. The justification of this view lies in the assumption that, since neither breach of confidence nor passing off create or protect monopolies, neither should be subject to monopoly regulation. Thus the owner of confidential information has only the right to compel others not to betray *him* by disclosure, and has no right to prevent others, who have not derived their information from him, from publishing or exploiting the identical secrets. Likewise the law of passing off stops 'Pimlico Pizza Parlour' from opening a High Street shop opposite the Pimlico Pizza Parlour which has traded there for the last five years, but it does not stop it from selling pizzas on that same site.

1.   See eg the Competition Act 1998, Ch 1; also the doctrine of restraint of trade, para **19.2** above and para **27.3**.
2.   Thus limits imposed by EC competition law affect the contractual licensing of technical secrets, but not the basic exercise of equitable rights to protect the information; Commission Regulation (EC) 240/96 of January 31, 1996, on the Application of Art 85(3) of the Treaty to certain categories of technology transfer agreement indicates acceptable forms of agreement.

19.10 It may be wondered why these justifications are valid in the light of commercial practice. So far as patents are concerned, for example, the published specification for a widget[1] will contain a description of a widget which enables one skilled in the art to understand what it is and how it works, and when the patent expires it is open to all widgeteers to manufacture the previously protected product. The most important information for would-be widgeteers is not, it is argued, what a widget actually is, but how one can establish a technique for the cheap and efficient manufacture of them in sufficient quantity and of a sufficient quality to provide effective competition for the holder of the expired patent, who already knows how to make widgets for the mass market and will keep its information secret till the end of time. It is true that, while the widget patent is still current, a compulsory licence or licence of right *may* be granted on terms which call for the divulgation of this valuable 'know-how',[2] but once the patent has expired the 'know-how' is safe from official interference.

1. The phrase 'widget' has been used by patent lawyers for many years to denote the archetypal mechanical invention; its use to describe a particular device for frothing beer is comparatively recent.
2. Patents Act 1977, s 48(4)(a) permits the Comptroller to order the grant of a patent licence on such terms as he thinks fit; this would presumably enable him to require that ancillary 'know-how' be furnished if it were necessary for curing the ills of the domestic market.

19.11 With regard to passing off, the economic implications are less easy to follow. Where wine-growers and importers cannot describe as 'Champagne' a product which, despite its chemical and aesthetic identity with Champagne wine, is grown outside the region in France to which 'Champagne' belongs exclusively as the appellation,[1] it may well be felt that it is not realistically possible for full and satisfactory competition to take place, and that the laws of passing off are unfairly conferring a perpetual market advantage. This view, however, misses the point. It is not because Champagne is described as 'Champagne' that it enjoys a strong market position, but because the term 'Champagne' has been promoted and advertised in a manner which appeals to the public. Rival traders in similar wines can still trade in their wines, and it is open to them to create and popularise a marketing image and get-up which competes with, or indeed supplants, that of 'Champagne'. In the *JIF lemons case* [2] it can be seen that the action in passing off gave the claimants a monopoly in lemon-sized plastic lemons as containers for lemon juice. But their competitors may still sell lemon juice, albeit in differently sized or shaped containers.

1. See *Bollinger v Costa Brava Wine Co Ltd* [1960] Ch 262, [1960] RPC 16; *Taittinger v Allbev Ltd* [1993] FSR 641 (use of 'Elderflower Champagne' restrained).
2. *Reckitt & Colman Products Ltd v Borden Inc* [1990] 1 All ER 873.

Unfair competition

19.12 The statutory intellectual property monopolies are all founded, in one form or another, on the principle that the unauthorised use of another's intellectual labour is an unfair exploitation of it.[1] Where the unauthorised user sells a product which incorporates intellectual property for which no actual payment is made, he can undercut the cheapest price at which his competitor who has paid for an authorisation can sell his product; this is a sort of unfair competition which patent and copyright law does much to inhibit,[2] if not prevent.

1. See eg *Millar v Taylor* (1769) 4 Burr 2303 at 2334-2335 (per Willes J); petition of Jacobo Aconcio for a patent, Calendar of State Papers, Domestic, 1601 to 1603 (Addenda 1547 to 1565), 495; *Perry v Truefitt* (1842) 6 Beav 66 at 73.
2. J Phillips *dubitante* as to copyright: see 'The Risk that Rewards: Copyright Infringement Today' [2001] Ent LR 103.

19.13 British law does not recognise a general tort of unfair competition,[1] which means that a party is quite entitled to embark upon a course of commercial action which will put a competitor, and possibly himself, out of business without running the risk of a civil action for damages.[2] The courts have been urged to recognise such a tort,[3] and academics and practitioners have from time to time postulated it,[4] but in vain.[5] Since most of the recent attempts to establish the existence of the tort have occurred in passing off cases, the interconnection between the concepts of intellectual property and unfair competition law has been emphasised. In this respect it may be helpful to consider the following points:

(i)   As a matter of domestic UK law it is not an actionable wrong for A to undercut B's prices in order to secure all B's customers, even if the result is that B goes out of business and A, without the threat of competition, can then put his prices up.[6] Such 'predatory pricing' may however lead to complaint to the Office of Fair Trading (UK) or to the Commission of the European Community, to censure and possibly to penalties by virtue of the Competition Act 1998[7] or Art 82 (formerly Art 86) of the EC Treaty if market dominance is thereby abused. The extent to which aggrieved parties may sue in national courts for damages (and other relief) for breaches of Community law remains uncertain.[8] There are dicta which indicate that damages and final injunctions are available and interlocutory injunctions have been obtained. However, it is undoubtedly actionable for A to dress up his business as B's so that A and B 'share' customers, even though competition is thereby enhanced, prices do not rise and no one goes out of business.[9] From this one may draw the conclusion that the customer's interest in knowing the source of his goods has been valued more highly than the customer's expectation of the benefits of competition.

(ii) It is not an actionable wrong for A to exploit for his own benefit a market created by B, in the manner established by B,[10] although it is an actionable wrong for A to exploit for his own benefit a set of facts compiled from B's research and which was compiled in order to benefit the market's consumers.[11] From this it may be argued that an intellectual property right will vest in a product or in information but not in a market as such. This may seem paradoxical if one considers that the damage inflicted upon an intellectual property right holder is usually measured in terms of loss or damage to his actual or potential market.[12]

1. The obligations under art 10*bis* of the Paris Convention being met by other laws, in theory at least. For commentary on other countries' unfair competition laws, see Clauss 'The French Law of Disloyal Competition' [1995] EIPR 550; Henning Bodewig 'International Protection against Unfair Competition' (1999) 30 IIC 166; Kamperman Sanders *Unfair Competition Law* (1997); Schricker 'Twenty Five Years of Protection against Unfair Competition' (1995) 26 IIC 166; World Intellectual Property Organisation *Protection against Unfair Competition: Analysis of the Present World Situation* (1994).
2. In *Hodgkinson & Corby v Wards Mobility Services* [1994] EIPR D-269, Jacob J stated:

    'There is no tort of copying. There is no tort of taking a man's market or customers. Neither the market nor the customers are the plaintiff's to own. There is no tort of making use of another's goodwill as such. There is no tort of competition.'

    See also *Bookmakers Afternoon Greyhound Services Ltd v Wilf Gilbert (Staffordshire) Ltd* [1994] FSR 723.
3. See *Mogul Steamship Co Ltd v McGregor Gow & Co* [1892] AC 25; *Cadbury-Schweppes Pty Ltd v Pub Squash Co Pty Ltd* [1981] 1 WLR 193, [1981] RPC 429.
4. See eg G Dworkin 'Unfair Competition – Is the Common Law Developing a New Tort?' [1979] EIPR 241 and articles cited in J Adams 'Unfair Competition: Why a Need is Unmet' [1992] EIPR 259; Robertson and Horton 'Does the UK or the EC Need an Unfair Competition Law?' [1995] EIPR 568.
5. In *Swedac Ltd v Magnet & Southern plc* [1989] FSR 243 Harman J stated 'Unfair competition is not a description of a wrong known to the law'.
6. *Mogul Steamship* case, n 1 above.
7. Ch II .

8. For a discussion of UK cases see R Whish 'The Enforcement of EC Competition Law in the Domestic Courts of Member States' [1994] ECLR 60; see also *Garden Cottage Foods v MMB* [1984] AC 130; *Francovich and Bonfaci v Italy* [1991] ECR I-5357; Case C-453/99 *Courage Ltd v Crehan* (2001) Times, 4 October.
9. See eg *Clock Ltd v Clock House Hotel Ltd* (1936) 53 RPC 269.
10. *Cadbury-Schweppes*, n 3, above.
11. *Elanco Products Ltd v Mandops (Agrochemical Specialists) Ltd* [1979] FSR 46.
12. For a helpful overview of damages policy see W Cornish *Intellectual Property* (4th edn, 1999) paras 2–39 to 2–42.

Chapter 20

Breach of confidence and passing off

Introduction

20.1 Although breach of confidence and passing off are very different remedies with entirely distinct historical backgrounds[1] they are discussed in the same chapter of this book for the following reasons: (i) both provide relief against business practices which are capable of being described as 'unfair competition'; (ii) both are of uncertain extent and application as a consequence of the protracted case-by-case evolution of their doctrines; (iii) both are therefore comparatively flexible and evolving;[2] (iv) both are 'adjuncts' of statutory rights, since breach of confidence law preserves the subject of patent application before the publication of an invention's specification puts it into the 'state of the art', while passing off protects the 'get-up' of a business even if it falls short of being an artistic work,[3] and the name of a trader even if it fails to be considered a literary work[4] and is not registrable as a trade mark; (v) both have been invoked so as to preserve both private individual and commercial interests;[5] and (vi) both have involved considerable speculation as to whether that which they protect is accurately described as 'property'.[6]

1. See paras **19.3-19.8** above.
2. For a perfect example of this evolution, see *British Telecommunications plc v One in a Million* [1999] ETMR 61, in which passing off was turned into a remedy even against 'cybersquatters' who did not seek to use the domain names they wrongfully registered.
3. *My Kinda Bones Ltd v Dr Pepper's Store Co Ltd* [1984] FSR 289, cf *Christine le Duc BV v Erochique Enschede VOF* [2001] ECDR 253.
4. *Exxon Corpn v Exxon Insurance Consultants International Ltd* [1982] Ch 119.
5. *Argyll v Argyll* [1967] Ch 302; *McCulloch v May* (1948) 65 RPC 58. Breach of confidence has often been invoked to protect State secrets, too. See, eg *A-G v Observer Ltd* [1990] 1 AC 109, sub nom *A-G v Guardian Newspapers Ltd (No 2)* [1988] 3 All ER 545; case comment by F Patfield [1989] 1 EIPR 27. Art 8 of the European Convention on Human Rights conferring a right to privacy and now enshrined in the Human Rights Act 1998, protects individuals but not corporations: *R v Broadcasting Standards Commission, ex p BBC* [2000] EMLR 587. The keeping and use of personal data is controlled by the Data Protection Act 1998, implementing Directive EC 95/46/EC on the protection of individuals

with regard to the processing of data and the free movement of such data [1995] OJ L281/31. See Baker 'New Data Protection Act' [2000] Ent LR 193;
6. See paras **19.4**, **19.7**, **19.8**, n 2 above and **20.2** below.

Breach of confidence

The nature of the obligation to keep a secret

20.2 An obligation not to disclose confidential information may arise from a person's express or implied agreement not to disclose it, as was mentioned in the previous chapter; in such circumstances the law of contract will govern it. It has been argued that some sort of consent to non-disclosure is inherent in every circumstance in which an obligation of confidence arises,[1] but it would seem contrived if the duty of a taxicab passenger not to publicise industrial secrets left in the cab by the previous passenger, or the telephone tapper's duty not to disclose that upon which he has eavesdropped, should depend upon the implication of some sort of tacit agreement between them. Another theory is that the possessor of a secret enjoys a right of 'property' in it, which is analogous to the rights which protect ordinary tangible property.[2] This theory may have had some support from civil law, but British criminal law does not regard information as 'property'– if it be stolen, there is no theft unless some tangible medium which incorporates it is also taken.[3] Perhaps the most satisfactory basis for the breach of confidence action is that it is a body of rules developed from the court's equitable jurisdiction[4] to restrain the performance of improper conduct which would be in bad faith.[5]

1. See *Mechanical and General Inventions Co Ltd and Lehwess v Austin* [1935] AC 346; *Nichrotherm Electrical Co Ltd, Cox, Drew and Francis v Percy* [1957] RPC 207.
2. For a good survey of 'property' in information see D Libling 'Property in Intangibles' (1978) 94 LQR 103.
3. See T Eisenschitz 'Theft of Trade Secrets' [1984] EIPR 89; *R v Absolon* (1983) Times, 14 September; *Oxford v Moss* [1979] Crim LR 119; despite these difficulties, the Law Commission's proposal, cited at para **19.4** above, to propertise trade secrets for the purposes of criminal law may not provide the ideal solution: J Hull 'Stealing Secrets: A Review of the Law Commission's Consultation Paper in the Misuse of Trade Secrets' [1999] IPQ 422; [1998] Crim LR 246.
4. For breach of confidence, see G Jones 'Restitution of Benefits Obtained in Breach of Another's Confidence' (1970) 86 LQR 463; *Coco v Clark (AN) (Engineers) Ltd* [1968] FSR 415, [1969] RPC 41; *Stephens v Avery* [1988] Ch 449; *Kitechnology v Unicor* [1995] FSR 765; *LAC Minerals v International Corona Resources* [1990] FSR 441; cf *A-G v Guardian Newspapers (No 2)* [1988] 3 All ER 545 at 658-659. The proprietary basis of passing off – goodwill in a business – has long been recognised – *IRC v Muller & Co's Margarine Ltd* [1901] AC 217 – but its attachment to a business rather than the business's identificatory signs sometimes causes conceptual difficulty.

5.   The duty of good faith, for example that owed by employee to employer, being of a lower order than a fiduciary duty: *Nottingham University v Fishel* [2001] RPC 367; C D Fredman 'Confidential Commercial Information and Breach of Fiduciary Duty' [2000] IPQ 208.

The ingredients of breach of confidence

20.3   There are three criteria[1] which must be satisfied before a breach of confidence action will succeed: (i) the information allegedly governed by the obligation of confidence must be of a sort which the law will protect, (ii) some party other than the 'owner' of that information must have obtained it in circumstances in which a duty of good faith will be imposed, (iii) that the other party must have acted (or be about to act) in a manner which was not consonant with that of a duty of good faith or which was a breach of some other duty. Let us look more closely at each of these.

(i)   *The information must be protectable.* It is often assumed that only information which is not in the public domain and which is not available for public scrutiny may be the subject of breach of confidence law, but this is not necessarily so. First, some information, such as the addresses of a milk roundsman's customers, can be obtained quite easily by watching the households at which the roundsman stops to deliver milk or collect money; yet the law will protect its unauthorised disclosure.[2] Second, information which is in the public domain but which has been forgotten, or the importance of which has not been previously recognised, can undoubtedly be protected.[3] Next, the information which is claimed to be confidential must be identified with reasonable precision. If the category of information is too general or vaguely defined, it will not be protected;[4] likewise if the information, when identified with reasonable precision, is trivial or lacks substance as a body of secret material.[5] Note also that the courts will not restrain or punish the disclosure of any information if it relates to an iniquity[6] such as a crime or civil wrong, or if there is a public interest in its disclosure.[7] What constitutes 'public interest' is a matter of doubt. In general any matter which pertains to the administration of justice, such as the accuracy of devices which purport to indicate the alcohol content (and therefore the criminal liability) of motorists,[8] or the misconduct of police officers,[9] is one of public interest. Lord Denning MR has indicated that 'public interest' may be more widely construed as embracing anything in which the public is interested, such as the alcoholic excesses and sexual activities of publicity-seeking entertainers who travel on aeroplanes.[10] However, a distinction may be drawn between what is in the public interest and what is of interest to the public.[11] Interestingly, the courts have evolved the notion that information may, in the public interest, be disclosed without permission to some parties but not others;[12] thus information relating to the commission of criminal offences should be disclosed to the police and not to the press, unless the criminal offences are committed by the police, in which case disclosure is permissible to the press in preference to the police.[13]

(ii) *A duty of good faith must be imposed.* Where A tells B a trade secret, a duty of good faith which requires B to keep that secret will be imposed where, for example, A first tells B that he is communicating a secret,[14] or where B is A's patent agent, solicitor or bank manager, in which case B has a duty towards A which is a consequence of their fiduciary relationship.[15] A duty of good faith will not be implied if the circumstances of the disclosure do not dictate it, such as where friends meet for an apparently social meal,[16] though such a duty is imposed upon an employee for the benefit of his employer.[17] Where secret information is disclosed to a recipient for a specific purpose, a duty may be imposed to use or disclose it only for that purpose.[18] Sometimes B will resist the imposition of the secrecy obligation, for example, by telling A that he will only receive information if it is *not* to be communicated in confidence, or by requiring A to execute a document in which the latter agrees to waive all rights to a breach of confidence action where B already possesses similar information and chooses to disclose or exploit it.[19] Where C casually overhears A's conversation with B, no obligation of confidence will exist,[20] but if C goes to some lengths to eavesdrop upon a conversation which A and B make an effort to keep private, C may, in an appropriate case, be under a duty of non-disclosure.[21] Where A is not communicating any information to anyone but keeps it locked up in a safe (like the famous Coca-Cola recipe), the authorities do not confidently indicate that B would be in breach of confidence if he obtained and disseminated it,[22] but justice would march to court hand-in-hand with commercial expediency in order to deny B an immoral benefit.[23]

(iii) *There must be an actual or imminent breach of good faith or other legal duty.* What a recipient may or may not do with another's information is a question of fact to be resolved in each case. The court's guidance is, however, extensive on this matter. An abuse of confidence need not be deliberate, but can take place quite subconsciously, and in good faith, according to the Court of Appeal in *Seager v Copydex Ltd.*[24] This decision would seem to indicate that a party which fails to take reasonable care to identify and look after the information communicated to it by another will commit breach of confidence through negligence, even in the absence of bad faith, if he inadvertently communicates it. A further point of guidance is that the use of information without its further disclosure may also be restrained by law, which means that if A passes a secret to B, who exploits it himself in an unauthorised manner, A may not only stop B doing so while that information remains secret but may stop B using the information as a 'spring-board' for deriving an otherwise premature benefit once that information has become public knowledge.[25] Where, however, the information passed by A to B is absorbed into the general stock of B's professional or vocational skill, public policy demands that B should not be restrained from performing his professional skills to the full;[26] since it is not in any event possible to separate B from his general stock of skill, it is fortunate that public policy has aligned itself with base necessity.

1. Identified in *Coco v A N Clark (Engineers) Ltd* [1969] RPC 41, citing *Saltman Engineering Co Ltd v Campbell Engineering Co Ltd* (1948) 65 RPC 203; the third element was qualified by detriment to the claimant, but this is often assumed.
2. *Wessex Dairies Ltd v Smith* [1935] 2 KB 80.
3. See *Coco v A N Clark (Engineers) Ltd* [1969] RPC 41 at 47 (per Megarry J); cf *Mustad & Son v Allcock (S) & Co Ltd and Dosen* [1963] RPC 41.
4. See eg *Amways Corpn v Eurway International Ltd* [1974] RPC 82; cf *Johnson & Bloy (Holdings) Ltd and Johnson & Bloy Ltd v Wolstenholme Rink plc* [1989] FSR 135.
5. *De Maudsley v Palumbo* [1996] FSR 447; *Balston v Headline* [1987] FSR 330; [1990] FSR 385.
6. See eg *Initial Services Ltd v Putterill* [1968] 1 QB 396.
7. See A Coleman *The Legal Protection of Trade Secrets* (1992), ch 5; A Coleman in C Reed (ed) *Computer Law* (4th edn 2000) pp 251-254; H Carty 'Employee Confidentiality and Disclosure in the Public Interest' [1985] EIPR 185.
8. *Lion Laboratories Ltd v Evans* [1985] QB 526.
9. *Cork v McVicar* (1984) Times, 31 October; Coleman '*Cork v McVicar*: Confidential Information and the Public Interest' [1985] EIPR 234.
10. *Woodward v Hutchins* [1977] 2 All ER 751. Having promoted a favourable public image, they could not complain when the public was disabused. Squires 'Striking the balance between kissers and tellers – the law of breach of confidence' [1999] Ent LR 240; *A v B and C*, Jack J (unreported).
11. *Lion Laboratories* n 6 above at 539. See also *Hyde Park Residence Ltd v Yelland* [2000] ECDR 275, in which neither the public's interest in the death of Diana, Princess of Wales, nor the public interest in the truthfulness of Mohammed Fayed overrode the latter's copyright in photographs taken by a security camera. cf *Ashdown v Telegraph Group Ltd* [2001] EMLR 1003.
12. *Imutran Ltd v Uncaged Campaigns Ltd* [2001] All ER 385 cites earlier cases.
13. *Cork* n 7 above.
14. All trade secrets licensed for use in manufacture fall within this category: eg *Ackroyds (London) Ltd v Islington Plastics* [1962] RPC 97.
15. On fiduciary relations see eg J McGhee *Snell's Equity* (30th edn 2000), pp 284-287. In *R v Department of Health, ex p Source Informatics* [2001] QB 424 information relating to patients passed to pharmacists under obligations of confidence but was held on appeal to have lost the quality of confidence when anonymised. Note that

the converse does not hold: non-confidential information does not become confidential when encrypted: *Mars v Teknowledge* [2000] FSR 138.

16. *De Maudsley v Palumbo* [1996] FSR 447.
17. For duties owed by *departing* employees, see A Stewart [1989] 3 EIPR 89.
18. Eg *Saltman Engineering Co Ltd v Campbell Engineering Co Ltd* (1948) 65 RPC 203; *Fraser v Thames Television Ltd* [1984] QB 44.
19. See T Arnold and D McGuire 'The Law and Practice of Corporation Information Security' (1975) 57 JPOS 169 and 237; A Coleman in C Reed *Computer Law* (4th edn 2000) at p 254. The dTi's useful booklets *Protecting Business Information: Keeping it Confidential* URN 96/938 and *Protecting Business Information: Understanding the Risks* URN 96/939 are reproduced in Hull *Commercial Secrecy: Law and practice* (1998).
20. See *Malone v Metropolitan Police Comr (No 2)* [1979] 2 All ER 620 at 645-646; *A-G v Guardian (No 2)* [1988] 3 All ER 545 at 658-659, per Lord Goff.
21. See *Francome v Mirror Group Newspapers Ltd* [1984] 1 WLR 892. In *Thomas v Pearce* [2000] FSR 718 honesty was said to be the relevant test in the case of a third party recipient of confidential information.
22. The authorities, and the satisfactory resolution of this problem in Australia in *Franklin v Giddins* [1978] Qd R 72, are discussed in S Ricketson *The Law of Intellectual Property* (1984), at pp 827-830. See, also, Wei 'Surreptitious Takings of Confidential Information' (1992) 12 Legal Studies 302; *Creation Records v News Group* [1997] EMLR 444.
23. In *Coco* n 3 above a subjective test was used – whether the recipient knew or ought to have known that information was confidential; see also Clark 'Circumstances importing an obligation of confidence: a subjective or objective test?' [1996] EIPR 632. Commercial expediency seems to underly the decision in *Douglas and Zeta Jones v Hello* [2001] EMLR 199 to enforce an exclusivity of wedding coverage granted by films stars to one magazine by using breach of confidence to enjoin coverage by another; Carey 'Hello to Privacy' [2001] Ent LR 120. This decision has been criticised as using breach of confidence to create a right of publicity rather than privacy: Jaffey 'Privacy, Publicity Rights and Merchandising' in Barendt and Firth (eds) *Yearbook of Copyright and Media Law* 2001.
24. [1967] RPC 349.
25. See *Terrapin Ltd v Builders' Supply Co (Hayes) Ltd* [1967] RPC 375 at 392; *Seager v Copydex Ltd* [1967] RPC 349.
26. Eg *Herbert Morris Ltd v Saxelby* [1916] 1 AC 688; *Poeton v Horton* [2001] FSR 169.

Remedies

20.4 Where a secret has not yet been divulged but looks as though it is in danger of being so, the person to whom the duty of secrecy is owed (and no one else[1]) can secure what for many years was known as a *quia timet* injunction (a restraining order in advance) to prevent unauthorised disclosure. It is not an inherently different type of injunction. *Quia timet* is the Latin for 'because he fears': fears, that is, what might occur were the defendant not restrained. In general, once confidential disclosure has become public as a result of an illicit disclosure no injunction will be granted.[2] This is a matter of common sense, since compelling a party not to use or disclose information which is now freely available to all will serve no useful purpose so far as the claimant is concerned. There are, however, two exceptions to this:

(i)   where there are only two parties in competition in a market in which confidential information is of commercial or industrial value, the fact that one of those parties has unlawfully made that information public will not prevent a court granting an injunction to restrain its use by him,[3] since in such a case the effect of the injunction will be to re-establish the claimant's market control over his information; and

(ii) the 'springboard' doctrine[4] permits the grant of an injunction which prevents a party from getting a 'head start' over his trade rivals in the case where he has sought to exploit his pre-disclosure familiarity with secret know-how which has, through his breach of confidence, fallen into the public domain. Since the injunction is an equitable remedy, the courts will consider its likely effect on third parties but, having done so, will not necessarily be deterred thereby from granting an injunction.[5]

1.   *Fraser v Evans* [1969] 1 QB 349.
2.   *A-G v Observer Ltd* [1990] AC 109, HL.
3.   *Speed Seal Products Ltd v Paddington* [1986] 1 All ER 91, CA.
4.   See para **19.5** n 6 above. The 'spring-board' injunction may be limited in time; see *Roger Bullivant Ltd v Ellis* [1987] FSR 172.
5.   In *PSM International v Whitehouse* [1992] FSR 489 the Court of Appeal upheld an interim injunction which prevented defendants fulfilling contracts (pending trial).

20.5   It is now clear that compensatory damages are available where a breach of confidence has taken place.[1] At one time it was thought that breach of confidence damages were awarded only in lieu of an equitable remedy such as an injunction,[2] perhaps in the sort of situation in which the granting of an injunction was not regarded as appropriate. However, since the Court of Appeal's decision in *Seager v Copydex Ltd (No 2)*,[3] damages have been available on the basis that an 'equitable tort' has been committed, and they may be assessed on the basis that they are analogous to damages for conversion (ie unlawful interference with another's chattels).[4] In at least one case breach of confidence damages have been immense,[5] which makes it surprising that they are not more frequently sought.

1.   *Seager v Copydex Ltd* [1967] RPC 349.
2.   See Chancery Amendment Act 1858 (Lord Cairns' Act). Such damages may be awarded in lieu of injunction to redress *future* loss in intellectual property cases, as discussed in G Harbottle 'Permanent injunctions in copyright cases: when will they be refused?' [2001] EIPR 154. Lord Goff, in *A-G v Guardian Newspapers Ltd (No 2)* [1990] 1 AC 109 regarded damages for *past* breaches of confidence as nonetheless stemming in some way from Lord Cairns' Act, by means of a 'beneficent interpretation'.

3. [1969] RPC 250.
4. Ibid at 256.
5. *Fraser v Thames Television Ltd* [1984] QB 44, see G Robertson and A Nicol *Media Law* (4th edn, 1999).

20.6   Two other available equitable remedies are an account of the defendant's profits[1] and an order for the destruction under oath (or delivery for destruction by the claimant) of information held or goods made as a consequence of the wrongful use of another's information.[2] Like the injunction, both of these remedies are awarded at the court's discretion, which means that the delivery up for destruction of an aberrant employee or ex-employee will not be ordered, no matter how earnestly his employer desires it. On the other hand, the duty of confidence owed by an employee to his employer is protected by the law of contract,[3] by the tort of unlawful interference with contractual relations[4] and by the criminal provisions of the Prevention of Corruption Act 1906,[5] which makes the bribing of employees for the purpose of securing employment information a criminal offence.

1. *Peter Pan Manufacturing Corpn v Corsets Silhouette Ltd* [1963] RPC 45. For the basis of the account of profits, see L Bently 'Accounting for Profits Gained by Infringement of Copyright: Where does it End?' [1991] EIPR 5. In *LAC Minerals v Corona International Resources* [1990] FSR 441, the Supreme Court of Canada went beyond a mere account of profits by deciding that the defendant held real property on constructive trust for the claimant.
2. *Industrial Furnaces Ltd v Reaves* [1970] RPC 605.
3. See eg *Littlewoods Organisation Ltd v Harris* [1977] 1 WLR 1472. Note that the duty of confidence owed by an ex-employee is more limited in scope than the implied duty of good faith owed during the course of employment: *Faccenda Chicken Ltd v Fowler* [1986] FSR 291. This is so even where the departing employee has received substantial benefits: *JA Mont (UK) Ltd v Mills* [1993] FSR 577 (restrictive covenant wider than necessary to protect confidential information and thus unenforceable). *Faccenda Chicken* is discussed by A Coleman in *The Legal Protection of Trade Secrets* (1992) at pp 11-13.
4. *Hivac Ltd v Park Royal Scientific Instruments Ltd* [1946] Ch 169.
5. Prevention of Corruption Acts 1906 and 1916, discussed by T Eisenschitz 'Trade Secrets and the Criminal Law' [1984] EIPR 266.

The tort of passing off

20.7   Until the House of Lords in the *Advocaat* case[1] (discussed below) laid down not one but two definitions of passing off, the nature of the tort was quite uncertain. It could always, however, be said with safety that the direct copying or use by one trader of another's name,[2] product get-up[3] or style[4] would constitute an actionable wrong if it caused confusion among the consuming public with a resulting loss of trade or goodwill to the injured party, without regard to the questions whether the party at fault had also committed an infringement of copyright[5] or of a registered trade mark.[6] Passing off was actionable without the need to prove that the act complained of was done fraudulently or with malicious intent, although the fact that one trader has deliberately and without apparent justification employed another's name has always been an important factor in the court's decision as to whether the act complained of should be stopped. Thus if a person who rejoices in the name of Harrod wishes to trade as a shopkeeper under the name 'Harrod's', he will probably be allowed to do so,[7] while Smith or Jones would not.[8]

1. *Erven Warnink BV v Townend & Sons (Hull) Ltd* [1979] AC 731.
2. *Eastman Photographic Materials Co Ltd v John Griffiths Cycle Corpn Ltd* (1898) 15 RPC 105.
3. *Edge v Niccolls* [1911] AC 693.
4. *My Kinda Town Ltd v Soll* [1982] FSR 147.
5. *Exxon Corpn v Exxon Insurance Consultants International Ltd* [1982] Ch 119.
6. *Jay v Ladler* (1888) 40 Ch D 649.
7. Cf *Boswell-Wilkie Circus (Pty) Ltd v Brian Boswell Circus (Pty) Ltd* [1985] FSR 434; *Guccio Gucci SpA v Paolo Gucci* [1991] FSR 89.
8. *Harrods Ltd v R Harrod Ltd* (1923) 41 RPC 74.

20.8 From the foregoing, it can be seen that passing off serves two functions: the protection of a trader against the unfair competition of his rivals, and the protection of consumers who would otherwise be confused as to the origins or nature of the goods or services which they are offered. In this second function passing off lays claims to fulfilling a role which breach of confidence does not, yet on a more abstract level the two apparently disparate remedies share another important similarity: both regulate the flow of information which is a necessary ingredient of the ideal and hypothetical perfect market to which all free market economies in theory aspire.[1] By making sure that the consumer can clearly distinguish the goods or services of market rivals, passing off law facilitates purchase decisions[2] on the basis of factors such as price or quality comparison rather than consumer confusion; breach of confidence law, on the other hand, determines which items of industrial know-how become part of the public domain and are thus available to all competing manufacturers. The greater the degree of manufacturer reliance upon the public domain, the greater the opportunity for the assimilation of the products of rival manufacturers, which means that consumer choice between rival products or services will be made more on the basis of price or quality comparison between like goods, and less upon the basis of consumer confusion as to the technical attributes of dissimilar goods.

1. On the role of information in the free market see eg D Lamberton (ed) *Economics of Information and Knowledge* (1971).
2. See A Kamperman Sanders and S Maniatis 'A Consumer Trade Mark: Protection Based on Origin and Quality' [1993] EIPR 406.

20.9 Where a person does not trade, passing off does not in general protect him against appropriation of his name by another. The reason for this legal failure to redress palpable injustice is explained below, where the relationship of goodwill to reputation is discussed. The effect of this rule can be damaging to well-known non-trading interests such as political parties[1] or media celebrities,[2] but it is mitigated by two important safeguards: (i) where the use of another's name is an intentional exercise in misleading the public,[3] or where it may lead the other to the risk of legal action being taken against him,[4] it may be restrained by a passing off action, and (ii) the trade interest which passing off protects is construed as broadly as possible, embracing such unlikely 'trade' as the British Medical Association's ability to attract members[5] or a charity's facility to raise money through voluntary donations.[6] Curiously, however, the courts have been reluctant to acknowledge that a well-known person 'trades' in his name when he licenses its use by others.[7]

1. *Kean v McGiven* [1982] FSR 119.
2. *McCulloch v May* (1947) 65 RPC 58.
3. *Lloyd's and Dawson Bros v Lloyd's, Southampton Ltd* (1912) 29 RPC 433.
4. *Routh v Webster* (1847) 10 Beav 561; *Walter v Ashton* [1902] 2 Ch 282.
5. *British Medical Association v Marsh* (1931) 48 RPC 565.
6. *Re Dr Barnardo's Homes, National Incorporated Association v Barnardo Amalgamated Industries Ltd* (1949) 66 RPC 103; *British Diabetic Association v Diabetic Society* [1996] FSR 1.
7. On character merchandising see ch 22.

Definition of passing off

20.10 In the *Advocaat* case in 1979, Lords Diplock and Fraser of Tullybelton both produced definitions of passing off.[1] Until 1984 the definition of Lord Diplock was usually employed in preference to that of Lord Fraser, because (i) he was the more distinguished jurist, or (ii) Lord Fraser's definition could be construed as applying to England to the exclusion of the rest of the UK, or (iii) Lord Fraser's judgment was obviously geared to the facts of the case before him, rather than being meant for all passing off cases. In *Budweiser*[2] the Court of Appeal indicated that both should be applied together. This was no great hardship since, in almost every factual instance one can think of, application of the two tests leads one to the same conclusion. Eventually, however, the Court of Appeal found it inconvenient to apply both tests cumulatively,[3] indicating that Lord Fraser was really talking about the facts of the case before him. More recently in the *Jif lemons* case[4] the House of Lords essayed a definition of passing off. It has been observed[5] that *Jif* does not offer a fundamental restatement of the *Advocaat* position, but it should be noted that the phraseology used in *Jif* more closely reflects the way in which passing off is often pleaded.

1.   *Erven Warnink BV v Townend & Sons (Hull) Ltd* [1979] AC 731.
2.   *Anheuser-Busch Inc v Budejovicky Budvar Narodni Podnik* [1984] FSR 413.
3.   *Bristol Conservatories Ltd v Conservatories Custom Built Ltd* [1989] RPC 455.
4.   *Reckitt & Colman Products v Borden Inc* [1990] 1 All ER 873; see case comment
     by C Wadlow 'Passing Off enters the Supermarket Age' [1990] 3 EIPR 104.
5.   C Wadlow, n 4 above.

20.11   According to Lord Diplock the characteristics of passing off are:

(i)   a misrepresentation
(ii)   made by a trader in the course of trade
(iii) to prospective customers or ultimate consumers
(iv)   which is calculated to injure the goodwill or business of another
       and
(v)   which causes actual damage to that other.

On these requirements some comments may be made.

(i)   a misrepresentation – which for the purposes of the law may be a
       true statement which subsequently becomes false[1] and a statement
       which, while literally true, nonetheless causes its recipient to be
       misled.[2] Note also that a misrepresentation can be effected by
       means other than a verbal falsehood; a nod, wink or other course
       of conduct is thus quite capable of being a misrepresentation.[3]
(ii)   made by a trader in the course of trade – which suggests that if
       A, a non-trader, makes a misrepresentation as to B's goods which
       damages C, then C will have no action for passing off against A[4]
       because he is not a trader and will have no remedy against B who
       has done him no wrong.
(iii) to prospective customers or ultimate consumers – it matters not
       which, since the confusion of both or either will equally tend to
       damage a business interest.
(iv)   which is calculated to injure the goodwill or business of another
       – the word 'calculated' here does not bear its meaning of
       'intended' but probably the meaning of 'having a reasonably
       foreseeable result'.[5] Likewise 'goodwill' does not here refer to
       what is shown to all men at Yuletide, but to the attractive force
       which brings in custom.[6]
(v)   which causes actual damage – but a serious likelihood of damage
       will also be prevented through a *quia timet* injunction.[7]

1.   *With v O'Flanagan* [1936] Ch 575.
2.   *Frank Reddaway & Co Ltd v George Banham & Co Ltd* [1896] AC 199.
3.   *Walters v Morgan* (1861) 3 De GF & J 718 at 723-724.
4.   An action for injurious falsehood may, however, lie: see *Ratcliffe v Evans* [1892]
     2 QB 524.
5.   [1980] RPC at 93; cf *Re Maeder's Application* [1916] 1 Ch 304.

The tort of passing off **20.13**

6. *IRC v Muller & Co's Margarine Ltd* [1901] AC 217.
7. On the *quia timet* injunction see para **20.4**.

20.12 Lord Fraser's test, the legal status of which has now been placed in question,[1] had these following components: the claimant must show that:

(i)   his business includes the sale in the United Kingdom[2] of a class of goods to which the name in question applies;
(ii) that class of goods is clearly defined;
(iii) the name applied to it distinguishes those goods from other goods;
(iv) because of his reputation in the goods there is goodwill in the name;
(v)   as a member of the class of people selling those goods, he is the owner of that goodwill;
(vi) he has suffered, or is really likely to suffer, damage to his property in the goodwill by reason of another's false use of the name which is applied to his goods.

For the purposes of this test, 'goods' must not be seen as excluding 'services' and 'name' must be taken to include any distinguishing mark or feature. The references to a class of persons using the mark are appropriate to passing off cases where a number of traders all complain that a mark used by them is being unfairly exploited by another; in this particular case all the manufacturers of real Advocaat were ganging up on the manufacturer of so-called Old English Advocaat, a drink of a different chemical composition, and in other cases the wine growers from the Champagne region of France ganged up on the distributors of 'Spanish Champagne' and the manufacturers of 'Elderflower Champagne',[3] but in the average passing off case the claimant is the only person in his 'class' (eg McDonalds as a producer of Big Mac hamburgers[4]) or is in a class which consists only of related companies which are controlled by a common seat of power.

1. Bristol Conservatories, para **20.10**, n 3 above.
2. Goodwill in the UK is essential – see *Budweiser*, para **20.10**, n 2 above and cases referred to in F Mostert 'Is Goodwill Territorial or International?' [1989] 12 EIPR 440. However, a customer base may suffice: *Pete Waterman v CBS* [1993] EMLR 27; *Jian Tools For Sale v Roderick Manhattan* [1995] FSR 924.
3. *Bollinger v Costa Brava Wine Co* [1960] Ch 262; *Taittinger SA v Allbev Ltd* [1993] FSR 641.
4. See *McDonalds Hamburgers Ltd v Burgerking (UK) Ltd* [1987] FSR 112.

20.13 In *Jif*,[1] Lord Oliver said that:

'...the law of passing off could be summarised in one short general proposition: no man might pass off his goods as those of another.'

More specifically, there were three elements which the claimant had to prove in order to succeed:

(i)   A goodwill or reputation[2] attached to the goods or services which he supplies in the mind of the market by association with the identifying 'get-up'(whether it consists simply of a brand name or a trade description, or the individual features of labelling or packaging) under which his particular goods or services are offered to the public, such that the get-up is recognised as distinctive specifically of the claimant's goods or services.

(ii) A misrepresentation by the defendant to the public (whether or not intentional) leading or likely to lead the public to believe that goods or services offered by him are the goods or services of the claimant. Whether the public is aware of the claimant's identity as the manufacturer or supplier of the goods or services is immaterial, as long as they are identified with a particular source which is in fact the claimant.

(iii) The damage or, in a *quia timet* action, the likelihood of damage by reason of the erroneous belief engendered by the defendant's misrepresentation that the source of the defendant's goods or services is the same as the source of those offered by the claimant.

Comparison with *Advocaat* indeed shows that this is a restatement rather than a reformulation. Although Lord Oliver refers to the goods or services of the claimant, the cases show that misrepresenting the defendant's goods, services or business as in some way connected with the claimant,[3] or creating confusion between the claimant's different lines of goods[4] may be actionable in passing off.

1.   Para **20.10**, n 4 above.
2.   Subsequent cases have stressed goodwill rather than reputation, eg *Hodgkinson & Corby v Wards Mobility Services* [1995] FSR 169, citing *Consorzio del Prosciutto di Parma v Marks & Spencer* [1991] RPC 351.
3.   Eg *Mirage Studios v Counter Feat Clothing Co Ltd* [1991] FSR 145; *Associated Newspapers plc v Insert Media Ltd* [1991] FSR 380; *Taittinger v Allbev* [1993] FSR 641. Cf the forms of misrepresentation alleged in *Hodgkinson & Corby*, n 2 above.
4.   *Spalding & Bros v AW Gamage Ltd* (1915) 32 RPC 273.

20.14   In passing off, damage may therefore be of various kinds. The most obvious manifestation is diversion of custom – misled by the misrepresentation, a customer buys the defendant's goods in substitution for the claimant's. Prejudice to reputation is another – the association of the defendant's inferior product or business methods may taint the claimant's image and ultimately lose him custom, even where their business spheres are distinct.[1] The claimant may be exposed to the risk of claims by consumers.[2] Opportunities to expand geographically[3] or into related products[4] may be diminished by the defendant's activities. There may be a loss of licensing opportunity, although the courts tend to look long and hard at this kind of claim.[5] 'Dilution' of a mark – its loss of freshness and attractive power when used by a non-rival – in circumstances where there is no confusion or misrepresentation is probably not actionable damage in passing off in the UK.[6] However, where there is a material misrepresentation, the damage to goodwill caused by loss of distinctiveness of the mark will be recognised.[7]

1. Eg *Annabel's (Berkeley Square) v Schock* [1972] FSR 261.
2. *Sony KK v Saray Electronics (London) Ltd* [1983] FSR 302; *Associated Newspapers plc v Insert Media Ltd* [1991] FSR 380.
3. *Chelsea Man Menswear Ltd v Chelsea Girl Ltd* [1987] RPC 189.
4. *Nationwide Building Society v Nationwide Estate Agents* [1987] FSR 579.
5. *Stringfellow v McCain Foods (GB) Ltd* [1984] RPC 501; cf *Mirage Studios v Counter Feat Clothing* [1991] FSR 145. In the case of a reputable defendant and product, a licensing argument may prejudice an interim injunction, royalty damages being adequate to compensate the claimant pending trial: *IPC Magazines Ltd v Black and White Music Corpn* [1983] FSR 348. For 'character merchandising' see Ch 22.
6. *Harrds v Harrodian School* [1996] RPC 697. See also C Wadlow *The Law of Passing Off* (2nd edn 1995) para 3-24; cf T Martino 'Trade Mark Dilution' in [1990] 4 EIPR 141 – a comment on US case law.
7. *Taittinger v Allbev* [1993] FSR 641.

Business goodwill and reputation

20.15 The simplest description of passing off is that, where A trades with the public by way of his business, B promotes himself in such a manner as to take away, or at any rate damage, a slice of A's business (see figure 5).

The 'before' and 'after' of passing off

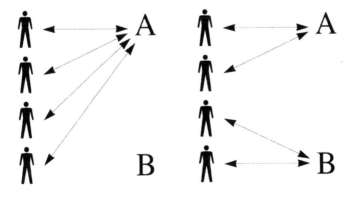

imposes two intangible variables between A and his customers. The first is 'reputation', or the fact that members of the public know of A's identity, while the second, 'goodwill' is (as mentioned in paragraph **20.11**) the attractive force which brings in custom. The relationship of these concepts may be seen from figure 6:

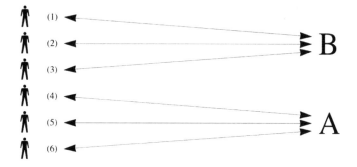

(1) has never heard of A, and trades with A's deceitfully look-alike competitor B; since he has not heard of A, the 'loss' of his custom to B is not actionable, however attractive B's business get-up may be as a result of his emulation of A, because there has been no diminution of A's reputation. (2) has heard of both A and B, is not confused by B's misrepresentation, and chooses B because he dislikes A's service; here there is no passing off because the customer has intimate knowledge of the market. (3) knows of A, does not know of B, and thinks that B is A; he has been confused with regard to A's reputation and is a lost sale to A which is remediable through passing off. (4) knows of A, does not know of B, thinks B to be A but goes to A because A's shop is geographically convenient; here there is damage to A's reputation but no damage to A's goodwill, so there is no passing off. (5) knows of both A and B, is not confused, and chooses A because he is angered by B's unfair trading policy; and (6) has no knowledge of either: he is just a casual customer. In respect of (5) and (6) there is no passing off. Note that once a claimant has established passing off against a defendant, the court in assessing damage is likely to base its calculations on all sales made under a misleading guise.[1]

1. *Lever v Goodwin* (1887) 36 Ch D 1.

20.16 A broad generalisation of the interrelation of these concepts may be drawn from figure 7, which puts in flow-diagram form the basic shape of the law which currently governs the unauthorised use of another's name, mark or other identificatory features. From this

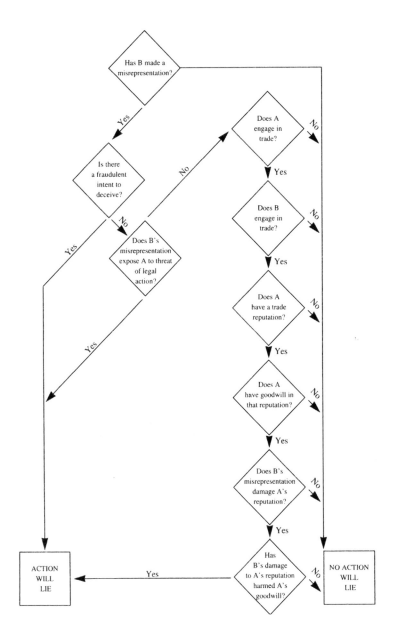

diagram it can be seen that there are numerous reefs upon which even a relatively simple passing off action may run aground. It is tempting to speculate that, at its current state of development, the law of passing off is rather too sophisticated for its users' needs.

Fields of activity

20.17 Where B 'borrows' A's name or identity tag, A's annoyance will not of itself lead to a passing off action: there must be an element of confusion of the public. This element is easily satisfied where the owner of the 'Taj Mahal' Indian restaurant, 15 The High Street, Anytown, objects to the establishment of another 'Taj Mahal' Indian restaurant at 17 The High Street, Anytown, since anyone who goes down the High Street in search of the 'Taj Mahal' restaurant will be uncertain as to which of the two establishments is that in which he is to meet his great aunt. If, however, one 'Taj Mahal' restaurant is in Plymouth and the other opens in Inverness, there is relatively little likelihood that anyone will be deceived, or that the Plymouth restaurateur will lose custom through the public's confusion of his premises with those of his Inverness competitor.

20.18 Aristotle once suggested that the ideal drama should possess three unities: of time, place and action.[1] The law of passing off takes all of these unities into account when considering whether an alleged misrepresentation is actionable. Let us look at each in turn:

(i) *Unity of time.* There is no doubt that a person wishing to trade in 1986 as the Carbolic Smoke-Ball Company would run no risk of a passing off action brought by the company of the same name which traded unsuccessfully a century ago. This is not because the nineteenth century corporation no longer trades,[2] but because it has no extant reputation and as a result of this there can be no goodwill in its reputation which brings in customers. As long as its reputation is not extinct and there is a sufficient interest for the law to protect, a business can satisfy the 'unity of time' requirement for bringing a passing off action even if it is some years since it last traded.[3] Similarly it may be possible, at least for an existing business, to protect the goodwill in its reputation even where it has not yet traded under a new sign, so long as there is evidence that its incipient goodwill exists (eg through extensive advertising of its forthcoming venture) and that it is in fact intending to trade.[4]

(ii) *Unity of place.* We have already discussed the 'Taj Mahal' phenomenon. In an appropriate case, however, the court will protect the British goodwill which the claimant enjoys in respect of his reputation in the UK, even though his place of business is abroad. This happened in *Maxim's Ltd v Dye*,[5] where the proprietor of Maxim's restaurant in Paris was able to secure an interlocutory injunction against the proprietor of Maxim's restaurant in Norwich (distant by 200 miles, one channel and several cultures, but within the European Community). Although the claimant traded only in Paris, its jet-set clientele often booked by telephone and then flew in from the UK. Since goodwill will generally exist where there is reputation, and reputation can only exist in the minds of men, it should follow that goodwill will be protectable wherever one's customers are reasonably to be found. So where a defendant has created a market in the UK by importing and supplying the claimant's goods, it will be restrained from passing off other goods as the claimant's.[6] Note that a person who does not trade in the UK in any shape or form,[7] or whose British trade is disregarded because it is, in legal terms, treated as trade abroad,[8] has no British business and therefore no British goodwill, even if he has ample reputation. The view that goodwill is localised in the United Kingdom can work in a claimant's favour when it comes to restraining 'parallel imports'[9] – goods connected with the claimant but first marketed abroad.[10] In many other jurisdictions a local reputation may be enough to enable a passing off type action to be brought.[11]

(iii) *Unity of action.* It has often been argued that, for a passing off action to succeed, the claimant and defendant must be engaged, however tangentially, in a 'common field of activity'.[12] In other words, the manufacturer of Steinway pianos might have an action against the manufacturer of Steinberg pianos, while he would not succeed in stopping the distribution of Steinway or Steinberg kiwifruit packing cases; this is because the typical member of the public would be likely to confuse Steinway and Steinberg pianos unless he looked carefully at the label or had a good ear for music, while no one would assume that a distinguished manufacturer of expensive and carefully-crafted musical instruments would have any connection with the moulding of plastic fruit trays. Unity of action does not, however, require the goodwill to be enjoyed by a single entity. As *Advocaat* and other cases[13] show, goodwill may be shared between a number of distinct traders legitimately using the name. Each may sue to restrain passing off and to recover the damages it has suffered.

1. Or 'plot': see Aristotle *Poetics.*
2. On the downfall of that company see *Carlill v Carbolic Smoke Ball Co* [1893] 1 QB 256.
3. *Ad-Lib Club v Granville* [1972] RPC 673; *Independent Newspapers Ltd v Irish Press Ltd* [1932] IR 615.

4. *My Kinda Bones v Dr Pepper's Store Co Ltd* [1984] FSR 289; cf *Elida Gibbs Ltd v Colgate-Palmolive* [1983] FSR 95 (use of 'tree' motif); *Labyrinth Media Ltd v Brave World Ltd* [1995] EMLR 38 (rival videos under the same title; arguable that one's pre-launch publicity might be adequate basis to restrain the other).
5. *Maxim's Ltd v Dye* [1977] 1 WLR 1155.
6. *Nishika v Goodchild* [1990] FSR 371.
7. *Athletes Foot Marketing Associates Inc v Cobra Sports Ltd* [1980] RPC 343; cf *C & A Modes Ltd v C & A (Waterford) Ltd* [1978] FSR 126.
8. *Anheuser-Busch Inc v Budejovicky Budvar NP* [1984] FSR 413.
9. *Colgate-Palmolive Ltd v Markwell Finance Ltd* [1989] RPC 497.
10. Special rules apply to goods first marketed in another Member State of the European Community – see Ch 27.
11. See, eg, the cases cited by F Mostert at [1989] 12 EIPR 440; .
12. This was first made a requirement by Wynn-Parry J in *McCulloch v May* (1947) 65 RPC 58.
13. Eg *Chocosuisse Union des Fabricants Suisses de Chocolat v Cadbury Ltd* [1999] RPC 826, CA in which particular Swiss chocolate manufacturers had standing to sue, but not their trade association.

20.19 The notion that there must be a 'common field of activity' was unknown before the *Uncle Mac* case[1] in 1947. Prior to that date the court had no problems in assisting the proprietors of *The Times* newspaper in stopping sales of 'The Times' bicycles;[2] likewise the makers of 'Kodak' cameras stopped the unauthorised sale of 'Kodak' bicycles for photographers[3]. In the *Uncle Mac* case, however, a children's programme broadcaster, affectionately known as Uncle Mac, was unable to prevent the defendants from selling 'Uncle Mac' puffed wheat breakfast cereal since he and they lacked a 'common field of activity'. The status of this rule is dubious. It is now clear that it will no longer apply where the claimant is seeking to protect a 'household name' such as 'Lego' (for toy bricks).[4] Perhaps it is safest to conclude for the while that, although common field of activity is not a necessary condition of a successful passing off action,[5] the existence of a common field is evidence of the likelihood of public confusion[6] and of damage[7] to goodwill. A related concept is that the actionable misrepresentation is seen as being made to the relevant public.[8]

1. Note 12, para **20.18** above.
2. *Walter v Ashton* [1902] 2 Ch 282.
3. *Eastman Photographic Materials Co Ltd v John Griffiths Cycle Corpn Ltd* (1898) 15 RPC 105.
4. *Lego Systems A/S v Lego M Lemelstrich* [1983] FSR 155. The Trade Marks Act 1994 confers special advantages on better known trade marks: ss 6(1)(c), 10(3)(c), 56(2).
5. See C Wadlow*The Law of Passing Off* (2nd edn 1995) paras 4.29-4.30.
6. This conclusion was accepted by Falconer J in *Lego* n 4 above.
7. Cf *Stringfellow v McCain Foods (GB) Ltd* [1984] RPC 501.
8. *Neutrogena v Golden* [1996] RPC 473; this case also demonstrates how a successful 'witness collection programme' may be achieved.

The wider dimensions of breach of confidence and passing off

20.20   In the UK the common law hatched the inbred laws of breach of confidence and passing off. The rules become more detailed and elaborate as the precedents of previously decided cases are woven into ever-increasingly intricate patterns. Other jurisdictions, notably in the United States, have in contrast tended towards the synthesis of different strands of these laws into new bodies of broad principles; these principles may be described as complementary to each other, for breach of confidence has been allowed to contribute towards the development of a general right of privacy,[1] while case law on the unauthorised appropriation of another's reputation has formed the basis for a right of publicity.[2] In essence the right of privacy is the right to prevent others from gaining access to and exploiting facts about oneself, while the right of publicity is the right to restrict the use by others of one's name, likeness or voice.[3] The right of publicity has been recognised at common law, assisted in particular by section 43(a) of the Lanham Act.

1. On privacy see S Warren and L Brandeis 'The Right of Privacy' (1890) 4 Harv LR 193.
2. See M Nimmer 'The Right of Publicity' (1954) 19 Law and Contemporary Problems 203; T Frazer 'Appropriation of Personality – A New Tort?' (1983) 99 LQR 281, cf the *Hello* case in the UK and the commentary it has attracted: note 23 to para **20.3** above.
3. For a criticism of the extent to which the right of publicity has been protected, see W M Borchard, 'The common law right of publicity is going wrong in the United States: *Waits v Frito-Lay* and *White v Samsung Electronics* [1992] 6 Ent LR 208.

20.21   In the UK the need to prevent illicit access to, or use of, personal information has been recognised for many years,[1] but it has been felt that the law, to a considerable extent, prohibits such undesirable activities in a number of ways which, if aggregated, would not fall short of a right of privacy.[2] Thus it has been suggested that the person who creeps into your garden so as to tape record your conversations (but not the man whose aeroplane flies over to take snapshots[3]) is a trespasser to property;[4] the person who gives away your secrets commits a breach of confidence; the bank which discloses your financial details to a casual enquirer is in breach of contract; the person who publishes your private correspondence is a copyright infringer, and so on. In *Kaye v Robertson*[5] the action for injurious falsehood was used to restrain publication of photographs and an interview obtained when the claimant was in hospital and unfit to consent. Such piecemeal protection does not, however, provide a person with a full, consistent and predictable legal basis for the remedy of his complaint. Since these diverse legal wrongs all share the common thread of invasion of privacy it is tempting to assimilate them into a unitary legal doctrine.

20.21 *Breach of confidence and passing off*

The European Convention on Human Rights[6] (to which the UK is party) contains provisions[7] to protect the privacy of individuals but only recently has the Convention been incorporated into domestic UK law, by way of the Human Rights Act 1998. Although the right is granted *vis-à-vis* public authorities, the courts, as public bodies, must take the Act into account in adjudicating the conflicting rights of citizens.[8] Legislation is construed in conformity with the Human Rights Act.[9] Prior to this, however, further pieces were added to the mosaic of protection: a moral right of privacy in photographs and films commissioned for private and domestic purposes was enacted in 1988[10] to compensate for changes in copyright ownership rules.[11] In 1990, a Report was published on privacy, with particular reference to the activities of the press.[12] The 'Calcutt Report' recommended prohibition of the most extreme forms of physical intrusion (such as the use of bugging, long-range cameras) extension of statutory restrictions on reporting and improvement on self-regulation by means of a new Press Complaints Commission. In a subsequent study of the Press Complaints Commission's effectiveness,[13] Calcutt recommended the creation of a statutory complaints tribunal, enactment of criminal offences in relation to the more blatant intrusive techniques and the introduction of a tort of infringement of privacy. In the event, the judiciary has responded to the challenge of creating such a general tort more quickly than the legislature. The decision in *Douglas & Zeta Jones v Hello*[14] that breach of confidence might provide a remedy against media coverage of the claimants' wedding, for which exclusive rights had been granted to a different magazine,[15] appears to take the action for breach of confidence into a new role, perhaps more akin to a right of publicity than to a right of privacy.

1. See *Report of the Committee on Privacy* Cmnd 5012, 1972.
2. Ibid, para 657. See, further, P Prescott 'Kaye v Robertson – a reply' (1991) 54 MLR 451; B Sherman and F Kaganas 'The Protection of Personality and Image: An Opportunity Lost' [1991] EIPR 340.
3. *Bernstein of Leigh (Baron) v Skyviews and General Ltd* [1978] QB 479.
4. See, generally, M Arnheim 'Trespass and Privacy' [1989] 133 SJ 1584; The Protection from Harrassment Act 1997 further protects individuals from the more extreme forms of intrusion, see M Davies 'Do we need our Privacy' [1997] Ent LR 286.
5. [1991] FSR 62.
6. European Convention on Human Rights 1950.
7. Art 8.
8. Eg *Ashdown v Telegraph Group Ltd* [2001] EMLR 1003, Ch D – copyright claims and defences.
9. Ibid; Tensions arise between the various rights conferred by the 1998 Act: J Griffiths 'The Human Rights Act, section 12 – Press Freedom over Privacy?'
10. Copyright, Designs and Patents Act 1988, s 85.
11. See para **18.14** above.
12. Report of the Committee on Privacy and Related Matters, June 1990 (Cm 1102) under the chairmanship of Sir David Calcutt QC.

13. January 1993, Cm 2135.
14. [2001] EMLR 199.
15. Cf *Times Newspapers v MGN Ltd* [1993] EMLR 442.

20.22 The long failure of case law to evolve from breach of confidence to right of privacy meant that there was no clear means by which a person could secure protection or compensation where another person holding information about him, such as a bank, a credit-rating agency or an employer, communicated to a third party information which was false. If the communication of such information was intentionally false and was calculated to cause damage, then an action for injurious falsehood might apply,[1] and if it were to cause its recipients to regard its subject with hatred, ridicule or contempt an action for defamation might lie; but most communication of misinformation is a consequence of clerical error (eg reading a credit balance of £10,000 as £1,000, or hitting an adjacent key on the word-processor) and would not in any event lead to a libel. It was therefore necessary for statute to intervene, in the form of the Data Protection Act 1984, and later the Data Protection Act 1998,[2] both to enable the 'data subject' to find what information is held about him,[3] and to give him a right to compensation for wrongful disclosure of information both true and false.[4] Until 2007,[5] however, Parliament has only accorded these statutory rights to data subjects whose good fortune it was to have their personal data stored in such electronic retrieval devices as are not excluded from the Act's ambit;[6] for those whose personal data is stored in manually accessed data-banks such as filing cabinets or card catalogues, no protection currently exist in excess of the common laws.[7]

1. *Ratcliffe v Evans* [1892] 2 QB 524.
2. Implementing EC Directive 95/46 on the protection of individuals with regard to the processing of personal data and on the free movement of such data [1995] OJ L281/31. M Jelf 'Not with a Bang but a Whimper: a Right to Privacy & the End of Voluntary Self-Regulation of the Press' [1999] Ent LR 244 has argued that the Data Protection Act will bring an end to the remaining areas of self-regulation.
3. Data Protection Act 1998, s 7.
4. Ibid. For a discussion of data protection see Baker 'New Data Protection Act' [2000] Ent LR 193; D Bainbridge and G Pearce 'Data Protection' [1995] NLJ 1505,1545, 1579, 1656; I Walden in C Reed (ed) *Computer Law* (4th edn), Ch 11. There are said to be eight Data Protection Principles: data should be (i) processed fairly and lawfully; (ii) for limited purposes; (iii) adequate, relevant and not excessive; (iv) accurate and kept up to date; (v) kept no longer than necessary; (vi) processing shall be in accordance with the data subject's rights; (vii) securely and (viii) the data shall not be transferred beyond the EEA without adequate protection. Compliance with these principles is required whether the data 'Controller' is required to notify under the Act or not.
5. Ibid, art 32; after July 2007, protection will extend to 'structured' manual records – see art 3.
6. See definitions of 'data' and 'data user' in s 1.

7. The Consumer Credit Act 1974, ss 157 to 160, does however, give the consumer ameans of checking on and correcting incorrect data held by a 'credit reference agency'.

20.23 The right of publicity, though not of so legally radical or politically sensitive a nature as the right of privacy, has far greater commercial value. Once a personal secret is disclosed to the public, it has lost its 'essence' and becomes mere fact; where no one knows that Nicole Kidman and Tom Cruise are separating, knowledge of the fact that this is so will have a high commercial value and its disclosure may attract a newspaper fee of £100,000. The week after, when the press has announced the separation, knowledge of that fact has a nil value even though the couple are every bit as estranged as before. In contrast, the commercial value of the right of publicity may be enhanced by overexposure. Once Tim Henman, say, has been paid £500,000 to let his name appear on tennis rackets, the fact that he is seen and heard constantly on television may raise to £600,000 the sum he can charge for endorsing tennis shoes.

20.24 In the UK the right of publicity has long been argued in academic circles[1] but has not been explicitly discussed in court. The wrongful exploitation of another's name, voice or likeness does not normally constitute a passing off,[2] even though it may be a defamation,[3] a criminal offence,[4] or a breach of statutory duty such as a false attribution of authorship.[5] Whether this legal state of affairs is unrealistic in a society which indulges in 'character merchandising' and recognises the practice of licensing[6] will be discussed in Chapter 22 below.

1. See T Frazer 'Appropriation of Personality – A New Tort?' (1983) 99 LQR 281.
2. *Sim v Heinz* [1959] RPC 75; *McCulloch v May* (1947) 65 RPC 58; *Lyngstad v Anabas Products Ltd* [1977] FSR 62; or give a ground for refusal of trade mark registration *ELVIS PRESLEY TM* [1997] RPC 543; affd [1999] RPC 567. Cf the fictional 'Teenage Mutant Ninja Turtles' in *Mirage Studios v Counter-feat Clothing* [1991] FSR 145; the real American chanteuse in *Midler v Ford Motor Co* 849 F 2d 460 (US 9th Cir 1988); T Frazer 'Vox Pop: US Law Finds a Voice in Sound-alikes' [1990] Ent LR 1 26 and citations in para **20.20**, above.
3. *Tolley v J S Fry & Sons* [1931] AC 333; or injurious falsehood *Kaye v Robertson* para **20.21** n 5, above.
4. *R v Collins* [1973] QB 100.
5. Copyright, Designs and Patents Act 1988, s 84. See para **18.14** above.
6. *Scandecor Development AB v Scandecor Marketing AB* [2001] ETMR 800.

Chapter 21

Registered trade marks

Introduction

21.1 A person who requires greater protection for his goodwill than passing off can provide may wish to seek the registration of his name or company name, trading names, brand names, logos and other badges of trade as trade marks under the Trade Marks Act 1994. The advantages of registering a trade mark are that (i) it is protected from the date of its registration,[1] even if it has not yet been used, (ii) there is no need to prove reputation in a mark which has been registered, which makes it easier to sue infringers,[2] (iii) it is less likely that a rival trader will employ a similar mark,[3] but (iv) if a rival trader does use the same or a similar mark, it will be difficult for him to justify a claim that he is entitled to continue to do so; (v) a proprietor who takes successful action against an infringer may recover damages on behalf of any licensees;[4] and (vi) filing for registration in the UK may facilitate an international registration programme.[5] Furthermore, (vii) the protection of a registered trade mark is nationwide, although that of passing off may be strictly local.[6] The disadvantages of trade mark registration are that (i) the initial application and subsequent renewals of registration cost money, (ii) a contested application for a trade mark may involve one in substantial expense and inconvenience, (iii) non-use of a registered trade mark may lead to the mark's being expunged from the register,[7] while non-use of an unregistered name or mark may well not be fatal to a later passing off claim[8] and (v) unjustified threats to sue for infringement of a registered trade mark may give rise to claims by parties affected by the threats,[9] whereas one may threaten with impunity to sue in passing off.

1. Trade Marks Act 1994, s 40(3). However proceedings for infringement can be commenced only once a mark has been registered: see s 2(2).
2. although proof of reputation can be relevant where the defendant is using the disputed sign on goods for which the claimant's mark is not registered: see below, para **21.22**.
3. Competitors can search the register of marks before adopting a new mark; registration of identical or similar marks is inhibited by the Trade Marks Act 1994, s 5(1)-(3).

21.1 *Registered trade marks*

4. Trade Marks Act 1994, s 30(6).
5. Using the priority date system of the Paris Convention or making an international application under the Madrid Protocol. See, further, ch 28.
6. On local reputation in passing off see *George Outram & Co Ltd v London Evening Newspaper Co Ltd* (1911) 28 RPC 308. Registration of a trade mark may be made subject to territorial limitations (Trade Marks Act 1994, s 13(1)(b)), but this rarely happens.
7. Trade Marks Act 1994, s 46(1)(a) and (b), unless there are proper reasons for non-use, such as the production difficulties in *MAGIC BALL TM* [2000] RPC 439.
8. See eg *Ad-Lib Club v Granville* [1972] RPC 673.
9. Trade Marks Act 1994, s 21.

The Trade Marks Act 1994

21.2 Prior to 1994, the Trade Marks Act 1938 held sway for nearly six decades, notwithstanding the increasingly unsuitable nature of many of its provisions. The 1994 Act made a number of changes to UK trade mark law. It brought it into line with the Trade Marks Harmonisation Directive, Council Directive No 89/104/EEC[1] and made provision for the Community Trade Mark system, which applies similar substantive rules for EC-wide registrations.[2] It enabled the UK to ratify the Madrid Protocol relating to the international registration of marks.[3] The most important changes were the relaxation and broadening of the criteria for registration, enlargement of the scope of protection conferred by registration of a mark and the removal of formalities previously associated with trade mark transactions. The propriety of transactions and consequent issues of validity are now a matter for the parties themselves, rather than the Registry. A new category of mark, the collective mark,[4] was introduced and certification[5] or 'quality' marks may now be registered for services as well as for goods. Useful information, services and links are available on the Patent Office's web site.[6]

1. First Council Directive of 21 December 1988 to approximate the laws of the Member States relating to trade marks, OJ 1989 L40/1. The UK complied with this directive rather belatedly; its extended implementation date was 31 December 1992.
2. Established by Council Regulation (EC) No 40/94 of 20 December 1993, OJ 1994 L11/1. Since the Directive and Regulation are drafted in closely similar terms, guidance on interpretation of the Directive and 1994 Act may be sought in decisions on the Regulation and *vice versa*. See, for example, the comments of the Advocate-General in the *BABY-DRY* case, *Procter & Gamble v OHIM* [2000] ETMR 580, esp para 9.
3. Of 27 June 1989, in fact a filing rather than a registration system. See, further, para **28.6**.
4. Trade Marks Act 1994, s 49.
5. Ibid, s 50.
6. www.patent.gov.uk. In particular, chapters of the Trade Marks Registry Work Manual give detailed guidance on the practice of examiners.

What is a registrable trade mark?

21.3   Three positive requirements must be met before a mark is registrable.[1] First, it must be a sign. Second, the sign must be capable of graphical representation, so that it may be entered on the register. Third, it must be capable of distinguishing the goods or services of one undertaking (the applicant) from those of other undertakings. If a mark satisfies these criteria, it may be registered unless prohibited by one or more specific grounds for refusal. The latter are divided into absolute grounds,[2] which depend upon the characteristics of the mark in question, and relative grounds,[3] which apply when there is conflict with prior marks on the register or in use, or other rights such as copyright[4] and rights in designs. There is also a prohibition on the registration of specially protected emblems, such as the Royal Arms and national flags.[5]

1.   Trade Marks Act 1994, s 1(1).
2.   Trade Marks Act 1994, s 3.
3.   Trade Marks Act 1994, ss 5-7.
4.   A two-dimensional or three-dimensional artistic work may also be a trade mark, such as the lady on the Sun-Maid raisin box, the striding infant on the Fairy washing up liquid bottle, the birds on Bird's Custard Powder containers and the 'Spirit of Ecstasy' adorning Rolls-Royce motor cars.
5.   Trade Marks Act 1994, s 4.

Goods, services and undertakings

21.4   The term 'trade mark' is used irrespective of whether the products it distinguishes are goods or services. Retailers had contended that they provided services which should be expressly provided for as 'retail services'. In carrying out its duties under the Trade Marks Act 1938[1] the Registry refused to register a service mark in respect of the selling of goods. This practice was upheld in *Dee Corpn's Applications*[2] and maintained under the 1994 Act. However, in *Giacomelli Sport SpA's Application*,[3] the Community Trade Mark Office, or Office for Harmonisation in the Internal Market, to give its correct title, decided to allow registration of retail service marks in suitably defined sectors. Subsequently, the UK Patent Office has followed suit.[4] The function of a trade mark in distinguishing goods or services *in the course of trade* is not spelt out in section 1. However, economic activity is implicit in the term 'undertaking'. This has a wide meaning in EC jurisprudence, where it has been interpreted particularly in the context of competition law; it embraces public and private undertakings, companies, individuals, sometimes unincorporated associations and charities.[5]

21.4 Registered trade marks

1. As amended by the Trade Marks (Amendment) Act 1984 to provide for the registration of service marks.
2. [1989] FSR 266.
3. [2000] ETMR 277, despite a statement to the contrary entered in the minutes of adoption of the Community Trade Mark Regulation in 1993. A remark at para 25 of *Giacomelli* suggests that a retail service mark should not be regarded as a substitute for registration of the mark for the range of goods or services in question:

   '25. That an imprudent applicant for registration of a trade mark for 'retail services' alone might have an expectation that it also covers its goods, cannot be a reason why retail sales service should be disallowed.'
4. PAC 13/00 *Change of Practice on 'Retail Services'* [2001] RPC 33.
5. See, for example, the cases cited in D M Raybould and A Firth *Law of Monopolies* (1991) pp 211-212.

Varieties of sign

21.5 Section 1(1) of the 1994 Act gives a non-exhaustive list of types of sign which may operate as trade marks:

'A trade mark may, in particular, consist of words (including personal names), designs, letters, numerals or the shape of goods or their packaging.'[1]

The following points may be noted:

(i) specific mention of the shape of goods or their packaging reversed the decisions in *James's Trade Mark*[2] and *Coca-Cola Trade Mark Applications*,[3] in which the shape of the product and the shape of the cola bottle were respectively refused registration. If the shape performs a technical or aesthetic function, however, it may not qualify as a registrable sign;[4]

(ii) colour is not included in the list. However, it has long been recognised that colours may be distinctive, especially in combination. In *Blue Paraffin Trade Mark*[5] the applicant sought registration of the words 'Blue Paraffin', since the characteristic colour of the product itself could not be registered under the Trade Marks Act 1938. Combinations of colours applied to semi-transparent capsules and granules comprising pharmaceutical dosages were held registrable in *Smith Kline & French Laboratories Ltd v Sterling-Winthrop Group Ltd*.[6] Those drafting the Trade Marks Directive took the view that a distinctive colour or combination of colours could be registered.[7] Case law shows that a even single colour may be registered if sufficiently distinctive[8] and provided its graphical representation is adequate.[9] On the other hand, where a colour or combination of colours is particularly apt for a class of product, registration will be refused.[10] If a colour scheme is not likely to be perceived as a trade mark, it will not be registered;[11]

(iii) Sounds are also not listed in the 1994 Act. They were, however, specifically mentioned in the context of the Community trade mark regulation[12] and in the White Paper *Reform of Trade Marks Law*.[13] Thus, a broadcaster's jingle[14] or the roar of the MGM lion[15] may be registered. The jingle may be represented graphically in musical notation,[16] while the lion's roar might simply be described as such;[17]

(iv) by the same token, marks perceived by taste and smell may be registered provided they are distinctive.[18] In the United States, the scent of a sewing yarn has been registered.[19] However, a scent or flavour which is the essential ingredient of the product itself, such as the scent of cologne or the flavour of a foodstuff, may not be registrable.[20] Again, difficulties may be encountered in representing the smell graphically.[21]

(v) it is questionable whether 'the shape of goods or their packaging' includes the tactile properties of a surface. Braille marks encoding a distinctive word may well be registrable as a word mark, but what about more generalised sensations of roughness or warmth to the touch?

(vi) It seems settled that distinctive slogans are registrable under the 1994 Act.[22] Indeed, despite refusal of registration to the Kit-Kat slogan 'Have a Break' in 1983,[23] the slogans 'I Can't Believe It's Yoghurt'[24] and a composite mark including the slogans 'My Mum's Cola' and 'Mum knows best'[25] were held registrable under the Trade Marks Act 1938.

1. The list of signs reproduces that in art 2 of the Trade Marks Harmonisation Directive (para **21.2**, n 1 above) and in art 4 of the Community Trade Mark Regulation (para **21.2**, n 2 above).
2. (1886) 33 Ch D 392.
3. [1985] FSR 315.
4. See para **21.11** below.
5. [1976] FSR 29.
6. [1975] 2 All ER 578, [1976] RPC 511.
7. The following statement regarding Art 4 of the Community Trade Mark Regulation was prepared for entry in the minutes of the Council meeting at which the regulation was adopted:

'The Council and the Commission consider that Article 4 does not rule out the possibility:
- of registering as a Community trade mark a combination of colours or a single colour;
- of registering in the future sounds as Community trade marks,
provided they are capable of distinguishing the goods or services of one undertaking from those of other undertakings.'

8. BP's mark, a particular shade of green applied to distinctively shaped surfaces, was registered pursuant to an application which pre-dated the 1994 Act: *BP Amoco plc v John Kelly Ltd* [2001] FSR 307; in that case the High Court of Justice in Northern Ireland took the view that the shade of green, on its own, would not have been sufficiently distinctive.
9. *Ty Nant Spring Water Ltd's Application* [2000] FSR 55, [1999] ETMR 981; *Orange Personal Communications Ltd's Application* [1998] ETMR 460.
10. *Procter & Gamble France's Application* [2001] ETMR 209 (OHIM): the colours white, blue and green, being associated with cleanliness and the environment, should be available for competitors to use in relation to cleaning products.
11. *Glaxo/Riker* [2001] ETMR 96 (pink/maroon inhalers).
12. See n 6 above.
13. Cm 1203 (1990) paras 2.06, 2.11 and 2.12, although scepticism was expressed as to the likelihood of sounds being unambiguously describable *and* distinctive.
14. Such as the musical motif in *Lawson v Dundas*, Falconer J, 12 June 1985, *The Times*, 13 June (see para **11.23**, n 1).
15. Referred to by the House of Lords Public Bill Committee, 2nd sitting, 18 Jan 1994, col 33.
16. Trade Marks Registry Work Manual, ch 6, para 2.3.6: 'Musical notation will be accepted as a graphical representation of a sound mark. If the instruments upon which the sound is played forms part of the mark, this should be stated. The names of pieces of music will not be accepted as a graphical representation of the sound.'
17. Ibid, col 34. A vague description of a commonplace class of sound will not be adequate as a graphical representation *Qlicksmart Pty Ltd* [1999] ETMR 190; 335 (OHIM, 'click').
18. White Paper Reform of Trade Marks Law 1990 Cm 1203, paras 2.11 and 2.12; in an explanatory memorandum to art 3 of the November 1980 draft of the Community Trade Mark Regulation, the European Commission stated:

> 'Depending on the circumstances, therefore, the Trade Marks Office, the national courts, or, in the last resort, the Court of Justice will be responsible for determining whether, for example, solid colours or shades of colours and signs denoting sound, smell or taste may constitute Community trade-marks'

Bulletin of the European Communities, Supplement No 5/80, p 56. A well-publicised example of a smell mark registered in the UK was the smell of roses for tyres.
19. *Re Celia Clarke* 17 USPQ 2d 1238 (Trademark Trial and Appeal Board 1990).
20. By analogy with the situation in the US: see n 19 above and M Sommers 'Extending the Boundaries of Trademark Protection in the US' *Trademark World*, September 1993, pp 18 and 29. However, the ground for refusal that a mark adds substantial value to the goods is spelt out only where the mark consists of the shape of goods: Trade Marks Act 1994, s 3 (2)(c) for which see para **21.11** below.
21. *Re John Lewis of Hungerford Ltd's Trade Mark Application* [2001] RPC 575 (the smell of cinnamon for furniture polish); *Vennootschap Firma Senta Aromatic Marketing's Application (Smell of fresh cut grass for tennis balls)* [1999] ETMR 429 (OHIM).
22. The reasoning in *MY MUM'S COLA* [1988] RPC 130 is still being applied: Registry Work Manual, ch 6, para 4.4.
23. Reported at [1993] RPC 217.
24. [1992] RPC 533.
25. [1988] RPC 130.

Level of distinctiveness

21.6 The words 'capable of distinguishing' appear to set a comparatively low threshold of distinctiveness.[1] The same words were used to define the level of distinctiveness required for registration in Part B[2] of the register under the 1938 Act.[3] At first glance one might suppose the same minimum threshold to apply under the 1994 Act. However, interpretation of these words in the UK was previously constrained by the decision of the House of Lords in *York Trailer Holdings v Registrar of Trade Marks*:[4] 'capable' meant 'legally capable' rather than capable in fact. The Irish Supreme Court had reached the opposite conclusion in *Waterford Trade Mark*.[5] Helpful guidance, often cited in decisions of the Trade Marks Registry, was given by The Appointed Person[6] in *AD 2000*.[7] Pointing out that a registrable sign possessed the qualities in section 1 of the Trade Marks Act 1994, and none of the defects in section 3, he held that 'capable' in section 1 had the limited meaning of 'not incapable'. Under section 3 it could then be decided whether a sign was adequately distinctive at the time of the application, whether by nature or by nurture, to go forward for registration. It should be noted that a mark of low distinctiveness is likely to enjoy protection only against the use of identical or closely resembling marks over a narrow range of products.[8]

1. Thus the European Court of Justice has opined that BABY-DRY was capable of distinguishing the applicant's disposable nappies from those of other traders; [2000] ETMR 580 (A-G), ECJ; [2001] ETMR 829; see, also *TRUSTEDLINK Harbinger v OHIM* [2001] ETMR 11; *DOUBLEMINT* [2001] ETMR 58.
2. The former division of the register into Parts A and B disappeared with the repeal of the 1938 Act. See *Reform of Trade Marks Law* 1990 Cm 1203, paras 4.03-4.05.
3. S 10.
4. [1982] FSR 111.
5. [1984] FSR 390. Contrast the earlier English decision at [1972] RPC 149, [1972] FSR 51.
6. The person appointed to hear appeals from the Registry under Trade Marks Act 1994, s 77, in this case Geoffrey Hobbs QC.
7. [1997] RPC 168; see also *BACH and BACH FLOWER REMEDIES Trade Marks* [2000] RPC 513, CA.
8. See, below, para **21.22**.

Absolute grounds for refusal of registration

21.7 Section 3 sets out the 'absolute' grounds upon which registration of a mark may be refused. The first group, in sub-section (1), may be paraphrased as follows:

(i)   the sign fails to satisfy the requirements of section 1;
(ii)   the sign is devoid of any distinctive character;
(iii)   the sign is wholly descriptive;
(iv)   the sign is generic in that it is used in common parlance or in the trade to describe the product, regardless of commercial origin.

All but the first ground may be circumvented by evidence that the trade mark has become distinctive in use prior to the date of the application for registration under the proviso to section 3(1). The categories are not mutually exclusive; (ii) embraces the more specific objections under (iii) and (iv).

21.8   Pausing here, the first ground is unlikely to inconvenience many applicants for registration. One may imagine a complex synthetic sound which is impossible to reduce to graphical form in a way that represents it adequately. However, the vast majority of applicants will have adopted – and wish to use – a mark in graphical form. As to the second, one may imagine a covetous applicant seeking to register an unadorned letter,[1] perhaps 'a' in the lower case representation of the indefinite article. This would undoubtedly be excluded as devoid of distinctiveness.[2] Very common surnames probably also fall into this category.[3] However, the less common the surname and the stronger the evidence of use, the more likely a surname is to be registered. This was the case under the 1938 Act, which allowed for the registration of BOOTS, THEAKSTONS and CIBA.[4] The number of appearances in telephone directories is used as an inverse measure of distinctiveness. Weight is given to non-surnominal meanings of names such as SWALLOW,[5] CANNON[6] or DENT.[7] Where surnames are registered, the possible discomfiture of other 'owners' of the name is alleviated by section 10(2)(a).[8]

1.   In claiming trade mark status for their 'double arches' logo, McDonalds assert exclusive rights in a stylised form of the letter 'M'.
2.   In *British Sugar v Robertson* [1996] RPC 281, Jacob J opined that a such mark, considered on its own and assuming no use, would be the sort of sign which could not do the job of distinguishing without first educating the public that it is a trade mark. Under the Community Trade Mark Regulation, INVESTORWORLD was held devoid of distinctive character for finance-related services *Community Concepts AG v OHIM* [2001] ETMR 176.
3.   See Registry Work Manual, ch 6, para 3.12.1; In *MISTER LONG* [1998] RPC 401, G Hobbs QC, decided that the mark could be registered for iced lollipops.
4.   All mentioned in *CIBA Trade Mark* [1983] RPC 75.
5.   *Swallow Raincoats' Application* (1947) 64 RPC 92.
6.   [1980] RPC 519.
7.   *Dent's Application* [1979] EIPR D-27.
8.   A defence to infringement under which permits the honest use of one's own name.

21.9   The next ground for refusal, descriptiveness, is likely to arise more frequently. Those adopting a new mark often plump for a suggestive or descriptive mark in order to minimise the trouble and expense of educating the public to recognise and remember it, especially where a new product is being introduced.[1] They should beware of sub-section 3(1)(c), which prohibits the registration of signs which consist exclusively of designations of kind, quality, quantity, intended purpose, value, geographical origin, the time of production of goods or rendering of services and other characteristics. The Trade Marks Registry Work Manual[2] gives examples of overly descriptive marks such as JUMBO, BEST, 454 for butter,[3] MARINE for paint, WORTH THEIR WEIGHT IN GOLD, EIGHT TIL LATE for restaurant services. Suggestive, rather than wholly descriptive, marks are likely to be registrable with, or even without, evidence of use under the 1994 Act, as they were under the 1938: CHUNKY[4] for dogfood, APHRODISIA for soaps and perfumes,[5] MOTHERCARE for books[6] and DUSTIC (pronounced dust-ic and not does-stick) for glue.[7] However, those attempting to register PERFECTION for soap,[8] and VAPO-RUB for vapour rubs[9] may still expect objection from the registry. These lack the 'minimum of imagination' held necessary in *Taurus-Film GmbH v OHIM*[10] to escape descriptiveness. The Registry's response to geographical indications will depend upon the importance of the geographical location in question, whether its use is fanciful or descriptive in relation to the services or goods in question, upon evidence of distinctiveness acquired through use and upon whether or not it would be right for the sign to be kept available to other traders.[11] For example, THE GLENLIVET was registered for whisky and for water prior to commencement of the 1994 Act.[12]

1. This habit was deplored by S A Diamond in his excellent book *Trade Mark Problems and How to Avoid Them* (1981, 2nd edn).
2. Ch 6, para 4.8.
3. Butter is often sold in 454 gram (1 lb) packs.
4. [1978] FSR 322.
5. *Aphrodisia Trade Mark* [1977] FSR 133.
6. *Mothercare v Penguin Books* [1988] RPC 113.
7. *RK Dundas Ltd's Application* (1955) 72 RPC 151.
8. *J Crosfield & Son's Application* [1910] 1 Ch 130.
9. *De Cordova v Vick Chemical Co* (1951) 68 RPC 103 at 108, cited with approval in *Oasis Stores Ltd's Application* [1999] ETMR 531 at 535.
10. [2001] ETMR 594; CFI - CINE ACTION could be registered for some activities in the entertainment and copyright field, but not for others such as broadcasting.
11. See *Windsurfing Chiemsee Produktions-und Vertriebs GmbH v Boots-und Segelzubehor Walter Huber* [1999] ETMR 585, ECJ.
12. *THE GLENLIVET Trade Marks* [1993] RPC 461.

21.10 A mark may be used in current language or in the trade to describe the product rather than to indicate its commercial origin. This can happen not only to descriptive marks, such as OVEN CHIPS,[1] which are used as product descriptions without ever becoming distinctive

of their originator, but also to initially distinctive marks such as
ASPIRIN or LINOLEUM. A sign which is thus used 'generically' by
the public or the trade cannot be registered by virtue of section 3(1)(d).[2]
JERYL LYNN was customarily used to describe a strain of vaccine
originating from a girl of that name; it could not be regarded as
distinctive of a particular producer of vaccines.[3] Sub-section 3(1)(d)
might also be used to prohibit the registration of common words which
honest competitors would need to promote their products.[4] Thus
ALWAYS and NEXT were refused registration under the 1938 Act on
the basis that others would wish to use the words in advertising.[5]

1. To the chagrin of the mark's originator in *McCain International Ltd v Country
   Fair Foods Ltd* [1981] RPC 69.
2. Once validly on the register, however, it can only be removed as generic if it is
   so used in the trade: s 46(1)(c).
3. [1999] FSR 491.
4. As with the geographical word 'Chiemsee' in *Windsurfing Chiemsee
   Produktions-und Vertriebs GmbH v Boots-und Segel-zubehor Walter Huber*
   [1999] ETMR 585, ECJ.
5. *ALWAYS Trade Mark* [1986] RPC 93; *NEXT Trade Mark* [1992] RPC 455.

Exclusions relating to the shape of goods

21.11   The next group of absolute grounds for refusal relates to marks
which consist of the shape of goods[1] and are set out in section 3(2).
These are not registrable if the sign consists exclusively of the shape
which (a) results from the nature of the goods themselves, such as the
general toroidal shape of a motor tyre; (b) is necessary to obtain a
technical result, as perhaps a tread pattern which is uniquely suitable
for ice or snow or the three-headed configuration of an electric shaver;[2]
or (c) which gives substantial value to the goods themselves, such as
the cut of a diamond.[3]

1. See A Firth, E Gredley and S Maniatis 'Shapes as Trade Marks: Public Policy,
   Functional Considerations and Consumer Perception' [2001] EIPR 86.
2. See *Philips Electronics NV v Remington Consumer Products* [1999] RPC 809,
   CA; cf *Ide Line Aktiebolaget v Philips Electronics NV* [1997] ETMR 377.
3. Or the 'designer' toaster shapes in *Dualit* [1999] RPC 890.

Immoral, deceptive and 'bad faith' marks

21.12   These are dealt with in the remaining subsections of section 3.

(i)   Marks which are felt to have a corrosive effect upon public
      morality or are otherwise contrary to public policy may not be
      registered,[1] even though they may be applied to goods and
      services without attracting any criminal penalty.[2] What constitutes

an immoral mark in the current climate is a matter for speculation, but it is unlikely that anything other than expletives,[3] terms of racial abuse or perhaps terms with connotations of drug-taking would fall foul of registration today. Cases such as *La Marquise Application*,[4] in which OOMPHIES was held registrable for footwear only after a strong challenge on the ground that the word 'oomph' was equated with sex appeal and thus created a risk of rampant foot-fetishism, are unlikely to be repeated.

(ii) Deceptive marks which are such as to deceive the public, for instance as to the nature, quality or geographical origin[5] of the product, are excluded from registration under sub-section 3(3)(b). Thus the result of the famous ORLWOOLA case,[6] in which the mark was held wholly descriptive if used in relation to all-wool goods and deceptive if the goods were not 100% wool, has been repeated under the 1994 Act, where EUROLAMB was held descriptive if used in relation to sheep meat and deceptive if used on other meats.[7]

(iii) The registration of marks the use of which is illegal under UK or Community law is precluded by sub-section 3(4).

(iv) Sub-section 3(6) prohibits registration if – or to the extent that – the application is made in bad faith. Bad faith involves falling short of acceptable standards of commercial behaviour: *Gromax Plasticulture v Don & Low Nonwovens Ltd.*[8] It includes applying for registration with no *bona fide* intention to use the mark, despite the statement of use or intention to use contained in the application form,[9] and a deliberate attempt to cash in on another's reputation.[10] One may wonder as to the circumstances in which the Registrar could make a finding of bad faith *ex parte*. Indeed, there is no corresponding provision for refusal of a Community Trade Mark on the ground of bad faith at any stage during examination of the application; such claims must be raised in cancellation proceedings.[11] For UK trade mark applications, bad faith as a ground for refusal will be most significant at the opposition stage,[12] although even after registration, the Registrar may apply to the court for a declaration of invalidity on this ground.[13]

1. Trade Marks Act 1994 s 3(3)(a).
2. Marks whose use is prohibited by any enactment or rule of law are dealt with separately in sub-s 3(4).
3. In *French Connection Ltd v Sutton* [2000] ETMR 341 at 346, the court indicated that it found the dispute over the mark FCUK 'unpalatable', although the mark had been registered by the claimant. Summary judgment was refused in a passing off action about a web site fcuk.com registered by the defendant.
4. (1947) 64 RPC 27.
5. S 3(3)(b) is an absolute ground of refusal; objection to a mark on the ground that it is deceptive as to commercial origin is the province of s 5, the relative grounds for refusal: *Reufach Marketing GmbH's Application* [1999] ETMR 412.

6. *ORLWOOLA Trade Mark* [1910] 1 Ch 130.
7. *BOCM Pauls Ltd and Scottish Agricultural College's Application* [1997] ETMR 420.
8. [1999] RPC 367.
9. In *DEMON ALE Trade Mark* [2000] RPC 345; the applicant had applied to register an anagram of LEMONADE for 'beer'.
10. *CA Sheimer (M) Sdn Bhd's Application* [1999] ETMR 519 (VISA for condoms).
11. Council Reg (EC) No 2100/94, art 51(1)(d).
12. Para **21.20** below.
13. Trade Marks Act 1994 s 47(4).

Relative grounds for refusal of registration

21.13 Sections 5-8 spell out the circumstances in which registration will be refused because of conflict with an 'earlier trade mark'. This phrase is defined in section 5 and includes earlier UK trade mark registrations, whether granted pursuant to a domestic or Madrid Protocol[1] filing, earlier Community Trade Marks,[2] registrations with earlier priority dates accorded under the Paris Convention[3] or Community trade mark systems and marks which at the application date are entitled to protection as 'well known trade marks' under the Paris Convention.[4]

Earlier applications also count, subject to their achieving registration,[5] as do marks of which the registration has expired. This effect lasts for a year after expiry, unless the mark was unused for at least two years immediately before that.[6] Section 5 sets out the rules for comparison between the application and the earlier marks. For conflict to impede registration, the marks must be identical or similar.[7] The products (goods or services) must be the same or similar,[8] unless the earlier mark has a reputation in the UK.[9] In the latter case registration is prohibited if use of the later mark without due cause would take unfair advantage of, or be detrimental to, the distinctive character or the repute of the mark.[10] For examples as to the operation of these rules, see paras **21.13** and **21.21,** below. The relative grounds for refusal mirror the infringement provisions, which have been described as 'conceptually indistinguishable'.[11]

At present the Trade Marks Registry carries out a search for conflicting earlier marks, and examines the application on relative grounds in the light of the search. A consultation exercise was carried out by the Patent Office in the first part of 2001 as to whether to retain examination on relative grounds; section 8 of the Trade Marks Act 1994 envisaged abandonment ten years into the operation of the Community Trade Mark system. At the time of writing, the results of the consultation exercise were not available.[12]

1. Trade Marks Act 1994, s 53 and para **28.6** below.
2. See para **27.9**.
3. See para **28.5**.
4. Art 6 *bis*.
5. Trade Marks Act 1994, s 6(2).
6. Ibid, s 6(3).
7. Ibid, s 5(1)-(3).
8. Ibid, s 5(1) and (2).
9. Or in the European Community, if the earlier mark is a Community trade mark.
10. Trade Marks Act 1994, s 5(3).
11. *Raleigh International Trade Mark* [2001] RPC 202, Geoffrey Hobbs QC. This decision also queried whether objections under subs 5(2) and 5(3) need be regarded as mutually exclusive.
12. However, a page on the patent office web site is devoted to 'Trade Marks: the future of examination on relative grounds' and may be accessed for further information through the home page at www.patent.gov.uk.

Identity and similarity

21.14   One might wonder whether, to be considered identical, the marks have to be the same in every respect. For example, the word marks SWALLOW HOLE and SWALLOW WHOLE are phonetically identical but their different spellings convey different ideas, one suggesting a geological feature or the entrance to a bird's nest, the other suggesting a snake devouring its prey. It may be the case that 'identical' means identical in every respect,[1] but there is uncertainty as to how to treat 'identical plus' marks , where the later mark contains additional elements. This was considered by Jacob J in the TREAT case,[2] where the judge suggested that added material which does not affect the distinctive character of the mark should be disregarded, whereas additions which change the mark's character take it out of the 'identical' category and into the similar. In Jacob J's example, only a crossword addict would discern 'TREAT' in 'THEATRE ATMOSPHERE and maintain that there was any true 'identity' between them. Yet, while the same judge has found that WILLIAM R. ASPREY ESQUIRE was identical to ASPREY,[3] the Appointed Person has concluded that 10 ROYAL BERKSHIRE POLO CLUB was not identical to POLO.[4] In *Decon Laboratories Ltd v Fred Baker Scientific Ltd*[5] the claimant had registered DECON for various cleaning and sterilising products in classes 3 and 5. It used the mark in combinations such as 'DECON90', 'DECON Acid Rinse'. Pumfrey J held that the defendant's use of DECON in conjunction with descriptive additions, such as DECON-AHOL, DECON-CLEAN, involved use of a sign identical to that registered.

The tests for similarity involve the likelihood of confusion on the part of the public, which is said to include the likelihood of 'association'.[6] This flows from the harmonisation directive.[7] The concept of association is said to stem from Benelux trade mark law.[8] Curiously, it seems clear that, in the Benelux, association is not a variety of confusion but occurs when a trade mark is brought to mind by use of a similar sign.[9] Thus, ANTI-MONOPOLY used in relation to an anti-capitalist board game, was held to infringe the mark MONOPOLY, as used for the traditional property trading game.[10] Both the English Court[11] and the European Court [12] have confirmed that 'association' in the 1994 Act, Directive and Regulation denotes an element of confusion as to commercial origin or connection, and not an alternative to confusion in its wider sense. The latter in turn may be compared with tests for passing off. Many kinds of misrepresentation in addition to the classic form of misrepresentation as to source are recognised as sufficient to establish passing off.[13] Operative confusion affects the 'average consumer', a 'reasonably well-informed', 'reasonably observant and circumspect' character.[14]

1. This is assumed by the rules for comparison of non-identical marks, taking into account their visual, aural and conceptual characteristics: *Sabel BV v Puma AG* [1998] RPC 199, [1998] ETMR 1; *Lloyd Schuhfabrik Meyer & Co GmbH v Klijsen Handel BV* [1999] All ER (EC) 587, [1999] ETMR 10, 690, [2000] FSR 77.
2. *British Sugar plc v James Robertson & Sons Ltd* [1996] RPC 281, [1997] ETMR 118; see, also *Société LTJ Diffusion v Sadas Vertbaudet* [2001] ETMR 854 (reference to European Court of Justice as to whether ARTHUR is identical to ARTHUR et FELICE)
3. *Asprey & Garrard Ltd v WRA (Guns) Ltd,* unreported, 18 May 2001.
4. *Royal Berkshire Polo Club's Application* [2001] ETMR 826.
5. [2001] RPC 17, [2001] ETMR 486.
6. Trade Marks Act 1994, s 5(2).
7. Para **21.2**, n 1 above, art 4(1)(b) and 10th recital, which in turn derives at this point from the draft Community Trade Mark Regulation, para **21.2**, n 2, above.
8. The following statement was made for entry in the minutes of the Council meeting at which the Community trade mark regulation was adopted:

   'The Council and Commission note that 'likelihood of association' is a concept which in particular has been developed by Benelux case-law.'

9. See C Gielen, 'Harmonisation of Trade Mark Law in Europe: the First Trade Mark Harmonisation Directive of the European Council' [1992] 8 EIPR 262; A Kamperman Sanders, 'Trade mark dilution – the parting of the ways?' *Managing Intellectual Property*, 1992, issue 3, p 42.
10. Decision of 24 June 1977 (Supreme Court) cited by Gielen n 4 above at p 267.
11. *Wagamama v City Centre Restaurants* [1995] FSR 713, [1996] ETMR 23.
12. *Sabel BV v Puma AG* [1998] RPC 199, [1998] ETMR 1; *Canon Kabushiki Kaisha v Metro-Goldwyn-Mayer Inc* [1999] RPC 117, [1999] ETMR 1

13. See paras **20.10-20.14** above and C Wadlow *The Law of Passing Off* (2nd edn 1995) paras 4.01-4.09.
14. *Lloyd Schuhfabrik Meyer & Co GmbH v Klijsen Handel BV* [1999] All ER (EC) 587 para 26 at 599, [1999] ETMR 10, 690 at 698; *BACH and BACH FLOWER REMEDIES Trade Marks* [2000] RPC 513.

21.15 The trade mark may also be refused on the grounds that it is liable to be prevented in the UK by an action for passing off, infringement of copyright or design or other rule of law.[1] Thus the owner of copyright in an original logo may prevent its registration as a trade mark. If a graphic designer has been engaged to create the logo for use as a trade mark by the applicant, she will, however, have impliedly consented to its registration. Section 5(5) allows registration where the proprietor of the earlier trade mark or other earlier right consents.

1. Trade Marks Act 1994, s 5(4); for an example of successful opposition based on passing off rights, see *NONOGRAM Trade Mark* [2001] RPC 355.

Honest concurrent user

21.16 Where an applicant who is faced with objection on the basis of an earlier mark can show that he has made concurrent use of his mark honestly, notwithstanding the earlier trade mark, the Registrar may allow the mark to proceed to registration, leaving it to the proprietor to object in opposition proceedings.[1]

1. Trade Marks Act 1994, s 7. Honest concurrent use, defined by reference to s 12(2) of the Trade Marks Act 1938, is merely a means of overcoming a Registry objection on relative grounds. If the proprietor of the other mark opposes, registration may still be refused. Likewise, honest concurrent use does not operate as a defence to infringement proceedings. Once the concurrently used mark is registered, however, a defence will lie under Trade Marks Act 1994, s 11(1).

Classification of registered marks

21.17 Once a registrable mark has been chosen, the applicant must decide what goods and services he wants his registration to cover. This is because the register is divided up by 'classes', each of which represents a conceptual grouping of similar trade interests. There are 34 classes in which goods may be registered and a further 8 which cover services.[1] The idea behind registration by classes is that traders' interests are not normally threatened by use of their marks in completely different markets and that, accordingly, the same mark can be used and registered by different proprietors in respect of their fields of activity. Thus the proprietor of the TAGOMAC mark for precision welding equipment is not likely to feel threatened by another's use of TAGOMAC hairgrips, plastic tablecloths or adhesive inner soles.

1.   Class 42, a 'miscellaneous' class for services not falling within classes 35 to 41, has no conceptual equivalent in the 34 goods classes. In 2003 a revision of the classification scheme will add another two classes for services.

21.18   The trade mark applicant can seek registration for goods or services in any or all of the classes in which he uses or proposes to use his mark, but he will be advised that he must pay filing fees[1] for the first and additional classes. If registration is obtained in respect of particular goods or services but the mark is not put to genuine use, the mark can be expunged from the register in respect of those goods or services.[2] Formerly it was possible to obtain a so-called 'defensive registration' of an invented word which is so well-known (eg OXO, BOVRIL, DULUX, BISTO) that its use by any other person in regard to any class of goods (but not services) would create a strong implication that the proprietor of that mark was engaged in his enterprise.[3] This category of registration disappeared with the repeal of the 1938 Act. However, such use may now be prohibited by the 'base' registration.[4]

1.   Trade Marks Act 1994, s 32(4).
2.   Trade Marks Act 1994, s 46(1)(a).
3.   Trade Marks Act 1938, s 27(1). Criteria for defensive registration were hard to satisfy: see *Ferodo's Application* (1945) 62 RPC 111; *Eastex's Application* (1947) 64 RPC 142. Once registered, however, the marks did not have to be used in the 'defensive' classes.
4.   See para **21.21** below. Some former 'defensive' registrations remain on the register. They are vulnerable to revocation on the ground of non-use. In *Premier Brands UK Ltd v Typhoon Europe Ltd* [2000] ETMR 1071, [2000] FSR 767, defensive registrations of TY.PHOO partially survived attack because they had been used on relevant products.

21.19   The division of the register into classes produces extra revenue for the Trade Marks Registry, but is open to criticism on the ground that the division of goods and services within classes is arbitrary and inconvenient, causing the applicant to register the same mark twice or more in respect of what seems to him to be the same business activity. For example, yarns and threads fall into class 23 while lace, embroidery, ribands and braids lie in class 26; artificial flowers lie in class 23, live flowers in class 31, plant pots in 21 (if earthenware) or 20 (if plastic); insecticides belong to class 1, while herbicides belong to class 5. The classification system is, however, used for searching the register for conflicting marks.[1] With the possibility that a registration may now operate to block a subsequent registration[2] or prevent use of a mark[3] even for dissimilar products, the difficulties of searching will be compounded. Wisely, perhaps, the Registry searches only for similar goods and services.

1. By third parties as well as by the Registry, *Altechnic Ltd's TM* [2001] RPC 227.
2. Trade Marks Act 1994, s 5(3) and para **21.13** above.
3. Ibid, s 10(3) and para **21.21** below.

Opposition

21.20   Once a mark has been accepted for registration, it is published in the *Trade Marks Journal*.[1] This gives warning to those who may be affected by the registration. Any person has the right, within three months of publication, formally to oppose the registration[2] or to make written observations as to its registrability.[3]

This is the phase in the application procedure where objections based upon 'outside' evidence as to the reputation of the mark[4] or the *bona fides* of the applicant,[5] may best be considered.

1. Trade Marks Act 1994, s 38(1); Trade Marks Rules 1994, rr 1 and 12.
2. Trade Marks Act 1994, s 38(2); Trade Marks Rules 1994, r 13. Once the Community trade mark system has been in operation for ten or more years, the Secretary of State may by order provide that relative grounds of refusal be raised in opposition and not as part of the registry's formal examination: s 8. See above, para **21.13**.
3. Trade Marks Act 1994, s 38(3).
4. Relevant to confusion under s 5(2) and essential for objection under s 5(3) of the Trade Marks Act 1994.
5. Ibid, s 3(6).

Trade mark infringement

21.21   The proprietor of a registered trade mark has exclusive rights in the mark which are infringed by its use in the UK without his consent.[1] The acts constituting infringement are elaborated in section 10. To summarise, infringing use involves the use in the course of trade of an identical or similar sign in relation to the goods or services for which it is registered, or similar goods, or even dissimilar goods if additional criteria are satisfied. There is also a form of contributory infringement, whereby those preparing labelling, packaging, business papers or advertising material are treated as party to infringing use if they knew or had reason to believe that use of the mark was not duly authorised.[2]

1. Trade Marks Act 1994, s 9.
2. Ibid, s 10(5).

Comparison of signs and products

21.22 This follows exactly the pattern outlined for conflict with earlier marks under section 5.[1] For identical marks and products there is no need to establish confusion.[2] This is useful in that it will enable cases of blatant infringement to be dealt with by way of summary judgment.[3] Where the marks or products are not identical, there must usually be sufficient similarity to give rise to confusion. Thus the owner of the KODAK mark could stop another's use of KODA, KOPAK or KODEK for photographic equipment, but probably not KAPAX, BOJAG or COWPAT. In each case the court will apply the law in relation to the facts of the appropriate market, and the standard by which confusingly similar marks are found to be so is similar to that which satisfies the criteria for a successful passing off action.[4] The 'average consumer' who is likely to be confused, or not, is reasonably well-informed, observant and circumspect, the degree to which these qualities are found being dependent upon the product or service in question.[5] Similarities which might lead to a finding of infringement in relation to sweets, breakfast cereals or 'impulse' goods would not render a motor car manufacturer liable for infringement.[6] In the past, the courts held OXOT, ELECTRIX and HANDI HANKI to be infringements of OXO, ELECTROLUX and HANDY ANDIES respectively,[7] while KOALA KOLA and BUTAZONG have not been regarded as infringements of COCA-COLA and BUTAZOLIDIN.[8] The necessary similarity of products will depend upon the 'strength' of the mark[9] and how closely the defendant has imitated it. Imitation of other indicia may affect the comparison. In *Pfizer v Eurofoods*,[10] the claimant's product was a pharmaceutical product, sold in pill form, for the treatment of impotency, whereas the defendant's product was a soft drink. However, considering that the defendant's drink was coloured blue like the claimant's pill, bore on its label a diamond motif in the shape of the claimant's pill and was sold in terms suggesting aphrodisiac qualities, the similarity of the products became apparent. Registration of a 'household name' such as LEGO or KODAK will enable its proprietor to prevent unauthorised use of the identical mark on a wide range of goods and services. The use of non-identical marks like KODA, KOPAK or KODEK could be restrained for products more closely resembling photographic articles or services.[11] With well-recognised marks, there is also the possibility that use in relation to dissimilar goods or services would be sufficiently detrimental to distinctiveness or reputation to infringe by virtue of section 10(3). Thus, where GODIVA has a reputation as denoting delicious and high-quality chocolates, the use of DOGIVA for dog biscuits is likely to take unfair advantage of the mark's distinctive character.[12] Using the sign VISA, well known for financial products, in relation to condoms is likely to have a similar effect.[13] It is hard to identify a 'due cause' for use of the mark. However, use of the sign EVER READY for condoms is more likely to be taken as a jokey allusion than to damage the mark EVER READY registered for batteries.[14]

1. See para **21.13** above.
2. Trade Marks Act 1994, s 10(1).
3. In the High Court this is effected under CPR 24. The claimant submits a statement testifying to belief that there is no defence to the action. Final judgment will be entered unless the defendant persuades the court to give leave to defend, which may be granted upon condition: for example that the defendant pay money into court. For a reported case where summary judgment was granted for trade mark infringement, see *Roadtech Computer Systems Ltd v Mandata (Management and Data Services) Ltd* [2000] ETMR 970.
4. See para **20.7** et seq above.
5. See para **20.13** above.
6. *LANCIA/LANCER* [1987] RPC 303.
7. See *Oxo Ltd v King* (1917) 34 RPC 165; *Electrix Ltd v Electrolux Ltd* [1960] AC 722; *Bowater-Scott Corpn Ltd v Modo Consumer Products Inc* [1969] FSR 330.
8. *Coca Cola Co v William Struthers & Sons Ltd* [1968] FSR 173; *Geigy AG v Chelsea Drug & Chemical Co Ltd* [1966] RPC 64.
9. In *Canon Kabushiki Kaisha v Metro-Goldwyn-Mayer Inc* [1999] RPC 117, [1999] ETMR 1 the European Court of Justice stressed the relevance of the 'distinctive character' of the mark to this enquiry; in that case similarity of the goods and services was the main issue, since the later mark CANNON was very close to the earlier mark CANON.
10. [2000] ETMR 896, [2001] FSR 17.
11. The reputation of the earlier mark is usually assumed to increase its power to block later applications and to prevent infringements. The above discussion suggests that this is certainly so where comparison of goods and services is concerned. However where a mark is really well known, the average consumer may be less rather than more likely to be confused by a similar but non-identical *mark*. A child is rarely fooled by a 'cheap imitation' of her favourite branded product. The decisions so far on the issue of reputation go to similarity of products. However, it is implicit in *Sabel BV v Puma AG* [1998] RPC 199, [1998] ETMR 1 that where marks are *not* well known, aspects such as conceptual similarity (in that case 'big cats') become important. As Jacob J has previously pointed out, in the case of a well-recognised mark, the public will be swift to spot differences.
12. In the US case of *Grey v Campbell Soup Co* 231 USPQ 562 (CD Calif 1986) it was held that use of DOGIVA on dog biscuits 'diluted' the mark GODIVA for chocolates; although there was little likelihood of confusion, the distinctiveness and prestige of the GODIVA mark would be diminished. A number of American states have had anti-dilution laws for some time and Federal anti-dilution provisions have been introduced into the Lanham Act, USC §1125.
13. *CA Sheimer (M) Sdn Bhd's Application* [1999] ETMR 519, a case decided under s 5(3).
14. *Oasis Stores Ltd's Application; Opposition of Ever Ready plc* [1998] RPC 631.

Use in the course of trade

21.23 Kinds of use that may be regarded as infringements include affixing the disputed sign to goods or packaging, dealing in marked goods, offering services under thesign, or using the offending sign on business papers or in advertising.[1] The use may be by way of graphic representation or otherwise.[2] Thus saying a word mark, playing a jingle or using a registered scent may infringe. The nexus between the products in relation to which the infringer uses the mark and the goods or services has already been considered. But does the trade have to be in the goods or services to which the mark refers? Common sense suggests the answer 'yes', which means that, where Andy Warhol depicts in his painting a can of Campbell's soup[3] or Manet depicts the celebrated red triangle of Bass Charrington beer,[4] no trade mark infringement is committed. Use of the Campbells or Bass marks is not trade mark use in relation to the *paintings* (the objects of trade) although they are recognisable as trade marks for soup or for beer. This question has now been referred to the European Court of Justice by Laddie J in *Arsenal Football Club v Reed*,[5] in which the court sought guidance as to whether the unauthorised affixation of the registered trade mark ARSENAL on football kit and memorabilia was a use of the trade mark as such or merely the use of the football club's name as a badge of support or affiliation.

In the Benelux, however,[6] a different analysis has been used. A variant of the Philips device mark used on electrical goods was used to illustrate an article about 'the terror of the Philips-Police' in the second world war. The usual stars were replaced by swastikas. Philips sued successfully for trade mark infringement; it was held that the use, to attract readers to the article, was 'in economic intercourse' as part of the defendant's commercial publishing activities.[7]

1. Trade Marks Act 1994, s 10(4).
2. Ibid, s 103(2).
3. Andy Warhol Campbell Soup Can 1965 (New York).
4. Edouard Manet *Un Bar aux Folies-Bergère* 1882 (London).
5. [2001] ETMR 860.
6. Benelux trade mark law has greatly influenced the EC draftsmen: see para **21.14** above.
7. Netherlands 1981; see M Knijff 'Selected Benelux Cases' Trademark World, July/August 1994, p 14.

Use to identify the proprietor's goods or services

21.24 Use to identify the proprietor's goods or services is permitted by section 10(6). However, such use must be 'in accordance with honest practices in industrial or commercial matters'; otherwise there will be infringement if the use of the mark without due cause takes unfair advantage of, or is detrimental to, the distinctive character or repute of the trade mark. This section is mainly designed to deal with the tricky issue of comparative advertising. Formerly the legitimacy of comparative advertising, where the advertiser compares his product with a successful product by reference to the latter's mark, often depended upon whether the mark in question was registered in Part A of the register,[1] or Part B,[2] or not at all.[3] It seemed absurd that, in a market in which A's (registered) ZING razor blades competed with B's (unregistrable) SMOOTH-SHAVE blades, A was able to advertise to the public that ZING blades were better, safer or cheaper than SMOOTH-SHAVE blades, while B could not claim that SMOOTH-SHAVE blades were better, safer or cheaper than ZING blades. It was also bad policy in terms of consumer choice: the perfect market requires that the consumer be in possession of all relevant information before he makes his purchase,[4] and trade mark law is supposed to aid his market decision by promising him that a particular mark will provide him with consistent information.[5] Since it is usually by the mark that he purchases goods (ie 'Give me three tins of CHOOSEY', not 'Give me three tins of the cod-flavoured cat-food made by Spillers Foods Ltd of Blagdon Road, New Malden') and it is by reference to those marks that goods are advertised, it defies logic, justice and commercial expediency to suggest that it is not by reference to such marks that competing goods be criticised. The European Commission and Council went so far as to express the view that 'the reference to advertising in paragraph 2(d) (of the draft community trade mark regulation) does not cover the use of a Community trade mark in comparative advertising'. However, the better view is probably that it does, hence section 10(6), whose wording followed the draft[6] of a subsequent amendment to EC legislation on misleading advertising.[7] Thus it seems that a comparative advertisement which is accurate and fair would be sheltered but an advertisement which was seriously misleading, or made unnecessary use of a rival's mark, could be restrained. The phrase 'honest practices in industrial or commercial matters' suggests a subjective view which might vary from industry to industry. Thus motor manufacturers and transport operators might take the view that comparative advertising was in accordance with honest practices, whilst computer manufacturers might not.[8]

In fact English judges have taken a robust view of comparative advertising under the 1994 Act, being slow to intervene to prevent advertisements which are not seriously misleading to the average consumer or grossly unfair.[9] Mere offensiveness was held not to take an advertisement 'beyond the pale' in *British Airways plc v Ryanair*

Ltd,[10] although the first Ryanair 'EXPENSIVE BA___DS' advertisement had been withdrawn after public complaint to the Advertising Standards Authority. This line of cases contrasts oddly with the humourless approach taken in the few cases on parody as a defence to infringement of intellectual property;[11] in *Schweppes Ltd v Wellingtons Ltd*,[12] the claimant was able to restrain the sale of 'SCHLURPPES' tonic water, a 'spoof' product.

1. In which case the use 'imported a reference to the proprietor of the registered mark: Trade Marks Act 1938, s 4(1)(b); *Bismag v Amblins (Chemists) Ltd* [1940] Ch 667.
2. In this case, actionability depended upon the presence of confusion. Since most comparative advertising is intended to encourage the public to buy the advertiser's product rather than the better-known brand, confusion is usually absent. See, for example, *Villa Maria Wines* (1984) 4 IPR 65 at 67, discharging the injunction reported at [1985] FSR 400.
3. Here, evidence of confusion could lead to a finding of passing off, as in *McDonald's Hamburgers Ltd v Burgerking (UK) Ltd* [1987] FSR 112. If the advertisement made false representations, an action for malicious or injurious falsehood might lie: *Wilts United Dairies v Thomas Robinson & Co Ltd* [1958] RPC 94.
4. On the perfect market see W Reekie and D Allen, *The Economics of Modern Business* (1938), pp 54-58.
5. On the functions of trade marks, see A Kamperman Sanders and S Maniatis 'A Consumer Trade Mark: Protection Based on Origin and Quality' [1993] 11 EIPR 407.
6. Directive 84/450/EEC; and see Hansard, vol 241 no 85 col 684, 18 April 1994; the wording also echoes art 5(3) of Directive 89/104/EEC, which allows Member States to prohibit the use of registered marks for purposes other than for distinguishing goods or services; in comparative advertising the purpose *is* however, to distinguish the advertiser's goods – to say that they are better, cheaper, more readily available than the better-known brand to which reference is made.
7. Now governed by Council Directive EC 97/55 and implemented in the UK Control of Misleading Advertisements (Amendment) Regulations 2000, SI 2000/914.
8. *Compaq Computer Corpn v Dell Computer Corpn* [1992] FSR 93.
9. *Barclays Bank plc v RBS Advanta* [1996] RPC 307; *Vodaphone Group plc v Orange Personal Communications Services Ltd* [1997] FSR 34; *Cable & Wireless plc v British Telecommunications plc* [1998] FSR 383.
10. [2001] FSR 541, where Jacob J held that the somewhat timid Directive 97/55 did not amend the Trade Marks Harmonisation Directive 89/104 or implementing national law: the Trade Marks Act 1994. The advertisements, headed 'EXPENSIVE BA___DS' and 'EXPENSIVE BA' compared fares.
11. See E Gredley and S Maniatis 'Parody: a fatal attraction?' [1997] EIPR 339, 412.
12. [1984] FSR 210. Summary judgment was given for infringement of copyright.

Defences

21.25 Apart from the defences already implicit in the definition of trade mark infringement or available under principles of general law, the Trade Marks Act provides statutory defences under sections 11, 12 and 13. By section 11(1), a registered trade mark is not infringed by use of another registered mark (subject to validity of the latter). Section 11(2)(a) allows the use of a person's own name or address, provided that the use is in accordance with honest practices in industrial or commercial matters.[1] The same proviso is applied to two other defences: that the use involves indications concerning the characteristics of the goods or services (section 11(2)(b)) and that the use is necessary to indicate the intended purpose of a product or service (as accessory or spare part). Thus the legend 'We supply spares for Rover cars' would be spared from infringement. Open to question, however, is the legend 'Rover spares supplied' in relation to spares for ROVER cars made by an unrelated manufacturer. In *BMW v Deenik*[2] it was held that the equivalent provision (Art 5(1)(a) of Directive 89/104) allowed a trader, without consent, to indicate that he carried out or maintained goods covered by the mark or specialised in their sales and repair. However, this did not hold good where the use of the mark created the erroneous impression that there was a commercial connection, affiliation or special relationship with the trade mark proprietor.[3] There is also a saving where an earlier unregistered mark is protected, for example by passing off, in a particular locality: section 11(3). This gives a right of continued use within the locality. Lastly, any goods which the trade mark proprietor or his licensee have put on the market under the mark in the European Economic Area[4] are free to circulate without infringement, unless there exist legitimate reasons to oppose further dealings.[5] This applied particularly where the condition of the goods has been changed or impaired and reflected the decision of the European Court in *Bristol Myers Squibb v Paranova*.[6]

1. For a passing off case where the defendant's lack of *bona fides* led to an injunction restraining use of his own name, see *Guccio Gucci SpA v Paolo Gucci* [1991] FSR 89. In relation to the Community trade mark, the Commission and Council of the European Communities took the view that 'his own name' applies only in respect of natural persons and therefore not companies: statement for entry in the minutes of the Council meeting at which the regulation was adopted. Although the logic of this is suspect, in practice the possibility of changing a company's name is usually taken into account by the courts in infringement and passing off cases.
2. *Bayerische Motorenwerke and BMW Nederland v Deenik* [1999] ETMR 339.
3. Reminiscent of the passing off decision in *Sony KK v Saray Electronics (London) Ltd* [1983] FSR 302, CA; see also *Aktiebolaget Volvo v Heritage (Leicester) Ltd* [2000] FSR 253, where the use of the phrase 'Independent Volvo Specialist' by a lapsed dealer was held to be an infringement, and not saved by s 11(2).
4. But not outside the EEA; the European Court rejected the concept of 'international exhaustion' in *Silhouette International Schmiedt GmbH v Hartlauer Handelsgesellschaft mbH* [1998] ETMR 286, 539; see further para **27.5** below.
5. Trade Marks Act 1994, s 12.
6. [1996] ETMR 1. See also *Glaxo v Dowelhurst* [2001] ETMR 96.

Certification and collective marks

21.26 The Trade Marks Act 1994 provides for the registration of what were formerly called standardisation marks[1] but what are now known as certification marks.[2] Such a mark is intended to be applied to goods or services,[3] but is not intended to indicate a trade connection between a person and a product he supplies; instead it indicates the origin, quality, means of manufacture or other inherent characteristics by which those goods, irrespective of their provider, are clearly identifiable or distinguishable from all others. A certification mark is usually registered by a trade association (*never* by a person who intends to trade with the mark himself[4]), and that association will be expected to 'police' its use for the benefit of those who are entitled to use it. Failure to observe the conditions or regulations upon which the registration is premised may result in the mark being expunged from the register, although this is a step which is not lightly taken.[5] The collective mark is a new creature. It is suitable to distinguish the goods or services of traders who belong to the proprietor association from those of non-members.[6] It, too, may consist of geographical indications. Its owner may trade but is again expected to police the use of the mark.[7] Collective purchasing and other associations are seen as an important ingredient of success for small and medium-sized enterprises in the European Union. The European Commission has stated:

> 'For small and medium-sized firms the use of a collective trade mark may often be the only means of extending their activities throughout the common market.'[8]

1. See *British Trade Mark Law and Practice* Cmnd 5601, 1974, para 189.
2. Trade Marks Act 1994, s 50(1). For an exhaustive account of certification marks under the 1938 Act, see Norma Dawson, *Certification Trade Marks – Law and Practice* (1988).
3. Prior to commencement of the 1994 Act, certification marks were registrable only for goods.
4. Trade Marks Act 1994, Sch 2, para 4.
5. *Erven Warnink BV v Townend & Sons (Hull) Ltd* [1979] AC 731; '*Sea Island Cotton' Certification Trade Mark* [1989] RPC 87; N Dawson, 'The West Indian Sea Island Cotton Association Certification Trade Mark: Application to Expunge' [1989] EIPR 375.
6. Trade Marks Act 1994, s 49.
7. Ibid, Sch 1, paras 5 and 13.
8. Bulletin of the European Communities, Suppl 8/76 at p 20.

Licensing of trade marks

21.27 When the owner of a trade mark allows another to use the mark, a licence is granted.[1] The licence may be express or implied, general or limited, informal or in writing, exclusive, sole or non-exclusive. Marks may be licensed for a number of reasons. The owner may not be able to provide all the relevant goods or services from its own resources and thus may meet market demand through licensees. The mark may be an important element of a franchised business format.[2] One company in a group may be responsible for owning and protecting the group's intellectual property, whilst other, operating, companies actually use the marks in trade. There may be tax advantages in vesting ownership of trade marks with a holding company, possibly off-shore. Because passing off protects the goodwill of a business carried on under a mark, rather than the mark itself, at common law the licensing of marks presents problems.[3] However, licensing registered trade marks has long been an activity blessed by statute.[4] The Trade Marks Act 1994 makes detailed provision for licensing in sections 28-31. Section 46 makes clear that use by another, with the owner's consent, will keep the registration valid by warding off an attack on the grounds of non-use. In order to enjoy the advantages of full statutory recognition, the licence must be in writing, signed by or on behalf of the person granting the licence.[5] That person may not actually be the proprietor, because sub-licensing is allowed for in section 28(4). If the licence is duly noted on the register,[6] a number of benefits follow: it is binding upon the grantor's successors unless it expressly provides otherwise;[7] a licensee may call on the proprietor to bring infringement proceedings, and in default bring them herself;[8] the proprietor may claim damages in infringement proceedings on behalf of licensees;[9] the exclusive licensee may have the rights and remedies of an assignee.[10] All these, together with the possibility of registering jointly owned marks,[11] collective and certification marks,[12] means that the 1994 Act caters fully for marks in multiple usership.[13]

1. See, generally, Wilkof *Trade Mark Licensing* (1995).
2. See para **22.4** below.
3. S Lane *The Status of Licensing Common Law Marks* 1991.
4. *Scandecor Developments AB v Scandecor Marketing AB* [2001] ETMR 800 provides an excellent history. The House of Lords referred questions to the European Court of Justice on the circumstances in which licensing may render trade marks deceptive.
5. S 28(2).
6. S 25.
7. Ss 28(3) and 29(2).
8. S 30(2), joining the proprietor; the licensee may apply on its own for interlocutory (or 'interim') relief: s 30(4).
9. S 30(6).
10. S 31.
11. S 23.
12. See paras **21.26** above.
13. See A Firth 'Collectivity, Control and Joint Adventure' in N Dawson and A Firth (eds) *Trade Marks Retrospective* (2000), Vol 7 Perspectives on Intellectual Property.

Other trade mark transactions

21.28   The registered mark is an object of property in its own right.[1] This means that it may be assigned, with or without the underlying business goodwill, bequeathed, transmitted by operation assigned by way of security, or made subject of a legal or equitable charge.[2] Such transactions should all be entered upon the register.[3]

1. S 22.
2. S 24 and 26(2). See J Fitzgerald and A Firth 'Equitable Assignments in Relation to Intellectual Property' [1999] IPQ 228; J Phillips 'Intellectual Property as Security for Debt Finance' [1997] EIPR 276 and citations therein.
3. S 25. However, express, implied or constructive trusts are not to be noted on the register: s 26(1).

Chapter 22

Character merchandising, franchising and sponsorship

Introduction

22.1 Where a label of identification has acquired a favourable reputation, it can be gainfully exploited in one of two ways short of actual sale by the original manufacturer or owner. It can be the subject of its proprietor's more vigorous market activity, or its *use* can be sold or hired to another person. An example of the former would be the opening up of a second or subsequent Baskin Robbins ice cream parlours once it was discovered that the first had substantial drawing power and therefore goodwill; an example of the second would be a famous footballer's consent to the use of his name in the endorsement of sports equipment or leisurewear. This chapter examines three typical and commercially significant situations in which the use of a name or personality is licensed to others: character merchandising, franchising and sponsorship. These three phenomena are not governed by purpose-designed codes of law, and are thus rarely treated in a cohesive fashion by British commentators. There now follows a brief account of each,[1] together with their distinguishing features and similarities.

1. For fuller treatments, see J Adams, K Prichard Jones and J Hickey *Franchising* (4th edn 1997); M Mendelsohn and R Bynoe *Franchising* (1995); J Pratt *Franchising* (looseleaf); Stallard, ed *Bagehot on Sponsorship, Merchandising and Endorsement* (1998); J Adams *Character Merchandising* (1996).

Character merchandising

22.2 The term itself was not used by any British judge prior to 1975,[1] although the practice is much older.[2] Since the law recognises no exclusive property in the name of a real[3] or fictional[4] character,[5] a person who wishes to protect his character may attempt to do so in one of three ways:

(i) If he seeks to apply the name, signature, or likeness of the character to his own goods or services, he may lay a claim to its protection as a registered trade mark or under passing off law. This approach is not popular, since the owner of a character frequently prefers to exploit it without dirtying his hands through direct trade or manufacture and, should the owner allow another to use his mark on goods similar to his own, will run the risk that the mark will no longer be associated with his own business.

(ii) An intent to use solely through the intermediary of licensees will provide sufficient standing for a trade mark application. Likewise the unlicensed use of a character may amount to a misrepresentation actionable in passing off.[6] However, the Registry and courts may be sceptical as to the trade mark significance of the name or likeness (see below) while a passing off action is only available to a claimant with goodwill, which is difficult to establish in the absence of trade in the goods or services in question.

(iii) He can draw or take photographs of likenesses of himself or of a fictitious character, and thus enjoy artistic copyright.

Once one of these simple steps has been taken, the legally protected character becomes a commodity which can be 'merchandised' through its commercial exploitation by its owner or, more usually, by a licensee who pays for the privilege of doing so. Typical examples which can be found in many British households are Barbie swimwear, Winnie the Pooh pencil cases, Pokemon pyjamas, Bob the Builder bean bags, Tweenies bedlinen. The higher the degree of public recognition or affection with regard to the persona so merchandised, the greater its commercial cachet; it is not possible for a real person or a work of copyright to become part of the public domain simply through prolonged over-exposure in the media or elsewhere, although a trade mark might die of dilution when it is so bandied about that the public no longer identifies it as a connecting factor which links its proprietor to his goods or services.[7]

1. *Tavener Rutledge Ltd v Trexapalm Ltd* [1975] FSR 479 at 485 (per Walton J).
2. See the dispute as to the entitlement to hold 'Richter Concerts' in *Franke v Chappell* (1887) 57 LT 141.
3. See A Coleman 'The Unauthorised Commercial Exploitation of the Names and Likenesses of Real Persons' [1982] EIPR 189, which contrasted the lack of protection under English law with the American and Australian positions.
4. *Conan Doyle v London Mystery Magazine Ltd* (1949) 66 RPC 312 (no property in 'Sherlock Holmes'), cf *Hepworth Manufacturing Co Ltd v Ryott* [1920] 1 Ch 1 and *Landa v Greenberg* (1908) 24 TLR 441 which indicate that, as between contracting parties, the user of a pseudonym may be entitled to regard it as part of his 'stock in trade'.
5. H Porter 'Character Merchandising: Does English Law Recognise a Property Right in Name and Likeness?' [1999] Ent LR 180.
6. *Mirage Studios v Counter-Feat Clothing* [1991] FSR 145. However, in *Halliwell v Panini*, Lightman J (6 June 1997, unreported), the court was

unconvinced that the public minded whether stickers depicting the Spice Girls were licensed or not.

7. *Linoleum Manufacturing Co v Nairn* (1878) 7 Ch D 834.

22.3 One of the most interesting facets of character merchandising is that, while it is a lucrative and long-standing commercial practice, the British judiciary has been painstakingly slow to recognise its significance. In *Lyngstad v Anabas*[1] the court thought it unlikely that members of the public who bought souvenir items and garments bearing the name and likeness of their favourite pop-stars would think that there was any connection between their idols and their purchases. The thought that a trade connection did exist between a celebrity and a product bearing his name was regarded as reasonable but erroneous.[2] Such views are alive and well, as evidenced by the *Spice Girls* case,[3] even though the widespread nature of the practice of character merchandising has been accepted by the courts.[4] With the decision in *Mirage Studios v Counter-Feat Clothing*,[5] fictional character merchandising achieved full judicial respectability. The defendants were enjoined from selling unauthorised 'Teenage Mutant Ninja Turtle' T-shirts. The plaintiff's case was argued both on the basis of passing off and copyright infringement; the Court took the view that members of the public today are conversant with the practice of licensing and were likely to assume that the plaintiffs had licensed the defendants to market the 'Turtles' clothing. However, real characters, particularly dead ones,[6] have not enjoyed such favour for their merchandising campaigns. The Registry and judges have shown reluctance to allow the names or likenesses of characters to be registered, preferring to allow the public free rein to indulge their desire for memorabilia, be it of the late Diana, Princess of Wales,[7] the late Elvis Presley,[8] or Jane Austen.[9]

1. *Lyngstad v Anabas Products Ltd* [1977] FSR 62.
2. Ibid per Oliver J at pp 65 ff.
3. *Halliwell v Panini*, Lightman J (6 June 1997, unreported); see para **22.2**, n 6.
4. *Stringfellow v McCain Foods* (GB) Ltd [1985] RPC 501 at 543-4 and 523, CA (per Whitford J).
5. [1991] FSR 145.
6. J Phillips 'Life after Death' [1998] EIPR 201; for the position in Germany see A Jooss 'Life after Death? Post-mortem Protection of Name, Image and Likeness under German Law with Specific Reference to "*Marlene Dietrich*"' [2001] Ent LR 141.
7. *Executrices of the Estate of Diana, Princess of Wales' Application* [2001] ETMR 254; C Waelde 'Commercialising the Personality of the late Diana, Princess of Wales – Censorship by the Back Door?', Ch 10 in Dawson and Firth (eds) *Trade Marks Retrospective* (2000), vol 7, Perspectives on Intellectual Property.
8. *ELVIS PRESLEY Trade Marks* [1999] RPC 567.
9. *JANE AUSTEN Trade Mark* [2000] RPC 879.

Franchising

22.4   Whereas character merchandising involves licensing another to exploit commercially a real or fictional character, franchising entails licensing another to exploit commercially the format and characteristics of a business. In both cases the key to the attraction of the licence lies in the public's consciousness of images and reputations. As far as character merchandising is concerned, the commodity manufacturer wishes to make his product more attractive by attaching to it the likeness of a popular and well-known character; it is illogical to conclude that a soap or toothpaste should provide greater consumer satisfaction on account of its bearing the imprimatur of Naomi Campbell rather than a more traditional trade mark, but it is a fact of commercial reality that more people will buy toothpaste if it is designated 'Naomi Campbell' rather than 'Kleen-O-Dent'. Similarly, in franchising, the licensee (or 'franchisee') takes a right to use a business format which is so advertised by its proprietor (the franchisor) as to be attractive to the general public, and endeavours thereby to make his enterprise, be it a fast food store or a drain-unblocking service, more viable.

22.5   In character merchandising, the licensee's adoption of the licensor's character says nothing about the character or quality of the product: the act of marking a chocolate bar 'Mickey Mouse' or 'Donald Duck' will convey little or nothing about the chocolate bar's inherent virtues. The case of franchising is in this respect quite different. Once a fast food store is labelled 'McDonalds' or 'Burger King', that label will convey a good deal more to the consumer – if he has been exposed to advertisements, personal experience or recommendations – as to the style and nature of the store and its services, the sort of price he can expect to pay, and so on. This difference between character merchandising and franchising is highlighted by the fact that, because the typical merchandised character is used promiscuously while the typical franchised reputation is not, the public expectation in respect of the standards maintained by franchised operations is very different to that in respect of goods bearing merchandised characters. For example, no one who has used Sooty bubble bath, and liked it, will have any necessary expectation that Sooty T-Shirts will be of good quality or that Sooty plastic beakers will be of a certain standard, while a customer of a Wimpy hamburger restaurant in London will assume that a restaurant bearing the same name in Manchester or Glasgow will provide an identical gastronomical environment. These expectations are not, of course, immutable and inevitable; they have, however, evolved in the course of long-standing commercial practice.

22.6 The essence of the franchise licence is that franchisor and franchisee exchange quite substantial mutual obligations, for their mutual benefit. The franchisor allows the franchisee to use his business format, but insists that the franchisee adhere rigidly to it – any deviation from the norm would result in the risk that consumers would find unacceptable any differences between the various franchisees of the same franchisor. In turn the franchisor has to ensure that each of his franchisees will enjoy a secure and continued supply of any items necessary for the preservation of their impression of consistency (eg serviettes, menus, receipts, bills, take-away food boxes, staff uniforms), and that sufficient advertising will be generated to ensure adequate publicity and to fend off competition from rival franchises. An element of quality control upon the franchisee's activities is normally vital, and a franchise agreement will be terminated if the franchisee cannot maintain his contractually-required standards of expertise, hygiene and so forth.

22.7 A franchisee may wish to sell his business. If so, he will find that he has a problem. Usually, the sale of a business includes not only the physical assets such as stock and machinery, and its commercial assets such as debts owed to it, but also its 'goodwill' – the attractive force of the business which brings in its custom. Since the name and likeness of the franchisee's business belongs to the franchisor, the franchisee obviously cannot sell the goodwill which is attached to his business. What he can do, since it is generally provided in the franchise contract, is to assign both his business and his right to use the franchise style to a purchaser approved by the franchisor; this enables the franchisee to receive a fair price for the sale of his business, while making sure that the franchisor can preserve quality by refusing to allow a sale to a potentially substandard franchisee.

Sponsorship

22.8 Like character merchandising and franchising, sponsorship is a contractual provision for the use by one party of another's name or reputation. Unlike the other two, however, sponsorship does not involve A's paying B to use B's name; instead it involves B's paying A to use B's name. Since sponsorship is a very different concept from character merchandising and franchising, the reader may find figure 8 (p 338 below) helpful in its breakdown of the main similarities and deviations between them.

22.9 The essence of sponsorship is simple: a wealthy and publicity-seeking party (for example, a brewery, tobacco manufacturer, insurance

Fig. 8 Broad Generalisations as to Contract Practice Between the 'Proprietor' and the 'User'

	Subject of the licence	Direction of payment	Aim of transaction	Controls exercised by proprietor?	Subject to be publicised by whom?	Is exclusivity of use sought within the market?	Can the user sub-license or assign this right?	Need the proprietor preserve the good reputation of the subject?
Character merchandising	Name of real or fictional character; trademark; artistic copyright; registered design	By user to proprietor	Enhancement of appearance and marketability of user's goods; licence royalties for proprietor; sale profit to user	Should be, so far as use of registered trademark is concerned; not necessary where copyright is licensed. Too rarely exercised even if reserved by contract	Proprietor	Usually	Rarely, unless assignment is of user's business	Yes
Franchising	Trademark; tradename; business 'get-up' and style	By user to proprietor	Enablement of user to achieve consistency of goods/services other franchisees; royalties to proprietor; trading profit to user	Should be, to ensure that goods and services of all franchisees are of similar and acceptable quality	Proprietor	Yes	No, unless proprietor is satisfied as to proposed user's standing	Yes
Sponsorship	Company name personal name; product name	By proprietor to user	Advertisement & enhancement of proprietor's name and goods/services; financial security for potentially unprofitable or low-profit ventures	Not usually	User	Not usually relevant	Rarely	No

company or bank) allows its name to be used either by the organiser of a sporting or cultural event or by a participant in such an event, in order to gain publicity and to create a favourable impression. In return, that body pays to the party which will bear its name a sum sufficient to enable either the event to take place or the participant to take part. A legal definition of such an arrangement is hard to come by, especially since 'sponsorship' is not a coherent term of art in British law.[1] The definition offered by Townley and Grayson is very wide:

> 'Sponsorship is a mutually acceptable commercial relationship between two or more parties in which one party (called the sponsor) acting in the course of a business, trade, profession or calling seeks to promote or enhance an image, product or service in association with an individual, event, happening, property or object (called the sponsee).'[2]

Indeed, so wide is this definition that it embraces both character merchandising and franchising; it should thus be taken, like the estate agent's measurements of an irregularly shaped room, as an indication of the widest dimensions of sponsorship rather than as a description of its typical appearance.

1. The term 'sponsorship' has not yet received a judicial definition in its commercial context.
2. *Sponsorship of Sport, Arts and Leisure* (1984), p 4.

22.10 In its most complex form, sponsorship can take on the dimensions of a cross-licence. For example with regard to the Olympic Games, a soft-drinks manufacturer or credit card company may be designated an official sponsor. In purely trade mark terms this will mean that the company's name will be prominently displayed at Olympic events; it will also mean that the Olympic symbol will be displayed in promotional literature, advertisements and sometimes also upon products made by the sponsor itself, often with the surprising result that the sponsor makes wider use of the sponsee's mark than vice versa. In these arrangements the sponsor will generally be accorded exclusive right to the sale or distribution (in the case of soft drinks) or use (in the case of eg credit cards) at Olympic events. Despite the elements of exclusivity, such arrangements do not usually have any undesirable anti-competitive effects, although an 'Official Supplier' arrangement between the Danish Tennis Federation and tennis ball manufacturers was modified after intervention by the European Commission under what are now Arts 81 and 82 of the EC Treaty.[1] Organisations vie with one another to sponsor different elements of an event, the losers often resorting to what is termed 'ambush marketing', a generally legal but arguably unethical practice whereby a non-sponsoring company's own advertising conveys the impression that it is in some way involved in the event itself.[2]

1. *DTF & Slazenger* Commission Press Release IP/98/355, 15 April 1998
2. On the steps taken by the organisers of the Sydney Olympics to prevent ambush marketing and thereby protect their sponsors' investment see M Roper-Drimie 'Sydney 2000 Olympic Games – the 'Worst Games Ever' for Ambush Marketers?' [2001] EntLR 150.

22.11   The owner of a mark or name which is being licensed out under a sponsorship arrangement should remember that, once his mark or name is associated with an event, he can lose control both of its use and its reputation. The manufacturers of GILLETTE razor blades were not pleased when they discovered that, after more than a decade of successful sponsorship of a cricket tournament, the public associated the name GILLETTE far more with the cricket trophy than with the product it was supposed to publicise. Sponsorship may also lead to tarnished reputations, eg where a sports event attracts unfavourable publicity through crowd trouble, poor sportsmanship or similar factors. The wise sponsee, too, will consider the effect of a loss of reputation on the part of the sponsor. For example, when the Canadian sprinter Ben Johnson was found to have taken drugs, he was estimated to have lost several millions of dollars through the abrupt termination of sponsorship contracts, presumably on the basis of frustration or fundamental breach.

Part VI

Some topics of current interest

Chapter 23

Problems with new technology

Introduction

23.1 It is an oft-repeated truism that the law lags behind technology. What is more rarely stated is that this does not usually matter. The law of homicide applies equally whether A bludgeons B over the head with a club or dematerialises him with a sci-fi ray gun; the parking meter bay accommodates in turn the 'T' model Ford and the latest Japanese import; the trade mark sits as comfortably upon the sixth generation computer as ever it did upon the child's abacus. There are, however, some areas of law in which modern science and technology pose new questions and require new applications. Most of these lie outside intellectual property and therefore fall beyond the scope of this book.

23.2 If this chapter may be permitted a non-legal excursion, it is submitted that the words 'new technology' often strike an irrational psychological response in the lawyer's mind. Faced with a law which he understands and a technology which he does not, he is frequently more willing to accept the need to amend the former than to make the effort to comprehend the latter. Attempts at amending the law in the light of the advance of technology sadly have the effect, given the tendency of British law to legislate with particularity and not in general sweeps of principle, of making the amended law less comprehensible and therefore less susceptible of easy and accurate application. For examples of such law one need look no further than the lego-technological latticework of section 7(1) and (2) of the Copyright, Designs and Patents Act 1988, which defines in no fewer than 394 words the term 'cable programme'.[1]

1. Interestingly, the provisions on cable programmes were pressed into the service of newer technology in *Shetland Times Ltd v Wills* 1997 SLT 669, [1997] FSR 604 – the Internet 'deep linking' case, see para **12.19**. T Drier 'The Cable and Satellite Analogy' in B Hugenholtz (ed) *The Future of Copyright in a Digital Environment* (1996) considered whether EC cable and satellite legislation would be a good model for digital copyright, either by direct application, or by analogy.

23.3 So far as intellectual property is concerned, copyright law is more adversely affected than patent law. This is because patent law is inherently designed to cope with new technology, on the principle of 'if it's new, protect it'.[1] Copyright law, on the other hand, suffers in two ways:

(i) Since copyright protection is conferred in terms of a work's form, not its content, the law has to pigeon-hole each new species of oeuvre within existing categories (ie literary, musical, dramatic, artistic works), or concede that they are unprotectable;[2] and

(ii) Since copyright infringement is in part determined by the vehicle of unauthorised transmission, the creation of new forms of transmission calls into question the appropriateness of the existing legal categories specified by the Act. It should not be thought that this problem is a new one. Every newly introduced technology, from printing, photography, the gramophone, cinema and television through to cable and satellite transmission and multimedia, has caught the law 'on the hop'.

1. On the criteria of patentability see ch 5 above.
2. See, for example, T Aplin 'Not in Our Galaxy: Why "Film" Won't Rescue Multimedia' [1999] EIPR 633.

23.4 In the rest of this chapter a number of branches of 'new technology' will be briefly examined. From this little survey one is tempted to conclude that it is not the new technologies but old techniques of statutory draftsmanship which cause the biggest problems.[1]

1. S Ricketson 'New Wine in Old Bottles' (1992) 10 Prometheus 53; cf J Perry Barlow 'Selling Wine Without Bottles' in B Hugenholz (ed) *The Future of Copyright in a Digital Environment'* (1996).

The computer

23.5 Whether computers may still be described as new technology is a matter of mystery to these writers; nonetheless there are many who are still suspicious of them. Most of the world's population has been born since the first electric-powered computer was put to use.[1] The principal legal problems of computers are obvious, and could have been dealt with long ago. That they were not is a sign of legislative indifference or ignorance, and that whole industries mushroomed in the teeth of a high degree of uncertainty as to the nature and extent of legal protection against unauthorised use and copying would suggest that, in commercial terms, intellectual property rights are not half as valuable as the market entry of a good product at the right time. The computer has also given rise to copyright's latest problems – the combination of many categories of work in digitised form, or 'multimedia' and that of on-line transmission of such material on information networks accessible to huge numbers of users. Copyright may eventually have coped with many of the problems raised by computer software [2] and, conversely, computer technology has been able to solve some problems related to copyright.[3] Other issues remain unresolved at the time of writing. A selection of computer law problems follows:

1. The first automatic computer was Howard Aikens's Automatic Sequence Controlled Calculator, made by IBM in 1937: see S Hollingdale and G Toothill *Electronic Computers* (1965), pp 58-60.

2. A Christie in 'Designing Appropriate Protection for Computer Programs' [1994] EIPR 486 argues that this is not the case. See, also, S Gordon 'The Very Idea! Why Copyright is an Inappropriate Way to Protect Computer Programs' [1998] EIPR 10.

3. For example, by facilitating the distribution of royalties by collecting societies and the Registrar of Public Lending Right. See ch 15 for efficiencies achieved by the Registrar. For music collecting societies, see M Hennessey 'Collection and Distribution of Royalties in Continental Europe and the United States' (1998) Copyright World, July p 21 and J Hutchinson 'Collection and Distribution of Performing and Mechanical Royalties: A View from the UK' (1999) 84 Copyright World, p 30. For literary applications, see C Clark 'The Answer to the Machine is in the Machine' in B Hugenholz (ed) *The Future of Copyright in a Digital Environment'* (1996).

(i) Is a computer program patentable?

23.6 Not as such, since the Patents Act 1977, section 1(2) and Art 52 of the European Patent Convention explicitly bar it from patent protection. This makes sense insofar as a computer program is a literary work protected by copyright. On the other hand it has long been accepted that a computer which has been programmed in a particular manner so as to perform a particular task may be patented.[1] In the European Patent Office and latterly the UK Patent Office, patent applications for software are sympathetically regarded: the approach is to look at the invention as a whole.[2] If a new technical effect is produced, the invention may be patented (subject to its satisfying other criteria).[3] If no such new technical result is obtained, or the result is itself excluded subject-matter, then the patent will be refused.[4] This approach has been followed in a number of decisions in the UK and the EPO.[5] The concentration on whether a computer program possesses any overall technical effect in United Kingdom and Europe may have resulted in a lack of discussion on what the phrase 'computer program' actually means.[6] The US patent office has been, if anything, even more generous to software-related inventions than its European counterparts.[7] This may be contrasted with the less generous scope of copyright protection afforded to computer programs by the US courts.[8]

23.6 *Problems with new technology*

Davies[9] has identified a trend in programming towards the use of 'object oriented' languages. This development, and others,[10] may mean that patent protection ultimately proves more apt to protect value in the programmer's art than copyright.[11] However, the prospect of 'patenteers charging across the cyberplains'[12] has its drawbacks, not least when their patents relate to the basic functioning of the Internet.[13]

1. See eg *Slee and Harris' Application* [1966] RPC 194; *Badger's Application* [1970] RPC 36.
2. *VICOM* (Case T208/84) [1987] 2 EPOR 74.
3. *IBM/Computer programs* [1999] EPOR 301; L Cohen 'The Patenting of Software' [1999] EIPR 607; UK Patent Office Practice Direction 'Claims to Programs for Computers' [1999] RPC 563; K Beresford *Patenting Software under the European Patent Convention* (2000).
4. See *Merrill Lynch's Application* [1989] RPC 561; *Fujitsu's Application* [1997] RPC 608.
5. For a fuller analysis, see T Press 'Patent Protection for Computer-related Inventions', ch 4 in C Reed and J Angel (eds) *Computer Law* (4th edn, 2000).
6. S Davies 'Computer Program Claims' [1998] EIPR 429. See also C Millard 'Copyright', ch 6 in C Reed and J Angel (eds) *Computer Law* (4th edn, 2000) at pp 188-189.
7. A Sharples 'The IT Patent Rush – the Stampede for Media Technology' [2001] ENT LR 195.
8. Denying protection on the grounds of functionality, as in *Lotus Development Corpn v Borland International Inc* 49 F 3d 807 (1st Cir, 1995); affd 516 US 233, 116 S Ct 804 (1996), or by strenuous application of an 'abstraction-filtration' test for infringement, as in *Computer Associates v Altai* 982 F 2d 693 (2nd Cir, 1992); cf *Ibcos Computers Ltd v Barclays Mercantile Finance Ltd* [1994] FSR 275. See DJM Attridge 'Protection for Computer Programs' [2000] EIPR 563 and para **23.14** below. Some comfort has been given to US owners – and users – of copyright in software by the Digital Millenium Copyright Act of 1998. J Bond 'The Digital Millennium Copyright Act: A Balance Result' [1999] EIPR 92.
9. N 5 above at 431.
10. Such the trend towards using interlocking software to speed up programming and to reduce file size.
11. Boudin J commented as such in relation to the LOTUS 1-2-3 command hierarchy in *Lotus v Borland*, n 7 above: see P Samuelson 'Economic an Constitutional Influence on Copyright Law in the United States' [2001] EIPR 409, at pp 416-417.
12. A Sharples, n 7 above.
13. See, eg, D Bender 'Business Method Patents: The View from the United States' [2001] EIPR 375.

23.7 Answers to the next series of questions all turn upon the status of temporary copies as potential infringements of copyright. Traditional criteria for copyright infringement have concentrated on the mode of dissemination of a work: for example by copying, publishing, or broadcasting. Since copyright may be justified as a means of increasing access to works by encouraging investment in infrastructure, such as printing capacity, distribution networks, television masts and cable networks, it is logical to give exclusive rights to those making copies, issuing them to the public, providing the content of broadcasts and so forth. This leaves the end user comparatively free from potential infringement. Computer technology and the development of the Internet have decentralised the focus of the exclusive rights and blurred the distinctions between the various acts restricted by copyright. This so-called 'convergence' between the media for dissemination of copyright has strained the traditional definitions and boundaries of infringement.

(ii) Is it a copyright infringement to feed a work into a computer?

23.8 According to the Copyright, Designs and Patents Act 1988 it is a 'restricted act' to copy a work, which includes 'storing' a work – including a computer program – 'in any medium by electronic means'.[1] This leads to the question of the meaning of the word 'store', since the word carries a connotation, if not of permanence, then at least of length of duration.[2] If I feed a work into a computer for only a brief period of time, depositing it in a RAM from which it can be eliminated at the depression of a key, have I 'stored' it there? What if, forgetting its presence, I neglect to remove it therefrom? Is that 'storage' any more than I 'store' a bus ticket in my pocket when I commence my ride and forget to throw it away when I debus? While accepting that depositing a work on a RAM is more likely than not to be regarded as copying, it is submitted that it would have been more sensible to explain that copying included the feeding of a work into a computer rather than its storage there. However, this result may be achieved if section 17(2) is considered together with section 17(6) which ensures that copying includes the making of transient copies. In this respect, UK legislation foreshadowed international developments. Directive 2001/29/EC on the harmonisation of certain aspects of copyright and related rights in the information society[3] which in turn implements 1996 WIPO treaties,[4] characterises the exclusive right of reproduction in wide terms for the digital environment:

> '… direct or indirect, temporary or permanent … by any means and in any form, in whole or in part.'[5]

However, Art 5.1 obliges Member States to permit temporary acts of copying which are transient or incidental, of no independent significance, and 'integral and essential' as part of a technological process to enable lawful use of a work.[6]

1. Copyright, Designs and Patents Act 1988, s 17(2).
2. See the various meanings listed in the Shorter Oxford English Dictionary which do not suggest mere transience.

3. [2001] OJ L167/10. EC Member States must implement the directive by 22 December 2002: see art 13.1.
4. The Copyright Treaty and Performances and Phonograms Treaty: see recital 15 of directive 2001/29/EC. A Mason 'Developments in the Law of Copyright and Public Access to Information' [1997] EIPR 636 expressed the view that these Treaties contribute towards achieving an appropriate balance between copyright owners and users. See also F W Grosheide 'Copyright Law from a User's Perspective': Access Rights for Users' [2001] EIPR 321.
5. Art 2.
6. A rather mysterious criterion, since the 'caching' of works by service providers to speed up internet use must surely have a distinct economic significance. At the time of writing the wording of the English version of directive 2001/29/EC was under linguistic review. Art 5.1 also excepts transmission by intermediaries: see below at para **23.11**.

(iii) Is the display of material on a computer screen an act restricted by copyright?

23.9 Not as such, unless the display amounts to a public performance. In practice, getting the display on to the screen will involve reproduction, as explained above. The possibility of a new right of display was raised in the context of a new Protocol to the Berne Convention;[1] this initiative led to creation of the WIPO copyright treaty, which did not include a display right. Note that the design of a screen display may involve the creation of artistic works, which can enjoy copyright distinct from that in the program itself.[2]

1. See 26 Copyright 62 at para 106; G Lea [1993] 9 CLSR 127.
2. *John Richardson Computers v Flanders* [1993] FSR 497.

(iv) Can using a computer program infringe copyright in the program?

23.10 It is not an infringement of copyright to read a book, listen to a sound recording of my favourite music, declaim the plays of Alan Ayckbourn in the bath or look covetously at a work of art. Why should using the program supplied free with this month's issue of PC World require consent from the copyright owner? The difference lies in the nature of a program. As Millard has pointed out,[1] a program is simultaneously 'symbolic' – it records instructions for carrying out a task – and 'functional' – it is the means by which the computer is instructed to carry out the task. Traditionally, copyright protects a literary work from reproduction but not execution of any instructions contained within it.[2] But in order to execute a program, it must be loaded,[3] reproduced and translated within the computer. Section 17(6) of the Copyright, Designs and Patents Act makes clear that transient or incidental copies may infringe; section 21(3)(ab) and (4) brings computer code conversion within the scope of a copyright owner's adaptation right.[4] The lawful use of a computer program put onto the market by the copyright owner must by necessary implication be licensed and section 50C of the 1988 act[5] expressly permits copying or adapting for lawful use, including error correction. But does the licence extend to use on different hardware or in different circumstances from those envisaged by the copyright owner? The latter may attempt to limit the scope of the user's licence by the technique known as 'shrink-wrap licensing' or its on-line cousin, 'click-wrap licensing', to which we turn next.

1. C Millard, 'Copyright' ch 6 in C Reed and J Angel (eds) *Computer Law* (4th edn, 2000) pp 203-204; See, also, B Fitzgerald 'Software as Discourse: The Challenge for Information Law' [2000] EIPR 47.
2. *Brigid Foley Ltd v Ellott* [1982] RPC 433.
3. See question (ii) above.
4. As amended by the Copyright (Computer Programs) Regulations 1992, SI 1992/3233, implementing Council Directive 91/250/EEC of 14 May 1991 on the legal protection of computer programs. This is in addition to s 50A, which permits the necessary making of backup copies, and s 50B, which deals with decompilation – see para **23.16** below.
5. Inserted by the Copyright (Computer Programs) Regulations 1992, n 4 above.

(v) Is it copyright infringement to transmit a work over the Internet?

23.11   This is really an amalgam of two, if not three, questions. First, does 'uploading' a work on to the Internet infringe copyright? This would be so if the acts of reproduction, issuing copies to the public or operating a cable programme service were taking place. Taking these possibilities in reverse order, we may first note that Parliament, in defining 'cable programme service', was careful to exclude intranet transmissions, whether domestic or business.[1] Fully interactive services are also excluded by section 7(2)(a), although 'demand' signals do not take cable operation out of the section. Section 7 does have the advantage to a copyright owner of controlling the act of transmission, so the tort is complete when a signal is sent, provided it is sent either for presentation to members of the public, or at two or more places. It does not matter whether the signals arrive at their destinations at the same time or at different times, in response to requests from users.[2] The act of issuing copies to the public is defined in section 18 of the 1988 Act. Although that section does not specify that the copies must be 'hard copy' reproductions, such a limitation is suggested by the presence in the Act of another provision, section 24(2), which reads:

> 'Copyright in a work is infringed by a person who without the licence of the copyright owner transmits the work by means of a telecommunications system (otherwise than by broadcasting

or including in a cable programme service), knowing or having reason to believe that infringing copies of the work will be made by means of the reception of the transmission in the United Kingdom or elsewhere.'[3]

Thus, it appears, uploading of content onto the Internet may be secondary infringement under section 24(2), actionable upon proof of knowledge, but is not primary infringement of copyright. Section 24(2) also undermines the next argument, that uploading is a direct infringement of the reproduction right. The uploader may enable or cause copies to be made, but does not (necessarily) make them himself. Could the uploader be liable for authorising reproduction?[4] This is a strong possibility, at least if copies are made or intended to be made in the United Kingdom. A related question is whether the activities of intermediaries like 'Napster', who match potential users of copyright music[5] with those who can upload the works, are liable for infringement by authorisation. Although held arguably liable for contributory infringement in the US, it is submitted that the reach of the tort of authorisation does not extend to this kind of service.[6]

1. Copyright, Designs and Patents Act 1988, s 7(2)(b)-(d).
2. Ibid, s 7(1).
3. The apparent power conferred by the words 'or elsewhere' is confounded by the UK-based definition of 'infringing copy' in s 27.
4. See ch 26.
5. For problems with music on the Internet see L Jones 'An Artist's entry into Cyberspace' [2000] EIPR 79.
6. U Suthersanen 'Napster, DVD and All That' in E Barendt and A Firth (eds) *Yearbook of Copyright and Media Law*, Vol V1, 2001.

23.12 Once a work has been made available for upload, what liability may be incurred by the intermediaries or service providers who enable Internet connections to be made? At the time of writing, the transmission of works on the Internet is achieved by sending data in comparatively small packets. Although temporary copies of the work are made during transmission, it might be difficult to show that a copy of a substantial part of a work exists at any one place or time. UK copyright law does not seem to provide protection against repeated insubstantial takings of works,[1] so infringement of the reproduction right will only occur if and when copies of works are 'cached' or stored in users' computers or on the servers of service providers, to speed up access. This inelegant argument will be superseded when the UK implements Directive 2001/29/EC.[2] The directive introduces two new rights, the distribution right of Art 4 and the right of communication to the public in Art 3. The distribution right is closely analogous to the UK issuing right and is intended to apply to hard copies and not online distribution. The right of communication to the public reflects the convergence of forms of delivery, and applies to online distribution (sometimes called 'webcasting') as well as to broadcasting and cable programme provision. It clearly applies to on-demand services, indeed it only applies to on-demand services where the rights of performers, film and phonogram producers and broadcasters are concerned. Private communications are excluded, although not defined.[3] Nor is the communication right infringed by those who simply provide the physical means to effect the communication. Internet service providers will therefore be protected from liability for 'passive' infringement by the exclusion from Art 3, by the exception of Art 5.1 and also by the 'e-commerce' directive.[4] A last question relates to the 'where' of infringement. The Internet gives rise to difficult questions of jurisdiction, applicable law and enforcement of judgments. Two areas of potential collaboration could obviate these problems. First, an agreed procedure for 'Notice and Take-Down' to Internet Service Providers could reduce the incidence of litigation.[5] Second, the use of unlicensed material on the Internet might be displaced if licensed material were readily available.[6]

1. See *Electronic Techniques (Anglia) Ltd v Critchley Components Ltd* [1997] FSR 401.
2. On the harmonisation of certain aspects of copyright and related rights in the information society: [2001] OJ L167/10.
3. K Weatherall 'An End to Private Communications in Copyright? The Expansion to Communicate Works to the Public' [1999] EIPR 342 and 398, examines the boundary between private and public uses of works by reference to Australian Cases. See, also, M Makeen *Copyright and Economic Theory* (2001).
4. Directive 2000/31 on legal aspects of electronic commerce, [2000] OJ L178/1, Art 4. Implementation date: 17 January, 2002. See F Macmillan and M Blakeney 'the Internet and Communications Carrier's Copyright Liability' [1998] EIPR 52; R Julia-Barcelo 'Liability for On-line Intermediaries: a European Perspective' [1998] EIPR 453.
5. 'Rightswatch', a pilot project for musical works, was under way at the time of writing (www.rightswatch.com). Under directive 2001/29/EC the remedy of injunction must be available against intermediaries even if their acts of transmission are excepted from liability for infringement – see recital 59 and art 8(3).
6. Such as the blanket licences granted by the US Harry Fox Agency for record stores to sell digital albums from its catalogue: S Hoare 'Let There Be Music on the World Wide Web', The Times, 23 October 2001, p 23.

(vi) What effect should be given to 'shrink-wrap' or 'click-wrap' licences?

23.13 Computer software houses do not like the fact that, once a purchaser buys software from a retailer, they lose effective control not only over the disks and manuals which embody their software but also the enforcement of their copyright. Under classical English contract theory the purchaser buys his software from the shop, not from the manufacturer – under the doctrine of privity of contract, purchaser and manufacturer have no legal relationship and the purchaser is not bound by any terms relating to the use of the software which the manufacturer seeks to impose upon him.[1] Many software packages are sold in shops with cellophane (or other) wrappers upon which there appears a notice indicating that, by opening the package, the purchaser agrees to be bound by various terms supplied alongside (or occasionally contained inside) it.[2] Typically the 'shrink-wrap' terms will include an undertaking by the purchaser not to claim against the manufacturer for consequential loss arising out of defective software, as well as restrictions upon the use of the software itself;[3] in return, the manufacturer agrees to replace defective disks. A transaction of this nature may be regarded as a collateral contract to the purchaser's contract of sale, thus avoiding the privity problem, but this hypothesis has not yet been fully tested in British courts.[4] Even if the contract is effective, however, it cannot prevent activities permitted by the 1988 Act.[5] Programs available online for download onto users' computers may be subject to 'click-wrap' licence terms. The situation is complicated by the availability of 'shareware'.[6] These programs may be the free-to-use output of a communally-minded programmer, but equally may be 'taster' versions of commercial software packages. Lastly, the click-wrap licence may have a role to play in negating any implied licence arising from the mere fact of making a work available on the Internet. Its very existence, read or unread, valid or unenforceable, may at least amount to evidence that the material was not intended for wholly free and unlimited use.

1. The Contracts (Rights of Third Parties) Act 1999 now allows for enforcement of contracts by persons for whose benefit the contract was made.
2. Eg 'Carefully read the Microsoft Licence Agreement inside before opening the pack! The program on the enclosed disk(s) is licensed to the user. By opening this packet, you indicate your acceptance of the Microsoft Licence Agreement'. The terms in which these licences are couched tend to be dominated by American usage and legal principle. On which, see P Samuelson and K Opsahl 'Licensing Information in the Global Information Market: Freedom of Contract Meets Public Policy' [1999] EIPR 387.
3. The possibility of restricting use by contract is envisaged by s 50C(1)(b) of the Copyright Designs and Patents Act 1988 as amended – see para **23.10**, n 5 above.
4. See, further, G Smith 'Software Contracts' in C Reed (ed) *Computer Law* (2nd edn, 1993) pp 57-59.
5. Making permitted backup copies: ss 50A(3) and 296A; decompilation: ss 50B(4), 296A; analysis: s 296A.
6. D Kelleher 'Shareware Licences for Software' [1998] EIPR 140.

(vii) Does copyright protect just the form of a computer program or does it also protect the underlying idea?

23.14 Under classical copyright theory,[1] copyright protects the form in which a work is expressed, but not the underlying notions (the 'content') which that form of expression conveys. The validity of this content/form dichotomy as a means of resolving disputes as to computer software infringement has been seriously questioned by judges and commentators alike, particularly in the United States where a substantial jurisprudence on 'non-literal copying' has arisen on this topic.[2] The argument is in many cases abstruse and difficult to follow but, in its simplest form, it ranges between those who maintain that, where two programs react vis-à-vis the computer user in similar or identical manner, there may be infringement of the first by the second even if, vis-à-vis the computer itself, the programs read as entirely different and distinct pieces of literature. Those who say that there is no infringement argue that, if two works have different logic structures, underlying architectures[3] and source and object codes, it is manifestly absurd to suggest that one should be regarded as an infringing copy of the other simply because it fulfils the same function as far as its user is concerned. In the US there was initially much support for the notion that the 'total concept and feel' (colloquially referred to as the 'look and feel') was protected even if the form was not copied,[4] but later cases suggested that the approach was not correct.[5] An alternative approach, which has become known as the abstraction/filtration test for infringement, was set forth in *Computer Associates v Altai*.[6] Structural elements of a program are identified; for each of these, mere ideas, forms of expression which are inevitable (given those ideas, so that expressions 'merges' with idea), and public domain material are filtered out. The remaining kernel (if any) is then used as the basis for comparison with the defendant's program. This test for infringement has found favour with judges in the US and was applied by Ferris J in the English case of *John Richardson Computers v Flanders*;[7] perhaps not surprisingly, given the tenor of recitals 13 and 14 of the software directive.[8] However, in *Ibcos Computers Ltd v Barclays Mercantile Highland Finance Ltd*,[9] Jacob J rejected the US approach and returned to UK first principles in deciding the issue of infringement. First, he identified the claimants' works in issue and decided whether they were original[10] and thus attracted copyright. The next question was whether they had in fact been copied. All similarities were relevant to this question. Last, it fell to be decided whether the part which was copied was substantial. Having heard expert evidence, he decided this point in the claimants' favour. It is submitted that this approach is correct. The test is not whether what is reproduced is itself protected by copyright,[11] but whether it forms a substantial part of a work which is.

1. Recited in the preamble to Council Directive 91/250/EEC of 14 May 1991 on the legal protection of computer programs OJ 1991 L122/42 ('the software directive'):

'13. Whereas, for the avoidance of doubt, it has to be made clear that only the expression of a computer program is protected and that ideas and principles which underlie any element of a program, including those which underlie its interfaces, are not protected by copyright under this directive;

14. Whereas, in accordance with this principle of copyright, to the extent that logic, algorithms and programming language comprise ideas and principles, those ideas and principles are not protected under this directive;'

2. See for example. D Karjala 'Recent United States and International Developments in Software Protection' [1994] EIPR 13 and 58; E Derclaye 'Software Copyright Protection: Can Europe Learn from US Case Law? [2000] EIPR 7 and 56 and citations therein.

3. In *Whelan Associates Inc v Jaslow Dental Laboratory Inc* 797 F2d 1222 (USCA, 1986) the taking of structure, sequence and arrangement was held to infringe.

4. *Whelan*, n 3 above, *Broderbund Software Inc v Unison World Inc* 648 F Supp 1127 (ND Cal, 1986); *Digital Communications Associates v Softklone Distributing Corpn* 659 F Supp 449 (ND Ga, 1987).

5. *Synercom Technology v University Computing Co* 462 F Supp 1003 (ND Tex, 1978); *Plains Cotton Co-operative Association v Goodpasture Computer Service* 807 F2d 1256 (5th Cir, 1987); *Computer Associates v Altai* 982 F2d 693 (2nd Cir, 1992). The importance of 'look and feel' to the user may be highly relevant to the issue of substantiality where expression has been copied. In *Lotus Development Corpn v Paperback Software International* 740 F Supp 37 (D Mass 1990) the menu command system of the 'Lotus 1-2-3' spreadsheet program was held substantial by a US district court. However, the 'abstraction-filtration' test was used to deny protection to the Lotus menu commands in *Lotus Development v Borland International* 49 F 3d 807 (1995).

6. N 5, above. See L J Zadra-Symes '*Computer Associates v Altai*: the Retreat from *Whelan v Jaslow*' [1992] EIPR 327.

7. [1993] FSR 497.

8. See n 1 above.

9. [1994] FSR 275.

10. There was formerly divergence within the European Community as to the level of originality required for a computer program to be protected by copyright. Germany, in particular, required a high degree of originality. Now, however, the level has been harmonised (at least in theory) at that of the personal intellectual creation of the author. See para **11.11** above.

11. Although if it is, the question of whether it forms a substantial part of a larger work becomes unnecessary.

(viii) Should computer software interfaces be legally protected?

23.15 There are usually reckoned to be two different species of computer program – systems programs and application programs. Systems programs enable a computer to operate as a computer, for example by enabling the computer's central processing unit to respond to keyboard instructions, or by instructing the pixels on the screen to respond by way of a visual image to the impulses directed from elsewhere in the computer. Applications programs, in contrast, enable the computer user to perform tasks through the operation of his computer, such as typesetting, graphic design or the preparation of accounts by means of spreadsheets. Only recently has a third species of program been recognised – though it has long existed – the interoperable[1] program, which enables the applications programs to talk to the systems software by providing an interface between them. Since the interoperable program is not normally a commodity in its own right but is generally a feature of what is normally regarded simply as a systems or applications program, it has been neglected despite its obvious importance. The software directive[2] refers to the exclusion from copyright protection of the ideas and principles underlying interfaces and goes on to recite[3] that circumstances may exist when reproduction of the code of a program may be indispensable to achieve inter-operability with an independently created program; for these purposes reproduction is permitted by Art 6. This aspect of Art 6 has not been expressly implemented in UK legislation; presumably it is thought to be fair dealing within the meaning of section 29 of the Copyright, Designs and Patents Act 1988.

1. Recital 12 to Council Directive 91/250/EEC of 14 May 1991 on the legal protection of computer programs OJ 1991 L122/42 (the 'software directive') defines interoperability as: 'the ability to exchange information and mutually to use the information which has been exchanged'.
2. Recital 13, set out in n 1 to para **23.14** above.
3. Recital 21.

(ix) To what extent should 'decompilation' or 'reverse engineering' be allowed?

23.16 This is closely related to the previous question, since a major purpose of decompilation (translating from object or machine code into higher level languages so that the program's operation may be examined or adapted) is to create interoperable programs. The Copyright (Computer Programs) Regulations 1992[1] amended section 29 of the Copyright, Designs and Patents Act 1988 to exclude decompilation from fair dealing in general and inserted a new section 50B. This permits decompilation if it is necessary (a) to obtain information not readily available elsewhere, and (b) is carried out by or on behalf of a licensed user, (c) for the purpose of creating an independent, interoperable but non-competing program. In the US, a court appears to have come to a similar conclusion on the basis of fair use. In *Sega Enterprises Ltd v Accolade Inc*[2] it was held fair to decompile Sega's programs to create video games compatible with Sega's 'Genesis' ('Mega Drive') hardware. *Sega and Accolade* was considered by the Singapore Court of Appeal in *Creative Technology v Aztech Systems*,[3] a decision which rejected the defence of fair dealing. A number of applications such as games had been produced to operate with plaintiff's sound card, an 'add-on' product which enhanced the sound processing capabilities of the user's computer. In order to compete with the plaintiff's 'Sound-blaster' card, the defendant wished to ensure that these games would run on its own card. It was held that the defendant's decompilation of the 'Sound-blaster' programs and the defendant's compatible card constituted infringements of the plaintiffs' copyright.

1. SI 1992/3233, implementing Council Directive 91/250/EEC, OJ No L122/42 1991, on the legal protection of computer programs.
2. 977 F 2d 1510 (9th Cir, 1992). See R H Stern 'Reverse Engineering of Software as Copyright Infringement – An Update: Sega Enterprises Ltd v Accolade Inc' [1993] 1 EIPR 34; P Samuelson 'Economic and Constitutional Influence on Copyright Law in the United States' [2001] EIPR 409, at 412-416.
3. [1997] 1 SLR 621, [1997] FSR 491. S Lai 'Recent Developments in Copyright Protection and Software Reverse Engineering in Singapore' [1997] EIPR 525.

(x) Should the exploitation of an employee's patent rights be inhibited by his employer's ownership of essential software?

23.17 An employer cannot utilise any express term in the contract of employment so as to diminish the employee's rights under the Patents Act 1977 in an invention made by and originally belonging to the employee.[1] No corresponding provision exists for copyright, which means that an employer can require an employee to vest in the employer even the rights in copyright works which the employee did not make in the course of his employment.[2] This means that where, outside his employment duties, an employee creates a new computer and writes applications software for it, he may find that he owns the invention and can patent it while his employer owns the copyright under a 'pre-assignment' clause in the employment contract. To counter this undesirable end, the 1988 Act[3] adds a new provision to the employment code of the Patents Act 1977 to the effect that, where an invention belongs to an employee, nothing done by the employee or anyone claiming under him for the purposes of obtaining a patent, and nothing done for the purpose of performing or working the invention, shall be taken to infringe any copyright or design right to which the employer is entitled in any model or document relating to the invention.

1. Patents Act 1977, s 42(2).
2. Copyright, Designs and Patents Act 1988, s 11(2). See J Angel and D Engel 'Employment Rights in an Information Society' ch 12 in C Reed and J Angel (eds) *Computer Law* (4th edn, 2000).
3. Copyright, Designs and Patents Act 1988, Sch 5, para 11, which created a new subsection, s 39(3), in the Patents Act 1977.

(xi) Who owns copyright in a computer's output?

23.18 Various suggestions have been offered over the years as to who the owner should be:

(i)   the person who programs the computer,[1]
(ii) the person who originates any data which, when processed by means of a program, leads to the output,[2]
(iii) the person who presses the button, as it were, and causes the output to be 'put-out' by running data through a programmed computer,[3]
(iv) the computer's owner,[4] and
(v)   the computer itself.[5]

Prior to the passage of the 1988 Act, British case law indicated that, since the computer is regarded as a rather sophisticated sort of pen, the person who operates it and runs a program through it so as to get the end result is analogised to the person who draws a pen across a piece of paper and thus creates a literary or artistic work; he is the 'author' and thus the first copyright owner, at least where he also writes the program and owns the computer. [6] Under the Act, this position changed. The possibility that the author of a work is the operator of the computer, the man who wields a big pen, has not been eliminated since 'author' means (in relation to a work) 'the person who creates it'.[7] However, where the work is a literary, artistic, musical or dramatic work, which is computer-generated, the author is taken to be 'the person by whom the arrangements necessary for the creation of the work are undertaken'.[8] The words 'computer-generated' are defined to mean a work 'generated by computer in circumstances such that there is no human author of the work'.[9] Unfortunately it is not clear who is meant by this formula. Is it the person by whom the physical, technical, financial or commercial arrangements must be taken?[10] And does 'necessary' suggest some sort of *sine qua non* arrangement?

1. *Copyright and Designs Law* Cmnd 6732, 1977, para 515. Even identifying this person can be problematic. See, eg, *Fylde Microsystems Ltd v Key Radio Systems Ltd* [1998] FSR 449 – client who gave detailed specifications and tested software was not a joint author.
2. *Copyright and Designs Law* Cmnd 6732, 1977, para 515.
3. S Hewitt 'Copyright Claims to Computer Output in the UK' [1983] EIPR 308.
4. *Reform of the Law Relating to Copyright, Designs and Performers' Protection* Cmnd 8302, 1981, ch 8, para 7.
5. Ibid.
6. *Express Newspapers plc v Liverpool Daily Post and Echo plc* [1985] FSR 306.
7. Copyright, Designs and Patents Act 1988, s 9(1).
8. Ibid, s 9(3).
9. Ibid, s 178.

10. Analogy may be drawn with sound recordings, where similar terminology as to authorship is used. See para **12.27**.

(xii) Should the use of computers be controlled?

23.19 This question goes beyond the scope of intellectual property law, and is properly dealt with elsewhere[1] since it raises matters of grave political concern. Suffice it here to say that the computer's capacity to do good, like that of the tin-opener, motor car and the automatic revolver, is as great as its capacity to inflict harm, and that, again like the car and the revolver, its power lies in its ability to do good or harm more perfectly than could those technologies which preceded it. Regulation of the computer without more general regulation of the wrongs which can be inflicted with or without its aid is capricious. It was inappropriate that the Data Protection Act 1984 applied to to personal information held in a computer[2] but not in a manual file.[3] Subject to transitional provisions, the Data Protection Act 1998 applies to manual as well as computer files, although persons processing personal data only have to register under the Act for computer activities. The problems of data protection and the Internet still exercise EC legislators: the European Commission has already proposed a new directive[4] concerning the processing of personal data and the protection of privacy in the electronic communications sector, to replace Directive 97/66. It has issued a number of decisions on the adequacy of data protection in countries outside the EC[5] for the purpose of ensuring security of data transfers and published a decision on standard contractual clauses for the transfer of personal data to third countries.[6]

1. See eg Weeramantry *The Slumbering Sentinels* (1983), J Rule *Private Lives and Public Surveillance* (1973).
2. Data Protection Act 1984, s 21(1). See I Walden 'Data Protection', in C Reed an J Angel (eds) *Computer Law* (4th edn, 2000) Ch 13, D Bainbridge *Data Protection* (2000).
3. The law recognised no general right of private access to one's personal data held by another: see the Younger Committee's report, Cmnd 5012, 1972.
4. COM (2000) 385.
5. Switzerland [2000] OJ 215/1; Hungary [2000] OJ L215/7; US [2000] OJ L215/7; all decisions under directive 95/46.
6. At europa.eu.int/comm/internal market/en/dataprot/news.

Copyright and databases

23.20 According to Ricketson, a database is:

'... a body of information organised or arranged according to some basic principle of compilation that enables a user to readily retrieve and use particular items.'[1]

The EC Council directive on databases defines an electronic database in these terms:

> '..."database" means a collection of independent works, data, or other materials arranged in a systematic or methodical way and individually accessible by electronic or other means...Protection under this Directive shall not apply to computer programs used in the making or operation of databases accessible by electronic means.'[2]

This wording was transposed almost *verbatim* into section 3A of the Copyright, Designs and Patents Act 1988.[3] Literary works are defined in section 3 of the Copyright, Designs and Patents Act to include compilations; it is clear from the quotations cited above that a database will normally constitute a compilation. However, not all compilations will necessarily constitute databases. For example, a manual detailing the operation of a particular piece of machinery, or a particular business method, may be 'compiled', but the data elements it contains are probably not 'independent'. As discussed earlier, the English courts have in the past provided generous protection for compilations as copyright literary works.[4] In the United States, however, the case of *Feist Publications Inc v Rural Telephone Service Co Inc*[5] showed that a comprehensive database of telephone numbers, arranged according to the simple alphabetic principle, was not susceptible to copyright protection, being mere 'sweat of the brow'. To qualify for copyright protection, a compilation had to enjoy originality of selection or arrangement. This approach was echoed in the EC Directive, which reserves copyright to databases whose selection or arrangement constitute their authors' own intellectual creations.[6] This copyright does not protect the database's contents,[7] which are protected instead either by their own copyright, if 'works', or by the *sui generis* right to prevent unfair extraction and utilisation.[8]

1. 'Copyright and Databases' in Hughes (ed) *Essays in Copyright Law* 1990, p 68, cited by G Lea, 'Databases and Copyright' [1993] 9 CLSR 68.
2. [1996] OJ L77/20, arts 1.2 and 1.3.
3. By the Copyright and Rights in Databases Regulations 1997 (SI 1997/3022).
4. See para **11.16** above.
5. 111 S Ct 1282 (1991).
6. Art 3.1.
7. Art 3.2.
8. Art 7. This right is a cousin of unfair competition: see paras **10.7** and **10.8** above.

23.21 The directive applies to non-electronic databases as well as electronic ones; this is consistent with Art 10(2) of the GATT/TRIPS agreement, which[1] obliges signatories to protect compilations generally, as to their selection and arrangement. However, a computer database differs from a paper compilation in three important respects:[2]

(i) indifference to the nature of the data. Anything that can be stored digitally can be included. This includes matter which is classified as one of the various types of work traditionally recognised by copyright law. The European Commission's definition clearly embraces this possibility;[3]
(ii) reconfigurability, whereby data may be reorganised, qualitatively and quantitatively, at will;
(iii) data efficiency, enabling storage and manipulation of quantities of data which would otherwise be physically impossible or economically impracticable.

Reconfigurability means that the arrangement of an electronic database may be somewhat arbitrary; this is recognised by Recital 21, which states that the materials do not have to be physically stored in an organised manner. Data efficiency enables truly comprehensive databases to be created, from which selections may be made by using a search program. In this case, the fact that a search produces a null result may be of great value. All this suggests that selection and arrangement are problematic vehicles for copyright in electronic databases. The directive provisions on the next question, that of ownership, are far from venturesome. In fact they do not really attempt to harmonise ownership provisions at all. Although this may be consistent with Art 295 (formerly Art 222) of the EC Treaty, it hardly serves the aim of ironing out legal differences to promote the functioning of the internal market.[4] Art 4 of the directive suggests that the author of a copyright database may be the group of people who actually compiled it, a legal person designated by national legislation, or the person regarded as holding copyright in collective works, where these are recognised in the Member State in question.

1. The agreement on trade-related aspects of intellectual property, concluded as part of the GATT Uruguay Round. See, further, para **28.2**. The text is reproduced as a supplement to [1994] 11 EIPR.
2. See G Lea 'Databases and Copyright' [1993] 9 CLSR 68 and 127.
3. Recital 17, which makes clear that the recordings as such do not fall within the scope of the directive; nor do compilation CDs: recital 19.
4. Recital 2.

Who owns a computer database?

23.22 This is a problem of great difficulty and of immense potential significance. If a database is regarded as being simply a quantity of data held in a computer's memory, one is tempted to conclude that the ownership of the database will run with the ownership of the material (be it tape, disk or chip) upon which it is recorded, subject to the right of the author of the database to restrict its use if he owns any copyright in it. Where a database has been compiled in the form of a literary work which is then loaded into a computer (for example an English-French dictionary or a set of law reports), the work as loaded into the computer is now an adaptation of the original work, and an unauthorised dealing with it may be a restricted act in respect of the work in its traditional form, and therefore an infringement of copyright. Where a database has had no effective existence as a separate literary work prior to its creation within the computer (eg where it is an accretion of the contributions of numerous computer-users, or where it is a compilation of survey forms), it may be difficult to describe it as a work of any particular author, and therefore to say that it is a work of authorship at all;[1] and this is where problems arise. For example, University A has a computer upon which Professor B stores coded data drawn from 120,000 questionnaires completed by adolescent cigarette smokers in Sussex. Assuming that there are no specific contractual provisions to be applied, consider the following issues:

(i) Can University A sell the database to cigarette manufacturer C?
(ii) Can Professor B take the data with him if he moves to University D?
(iii) Who is the owner of the copyright in the database, which may have been stored in the computer by a variety of different persons, at different times?
(iv) Who is the author of the database for the purposes of calculating the duration (if any) of the copyright term?

Neither the directive nor the 1988 Act has erased the problem. At first glance the Act's recognition of a 'computer-generated' work[2] may seem to be applicable here, – but our examples are not 'computer-generated', they are 'people-generated' with the assistance of computers. Nor can such works be described as works of 'unknown authorship'[3] unless the identity of none of the contributors is known. The copyright provisions of the Copyright and Rights in Databases Regulations 1997[4] make no mention of authorship and ownership of copyright in databases, presumably leaving this matter to the general provisions of the 1988 Act. However, the 'maker' of the database is defined in the Regulations for the purposes of the *sui generis* database right as 'the person who takes the initiative in obtaining, verifying or presenting the contents of a database and assumes the risk of investing in that [activity]'.[5] Where the actual maker creates the database in the course of his employment, the employer is regarded in law as its maker.[6]

23.22 *Problems with new technology*

1. On the concept of authorship see ch 10 above.
2. Copyright, Designs and Patents Act 1988, s 9(3).
3. Ibid, s 9 (4).
4. SI 1997/3022.
5. Reg 14(1).
6. Reg 14(2). This is permitted by the directive – see recital 29 – but again not harmonised.

23.23   The scope of database right was at issue in *British Horseracing Board Ltd v William Hill Organisation Ltd*.[1] The Board was responsible for the horse-racing calendar. It compiled and published lists of race fixtures, using its computerised database. The database not only contained information on race fixtures, but also on racehorses, jockeys, trainers and owners, with details of the racehorse owners' distinctive racing colours. The Board spent substantial sums each year in collecting and checking information and keeping the database up-to-date. The Board made the information available to subscribers to an online service. William Hill began to offer an on-line betting service, making use of information derived from the Board's database. The Board sued William Hill for infringement of their database right by extraction or re-utilisation of substantial parts of their database,[2] and/or by repeated and systematic extraction or re-utilisation of insubstantial parts.[3] Laddie J held that the Board enjoyed database right and that their right was infringed by William Hill's use of the data in its online betting business. Although the information used did not at any time represent a high proportion of the information in the database, it was the most recent data and a substantial part. The Court of Appeal has referred to the European Court a number of questions on interpretation of the database directive.[4]

1. [2001] ECLR 257.
2. Contrary to reg 16(1) of the Copyright and Rights in Databases Regulations 1997 (SI 1997/3032), which implemented art 7(1) of Directive 96/9/EC on the legal protection of databases.
3. Ibid, reg 16(2) and art 7(5) respectively.
4. For a discussion of the issues, see S Chalton 'Database Right: Stronger Than it Looks?' [2001] EIPR 296.

Electronic publishing, electronic networks and the 'information superhighway'

Some economic effects

23.24   In the long term, the repercussions of computer use for traditional information-based industries such as publishing and librarianship will probably be more profound than are the important but ephemeral questions listed under the previous headings. This is because traditional book publishing and librarianship, and conventional means of distribution of other works such as music and films, are likely to be victims rather than beneficiaries of new computer uses.

23.25 At the time of writing this chapter, book publishing is costly and wasteful.[1] Publishers produce a 'hard copy' in the form of books printed in volume format; the publisher's profit, and that of the author, depend upon the number of copies sold. The sale of books is dependent upon a number of factors such as advertising and the securing of favourable reviews following a distribution of review copies, and is inhibited by library acquisitions which may result in multiple readership of a single copy. The manufacture, transport and storage of books is a costly affair, which undermines the commercial viability of publishing ventures; it is also an essentially wasteful operation, as the number of books remaindered each year has testified. The library is also costly and inefficient as a means of acquiring and distributing information to its users.[2] Even in research institutions where users determine the books to be stocked, libraries hold a large proportion of books which are not used at all.[3] Library stocks are frequently underutilised or over-duplicated and institutionalised inter-library loan facilities are (so far) cumbersome, expensive and delay-inducing.[4]

1. On the economics of traditional book publishing see Sir Albert Plant's substantially out-of-date 'The Economic Aspects of Copyright in Books' (1934); *Economica* (ns); see also F E Dowrick' Law Book Publishing' (1974) JSPTL 27.
2. On the waste inherent in the library system see J Thompson *The End of Libraries* (1982), ch 1 ('The Unusable Library').
3. J Thompson, op cit, pp 8-9. The new British Library building is already full.
4. For a general account of the inter-library loan system see D Wood, 'Reprography and Copyright with Particular Reference to Document Supply – A view from the British Library Lending Division' [1983] EIPR 323.

23.26 Consider in contrast the following scenario. A 'publisher' will produce not thousands of print-and-paper books, but a single computer file upon which a work is encoded. He will not be a 'publisher' in the traditional sense, but the author of the work.[1] The contents of the file will be available for consultation on the Internet,[2] on which all literature, drama, music, films, sound recordings and scientific research are stored as a resource accessible to all. The end consumer or reader of the work thus stored will be able to access it from the computer in his own home or workplace, without the necessity (or pleasure) of a trip to Foyles' Bookshop or to the library; he can either 'browse' or read through it on his visual display unit, and he may obtain a printout if he wants a 'hard copy'. The economics of the scheme are easy to predict: the authors will pay for the placing on file of their works, and they will be remunerated for consumer use on a per-scan or per-print basis. This means that publication cost and, more importantly, publication time is reduced, and that the author's remuneration is directly proportional to the use of his works. Libraries are avoided, but librarianship – in the guise of information science – becomes a precise discipline for the identification and location of information, and will never again be a euphemism for the dusting of shelves in Victorian Gothic municipal buildings.

1. The definition of 'publication' in s 175 of the Copyright, Designs and Patents Act 1988 already caters for electronic retrieval.
2. Also dubbed the 'information superhighway' in the European Union and the 'national information infrastructure' in the US. See R B Rich and K J Daniels 'Intellectual Property and the National Information Infrastructure' (1994) 6 J Prop R 2.

23.27 The impact of such an end result for traditional copyright concepts is immense, but is of far less importance than the sensitive (and possibly insoluble) problems of determining (i) who should be accorded access,[1] (ii) the terms – if any – under which access should be permitted, (iii) the computation of scale of remuneration for access to works, (iv) the means of remuneration of authors whose works are distributed, in particular whether collective licensing mechanisms are adequate,[2] (v) whether and how the moral rights of those authors may be protected (vi) administering and regulating the all-powerful Internet. Furthermore, the Internet is not national – and thus governed by one set of copyright laws – but international. It is clearly recognised that all this has serious implications for copyright.[3]

1. In *R v Whiteley* [1993] FSR 168 the accused 'hacker' who obtained unauthorised access to JANET, the UK universities Joint Admissions Network, and corrupted files was convicted of criminal damage. However, it is even more difficult to detect an unauthorised user who does no damage to the facilities available to network users.
2. The implications for musical works are discussed in H Rosenblatt 'The Impact of New Technology on Composers and Music Publishers: Policing the Superhighways' [1994] Ent LR 73; L Jones 'An Artist's Entry into Cyberspace' [2000] EIPR 79.
3. A N Dixon and L C Self 'Copyright Protection for the Information Superhighway' [1994] EIPR 465.

What is the legal status of Internet domain names?

23.28 A domain name is a mnemonic for the electronic address of a site on the world wide web. There is a hierarchical system of domain names. The suffix of names in the highest level domains, such as .com or .org denote the kind of organisation which has registered the name with the relevant domain registry. Country suffixes are assigned to the state concerned, although some countries with commercially desirable suffixes, such as Tobago (.to) or Tuvalu (.tv) have sold their national allocation *en bloc*. The sub-classes within a national domain, such as .ac.uk or .co.uk, are used for academic institutions, companies, etc. In front of the suffix may come the name of an individual, company, professional grouping or perhaps a generic term such as 'housingagency'.[1] It is at this position within the domain name that trade mark disputes tend to arise. Internet users recognise domain names as indicating a connection with the person named. Confusion can occur when the identity of the person 'behind' the name does not correspond with the public's expectations. Whether by accident or design, such domain names can effect a misrepresentation. A user may guess at a domain name but reach an address quite unconnected with the desired organisation. The phrase 'cyber-squatting' is used to describe the activities of those who deliberately register domain names corresponding to reputed companies or individuals. The registrant will often try to sell the domain names to the 'true owner'. The latter may bring an action for passing off.[2] If the name in question is registered as a trade mark, the owner may sue for infringement, at least where the user trades in relevant goods or services over the Internet.[3] These classic forms of action have several drawbacks. They can be slow, cumbersome and expensive. But most of all, passing off rights are national and trade mark registrations are national or regional. The Internet is global.[4] Accordingly, internationally respected mechanisms are needed to resolve disputes. A number of schemes exist. Domain name registries[5] may offer such services within their domains, in accordance with a Uniform Dispute Resolution Policy ('UDRP') devised by ICANN on the recommendations of the World Intellectual Property Organization.[6] WIPO's Arbitration and Mediation Center and other bodies offer domain name dispute resolution under the UDRP. An application has to satisfy three criteria:

a. the disputed domain name is identical or similar to a trade mark in which the complainant has rights; unregistered rights are recognised, including the names of authors and other well-known personalities;

b. the respondent has no legitimate interest or rights in the domain name;

c. the domain name must have been registered and be used in bad faith; this includes speculative buying of names which are offered for sale, blocking registration of the complainant and diversion of 'hits'.

A disadvantage of these schemes is that they tend to deal with single names, one at a time, so many applications may have to be made to deal with a dedicated cybersquatter. Furthermore, the application and extension by dispute resolution services of trade mark principles worked out for a diferent environment may distort the principles themselves.[7]

1. The German Federal Supreme Court, reversing a decision of a lower court, has held that Mitwohnzentrale.de (German for housing agency) could be appropriated by registration as a domain name without contravening unfair competition laws or a need to keep the term free for general use. [decision of 17 May 2001]. The German language, with its custom of composite words, lends itself to such registrations.
2. As in *British Telecommunications plc v One in a Million* [1999] FSR 1; for passing off, see para **20.**7 ff.
3. H Hurdle 'Domain Names – the Scope of a Trade Mark Proprietor's Monopoly *Avnet Inc v Isoact Ltd* [1998] EIPR 74. *Avnet* is reported at [1998] FSR 16.
4. C Elliott and B Gravatt 'Domain Name Disputes in a Cross-border Context' [1999] EIPR 417.
5. Such as Nominet UK, the registry responsible for domain names ending in .uk; see www.nominet.org.uk for examples.
6. ICANN is the Internet Corporation for Assigned Names and Numbers. For details, see S Jones 'A Child's First Steps: The First Six Months of Operation – the ICANN Dispute Resolution Procedure for Bad Faith Registration of Domain Names' [2001] EIPR 66; G Evans 'Comment of the Terms of Reference and Procedure for the Second WIPO Internet Domain Name Process' [2001] EIPR 61.
7. C Thorne and S Bennett 'Domain Names – Internet Warehousng: Has Protection of Well-Known Names on the Internet Gone Too Far?' [1998] EIPR 468; N Wilkof 'Trade Marks and the Public Domain'[2000] EIPR 571.

23.29   The above suggests that domain names may operate as trade marks. If so, we may expect trade mark registries to have policies on the registration of Domain names. This is indeed the case. The UK Registry and the Community Trade Mark Office have announced[1] their willingness to register domain names as trade marks provided they otherwise satisfy the requirements for registration. [2]

1. UK Trade Marks Journal No 6166, Marcg 12 1997, J Olsen and S Maniatis *Domain Names* (2000); GN Vergani 'Electronic Commerce and Trade Marks in the United States: Domain Names, Trade Marks and the 'Use in Commerce Requirement' on the Internet' [1999] EIPR 450.
2. See ch 21.

Interactive multimedia

23.30   A related area is the development of interactive 'multi-media'[1] products,[2] whereby a user can access, manipulate and combine text, sound and images. The use of video computer games and music sampling devices has already been considered by the courts, but the current generation of multi-media products is characterised by the enormous volume of original and copied works in packages which can be supplied to the user in CD form and the sophistication of the systems that allow for their manipulation. This raises questions of ownership[3] and infringement of copyright[4] which are likely to be litigated whilst this edition is current.

1. P-Y Gautier 'Multi-media Works in French Law' RIDA(1994) 159/8 p 90 defines a multi-media work as

    'a complex creation which, after being given a form by a computer, is made up of an ensemble of texts, fixed and/or moving images and/or music accessible on 'Compact disc' (CD ROM for reading only, CDI for dialogue) which requires the use of equipment (an independent player/reader or one that is incorporated in a television, etc) to enable users to become acquainted with it'.

    For meanings of reproduction and meanings of acronyms, see PRS Yearbook 1993-94, p 55.
2. M D Scott and J L Talbott 'Interactive Multimedia: What is it, Why is it important and why does one need to know about it?' [1993] EIPR 284.
3. See D L Gersh and S Jeffrey 'Structuring the multi-media deal: legal issues' [1992] Ent LR 196 and A White 'Multimedia and Copyright laws: Practical Options for Producers' Copyright World, September 1993, p 20 for suggestions which may avoid some potential problems.
4. Which can be avoided in relation to included works by taking appropriate licenses: see, eg, M Schippan 'Purchase and Licensing of Digital Rights: the Verdi Project' [2000] EIPR 24.

Broadcasts

23.31   The technology of broadcasting is not in itself new,[1] nor is the currency of its widespread exploitation.[2] More recent, however, is the harmonisation of techniques of broadcasting, relay and reception so that a 'broadcast' work can be directed for simultaneous reception across the world or for 'narrowcasting' to individual subscribers of a programme provider.[3] Once broadband connection is available on the Internet, the 'webcasting' of film and other works may become widespread. Purely from the perspective of intellectual property the technology of broadcasting offers relatively few problems; but as a political and commercial phenomenon, broadcasting has attracted a good deal of legal commentary.[4] Of particular interest to copyright lawyers has been the issue of spillage – the inevitable consequence of having irregularly-shaped countries. When a broadcast is made in one country, it may be picked up by radio or television audiences in another. In a non-ideal world every 'spillage' would result in copyright infringement, since the party which pays for a licence to broadcast a work in country A also has to broadcast it, without benefit of royalties, to an audience in countries B, C and D. So far as British law is concerned, a broadcast takes place in the country in which it is made, not in the country or countries in which it is received;[5] thus the originator of a French broadcast would not, on the sole ground that the good folk of Dover could tune into it, be liable as a copyright infringer in the UK. On the other hand, anyone who includes such a broadcast in a cable programme which he relays to others will be infringing the copyright of both the broadcast[6] and any underlying literary works it contains. As satellites became increasingly diversified in the types of information they transmit, and de-regulation of broadcasting led to a large number of programme providers and potential infringers, the old distinctions between different kinds of work and different modes of exploitation of work are breaking down. This phenomenon, known as 'convergence', has been particularly studied in the context of broadcasting[7] but is evident in all areas of copyright.[8]

1. See eg Briggs *The BBC: The First Fifty Years* (1985).
2. Ibid, ch 2 et seq.
3. On the sophistication of broadcasting techniques for small audiences see eg E Noam (ed) *Video Media Competition* (1985).
4. See eg I de Sola Pool *Technologies of Freedom* (1983), D Brenner and W Rivers (eds) *Free but Regulated* (1982).
5. Copyright, Designs and Patents Act 1988, s 6(3), (4).
6. Ibid, s 20.
7. See M Ryan 'Highways to change – Report of the Australian Copyright Convergence Group' Copyright World, November 1994, p 17; Results of EC consultation on convergence of the telecoms, media and technology sectors, COM (99) 108.
8. S Perlmutter 'Convergence and the Future of Copyright' [2001] EIPR 111.

Copying and anti-copying devices

23.32   Copyright infringement can best be done at home, where the risk of detection is minimal and the quantum of damage from each individual act of infringement is usually thought to be too small to make it worth suing the infringer. The advent of the audio-cassette and the video-cassette recording machines brought infringement within everyone's means; copyright infringement at last became a proletarian activity from which few if any were disqualified by personal resources. Once this was recognised to be the case, attention turned once more to the employment of technical means, in place of legal remedies, as a way of inhibiting widescale casual domestic infringement. The principal problem faced in selecting an appropriate technology was that of its reversibility – gadgets designed to prevent copying could be removed, neutralised or circumvented at little cost. With the arrival of DAT (digital audio tape) technology, the prospect of the ordinary man in the street being able to make technically perfect copies of recorded works posed so much of a threat to the established interests of the recording industry that refuge to a technical solution had once again to be considered. Following an agreement between representatives of the recording industry and the Japanese, US and European hardware manufacturers, it was decided that all DAT recorders would be fitted with a Serial Copy Management System (SCMS) which would mean that all digital recordings (be they digital *ab initio* or digital recordings made from traditional analogue technologies) would be encoded with information buried in a sub-code channel. This information would enable the DAT recorder to 'read' whether a single digital-to-digital recording had already been made. Once that single recording (disliked by the recording industry but so widely made as to be nearly the norm) has been made, no further copy can be made from it.[1] The agreement to utilise SCMSs did not, of course, supplant copyright law and may have caused the scant take-up of DAT technology. At the time of writing, CD writers have become commonplace components of domestic personal computers, enabling countless teenagers to compile CDs from borrowed recordings or from the Internet. In the UK the position of the copyright owner was strengthened by the statutory provision that a person who issues copies of a work in electronic form to the public enjoys in certain circumstances the rights of the copyright owner against a person who makes, sells, hires out or imports 'any device or means specifically designed or adapted to circumvent the form of copy-protection employed', and against the person who publishes information intended to enable or assist another to circumvent any form of copy-protection.[2] A similar provision protects the broadcasters of encrypted broadcasts against those who make and sell unauthorised decoding equipment by means of which viewers can watch television programmes for which they have not subscribed.[3] These and similar provisions will become the norm in Europe as EC Member States implement the 'Copyright' Directive, 2001/29/EC.[4] Art 6 of that directive requires Member States to provided adequate protection against the circumvention of effective technological measures by a defendant who knows, or has reason to know, the nature of their activity. Art 7 further requires protection for rights management information against removal or tampering. Rights management information is embedded in works for the purpose of tracking use and facilitating reward, normally through a copyright collecting society. When Art 7 is implemented, this will enjoy protected status.

1. On SCMS and DAT technology see T Faure, 'Digital Equals Exponential', (1990) Copyright World No 9, p 45.
2. Copyright, Designs and Patents Act 1988, s 296(2).
3. Ibid, s 298(1).
4. On the harmonisation of certain aspects of copyright and related rights in the information society; 22 May 2001; [2001] OJ L167/10.

Chapter 24

Protection of industrial designs

Introduction

24.1   The patent system evolved as a means of protecting the development of inventions, while artistic copyright derived its vital force from its role as a safeguard of rights in largely aesthetic works. As the two systems became more specialised and gradually grew apart, it became inevitable that a sort of intellectual property no man's land should separate them.[1] The prime occupants of this no man's land were industrially exploited designs. These designs, applied to manufactured products, would govern their shape and appearance and thus add aesthetic appeal to their otherwise functional form. Some designs so dictate the physical character of goods that one might claim with justification that their employment resulted in the creation of an entirely new product. A design, however, is only a design, though it may be novel, it is not a patentable invention and cannot therefore claim the protection of the patent system. However, many industrialists would wish to rely upon secure legal protection before investing funds and effort in the development, tooling and staff training necessary to launch a new production on to the market. Accordingly, from the early nineteenth century, and particularly during the era of the Great Exhibition of 1851, there grew an awareness of the need to provide special protection for what, in effect, were aesthetically appealing non-inventions exploited industrially in like manner to the development of inventions.[2] Indeed, plagiarism of exhibited products and inventions was a spur to the establishment in 1883 of the Paris Convention for the Protection of Industrial Property.[3] It is not surprising, therefore, that the registration system which evolved in the UK for designs with visual appeal came to resemble the patent system which protects functional invention. Like the Patents Act 1977, the Registered Designs Act 1949 provided for the grant of an absolute monopoly, renewable for a fixed and limited period only. It required some degree of novelty as a criterion of registrability and it legislated for the grant of rights only as a consequence of a successful examination of the application. The design to be registered had also to be capable of industrial application. The 1949 Act is being amended[4] to comply with EC directive 98/71/EC on the legal protection of design.[5]

These amendments have removed the requirement of industrial application, so that design protection extends to handicraft items. A requirement of individual character has been added to that of novelty and the standard of novelty has been revised. The criterion of eye-appeal has been dropped, although a design still needs to be visible in normal use. Registration is no longer product-specific, so that infringement rights are extended. These changes may make registration more popular in the UK. However, for many years copyright provided a vastly more powerful and convenient form of protection for industrial designs in the UK and the registration system was little used. So few designs were recorded on the register that, eventually, the UK Registry stopped searching and examining designs for novelty.

1. On questions of overlap and lacunae within intellectual property, see U Suthersanen 'Breaking down the Intellectual Property Barriers' [1998] IPQ 56.
2. For the history and development of design registration see the *Report of the Departmental Committee on Industrial Designs* Cmnd 1808, 1962; L Bently 'Requiem for Registration: Reflections on the history of the UK registered designs system' in A Firth (ed) *The Prehistory and Development of Intellectual Property Systems* (1997), Vol 1, Perspectives on Intellectual Property.
3. See para **28.5** below.
4. By the Registered Designs Regulations 2001.
5. [1998] OJ L289/28.

The role of copyright

24.2   Copyright in a two-dimensional work may be infringed by reproduction in three dimensions and vice versa.[1] Thus the owner of copyright in cartoon drawings depicting 'Popeye' the sailor could prevent the unlicensed sale of 'Popeye' dolls.[2] Prior to 1968, copyright and design registration were viewed as alternative forms of protection – registrability ousted copyright. Had the original Popeye drawings been designs for dolls, the claimants' copyright action would have failed. In the 1960s it was realised that, where a design was functional and lacked the visual appeal necessary to secure registration, copyright in design drawings could be used to prevent copying of the articles depicted.[3] Thus unregistrable designs were protected by copyright where registrable designs were not. The Design Copyright Act 1968 improved matters a little for aesthetic design by amending section 10 of the Copyright Act 1956 so that copyright was retained for industrial designs with eye-appeal, but with a reduction in effective term to match the maximum duration of registration – 15 years. Thus copyright in design drawings was limited when the design was registrable but endured with full force for the author's life plus 50 years when the design was not registrable. This had the curious effect that claimants would argue that their designs were unregistrable whilst defendants would argue that they were registrable.[4] This anomalous situation was widely criticised, ultimately in *British Leyland Motor Corpn Ltd v Armstrong Patents Co Ltd*.[5] In that case, the House of Lords held that the claimants' computer-aided design drawings for motor exhausts were original artistic works, copyright in which would prima facie enable them to prevent unlicensed 3-D reproduction of BL exhausts by independent spare parts manufacturers. Motor cars need replacement exhausts regularly throughout their useful lives. In order to avoid finding for the claimants and confirming their monopoly over spares,[6] the House of Lords drew an analogy with the law of real property. They held that copyright in the exhaust drawings could not be exercised by BL against parts manufacturers as this would amount to derogation from BL's grant to motorists of property in the cars. Although *British Leyland* has been held of limited application, notably by the Privy Council in *Canon Kabushiki Kaisha v Green Cartridge Company (Hong Kong) Ltd*,[7] these legal anomalies shaped legislative reform in 1988.

1. Copyright, Designs and Patents Act 1988, s 17(3). See also para **13.2** above.
2. *King Features Syndicate Inc v O and M Kleeman Ltd* [1941] AC 417.
3. *Dorling v Honnor Marine Ltd* [1965] Ch 1.
4. Eg *Interlego AG v Tyco Industries Inc* [1989] AC 217 where the claimants argued against the registrability of their own designs, having already enjoyed design registration for 15 years!
5. [1986] AC 577.
6. H MacQueen *Copyright, Competition and Industrial Design* (1995).
7. [1997] FSR 817. In that case the Privy Council declined to apply *British Leyland* where purchasers of photocopiers had been free to choose initially cheap models with expensive consumables over dearer purchases with lower on-going costs. J Rawkins 'Copyright, Designs – *British Leyland* Spare Parts Defence' [1997] EIPR 674.

The 1988 reforms

24.3 Under the Berne Convention,[1] countries are free to choose how to protect industrial design. Parliament chose to reduce the scope of copyright protection for industrial designs in the UK by enacting section 51 of the Copyright, Designs and Patents Act 1988. Where copyright subsists in a drawing or other design document for[2] an article which is not an artistic work in its own right,[3] the copyright is not infringed by making an article to the design or by copying an article made to the design (the process often referred to as 'reverse engineering'). 'Design' is defined[4] as meaning any aspect of the shape or configuration of the whole or part of an article, but not surface decoration. Thus copyright in design drawings for motor exhausts is not infringed by the manufacture of spare parts. Copyright in design drawings for 'Teletubbies' cartoon characters could not be used to prevent the manufacture of unlicensed 'Teletubbies' merchandise.[5] Copyright in design drawings for a bank headquarters , however, is not affected by section 51. 'Article' is not defined in this part of the 1988 Act but its meaning is unlikely to include a building.[6] Even if the building is an 'article', it is an artistic work – of architecture[7] – and so is excluded from section 51. The difference in treatment between surface decoration (for which copyright protection is not denied) and shape was held to be unsatisfactory in *Jo-y-Jo Ltd v Matalan Retail Ltd,*[8] a case concerning embroidered clothing. The operation of section 51 is illustrated in Figure 9, below.

Figure 9   The copyright/UDR interface I

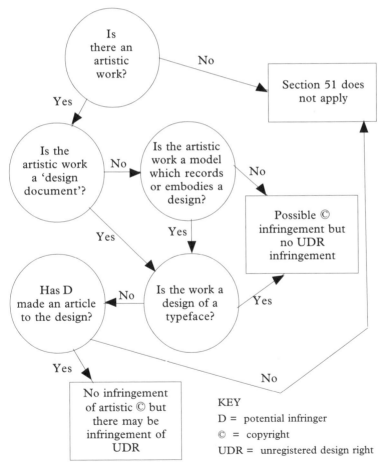

373

24.3 *Protection of industrial designs*

1. Berne Convention for the Protection of Literary and Artistic Works 1886 Art 2(7), see para **28.**5; H Cohen Jehoram 'Design Laws in Continental Europe and their Relation to Copyright' [1981] EIPR 235; A Firth, 'Aspects of Design Protection in Europe' [1993] EIPR 42.
2. G Dworkin and A Christie 'By Accident or Design' [1990] EPR 33.
3. Or typeface.
4. Copyright, Designs and Patents Act 1988, s 51(3).
5. *BBC Worldwide Ltd v Pally* [1998] FSR 665.
6. *Pensher Security Door Co Ltd v Sunderland City Council* [2000] RPC 249.
7. Ibid, s 4(1)(b).
8. See S Clark '*Jo-y-Jo v Matalan Retail Ltd*' [1999] EIPR 627.

24.4   Some of the protection removed by section 51 was replaced by the creation of a new unregistered design right.[1] This goes further than copyright in that no 'work' is required, although the design must be recorded in a design document[2] or embodied in an actual article. The claimant furniture makers in *George Hensher Ltd v Restawile Upholstery (Lancs) Ltd* whose copyright action failed when the House of Lords confirmed that their prototype was not a work of artistic craftsmanship[3] would today enjoy unregistered design right. The 1988 Act also amended the Registered Designs Act 1949, the most significant change being an increase in maximum term from 15 to 25 years. This is reflected in section 52 of the 1988 Act, which applies where copyright exists in a work which is exploited by making[4] and selling licensed copies. Section 52 limits 3-D protection to 25 years from first marketing. Neither section 52 nor section 51 have been affected by the reform of registered design law. The operation of section 52 is illustrated in Figure 10 opposite.Before looking further at registered designs and (unregistered) design right, turn to pp 376-377 where we shall compare them with copyright [Table A].

1. Copyright, Designs and Patents Act 1988, s 213 et seq. See, below, para **24.10**.
2. Ibid, s 213(6).
3. [1976] AC 64.
4. By an industrial process – more than 50 articles or continuous 'piece' goods – SI 1989/1070.

Registered designs

The design of 'products'

24.5   Now that a design need not be registered in relation to a specific product, it is not surprising that the Registered Designs Act 1949[1] defines in purely general terms the kind of product the design of which can be protected. According to section 1(3), 'product' means:

'...any industrial or handicraft item other than a computer program;[2] and, in particular, includes packaging, get-up, graphic

Figure 10   The copyright/UDR interface II

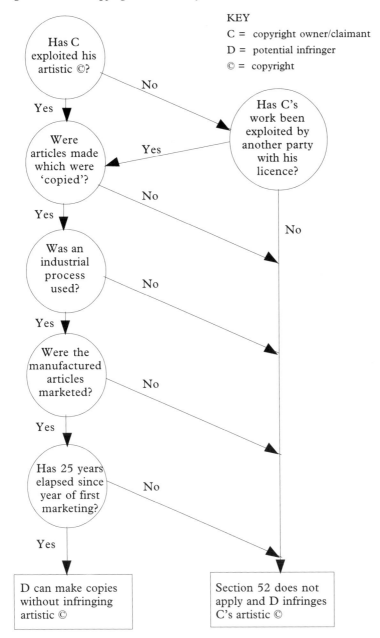

KEY
C = copyright owner/claimant
D = potential infringer
© = copyright

375

Table A

Topic covered	Artistic copyright	Unregistered design right	Registered design
Type of work protected	'Artistic work', in whatever form	'Design' contained in a 'design document'	'Design' described in an application
Duration of protection for unpublished works	Life plus 70	15 from creation	Not applicable; 'grace period' means that design can be registered up to 12 months after marketing
Duration of protection for published works	Life plus 70	10 from publication	5 + 5 + 5 + 5 + 5
Statutory source	CDPA Part I	CDPA Part II	RDA 49, as amended
Relation to prior art	Must be original	Must be original and not commonplace	Must be new and have individual character
Formalities	None	None	Application must be in accordance with Design Rules
Classification	No	No	Voluntary
Aesthetic appeal	No aesthetic quality required	No aesthetic quality required	No aesthetic quality required but parts of complex product must be visible in normal use. No registration if design dictated solely by function.
Form of recordal	2D or 3D	2D or 3D	2D only
Infringement damages	Compensatory and exemplary	Compensatory and exemplary	Compensatory only
Creator	Author	Designer	Designer

TOPIC COVERED	ARTISTIC COPYRIGHT	UNREGISTERED DESIGN RIGHT	REGISTERED DESIGN
Relational derogation of protection	No exception relating to other works	Must fit/match exceptions	Must fit exception
Infringement	Restricted acts, whether manufactured or not, in 2D and 3D	Making 3D articles	2D and 3D
Criminal infringement	Yes	No	No
Inalienable rights	Moral rights	No moral rights	No moral rights
First entitlement	Author's employer	Commissioner, employer or designer	Commisioner, employer or designer
Is it safe to warn off infringers?	No threats action	No threats action	Threats action
Risk of non-use	No compulsory licence	Compulsory licence	No compulsory licence
Fair dealing defence	Yes	No	For teaching or citation
How much must be copied?	'Substantial part'	Whole work, but UDR may subsist in part(s)	Whole work, or enough to ensure overall impression not different
Office proceedings	Not available	Controller has jurisdiction	Controller has jurisdiction
International protection	Berne, UCC	Paris	Paris
Licence of right?	No	Yes	No

> symbols, typographic type-faces and parts intended to be assembled into a complex product.'

This is a broad definition and embraces many items formerly excluded from design registration in the UK, such as hand-made wallpaper, wall plaques, medals and the graphic design of greetings cards.

1. As amended by Registered Designs Regulations forthcoming in 2001, implementing Directive 98/71/EC on the legal protection of design. References in this chapter are to the Patent Office's 'unofficial' consolidation of the Registered Design Act, as proposed to be amended. It is understood the changes will be in place by the end of 2001.
2. Which enjoys copyright: see paras **11.16** and **23.5** ff.

Definition of 'design'

24.6 A design which is proposed for registration must satisfy the statutory criteria of a design before one need consider the requirements of its registrability. Again, these are now couched in very broad terms. 'Design' is defined as:

> '... the appearance of the whole or part of a product resulting from the features of, in particular, the lines, contours, colours, shape, texture or materials of the product or its ornamentation.'[1]

Thus design is not regarded as merely the ornamentation of an otherwise complete product, but rather as the aggregate of a product's tangible three-dimensional and surface characteristics. The only features excluded from protection are those dictated solely by function,[2] those necessary to achieve interconnection with another product so that either may perform its function,[3] and those components of a complex product which are invisible in normal use.[4] Directive 98/71/EC on the legal protection of designs did not purport to harmonise 'must-match' provision of national design;[5] it is still possible for 'must-match' spares to be made in the UK. This is achieved by way of an exception from infringement[6] rather than denial of registration.[7] Designs which are contrary to public policy or accepted principles of morality do not enjoy registered design right,[8] but case law suggests that this objection will seldom be used to deny registration.[9]

1. Registered Designs Act 1949, s 1(2), as amended.
2. Ibid, s 1C(1).
3. Ibid, s 1C(2)(2), an exclusion usually dubbed 'must-fit'. This is intended to keep connecting elements free from protection under registered design law, but s 1C(3) makes clear that this does not apply to the design of a modular assembly.
4. Ibid, s 1B(8) and (9); such as under-the-bonnet motor spares.
5. This difficult matter being left for later review: art 18.

6. Registered Designs Act 1949, s 7A(5) – see below, para **24.9**.
7. Cf s1(1)(b) of the 1949 Act prior to the 2001 amendments.
8. Ibid, s 1D.
9. *Masterman's Design* [1991] RPC 89 (design registered for doll of Scotsman wearing nothing under the kilt). See, also, para **14.5** (copyright), para **5.29** (patents); para **21.12** (registered trade marks).

Registrable designs

24.7 A design is registrable under the Registered Designs Act 1949 if it is 'new' and has 'individual character'.[1] 'New' is a criterion which has some similarity to that of novelty in patent law.[2] Prior disclosure,[3] of an identical design[4] or one differing only in immaterial detail, will in principle be novelty-destroying wherever it occurred. However, some disclosures do not rob a design of novelty.[5] These include activities which could not reasonably have been known to EEA businessmen in the sector concerned, disclosures made in confidence, and disclosures made by the designer within the twelve months preceding the relevant date.[6] Individual character' is a concept which bears some resemblance to the criterion of 'originality' in UK unregistered design right.[7] A design has individual character if it produces an overall impression on an informed user which is different from the impression produced by designs already available to the public.[8]

1. Registered Designs Act 1949, s 1B(1).
2. See para **5.2** above.
3. by publication, exhibition, use in trade or otherwise: Registered Designs Act 1949, s 1B(5)(a).
4. A combination of previously known design features may be novel: *Household Article Ltd's Registered Design* [1998] FSR 676.
5. Ibid, s 1B(5)(b) and (6).
6. Ibid, s 1B(7) – usually the application date or priority date under the Paris Convention, see para **28.5**.
7. Registered Designs Act 1949, s 1B(3).
8. In this respect 'individual character' resembles non-obviousness or inventive step under patent law; see para **5.11** ff.

The consequences of registration

24.8 If, as usually happens, registration is granted, the proprietor of the design has a monopoly over its use for a period of five years from the date of first registration.[1] Infringing use may be by way of commercial manufacture, importing, exporting, stocking or dealing.[2] Note that the concept of infringement by authorisation is absent here.[3] Nor is there any need to prove copying.[4] The exclusive right of the proprietor may be exercised in relation to any article, as long as the test for infringement is satisfied – that the defendant's design is either identical or does not produce on the informed user a different overall impression. This sets practical limits on the scope of protection. Furthermore, allegations of infringement in a design field distant from that of the right owner may expose the registration to greater risk of attack for invalidity. This is because the 'prior art' against which novelty and individual character are measured is dependent on design sector.[5] The initial five-year period of registration may be extended four times by renewal, up to a maximum term of twenty-five years.[6]

1. This is usually the date of application: Registered Designs Act 1949, s 3C, but this only applies if and when the design is registered. See also ibid, s 7A(6).
2. Registered Designs Act 1949, s 7(1).
3. Cf Copyright, Designs and Patents Act 1988, ss 16(2) (copyright) and s 226(3) (design right). See, further, para **26.1** below.
4. *Thermos Ltd v Aladdin Sales and Marketing Ltd* [2000] FSR 402; appeal dismissed (10 May 2001, unreported).
5. Registered Designs Act 1949, s 1B(6)(a), see para **24.7** above. The court's approach to novelty determination. as developed in *Household Articles Ltd's Registered Design* [1998] FSR 676 is likely to prove helpful under the 1949 Act as amended.
6. Registered Designs Act 1949, s 8.

Defences to infringement

24.9 Section 7A(2) lists a number of activities that do not infringe a registered design. These include private and non-commercial acts, experiments, fair and acknowledged[1] reproduction in teaching or citation and uses related to visiting ships or aircraft. The free movement of goods within the European Economic Area is preserved by sub-section 7A(5), which ensures that a product previously marketed within the EEA by the owner of the design or with his consent does not infringe by further circulation in the UK. The need for spare parts to match the product to which they are fitted is recognised by sub-section 7A(5), which negates infringement in the context of repair.

1. Registered Designs Act 1949, s 7A(3).

Design right (unregistered)

24.10 This internationally anomalous[1] right was introduced in 1988 for qualifying designs created on or after 1 August 1989. 'Design' is defined[2] as meaning 'the design of any aspect of the shape or configuration (whether internal or external) of the whole or part of an article'. Surface decoration is excluded. This may be two-dimensional decoration, such as a painted design. It may also be relief embellishment, as in *Mark Wilkinson Furniture Ltd v Woodcraft Designs (Radcliffe) Ltd,*[3] where decorative grooves on kitchen units were held to be 'surface decoration'. However, in *Parker v Tidball,*[4] holes punched through the leather of cases for mobile telephones were held not to be 'surface decoration'. The design must be specific, a method or principle of construction is not protected by design right.[5] In *A Fulton Co Ltd v Grant Barnett Ltd,*[6] Park J held that the claimant's rectangular 'Miniflat' umbrella case was a shape produced by the method of construction, it was a design and not the method of construction as such. Also excluded from design right are features of shape or configuration which enable the article to fit on to, into, around or against another for functional purposes – the 'must-fit' exception.[7] Thus the contours of an exhaust pipe which enable it to fit snugly and aero-dynamically under a motor car will not be protected by design right. 'Must-match' features are excluded – those dependent upon the appearance of another article of which the article is intended by the designer to form an integral part. Accordingly car door panels will not enjoy design right as separate components, since they are intended to form a coherent design when connected to the rest of the car. However, this exception was not applied to the 'modular' kitchen units in *Mark Wilkinson Furniture.*[8]

1. A similar concept appears in the European Commission's proposals on design protection, the possibility of registering a Community Design is to be supplemented by an unregistered design right to protect a design for a period of three years: see OJ 1994 C29/20, art 12, an amended version of which was adopted in 2000: COM (2000) 660.
2. Copyright, Designs and Patents Act 1988, s 213(2).
3. [1998] FSR 63; see C Skyrme and I Rosenblatt '*Mark Wilkinson Furniture v Woodcraft Designs (Radcliffe) Ltd*' [1998] EIPR 111.
4. [1997] FSR 680.
5. See U Suthersanen 'Exclusions to Design Protection – a New Paradigm' in J A L Sterling, ed, *Intellectual Property and Market Freedom* (1997), Vol 2, Perspectives on Intellectual Property.
6. [2001] RPC 257. For comment see S Ashby 'Protection of Designs: UK Design Right under the Copyright Designs and Patents Act 1988' [2001] EIPR 255.
7. This exception was argued in *Ocular Sciences Ltd v Aspen Vision Care Ltd* [1997] RPC 289 and *Parker v Tidball* [1997] FSR 680. Both decisions are discussed by J Radcliffe and N Caddick in 'Abbreviating the Scope of Design Right' [1997] EIPR 534 and by L Bently and A Coulthard 'From the Commonplace to the Interface' [1997] EIPR 401. See, also, references at n 6 above.
8. Above, n 3.

24.11 Design right is an automatic right; like copyright, it springs into being when a qualifying design is created. The qualification provisions are more limited[1] than for copyright. In order for design right to be enjoyed, the design must be connected with the UK in an appropriate way. That requirement is satisfied if the designer is a citizen or resident of the UK, another member state of the European Community or a country which affords reciprocal protection to British designs.[2] Alternatively the design's commissioner or the designer's employer may qualify the design for protection.[3] Lastly, by being marketed for the first time in one of the countries mentioned, the design may gain the protection of design right.[4] However, many designs, for example those designed and first marketed in the USA, do not qualify.[5] The duration of design right depends upon when the design is exploited commercially. It expires upon the earlier of *either* fifteen years from the end of the calendar year in which the design was first recorded or incorporated into an article *or* ten years from the end of the calendar year in which articles made to the design were first made available for sale or hire, anywhere in the world, by or with the licence of the design right owner.[6]

1. But see extension powers in Copyright, Designs and Patents Act 1988, s 221, to comply with international obligations, eg Paris Convention, n 1 to para **28.5**.
2. Copyright, Designs and Patents Act 1988, ss 255-256.
3. Ibid, s 219.
4. Ibid, s 220.
5. *Mackie Designs Inc v Behringer Specialised Studio Equipment (UK) Ltd* [1999] RPC 717; R Spavin 'the Absence of Effective UK Protection for Non-European Designs under the Copyright Designs and Patents Act 1988' [2000] EIPR 30.
6. Copyright, Designs and Patents Act 1988, s 216. D Bainbridge criticises the duration of design right as being too short, in his opinion 'Why the Design Right is Failing Innovators' [1999] EIPR 423.

Originality

24.12 To qualify for design right the design must be 'original'. This is elaborated in section 213(4) which provides that a design is not 'original' if it is commonplace in the design field in question at the time of its creation. In *C & H Engineering v Klucznik*[1] this was held to be a requirement in addition to the copyright test of 'not copied'. In *Ocular Sciences Ltd v Aspen Vision Care Ltd,*[2] Laddie J observed:

> 'Any design which is trite, trivial, common or garden, hackneyed or of the type which would excite not particular attention in those in the relevant art is likely to be commonplace.'

He went on to point out that commonplace features may be put together in an original combination, a point confirmed by the Court of Appeal in *Farmers Build Ltd v Carier Bulk Materials Handling Ltd.*[3] In *Farmers Build*, Mummery LJ gave guidance as to how originality should be assessed for design right. First, comparison should be made at the time of creation of the relevant design and with other designs in the same field.[4] Second, the design must be original in the usual copyright sense. Third, the Court assesses the degree of similarity between the claimant's design and others in the field.[5] This is done objectively possibly with the help of expert evidence. If the design is very similar to others in the field, it is likely to be commonplace, if not copied. However, the differences which take a design beyond the commonplace may be quite subtle.[6]

1. [1992] FSR 421.
2. [1997] RPC 289.
3. [1999] RPC 461. N Caddick and J Racliffe, 'When is a Design Commonplace?' [1999] EIPR 264.
4. In *Scholes Windows Ltd v Magnet Ltd* [2000] FSR 432, the decorative horns used by Victorian carpenters to embellish sash windows were still commonplace a century later.
5. *Guild v Eskander* [2001] FSR 645.
6. Also noted by the judges in *Scholes Windows Ltd v Magnet Ltd*, above, n 4, and *A Fulton Co Ltd v Grant Barnett Ltd,* para **24.10**, n 6.

Infringement

24.13   Design right preserves to its owner the exclusive right to reproduce the design, exactly or substantially, for commercial purposes – making articles to the design or making a design document for the purpose of manufacture.[1] Design right is a relative monopoly, dependent upon proof of copying, or at least a strong inference of copying. Where design right subsists in part of an article, the phraseology of section 226 tends to encourage the courts to compare the whole of the defendant's article with the claimant's.[2] This was the case in *C & H Engineering v Klucznik*, where Aldous J seems to have applied a test more akin to the 'difference' test familiar from infringement of registered designs.[3] This may be limiting the scope of design right too far. In *Electronic Techniques (Anglia) Ltd v Critchley*,[4] Laddie J deemed it unlikely that designs were intended only to be protected by design right in relation to precisely the same type of article. However, a design might have different impact if applied to a different article. Doing or authorising[5] these acts constitutes infringement. Once infringing articles come into being, commercially importing, possessing or dealing with them will infringe if the doer knows or has reason to believe that they are infringing articles.[6] There are a number of provisions which limit the monopoly conferred upon the design right owner. Licences are to be available as of right during the last five years of design right term,[7] the Crown may use designs for defence and health service purposes or in emergencies[8,9] and compulsory licences may be granted after an adverse report of the

Competition Commission.[10] Anything which is an infringement of copyright does not infringe design right,[11] so copyright and design right provide exclusive remedies. This would not matter too much if the ownership provisions were identical. However that is not the case.

1. Copyright, Designs and Patents Act 1988, s 226.
2. D Bainbridge 'Why the Design Right is Failing Innovators' [1999] EIPR 423.
3. [1992] FSR 421. See B Turner 'A True Design Right: *C & H Engineering v F Klucznik & Sons*' [1993] 1 EIPR 24, U Suthersanen 'Pig Fenders "Commonplace"' Managing Intellectual Property, Jan/Feb 1993, p 35.
4. [1997] FSR 401.
5. See paras **26.1** ff for the meaning of 'authorise'.
6. Copyright, Designs and Patents Act 1988, s 227. In A *Fulton Co Ltd v Grant Barnett* [2001] RPC 257, the defendant's awareness of a related design registration was 'reason to believe'. See S Ashby 'Protection of Designs' [2001] EIPR 255.
7. Ibid, s 237, a provision criticised by D Bainbridge 'Why the Design Right is Failing Innovators' [1999] EIPR 423. During this period an unlicensed defendant will not be restrained by injunction if he undertakes subsequently to take a licence: s 239.
8. Ibid, ss 240-244.
9. And see Registered Designs Act 1949, s 12 and Sch 1 (defence and emergencies).
10. See para **14.23** above.
11. Copyright, Designs and Patents Act 1988, s 236.

First ownership of design right and registered designs

24.14   The author of an original work is first owner of copyright,[1] subject to two exceptions. First, if the work is created in the course of employment, copyright belongs to the employer. Second, it is open to the author to make a prospective assignment, vesting copyright in, for example, a person who commissions the work before it is created. There are no special provisions which vest copyright in a commissioner for value who pays for creation of the work.[2] In the case of designs, however, design right and the right to apply for registration will vest in a commissioner who pays for the design to be created.[3] Next in priority comes the designer's employer and last comes the creator or author of the design. Where more than one person contributes to the creation of a design, authorship and hence ownership may be disputed. In deciding disputes between contributors of ideas and those who translate the ideas into a particular expression, the court might use the copyright paradigm, whereby the one who gives expression is regarded as the author.[4] Alternatively the contributor of creative concept might be given the status of 'author', by analogy with patent cases.[5] Aldous J tended towards a patent model in *C & H Engineering v Klucznik*,[6] whereas in *Farmers Build Ltd v Carier Bulk Materials Handling Ltd*[7] the court rejected an argument that contributors of ideas were joint authors. In *Parker v Tidball*,[8] the judge adopted the approach that someone contributing a significant degree of skill and labour to the design process might be a joint author even if they did not contribute to its fixation. Although the statutory provisions do not favour the designer, design right can be prospectively assigned,[9] so that it is in theory open for a designer to agree contrary terms with a commissioner (or employer).

1. For more details, see paras **11.12** and **12.26** above.
2. See *Ray v Classic FM plc* [1998] FSR 622, where the radio station was not assignee but merely licensee of copyright in commissioned work.
3. Copyright, Designs and Patents Act 1988, s 215; Registered Designs Act 1949, s 2. Provided the commission is for money or money's worth, the courts are reluctant to consider whether the consideration for creation of the design is adequate: *Farmers Build Ltd v Carier Bulk Materials Handling Ltd*, para **24.12**, n 3.
4. See paras **11.12** and **11.14**.
5. See paras **6.4-6.5**.
6. [1992] FSR 421, *obiter*.
7. Above, n 3.
8. [1997] FSR 680, referring to *Cala Homes (South) Ltd v McAlpine* [1995] FSR 818.
9. Copyright, Designs and Patents Act 1988, s 223.

Cumulative or exclusive protection?

24.15   As may be seen from the table on pp 376-377, copyright, design right and design registration do overlap in scope, so that an industrial design may be protected by more than one right. A colour or relief pattern to be applied to the surface of a teapot may be protected by copyright and design registration (if a design drawing exists and if the design is new and has individual character). The new and unusual shape of a teapot may be protected by design right and by a registered design, indeed section 3(3) of the Registered Designs Act 1949, as amended, states that an application for registration shall be made by the person claiming to be the owner of national design right.[1] Copyright and design right may co-exist but infringement of copyright ousts infringement of design right.[2] The possibility of dual protection has provoked mixed judicial response. In *Werner Motors Ltd v Gamage*,[3] the Court of Appeal rejected the argument that a product could not be protected by both patent and registered design. However in *Catnic Components v Hill and Smith*,[4] Whitford J held that publication of a patent specification disentitled the patentee from relying upon copyright in drawings included in the patent specification. This finding was not disturbed upon appeal in *Catnic*, although in subsequent cases judges have distinguished or refused to follow *Catnic*.[5] Since the various rights each protect a rather different aspect of industrial design, it is submitted that cumulative protection, where it occurs, is desirable.[6] Overlapping is preferable to *lacunae*, which are often unforeseen. It is clear from the design directive that design registration should be available in parallel with other rights, including copyright.[7]

1. If such claim is inaccurate, the true owner may apply for a declaration of invalidity of the registration: Registered Designs Act 1949, ss 11ZA and ZB
2. See para **24.13** above.
3. (1904) 21 RPC 621 at 629.
4. [1982] RPC 183.
5. Eg *Wham-O Manufacturing Co v Lincoln Industries Ltd* [1982] RPC 281 (NZ), *Gardex Ltd v Sorata Ltd* [1986] RPC 623 (Falconer J).
6. For a European viewpoint see H Cohen Jehoram [1989] 3 EIPR 83. Prof Cohen Jehoram has been a leading proponent of the view that design is best protected by copyright. See, also, H Cohen Jehoram 'The EC Green Paper on the Legal Protection of Industrial Design' [1993] EIPR 75; J Lahore [1992] EIPR 428; A Kur 'The Green Paper's Design Approach – What's Wrong with It' [1993] EIPR 374.
7. Directive 98/71/EC on the legal protection of design, arts 16 and 17.

Semiconductor topographies

24.16 A semiconductor chip is a small piece of mineral, usually silicon or gallium arsenide, upon which is etched an electronic circuit (a 'mask work') which, like the traditional circuit-board, can obtain certain end results by means of the regulation and redirection of electrical impulses which are passed through it. The chip may contain a computer program, or may contain nothing more than a storage facility for information to be deposited in it until it is either moved elsewhere or erased. In the United States the semiconductor chip was accorded *sui generis* protection on the assumption that it was not within the true ambit of either patent or copyright protection.[1] The Semiconductor Chip Protection Act 1984 provided for the protection of all chips registered at the United States Copyright Office, protection lasts for ten years from the date of registration or from the date of first commercial exploitation, whichever is the earlier. Exact copying and unauthorised importation are prohibited, but the 'reverse engineering' of a chip so as to produce a new and non-identical mask work is not. Since the US statute only offered protection to US nationals and to nationals of states offering equivalent protection to US nationals, it was not surprising that the US promptly became a model to be emulated by legislatures in the European Community and further afield, including Japan. The European Community issued a harmonisation directive to which the current British response is a statutory instrument[2] which provides for the protection of topographies under the general regime, *mutatis mutandis*, of design right. Duration of design right in topographies is fifteen years (or ten years from the end of the year in which the first sale or hire was made, if that fifteen year period has not yet expired).[3] As in the US, reverse engineering of other people's chips in order to evaluate or analyse them does not constitute an infringing act.[4] If the 'reverse engineer' proceeds to develop the chip, devoting sufficient creative input to produce a further original, if derivative, chip, the latter will not infringe the earlier topography right.[5]

1. See R Hart and C Reed 'Design right and semiconductor chip protection', ch 6 in C Reed and J Engel (eds) 'Computer Law' (4th edn, 1993) at pp 166-169.
2. Design Right (Semiconductor Topographies) Regulations 1989 (SI 1989/1100), replacing the Semiconductor Products (Protection of Topography) Regulations 1987.
3. Ibid, reg 6(1).
4. Ibid, reg 8(1).
5. Ibid, reg 8(1) and (4).

The Community Design

24.17 Harmonisation of many aspects of national design laws of EC Member States has now been achieved by Directive 98/71/EC. However, the existence of separate national rights and the possibility of their being in different ownership are still regarded as obstacles to the free movement of goods within the Single Market.[1] The European legislators are still working on a draft Community Design Regulation.[2] In November 2000, political agreement was reached on all substantive aspects of the proposal except for one thorny question – the language regime for design registration at the Office for Harmonisation in the Internal Market in Alicante. The proposed Regulation provides for Community-wide protection for the same range of design as in the Directive, and hence the UK Registered Designs Act 1949, as amended.[3] The potential for protection of a design by registration, for a five-year term renewable to a total of 25 years,[4] is to be reinforced by a short-term unregistered design right to prevent copying.[5] The term of three years for unregistered design right was agreed at an early stage, but the event triggering commencement of the term proved more intractable. Since the term is relatively short, three years from creation of the design would barely suffice to protect many designs for a reasonable period after market launch. Consequently, the legislators preferred a point later than creation – that of availability of the design to the public, whether by publication, exhibition or use in trade. This has the virtue of corresponding to the start of the grace period for design registration already laid down by the Directive. However, it begs the question as to how a design should be protected by the Community prior to disclosure to the public. Luckily, Community design rights are without prejudice to other forms of protection at the Community or national level,[6] such as unregistered design right, trade mark rights, patents, utility models, typefaces, 'civil liability'[7] or unfair competition. The applicant for registration of Community design may ask for deferment of publication, for 30 months.[8]

1. Amended proposal for a Council Regulation on Community Design COM(2000) 660; [2000] OJ C248/3, recital 4.
2. An earlier (amended) draft was published at OJ 1994 C29/20. For commentary on the obstacles to Community design legislation, see A Horton 'Industrial Design Law: the Future for Europe' [1991] EIPR 442; A Horton 'European Design Law and the Spare Parts Dilemma' [1994] EIPR 51.
3. Art 3 of the draft regulation defines 'design' and 'product' in terms discussed above at paras **24.5-24.6**.
4. Arts 13 and 13a of the draft regulation.
5. Ibid, art 12.
6. Ibid, art 100.
7. The basis of 'concurrence déloyale' in France.
8. Art 52 of the draft regulation. The usual publication of registration will be limited to the fact of deferment and the identity of the proprietor, but will not disclose details of the design itself.

24.18 Art 84 of the draft Regulation requires Member States to designate courts of first instance – 'as limited a number as possible' – to act as Community Design Courts in hearing disputes as to infringement and validity. The Brussels Convention on civil jurisdiction and judgments[1] applies.[2] As well as findings of infringement, a court properly seised may make a declaration of invalidity which is binding for the Community as a whole. Invalidity proceedings may also be brought in the Office.[3] If one of the various initiatives to create a European Intellectual Property Court is successful, the resulting tribunal will be available to hear design disputes.[4] Pending availability of Community-wide rights, designers may consider using the revised mechanism of the Hague Convention on the International Registration of Designs to seek protection in those EC member states which also belong to the Convention.[5]

1. Convention on Jurisdiction and Enforcement of Judgments in Civil and Commercial Matters, Brussels, 27 September 1968 and its successor, Reg 44/2001, [2001] OJ L12/1.
2. Art 83 of the draft regulation.
3. Ibid, art 56.
4. See para **9.19**.
5. J Phillips 'International Design Protection – Who Needs It?' [1993] EIPR 431; U Suthersanen *Design Law in Europe* (2000) Ch 23.

Chapter 25

The protection of plant varieties

Introduction

25.1 The creation of new plant forms is an intellectual feat of great significance for at least two reasons. Where it involves the production of a new food crop it increases mankind's options for feeding its ever-increasing population, and may do so by techniques of genetic manipulation which combine the virtues, or minimise the weaknesses, of pre-existing strains; while the establishment of new ornamental flower strains enhances our aesthetic appreciation. From this it can be seen that a new plant variety can be analogised to an industrially applicable invention or to a work of aesthetic design, which would lead one to suppose that it should be protectable either by taking out patent protection or by reliance on the laws of copyright and designs. Perhaps curiously, this has not been so.

25.2 Even in the heyday of copyright protection for useful products,[1] no attempt seems to have been made to use copyright in drawings of a plant or flower to prevent copying of the new variety depicted. It seems unlikely that design right[2] or design registration[3] would be available to protect the appearance of a new plant or flower. As for patents, patent law both in the UK and in the other European Patent Convention countries explicitly excludes from patentability:

> '... any variety of animal or plant or any essentially biological process for the production of animals or plants, not being a microbiological process or the product of such a process.'[4]

This seemed to prevent, unequivocally, the patenting of plant varieties but the reality was ambiguous, partly because the terms 'essentially biological process' and 'microbiological process' were not defined[5] and also because it is possible that the *product* of a microbiological process is itself a new plant variety.[6] A related question is whether a plant or animal whose characteristics have been altered by genetic engineering[7] is a 'variety'. The European Patent Office granted a patent application relating to a 'transgenic' mammal,[8] construing 'variety'

389

narrowly. These questions have been addressed in Directive 98/44/ EC on the legal protection of biotechnological inventions.[9] This has taken effect by implementation in the patent laws of EC Member States[10] and by incorporation of relevant provisions in the Implementing Regulations of the European Patent Office.[11] 'Variety' has a definition in relation to plant breeders' rights,[12] and this definition was adopted in the 'biotech' directive.[13] The exception of plant varieties from patent protection arose originally from a provision against cumulative protection in the International Convention for the Protection of New Varieties of plants.[14] That exception has been removed from the latest revision.[15] Although plant varieties remain unpatentable, elucidating the meaning of 'variety' in patent law has removed uncertainty. Furthermore, the phrase 'essentially biological process' has now been defined as 'a process for the production of animals and plants which consists entirely of natural phenomena such as crossing and selection'.[16] Finally, we may note that the protection conferred by a process patent resulting in biological material[17] with specific characteristics extends not only to the direct product of the process but to subsequent propagations of that material which possess those same characteristics.[18] This means that 'farmers' privilege' and other defences relating to plant breeders' right[19] had to be introduced into the patent system.[20]

1. See para **24.2** above.
2. See para **24.10** above.
3. See para **24.6** above.
4. Patents Act 1977, Sch A2, para 3(f); European Patent Convention, art 53(b).
5. In *Lubrizol Genetics Inc* 1988 T320/87, [1990] EPOR 173, an EPO Technical Board of Appeal took the view that a non-microbiological plant breeding process was more than 'essentially biological' and hence patentable.
6. See, eg, A Christie 'Patents for plant innovation' [1989] 11 EIPR 394.
7. For an extensive description of processes involved in reproducing a naturally occurring protein by genetic engineering, see *Genentech Inc's Patent* [1989] RPC 147.
8. *Onco-mouse/HARVARD* [1992] 10 OJ EPO 590, [1990] EPOR 4. Inventions which concern plants or animals may be patented if the technical feasibility of the invention is not confined to a particular plant or animal variety: Patents Act 1997, Sch A2, para 4; Directive 98/44/EC, art 4.2.
9. [1998] OJ L213/13. M Llewelyn 'The Legal Protection of Biotechnological Inventions: an Alternative Approach' [1997] EIPR 115; J Funder 'Rethinking patents for plant innovation' [1999] EIPR 551; M Llewelyn 'The Patentability of Biological Material: Continuing Contradiction and Confusion' [2000] EIPR 191.
10. In the UK by the Patents Regulations 2000 (SI 2000/2037) with effect from 28 July 2000. Provisions on biotechnological inventions are consolidated in Sch A2.
11. New Ch VI, Rules 23b-e, in force from 1 September 1999, inserted by decision of the Administrative Council of the European Patent Office.
12. See para **25.4** below.

13. Art 2(3), by reference to art 5 of Regulation EC No 2100/94 on Community Plant Variety Rights; incorporated in Patents Act 1977, Sched A2, para 11.
14. Known as the UPOV (Union pour la Protection des Obtentions Végétales, or Union for the Protection of Plant Varieties) Convention, of 2 December 1961 and subsequently revised.
15. Geneva, 19 March 1991. B Greengrass ' The 1991 Act of the UPOV convention' [1991] EIPR 466.
16. Patents Act 1997, Sch A2, para 11; Directive 98/44/EC, art 2.2. 'Microbiological process' has been defined (ibid) as 'any process involving or performed upon or resulting in microbiological material', a definition which adds little to our understanding of the phrase.
17. Itself defined as 'any material containing genetic information and capable of reproducing itself or being reproduced in a biological system': Patents Act 1977, s 130, as amended by the Patents Regulations 2000 (SI 2000/2037), Reg 7.
18. Patents Act 1977, Sch A2, para 8; see also paras 7 and 9 in relation to product patents.
19. See para **25.7.**
20. Patents Act 1977, s 60(5)(g)-(h) and Sch A1; Directive 98/44/EC, art 11.

25.3 The relationship between the patent system and that of plant breeders' rights was placed under great strain by developments in biotechnology. European Community secondary legislation was drafted in the hope both of harmonising the two systems and of extending protection for biological and microbiological innovation. Unusually, the Community did not attempt to harmonise national plant variety laws by directive. This was probably sensible, given the climatic variations within the EU, the need for plant breeders' right protection systems to test varieties and the existing cooperation between some national offices in relation to testing. The Regulation on Community Plant Variety rights[1] was promulgated in such a way as to prevent cumulation with national plant breeders' rights or with patent protection.[2] The United Kingdom had been the first to ratify the UPOV Convention of 1961 under the guise of the Plant Varieties and Seeds Act 1964, later amended by the Plant Varieties Act 1983.[3] These relatively recent Acts represented the first conscious recognition by Parliament of plant varieties as a separate subject for legal protection, even though inventions and authors' works have been protected in one form or another for hundreds of years. Considering that the selective breeding of plant and animal strains is an ancient act,[4] it is surprising that plant breeding took so long to obtain legal recognition and that the creation of new animal varieties, at least in the UK,[5] remains to be accorded legal protection *per se*. The probable reasons for this late development are (i) the relatively recent advent of sophisticated technology for the breeding and testing of new plant strains, (ii) recognition of seeds and plant cultures as a commercial market of their own, and not merely as a supplementary market which served the primary markets for crops, and (iii) a certain degree of inhibition against the granting of even temporary proprietary rights in the products of a form of intellectual activity which so closely resemble the role of an omnipotent deity in the creation of the world.[6]

1. Council Regulation (EC) No 2100/94 of 27 July 1994 on Community Plant Variety Rights OJ [19944] L227/1. For a critical account of an earlier draft, see M Llewelyn, 'Future Prospects for Plant Breeders' Rights within the European Community' [1989] 9 EIPR 303. The Community Plant Variety Office has been established at Angers, France. Applications may be made directly to that Office or via national offices by persons with standing within the EC or under the UPOV Convention. The Office's website at www.cpvo.eu.int describes the administrative arrangements for obtaining Community plant breeders' rights.
2. Art 92 renders national plant breeders' rights and patents ineffective where a Community plant variety right may be relied upon. However, a national plant breeders' right does not have to be surrendered if Community protection is later obtained. See also M Llewelyn, n 1.
3. See G Dworkin 'The Plant Varieties Act 1983' [1983] EIPR 270.
4. See eg *Genesis*, ch 30, vs 31-43.
5. Cf USA: *Diamond v Chakrabarty* 65 L Ed 2d 144 (1980); Australia: *Rank Hovis McDougall Ltd's Application* (1976) 46 AOJP 3915; and see para **25.2** above.
6. For criticisms of plant variety protection , see C Correa 'Biological Resources and Intellectual Property Rights' [1992] EIPR 154; S Verma 'TRIPs and Plant Variety Protection in Developing Countries' [1995] EIPR 281.

What is a plant variety?

25.4   The current statutory definition[1] is based on Art 1(iv) of the revised UPOV Convention[2] and defines 'variety' as:

'a plant grouping within a single botanical taxon of the lowest known rank, which grouping, irrespective of whether the conditions for the grant of a breeder's right ...are met, can be
  – defined by the expression of the characteristics resulting from a given genotype or combination of genotypes,
  – distinguished from any other plant grouping by the expression of at least one of the said characteristics and
  – considered as a unit with regard to its suitability for being propagated unchanged.'

A closely similar definition was adopted in the Community Plant Variety Right Regulation.[3] A plant which cannot be reproduced by following its inventor's instructions,[4] rather like an invention which cannot be put into action through following the information contained in its specification, is a 'variant' but not a variety and cannot be protected.

1. Plant Varieties Act 1997, s 1(3); J Ardley 'The New United Kingdom Law on Plant Variety Rights' [1997] Bioscience Law Rev 146.
2. Para **25.2**, nn 14 and 15 above.
3. Reg 2100/94, art 5.2.
4. Supplemented by commercial practice; see eg *Moulin Winter Wheat* [1985] FSR 283.

What can be protected?

25.5   However great its merit, no plant could be protected under the 1964 and 1983 Acts if its genus or species did not fall within the category of any one of some fifty-odd 'schemes' laid down by the relevant minister. The justification of these 'schemes' was that each could be tailor-made to suit the biological and commercial requirements of plant varieties which fell therein so that, for example, the terms of protection could be varied from 20 to 30 years.[1] Under the Plant Varieties Act 1997, all genera and species of plant may be protected,[2] for maximum periods of time which have been set at 30 years for potatoes,[3] trees and vines, and 25 years for other plants.[4] However, the Act and Regulations allow the Minister to increase the term in specific cases, up to 35 and 30 years respectively.[5] If a variable term is accepted for plants, it should be equally applicable to patent law too, because the requirements of different industrial sectors, and the ease or difficulty with which they re-coup development expenses and derive monopoly profits can also be 'tailored'. Indeed, on a wider consideration of intellectual property, 'tailoring' may be seen as an ideal compromise between having (as we now do) one set of laws to govern all cases and having (as has been advocated[6]) an ad hoc evaluation of each monopoly claim on its own merits.

1. Plant Varieties Act 1983, s 1.
2. Plant Varieties Act 1997, s 1(2); UPOV, art 3. Reg 2100/94, art 5.1 also refers to hybrids.
3. See Council Regulation EC No 2470/96 providing for an extension of the terms of the Community plant variety right in respect of potatoes, OJ [1996] L335/10.
4. Plant Varieties Act 1997, s 11(1); Reg 2100/94, art 19.1.
5. Plant Varieties Act 1997, s 11(2); Reg 2100/94, art 19.2.
6. See eg W Kingston 'An "Investment" Patent' [1981] EIPR 207.

Criteria of protectability

25.6   Once it is shown that a plant variety exists, it further remains to establish the following technical criteria for protection:

25.6 *The protection of plant varieties*

(i) *The plant variety must be new*[1]   The concept of novelty in plant-breeding terms is very much narrower than the absolute concept of novelty which pertains in patent law[2] since the only way a plant variety will be held *not* to be novel is if propagating or harvested material of the variety has been sold or otherwise disposed of, with the consent of the applicant. There is a 'grace period' of one year within the UK and four years outside the UK.[3] Commercialisation of the variety during the grace period does not destroy novelty. If competing applicants for the same plant variety have bred or discovered and developed the variety independently, the first to file gains precedence. As between such applications made on the same day, the earlier to gain the right to apply will prevail.[4] If the requirement of novelty is adhered to in patent law on the basis that it is wrong in principle to grant a private monopoly in respect of that which is already, in theory, publicly available, it is difficult to see what principle is served, or what public interest protected, by so weak a requirement of novelty; and if the standard of novelty in plant variety law is felt to be the more desirable, in that it protects the applicant more generously against the consequences of his own non-commercial publication or disclosure of his product, then should not a similar standard be adopted for patent law? The concept of commercial rather than absolute novelty is retained in the revised UPOV Convention and is used in the Regulation texts.[5]

(ii) *The plant variety must be distinct*[6]   As the text of the statute says, the applicant's variety must be:

'...clearly distinguishable by one or more characteristics which are capable of a precise description from any other variety whose existence is a matter of common knowledge at the time of application.'

The description of distinctness is thus analogous to the claims in a patent specification, which serve to distinguish the applicant's invention from the prior art. The reference to 'common knowledge' as the measuring stick of distinctiveness may be seen as occupying an inexact correspondence to the patent law notion of 'prior art'. Distinctive factors, it should be noted, include colour, shape, leaf-length and mildew-resistance[7] but not, it seems, winter-hardiness[8] (which is difficult to verify) and, it is suggested by one commentator,[9] characteristics which can only be subjectively verifiable such as taste and smell. It should be noted that there is no requirement akin to the 'inventive step' necessary to patent an invention, although a 'minimum distance' from known varieties has been advocated as a spur to development.[10]

(iii) *The plant variety must be uniform*   The absolute identity of all plants belonging to the new variety is not required, even if it were possible to achieve it; instead, it is a degree of uniformity, in the characteristics which distinguish the variety, which might be expected from the particular features of its propagation.[11]

(iv) *The plant variety must be stable*[12]   The relationship between stability and uniformity is likely to be a consequence of a plant's inherent instability.[13] Stability is, however, a more long-term requirement than uniformity: it is that a variety must remain true to its description even after repeated propagation or at the end of each cycle of propagation.[14] It is a matter of common sense that characteristics which distinguish the variety must remain stable.

Unlike the Patent Office in respect of inventions, the Plant Variety Rights Office[15] tests all the plant variety applications which are made to it;[16] if any of the four criteria listed above are found to be unsatisfied, the monopoly right will be refused, nullified[17] or cancelled.[18] Since all applications are tested, there is no need to impose a requirement, similar to that of the Patents Act 1977 section 1(1), of 'industrial applicability'.

1. Plant Varieties Act 1997, s 4(2)(d) and Sch 2, Pt I, Para 4.
2. See para **5.2** above.
3. Plant Varieties Act 1997, Sch 2, Pt I, para 4(2) and (3). The grace period outside the UK is six years for trees or vines.
4. Ibid, Sch 2, Pt II, para 5. There is also a 12 month international priority system, whereby an application may be treated as being made on the date of an EC or Convention filing within the previous 12 months: ibid, paras 6 and 7.
5. Arts 6 and 10 respectively.
6. Plant Varieties Act 1997 s 4(2)(a) and Sch 2, Pt I, para 1.
7. See eg *Maris Druid Spring Barley* [1968] FSR 559.
8. *Daehnfeldt v Controller of Plant Varieties* [1976] FSR 95.
9. See Noel Byrne *The Scope of Intellectual Property Protection for Plants and Other Life Forms* (1989) para 6.1.
10. N Byrne, n 6 above, para 16.
11. Plant Varieties Act 1997, s 4(2)(b) and Sch 2, Pt I, para 2; *Moulin Winter Wheat* [1985] FSR 283. See also art 8 of Reg 2100/94.
12. Plant Varieties Act 1997, s 4(2)(c) and Sch 2, Pt I, para 3.
13. See *Zephyr Spring Barley* [1967] FSR 576.
14. See para **25.9** below.
15. Or a sister office in another country; mention of this and other administrative matters may be found in web pages on plant breeders' rights at www.defra.gov.uk, where visitors may consult the *Plant Breeders' Rights Handbook* 1998. Where the Plant Variety Rights Office has not established a suitable testing regime, it may ask the applicant to propose one.
16. Even if it did not, the right owner would have to test it by keeping the new variety going and by giving reproductive material test results or other data to the Controller if required to do so: Plant Varieties Act 1964, ss 3(2), 16. Failure to supply such material or provide information upon request may result in refusal or cancellation of the plant breeder's right: s 3(3) and 22(1)(b).
17. See para **25.9**.
18. See para **25.9**.

25.7 *The protection of plant varieties*

What is the plant breeder's right?

25.7 The holder of a plant breeder's right enjoys an absolute monopoly to sell, offer for sale, otherwise market, import or export or to stock for these purposes the 'propagating material' for his plant variety, and to produce, multiply or condition such material.[1] Allied to this is his duty and exclusive right to apply the registered name to that protected variety.[2] Where the holder dos not have a reasonable opportunity before harvest to exercise his rights, they may be pursued against harvested material[3] and even (in certain cases if prescribed) against products obtained directly from the harvested material.[4] This represents an extension in the scope of plant breeders' rights over the previous statutes.[5] Formerly it was not infringement for a farmer to retain a proportion of one crop as seed for subsequent crops. This 'farmer's privilege' was diminished by revision of the UPOV Convention.[6] The Plant Varieties Act 1997, section 9, contains a number of enabling provisions to support schemes for royalty payments, or 'equitable remuneration' to be paid on farm saved seed, at a rate 'sensibly lower' than for new propagating material. For small farmers, no remuneration may be levied. There are general exceptions to plant breeders' rights: section 8 provides that the rights do not extend to private and non-commercial use, or use for experimental purposes or to develop another variety. These exceptions have their counterparts for patents.[7] Section 10 provides that plant breeders' rights in relation to propagating material are 'exhausted' by marketing the material, but this does not extend to further propagation.

1. Plant Varieties Act 1997, s 6; see *Germinal Holdings Ltd v H R Fell & Sons Ltd* [1993] FSR 343.
2. Ibid, ss 19 and 20.
3. Ibid, s 6(3); UPOV, art 13.
4. Plant Varieties Act 1997, s 6(4). For a system of notices and presumptions relating to these forms of infringement, see ss 14 and 15.
5. Previously certain schemes had more extensive rights, eg in relation to cut blooms.
6. Under art 15(2), this exception is now optional and is subject to the legitimate interest of the plant breeder. For a discussion of this issue, see B Greengrass 'The 1991 Act of the UPOV Convention' [1991] EIPR 466. The 1997 Act follows EC Regulation 2100/94 which made farmers' privilege subject to agricultural species and farm size: art 14.
7. See para **8.8**.

How much does it cost to obtain and maintain plant breeders' rights?

25.8 At the time of writing,[1] application fees for most categories are £275, exceptions being roses (£75) and other decorative varieties.

Standard annual test fees range from £120 (roses) to £745 (cereals). Renewal fees range from £435 to £70, depending on variety.

1. The Plant Breeders' Rights (Fees)(Amendment) Regulations 1999 (SI 1999/1089).

Further legal points to note

25.9 The plant breeder's right is transmissible like any other intellectual property, and may be bought or sold.[1] Where propagation of one variety is dependant upon another, for example a mutant or genetically engineered variety and its parent, the rights may not be assigned separately.[2] There is no provision for the extension of such rights, but they may be surrendered.[3] Plant breeders' rights are vulnerable to cancellation, which may be ordered by the Plant Variety Rights Office if, at any time after a right is granted, continued testing reveals that the strain is unstable or not uniform.[4] The Controller (not Comptroller) of that Office can also terminate a right if it appears that the proprietor is not maintaining the variety.[5] The controller can declare a right null and void *ab initio* if she is satisfied that the variety was not new or distinct,[6] that the subject matter of the right already belonged to someone else,[7] that the variety is not distinct or that the grant was secured through the supply of false information as to uniformity and stability.[8]

1. Plant Varieties Act 1997, s 12.
2. Plant Varieties Act 1997, ss 7 and 12.
3. Ibid, s 22(1)(d).
4. Ibid, s 22(1)(a).
5. Ibid, s 22(1)(b) and (c).
6. Ibid, s 21(1)(a). For retroactive nullity under the UPOV Convention see N Byrne, n 9 to para **25.6** above, at para 15.2.
7. Ibid, s 21(c). Nullity may be avoided by transferring the rights to the person entitled.
8. Ibid, s 21(1)(b).

Patents or plant breeders' rights?

25.10 With the possibility of choice[1] between patents and plant variety rights, much will depend upon user perceptions of the two systems. The patent system being perceived as legalistic and oppressively expensive; the plant breeders' right was designed as an easier option for its users and yet, particularly in the case of firms which employ advanced biotechnological techniques, there is a move afoot to seek the wider protection of the industrial patent. The attractions of a patent, apart from the broader definition of infringement, are that:

(i)   patented microbiological techniques will be protected against all
       types of industrial uses,
(ii)   protection does not depend upon the development of an end-
       product, and
(iii) protection can be granted without the necessity of testing.

Advocates of the patent system may forget, however, that it is not
without its risks. For example, the criteria of novelty and obviousness
are difficult to satisfy and pose a constant threat to the stability of the
granted patent; the Patents Act's compulsory licence provisions would
apply to the right owners,[2] and so would its employee inventions code.[3]
Whatever form of protection is chosen, problems of licensing as
between patentees and plant breeders are likely to arise.[4]

1. See paras **25.2** and **25.3**.
2. Compulsory licensing is in fact available under the Plants Varieties Act 1997,
    s 17.
3. See para **9.8**.
4. See M Llewelyn 'Future Prospects for Plant Breeders' Rights within the
    European Community' [1989] 9 EIPR 303.

25.11   Critics of the patent system, such as William Kingston, propose
reforms for it which would, in fact, draw it closer to the plant rights
systems by:

(i)   making protection contingent upon the existence of a marketable
       product, not on the disclosure of a 'drawing-board' specification,
       and
(ii)   relating the degree of protection more closely to the product's
       market.[1]

If those features of the plant breeders' right do not particularly
commend themselves to their intended users, their incorporation into
the patent system should not be effected without the most careful
consideration.

1. W Kingston 'An "Investment" Patent' [1981] EIPR 207, 'Innovation Patents
    and Warrants' in J Phillips (ed) *Patents in Perspective* (1985).

Chapter 26

Copyright infringement: authorisation and secondary infringement

Authorisation as infringement

26.1 'Copyright', according to section 16(2) of the Copyright, Designs and Patents Act 1988, 'is infringed by a person who without the licence of the copyright owner does, or authorises another to do, any of the acts restricted by copyright'. Those acts – copying the work, issuing copies to the public, performing in public, broadcasting, adapting[1] may lawfully be done only by the owner of that copyright. The meaning of the word 'authorise' in this context for a long time troubled the courts, which drew contradictory conclusions as to its significance. For example in *A & M Records Inc v Audio Magnetics Inc (UK) Ltd*[2] Foster J held that a supplier of blank cassette tapes, despite an advertising campaign in which it alluded to the beneficial results of recording certain well-known copyright works on its own brand of tapes, had not authorised the infringement of the copyright in those works. By contrast, in the Australian case of *Moorhouse and Angus and Robertson (Publishers) Pty Ltd v University of New South Wales*[3] a university made available for use in its library an unsupervised photocopy machine. This machine, which bore no warning as to copyright implications of its use, was used by a student for the purposes of making an infringing copy of a literary work. The university was held by the High Court of Australia to have authorised the infringement on the ground that it had the power to control the use of the machine but failed to take reasonable steps to avoid the infringements of others. What, then, does 'authorise' mean? Let us look at some possible meanings of the word.

1. These forms of 'primary' infringement of copyright are discussed in Ch 13. Authorisation is also a mode of design right infringement see para **24.13** – but not of database right See para **23.23**.
2. [1979] FSR 1.
3. [1976] RPC 151.

'Authorise' as 'to make lawful that which would otherwise be unlawful'

26.2 In this sense of the word only the copyright owner can 'authorise' the use of copyright material, since it is plain that no one but the owner can vest with legitimacy those acts which would otherwise be infringements of a legal right. If this sense of the word were adopted as that intended by Parliament, the authorisation of an infringement, being an act that only the copyright owner could perform, would only be an infringement when it was done by one of two or more joint copyright owners without the consent of his colleague(s). This is clearly not what the legislature intended.

Or purporting to do so

26.3 A slightly wider variant of the above definition was formulated by Atkin LJ in *Falcon v Famous Players Film Co Ltd*:[1] 'to grant or purport to grant a right to do the act complained of'. While, as we have seen, the grant of a right is something that can only be done by its owner, purporting to grant it is something which can only be done by someone who is not the owner and is therefore capable of being regarded as an infringement of the owner's property right. Atkin LJ derived support for his formulation from what he understood to have been the application of the word to the facts by Tomlin J in *Evans v Hulton & Co Ltd*,[2] and from the dictum of Buckley LJ in *Monckton v Pathé Frères Pathephone Ltd*[3] upon which Tomlin J's decision was based. There would appear to be no inherent objection to Atkin LJ's explanation of the word, but it took until 1988 for his decision to gain the approval of the House of Lords;[4] in the meantime several other interpretations of 'authorise' were canvassed and adopted.

1. *Falcon v Famous Players Film Co Ltd* [1926] 2 KB 474 at 499.
2. *Evans v Hulton & Co Ltd* (1924) 131 LT 534.
3. *Monckton v Pathé Frères Pathephone Ltd* [1914] 1 KB 395.
4. In *CBS Songs Ltd v Amstrad Consumer Electronics plc* [1988] RPC 567.

Competing formulations

26.4 In *Evans v Hulton & Co Ltd*,[1] Tomlin J cited the Oxford English Dictionary definition of 'authorise' as 'to give formal approval to, sanction or countenance'. He did not give judicial approval to the dictionary definition, but in subsequent cases [2] a great many judges did. By contrast, in *CBS Inc v Ames Records and Tapes Ltd*[3] the defendants, owners of a chain of record shops, opened a lending library. Subscribers to the library paid an initial subscription fee, plus a small per-record borrowing fee. The economics of the library were such that a member who borrowed records and made pirate tape recordings at home would acquire his copies for substantially less than their retail purchase price. The defendants were well aware of the likelihood of home taping, but did nothing about it. The claimant alleged that this was an 'authorisation' of the infringement of its copyright, but Whitford J disagreed. What the defendants had done, he said, was to enable acts of infringement to take place – but enabling and authorisation are not synonymous, and something more is required before an authorisation has occurred. This reasoning, applied in the *University of New South Wales* case, would clearly have resulted in a different decision, for there the provision of a photocopying machine could well be said to have 'enabled' rather than 'authorised' the infringement. Note that there are torts of enabling infringement, but these are 'secondary' and actionable only upon proof of knowledge.[4]

1. (1924) 131 LT 534.
2. See eg *A & M Records* [1979] FSR 1; *Moorhouse and Angus and Robertson (Publishers) Pty Ltd v University of New South Wales* [1976] RPC 151, and cases cited therein.
3. [1982] Ch 91.
4. See para **26.9**.

The Amstrad decision

26.5   In *CBS Songs Ltd v Amstrad Consumer Electronics plc*,[1] the defendants were manufacturers of high-speed twin deck tape recorders. They promoted the recorders by means of advertisements which stated that purchasers could 'tape tapes at twice the normal speed', 'record from any record and make copies in half the time' and 'make copies of favourite cassettes'; attached to each machine was a notice which informed the purchaser that the recording and playback of certain material may only be possible by permission, referring the purchaser to the Copyright Act 1956 and the Performers' Protection Acts 1958-1972. After a complicated series of skirmishes, the Court of Appeal struck out CBS's writ and statement of claim. CBS appealed to the House of Lords, arguing that Amstrad had infringed copyright by 'authorising' purchasers to infringe; that Amstrad contributed to purchasers' infringement or was jointly liable with purchasers; that Amstrad was negligent in providing purchasers with the means to infringe where it was inevitable that purchasers would do so; that Amstrad had incited purchasers to infringe, which incitement was actionable in the civil courts; and that Amstrad was in breach of an equitable duty to copyright owners. The House of Lords rejected all these arguments, holding that 'authorise' meant 'to grant or purport to grant expressly or by implication the right to do the act complained of'. Amstrad had given purchasers the ability to copy but could not be said to have granted the right to copy or purported to do so.

1. Para **26.3**, n 4, above.

The when and where of authorisation

26.6   *CBS v Amstrad* has been credited with leaving the meaning of authorisation 'tolerably clear'.[1] Authorisation has to refer to specific works, or at least an identifiable class of works, such as a music copyright owner's 'catalogue' of songs. But two issues remained unclear – when is the tort of authorisation complete, and where does authorisation occur? In most cases the exact location does not matter, but if an order is given outside the UK for restricted acts to be performed within the jurisdiction, would the authorisation be actionable here? In *Wilden Pump Engineering Co v Fusfeld*,[2] Whitford J held that an order sent from Germany and accepted in England amounted to an authorisation. It was intended to be acted upon in the UK and was an infringement of UK copyright. In *ABKCO Music & Records Inc v Music Collection Ltd*,[3] the Court of Appeal confirmed that an authorisation abroad, to do acts in this country, was actionable here. From these cases one might infer that an authorisation takes place when acted upon, whether by making an infringing copy or at least by concluding a contract. The latter gains some support from *Pensher Security Door Co Ltd v Sunderland City Council*.[4] In that case, authorisation occurred when the Council accepted a tender, knowing that it involved a close approximation to the claimant's copyright door. However, in *MCA Records Inc v Charly Records Ltd*,[5] Rimer J held that the authorisation tort was complete when authorisation was given – as a 'once-and-for-all event'.[6] This was so even though the authorisation purported to permit a period of exploitation of the copyright work. As a result, some of the acts of authorisation in *MCA v Charly* were 'statute-barred'; having occurred more than six years before proceedings were issued against the defendant concerned. For these acts, the Limitation Act 1980 provided a complete defence. This decision has been criticised,[7] not least because if the authorisation is complete when given, revocation of the authorisation – for example because the authoriser belatedly realises that there is a copyright problem – cannot be effective. In *MCA Records Inc v Charly*, the judge criticised the defendant in question for giving encouragement to a company to continue the infringing course of action after an adverse decision of the Californian court; this went to the question of additional damages.[8]

1.   P Dickens 'When is an Authorisation an Authorisation?: *MCA Records Inc v Charly Records Ltd* [2000] EIPR 339
2.   (1985) 8 IPR 250, [1985] EIPR N-86.
3.   [1995] EMLR 449.
4.   [2000] RPC 249, CA.
5.   [2000] EMLR 743.

6. Ibid at 807
7. P Dickens, n 1; H Laddie et al *The Modern Law of Copyright* (3rd edn, 2000), para 39.20.
8. See para **14.12**.

Joint infringement

26.7   Another possible argument in *MCA v Charly* and *CBS v Amstrad* was that of joint infringement – could the authorising party be held liable as joint tortfeasor with the person who carried out the copying? In neither case was this established. Joint infringers are two or more persons who act in concert with one another pursuant to a common design in infringement. In *CBS v Amstrad* there was no common design. Amstrad were not liable for procuring or inciting infringement, nor in negligence nor equity. The *Amstrad* decision was referred to in a performer's rights case,[1] *Grower v BBC*.[2] The BBC had a recording of a performance by the late Alexis Korner, a popular musician and disc jockey. It had licensed a third party to use the recording subject to obtaining consents from performers and other copyright owners. The licensees made records without the consent of Korner's personal representatives. Scott J rejected the submission that the BBC was a joint tortfeasor with its licensees. In *MCA Records Inc v Charly*[3] there was a finding of authorisation – primary but indirect infringement – but not of joint tortfeasorship with the companies who made the infringing copies. The court also considered the extent to which the director of a company (a shadow director on the facts) could be liable for the company's tort. As Rimer J pointed out, this is the reverse of vicarious liability. The judge reviewed the authorities and held this to be an 'elusive' question, to be decided in each case on the degree of involvement of the director concerned.

1. For rights in performances, see ch 17.
2. [1990] FSR 595.
3. [2000] EMLR 743.

26.8   One might imagine that the ghost of *Moorhouse* had been laid to rest in the United Kingdom by *Amstrad*. But this is not so. Distinguished authors[1] refer to it; librarians act as if *Moorhouse* still represented the law. And there may be at least one respect in which *Moorhouse* can still be applied, because the meaning of 'authorise' in copyright may influence the interpretation of 'permit'.[2] In *Moorhouse*, Gibb J pointed to the fact that in *Adelaide Corpn v Australasian Performing Right Association Ltd*[3] the words 'permit' and 'authorise' were used synonymously. There are indeed reasons why 'authorise' and 'permit' might be treated in this way:

(i) It is not possible to authorise an act without also permitting it, and vice versa, if the words refer not to the doing of an act but to the legal consequences of it. Thus if A authorises B to pick the apples in his orchard he also permits B to pick them. However, the words do not enjoy this close relationship if they are applied to a more physical end: if A authorises B to pick the apples in his orchard but refuses to unlock the orchard gate, he does not permit the doing by B of that which B is authorised to do.

(ii) Both authority and permission may be established by the same proofs, ie by express words or by inference drawn from the conduct of the parties. But this does not render the two words synonymous. As Bankes LJ said in *Performing Right Society Ltd v Ciryl Theatrical Syndicate Ltd*:[4] 'The indifference from which permission or authority is to be inferred is of a very different character...'.

1. Eg W R Cornish 'Intellectual Property' (4th edn, 1999), paras 11-19 and 20.
2. Which appears in s 25 of the Copyright, Designs and Patents Act: see para **26.9**.
3. (1928) 40 CLR 481 at pp 489, 497.
4. [1924] 1 KB 1 at 9.

Secondary infringement of copyright

26.9 As well as primary infringement – doing or authorising the acts restricted by copyright[1] – the Copyright, Designs and Patents Act 1988 specifies other activities which constitute 'secondary' infringement of copyright.[2] There are various forms of secondary infringement, such as importing or dealing commercially with infringing copies, permitting premises to be used for infringing performances, supplying a copy of a film used for infringement. All have one thing in common: actual or constructive knowledge on the part of the infringer, who knew or had reason to believe that the copies were infringing, and so on. The sufficiency of proving constructive knowledge represents an improvement in the position of copyright owners. Under the Copyright Act 1956, secondary infringement was actionable only on proof of actual knowledge by the infringer. The Whitford Committee recommended[3] that where knowledge was material, a claimant should succeed on proof of constructive knowledge. Shortly before the reforms of 1988, Scott J held that a defendant who shut his eyes to the obvious and deliberately refrained from enquiry could not be heard to say that he lacked the requisite knowledge.[4] It should be noted that many types of secondary infringement are criminal offences[5] as well as torts and carry heavy penalties. It seems that a defendant who is possessed of information which suggests that copies, performances and so forth are liable to infringe, cannot shelter behind the reassuring advice of a lawyer.[6]

1. See Ch 13 and paras **26.1-26.6** above.
2. Ss 22-26. Note that authorising these infringements is not actionable.
3. *Copyright and Designs Law* Cmnd 6731 (1977) paras 749(1), 750.
4. *Columbia Picture Industries Inc v Robinson* [1986] FSR 367 at 424.
5. Copyright, Designs and Patents Act 1988, s 107.
6. *ZYX Music Ltd v King* [1997] 2 All ER 129, [1997] EMLR 319, CA.

Dealings with infringing copies

26.10   Copyright is infringed by importing an infringing copy of a work into the United Kingdom, other than for private and domestic use.[1] But the Act only regulates the right to copy in the United Kingdom.[2] The imported copy was presumably manufactured outside the United Kingdom. How then can it be 'infringing'? This is explained by section 27, which provides that an article is an infringing copy not only when its making constituted an infringement of (UK) copyright, but also:

'(3)... if –
(a) it has been or is proposed to be imported into the United Kingdom, and
(b) its making in the United Kingdom would have constituted an infringement of the copyright in the work in question, or a breach of an exclusive licence agreement relating to that work.'

In applying section 27(3)(b) one imagines the person who actually made the copy abroad making it in the UK.[3] If that person is not the UK copyright owner, or his UK licensee, and making the copy would not otherwise be permitted in the UK,[4] the copy is infringing. Further, if the copyright owner has put it out of his power in the UK to make or license legitimate copies by granting an exclusive licence, making the copy in question in the UK would breach the licence agreement, bringing the second limb of section 27(3)(b) into play.[5]

Section 27(5) then goes on to preserve the principle of free movement of goods and services within the European Community by ensuring that section 27(3) does apply to an article which may lawfully be imported as a matter of EC law.[6]

1. Copyright, Designs and Patents Act 1988, s 22.
2. Ibid, s 16(1).
3. *CBS United Kingdom Ltd v Charmdale Record Distributors Ltd* [1981] Ch 91.

4. Eg because it was made for the purpose of research – see s 29 of the Copyright, Designs and Patents Act 1988.
5. In this respect the 1988 Act reverses *CBS v Charmdale*, n 3 above.
6. See ch 27.

26.11 A person who knows or has reason to believe that a copy is infringing, will infringe copyright if, in the course of a business, he possesses it, sells it, lets it for hire, offers or advertises it for sale or hire, exhibits or distributes it, or if he distributes it otherwise than in the course of a business to such an extent as to prejudice the copyright owner.[1]

1. Copyright, Designs and Patents Act 1988, s 23.

Enabling torts

26.12 In the light of the House of Lords' opinions in *CBS v Amstrad*,[1] the 1988 Act has introduced or revised a number of specific torts the commission of which aids a primary infringer. Section 24(1) outlaws the manufacture, import, commercial possession or supply of an article specifically designed or adapted for making copies of a work (where the actor knows or has reason to believe that it is to be used to make infringing copies). A master for pressing CDs would be an obvious example of this type of article. Sending a fax so that an infringing copy will be made at the receiving end is caught by section 24(2). Permitting premises to be used for an infringing public performance is rendered infringing[2] unless the person giving permission believed on reasonable grounds that the performance would not infringe.[3] Section 26 creates a number of forms of secondary infringement which facilitate infringing performances or public showings of works by means of films, sound recordings or other audio-visual media. The projectionist who 'borrows' a film overnight to enable his friends to make pirate videos is liable to be sued under section 26(4).[4]

1. Note 4, para **26.3** above.
2. By s 25(1), provided that the premises are from time to time made available for hire for the purposes of public entertainment.
3. Eg because the person giving the performance had promised to obtain a licence from the Performing Right Society.
4. Cf *R v Lloyd* [1985] QB 829. An advantage of suing in tort rather than relying upon the protection of the criminal law is that the claimant's case of infringement is proved on the balance of probabilities rather than beyond reasonable doubt.

Chapter 27

Intellectual property rights and the European Community

Introduction

27.1　On 1 January 1973[1] the United Kingdom became a member of the European Economic Community (EEC), later retitled the European Community (EC). In 1992, at Maastricht, the Treaty on European Union established a further level of cooperation between EC countries, creating the European Union (EU). The title EC will be used in this chapter. Rationalisation and consolidation of the Treaties was achieved by the Amsterdam Treaty of 1997. The Treaty Establishing the European Economic Community (Treaty of Rome), as amended, is now referred to as the EC Treaty; many of its articles have been renumbered. Some of the main provisions are listed in Table 1, which shows the old and the new numbers. The stated aims of the EC include the harmonisation of national laws[2] and the creation of a unified market,[3] consisting of all member states, within which there are no unjustifiable barriers to free trade.[4] Since the rules of the EC, as a matter of UK[5] and Community[6] law, take precedence over conflicting national law, it is obvious that no description of UK law can be complete if it fails to take into account the impact of any relevant EC law and, in particular, the EC Treaty and the many European Court of Justice decisions and Commission rules which seek to explain and implement it. An example of the powerful and sometimes unexpected effect of EC law on intellectual property is the decision in *Collins v Imtrat*.[7] In that case, what is now Art 12 of the EC Treaty, which prohibits discrimination within the EC on the grounds of nationality, was invoked so as to prevent German performers' right legislation granting rights over performances by German artists while withholding them from nationals of other EC Member States. From time to time other Community rights are invoked in intellectual property matters.[8] In *Metronome Musik GmbH v Music Point Hokamp GmbH*,[9] the European Court of Justice rejected an argument that rental right was inconsistent with a fundamental right of freedom to pursue a trade or profession. In that case, the court balanced freedom of trade with the economic and competitive benefits of copyright protection.

27.1 Intellectual property rights and the European Community

At present the role of the European Court of Justice in intellectual property matters is limited to references on points of Community law,[10] and appeals from decisions of Community Institutions, including the Commission and the Office for Harmonisation in the internal market. These latter are heard by the Court of First Instance, a somewhat misleading title because it does not hear disputes between companies and individuals.[11]

1. The date of coming into force of the European Communities Act 1972.
2. EC Treaty, art 3, particularly 3(h).
3. Ibid, art 2. As of 2001, this market includes Belgium, Germany, France, Italy, Luxemburg, the Netherlands, Denmark, Greece, Spain, Ireland, Portugal, Sweden, Finland and Austria. EC countries plus Iceland, Norway and Liechtenstein constitute the European Economic Area (EEA) and all those countries plus Norway make up the European Free Trade Area (EFTA). Agreements with countries scheduled to join the Common Market, such as Poland, contain many terms which reflect the EC Treaty.
4. Ibid, art 3(c); the phrase 'internal market' used in this article has supplanted the 'common market' of art 2 in common parlance.
5. European Communities Act 1972, s 2.
6. See eg *Algemene Transport-en Expeditie Onderneming van Gend en Loos NV v Nederlands Administratie der Belastingen* 26/62: [1963] ECR 1, ECJ; *Application des Gaz SA v Falks Veritas Ltd* [1974] 2 CMLR 75.
7. [1993] 3 CMLR 773, [1994] FSR 166. See G Dworkin and J A L Sterling 'Phil Collins and the Term Directive' [1994] 5 EIPR 187. For a case in which it was held that favouring nationals of other Member States over home nationals did not contravene the Treaty, see N Mout-Bouwman 'Phil Collins Revisited' [2001] EIPR 100.
8. See J Phillips 'Piranha, Pariah or Partner: The New View of Intellectual Property in Europe' [1998] IPQ 107.
9. [1999] FSR 576.
10. Including those under art 234 of the EC Treaty.
11. Various proposals for the creation of a pan-European Court of first instance for patent and other intellectual property disputes are considered in para **9.21**.

A brief overview of EC competition and 'free movement' law[1]

27.2 The EC Treaty is founded upon the assumption that competition within any given market for goods or services is the most effective way of keeping prices down, of ensuring that industrial output keeps pace with existing consumer demand and of fostering the creation and exploitation of new markets. Market competition itself has a tendency towards that market's self-destruction, as one competing concern succeeds in winning the market from its rivals, and competition can neither be protected from itself nor enhanced by means of competition; for this reason it is accepted that legal rules are desirable in order to establish an artificial economic environment within which competition is preserved, and that these rules should be

Table 1: EC Treaty: selected provisions

Treaty of Rome	EC Treaty, as amended	Provision
Art 6	Art 12	Non-discrimination on ground of nationality
Art 30	Art 28	Free movement – no quantitative restriction on imports
Art 34	Art 29	Free movement – no quantitative restriction on exports
Art 36	Art 30	Free movement – justified restrictions on imports, exports and goods in transit
Art 59	Art 49	Free movement of services
Art 73b	Art 56	Free movement of capital
Art 85	Art 81	Competition – no restrictive practices
Art 86	Art 82	Competition – no abuse of dominant position
Art 100	Art 94	Approximation of laws – Commission proposal, consult Parliament, Council issue directives
Art 100a	Art 95	Special qualified majority procedure for internal market harmonisation directives (Art 14)
[new][1]	Art 133(5)	International negotiations and agreements on intellectual property
Art 177	Art 234	Referrals to European Court of Justice for preliminary rulings on interpretation of Treaty, validity and interpretation of EC secondary legislation, etc
Art 249	Art 189	Status of Council, Commission and European Parliament output: Regulations (generally and directly applicable), Directives (binding on Member States as to the result to be achieved), Decisions (binding on those to whom addressed) Recommendations (not binding) Opinions (not binding)
Art 222	Art 295	'This Treaty shall in no way prejudice the rules in Member States governing the system of property ownership.'

1. Cf *Re Agreement Establishing World Trade Organization* 1/94 [1994] ECR I-5267.

enforceable both by market competitors and by the intervention of the EC Commission in Brussels.

1. For a more detailed view see R Whish *Competition Law* (4th edn, 2001); see also V Korah's popular *An Introductory Guide to EC Competition Law and Practice* (7th edn 2001) and Ulrich 'Patents and Know-How, Free Trade, Interenterprise Cooperation and Competition within the Internal European Market (1992) 23 IIC 583.

27.3 The intended function of these rules is basically to interfere with competition no more than is necessary in order to keep competition alive. Thus Arts 28 to 30 of the EC Treaty seek to prohibit unjustifiable restrictions upon what can be imported into or exported from one member state to another, while Art 81 prohibits the operation of cartels and concerted undertakings which have, as their object or effect, the distortion or prevention of competition. Art 82 prohibits the abuse of a position of dominance within the Community by any commercial undertaking. Since the exercise of national intellectual property rights is ideally suited to the preservation of market exclusivity, and to the elimination or selective preservation of competition, it is natural that the EC competition policy and the exploitation of intellectual property rights should come into conflict.

'Existence' v 'exercise' of rights[1]

27.4 The key to the European Court of Justice's resolution of the conflict between pro- and anti-competitive laws lay in its distinction of the *existence* of intellectual property rights from the *exercise* of them. All national property rights – including those of an intellectual nature – are expressly preserved by Art 295 of the Treaty; this is so even where a form of property, such as copyright in a sound recording, subsists in only some of the member states of the Community.[2] But there is a world of difference between recognising a property right (and not vitiating or expropriating it) and allowing its unfettered exercise. Art 295 does not therefore render the exercise of intellectual property rights invulnerable from the provisions of Arts 28 to 30, 81 and 82. In a similar manner, Art 30, which permits restrictions upon imports if they are justified as protection of industrial or commercial property, does not allow an 'arbitrary discrimination' or 'disguised restriction' of otherwise legitimate trade between Member States.

1. G Tritton, in 'Arts 28-30 and Intellectual Property: is the Jurisprudence of the ECJ now of an Ideal Standard' [1994] 10 EIPR 422 argues that this distinction is moribund. See also C Miller 'Magill: time to abandon the 'Specific subject-matter' Concept [1994] 10 EIPR 413.
2. *EMI Electrola GmbH v Patricia Im- und Export GmbH*: 341/87 [1989] 2 CMLR 413.

410

EC competition and free movement law in action

27.5 This book is not the place for a detailed account of EC competition law,[1] or for an analysis of its complex interrelations with intellectual property rights;[2] the following is a brief and necessarily superficial survey of the main features of the subject.

(i)   The abuse of a dominant position[3] within the Common Market, or in a substantial part of it, is prohibited to the extent that it affects trade between the various Member States.[4] This prohibition applies without reference to the means by which the abuse is carried out, and has been held to apply to the exercise of intellectual property monopolies.[5] Art 82 identifies four particular activities which the Treaty of Rome regards as abusive, of which three (the imposition of unfair purchase or sale conditions,[6] the limitation of production output[7] and the imposition of conditions relating to unconnected transactions[8]) were formerly echoed in the UK Patents Act 1977.[9] These are now presumably the preserve of the UK Competition Act 1998.[10] Art 82 has been applied to the acquisition and exercise of intellectual property, notably in the Magill television listings cases;[11] it has been argued that exercise of intellectual property can never constitute an abuse of dominant position.[12]

(ii)   Agreements and concerted practices entered into between, or conducted by, two or more parties are prohibited if they affect trade between member states and have as their object or effect the prevention, restriction or distortion of competition.[13] This means that many types of clause once favoured in patent licences, such as those which prohibited a licensee from challenging the validity of the licensed patent or which divided a geographical market between licensor and licensee, are no longer of utility within the context of European trade. Agreements in settlement of intellectual property disputes may also fall foul of Art 81.[14]

(iii) Quantitative restrictions on imports, and all measures which have that effect, are prohibited.[15] National intellectual property laws, and especially trade mark laws, are ideally suited to the restriction of imports from one member state to another since the same person, holding the identical trade mark in each member state in respect of the same goods, could otherwise charge different prices for those goods in different countries and then prevent the export of his lawfully manufactured and marketed goods from a 'cheap' country to an 'expensive' one.[16]

(iv) So far as concerns (i) and (ii), but not (iii), it is possible for one or more traders to obtain 'negative clearance' from the Commission in respect of their prima facie unlawful acts.[17] 'Negative clearance' is simply certification by the Commission's

Directorate-General IV (which administers the Treaty's competition policy) that, on the basis of facts known to it, usually being facts communicated to it by interested parties, there are no grounds for initiating proceedings against the practices or agreement in question. It is therefore an expression of opinion, and is not immutable. There is no duty to apply for 'clearance' or to disclose one's possibly wrongful trading practices but, if one did so, one enjoyed an immunity from the possibly huge fines which the Commission can impose upon reluctant competitors.[18] The Commission has traditionally been slow to give negative clearances but may indicate informally in a 'comfort letter' that it does not intend to pursue an agreement or practice notified to it. Since no 'comfort letter' is irrevocable, parties may embark upon a course of action which initially appears to be commercially neutral and only later turns out to be objectionable. DGIV's heavy workload has led it to discourage applications for clearance in many cases.[19]

(v) Some types of agreement – including patent and know-how licences,[20] and distribution agreements with ancillary IP provisions[21] – are exempt from Art 81(1) if they consist wholly of clauses which are approved by the Commission. It cannot, however, be inferred from this that a patent licence is objectionable simply because its terms do not qualify it for such an exemption, although the 'block exemption' Regulations do contain lists of objectionable clauses.[22]

(vi) As a guiding principle, the EC's free movement rules will not permit the holder of any national intellectual property right to exercise that right in respect of goods or any other facilities once they have been made and commercially exploited by him or with his permission,[23] within the single market.[24] This is known as the principle of 'exhaustion of rights'.[25] It applies to manufacturing and distribution rights, but not to performing rights and the like.[26] Thus a performing right society or record company can exercise their copyrights and neighbouring rights so as to prevent any unauthorised performance or broadcast of a work. The record company may not, however, prevent an unauthorised transaction with regard to a CD which has been legitimately made and sold in the EC in consequence of their own exploitation of those rights. By way of a further example, the UK manufacturer of *Succo* chocolate bars can use his trade mark to stop the import of *Succo* bars made by a rival in Italy, in which *Succo* has not been registered[27] and may be used by any manufacturer; but he cannot use it in order to stop legitimate *Succo* bars being imported from Belgium, where they were made and sold by his subsidiary company. If the *Succo* bars had been made and marketed in Brazil under licence before import to the UK, however, it seems that the UK manufacturer could use his trade mark rights to keep them out of circulation.[28] The latter variety of exhaustion, known as 'international exhaustion', has not been endorsed by the European Court of Justice, although it has found favour with the EFTA court.[29] The parallel importation and repackaging of pharmaceuticals has led to an especially voluminous case law.[30]

(vii) These rules are naturally beloved of defendants in actions for infringement of intellectual property rights. The pleading of 'Euro-defences' has become more and more common of late, although the courts will strike out 'Euro-defences' which are wholly lacking in merit.[31]

1. See works cited at para **27.2**, n 1 above and C Bellamy and G Child *European Competition Law* (9th edn 2001).
2. On which see D Guy and G Leigh *The EEC and Intellectual Property* (1981). See also V Korah *An Introductory Guide to EEC Competition Law and Practice* (7th edn 2001); J Flynn 'Intellectual Property and Anti-trust: EC Attitudes' [1992] 2 EIPR 49; V Korah 'Patents and Anti-trust' [1997] IPQ 395.
3. EC Treaty, art 82.
4. The effect upon trade between member states is determined not just by geographical but, more importantly, by economic factors such as the proportion of market share affected: see eg *Felixstowe Dock and Rly Co and European Ferries Ltd v British Docks Board* [1976] 2 CMLR 405. For a critique of market share tests in the context of intellectual property, see O Vrins 'Intellectual Property Licensing and Competition Law: Some News from the Front' [2001] EIPR (forthcoming).
5. See eg *Volvo v Veng* [1989] 4 CMLR 122; mere refusal to license was held not to amount to abuse. See also *Chiron Corpn v Murex* [1993] FSR 324.
6. EC Treaty, art 82(a).
7. Ibid, art 82(b).
8. Ibid, art 82(d).
9. M Heal 'Loosening the Ties: Tie-in Clauses to be Assessed under "Effects"-based Competition Act 1998' [1999] EIPR 414.
10. At time of writing, the Office of Fair Trading's long-promised Guidelines on the application of the Competition Act 1998 to intellectual property had not been published.
11. *RTE, BBC and ITP v EC Commission* [1991] 4 CMLR 586, 669, 745, [1995] 4 CMLR 718.
12. C Miller, para **27.4**, n 1 above; R Greaves 'Article 86 of the EC Treaty and Intellectual Property Rights' [1998] EIPR 379.
13. EC Treaty, art 81.
14. S Singleton 'Intellectual Property Disputes: Settlement Agreements and Ancillary Licences under EC and UK Competition Law' [1993] EIPR 48.
15. EC Treaty, art 28.
16. See *Deutsche Grammophon Gesellschaft GmbH v Metro-SB-Grossmarkte GmbH & Co KG*: 78/70 [1971] ECR 487; *Centrafarm BV v American Home Products Corpn*: 3/78 [1979] FSR 189.
17. Council Regulation 17/62, art 2.
18. Ibid, art 15(5).
19. In cases where the parties concerned are too small for their agreements seriously to affect competition, they may rely upon the Commission's *'De Minimis'*

Notice, or Notice on Agreements of Minor Importance. The notice is currently under review, with a new draft published on 19 May 2001: OJ 2001 C 149/18.
20. Commission Regulation No 240/96 of 31 January 1996 on the Application of Art 85(3) [now 82(3)] of the Treaty to Certain Categories of Technology Transfer Agreement, usually dubbed the 'technology transfer block exemption'. See R Whaite 'The Draft Technology Transfer Block Exemption' [1994] 5 EIPR 259; V Korah 'The Preliminary Draft of a New EC Group Exemption for Technology Licensing' [1994] 5 EIPR 263.
21. Commission Regulation No 2790/1999 of 22 December 1999 on the application of Article 81(3) of the Treaty to categories of vertical agreements and concerted practices, often described as 'the verticals block exemption'.A Gagliardi 'Territorial Restraints in Pure Trade Mark Licence Agreements: An Unsettled Issue' [1997] EIPR 723.
22. Reg 240/96, art 5; Reg 2790/1999, arts 4, 5.
23. See eg *Deutsche Grammophon*, n 16.
24. *Silhouette International Schmied GmbH & Co KG v Hartlauer Handelsgesellschaft mbH*: C-355/96 [1998] All ER (EC) 769; [1998] ETMR 539, [1998] ECR I-4799.
25. For discussions of 'exhaustion' within its wider EC context see V Korah *An Introductory Guide to EEC Competition Law and Practice* (7th edn 2001).
26. *Compagnie Générale pour la Diffusion de la Télévision, Coditel SA v Cine Vog Films SA*: 62/79 [1980] ECR 881; *Warner v Christiansen*: 158/86 [1988] ECR 2605.
27. *Merck & Co v Stephar BV*: 187/80 [1981] ECR 2063; I Britton and I Karet 'Parallel Imports Continue: The Patent Exhaustion Principle Upheld' [1997] EIPR 207.
28. *Sebago and Ancienne Maison Dubois et fils SA v GB-Unic SA* [1999] ETMR 681. H Norman 'Parallel Importation from Non-EEA Member States: The Vision Remains Unclear' [2000] EIPR 159.
29. *Mag Instrument v California Trading Co Norway* [1998] ETMR 85; A Carboni 'Cases about Spectacles and Torches: Now, Can We See the Light?' [1998] EIPR 470. In *Zino Davidoff SA v A & G Imports Ltd* [1999] ETMR 700; [2001] ETMR 67 and *Zino Davidoff SA v M & S Toiletries Ltd* [2000] ETMR 622; [2001] ETMR 112, the English High Court and Scots Court of Session took differing views as to whether consent to sale in the EC could be implied from the fact of marketing in Singapore. N Gross 'Trade Mark exhaustion: the UK Perspective' [2001] EIPR 224. On reference to the European Court of Justice, [2001] ETMR 723, A-G Stix-Hackl expressed the opinion that consent should not be readily implied and was a matter for Community, rather than national, law.
30. *Bristol-Myers Squibb v Paranova* [1996] ECR I-3457, [1997] FSR 102, ECJ; D Rosenburg and M van Kerckhove *'Upjohn v Paranova*: Utterly Exhausted by a Trip Too Far?' [1999] EIPR 223; *Glaxo Group v Dowelhurst Ltd* [2000] FSR 529, Ch D; *Boehringer Ingelheim/Glaxo v Swingward & Dowelhurst* (A-G Jacobs, 12 July 2001)
31. *Philips v Sony* [1999] FSR 112; M Cunningham 'How Far Can a Patent Holder Go?' [1999] EIPR 469; *Sandvik Aktiebolaget v KB Pfiffner (UK) Ltd* [2000] FSR 17; amended defences were allowed. cf *Glaxo Group Ltd v Dowelhurst Ltd* [2000] FSR 371.

Approximation and assimilation of national laws

27.6 The Commission of the EC has in mind two ideals towards which future legal developments should, it feels, be aimed. One is that each member state should employ, as far as is possible, the same substantive intellectual property rules; the other is that intellectual property monopolies should run the length and breadth of the Community, irrespective of the country of their origin.[1] The remainder of this chapter will indicate the extent to which these aims have been, and remain to be, fulfilled.[2]

1. H Laddie 'National IP Rights: A Moribund Anachronism in a Federal Europe?' [2001] EIPR 402.
2. Useful tables of Community measures on intellectual property are published in the blue digest pages of EIPR. A selected list appears in Table 2 at the end of this chapter.

Patents and plant variety rights

27.7 Member states have broadly identical laws governing the criteria of patentability and the patent term. That they do so is not, however, attributable to their membership of the EC; it is instead a by-product of their membership of the European Patent Convention (discussed in Chapter 28 below). A Community Patent Convention,[1] which would provide inter alia that one unitary patent would cover the entire territory of the Community,[2] and that the EC be treated as one country for the purposes of the European Patent Convention,[3] has been waiting many years for implementation. The Community Patent is intended to offer an additional tier of patent protection, running in parallel with existing national systems. It is however a moot point whether national patent systems will be financially viable or economically justifiable if and when the unitary system comes into force.[4] In the meantime, patent measures[5] have been adopted to make extensions available for pharmaceutical patents and 'plant protection products', the effective life of which is reduced by long delays in obtaining product approvals under medicines legislation. Supplementary Protection Certificates can extend the patent monopoly for up to five years in an appropriate case.[6] The Directive on the legal protection of inventions in biotechnology has ostensibly harmonised the interpretation of the EPC in this field,[7] although it has led to amendment of the EPC Implementing Regulations, so has a wider reach than might be supposed. The Community Plant Variety Regulation has paved the way for unitary plant breeders' rights.[8] The Commission has proposed harmonisation of the protection of inventions by utility model.[9] When this proposal was originally launched, the Commission indicated that a Community-wide utility model was not in prospect.[10] However, a consultation as to a Community utility model has subsequently been set in train.[11]

1. The Convention for the European Patent for the Common Market, Luxembourg, 15 December 1975 (Cmnd 6553, 1976); Agreement of 15 December 1989 relating to the Community Patents OJ 1989 L401/1; Proposal for a Council Regulation on the Community Patent COM (2000) final, 1 August 2000.
2. Convention for the European Patent for the Common Market, art 1.
3. Ibid, art 2.
4. See J Phillips 'Time to Close the Patent Office Doors' [1990] 5 EIPR 151.
5. Council Regulation No 1768/92/EEC of 18 June 1992; Council Regulation EC No 1610/96 of 23 July 1996; see Table 2.
6. Within the EC. See J Adams 'Supplementary Protection Certificates: the Challenge to EC Regulation 1768/92' [1994] EIPR 323.
7. See R Nott 'The Proposed EC Directive on biotechnological inventions' [1994] 5 EIPR 191.
8. Regulation 2100/94 of 27 July 1994; OJ 1994 L227/1.
9. COM (1999) 309 final; OJ 2000 C248 E/03.
10. COM (97) 691 final: para 26 of explanatory memorandum.
11. http://europa.eu.int/comm/internal market/en/intprop/indprop/index htm. See J Beton 'The Community Utility Model' (2001) CIPA Journal, p 508, for discussion of the likely effects of a Community utility model.

Copyright

27.8 This area at first sight is the most resistant to harmonisation, since the nature and extent of the variation of national laws, both between common law and civil law systems and within the different civil law systems, is so great that it is in many cases difficult to identify common conceptual ground between them. A preliminary comparative study of the state of national copyright law,[1] conducted when the Community had only nine Member States, served mainly to highlight the extent of national variation. One cannot escape the observation that, just as the laws of science are the same throughout Europe, patent systems run largely in parallel with each other but that, just as the culture of each European country is uniquely personal to it, so too are the copyright laws which govern the protection and exploitation of cultural products. In 1988 a Green Paper was published on copyright and the new technologies.[2] This Green Paper was criticised as seeking to solve European copyright problems by employing the British 'copyright' approach in preference to the continental 'droit d'auteur' philosophy[3] – indeed, it did seem to advance practical solutions in preference to moral principles. It has been followed by a remarkable stream of legislative drafts and texts, which were all aimed, in a rather piecemeal fashion, at harmonising the copyright laws of Member States. At the time of writing, measures are in force as to computer software,[4] rental and lending rights,[5] cable and satellite,[6] the term of copyright,[7] databases,[8] and copyright in the information society.[9] In the future, one may expect attempts to harmonise the arrangements for collective administration of copyright.[10]

1. A Dietz *Copyright Law in the European Community* (1978).
2. Green Paper on *Copyright and the Challenge of Technology* (1988).
3. Margaret Möller *Urheberrecht oder Copyright?* (1988).
4. Directive 91/250 of 14 May 1991 on the Legal Protection of Computer Programs OJ 1991 L122/42
5. Directive 92/100 of 19 November 1992 on rental and lending rights and certain rights relating to copyright; OJ 1992 L346/61, as amended by directive 93/98/EEC.
6. Directive 93/83 of 27 September 1993 on copyright and neighbouring rights relating to satellite broadcasting and cable retransmission; OJ 1993 L248/15.
7. Directive 93/98/EEC of 29 October 1993 harmonising the term of protection of copyright and related rights; OJ 1993 L290/9.
8. Directive 96/9/EC of 11 March 1996 on the legal protection of databases; OJ L77/20.
9. Directive 2001/29/EC of 22 May 2001 on the harmonisation of certain aspects of copyright and related rights in the information society; OJ 2001 L167/10
10. H Cohen Jehoram 'The Future of Copyright Collecting Societies' [2001] EIPR 134.

Trade marks and designs

27.9   It is in the field of trade mark law that the greatest degree of progress has been made towards the goal of a law common to all Member States. The Trade Marks Approximation Directive of 1988 laid down principles common to the Community's national or regional trade mark systems.[1] The Community Trade Mark Regulation[2] provides for a single standard of registrability for a trade mark which gives protection to its proprietor throughout the Community's extensive territory, in addition to the protection provided by registration and unfair competition rules under national laws.[3] Because many marks currently used in Europe could be owned by different, and possibly quite unrelated, proprietors in a number of countries, opposition to the majority of Community trade mark registrations were predicted by commentators; at the date of writing this had not materialised.[4] It is also inevitable that nuances of meaning in the different languages used within the Community will make questions of whether a mark is descriptive of the goods to which it is applied a matter of comparative semantics.[5] The Community Trade Marks Office[6] is established in Alicante, Spain, and opened its doors to applicants in April 1996. Certification marks[7] for foodstuffs (but not wines[8]) may be affected by Regulation 2081/92 on the protection of geographical indications.[9] The blocking of counterfeit goods is also subject to a Regulation,[10] while the comparative advertising is the subject of amendments to a Directive on Misleading Advertising.[11] Lastly, Directive 98/71/EC harmonises national laws on the registration of designs and proposals for a Community Design (registered and unregistered) are under debate.[12]

27.9 *Intellectual property rights and the European Community*

1. 89/104/EEC of 21 December 1988.
2. Council Regulation (EC) No 40/94 of 20 December 1993 on the Community Trade Mark; OJ 1994 L 11/1.
3. See eg *Re Persil Trade Mark* [1978] 1 CMLR 395.
4. OHIM Annual Report for 1999 showed that 22,016 oppositions were received in 1996-99, of which 42% had been resolved. This compared with totals of 24,881 registrations in 1996-98 and 34,266 in 1999, giving an opposition rate of less than 40%.
5. In *BABY-DRY* [2001] ETMR 829, the European Court of Justice has recommended a permissive approach to registration of arguably descriptive terms.
6. Called the Office for Harmonisation of the Internal Market: art 2; this will also be the seat of the proposed Community Design office.
7. R Rozas and H Johnson 'Impact of Certification Marks on Innovation and the Global Market-place' [1997] EIPR 598.
8. Which have their own Regulation 823/87, as amended. See *Taittinger SA v Allbev Ltd* [1993] FSR 641 at 656-658.
9. OJ 1992 C69/15; see M Kolia 'Monopolising Names of Foodstuffs: the New Legislation' [1992] EIPR 333.
10. Regulation 3295/94; OJ L341/8. *Re Adidas AG* [2000] FSR 227. For (proposed) amendments, see J Phillips 'Fakin' It' [1999] EIPR 275; A Clark 'The Use of Border Measure to Prevent International Trade in Counterfeit and Pirated Goods: Implementation and Proposed Reform of Council Regulation 3295/94' [1998] EIPR 414. See also, A Clark 'Trade Marks and the Relabelling of Goods in the Single Market: Anti-counterfeiting implications of *Loendersloot v Ballantine*' [1998] EIPR 328.
11. See OJ 1994 C136/4 for an amended proposal.
12. See para **24.17**.

Table 2: Some European secondary legislation relating to intellectual property

Measure	Subject-matter	OJ ref
Dir 84/450	Misleading and unfair advertising	[1984] L250/17
Dir 87/54	Semi-conductor chips	[1987] L24/36
Dir 89/104	Trade marks	[1989] L40/1
Dir 91/250	Computer programs	[1991] L122/42
Dir 92/100	Rental and lending rights	[1992] L346/1
Reg 1768/92	Supplementary protection for pharmaceutical products	[1992] L182/1
Dir 93/83	Satellite broadcasting and cable retransmission	[1993] L248/15
Dir 93/98	Copyright term	[1993] L290/9
Reg 40/94	Community trade mark	[1994] L11/1

Reg 2100/94	Community plant variety right	[1994] L227/1
Reg 3295/94	Prohibition on release of counterfeit and pirated goods	[1994] L341/08
Reg 240/96	Technology transfer block exemption	[1996] L31/2
Reg 1610/96	Supplementary protection certificates for plant protection products	[1996] L198/30
Dir 96/9	Databases	[1996] L77/20
Dir 97/55, amending 84/450	Comparative advertising	[1997] L290/18
Dir 98/44	Biotechnological inventions	[1998] L213/13
Dir 98/71	Designs	[1998] L289/28
Dir 98/84	Conditional access	[1998] L320/54
Reg 2790/1999	Vertical agreements block exemption	[2000] L336/21
Dir 2000/31	Electronic commerce	[2000] L11/48
Reg 1334/2000	Dual use goods (incl cryptography)	[2000] L159/1
Reg 2658/2000	Specialisation agreements block exemption	[2000] L304/3
Reg 2659/2000	Research and development block exemption	[2000] L304/7
Dir 2001/29	Copyright in the information society	[2001] L167/10
Reg 44/2001	Civil jurisdiction and judgments [to replace Brussels Convention; not Denmark]	[2001] L00/00
Guidelines	On the applicability of Art 81 to horizontal cooperation	[2001] C3/2

Chapter 28

Intellectual property on the international stage

Introduction

28.1 One of the most significant and distinctive features of intellectual property is its ability to transcend national boundaries in a way which is simply not open to real property. A book, film or song enjoyed in one country may well take root within the culture of another with very little effort; the pharmaceutical compound which treats a skin ailment in Germany will be equally efficacious in Austria; the customer at a McDonald's fast food outlet in Geneva will bring with him the expectations drawn from his experiences of similar establishments in London, New York or Tokyo, and so on. It is not therefore surprising that there has been much activity in the international field with regard to both the protection of intellectual property and the dissemination of the information protected by it. This chapter will give a brief overview of this international activity, in the hope that the reader will be able to derive a general impression of it. The subject is of very much more legal, political and economic importance than this brief treatment suggests.

The players

28.2 The international stage is occupied by the following players:

(i) *Sovereign states* Techniques for counting sovereign states vary as to one's preparedness to recognise particular countries for particular purposes, but a rough and non-political estimate is that there are now over 200 of them, *de facto* or *de jure*. These countries may be categorised accordingly:

(a) Developed capitalist economies (United States, Japan, the countries occupying the European Economic Area, Switzerland, Canada, Australia and quite a few others), which both produce and consume great quantities of intellectual property. These countries generally perceive their interest as being served by the greatest degree of protection and enforcement of intellectual property rights, of which they create most of the world's current stock.

(b)   The formerly socialist economies (the Russian Federation and other former members of the USSR, Poland, Hungary, the Czech and Slovak Republics, Bulgaria, the Baltic states and others), which may be industrially advanced or not, and which are torn between their desire to create products and stimulate production on the one hand, and their recently discarded but still influential practice of supporting state enterprise and public trusteeship of the means of production on the other. In general these countries are neither conspicuous producers nor consumers of intellectual property, at least in comparison with the developed capitalist economies. Those which desire closer links with the European Union have engaged in impressive legislative activity in the fields of intellectual property and competition law; indeed Hungary, the Czech Republic, Poland, Estonia and Slovenia are lining up for the next round of admissions to the European Union.

(c)   Developing countries (most of the world's nations), which currently consume far more intellectual property than they can produce or pay for, and which they can obtain largely through foreign aid and co-operation, charity or theft.[1] Within this group is a large body of countries which are often termed LDCs ('Least Developed Countries'). The LDCs are generally the poorest in terms of money, physical resources and qualified manpower, and usually the least able to assist themselves.

(d)   The Islamic world (largely the Middle Eastern states) which, with some honourable exceptions, has until recently taken relatively little interest in the phenomenon of intellectual property. In some cases this lack of interest results from the strong national or cultural homogeneity that makes several of the countries of this group culturally self-sufficient; in other cases it is a consequence of the fact that the wealth-creating possibilities of intellectual property have failed to shine beneath the brilliant light of the petro-dollar. This group has also enacted a number of intellectual property statutes in the last few years. In recent years, possibly in result of the spread of the Internet and advances in telecommunications services, most countries within this group have taken a more positive attitude towards intellectual property and have shown themselves adept in both adopting and adapting its norms to local conditions.

These various sovereign states sometimes form themselves into groupings which have great significance for intellectual property. The

European Union, for example, has aimed to harmonise divergent national laws and to establish pan-Union rights;[2] the countries of the Andes, most former states of the USSR and groups of French- and English-speaking African countries have also demonstrated some successful collaboration in the establishment of laws and granting of rights. In result, there is currently a greater tendency for countries to work in groups and through regional consensus than to enter into bilateral agreements with each other (the predominant practice until the late nineteenth century).

(ii) *International bodies* Sovereign states have, during the last half-century, shown a marked tendency to establish international bodies which, while deriving their status and authority only from the consensus of sovereign states, often appear to wield more power and influence than such states. The United Nations Organization is the best known example of such a body, but the three which most greatly occupy the international stage of intellectual property law are WIPO (the World Intellectual Property Organization), UNESCO (the United Nations Educational, Scientific and Cultural Organisation) and WTO (the World Trade Organization) established as a result of the General Agreement on Tariffs and Trade (GATT) Uruguay Round.[3] In short the organisations' roles are as follows:[4] WIPO seeks to establish intellectual property laws which maintain at least a minimum standard of protection in all countries, without taking specific regard to the economic or cultural necessity to do so in any individual case; UNESCO seeks to encourage the widest exploitation of educational and scientific materials on reasonable terms, unshackled from any obligation to consider the proprietary implications of so doing,[5] while the WTO is at work in establishing intellectual property licensing norms which will give equal weight to the claims of both owners and users of intellectual property that they be allowed to determine the terms under which it may be protected or exploited. WTO's stewardship of the Agreement on the Trade Related Aspects of Intellectual Property Rights (the so-called TRIPs Agreement)[6] also focuses on the issue of whether countries are justified in applying punitive trade sanctions against other countries – whatever their state of development – who fail to provide adequate domestic remedies against counterfeiting and other infringements of rights. If the provisions of the TRIPs Agreement are not respected by any WTO member state, the WTO's complaint resolution system provides for enforcement measures which ultimately include trade sanctions against offending countries.

(iii) *International pressure groups* Intellectual property rights owners, and those who make it their business to service them, have organised themselves into cogent and articulate exponents of the case for promoting intellectual property rights. Of these the best-known are ALAI (L'Association Littéraire et Artistique Internationale), which speaks for authors and creators in numerous countries, AIPPI (L'Association Internationale pour la Protection de la Propriété Industrielle), which speaks for those who deal in industrial property rights, FICPI (Fédération Internationale des Conseils en Propriété Industrielle), IFPI (the International Federation of Producers of Phonograms and Videograms), LES (the Licensing Executives' Society), CISAC (La Confédération Internationale des Sociétés des Auteurs et des Compositeurs), which represents the interests of the world's most important copyright collecting societies, and INTA (the International Trademark Association), which has a powerful and well-informed membership, a large and capable secretariat, a cogent lobbying facility and a healthy budget with which to further its aims.

1. For a sympathetic account of the position of developing countries see Aruda 'Third World View of Technology Transfer' (1984) Les Nouvelles 12.
2. The European Court of Justice held that the EU and its Member States shared competence in international treaty making in relation to intellectual property: Opinion 94/1. Art 113(5) of the EC Treaty as amended strengthens the region's competence in intellectual property matters. See, also, D Rose 'The EU Trade Barrier Regulation: An Effective Instrument for Promoting Global Harmonisation of Intellectual Property Rights? [1999] EIPR 313.
3. See below.
4. P Samuelson 'Challenges for the World Intellectual Property Organization and the Trade-related Aspects of Intellectual Property Rights Council in Regulating Intellectual Property Rights in the Information Age' [1999] EIPR 578 reviews the activities of WIPO and WTO.
5. On the attitude of UNESCO towards the New International Economic Order see its General Conference Resolution 9.1.1978, much of which may seem incompatible with its stewardship of the Universal Copyright Convention of 1952.
6. The text of the TRIPs agreement is reproduced as a supplement to [1994] 11 EIPR. See J Worthy 'Intellectual Property after GATT' [1994] 5 EIPR 195.

Types of international activities

28.3 Now that some account has been given of the various parties to international agreements and activities, it falls to describe some of the types of activity in question.

Reciprocity of protection

28.4 In the early nineteenth century any English author would have found, to his annoyance, that anyone in France who wished to publish there an issue of his work could do so without the fear of any legal reprisals; it would be of little comfort to him, especially in the light of English 'Francophobia' and ignorance of the French language, to know that he could, with impunity, publish in the UK the work of any of France's leading authors. The solution to this problem was for the UK and French governments to get together and to do a deal with each other: French authors would thus be protected by UK copyright law if the French protected UK authors in return.[1] By the mid- to late-nineteenth century there were numerous such reciprocal treaties, despite the potential problems of balancing out inequalities of protection (eg if country A, but not country B protects a particular right, should an author from country B be able to enjoy that right in country A, or vice versa?).

1. Such treaties were brought into domestic law by orders made under the International Copyright Acts 1844, 1852 and 1875.

28.5 Bilateral treaties of this nature did much to ease the immediate needs of the then most developed countries, but the preparation and negotiation of a multiplicity of bilateral agreements requires an inefficient duplication of skilled labour and does not of itself result in any establishment of general norms of protection. That is why it was felt necessary to replace bilateral treaties, where possible, with international treaties made between as many as possible of the economically significant nations. Two such international treaties, the Paris Convention for the Protection of Industrial Property in 1883[1] and the Berne Convention for the Protection of Literary and Artistic Works of 1886,[2] contributed greatly to the establishment of principles of reciprocity by requiring that signatory nations adhere to the obligation to treat nationals of other Member States as they would their own. The importance of the principle of reciprocity may be drawn from the number of countries signatory to one or other of the various texts of the Paris and Berne Conventions (162 and 148 respectively, on 1 November 2001); most of these countries have little or nothing to gain from joining them apart from the resulting protection of their nationals overseas.[3]

1. Revised to the Stockholm text of 14 July 1967.
2. The most recent revision is the Paris text of 24 July 1971.
3. Contrast adherence to TRIPs, which has economic consequences.

Economies of labour or scale

28.6 Some international agreements are not designed to establish principles of reciprocity or to establish new norms of protection (discussed below); they are primarily intended to give their member states (or their nationals) the benefits of economies of labour or of scale. For example, in the absence of the Patent Cooperation Treaty (PCT) of 1970,[1] a person who wanted worldwide patent protection for his invention would have to pay fees for the filing, examination and novelty search conducted in each of over one hundred countries which have patent systems. This is useless, repetitive labour for which the applicant would have had to pay a hundredfold. The PCT, however, provides that a single application, a single partial search and examination, will cover all the countries which adhere to it. By November 2001 as many as 115 countries (including the UK) belonged to the PCT, which means that the saving in terms of liberated bureaucratic time and application funding is immense for any applicant considering patent protection in a multiplicity of those countries. Along the same lines as the PCT but of a rather more advanced nature is the European Patent Convention (EPC), by which an applicant to the European Patent Office (EPO) in Munich can designate his patent application to cover one or more of its 20 Member States. The EPO processes each application at a fraction of the cost of making separate applications in all the signatory states (both under the PCT and EPC the cost of a treaty application is cheaper than the cost of three separate national applications). Similarly, savings can be made in trade mark applications under the terms of the Madrid Agreement on the International Registration of Trade Marks of 1891 to which some 52 countries[2] (but not the UK) adhere. Under this Agreement a person who has successfully registered a trade mark in his own country can deposit that mark with WIPO; the mark will then be registered in any Member State designated by the trade mark's proprietor and which does not within twelve months object to its registrability under the provisions of its national law. A revised and more versatile version of the Madrid Agreement, is known as the Madrid Protocol; it contains fewer idiosyncrasies than the Madrid agreement and allows English as a working language besides French.[3] The Protocol, which came into force on 1 April 1996, now has 56 members, including the UK, China and Japan (with the United States expected to follow shortly).

1. Washington 1970; amended and modified to 3 February 1984. For a usefully simplified view of PCT procedure see B Reid *A Practical Guide to Patent Law* (2nd edn 1993), p 160 and appendix 4C.
2. As at 15 April 2000.
3. Rule 6, 1998 WL 1742558.

28.7 Economies of scale, as distinct from labour, are achieved by two African treaties of relatively recent provenance which established OAPI[1] and ARIPO.[2] OAPI is a group of French-speaking African states and ARIPO contains 13 of its English-speaking counterparts. In each group of countries a single patent application and grant procedure will result in the applicant obtaining a single patent to cover each set of territories (OAPI), or as many member states as the applicant designates (ARIPO). This makes great sense from an economic point of view. If lots of small and relatively disadvantaged African states each maintain their separate patent systems, they must establish and pay for the infrastructure of patent systems which will be substantially under-utilised, given that in a small jurisdiction one can often secure a powerful *de facto* monopoly by being first on the market without ever needing patent protection. OAPI and ARIPO both offer attractively large and thus more viable markets for would-be patentees and free their member states from the financial burdens of running a whole Patent Office.

1. The African Intellectual Property Organisation (established in March 1977).
2. Formerly ESARIPO, Industrial Property Organisation for English-speaking Africa (established in December 1982).

Establishment of norms of protection

28.8   While the Paris and Berne Conventions both encouraged the adoption in many countries of higher levels of legal protection than had been enjoyed within them previously, that improvement in general standards might be viewed as a fortunate, if important, by-product of the reciprocity-seeking process. In modern conventions, however, the setting of new standards of protection and the identification of new subject matter for protection have supplanted reciprocity as their most important object. Much of the groundwork in the examination of norms and the identification of subject matter has been done by WIPO which administers, or is at least associated with, almost all the major modern world intellectual property conventions. Early examples of such agreements are the Rome Convention of 1961 for the Protection of Performers, Producers of Phonograms and Broadcasting Organisations, which attempted to set new standards for the protection of 'neighbouring rights', the Geneva Convention of 1971 for the Protection of Producers of Phonograms Against Unauthorised Duplication of their Phonograms, and the Union for the Protection of Plant Varieties Convention (the 'UPOV Convention') of 1961.[1] More recently WIPO has pioneered normative agreements on copyright and neighbouring rights in the form of the WIPO Copyright Treaty and the WIPO Neighbouring Rights Treaty, both of 1996.

1. Revised in 1972, 1978 and 1991.

28.9   Not all of the conventions set up to establish norms are successful. For example, the Brussels Convention of 1974 on the Protection of Satellite Transmission only attracted 24 members to November 2001, which is perhaps a reflection on the small number of countries whose 'point-to-point' satellite broadcasts are in danger of being intercepted by pirates, and the Vienna Agreement for the Protection of Typefaces and their International Deposit (1973), has attracted little international support, with just 15 adherents. This is not a consequence of hostility but of indifference, since its subject matter so rarely arises even as a national issue.

Harmonisation and integration

28.10   Since the European Union has as one of its aims the integration of separate markets into one large market within which there are no artificial barriers, it is not surprising that the European Commission has promoted the causes of harmonisation of intellectual property laws,[1] and the Community Patent, Utility Model, Trade Mark, Design and Plant Variety Right.[2] When the respective proposals are implemented, pan-European rights may be secured in result of the making of just one single application to one Office, following one registration procedure. On a less grand scale, international co-operation can determine even standards of an arbitrary or bureaucratic nature which are subservient to the law. Of such a nature are the Nice Agreement of 1957 on the Classification of Goods and Services, which fixed internationally recognised categories of registration for trade marks, the Trade Mark Law Treaty reached under the auspices of WIPO in November 1994[3] and the International Patent Classification which provides formulaic descriptions of fields of science in order to render the prior art accessible to researchers in any language.[4]

1. See paras **27.6** to **27.9**.
2. Ibid.
3. J Adams 'Adoption of the Trade Mark Law Treaty' [1995] EIPR D-24.
4. The International Patent Classification Agreement of 24 March 1971.

The facilitation of the greater dissemination of intellectual property

28.11   Until the mid-1960s the voice of the developing world was scarcely heard in the auditorium of intellectual property debate. Most of today's poorest and least privileged regimes were still subject to colonial rule or protection; those which had achieved independence had yet to find their voice. The only thing they sought was independence and it was assumed that, with independence, they could without further assistance harness their indigenous potential and develop themselves. Whatever the merits of this assumption, the factual basis for it was swept aside by the sudden surge in technological growth experienced by the developed nations in the mid-1960s. From that time onwards it has become increasingly apparent that technological information in the form of both pure and applied science is a necessary ingredient, if not a sufficient one, of sustained industrial and agricultural growth.[1]

1. See, for example, the final report of the ad hoc working group on the interrelationship between investment and technology transfer to the trade and development board, UNCTAD TD/B/40(2)/17 which reflects on changes in world trends.

28.12 The demand made by developing countries for greater access to intellectual property on reasonable terms has been reflected by international developments in at least three ways. First, the Berne Convention,[1] and its 'shadow', the Universal Copyright Convention,[2] relaxed their standards of protection, in their Paris revision in 1971, so as to allow developing countries to institute in their own laws a regime of non-exclusive, non-transferable licences to translate, broadcast and reproduce works for educational purposes, on payment of reasonable royalties. Second, the UNCTAD Transfer of Technology Code, in its sixth draft,[3] aimed at establishing model terms under which developing countries could enjoy the technological benefits of co-operation with sophisticated corporations based in developed countries. Although work on this Code has ceased, many of the issues raised in the course of its discussion have remained live. Third, developing countries were given a somewhat longer time-scale in which to implement TRIPs,[4] in recognition of the difficulties they faced in establishing a viable intellectual property infrastructure in what may be an economically or socially hostile environment.

1. Appendix to the Paris text of 24 July 1971.
2. Para **28.2**, n 3 above, articles V *bis* to V *quater*.
3. *Draft International Code of Conduct on the Transfer of Technology*, on which see M Blakeney *Legal Aspects of the Transfer of Technology to Developing Countries* (1989), pp 131-161.
4. See C Correa 'The GATT Agreement on Trade-Related Aspects of Intellectual Property Rights: New Standards for Patent Protection' [1994] 8 EIPR 327.

Index

Index

Index

Index

Index

442